MILITARY Living's™

Temporary Military Lodging
Around the World

by
L. Ann Crawford
Vice President, Military Marketing Services, Inc.
and Publisher Military Living Publications
and
William "Roy" Crawford, Sr., Ph.D.
President, Military Marketing Services, Inc.
and Military Living Publications

Vice President - Marketing - R. J. Crawford

Editor - Donna L. Russell
Cover Design - Ann Crawford and R.J. Crawford

Office Staff:
Timothy Brown, TSgt, USAF (Ret), Eula Mae Brownlee, Nicole Clark, Michael Druzak, Susan Druzak, Nigel Fellers, Maureen Fleegal, Irene Kearney, Lourdes Medina, Keisha Perry, Kathie Russell, Joel Thomas, MSgt, USA(Ret), Larry Williamson.

Military Living Publications
P. O. Box 2347
Falls Church, Virginia 22042-0347
TEL: (703) 237-0203 - FAX: (703) 237-2233

NOTICE

The information in this book has been compiled and edited either from the activity/installation listed, its superior headquarters, or from other sources that may or may not be noted by the authors. Information about the facilities listed, including contact phone numbers and rate structures, could change. This book should be used as a guide to the listed facilities with this understanding. Please forward any corrections or additions to: **Military Living Publications, P. O. Box 2347, Falls Church, Virginia 22042-0347. TEL: 703-237-0203, FAX: 703-237-2233.**

This directory is published by Military Marketing Services, Inc. T/A Military Living Publications, a private business in no way connected with the U.S. Federal or any other government. This book is copyrighted by L. Ann and William Roy Crawford, Sr. Opinions expressed by the publisher and authors of this book are their own and are not to be considered an official expression by any government agency or official.

The information and statements contained in this directory have been compiled from sources believed to be reliable and to represent the best current opinion on the subject. No warranty, guarantee, or representation is made by Military Marketing Services, Inc., as to the absolute correctness or sufficiency of any representation contained in this or other publications and we can assume no responsibility.

Copyright 1995
L. Ann and William "Roy" Crawford
MILITARY MARKETING SERVICES, INC.,
(T/A MILITARY LIVING PUBLICATIONS)
First Printing - June 1995
Second Printing - March 1996
Third Printing - August 1996

All rights reserved under International and Pan-American copyright conventions. No part of this book may be reproduced in any form without permission in writing from the publisher, except by a reviewer who wishes to quote briefly from listings in connection with a review written for inclusion in a magazine or newspaper, with source credit to **MILITARY LIVING'S *TEMPORARY MILITARY LODGING AROUND THE WORLD*.** A copy of the review, when published, should be sent to Military Living Publications, P. O. Box 2347, Falls Church, Virginia 22042-0347.

Library of Congress Cataloging-in-Publication Data

Crawford, Ann Caddell.
    Military livings' temporary military lodging around the world / by L. Ann Crawford, and William "Roy" Crawford, Sr. ; editor, Leon G. Russ.
      p. cm
    W.R. Crawford's name appears first on the earlier editions.
    Includes index
    ISBN 0-914862-57-X (alk. paper)
    1. United States--Armed Forces--Barracks and quarters--Directories. 2. Military bases, American--Directories.
I. Crawford, William Roy, 1932- . II. Russ, Leon G. III. Title.
UC403.C712 1995
649.94'088'355--dc20   95-22342
                                                                                                 CIP

ISBN 0-914862-57-X

INTRODUCTION

This book will pay for itself many times over. All you have to do is use it! There are places to stay on military installations for as little as $4 or $5 per night. The most common charges we found quoted were in the $25-$35 price range for a family of five sharing one unit in a transient lodging facility, or $35-$45 for a Navy Lodge unit, many of which have sleeping space for five, wall-to-wall carpeting, color TV, kitchenette with all utensils, and more. Since our last edition, inflation has caused some military lodging prices to increase; however, they have not increased to the same degree or at the same rate as prices in the civilian sector. In some large cities, the cost of lodging has risen to $200 per night, or more. Clearly, *Temporary Military Lodging Around the World* can greatly reduce the high cost of travel experienced by military families.

Before the first edition of this book was published in 1971, there was a big "catch" involved in getting to use temporary lodging facilities. The problem was finding out which installation had what. Military Living Publications has solved that problem by doing the leg work for you. Just glance through the hundreds of listings that follow and you will find out why this book is indispensable if you want to "travel on less per day...the military way."

L. Ann & William "Roy" Crawford, Sr

AREA VOICE CODES FOR THE DEFENSE SWITCHED NETWORK (DSN) TELEPHONE SYSTEM

ALASKA -	317
CARIBBEAN -	313
CONTINENTAL UNITED STATES -	312
EUROPE -	314
PACIFIC -	315

STANDARD EMERGENCY & SERVICE NUMBERS FROM ALL DEFENSE SWITCHED NETWORK EUROPE TELEPHONE (DSN-E)

EMERGENCY	NUMBER
Ambulance/Hospital/Clinic	116
Engineer	115
Fire	117
Military Police	114

SERVICE	NUMBER
Operator	0 or 1110
CONUS DSN	312
Booking	112
Information	113
Civilian Access	133
AFN-TV Trouble	113
Telephone Repair	119

NOTE: The United States Army, Europe Telephone Directories list "Civilian to Military prefixes", "Telephone Exchange DSN-E prefixes" and "Numerical Military Dial prefixes" all of which are too numerous to list here!

Note: * The Direct Distance Dial (DDD) system (also known as the Military system) has been replaced with the Defense Switched Network - Europe (DSN-E).

HOW TO USE THIS DIRECTORY

Each listing has similar information, listed in the following order:

Name of Installation (AL01R2)
Temporary Lodging Mailing Address
Street / PO Box / Bldg No. (as required)
City/APO/FPO,/ Region/ State, ZIP Code
Scheduled to close month/day/year (if applicable)

TELEPHONE NUMBER INFORMATION: C- This is the commercial telephone service for the installation's main or information/operator assistance number, the designation has also been used for other commercial numbers in this directory, including the number to be called for billeting reservations. Within the U.S. Area Code System, the first three digits are the area code. For foreign country locations, we have provided full telephone numbers for dialing from the U.S. and in-country. The first two digits, after direct dial long distance (011), are the Country Code, the next one or two digits is the city code, if used (consult your local directory or operator for specific dialing instructions). The next three digits are the area telephone exchange/switch number. For foreign countries, the exchange number can be either fewer or more digits than in the U.S. system. The last four digits are usually the information or operator assistance number or the individual telephone line number. In the United Kingdom (UK), dialing instructions are given from the telephone exchange serving the installation. These numbers are different for each location in the UK from which you are dialing. Consult the local directory or operator for specific dialing instructions.

D- This is the Department of Defense, worldwide, Defense Switched Network (DSN). We have, at the request of our readers, included the DSN prefix (area voice codes) with most numbers in each listing. In most cases, the number given is for information/operator assistance.

DSN-E: (Defense Switched Network - Europe) which replaced the European Telephone System (ETS). See standard DSN-E emergency and service numbers listed on the previous page.

FAX: Telefax numbers are listed for reservations when available.

FTS: (Federal Telephone System) The number given is for information/operator assistance. On smaller installations the information/operator assistance number may be the contact number for Temporary Military Lodging. FTS telephone numbers are at U.S. Coast Guard installations.

Location Identifier: Example (AL01R2). The first two characters (letters) are Country/State abbreviations used in Military Living's books (Appendix A). The next two characters are random numbers (00-99) assigned to a specific location. The fifth character is an R indicating region and the sixth character is the region number.

LOCATION: Here you'll find specific driving instructions to the Temporary Military Lodging location from local major cities, interstate/country highways and routes. More than one routing may be provided. **USMRA**: Coordinates in *Military Living's UNITED STATES MILITARY ROAD ATLAS* which are given for each CONUS and OCONUS location. **HE**: is the Hallwag Europe Road Atlas reference to the location. **NMC**: is the nearest major city. Distance in miles and directions from the temporary military lodging (TML) location to the nearest major city are provided.

Lodging Office: In most cases the lodging/billeting address is the address we have provided at the beginning of the listing. In those cases that it is not at the beginning of the listing, it will be listed here. The building number, street address, etc., are listed to provide you the physical location of the lodging office. The C-, D-, and/or FTS telephone numbers and FAX numbers of the billeting office are given when provided to us. **We have "bolded" (darkened) reservation numbers for the convenience of our readers - this should help, particularly when making expensive overseas**

calls. Hours of operation of the billeting office, main desk, or contact office are listed. Check in/check out points and times are given. Use of TML by government civilian employees on duty is specified. Other helpful general billeting information is detailed.

TML: (Temporary Military Lodging) Each category of TML, i.e., Guest House, Hotel, Army/Navy/Air Force/Marine Corps Lodge, and so on, is listed separately in most cases. The category of occupancy, i.e. all ranks, specific grades, officer, enlisted, male, female, is given. Occupancy by leave or duty status is given. Reservation requirements and some contact telephone numbers are listed. The accommodations (bedroom, two bedroom, three bedroom, separate bedroom, suite), and amount of each category of accommodation is given last in parenthesis. Appointments, services and supporting facilities such as kitchens, utensils, television, air conditioning, maid service, cribs, cots, washer/dryer, ice, vending machines, handicapped facilities, etc., are given where they were provided to us. Where there is a charge for services it is noted, otherwise it is free. Whether the structure is older or modern, its condition, and if renovations or improvements have taken place since 1990 are specified. The per day rates are listed for each category of occupant. Please note that rates can change often. Priorities and restrictions on occupancy are listed. **NOTE:** Pets are not allowed in temporary lodging facilities unless otherwise noted, but for the convenience of our readers we have noted where kennel facilities are available. Also, all facilities are open to men and women unless otherwise noted.

DV/VIP: (Distinguished Visitor / Very Important Person) The contact office or person, building, room and telephone number for DV/VIP lodging and other support is given where available. The grade/status for DV/VIPs at the installation is specified. The use of DV/VIP facilities/services by retirees and lower grades is indicated.

TML Availability: The best and most difficult times for TML are listed as reported. If possible, call, FAX or write regarding availability before you travel or take your chances on space-available use.

Points of Interest for visitors are indicated and are bolded near the bottom of the installation listing. Some listings carry military information of interest to visitors such as famous units stationed, or on post/base military museums. Post/base/station locator, medical emergency and police telephone numbers are provided where available. Other Military Living publications carry many support facility telephone numbers are used on listings that are closing or expanding in some manner, "inside information" may also be included here.

Please review Appendix A, Country and State Abbreviations, and Appendix B, General Abbreviations, Appendix D, Billeting regulations and Navy Lodge Information. Also read the other appendices and the questions and answers about TML Regulations that supplement the basic TML listings.

Roy, Ann, & R.J. Crawford, Publishers, thank you for buying our book. We hope it will save you many dollars on your travel and bring more fun into your life.

A Few Words About Telephone Systems in Germany

Each of the commercial/civilian telephone numbers at the top of all listings in Germany follow the same pattern. When dialing from the USA, the first set of digits is the international access, 011, the second set of digits is the country code (49 in Germany), and the third set of digits is the city code (631 - Kaiserslautern). The fourth set of digits is the local area civilian prefix. The next set of digits is the civilian-to-military conversion code. The last set of digits is the line number/extension (or a set of Xs indicating line number/extension). Telephone calls originating on civilian instruments and terminating on military instruments require the conversion code. Telephone calls originating and terminating on civilian instruments do not require the conversion code. Commercial-to-commercial or commercial-to-military telephone calls originating and terminating in the same local area do not generally require the use of the civilian prefix either. Also, local area civilian prefixes all begin with a "0". The "0" is only used in-country. Drop the "0" if dialing from outside the country.

Some Words About Our Changing World

The military is undergoing sweeping changes which have made this book both challenging and interesting to publish. Some installations are closing, and others are realigning. We have included the dates of expected closure as provided to us at the beginning of each listing. Installations which will close prior to 31 December 1995 have been excluded from this book. The information in this book is as accurate as we can make it. It has been provided by billeting facilities worldwide. However, as with all directories, there are changes that happen daily that cause inaccuracies. **Military Living Publications** has always relied on its readers to write or call when information has become outdated. It is the secret of our success. Please do not hesitate to let us know when information is incorrect, or if we have missed a lodging opportunity for your fellow travelers. Enjoy.

EDITOR'S NOTE: Most installations that replied to our request have furnished FAX numbers for reservations and/or which credit cards are accepted at their lodging facilities. If you come across a listing which does not have either FAX numbers or credit cards listed, it is suggested that you phone before you go as there is a good chance that this installation did not respond to our request for information. If you do stay at a facility which did not respond to our request, we would appreciate it if you could forward any information on that facility to us at:

Military Living Publications
ATTN: Editor - TML
P.O. Box 2347
Falls Church, VA 22042-0347

COVER PHOTO CREDITS

1. FRONT COVER: *All photographs courtesy of Hale Koa Hotel, Honolulu, HI.*

2. INSIDE FRONT COVER: ***Top right:*** *Chiemsee AFRC, Germany (courtesy of Chiemsee AFRC);* ***Center:*** *Shades of Green on Walt Disney World Resort, FL (courtesy of Shades of Green on Walt Disney World Resort);* ***Bottom right:*** *Dragon Hill Lodge, Korea (courtesy of Dragon HIll Lodge).*

3. INSIDE BACK COVER: *Ann & Roy Crawford, publishers (courtesy of Military Living Publications).*

UNITED STATES

LOCATION IDENTIFIER	INSTALLATION	PAGE

ALABAMA

AL07R2	Dauphin Island Recreational Complex	1
AL01R2	Fort McClellan	1
AL02R2	Fort Rucker	2
AL04R2	Gunter Annex/ Maxwell Air Force Base	3
AL03R2	Maxwell Air Force Base	4
AL06R2	Redstone Arsenal	5

ALASKA

AK04R5	Adak Naval Air Facility	6
AK18R5	Clear Air Force Station	6
AK15R5	Eielson Air Force Base	7
AK09R5	Elmendorf Air Force Base	8
AK10R5	Fort Greely	8
AK03R5	Fort Richardson	9
AK07R5	Fort Wainwright	10
AK08R5	Kodiak Coast Guard Support Center	11
AK25R5	Sitka Coast Guard Air Station	11

ARIZONA

AZ01R4	Davis-Monthan Air Force Base	13
AZ02R4	Fort Huachuca	14
AZ16R4	Gila Bend Air Force Auxiliary Field	14
AZ03R4	Luke Air Force Base	15
AZ05R4	Yuma Army Proving Ground	16
AZ04R4	Yuma Marine Corps Air Station	17

ARKANSAS

AR04R2	Fort Chaffee	18
AR02R2	Little Rock Air Force Base	18
AR03R2	Pine Bluff Arsenal	19

CALIFORNIA

CA33R4	Alameda Naval Air Station	20
CA13R4	Barstow Marine Corps Logistics Base	21
CA47R4	Beale Air Force Base	22
CA30R4	Camp Pendleton Marine Corps Base	23
CA83R4	Camp San Luis Obispo	24
CA34R4	China Lake Naval Air Warfare Systems Center, Weapons Division	25
CA03R4	Club Del Cottages (Camp Del Mar Beach)	26
CA38R4	Coronado Naval Amphibious Base	26
CA48R4	Edwards Air Force Base	27
CA09R4	El Centro Naval Air Facility	28
CA22R4	El Toro Marine Corps Air Station	29
CA37R4	Fort Hunter Liggett	30

CALIFORNIA, continued

CA01R4	Fort Irwin National Training Center	31
CA46R4	Fort MacArthur	31
CA45R4	Fort Mason Officers' Club	32
CA06R4	Lemoore Naval Air Station	32
CA55R4	Long Beach Naval Shipyard	33
CA39R4	Los Alamitos Armed Forces Reserve Center	34
CA25R4	Los Angeles/Long Beach Coast Guard 11th Coast Guard District	35
CA08R4	March Air Force Base	35
CA56R4	Mare Island Naval Shipyard	36
CA20R4	Marines' Memorial Club	36
CA35R4	McClellan Air Force Base	37
CA14R4	Miramar Naval Air Station	38
CA15R4	Moffett Federal Air Field	39
CA16R4	Monterey Naval Postgraduate School	39
CA43R4	North Island Naval Air Station	40
CA18R4	Oakland Army Base	41
CA23R4	Petaluma Coast Guard Training Center	41
CA40R4	Point Mugu Naval Air Weapons Station	42
CA32R4	Port Hueneme Naval Construction Battalion Center	43
CA57R4	San Diego Marine Corps Recruit Depot	44
CA26R4	San Diego Naval Station	45
CA79R4	San Diego Naval Submarine Base	46
CA54R4	San Diego Naval Training Center	47
CX01R4	San Diego YMCA Inns	47
CA44R4	Sierra Army Depot	48
CA51R4	Stockton Naval Communications Station	49
CA50R4	Travis Air Force Base	49
CA21R4	Treasure Island Naval Station	50
CA86R4	Tustin Marine Corps Air Station	51
CA27R4	Twentynine Palms Marine Corps Air/Ground Combat Center	51
CA29R4	Vandenberg Air Force Base	52

COLORADO

CO10R3	Fitzsimons Army Medical Center	54
CO02R3	Fort Carson	54
CO06R3	Peterson Air Force Base	55
CO07R3	United States Air Force Academy	56

CONNECTICUT

CT01R1	New London Naval Submarine Base	58

DELAWARE

DE01R1	Dover Air Force Base	59

DISTRICT OF COLUMBIA

DC01R1	Bolling Air Force Base	60
DC05R1	Fort Lesley J. McNair	60
DC03R1	Walter Reed Army Medical Center	61

DISTRICT OF COLUMBIA, continued

DC04R1	Washington Navy Yard	62

FLORIDA

FL42R1	Camp Blanding Training Site	64
FL06R1	Cecil Field Naval Air Station	64
FL27R1	Eglin Air Force Base	65
FL18R1	Hurlburt Field	66
FL08R1	Jacksonville Naval Air Station	66
FL15R1	Key West Naval Air Station	67
FL02R1	MacDill Air Force Base	68
FL13R1	Mayport Naval Station	69
FL09R1	Oak Grove Park	70
FL11R1	Orlando Naval Training Center	70
FL35R1	Panama City Naval Coastal Systems Station Naval Surface Warfare Center	71
FL03R1	Patrick Air Force Base	72
FL14R1	Pensacola Naval Air Station	72
FL49R1	Shades of Green on Walt Disney World Resort	73
FL04R1	Tyndall Air Force Base	74
FL05R1	Whiting Field Naval Air Station	75

GEORGIA

GA17R1	Albany Marine Corps Logistics Base	76
GA12R1	Athens Naval Supply Corps School	77
GA16R1	Atlanta Naval Air Station	77
GA13R1	Dobbins Air Reserve Base	78
GA11R1	Fort Benning	79
GA21R1	Fort Gillem	80
GA09R1	Fort Gordon	81
GA08R1	Fort McPherson	82
GA15R1	Fort Stewart	83
GA10R1	Hunter Army Airfield	84
GA03R1	Kings Bay Naval Submarine Base	84
GA02R1	Moody Air Force Base	85
GA14R1	Robins Air Force Base	86

HAWAII

HI10R6	Barbers Point Naval Air Station	88
HI01R6	Barbers Point Recreation Area	88
HI04R6	Barking Sands Pacific Missle Range Facility	89
HI02R6	Bellows Recreation Area	90
HI09R6	Fort Shafter	91
HI08R6	Hale Koa Hotel AFRC	91
HI11R6	Hickam Air Force Base	93
HI06R6	Kaneohe Bay Beach Cottages	94
HI12R6	Kaneohe Marine Corps Base	94
HI17R6	Kilauea Military Camp AFRC	95
HI23R6	Lualualei Naval Magazine	96
HI20R6	Pearl Harbor Naval Station	96
HI13R6	Schofield Barracks	97
HI03R6	Tripler Army Medical Center	98

HAWAII, continued

HI05R6 Waianae Army Recreation Center 98

IDAHO

ID01R4 Mountain Home Air Force Base 100

ILLINOIS

IL04R2 Charles Melvin Price Support Center................................. 101
IL07R2 Great Lakes Naval Training Center 101
IL08R2 Rock Island Arsenal... 102
IL02R2 Scott Air Force Base 103

INDIANA

IN03R2 Crane Division Naval Surface Warfare Center 105
IN02R2 Fort Benjamin Harrison.. 105
IN01R2 Grissom Air Reserve Base.. 106

IOWA

IA02R2 Camp Dodge... 107

KANSAS

KS04R3 Fort Leavenworth 108
KS02R3 Fort Riley 108
KS03R3 McConnell Air Force Base 109

KENTUCKY

KY02R2 Fort Campbell 111
KY01R2 Fort Knox 111

LOUISIANA

LA01R2 Barksdale Air Force Base 113
LA07R2 Fort Polk... 114
LA13R2 Jackson Barracks.. 114
LA11R2 New Orleans Naval Air Station/Joint Reserve Base 115
LA06R2 New Orleans Naval Support Activity.................................. 116

MAINE

ME10R1 Bangor Air National Guard Base...................................... 118
ME07R1 Brunswick Naval Air Station... 118
ME08R1 Cutler Naval Computer and Telecommunications Station................. 119
ME09R1 Winter Harbor Naval Security Group Activity......................... 120

MARYLAND

MD11R1 Aberdeen Proving Ground... 121
MD02R1 Andrews Air Force Base 122
MD01R1 Curtis Bay Coast Guard Yard... 123

MARYLAND, continued

MD07R1	Fort Detrick	123
MD08R1	Fort George G. Meade	124
MD13R1	Fort Ritchie	125
MD04R1	Indian Head Naval Surface Warfare Center	126
MD06R1	National Naval Medical Center	127
MD09R1	Patuxent River Naval Air Warfare Center	128
MD05R1	Solomons Navy Recreation Center	129
MD10R1	United States Naval Academy/Annapolis Naval Station	129

MASSACHUSETTS

MA16R1	Armed Services YMCA of Boston	131
MA07R1	Boston Coast Guard Support Center	131
MA10R1	Cape Cod Coast Guard Air Station	132
MA09R1	Fort Devens	132
MA02R1	Fourth Cliff Family Recreation Area	133
MA06R1	Hanscom Air Force Base	134
MA05R1	South Weymouth Naval Air Station	134
MA03R1	Westover Air Reserve Base	135

MICHIGAN

MI10R2	Camp Grayling	137
MI01R2	Selfridge Air National Guard Base	137

MINNESOTA

MN01R2	Minneapolis-St. Paul Air Reserve Station	139

MISSISSIPPI

MS01R2	Columbus Air Force Base	140
MS03R2	Gulfport Naval Construction Battalion Center	141
MS02R2	Keesler Air Force Base	142
MS04R2	Meridian Naval Air Station	143
MS06R4	Pascagoula Naval Station	144

MISSOURI

MO03R2	Fort Leonard Wood	145
MO01R2	Lake of the Ozarks Recreation Area	146
MO04R2	Whiteman Air Force Base	146

MONTANA

MT03R3	Malmstrom Air Force Base	148

NEBRASKA

NE02R3	Offutt Air Force Base	149

NEVADA

NV02R4	Fallon Naval Air Station	151

NEVADA, continued

NV01R4	Nellis Air Force Base	151
NV03R4	Indian Springs Air Force Auxiliary Field	152

NEW HAMPSHIRE

NH02R1	Portsmouth Naval Shipyard	154

NEW JERSEY

NJ01R1	Armament Research, Development and Engineering Center	155
NJ10R1	Bayonne Military Ocean Terminal	155
NJ13R1	Cape May Coast Guard Training Center	156
NJ11R1	Earle Naval Weapons Station	157
NJ03R1	Fort Dix Army Training Center	157
NJ05R1	Fort Monmouth	158
NJ08R1	Lakehurst Naval Air Warfare Center	159
NJ09R1	McGuire Air Force Base	160

NEW MEXICO

NM02R3	Cannon Air Force Base	161
NM05R3	Holloman Air Force Base	161
NM03R3	Kirtland Air Force Base	162
NM04R3	White Sands Missile Range	163

NEW YORK

NY06R1	Fort Drum	165
NY02R1	Fort Hamilton	165
NY07R1	Gateway National Park	166
NY01R1	New York Coast Guard Support Center	167
NY12R1	Niagara Falls Air Reserve Base	167
NY03R1	Seneca Army Depot	168
NY17R1	Soldiers', Sailors' and Airmen's Club	169
NY09R1	Stewart Army Sub-Post	170
NY16R1	United States Military Academy, West Point	170

NORTH CAROLINA

NC10R1	Camp Lejeune Marine Corps Base	172
NC09R1	Cape Hatteras Coast Guard Recreational Quarters	173
NC02R1	Cherry Point Marine Corps Air Station	173
NC03R1	Elizabeth City Coast Guard Support Center	174
NC05R1	Fort Bragg	175
NC13R1	Fort Fisher Air Force Recreation Area	176
NC06R1	New River Marine Corps Air Station	177
NC01R1	Pope Air Force Base	177
NC11R1	Seymour Johnson Air Force Base	178

NORTH DAKOTA

ND03R3	Camp Gilbert C. Grafton	180

NORTH DAKOTA, continued

ND04R3 Grand Forks Air Force Base 180
ND02R3 Minot Air Force Base 181

OHIO

OH06R2 Camp Perry Clubhouse 183
OH05R2 Defense Construction Supply Center 183
OH01R2 Wright-Patterson Air Force Base 186

OKLAHOMA

OK02R3 Altus Air Force Base 188
OK03R3 Camp Gruber 188
OK01R3 Fort Sill 189
OK09R3 McAlester Army Ammunition Plant 190
OK04R3 Tinker Air Force Base 191
OK05R3 Vance Air Force Base 192

OREGON

OR03R4 Kingsley Field 193

PENNSYLVANIA

PA08R1 Carlisle Barracks 194
PA06R1 Defense Distribution Region East 194
PA04R1 Fort Indiantown Gap 195
PA03R1 Letterkenny Army Depot 196
PA05R1 Tobyhanna Army Depot 196
PA01R1 Willow Grove Naval Air Station/Joint Reserve Base 197

RHODE ISLAND

RI01R1 Newport Naval Education & Training Center 198

SOUTH CAROLINA

SC01R1 Beaufort Marine Corps Air Station 199
SC06R1 Charleston Air Force Base 199
SC09R1 Fort Jackson 200
SC08R1 Parris Island Marine Corps Recruit Depot 201
SC10R1 Shaw Air Force Base 202
SC02R1 Short Stay Navy 203

SOUTH DAKOTA

SD01R3 Ellsworth Air Force Base 205

TENNESSEE

TN02R2 Arnold Air Force Base 206
TN01R2 Memphis Naval Air Station 206

TEXAS

TX50R3	Armed Services YMCA	208
TX07R3	Belton Lake Recreation Area	208
TX27R3	Bergstrom Air Reserve Base	209
TX26R3	Brooks Air Force Base	210
TX10R3	Corpus Christi Naval Air Station	211
TX12R3	Dallas Naval Air Station	212
TX14R3	Dyess Air Force Base	212
TX06R3	Fort Bliss	213
TX02R3	Fort Hood	214
TX18R3	Fort Sam Houston	215
TX21R3	Fort Worth NAS/Joint Reserve Base	216
TX24R3	Goodfellow Air Force Base	217
TX03R3	Kelly Air Force Base	218
TX22R3	Kingsville Naval Air Station	218
TX25R3	Lackland Air Force Base	219
TX05R3	Laughlin Air Force Base	220
TX19R3	Randolph Air Force Base	221
TX09R3	Red River Army Depot	222
TX20R3	Reese Air Force Base	223
TX37R3	Sheppard Air Force Base	224

UTAH

UT11R4	Camp W.G. Williams	226
UT04R4	Dugway Proving Ground	226
UT02R4	Hill Air Force Base	227
UT05R4	Tooele Army Depot	228

VERMONT

NONE

VIRGINIA

VA50R1	Camp Pendleton Virginia National Guard	229
VA02R1	Cheatham Annex Fleet Industrial Supply Center	229
VA06R1	Dahlgren Naval Surface Warfare Center	230
VA25R1	Dam Neck Fleet Combat Training Center Atlantic	231
VA17R1	Fort A. P. Hill	232
VA12R1	Fort Belvoir	233
VA10R1	Fort Eustis	234
VA15R1	Fort Lee	234
VA13R1	Fort Monroe	235
VA24R1	Fort Myer	236
VA16R1	Fort Pickett	237
VA08R1	Fort Story	238
VA01R1	Judge Advocate General's School	239
VA07R1	Langley Air Force Base	239
VA19R1	Little Creek Naval Amphibious Base	240
VA18R1	Norfolk Naval Base	241
VA26R1	Norfolk Naval Shipyard	243
VA09R1	Oceana Naval Air Station	244
VA11R1	Quantico Marine Corps Base	244
VA03R1	Vint Hill Farms Station	245

VIRGINIA, continued

VA46R1	Wallops Island AEGIS Combat Systems Center	246
VA14R1	Yorktown Naval Weapons Station	247

WASHINGTON

WA08R4	Bangor Naval Submarine Base	248
WA02R4	Fairchild Air Force Base	249
WA09R4	Fort Lewis	250
WA15R4	Madigan Army Medical Center	251
WA05R4	McChord Air Force Base	251
WA16R4	Pacific Beach Resort	252
WA11R4	Puget Sound Naval Shipyard	253
WA06R4	Whidbey Island Naval Air Station	254

WEST VIRGINIA

NONE

WISCONSIN

WI02R2	Fort McCoy	255

WYOMING

WY01R4	Francis E. Warren Air Force Base	256

UNITED STATES POSSESSIONS

GUAM

GU01R8	Andersen Air Force Base	257
GU02R8	Guam Naval Station	258

PUERTO RICO

PR03R1	Borinquen Coast Guard Air Station	259
PR01R1	Fort Buchanan	259
PR02R1	Roosevelt Roads Naval Station	260

FOREIGN COUNTRIES

BELGIUM

BE01R7	NATO/SHAPE Support Group (US)	262
BE02R7	Tri-Mission Association	262

CANADA

CN04R1	8th Wing Trenton	264
CN08R1	Royal Road Military College	264

CUBA

CU01R1	Guantanamo Bay Naval Station	265

GERMANY

GE60R7	Ansbach Base Support Battalion	266
GE39R7	Augsburg Base Support Battalion	266
GE90R7	Babenhausen Kaserne	267
GE91R7	Bad Aibling Station	268
GE01R7	Bad Kreuznach Community	268
GE34R7	Bamberg Base Support Battalion	269
GE54R7	Baumholder Annex (Bieuenfeld)	270
GE03R7	Baumholder Base Support Battalion	270
GE08R7	Chiemsee AFRC	271
GE37R7	Darmstadt Base Support Battalion	272
GE10R7	Garmisch AFRC	272
GE23R7	Giessen Base Support Battalion	274
GE11R7	Grafenwöhr Community	274
GE13R7	Hanau Community	275
GE33R7	Heidelberg Community	276
GE30R7	Kaiserslautern Community	277
GE40R7	Landstuhl Army Medical Center	278
GE43R7	Mannheim Base Support Battalion	278
GE42R7	Pirmasens Base Support Battalion	279
GE24R7	Ramstein Air Base	280
GE16R7	Rhein Main Air Base	281
GE48R7	Schweinfurt Base Support Battalion	281
GE18R7	Sembach Air Base	282
GE19R7	Spangdahlem Air Base	283
GE20R7	Stuttgart Community	284
GE85R7	Vilseck Base Support Battalion	284
GE27R7	Wiesbaden Base Support Battalion	285
GE86R7	Wildflecken Community	286
GE31R7	Worms Community	287
GE21R7	Wurzburg Community	287

ICELAND

IC01R7	Keflavik Naval Station	289

ITALY

IT03R7	Admiral Carney Park	290
IT04R7	Aviano Air Base	290
IT10R7	Camp Darby	291
IT13R7	La Maddalena Naval Support Activity	292
IT05R7	Naples Naval Support Activity	292
IT01R7	Sigonella Naval Air Station	293
IT06R7	Vicenza Community	294

JAPAN

JA14R8	Atsugi Naval Air Facility	295
JA07R8	Camp S. D. Butler Marine Corps Base	297
JA06R8	Camp Zama	298

JAPAN, continued

JA12R8	Iwakuni Marine Corps Air Station	299
JA08R8	Kadena Air Base	300
JA03R8	Misawa Air Base	301
JA01R8	New Sanno US Forces Center	302
JA09R8	Okuma Beach Resort - Okinawa	303
JA15R8	Sasebo Fleet Activities	304
JA10R8	Tama Lodge Recreation Area	305
JA02R8	Tokyo Administration Facility	305
JA05R8	Yokosuka Fleet Activities	306
JA04R8	Yokota Air Base	307

KOREA

RK08R8	Camp Henry	309
RK03R8	Camp Page	309
RK08R8	Camp Humphreys	310
RK06R8	Chinhae Fleet Activities	310
RK09R8	Dragon Hill Lodge	311
RK05R8	Kunsan Air Base	312
RK04R8	Osan Air Base	312
RK07R8	Yongsan Army Garrison	313

NETHERLANDS

NT02R7	Brunssum Officers' Club	315

NEW ZEALAND

NZ01R8	Christchurch Naval Antarctic Support Unit	316

PANAMA

PN02R3	Fort Clayton	317
PN01R3	Howard Air Force Base	318
PN09R3	Panama Canal Rodman Naval Station	319

PORTUGAL

PO01R7	Lajes Field, Azores	320

SINGAPORE

SI01R1	Sembawang	320

SPAIN

SP01R7	Moron Air Base	321
SP02R7	Rota Naval Air Station	321

TURKEY

TU03R9	Incirlik Air Base	323
TU04R9	Izmir Air Station	324

UNITED KINGDOM

UK01R7	RAF Alconbury	325
UK05R7	Diego Garcia, U.S. Navy Support Facility	325
UK06R7	Edzell Naval Security Group Activity	326
UK11R7	RAF Fairford	327
UK07R7	RAF Lakenheath	328
UK13R7	London Service Clubs	329
UK08R7	RAF Mildenhall	330
UK10R7	Portsmouth Royal Sailors Home Club	331

APPENDICES

APPENDIX A - Country & State Abbreviations 332
APPENDIX B - General Abbreviations 333
APPENDIX C - Temporary Military Lodging Questions & Answers 335
APPENDIX D - Billeting Regulations and Navy Lodge Information 338

TOO LATE TO COPY

The following pages contain information on facilities noted as "Too Late To Copy": 12, 53, 58, 63, 87, 99, 100, 117, 144, 147, 187, 193, 204, 207, 225, 254, 263, 288, 308, 314, 331, 346, and 348. When possible, information on these facilities was listed at the end of their respective states/countries, otherwise, they may be found on pages 346 and 348.

INFORMATION ON MILITARY LIVING

MILITARY LIVING PUBLICATIONS T/A
(MILITARY MARKETING SERVICES, INC.)

Military Living was founded in 1969. The company publishes **Military Living**, a 50,000-copy circulation quarterly magazine distributed on more than twenty military installations in the Washington, D.C. area.

Our travel newsletter, Military Living's **R&R Space-A Report®**, has been published since 1971 and is available worldwide by subscription. In addition, we currently publish nineteen travel atlases, books, and maps and are researching more topics to improve the quality of life for military personnel and their families. See Central Order Coupon on page 347.

HOW TO RECOGNIZE MILITARY LIVING'S BOOKS

All of Military Living's books carry the famous Military Living logo. Military Living is known as "The Morale Booster Publisher." The slogan, "Travel on Less Per Day...The Military Way," is copyrighted by Military Living; L. Ann Crawford, the founder of Military Living, is a well-known travel writer whose articles reach military families around the world. The president of Military Living Publications and the parent company, Military Marketing Services, Inc., is William "Roy" Crawford, Sr., Ph.D. The Vice President - Marketing is R.J. Crawford.

BASE CLOSURES

The first Department of Defense domestic (United States and Possessions) base closure actions since the 1960's was authorized in October 1988, when the Congress enacted Public Law 100-526 which created the Secretary of Defense Commission on Base Realignment and Closure (BRAC). In 1990 Congress created an independent five-year Defense Base Closure and Realignment Commission with the passage of Public Law (PL) 101-510 under Title XXIX. The amendment of PL 101-510 provides for the Defense Base Closure and Realignment Commission to meet in 1991, 1993 and 1995. The findings of the 1991, 1993 and 1995 commissions have been finalized in public law as reported to the DoD and the Congress.

We have noted in the listings the bases which are remaining for closure and the scheduled dates of the closure (if available). Bases which have been previously closed are not listed. When the DoD acts on The 1993 and 1995 Base Closure Laws and the final action on bases which are in the process of closing is taken, this information will be published in upcoming editions of *Military Living's R & R Space-A Report*®. We have only reported on bases which have significant base support facilities and the related loss of support services for all military members and their families.

Lastly, it should be noted that the 1995 Defense Base Closure law and previous Base Closure Laws only apply to domestic United States Bases (CONUS & OCONUS not foreign countries). The Secretary of Defense, acting within his authority, announced on 24 February 1994 the further reduction or realignment of United States Military Sites Overseas (in Foreign countries).

ATTENTION!!!

Army lodging to be booked through toll free numbers.

DoD travelers, even those overseas, can call a toll-free number and make TML reservations at most (approximately 160) Army installations worldwide. The toll free numbers are:

CONUS-1-800-GO-ARMY-1 (1-800-462-7691)
GERMANY-0130-81-7065
ITALY-678-70-555
PANAMA-001-800-462-7698
KOREA-0078-11-893-0828

The Navy Lodge central reservations number for lodges in the United States is:

1-800-NAVY-INN (1-800-628-9466)

Overseas Navy Lodges must be called directly (see listings in this book).

No central lodging reservation numbers for USMC, USAF or USCG. US Navy personnel, **on duty only**, can make lodging reservations by calling the Bachelor Quarters Central Reservations number at 1-800-576-9327.

Call 1-800-800-4000. Get a military rate by using your Military Living ID # ML3009. Retirees/Active Duty/Reserve/Guard.

The Value Of A Dollar Is Even Greater with Dollar Rent A Car:

Call Us Anytime, Anywhere.

Through our state-of-the-art automated computer reservation center, you can reserve a Dollar Rent A Car. Just contact our 24 hour toll-free worldwide reservation center at 1-800-800-4000 and give your Military Living ID #ML3009.

Temporary Military Lodging Around the World - 1

UNITED STATES

ALABAMA

Dauphin Island Recreational Complex (AL07R2)
PO Box 436, Mobile Coast Guard Base
Mobile, AL 36615-1390

TELEPHONE NUMBER INFORMATION: Main installation numbers: C & FTS-205-441-5240.

Location: Off base. On the Gulf of Mexico approximately 40 miles south of Mobile. I-10 to AL-193 (Exit 17). South approximately 35 miles to Dauphin Island. Left at dead end to east end of island. Follow signs to complex. NMI: Mobile CG Base, 40 miles north. *USMRA: Page 36 (B-10).* NMC: Mobile, 40 miles north.

Lodging Office: None. Reservations required, by application only, with advance payment. Summer (1 May-30 Sep): up to 60 days in advance for active CG; up to 30 days, all others. Fall/winter (1 Oct-30 Apr): 15-30 days in advance. Address: Dauphin Island Recreational Complex, PO Box 436, Dauphin Island, AL 36528-0436. **C-205-861-7113.**

TML: TLF. Three bedroom cottages, private bath (13). Bedding and linens provided. Seven day maximum stay for cottages during summer. Rates: weekend (Fri afternoon-Sun afternoon) $45-$75; weekly (Sun afternoon-Fri afternoon) $55-$100. Reservations as outlined above.

Gulf beaches, visits to historic Fort Gaines and Mobile, serious bird watching, wading for flounder and crab at night, or deep sea fishing are all a part of the simple, unhurried relaxation that is Dauphin Island.

Fort McClellan (AL01R2)
Bldg 3295
14th Street & Summerall Road
Fort McClellan, AL 36205-5000
Scheduled to close. No closure date has been established.

TELEPHONE NUMBER INFORMATION: Main installation: C-205-848-4611, D-312-865-1110.

Location: Nine miles north of I-20. Take AL-21 north to fort. Also located 25 miles southeast of I-59. Take US-431 to fort. *USMRA: Page 36 (F-3).* NMC: Anniston, 3 miles southeast.

Lodging Office: Building 3295, Welcome Center, 14th Street & Summerall Road, 24 hours daily. **C-205-848-4338/3546,** D-312-865-4338/3546, FAX 205-848-4920, D-312-865-4920. Check in billeting 1400 hours, check out 1100 hours.

TML: Fort McClellan Lodge. Building 3127, all ranks, leave or official duty. Check in at lodge. Handicapped accessible. C-205-848-4916. Rooms, two double beds/queen size sofa sleeper, private bath (50). A/C, cribs, essentials, ice vending, kitchenette, complete utensils, housekeeping service, special facilities for DAVs, color TV in room & lounge, coin washer/dryer. New structure. Rates: $31.50 per night. Maximum 6 persons. DAVs (hospital patients) and dependents, and PCS can make reservations, others Space-A.

TML: VEQ. Buildings 269, 940, 941, 943-946, enlisted, all ranks, official duty only. C-205-848-4338/3546. Rooms, private and semi-private baths (640); three bedroom cottage, private bath (1).

ALABAMA
Fort McClellan, continued

A/C, ice vending, housekeeping service, refrigerator, color TV, washer/dryer. Modern structures. Rates: $8.00 per person. Maximum 1 per room.

TML: VOQ. Buildings 2275-2277, 3136, 3137, officers all ranks, official duty only, C-848-4338/3546. Bedroom, private bath (179); bedroom, semi-private bath (177). A/C, community kitchen, essentials, refrigerator, kitchenette (some units), color TV in room & lounge, washer/dryer, ice vending. Older structures. Renovated '90. Rates: $11.00 per person. Maximum 1 per room.

TML: DV/VIP. Buildings 57, 300, 900, 1026, leave or official duty, officers O6+. Bedroom, private bath (4); two bedroom, private bath (5); three bedroom cottages, private bath (3). A/C, essentials, ice vending, kitchenette, complete utensils, housekeeping service, refrigerator, color TV, washer/dryer. Older structures, remodeled. Rates: Cottages $32.50 daily, Suites (2 bedroom) $23, Single rooms $11.50. Duty can make reservations Mon-Fri C-205-848-5616. Retirees, lower ranks Space-A.

DV/VIP: Protocol, USACML+MPCEN+FM, C-205-848-5616, O6+, GS-13+. Retirees and lower ranks Space-A.

CREDIT CARDS ACCEPTED: Visa, MasterCard, and American Express.

TML Availability: Best Nov-Dec. Difficult, other times.

For military history buffs, trace the history of women in the Army in building 1077, the role of chemical and biological weapons in building 2299, and the history of the military police corps in building 3182.

Locator 848-3795   Medical 848-2345   Police 848-5555

Fort Rucker (AL02R2)
Billeting Branch, Bldg. 308
6th Avenue
Fort Rucker, AL 36362-5000

TELEPHONE NUMBER INFORMATION: Main installation numbers: C-334-255-6181, D-312-558-1110.

Location: Ninety miles southeast of Montgomery, midway between the capital city and Florida Gulf Coast, and 7 miles south of Ozark, off US-231 on AL-249. Clearly marked. *USMRA: Page 36 (F,G-8)*. NMC: Dothan, 22 miles southeast.

Lodging Office: Building 308, 6th Ave, 24 hours daily. Reservations: **C-334-598-5216, 334-255-3780/3782,** D-312-558-3780, FAX 334-598-3595. All travelers report to billeting. Check in between 1400-1800, check out 1100 hours daily. Government civilian employee billeting in VOQ. All TDY report to Bldg. 308.

TML: VOQ/VEQ/DVQ. Bldg: 308, for all ranks on TDY. Efficiency suites, family suites, kitchen and non-kitchen rooms, and six lake cottages for TDY clientele. Rates: $20, $18 and $16. TDY reservations 60 days in advance, Active Duty reservations 21 days in advance, others 7 days in advance.

DV/VIP: ATTN: Protocol, building 114 (Post HQ). C-334-255-3100, D-312-558-3100. O6/GS-15+. Retirees and lower ranks one night only, Space-A.

ALABAMA
Fort Rucker, continued

GUEST HOUSE: Building 124, all ranks, leave or official duty, 0600-2200 daily. C-334-598-6352, D-312-558-4432. Two double beds, sofa bed, private bath (38). A/C, kitchen, housekeeping service, color TV, washer/dryer, ice machine. Rates: $30 per unit PCS, $32 Space-A. Official PCS orders and hospital visitors have priority.

TML Availability: Best, Oct-Apr. Limited, May-Sep.

CREDIT CARDS ACCEPTED: Visa, MasterCard and American Express can be used to secure/confirm room.

"Dixie's Heartland" is sprinkled with fine fresh water fishing. Landmark Park has sixty acres of shady nature trails and boardwalks, picnic sites and historic restorations. Waterworld in Dothan is good family entertainment.

Locator 334-6181   Medical 334-7900   Police 334-2222

Gunter Annex, Maxwell Air Force Base (AL04R2)
Gunter Lodging
100 S. Turner Blvd, Bldg 826
Gunter Annex, AL 36114-3011

TELEPHONE NUMBER INFORMATION: Main installation numbers: C-334-416-3360/4611, D-312-596-1110.

Location: Take I-65 to Northern bypass, 6 miles to exit on AL-231, continue west 1 mile to AFB. Coming from the opposite direction, from I-85, follow signs and take eastern bypass north 1 mile to AL-231. Then west 1 mile to AFB. *USMRA: Page 36 (E,F-6)*. NMC: Montgomery, 2 miles southwest.

Lodging Office: Building 826, 24 hours daily, **C-334-416-3360/4611**, FAX 334-416-3945, DSN FAX 312-596-3945, D-312-596-3360/4611. Check in 1400, check out anytime.

TML: VAQ. Buildings 1014/15/16/17, enlisted all ranks, leave or official duty. Check in at Lodging Office. Separate bedroom, semi-private bath (247); bedroom, private bath (250); chief suites, private bath (6). Refrigerator, A/C, color TV, housekeeping service, washer/dryer. DAV facilities, modern structure. Check out 1200 hours daily. Rates: $4 per person; suites $10. Duty can make reservations, others Space-A.

TML: VOQ. Buildings 301, 314, 315, 872/3/4 & 1503, officers all ranks, leave or official duty. Handicapped accessible. Buildings 301-315: suites with private bath (33). Building 1503: rooms with semi-private bath (enlisted use this facility) (69). Building 872: rooms, private bath (40), suites (4). Refrigerator, A/C, color TV, housekeeping service, cribs & cots, washer/dryer, DAV facilities, older buildings. Check out 1200 hours daily. Rates: $4 per person (rooms); $10 per person (suites). Duty can make reservations, others Space-A.

TML: TLF. Building 200, all ranks, leave or official duty. Two bedroom, private bath (3); three bedroom apartment, private bath (1). Kitchen, utensils, A/C, color TV, housekeeping service, cribs & cots, washer/dryer. Modern structure. Check out 1200 hours daily. Rates: $20 per night. Maximum $20 per family. Duty can make reservations, others Space-A.

DV/VIP: Buildings 873, 874. O6+, leave or official duty. Separate bedroom, private bath, kitchenette (17). Rates: $10.

4 - Temporary Military Lodging Around the World

ALABAMA
Gunter Annex, Maxwell Air Force Base continued

TML Availability: Good, except for enlisted quarters (SNCOA expansion).

CREDIT CARDS ACCEPTED: Visa, MasterCard and American Express.

Visit Oak Park's W.A. Gayle Planetarium, the Montgomery Zoo, and the state capital building where Jefferson Davis took the oath of office as President of the Confederate States of America.

Locator 270-4000   Medical 416-5816   Police 416-4250

Maxwell Air Force Base (AL03R2)
Services SQ SVML
351 West Drive
Maxwell AFB, AL 36112-6024

TELEPHONE NUMBER INFORMATION: Main installation numbers: C-334-953-1110, D-312-493-1110.

Location: Take I-85 South to I-65, exit on Day St which leads to main gate of base. *USMRA: Page 36 (E-6).* NMC: Montgomery, 1.5 miles southeast.

Lodging Office: Building 157, 351 West Drive, **C-334-953-2401/2055**, D-312-493-2401/2055, FAX 334-953-5696. DSN FAX 312-493-5696, 24 hours daily. Check in billeting 1400, check out 1200 hours. Government civilian employee billeting.

TML: TLF. Buildings 46, 47, 48, 49, all ranks, leave or official duty. Bedroom apartments, private bath (30). Kitchen, limited utensils, A/C, color TV, housekeeping service, cribs/cots, washer/dryer, ice vending. Modern structure. Rates: $20 per apartment. Maximum 5 persons. Duty can make reservations, others Space-A.

TML: VAQ. Building 695, enlisted all ranks, leave or official duty. SNCO suites, private bath (6); single rooms, shared bath (38); double rooms, shared bath (24). Rates: $5 per person, maximum $10.

TML: VOQ. Buildings 680, 1415-1419, 1428, 1429, 1430-1434, all ranks, leave or official duty. Bedroom, semi-private bath (816); separate bedroom, private bath (342); Suites with kitchenette, private bath (99). Kitchen, A/C, color TV, housekeeping service, cribs/cots, washer/dryer, ice vending. Modern and older structures. Complete renovations in process 1412-1419, 1430-1434. Rates: sponsor $5, adult $5, maximum charge $10. Max 3 persons per unit. Duty can make reservations, others Space-A.

TML: Chief Suites. Building 697, enlisted to E-9, leave or official duty. Separate bedrooms, private bath (5). A/C, essentials, ice vending, housekeeping service, refrigerator, color TV, washer/dryer, wet bar, microwave. Renovated. Rates: sponsor $10, adult $10, maximum charge $20. Maximum 3 persons per unit. Duty can make reservations, others Space-A.

TML: DVQ. Buildings 117, 121, 142, 143, 157, 1422, 1468, 1470. Bedroom, private bath, shared kitchenette (84). Rates: sponsor $10, adult $10, maximum $20.

DV/VIP: AU Protocol Office, building 800. C-334-953-2095. O7+. Retirees Space-A.

TML Availability: Extremely limited year-round.

Temporary Military Lodging Around the World - 5

ALABAMA
Maxwell Air Force Base, continued

While here be sure to visit the Civil Rights Memorial, Montgomery Zoo, W.A. Gayle Planetarium, Executive Mansion, State Capitol Archives & History Museum, and the first White House of the Confederacy.

Locator 953-5027   Medical 953-2333   Police 953-7222

Redstone Arsenal (AL06R2)
ATTN: AMSRI-RA-DPW-HM-BF
Bldg 244, Goss Road
Redstone Arsenal, AL 35808-5099

TELEPHONE NUMBER INFORMATION: Main installation numbers: C-205-876-2151, D-312-746-0011.

Location: Off US-231 West on Martin Rd to main gate with visitor control. For uniformed personnel, Gate 8 is on Drake Ave. Take US-72 East to Jordan Lane, south to Drake. Drake becomes Goss Road at the Arsenal. *USMRA: Page 36 (E-1)*. NMC: Huntsville, adjacent north and east sides. Huntsville International Airport off I-565 is just 10 miles from Redstone Arsenal.

Lodging Office: Building 244, Goss Rd, **C-205-876-5713/8025,** FAX 205-876-2929, DSN FAX 312-246-2929, 24 hours daily. Check in facility, check out 1100 hours daily. Government civilian employee billeting.

TML: The Trail Blazer. Building 244, all ranks, leave or official duty. C-205-837-4130. Bedroom, private bath (17); bedroom, kitchen, private bath (4). Refrigerator, community kitchen, limited utensils, A/C, color TV, housekeeping service, cribs, coin washer/dryer, ice vending. Modern structure, redecorated. Buildings 238 & 239 accommodate those traveling with pets. Rates $22 per person. Duty can make reservations, others Space-A.

TML: VOQ. Buildings 55, 60, 62, 131, 132, 133, 135 all ranks, official duty only. Bedrooms, private bath (25); two bedroom, semi-private bath (86). Three bedroom cottages fully equipped (3). All units have color TV, A/C and housekeeping service, other amenities. Rates: $24.50 per person. Duty can make reservations. Duty on leave Space-A. Check with billeting for availability.

TML: DVQ. Buildings 56, 58. Field grade and General Officers. Decorated and fully equipped 3 bedroom cottages. Rates: sponsor $24.50, $5 each additional person, maximum $34.50 per family. Duty can make reservations, others Space-A.

DV/VIP: Contact billeting office. O6+. Retirees and lower ranks Space-A.

CREDIT CARDS ACCEPTED: Visa, MasterCard, and American Express.

TML Availability: Very good, Nov-Feb. More difficult, other times.

Visit the Alabama Space & Rocket Center, I-565 West of Huntsville.

Locator 876-3331   Medical 876-8621   Police 876-2222

ALASKA

Adak Naval Air Facility (AK04R5)
PSC 486 Box 1202
FPO AP 96506-1202
Scheduled to close. No closure date has been established.

TELEPHONE NUMBER INFORMATION: Main installation numbers: C-907-592-8001, D-317-692-8001.

Location: On Adak Island of the Aleutian Island chain, accessible only by air or ship. *USMRA: Page 128 (H-8)*. NMC: Anchorage, 1200 air miles northeast. *Note: Closed Station, only assigned personnel and cleared/sponsored guests are allowed on base.* Write to Security Office for clearance.

Lodging Office: Housing Office, **C-907-592-8277**, D-317-692-8287, FAX 907-592-4468, 0800-1700 hours duty days. Check in facility 1100, check out 1200 hours daily. Government civilian employee billeting.

TML: TLQ. All ranks, leave or official duty. Two bedroom, living room, private bath (2); three bedroom, living room, private bath (10). Kitchen, color TV, coin washer/dryer, vending machine. Modern structure. Rates: BAQ/VHA rates. PCS only.

TML: TTL. Officers, all ranks, enlisted E4-E9. Duty only. Two bedroom apartments, private bath (8). Kitchen, complete utensils, color TV, cribs/cots, washer/dryer. Modern structures. Rates: same as above. Married enlisted quarters.

TML Availability: Extremely limited.

CREDIT CARDS ACCEPTED: Visa, MasterCard and American Express.

The former Navy Lodge has become the TLQ. There's little opportunity to come here, but for those who need to visit someone stationed here, it may be an opportunity to see a far flung area of spectacular beauty.

Locator 592-4201   Medical 592-8383   Police-555

Clear Air Force Station (AK18R5)
13 SWS/SV
AK 99704-5000

TELEPHONE NUMBER INFORMATION: Main installation numbers: C-907-585-1110, D-317-585-1110.

Location: 78 miles south of Fairbanks, 35 miles north of Healy, on the Parks Highway. Road is on the right as you travel south. Watch for the sign. *USMRA: Page 128 (F-4)*. NMC: Fairbanks, 78 miles northeast.

Lodging Office: Building 200, **C-907-585-6224**, FAX 907-585-6549, DSN FAX 317-585-6549, D-317-585-6224, 0700-1700, hours M-F. Other times Duty Manager, 585-6351. Check in billeting, check out 1200 hours daily. Reservations required. Government civilian employee billeting.

TML: BOQ, BEQ. Buildings 202, 204. Officers and enlisted all ranks, official duty. Bedroom, private bath (8); bedroom, common bath (12). Refrigerator, color TV in room and lounge, housekeeping

ALASKA
Clear Air Force Station, continued

service, washer/dryer. Barracks, renovated. Bldg 204 has (2) DV/VIP suites for O6+. Rates: not provided. Reservations required.

TML: TLQ. Building 3. Officers and enlisted all ranks, official duty. **C-907-585-6576/6487**, D-307-585-6576, 0730-1630 hours, after hours report to consolidated club, Bldg. 209. Check out 1200 hours. Bedrooms, shared bath (10); separate bedroom, private bath (2). Community kitchen, limited utensils, color TV in room and lounge, housekeeping service, washer/dryer, ice vending. Wood frame building. Rates: not provided. Reservations required.

TML Availability: Extremely limited from May-Sept

This facility is in the heart of Alaska, very near to Denali (Mount McKinley) National Park and wonderful fishing, hunting and a full range of other outdoor activities.

Locator 585-1110   Medical 585-6414   Police 585-1110

Eielson Air Force Base (AK15R5)
354 SVS/SVML
3112 Broadway Ave. Ste. 4
Eielson AFB, AK 99702-1870

TELEPHONE NUMBER INFORMATION: Main installation numbers: C-907-377-1110, D-317-377-1110.

Location: On the Richardson Highway (AK-2), AFB is clearly marked. *USMRA: Page 128 (F,G-4)*. NMC: Fairbanks, 26 miles northwest.

Lodging Office: Gold Rush Inn, building 2270, Central Ave, **C-907-377-1844**, D-317-377-1844, FAX 907-377-2559, 24 hours daily. Check in billeting, check out 1200 hours daily. Government civilian employee billeting.

TML: TLF. Building 3305, all ranks, leave or official duty. Separate bedrooms, private bath (living room has sleeper sofa & chair) (40). Kitchen, complete utensils, color TV, housekeeping service, cribs, washer/dryer, VCR, microwave, accessible to handicapped. Modern structure. Rates: $25.50 per room. Maximum 5 per room. Duty can make reservations, others Space-A.

TML: VOQ/VAQ. Buildings 2270-2272. All ranks in respective quarters. Leave or official duty. All buildings accessible to handicapped. One bedroom, private bath (VOQ) (207). One bedroom, private bath (VAQ) (179). Refrigerator, microwave, VCR, cribs, essentials, ice vending, color TV in room & lounge, housekeeping service, washer/dryer. New 3 story structures. Rates: $9.50 per person. Duty can make reservations, others Space-A.

DV/VIP: Protocol Office, 354 FW/CCP, building 3112, room 5, C-907-377-7686. E9/O6+. Retirees Space-A. Rates: $14.00.

TML Availability: Good, Sep-Apr. Note: Space-A May-Oct limited to non-existent.

CREDIT CARDS ACCEPTED: Diners.

Enjoy Denali National Park, historical Fairbanks, hunting, fishing and skiing in season. All outdoor activities are available both on and off base.

Locator-377-1841   Medical-377-2296   Police-377-5130

ALASKA

Elmendorf Air Force Base (AK09R5)
North Star Inn
Bldg 31-0250, Acacia St.
Elmendorf AFB, AK 99506-3565

TELEPHONE NUMBER INFORMATION: Main installation numbers: C-907-552-1110, D-317-552-1110.

Location: Off Glenn Highway. Take Muldoon Gate, Boniface Gate, Post Road Gate or Government Hill Gate exits. The AFB is next to Ft Richardson. *USMRA: Page 128 (F-5) & Page 131 (B,C,D,E-1).* NMC: Anchorage, 2 miles southwest.

Lodging Office: North Star Inn, building 31-0250, Acacia St, **C-907-552-2454,** D-317-552-2454, FAX 907-552-8276, 24 hours daily. Check in facility, check out 1200 hours daily.

TML: TLF. Buildings 21-400 and 2-700 areas, all ranks, TDY or official duty. 21-400: one bedroom, private bath (100). Sofa roll-away bed, fully equipped kitchen, refrigerator, microwave, color TV, housekeeping service, washer/dryer. 2-700: three bedrooms, private bath, fully equipped kitchen, refrigerator, microwave, color TV, housekeeping service, washer/dryer. Older structures. Rates: $25.50 per unit. Personnel on orders can make reservations, others Space-A.

TML: VOQ. Officer all ranks, TDY or official duty. Bedroom, private bath (87); bedroom, private bath, kitchenette (20). Rates: $9.50 per person. Personnel on orders can make reservations, others Space-A.

TML: VAQ. Enlisted all ranks, TDY or official duty. (E1-E3) Shared bedroom and bath (258 rooms 464 beds); E4 and above single room, shared bath (15); DV suites (9). Lounge, reading room, exercise room, conference room. Rates: $9.50 per person. Personnel on orders can make reservations, others Space-A.

DV/VIP: Protocol Office. Reservations for O-6 and above C-907-552-3210.

TML Availability: Fairly good. Best, Nov-Jan. Extremely limited May-Sep.

CREDIT CARDS ACCEPTED: Visa, MasterCard and American Express.

Alaska's largest city boasts many cultural events, museums, sporting events (the Anchorage Bowl is a world class ski resort), and restaurants in a spectacular setting. Outdoor activities abound.

Locator 552-4860   Medical 552-5555   Police 552-3421

Fort Greely (AK10R5)
Billeting Office
P. O. Box 1023
Delta Junction, AK 99737-5000

TELEPHONE NUMBER INFORMATION: Main installation numbers: C-907-873-4113, D-317-873-4113.

Location: Off AK-4, 5 miles south of junction of AK-2 & AK-4. Five miles south of Delta Junction. *USMRA: Page 128 (F,G-4).* NMC: Fairbanks, 105 miles northwest.

ALASKA
Fort Greely, continued

Lodging Office: ATTN: Billeting. Building 663, First St, **C-907-873-3285**, D-317-873-3285, FAX 907-873-3707, 0730-1530 hours M,T,Th,F, 0730-1130 hours W. Others hours, call, or report to SDO, Building 501, C-907-873-4120. Check in 1300 hours, check out 1100 hours daily. Government civilian employee billeting.

TML: VOQ. Building 702, 801, all ranks, leave or official duty. Sitting room, double bed, private bath (14); family quarters, 2 single beds, 1 double, separate bedrooms, private bath (5). Refrigerator, color cable TV, housekeeping service, cribs/cots, washer/dryer. Building 801, double bed, sitting room, telephone, private bath, kitchenette, cable color TV (16). DVQ, same as above, but larger (4). Older structures. Rates: $20 1st person, $7 each additional person. DVQ $32 1st person, $7 each additional person. Unofficial visitors $40 1st person, $7 each additional person. TDY or PCS can make reservations 60 days in advance, unofficial, 3 days, others Space-A. No pets.

TML Availability: Good. Best, Mar-Apr, Dec. More difficult, Jan-Feb.

CREDIT CARDS ACCEPTED: Visa, MasterCard and American Express.

Hunting, fishing, all outdoor summer and winter sports are part of living in Alaska. A visit to nearby Delta Junction and Fairbanks, farther north, will give a visitor a taste of life on "the last frontier."

Locator 873-3255   Medical 873-4498   Police 873-1111

Fort Richardson (AK03R5)
P.O. Box 240373 ATTN: APVR-RPW-HB
Fort Richardson, AK 99505-0373

TELEPHONE NUMBER INFORMATION: Main installation numbers: C-907-384-1110, D-317-864-1110.

Location: Main gate is on Glenn Highway, 5 miles south of Eagle River. *USMRA: Page 128 (F-5) & Page 131 (E-1).* NMC: Anchorage, 8 miles northeast.

Lodging Office: Building 600, Room 105A, 5th St and Richardson Dr, **C-907-384-0436**, D-317-384-0436, FAX 907-384-0470, 0600-2230, hours M-F, 1000-1730 Sa, Su. Other times SDO, building 1, 384-0104. Check in billeting, check out 1100 hours daily. Reservations check in after 1300. Government civilian employee billeting in VOQ/DV/VIP.

TML: VOQ. Buildings 57, 58, 345, 347, 1107, 1113, 1114, officers and enlisted all ranks, leave or official duty. Separate bedroom, private bath (111). Kitchen (some), refrigerator, microwave, CATV, housekeeping service, cribs/cots, washer/dryer, ice vending. Older structure, renovated. Rates: $20, each additional person $7, unofficial visitors $40, each additional person $7. Reservation 60 days in advance for official PCS, TDY or ADT, 3 days in advance for Space-A.

TML: DV/VIP. **The Igloo**, building 53. Officers O5+, leave or official duty. **C-907-384-1586.** Bedroom, private bath (1); separate bedroom suites, private bath (13); bedroom, kitchen, private bath apartments (2). Refrigerator, limited utensils, color TV, housekeeping service, cribs/cots, washer/dryer, ice vending. Older structure, renovated. Rates: suites $32, $7 each additional person, unofficial visitors $40, $7 each additional person. Reservation policy same as VOQ.

DV/VIP: ATTN: APVR-CS-P, Protocol Office, building 1, Room 111, C-907-384-2067, O6+. Retirees and lower ranks Space-A 3 days in advance.

10 - Temporary Military Lodging Around the World

ALASKA
Fort Richardson, continued

TML Availability: Good, Oct-Apr. Difficult, other times.

CREDIT CARDS ACCEPTED: Visa, MasterCard and American Express.

Visit the Fish and Wildlife Museum in Building 600. The Earthquake Park in Anchorage commemorates the violence of the far North, while towering mountains, wildlife parks, the Cook Inlet and great downhill skiing welcome visitors nearby.

Locator 384-0306   Medical 552-5555   Police 384-0823

Fort Wainwright (AK07R5)
Fort Wainwright Billeting
P.O. Box 35086
Fort Wainwright, AK 99703-0086

TELEPHONE NUMBER INFORMATION: Main installation numbers: C-907-353-6113/7500, D-317-353-6113/7500.

Location: From Fairbanks, take Airport Way East which leads to the main gate of the post. *USMRA: Page 128 (F-4)*. NMC: Fairbanks, 3.5 miles west.

Lodging Office: Building 1045 (**Murphy Hall**), Gaffney Rd, **C-907-353-7291**, 0630-2230 hours M-F, 1030-1730 hours, Sa. Other hours SDO, building 1555, C-907-353-7500. Check in billeting, check out 1200 hours daily.

TML: VEQ/VOQ. Building 4056, enlisted and officer all ranks, leave or official duty. Bedroom, private bath (27, 12 suites). Refrigerator, microwave, color TV, housekeeping service, cribs/cots, washer/dryer, food/ice vending. Older structure. Rates: singles, sponsor, $20, suites - $25, each additional person $13. Duty, TDY can make reservations 60 days in advance, others 3 days.

TML: VEQ/VOQ. Building 4063, enlisted and officer all ranks, leave or official duty. Two bedroom, private bath (4); single bedroom, private bath (4); bedroom, private bath (16) (12 suites). Refrigerator, microwave, color TV, housekeeping service, cribs/cots, washer/dryer, ice vending. Rates: sponsor $20, each additional person $13. Duty, TDY can make reservations 60 days in advance.

TML: VEQ/VOQ. Buildings 4064, enlisted and officers all ranks, leave or official duty. Two bedroom, private bath (8); bedroom, private bath (8). Refrigerator, color TV, housekeeping service, essentials, cribs/cots, washer/dryer, food/ice vending. Older structures. Rates: sponsor $20, each additional person $7. Duty, TDY can make reservations 60 days in advance, others 3 days.

TML: VEQ/VOQ. Building 1045, enlisted and officers, all ranks. Leave or official duty. Bedroom, private bath (26). Refrigerator, microwave, color TV, housekeeping service, cribs/roll away, washer/dryer, food/ice vending. Rates: sponsor $20, each additional person $7. Duty, TDY can make reservations 60 days in advance, others 3 days.

DV/VIP: Building 1045. Officers O6+, leave or official duty. Protocol C-907-353-6671. Bedroom deluxe suite (4). Refrigerator, microwave, color TV, housekeeping service, cribs/roll away, washer/dryer, food/ice vending. Rates: sponsor $32, each additional person $7. Duty, TDY can make reservations 60 days in advance, others 3 days.

TML Availability: Difficult year round.

Temporary Military Lodging Around the World - 11

ALASKA
Fort Wainwright, continued

In summer Fairbanks hosts Midnight Sun baseball games, in winter (Feb-Mar) the North American Championship Sled Dog Race (and others), University of Alaska Eskimo Olympics. New shopping malls belie wilderness nearby.

Locator 353-6815   Medical 353-5143/5172   Police 353-7535

Kodiak Coast Guard Support Center (AK08R5)
MWR, P.O. Box 195027
Kodiak CGSC, AK 99619-5027

TELEPHONE NUMBER INFORMATION: Main installation numbers: C-907-487-5267, D-317-487-5267.

Location: From city of Kodiak, take main road southwest for 7 miles. Base is on the left side. *USMRA: Page 128 (E-7)*. NMC: Kodiak, 7 miles northeast.

Lodging Office: Guest House, Bldg N-30, **C-907-487-5446**, 0700-2200 daily. Check in at facility, 1400 hours, check out 1200 hours. Government civilian employee billeting Space-A.

TML: Guest House. Building N-30, all ranks, PCS or official duty, 0800-1630 hours weekdays for reservations. Bedroom, private bath (3); Bedrooms, shared bath (39), family suites, shared bath (2), Community kitchen, CATV, housekeeping service, cribs, washer/dryer, ice vending, children's play area. Older structure, renovated. Rates: $28 single, $38 double, $44 family suite. PCS In/Out have priority; TAD/TDY can make reservations except during PCS season, others Space-A.

TML: BEQ. Rooms, (250), E1-E6 on duty only, **C-907-487-5265**. Rates: no charge.

TML: DV/VIP. Guesthouse. Officer O5+. PCS or official duty, others Space-A. Reservations accepted. VIP suites (3), 2 interconnecting. C907-487-5446, same facilities and rates as Guest House above.

TML Availability: Good, Oct-Apr. Difficult, May-Sep.

CREDIT CARDS ACCEPTED: Visa, MasterCard and American Express.

Kodiak is known for its big bears (the biggest in the world), which are tourist attractions in themselves, great scenery, wonderful king crab and salmon, which is not so threatening, and more tasty.

Locator 487-5267   Medical 487-5227   Police 487-5266

Sitka Coast Guard Air Station (AK25R5)
611 Airport Road
Sitka, AK 99835

TELEPHONE NUMBER INFORMATION: Main installation numbers: C-907-966-5420, D-none.

Location: At end of Airport Rd. on Jponski Island, .5 mi N. of airport terminal. *USMRA: Page 128 (I-7)*. NMC: Juneau, 90 miles northeast, by air.

ALASKA
Sitka Coast Guard Air Station, continued

Billeting Office: 611Airport Road, **C-907-966-5591**, 0800-1600 hours M-F. Other times SDO, 907-966-5420. Check in at facility, check out 0800-1600. After hours, SDO in Flight Operations Center. Government civilian employee billeting.

TML: BEQ. Enlisted all ranks, official duty. Rooms, semi-private bath (2). Color TV, washer/dryer. Rates: $6. Maximum 2 persons per unit. Modern structure. Reservations for active duty on orders and reservists and National Guard on orders, others Space-A. No pets.

DV/VIP: Public Affairs office, USCG Air Station, Sitka, AK 99835, C-907-966-5422.

TML Availability: Extremely limited. Best Fall to spring, difficult in summer.

This small island community has an abundance of sport fishing and hunting. Sitka Historical Park, totem poles and the Sitka shoreline are picturesque. Visit the Russian Bishop's House; St. Michaels Russian Orthodox Church, and Castle Hill, site of the 1867 transfer of Alaska Territory to the US.

Locator 966-5420   **Medical 966-5555**   **Police 747-3245**

Too Late To Copy
Seward Army Recreation Camp, ITR Office, P.O.Box 5-367, Fort Richardson, AK 99505-5100. **C-907-384-1649, 1-800-770-1858**, D-317-384-1649. Call for more information 0800 - 1700 local time. Rates: $50 for motel room with microwave and refrigerator, $75 for duplex (sleeps 6-8) with kitchen, $250 (AD only) and $350 (others) for premier duplex (duplex comes with 6 passenger boat). The camp opens in May 1996 after having undergone a $9.2 million renovation. Old Quonset hut cabins have been replaced with a 56-unit motel complex, and six duplexes. The recreation camp is located on Resurrection Bay near Seward. Pine trees throughout picturesque 12 acre site surrounded by mountains on three sides. Superb fishing for salmon, halibut, snapper, ling cod, sea bass and flounder. Nearby streams and lakes also offer outstanding fishing. Abundant wildlife includes: porpoise, whale, puffin, sea otter, and much more. Area is a photographer's dream. Travelers in late Jul to mid-Aug see active salmon spawning areas on drive to Seward. Full range of support facilities at Fort Richardson and Elmendorf AFB.

ARIZONA

Davis-Monthan Air Force Base (AZ01R4)
Inn on Davis-Monthan
355 SVS/SVML
3375 S. Tenth Street
Davis-Monthan AFB, AZ 85707-4237

TELEPHONE NUMBER INFORMATION: Main installation numbers: C-520-228-3900, D-312-228-1110.

Location: Exit Alvernon Way #265 off I-10, proceed left at traffic light. Alvernon Way eventually becomes Golf Links Road. After about two miles you will turn right on Craycroft road and proceed to main gate. *USMRA: Page 108 (F-9).* NMC: Tucson, 3 miles southwest.

Lodging Office: Inn on Davis-Monthan, building 2350, 3375 S. Tenth St, ATTN: Inn on Davis Monthan, P.O. Box 15013. **C-520-228-1500 ext 1, or C-520-228-3309**, D-312-228-3309, 24 hours daily. Check in billeting after 1300, check out 1100 hours daily except TLFs check out 1000 hours. Government civilian employee billeting.

TML: TLF. Various buildings, all ranks, official duty, C-520-228-3309/3230. Two bedroom, private bath (15); four bedroom, private bath (1). Kitchen, complete utensils, A/C, color TV, housekeeping service, cribs/cots, washer/dryer. Modern structure. Rates: Vary depending upon rank, will not exceed $24. PCS in/out can make reservations, others Space-A.

TML: VAQ. Buildings 3511, 4210, enlisted E1-E6, official duty, C-520-228-3309/3230. Bedroom, double occupancy, common bath (139); Senior Non-commissioned Officer suites (4), kitchen, private bath; separate bedroom, private bath (E7-E9) (4). Refrigerator, A/C, color TV, housekeeping service, washer/dryer, ice machine. Modern structure. Rates: $8 per person; suites $10 per person. Maximum $20 per family. Official duty can make reservations, others Space-A.

TML: VOQ. Buildings 2350, 2550, 4065, officer all ranks, Enlisted E7-E9, leave or official duty, C-520-228-3309/3230. Bedroom, shared kitchen, private bath (144); two room suites, separate bedroom, kitchen, private bath (24); Two bedroom, living room, kitchen, private bath (8). Senior NCO suites, kitchen, private bath, separate bedroom, E7-E9 (4). Refrigerator, microwave, A/C, CATV, housekeeping service, washer/dryer, ice machine. Modern structure. Rates: rooms $8 per person, maximum $16 per family; NCO suites $14 per person, maximum $28 per family. Official duty can make reservation, others Space-A.

TML: DV/VIP. Building 4065, officer O6+, leave or official duty, C-520-228-3600. Two bedroom suites, O6+, private bath (6); One bedroom deluxe suites (two special for general/flag officers). Refrigerator, microwave, complete utensils, A/C, CATV, stocked bar/refrigerator, housekeeping service, ice vending. Modern structure. Rates: $14 per person. Maximum $28 per family. All categories can make reservations. Protocol may cancel reservations for non-AD if AD requires space.

DV/VIP: 355th WG Protocol. C-520-228-3600. O6+. Retirees Space-A.

TML Availability: Difficult. Best, Aug-Dec.

CREDIT CARDS ACCEPTED: Visa, MasterCard and American Express.

Visit Old Tucson; Reid Park & Zoo; Arizona-Sonora Desert and Pima Air Museum. Nearby Mt Lemmon is the site of local snow sports in winter.

Locator 228-3347   **Medical** 228-3878   **Police** 228-3200

14 - Temporary Military Lodging Around the World

ARIZONA

Fort Huachuca (AZ02R4)
Billeting Office
P.O. Box 12775
Fort Huachuca, AZ 85670-2775

TELEPHONE NUMBER INFORMATION: Main installation numbers: C-520-538-7111, D-312-879-0111.

Location: From I-10 take AZ-90 south to Sierra Vista and main gate of fort. *USMRA: Page 108 (F,G-9,10).* NMC: Tucson 75 miles northwest.

Lodging Office: Building 43083, Service Road, **C-520-533-2222/5361**, FAX 520-458-0459, 24 hours daily. Check in 1400, check out 1100 hours. Government civilian employee billeting.

TML: Guest House. Buildings 42017, 52054, all ranks, leave or official duty. Bedroom, 2 double beds, private bath (21); separate bedroom, double bed, private bath (6); two bedroom, double beds, private bath (3); three bedroom, double beds, private bath (3). Community kitchen, refrigerator, A/C, color TV, housekeeping service, cribs, washer/dryer. Modern structure. Rates: $30.50 - $34.50 per unit. Maximum eight persons in 42017, five persons in 52054. Duty can make reservations, others Space-A. Pets OK first night only. Must be boarded by second day. On-post kennels usually available.

TML: DVQ. Building 22104, officers O4+, official duty. Suites - separate bedroom, private bath (6); two bedroom, private bath (2). Kitchen, A/C, color TV, housekeeping service, cribs, washer/dryer. Older structure. Rates: sponsor $33.50, $2 each additional person. Duty can make reservations, others Space-A.

TML: VOQ/VEQ. Buildings 43083-43086, all ranks. Bedroom, private bath or semi-private bath (210). Kitchen & refrigerator in most units, A/C, color TV, housekeeping service, washer/dryer. Modern structure. Rates: VOQ $18.00 VEQ $16, $2 for spouse. *Active duty can make reservations, others Space-A.*

TML Availability: Best, Dec. Difficult, other times

CREDIT CARDS ACCEPTED: Visa, MasterCard, American Express, and Discover.

Visit historic Bisbee and Tombstone, the "Town too tough to die". The ITR office on post is the information office on local activities. Hunting and fishing are good. How about a picnic on Reservoir Hill with a view of 100 miles!

Locator 538-7111   Medical-533-9200   Police-533-2181

Gila Bend Air Force Auxiliary Field (AZ16R4)
HC01 Box 22
Gila Bend AFAF, AZ 85337-5000

TELEPHONE NUMBER INFORMATION: Main installation numbers: C-520-683-6200, D-312-896-6200 (Security Police).

ARIZONA
Gila Bend Air Force Auxiliary Field, continued

Location: From Phoenix, take I-10 West to AZ-85 south to Gila Bend. The field is four miles out of town. Also off I-8 between Yuma and Casa Grande. *USMRA: Page 108 (C-7,8).* NMC: Phoenix, 65 miles northeast.

Lodging Office: ATTN: **Desert Hideaway Inn**, building 4300, Gila Bend AFAF, AZ 85337, **C-520-683-6238**, D-312-853-5238, FAX 520-683-6239, DSN FAX 312-896-5239, 0700-1600 or 0700-2000 depending on occupancy M-F, after hours and weekends check at Security bldg 300. Check in billeting, check out 1200. Government civilian employee billeting.

TML: Desert Hideaway Inn, all ranks, leave or official duty. Two beds per unit, semi-private bath (22); separate bedrooms, semi-private bath (5); Two bedroom, semi-private bath (4). Three bedroom, private bath (3). A/C, community kitchen, cribs, essentials, housekeeping service, refrigerator, color TV in lounge & room, washer/dryer. Older structure, remodeled. Rates: $5.50 per night, maximum charge $18. Maximum 2 persons. Duty can make reservations, others Space-A.

TML: VAQ. Building 4250, enlisted, all ranks, leave or official duty. Bedroom, private bath (50); bedrooms, semi-private bath (5). A/C, refrigerator, color TV, laundry room. Older structure, renovated, remodeled. Rates: $5.50 per person. Maximum 2 persons. Duty can make reservations, others Space-A.

TML: VOQ. Buildings 2358 A, B, C, D, officer, all ranks. Handicapped accessible. Two bedroom, semi-private bath (4). A/C, essentials, fully equipped kitchen, housekeeping service, refrigerator, color TV in lounge. Older structure. Rates: $8 per person. Maximum 2 persons. Duty can make reservations, others Space-A.

DV/VIP: Protocol Office, 58 SG/CC, C-520-683-6262, D-312-853-5262. O6+. Retirees and lower ranks Space-A.

TML Availability: Very good. Difficult Oct-Jan.

CREDIT CARDS ACCEPTED: American Express.

Hunting, fishing, boating, and trips to Tucson, the Organ Pipe National Monument, and Rocky Point Mexico are favorite activities in this area.

Locator 683-6200   Medical 683-6200   Police 683-6200

Luke Air Force Base (AZ03R4)
Fighter Country Inn
7012 N. Bong Lane
Luke AFB, AZ 85309

TELEPHONE NUMBER INFORMATION: Main installation numbers: C-520-856-7411, D-312-853-0111.

Location: From Phoenix, west on I-10 to Litchfield Rd, north on Litchfield Rd approximately 5 miles. Also, from Phoenix, on I-17 to Glendale Ave, west on Glendale Ave to intersection of Glendale Ave and Litchfield Rd, approximately 16 miles. *USMRA: Page 108 (D-6,7).* NMC: Phoenix, 20 miles southeast.

Lodging Office: ATTN: **Fighter Country Inn**, 7012 N. Bong Ln. **C-520-935-2641**, D-312-896-3941, Fax 520-856-3332, 24 hours daily. Check in billeting, check out 1200 hours daily.

ARIZONA
Luke Air Force Base

TML: VOQ. Five buildings, officers all ranks, leave or official duty. Bedroom, private bath (68); shared suites, private bath (28). Kitchen, refrigerator, A/C, color TV, housekeeping service. Modern structure. Rates: $8.50 per night, per person.

TML: TLF. Four buildings, all ranks, leave or official duty. Bedroom, private bath (40). Kitchen, utensils, A/C, color TV, housekeeping service, washer/dryer. Modern structure. Rates: $20 per night.

TML: VAQ. Three buildings, enlisted all ranks, leave or official duty. Bedroom, private bath (6); two bedroom, semi-private bath (70). Kitchen, utensils, A/C, color TV, housekeeping service, washer/dryer. Older structure. Rates: Maximum $5.50 per night per person.

TML: DV/VIP. Two buildings, officer O7+, leave or official duty. Two bedroom suites, private bath (2). Kitchen, utensils, A/C, color TV, housekeeping service. Older facility. Rates: $10 per night, per person. Duty can make reservations, others Space-A.

DV/VIP: Protocol Officer, 58th FW, C-520-856-5840, ranks O6+. Retirees and lower ranks Space-A on a day-by-day basis.

TML Availability: Best, Dec. Difficult, other times.

See Phoenix State Capital Building murals, the Desert Botanical Garden in Papago Park. Pioneer Arizona, a living history museum, and the Phoenix Zoo are worth a visit.

Locator 856-6405   **Medical 856-7506**   **Police 856-6349**

Yuma Army Proving Ground (AZ05R4)
ATTN: STEYP-EH-H
Bldg 1000, Seventh St
Yuma, AZ 85365

TELEPHONE NUMBER INFORMATION: Main installation numbers: C-520-328-2151, D-312-899-2151.

Location: Northeast of I-8 turn right on US-95. Southwest of I-10 turn left on US-95. US-95 is north/south route which bisects APG. *USMRA: Page 108 (A-6,7,8; B-7,8).* NMC: Yuma, 27 miles southwest.

Lodging Office: Building 1003, Seventh St, **C-520-328-2129/2127**, 0630-1700 hours. Mon-Thurs. Other hours, SDO, building 506, C-520-328-2020. Check in billeting, check out 1100 hours daily. Government civilian employee billeting.

TML: Guest House. Building 538, all ranks, leave or official duty. Bedroom, private bath (10). Kitchen, utensils, A/C, color TV in room & lounge, housekeeping service, cribs/cots, washer/dryer, ice vending. Modern structure. Rates: sponsor $18, each additional person $3. Maximum 4 per room. Reservations required. One room handicapped accessible.

TML: VOQ. Building 1004, all ranks, official duty only. Bedroom, semi-private bath (16); Two bedroom, kitchen, private bath (5). Community kitchen, A/C, color TV in room & lounge, housekeeping service, washer/dryer, ice vending. Modern structure. Rates: sponsor $21, each additional person $4. All categories can make reservations.

ARIZONA
Yuma Army Proving Ground, continued

TML: DV/VIP. Building 944 A/B, officer O6+, official duty. Suites, private bath (2). Refrigerator, community kitchen, A/C, color TV, housekeeping service, cribs/cots, washer/dryer, ice vending, coffee machine, beverages. Older structure. Rates: sponsor $25, each additional person $7. O6/GS-15+.

TML Availability: Fairly good, Apr-Sep. More difficult, Oct-Mar.

CREDIT CARDS ACCEPTED: American Express.

Visit the Century House Museum for local history, Fort Yuma and the St Thomas Mission, Yuma Territorial Prison and Museum, and the Quechan Indian Museum in Old Fort Yuma to get a taste of this pre-old west town.

Locator 328-2151   Medical 328-2911   Police 328-2720

Yuma Marine Corps Air Station (AZ04R4)
MCAS Yuma Billeting Fund
Box 12776 MCAS Yuma
Yuma, AZ 85369-5000

TELEPHONE NUMBER INFORMATION: Main installation numbers: C-520-341-2011, D-312-951-2011.

Location: From I-8 take Ave 3E south for 1 mile to MCAS on the right. Adjacent to Yuma IAP. *USMRA: Page 108 (A-8)*. NMC: Yuma, 3 miles northwest.

Lodging Office: Building 1058 Martini Ave, **C-520-341-3094,** D-312-951-3094, 24 hours daily. Check in billeting, check out 1000 hours.

TML: TLQ. **Hostess House,** building 1020, all ranks, leave or official duty, C-520-341-2262. Separate bedroom, private bath (13). Refrigerator, community kitchen, A/C, color TV, housekeeping service, cribs/cots, ice vending. Older structure. Rates: station personnel $16 per unit, transient personnel $23. Seven day limit, then daily. All categories can make reservations.

TML: BEQ. Building 1058, E6-E9, leave or official duty. Bedroom, semi-private bath (52); Refrigerator, A/C, color TV in room & lounge, housekeeping service, washer/dryer, microwave in lounge. Older structure. Rates: $10 per person. All categories can make reservations on Space-A basis.

TML: BOQ. Building 1058, officers all ranks, leave or official duty. Bedroom, semi-private bath (78); separate bedrooms, private bath (4). Refrigerator, A/C, color TV in room and lounge, housekeeping service, washer/dryer, ice vending. Older structure. Rates: $12 per person. All categories make reservations on a Space-A basis.

DV/VIP: None.

TML Availability: Extremely limited. **Note: It is almost impossible to get Space-A lodging.**

Located on the Colorado River, fine water recreation is available, as well as hunting, golf, and trips to nearby Mexico for shopping, festivals and restaurants.

Locator 726-2011   Medical 726-2772   Police 726-2361

ARKANSAS

Fort Chaffee (AR04R2)
ATTN: Billeting Office
Bldg 1377, Fort Smith Blvd.
Fort Chaffee, AR 72905-5000
Scheduled to close 10/31/97.

TELEPHONE NUMBER INFORMATION: Main installation numbers: C-501-484-2141, D-312-962-2111. Police 484-2666

Location: From I-40, take the I-540 spur to Fort Smith. From I-540, exit at Ft Chaffee exit sign. Take state highway 59 south across Arkansas River to highway 22. It goes past Ft Chaffee main gate. Five to six miles total. *USMRA: Page 76 (A,B-4,5)*. NMC: Fort Smith, 6 miles southwest.

Lodging Office: Building 1377, Fort Smith Blvd, **C-501-484-2252**, D-312-962-2252, M-Th 0730-1600, F 0730-2200, Sa 0930-1600.

TML: VEQ/VOQ. Various buildings. All ranks, TDY have priority, limited Space-A availability. Rooms, private/shared baths; suites, private bath. A/C, refrigerator, community kitchen, in room telephones (suites), washer/dryer, color TV, housekeeping service. Older structures, some renovated. Rates $6-$15. No pets.

TML: DVQ. Cottages (9). All ranks, TDY have priority, limited Space-A availability. A/C, kitchen (2), refrigerator, telephones, washer/dryer, color TV, housekeeping service. Older structures, some renovated. Rates: $22 single; $29 married. No Pets.

TML Availability: More difficult, summer.

CREDIT CARDS ACCEPTED: Visa, MasterCard, American Express and Discover.

Historic Fort Smith, on the Arkansas River, 5 miles. Gateway to the Ozarks. Fayetteville - University of Arkansas is an opportunity for sporting events. Wildlife management area, excellent hunting and fishing.

Little Rock Air Force Base (AR02R2)
P.O. Box 1192
Little Rock AFB, AR 72099-0001

TELEPHONE NUMBER INFORMATION: Main installation numbers: C-501-988-3131, D-312-731-1110.

Location: Use US-67/167 to Jacksonville, take AFB exit to main gate. *USMRA: Page 76 (D,E-5)*. NMC: Little Rock, 18 miles southwest.

Lodging Office: Building 1024, Cannon Circle, **C-501-988-6753/1141** 24 hours daily, D-312-731-6753 during normal duty hours, FAX 501-988-7769, after duty hours 501-988-6200, DSN FAX 312-731-7769. Check in billeting, check out 1200 hours daily.

TML: VOQ/VAQ. **Razorback Inn**, building 1024, all ranks, official duty, C-501-988-6652. Spaces available (290). No TLF. Refrigerator, A/C, color TV, housekeeping service, washer/dryer, ice vending. Modern structure, remodeled. Rates: VAQ/VOQ $7, DV $14. Children not authorized. Duty can make reservations, others Space-A.

ARKANSAS
Little Rock Air Force Base, continued

DV/VIP: 314 AW/CCE. C-501-988-6828/3588. O6+. TDY to base only. Retirees and Space-A call lodging direct for availability.

TML Availability: Extremely limited. Best, Dec. 20-31.

CREDIT CARDS ACCEPTED: Visa, MasterCard and American Express.

See War Memorial Park, Arkansas Traveller's Baseball, Burns Park, and Governor's Mansion.

Locator 988-6025   Police 988-3221   Medical 988-7333

Pine Bluff Arsenal (AR03R2)
ATTN: SMCPB-EHH
Bldg 15-330, Room 6
Sibert Road
Pine Bluff Arsenal, AR 71601-9500

TELEPHONE NUMBER INFORMATION: Main installation numbers: C-501-540-3000, D-312-966-3000.

Location: Off US-65 northwest of Pine Bluff. Take AR-256, cross AR-365 into main gate of Arsenal. Or south on US-65 from Little Rock, 35 miles, follow signs. *USMRA: Page 76 (E-6)*. NMC: Pine Bluff, 8 miles southeast.

Lodging Office: Building 15-330, Room 6, Sibert Rd, **C-501-540-3008**, 0730-1600 hours daily. Other hours OC, C-501-540-2700. Check in billeting, check out 1200 hours daily. Government civilian employee billeting.

TML: TQ & BOQ. Buildings 15-330, 15-350, all ranks, leave or official duty. Bedroom, private bath (6); separate bedroom, private bath (14); two bedroom, private bath (1). Refrigerator, community kitchen, utensils, A/C, color cable TV, housekeeping service, iron/ironing board, washer/dryer. Older structure, Rates: sponsor $20, DV/VIP $25, adults $1, children (12+) $1.00, under 12 free. Duty can make reservations, others Space-A.

TML Availability: Extremely limited.

CREDIT CARDS ACCEPTED: Visa, MasterCard, American Express.

Great hunting and fishing. Also a nine hole golf course and a recreation area.

Locator 540-3000   Medical 540-3409   Police 540-3506

CALIFORNIA

****

ATTENTION!
THERE IS A FIRST CLASS HOTEL WITH LOW RATES IN THE HEART OF DOWNTOWN SAN FRANCISCO!

Why not enjoy the very best in America's favorite city? Only one block from Union Square, cable cars, theaters and great shopping.

MARINES' MEMORIAL CLUB

Our first class rooms are from $70 and luxurious Suites from $100. You'll enjoy fine dining in our Skyroom Dining Room and Lounge. Our facilities also include Banquet and Meeting Rooms and a Health Club and pool.

609 Sutter Street - San Francisco, CA 94102   Phone (415) 673-6672

For Reservations & Membership Information Call
1-800-5-MARINE

Membership in this unique organization is available to former and retired members of all branches of the U.S. Armed Services.

****

Alameda Naval Air Station (CA33R4)
Combined Bachelor Quarters
Bldg 17, B Street
Alameda, CA 94501-5083
Scheduled to close 3/31/97.

TELEPHONE NUMBER INFORMATION: Main installation numbers: C-510-263-0111, D-312-993-0111.

Location: From Nimitz Freeway, I-880 south, take the Broadway/Alameda exit, turn left at first light, left at next light through tunnel to Alameda. From I-880 north take 12th/11th exit, follow to 5th Street, turn left, follow through tunnel to Alameda. NAS clearly marked. *USMRA: Page 119 (D-5)*. NMC: Oakland, 2 miles northwest.

Lodging Office: Building 17, B St, **C-510-263-3649**, FAX (BOQ) 510-263-3653, 24 hours daily. Check in 1500 at facility, check out 1200 hours daily. Government civilian employee billeting.

Temporary Military Lodging Around the World - 21

CALIFORNIA
Alameda Naval Air Station, continued

TML: Navy Lodge. Buildings 531, 532 533. All ranks, leave or official duty. Reservations call **1-800-NAVY-INN**. Lodge number 510-523-4917, D-312-993-2755, FAX 510-748-8224. Check in 1500-1800, check out 1200 hours daily. Bedroom, 2 double beds, living room, private bath (56). Single bedroom (10), Handicapped accessible (2). Forty-six non-smoking units. Kitchenette, utensils, A/C, CATV, complimentary coffee/tea, cribs, phones, housekeeping service, mini-mart, playground, snack vending, coin washer/dryer, ice vending. Modern structure. Rates $41.50 per unit. Maximum 5 persons. All categories can make reservations.

TML: BOQ. Building 17, officers, all ranks, leave or official duty. Bedroom, semi-private bath (129); separate bedrooms, private bath (9); suites, private bath (46); suites (VIP, O7+), private bath (4). Refrigerator, color TV in room & lounge, washer/dryer, ice vending, telephone in room. Older structure, renovated. Rates: regular room $8, suites $15, VIP suites $20, add $10 for dependents. VIP suite reservations made through CO's secretary at 510-263-3000.

TML: BEQ. C-510-263-3673, FAX 510-263-3674. Rates: E1-E6 $4 per day; E7+ $8 per day. Enlisted DV/VIP $10. DV/VIP reservations made through Command Master Chief at 510-263-3005.

DV/VIP: CO, building 1, O7+. Retirees, Space-A.

TML Availability: Good, all year.

CREDIT CARDS ACCEPTED: Visa, MasterCard and American Express. The Navy Lodge accepts Visa, MasterCard, American Express and Discover.

Within easy access of San Francisco, Berkeley, and the California wine country. Visit Lake Merritt in the heart of Oakland, the Oakland Art Museum, and Joseph Knowland Arboretum.

Locator 263-0111   Medical 263-4400   Police 263-3767

Barstow Marine Corps Logistics Base (CA13R4)
Food & Hospitality Branch
Bldg. 171
Barstow MCLB, CA 92311-5047

TELEPHONE NUMBER INFORMATION: Main installation numbers: C-619-577-6211, D-312-282-6611/6612.

Location: On I-40, 1.5 miles east of Barstow. Take I-15 northeast from San Bernardino, or west from Las Vegas, NV. Signs mark direction to MCLB. *USMRA: Page 111 (G-12,13)*. NMC: San Bernardino, 75 miles southwest.

Lodging Office: Building 171. **C-619-577-6418,** D-312-282-6418, FAX 619-577-6542, 0700-1530 hours daily. Other hours OD, Building 30, Room 8, C-619-577-6611. Check in/out at billeting.

TML: TLF. **Oasis Lodge.** Buildings 114, all ranks, leave or official duty. Food and Hospitality Building 171, C-619-577-6418. Bedroom, private bath (2); two bedroom, private bath (2). Kitchen, utensils, A/C, color TV. Older structure. Reservations accepted. Rates: $25. Check out 1100 hours daily. All categories can make reservations in advance.

CALIFORNIA
Barstow Marine Corps Logistics Base, continued

TML: VIP. Building 11-A, O6+, leave or official duty. C-619-577-6555, D-312-282-6418. Two bedroom, private bath (1). Kitchen, utensils, A/C, color TV, housekeeping service, washer/dryer. Older structure. Rates: $25 per unit. All categories can make reservations. Check out 1100 hours daily.

DV/VIP: Commanding General, Building 15, C-619-577-6555, D-312-282-6555, FAX 619-577-6058. O6+. Retired & lower ranks Space-A. Rates: $35 per unit.

TML Availability: Good, Oct-Apr. Difficult, other times.

CREDIT CARDS ACCEPTED: Visa, MasterCard, and American Express (government card only.).

Visit Calico Ghost Town, 8 miles east. Lake Delores is 13 miles east for water recreation. . Southern California is in easy reach, and Las Vegas not too far east

Locator 577-6211   Medical 577-6591/6592   Police 911

Beale Air Force Base (CA47R4)
Gold Country Inn
9 SVS/SVML
Building 24112, A Street
Beale AFB, CA 95903-1615

TELEPHONE NUMBER INFORMATION: Main installation numbers: C-916-634-3000, D-312-368-3000

Location: From CA-70 North exit south of Marysville, to North Beale Rd, continue for 10 miles to main gate of AFB. *USMRA: Page 110 (C,D-5,6)*. NMC: Sacramento, 40 miles south.

Lodging Office: Gold Country Inn. Building 24112, B Street, C-916-634-2953, D-312-368-2953, FAX 916-634-3674, DSN FAX 312-368-3674, 24 hours daily. Check in billeting, check out 1200 hours daily. Government civilian employee billeting.

TML: TLF. Buildings 5109-5112, all ranks, official duty, Space-A. Two bedroom, private bath (3); three bedroom, private bath (6); four bedroom, private bath (8). Kitchen, complete utensils, A/C, color TV in room & lounge, housekeeping service, cribs/cots, washer/dryer, microwave. Older structure. Rates: Range from $18-$24 for two bedroom, three bedroom, four bedroom. All Space-A is $24. All must make reservations.

TML: VOQ. Buildings 2350-2360, officer all ranks, official duty, Space-A. Bedroom, private bath (47). Kitchen, A/C, limited utensils, color TV in room & lounge, housekeeping service, cribs/cots, washer/dryer, microwave. Older structure. Rates: $8 per person.

TML: VAQ. Building 18000, enlisted all ranks, official duty, Space-A. Bedroom, semi-private bath, (18); Two bedrooms, semi-private bath (34); SNCO suites, private bath (3). Refrigerator, A/C, color TV in room & lounge, housekeeping service, cribs/cots, washer/dryer, ice vending, microwave. Older structure, remodeled. Rates: $7 per person, $14 per couple. SNCO rates: $8 per person, $16 per couple. Reservations accepted.

DV/VIP: Protocol Office, C-916-634-2954, O6+, retirees. Reservations required.

TML Availability: Good, Sep-May. Difficult, other times.

CALIFORNIA
Beale Air Force Base, continued

CREDIT CARDS ACCEPTED: Visa, MasterCard and American Express.

In the center of historic California gold rush country, east of Marysville and north of Sacramento. Outdoor sports are popular.

Locator 634-2960   Medical 634-4444   Police 634-2000

Camp Pendleton Marine Corps Base (CA30R4)
Billeting/Bachelor Housing Office
Bldg 1341, Box 555013
Camp Pendleton MCB, CA 92055-5013

TELEPHONE NUMBER INFORMATION: Main installation numbers: C-619-725-4111, D-312-365-4111.

Location: On I-5 which is adjacent to main gate. Take Camp Pendleton off ramp from I-5 at Oceanside. *USMRA: Page 111 (F-14,15).* NMC: Oceanside, adjacent to base.

Billeting Office: Building 1341, **C-619-725-3718/3451/3732,** 24 hours daily. Check in as indicated, check out 1200 hours daily. Government civilian employee billeting.

TML: TOQ. Buildings 1341, 1342, Mainside, officers all ranks, WO1-O6. Check in at billeting. Bedroom, single occupancy, semi-private bath (20); separate bedrooms, private bath (20). Refrigerator, coffee maker, CATV, essentials, community kitchen, housekeeping service, cribs and rollaways ($1 each), washer/dryer. Older structure, renovated. Rates: building 1341 TAD/TDY $18, others $22; building 1342 TAD/TDY, $20, others $28, $5 each additional person. TAD/TDY and PCS in/out can make reservations, others Space-A.

TML: TEQ. Building 16146, enlisted all ranks, leave or official duty. Check out 1200. Bedroom, community bath (42). Refrigerator, CATV, essentials, housekeeping service, cribs and rollaways ($1 each), washer/dryer. Older structure. Rates: TAD/TDY, $17-$20, others $18-$22, $5 each additional person. Duty can make reservations, others Space-A.

TML: BOQ. Building 210440 (Del Mar). From main gate, 1 block, left to fire station, left to stop sign, left to BOQ on the left. Check in at facility. Call for reservations. Officers, WO1-O6, leave or official duty. Suites, kitchenette, private bath (4); studio, private bath (8); bedroom, shared living, private bath (40). Refrigerator, microwave, utensils, coffee maker, washer/dryer, housekeeping service, CATV, cribs and rollaways ($1 each). New structure. Rates: TAD/TDY $17-$20, others $19-$27, $5 each additional person. Duty can make reservations, others Space-A.

TML: DV/VIP. Building 1751. Officer O6+, leave or official duty, C-619-725-5080/5780 (Joint Protocol Officer). Two bedroom suites (3), living room, dining room, den, private bath. Kitchen, utensils, A/C, CATV, essentials, housekeeping service, cribs and rollaways ($1 each), washer/dryer, dishwasher. Older structure, Rates: TAD/TDY $20-$30, others $27-$52, $5 each additional person. Maximum 6 per suite. TAD/TDY can make reservations, others Space-A. General/Flag rank have priority.

DV/VIP: ATTN: Joint Protocol Officer, building 1160, C-619-725-5194. O5+. Retirees and lower ranks Space-A.

MWR TML: Guest House. **Ward Lodge.** Fifteen miles from main gate. Building 1310, all ranks, leave or official duty. Reservations accepted, C-619-725-5304. Check in at facility. Bedroom, private

CALIFORNIA
Camp Pendleton Marine Corps Base, continued

bath (64). Kitchen (36 units), limited utensils, A/C, color TV in room & lounge, VCR, housekeeping service, cribs ($1), cots ($1), coin washer/dryer, ice vending, facilities for DAVs, swimming pool. Modern structure. Rates for PCS/leave personnel: $30 with kitchen, $25 without kitchen. All categories can make reservations.

TML: Club Del Cottages, (Camp Del Mar Beach) mobile homes, reservations by phone or in person, **C-619-725-2134.** Leave or official duty. Cottages, one bedroom, private bath (48); mobile homes, two bedrooms, 2 sets bunk beds, sleeps 6, private bath (14); mobile home, four bedrooms, double wide, sleeps 16, private bath (1). Kitchen, fully equipped, no housekeeping service, bring bed linens, blankets, pillows, towels, etc. Recreation area with many amenities, ITT Office has tickets to Southern California attractions. Summer package, minimum stay 7 days. Mon-Th, leave Fri., Fri-Su, leave Mon. Rates: cottages $30 daily; 2 bedroom mobile home $30; 4 bedroom mobile home $60. Winter rates available. No pets. All categories can make reservations. **Note: See complete lodging listing in this book under Club Del Cottages, and also in** *Military RV, Camping & Rec Areas Around the World.*

TML Availability: Fairly good, Oct-Mar. More difficult, other times.

CREDIT CARDS ACCEPTED: Visa, MasterCard and American Express.

Beaches, all forms of water recreation, Mission San Luis Rey, and 72 golf courses are within easy reach of Camp Pendleton.

Locator 725-4111   Medical 725-6308   Police 911

Camp San Luis Obispo (CA83R4)
ATTN: Billeting Manager
P.O. Box 8104
San Luis Obispo, CA 93403-8104

TELEPHONE NUMBER INFORMATION: Main installation numbers: C-805-549-3800, D-312-878-9800, FTS-629-3800.

Location: Take Highway 1 five miles northwest of the city of San Luis Obispo. *USMRA: Page 111 (C-11).* NMC: San Luis Obispo, five miles southeast.

Lodging Office: Building 738, San Joaquin Avenue, **C-805-549-3800**, 0800-1630 hours daily. After duty hours C-805-549-3806, Operations. Check in 0800-1630, check out 1200 hours. Government civilian employee billeting.

TML: BOQ. Transient housing. Rooms, apartments, cottages, officers all ranks, E-7 thru E-9, leave or official duty. Bedroom, community bath (101); bedroom, hall bath (39); two bedroom, private bath (3); three bedroom, private bath (3); various bedroom/bath combinations (4). Refrigerator, kitchen (some units), limited utensils, color TV, housekeeping service. Older structure, redecorated. Rates: leave/official duty, sponsor $14, adult, child $15 each. Maximum varies with unit. Duty can make reservations, others Space-A. No pets allowed.

DV/VIP: No separate office, call billeting, O6+. Retirees, lower ranks Space-A.

TML Availability: Fairly good. Best Sept thru Mar. Difficult other times.

CALIFORNIA
Camp San Luis Obispo, continued

There is a small aircraft museum on post, and don't miss local state beaches. Visit local wineries, Hearst Castle, San Luis Obispo Mission Plaza and Farmers Market.

Locator 549-3800   Police 911

China Lake Naval Air Warfare Systems Center, Weapons Division (CA34R4)
Central Billeting, Bldg 1395
China Lake NWC, CA 93555-6100

TELEPHONE NUMBER INFORMATION: Main installation numbers: C-619-939- 9011, D-312-437-9011.

Location: From US-395 or CA-14, take CA-178 east to Ridgecrest and the main gate. *USMRA: Page 111 (G-10,11,12; H-11).* NMC: Los Angeles, 150 miles southwest.

Lodging Office: Bldg. 1395, **C-619-939-3146**, 24 hours daily. Check in after 1500, check out 1200 hours daily. Government civilian employee billeting.

TML: Transient House. Ten buildings, all ranks, leave or official duty. Three bedroom, private bath, kitchen (utensils on request). A/C, CATV, housekeeping service, telephone, washer/dryer. Rates: $25 per family of 3, $4 each additional person. Duty can make reservations, others Space-A.

TML: BOQ. 00496, 00499, officers all ranks, leave or official duty. Bedroom, private bath (24). Refrigerator, central cooling, color TV, CATV in lounge, individual heaters, hall phones, housekeeping service. Older structure. Rates: $12 per person, 1 per room. Personnel on orders can make reservations, others Space-A.

TML: BEQ. 1915 Mitscher, enlisted, all ranks, leave or official duty. Three bedroom, private bath (4). Kitchen, utensils on request, A/C, CATV, housekeeping service, washer/dryer. Older structure. Rates: $15 per family of 3, $4 each additional person. Reservations PCS in/out only. Personnel on orders can make reservations, others Space-A. Pets allowed at extra cost.

TML: BEQ. 1805 Harpoon, building 02340, E1-E6, leave or official duty. Bedroom, shared bath (39). A/C, color TV, CATV in lounge, housekeeping service, washer/dryer. Older structure. Rates: $6 per person. Unaccompanied personnel only. Duty can make reservations, others Space-A.

TML: BEQ. Building 1395, E7-E-9, leave or official duty. Bedroom, shared bath (12). A/C, color TV, CATV in lounge, housekeeping service, washer/dryer. Older structure. Rates: $8 per person. Unaccompanied personnel only. Duty can make reservations, others Space-A.

TML: DV/VIP. Buildings 00662, 00663, officers O6/GS-15+, leave or official duty. Three bedroom suites, private bath (4). Kitchen, utensils, A/C, CATV, housekeeping service. Older structure. Rates: $34 family of three, $4 each additional person. Duty can make reservations, others Space-A.

DV/VIP: Protocol Office, C-619-939-2383/3039, D-314-437-2383/3039, O6+. Retirees and lower ranks Space-A.

TML Availability: Good.

26 - Temporary Military Lodging Around the World

CALIFORNIA
China Lake Naval Air Warfare Systems Center, Weapons Division, continued

Four wheelers enjoy hundreds of trails nearby, while popular mountain areas (Mammoth, June and the Greenhorn Mountains) draw other enthusiasts year round. Visit Red Rock Canyon, and Fossil Falls.

Locator 939-2303   Medical 939-2911   Police 939-3323

Club Del Cottages (Camp Del Mar Beach) (CA03R4)
Lodging Office, Bldg 210595
Camp Pendleton, CA 92055-5018

TELEPHONE NUMBER INFORMATION: Main installation numbers: C-619-725-7935, D-312-365-2463.

Location: Exit I-5 on Harbor Drive/Camp Pendleton. Enter either the Del Mar Gate or the Main Gate on Camp Pendleton. Approximately 2.5 miles from either gate. *USMRA: Page 111 (F-14,15)*. NMC: Oceanside, 1 mile south.

Lodging Office: Building 210595, **C-619-725-2134**, 0800-2200 hours. Check in facility 1400-1630 hours daily. Late arrival should be pre-arranged. Check out 1200 hours daily. No government civilian employees billeting.

TML: Club Del, mobile homes, officer, enlisted E6+, leave or official duty. Two bedroom, private bath, beach front, sleeps 6 (12). Four bunk beds, 1 double, full bath, living room, kitchen w/refrigerator, microwave, stove, coffee maker, cooking utensils, TV. No. 7 is doublewide, 4 bedrooms, sleeps 16 with 8 beds, 4 sleeper couches, 2 baths, fully equipped kitchen. One bedroom, double bed and sleeper couch sleeps 4 (47). Fully equipped kitchen and bath. Housecleaning aids furnished, bring bed linens, pillows, dish soap, towels, food and firewood, Ice vending, washer/dryer. Rates: $30, winter/summer, 1-2 bedroom units; $30, 4 bedroom units $60. Trailer #9/E9 only, #10/O6 only, #11/O7 only. If checkout occurs during non-working hours, patron forfeits the right to be present for inspection. Reservations all categories, must be paid 4 weeks prior to occupancy. Duty and Reservists, Camp Pendleton, can make reservations 12 weeks in advance, duty and Reservists (other stations) 10 weeks, retirees, 8 weeks. No bumping, mail in reservations not accepted. Call 619-725-2134 for further information. No Pets.

TML Availability: Good, Oct-Apr. Difficult, other times.

CREDIT CARDS ACCEPTED: Visa, Mastercard and Discover.

All ocean activities available in the area, a 26 mile Ocean shoreline. Oceanside, San Clemente, and Carlsbad nearby.

Coronado Naval Amphibious Base (CA38R4)
Combined Bachelor Quarters
BOQ Bldg #500
San Diego, CA 92155

TELEPHONE NUMBER INFORMATION: Main installation numbers: C-619-437-2011, D-312-577-2011.

Location: From San Diego, I-5 south to Palm Ave (CA-75) west 10 miles. Follow signs to Naval Amphibious Base, Coronado. *USMRA: Page 118 (C,D-7,8)*. NMC: San Diego, 5 miles north.

CALIFORNIA
Coronado Naval Amphibious Base, continued

Billeting Office: Building 504, Tulagi St, **C-619-437-3860**, FAX 619-437-3475 (BOQ); building 302, **C-619-437-3494**, D-312-577-3494, FAX 619-437-2556 (BEQ), 24 hours daily. Check in billeting 1500, check out 1200 hours daily. For group reservations call C-619-437-5268, D-312-577-5268.

TML: BOQ. Buildings 500, 504, 505, officers all ranks, leave or official duty. Accessible to handicapped. Bedroom units, private bath (374); separate bedroom, private bath (90). Refrigerator, color TV, housekeeping service, washer/dryer, ice vending. Modern structure. Rates: sponsor $11, guests $2.75. Duty can make reservations, others Space-A reservations 24 hours in advance.

TML: BEQ. Building 302, enlisted all ranks, leave or official duty. Handicapped accessible. DV suite private bath (4), DV suite, common bath (2), E7-E9 common bath (10), E5-E6 common bath (87), E1-E4 common bath (36). Housekeeping service, refrigerator, color TV, washer/dryer. Rates: DV $12 per person, E1-E9 $6 per person. Duty can make reservations, others Space-A after 1800 hours.

TML: DV/VIP. Building 504. Officers O6-10, leave or official duty. Separate bedroom suites, private bath (20). Refrigerator, color TV, housekeeping service, washer/dryer, ice vending. Modern structure. Rates: Sponsor $25, guests $6.75. Duty can make reservations, others Space-A 24 hours in advance.

DV/VIP: Reservations: C-619-437-3860, O6+/civilian equivalent. Retirees Space-A.

TML Availability: Good most of the year.

CREDIT CARDS ACCEPTED: Visa, MasterCard and American Express.

Coronado Bay and the Pacific Ocean offer all water sports; Seaport Village and Sea World are good family fun. There are a multitude of attractions in San Diego.

Locator 437-2011   Medical 437-2375/2376   Police 437-3432

Edwards Air Force Base (CA48R4)
95 SVS/SVMH
115 Methusa Avenue
Edwards AFB, CA 93524-5000

TELEPHONE NUMBER INFORMATION: Main installation numbers: C-805-277-1110, D-312-527-1110.

Location: Off CA-14, 18 miles east of Rosamond and 30 miles northeast of Lancaster. Also, off CA-58, 10 miles southwest of Boron. *USMRA: Page 111 (F,G-12)*. NMC: Los Angles, 90 miles southwest.

Lodging Office: Building 5602, **C-805-277-4101/3394**, FAX 805-277-2517, DSN FAX 312-527-2517, 24 hours daily. Check in 1400, check out 1200 hours daily.

TML: VOQ. Buildings 5601, 5602, officers all ranks, leave or official duty. Bedroom, semi-private bath (81). Fully furnished, A/C, color TV, housekeeping service, washer/dryer, ice vending. Older structure, newly furnished. Rates: $8 per person. Duty can make reservations, others Space-A.

TML: VAQ. Buildings 5603, 5604, all ranks, leave or official duty. Building 5603: Rooms (54). Building 5604: One bedroom SNCO suites (9). Rates: $14 per person **(Note: No SNCO suites until**

CALIFORNIA
Edwards Air Force Base, continued

March 1996 due to ongoing renovations). A/C, color TV, housekeeping service, washer/dryer. Older structure. Rates: $8 per person. Duty can make reservations, others Space-A.

TML: TLF. Bldgs 7022-7031, all ranks. One bedroom suite/family quarters, private bath (51). Double & single bed, sleeper couch in living room, A/C, color TV, washer/ dryer, kitchen. Rates: $21. PCS personnel can make reservations, others Space-A.

TML: DV/VIP. Building 5601, officer O6+. One bedroom suites, private bath (10). A/C, color TV, housekeeping service. Older structure. Rates: $14 per person. Duty can make reservations, others Space-A.

DV/VIP: Protocol, ATTN: AFFTC/CCP, Bldg 2650, room 200, C-805-277-3326. O7+/SES.

TML Availability: Good, all year.

CREDIT CARDS ACCEPTED: Visa, MasterCard and American Express.

Los Angeles, 90 miles southwest, many Southern California attractions are nearby.

Locator 277-2777   Medical 277-4427   Police 277-3340

El Centro Naval Air Facility (CA09R4)
Bldg 401
El Centro NAF, CA 92243-5001

TELEPHONE NUMBER INFORMATION: Main installation numbers: C-619-339-2524, D-312-958-8408

Location: Take I-8, 2 miles west of El Centro, to Forrester Rd exit, 1.5 miles to Evan Hewes Highway left west for 4 miles, right on Bennet Rd to main gate. *USMRA: Page 111 (H-15,16).* NMC: El Centro, 7 miles east.

Lodging Office: Building 401, **C-619-337-4645/4918,** D-312-958-4645/4918, FAX 619-337-4936, 24 hours daily. Check in billeting, check out 1000 hours daily. Government civilian employees on orders billeted.

TML: Navy Lodge. Building 388, 392 all ranks, leave or official duty. Reservations: **1-800-NAVY-INN.** Lodge number is 619-339-2478. Two bedroom trailers, one queen, one double bed, private bath (5), one handicapped accessible unit. Kitchenette, utensils, microwave, coffee/tea, A/C, CATV, housekeeping service, cribs, mini mart, free washer/dryer, picnic grounds, playground. Rates: $39 per unit. All categories can make reservations.

TML: BOQ. Building 270, officers, leave or official duty. Bedroom, 2 beds, private bath (36); separate bedrooms, private bath (2); bedroom suite, private bath (DV/VIP) (2). Refrigerator, limited utensils, A/C, color TV in room & lounge, housekeeping service, ice vending. Older structure, remodeled. Rates: $12 per person, VIP $15. Duty can make reservations, others Space-A. Also TVQ rooms ($3). Inquire.

TML: BEQ. Building 4001. Enlisted, all ranks, leave or official duty. Bedroom, 2 beds, shared bath (48); suites, private bath E7+ (6); single bed, shared bath (24). Refrigerator, CATV, A/C,

CALIFORNIA
El Centro Naval Air Facility, continued

housekeeping services, M-Sa., TV lounge, arcade games, snack machines, non smoking lounge. New structure Rates: $4 - $8. Duty, reservists on orders, retired Space-A.

DV/VIP: Contact billeting, O6+, retirees Space-A. C-619-339-8535.

TML Availability: Fair. Sep-Jun, more difficult.

CREDIT CARDS ACCEPTED: Visa, MasterCard and American Express.

Hunting, fishing, golf, tennis, hiking and camping are all available in the Imperial Valley, it is also the winter home (Jan-Mar) of the "Blue Angels".

Locator 339-2555   Medical 339-2675/2666   Police 339-2525

El Toro Marine Corps Air Station (CA22R4)
Lodging Office, Bldg 58
El Toro MCAS, CA 92709-5001
Scheduled to close 12/31/99.

TELEPHONE NUMBER INFORMATION: Main installation numbers: C-714-726-3011, D-312-997-3011.

Location: Off I-5, take the Sand Canyon Rd exit. Follow signs to MCAS. *USMRA: Page 111 (F-14); Page 117 (G,H-7,8).* NMC: Los Angeles, 40 miles northwest.

Lodging Office: Building 58, **C-714-726-2381/6000/3001,** D-312-977-2381/6000/3001, FAX-726-3308, 0700-2400 hours daily. Check in facility, check out 1200 hours daily. Government civilian employee billeting.

TML: TLF. Building 823, four blocks from main gate. All ranks, leave or official duty. C-714-726-3500/2084, 0700-2000 hours daily. Suites, sitting room, bedroom, queen size bed, sofa bed (24). Kitchen, complete utensils, A/C, color TV in room & lounge, housekeeping service, coin washer/dryer, ice vending, facility for DAVs. Modern structure. Close to exchange, 7 day store and commissary. Rates: $33 per unit. Maximum 4 per unit. Duty can make reservations, others Space-A.

TML: TOQ/DVQ. Buildings 33, 35, 248, 249, 250 (DGQ), 375 officers all ranks, leave or official duty. C-714-726-3001. Bedroom, shared bath; separate bedrooms, private bath (17); two bedroom suite, private bath (2); three bedroom suite, private bath (3). Kitchen (5 units), refrigerator, A/C, color TV in room & lounge, housekeeping service, cots, washer/dryer, ice vending. Rates: common bath rooms $6.50; private bath rooms, $9.50, $4 each additional guest; civilians $7; suites $15, $4 each additional guest; DVQ rooms $20, each additional guest $5, maximum $30.

TML: TEQ, EFQ (Enlisted Family Quarters). Buildings 660, 668. Bedroom, queen bed, private bath (E6+) (28); bedroom, shared bath (to E5, 4 persons per room); EFQ bedrooms, private bath (43). Refrigerator, microwave, cooking facilities, washer/dryer, housekeeping service, color TV in room (EFQ in lounge). Rates: $7 TEQ, $4 each additional guest; $4-$5 EFQ.

TML: Big Bear Recreation Area. Write to: The Lodge, building 823, MCAS El Toro, Santa Ana, CA 92709, **C-714-726-2626/2572,** D-312-997-2626/2572. All ranks, leave or official duty. Chalets, one bedroom, sofa bed, living room, loft (2 double beds) (8). Kitchen, microwave, utensils, fireplace, color TV, bring personal items, many recreational facilities.

30 - Temporary Military Lodging Around the World

CALIFORNIA
El Toro Marine Corps Air Station, continued

All categories may make reservations, active duty MCAS El Toro and Tustin have priority. See *Military Living's Military RV, Camping and Rec Areas Around the World* for additional information and directions.

DV/VIP: Building 250, C-714-726-3624, O6+. Retirees and lower ranks Space-A.

TML Availability: Good, winter months. Difficult, summer months.

Orange County, Mission Viejo, Laguna Hills, Laguna Niguel and San Juan Capistrano Mission are all nearby.

Locator 726-2100   Medical 911   Police 726-3527/8

Fort Hunter Liggett (CA37R4)
ATTN: AFRC-FMH-PWH
P.O. Box 631
Jolon, CA 93928-5000

TELEPHONE NUMBER INFORMATION: Main installation numbers: C-408-386-5000, D-312-949-2291.

Location: From US-101 south exit at King City to CA-G-14, south to main gate. *USMRA: Page 111 (C-10)*. NMC: San Luis Obispo, 60 miles south.

Lodging Office: Building 205, **C-408-386-2511,** D-312-686-2511, FAX 408-386-2209, DSN FAX 312-686-2209, 0800-1630 hours duty days. Other hours SDO, building 205, C-408-386-2503. Check in 1200, check out 1000 hours daily. Government civilian employee billeting.

TML: Hacienda Guest House. Building T-101, all ranks, leave or official duty. Bedroom, private bath (6); bedroom, hall bath (5). Refrigerator, microwave, color cable TV, housekeeping service. Older structure. Rates: $25-$30 with bath, $15 without bath, $2 each additional person. Reservations accepted for duty only, others Space-A.

TML: VOQ/VEQ. Building T-128, officers and enlisted all ranks. Separate bedrooms, private bath (30). Share kitchen with adjoining room, refrigerator, A/C, color/cable TV, housekeeping service. Modern structure. Rates: officers, $23 per room, $5 each additional person. Reservations accepted duty only, others Space-A.

TML Availability: Good, most of the year.

CREDIT CARDS ACCEPTED: Visa, MasterCard, American Express, and Diners.

Famous for the yearly return of the swallows—just like Capistrano. The old California Hacienda formerly belonged to the Hearst family. Nearby is Mission San Antonio de Padua. Hunting and fishing available on post in season.

Locator 386-2533/2520   Medical 386-2570   Police 386-2613

Temporary Military Lodging Around the World - 31

CALIFORNIA

Fort Irwin National Training Center (CA01R4)
Lodging Office, Bldg 109
Fort Irwin, CA 92310-0041

TELEPHONE NUMBER INFORMATION: Main installation numbers: C-619-380-4111, D-312-470-4111.

Location: Take I-15 east from Los Angeles for 125 miles or I-15 west from Las Vegas, NV, for 150 miles. Fort is north of I-15 near Barstow, watch for signs. *USMRA: Page 111 (G,H-11,12)*. NMC: San Bernardino, 60 miles southwest.

Lodging Office: Building 109, Langford Lake Rd, **C-619-380-4599/1428**, 24 hours daily. Check in 1400-1800 hours, check out 1200 hours daily.

TML: Guest House. All ranks, leave or official duty. Mobile homes, private bath. Kitchen, utensils, A/C, color TV, housekeeping service, washer/dryer. Reservations accepted. Rates: moderate. Maximum 6 per unit. All categories eligible, early reservations suggested.

TML: DVQ. Building 28, officers O6+, C-EX-3000. Bedroom, private bath (8). Refrigerator, A/C, color TV, housekeeping service. Modern structure. Rates: moderate. Maximum 1-3 per unit. Reservations required.

DV/VIP: Protocol, building 151, C-619-380-3000, O6+. Lower ranks Space-A.

TML Availability: Good, winter. Difficult, summer.

Visit NASA's Goldstone Deep Space Tracking Station for a group tour. Rainbow Basin has many interesting fossils (<u>not</u> collectable!), and Park Moabi Marina in a quiet cove off the Colorado river are of interest to visitors.

Locator 380-3369   Medical 380-3242   Police 380-4444

Fort MacArthur (CA46R4)
Fort MacArthur Inn
2400 South Pacific Avenue Bldg 37
San Pedro, CA 90731-2960

TELEPHONE NUMBER INFORMATION: Main installation numbers: C-310-363-8296, D-312-833-8296.

Location: At the end of Harbor 110 Freeway south, left on Gaffey Ave to 22nd St, left to Pacific Ave, right two blocks, left to gate. *USMRA: Page 117 (C-7)*. NMC: Los Angeles, 18 miles north.

Lodging Office: Fort MacArthur Inn, Building 37, Sout Pacific Avenue, **C-310-363-8296**, 24 hours. Check in 1800, check out 1100 hours.

TML: TLF. Building 40, all ranks, leave or official duty. Reservations only for official duty, others Space-A. Separate bedrooms, private bath (22). Sofa becomes double bed, chair, single bed. Kitchen, utensils, color TV, HBO, housekeeping service, cribs/cots, washer/dryer, ice vending. Older structure. Renovated '92. Rates: based on rank, $24 per night. Maximum 3-5 per room.

CALIFORNIA
Fort MacArthur, continued

TML: VOQ/VAQ. Building 36, all ranks. Reservations only for official duty, others Space-A. Bedroom, private bath (27). Microwave, complete utensils, color TV, HBO, housekeeping service, cribs/cots, washer/dryer, ice vending. Older structure. Rates: $8 per person, maximum $16.

TML: DV/VIP. Cottages 14-17, officers O7+, leave or official duty. Two bedroom units, private bath (2); bedroom, private bath (2). Kitchen, utensils, color TV, housekeeping service, cribs/cots, washer/dryer. Older structure, renovated. Rates: sponsor $14, maximum $28 per family. Maximum 4 per cottage. Must make reservations through Protocol **C-310-363-3751.**

COTTAGES: 14-16 available to O6+ on a Space Available basis.

TML Availability: Best, Nov-Apr. Difficult, other times.

Locator 363-1876   Medical 363-8301   Police 363-8385

Fort Mason Officers' Club (CA45R4)
Bldg #1, Bay & Franklin Sts.
San Francisco, CA 94123-5000

TELEPHONE NUMBER INFORMATION: Main installation numbers: C-415-441-7700.

Location: Entrance on Bay and Franklin Sts, 3 blocks north of US-101 (Lombard Street). *USMRA: Page 119 (C-5).* NMC: San Francisco, in the city.

Lodging Office: Reservation Office: Building #1, Bay and Franklin Sts. **C-415-441-7700**, FAX 415-441-2680. Tu-Sa 0900-1700 hrs. Check in 1200 hrs, checkout 1100 hours daily.

TML: VIP Guest Quarters, historic building, officers all ranks, leave or official duty. Reservations advised up to 30 days in advance. Suites, private bath (2); bedroom, private bath (3); CATV, telephone, refrigerator, bar, housekeeping service, ice available, continental breakfast, morning paper and other amenities. Lunch and dinner available on scheduled days. Older structure, remodeled '90. Rates: Single or double, 1 bedroom $55; suites $65. Additional persons $10 extra, deposit required. Active duty, reserves, retirees or GS-7 DOD employees on official business.

TML Availability: Difficult, all year. Reservations accepted 30 days in advance. See listing for Marines' Memorial Club for additional lodging in San Francisco.

Fort Mason is a National Park. It offers a magnificent view of Alcatraz Island and San Francisco Bay. Close to North Beach, Fisherman's Wharf and Chinatown. Convenient location, good public transportation. Superb Officers' Club.

Lemoore Naval Air Station (CA06R4)
CBQ Billeting Fund
Bldg 852 (Code 4400)
Lemoore, CA 93246-5001

TELEPHONE NUMBER INFORMATION: Main installation numbers: C-209-998-0100, D-312-949-1110.

Location: On CA-198, 24 miles east of I-5, 30 miles west of CA-99 in the south central part of the state. *USMRA: Page 111 (D-10).* NMC: Fresno, 40 miles north northeast.

CALIFORNIA
Lemoore Naval Air Station, continued

Lodging Office: Barracks 7, building 852, Hancock Circle, **C-209-998-4784**, FAX 209-998-3236, 24 hours daily.

TML: Navy Lodge. Building 908/909, all ranks, leave or official duty. For reservations call **1-800-NAVY-INN**. Lodge number is 209-998-5791, D-312-949-4861, FAX 209-998-6149. Check out 1200 hours daily. Efficiency rooms, private bath, 2 queen beds (38), 1 queen bed and 1 sofa (6), handicapped accessible (2). Kitchenette, complete utensils, A/C, CATV, housekeeping service, coin washer/dryer, ice vending. Completely renovated '93. Rates: sponsor $36. Maximum 5 per room. All categories can make reservations. Military member may sponsor guest. Non smoking rooms available.

TML: BEQ. Building 852, enlisted all ranks, leave or official duty. Check in/out (1200 hours daily) at billeting office. Rooms (48), two persons per room. Refrigerator, microwave, A/C, CATV, VCRs, housekeeping service, ice vending, washer/dryer, sauna, jacuzzi, weight room, library, BBQ area. Modern structure. Rates: Sponsor $4. Duty can make reservations, retirees & DAVs Space-A.

TML: BOQ. Building 800, officer all ranks, leave or official duty, C-209-998-4609. Check in/out (1200 hours daily) front desk of facility. Rooms, private bath (60). Refrigerator, microwave, A/C, CATV, VCRs, housekeeping service, washer/dryer, ice vending, 50" TV in lounge, sauna, jacuzzi, weight room, library, BBQ area. Modern structure. Rates: On orders $8. Retirees, DAVs, reservists Space-A, others can make reservations.

DV/VIP: Commanding Officer, C-209-998-3344, O6+. Retirees Space-A.

TML Availability: Good all year.

CREDIT CARDS ACCEPTED: Visa, MasterCard and American Express. The Navy Lodge accepts Visa, MasterCard, American Express and Discover.

In the San Joaquin Valley, near Sequoia and Yosemite National Parks, two hours from the coast or mountains, and three hours from Los Angeles and San Francisco. Excellent base facilities.

Locator 998-3789   Medical 998-4435   Police 998-4749

Long Beach Naval Shipyard (CA55R4)
CBQ, Bldg 422
300 Skipjack Road
Long Beach, CA 90822-5099
Scheduled to close 9/30/97

TELEPHONE NUMBER INFORMATION: Main installation numbers: C-310-547-6202, D-312-360-6202.

Location: Take Long Beach Freeway, CA-710 south, to Terminal Island exit to NS. Clearly marked. *USMRA: Page 117 (C,D-7).* NMC: Long Beach, 2 miles east.

Lodging Office: Building 422, Skipjack Road, **C-310-547-7924/7928**, D-312-360-7928, FAX 310-521-0287, 24 hours daily. Check out 1200 hours.

CALIFORNIA
Long Beach Naval Shipyard, continued

TML: Navy Lodge. All ranks, leave or official duty. Check in 1500-1800 hours daily, check out 1200. For reservations call **1-800-NAVY-INN**. Lodge number is 310-833-2541, FAX (For group reservations only) 310-519-5197. Bedroom, 2 double beds, private bath (50). Six interconnecting, 2 handicapped accessible and 25 non-smoking. Kitchenette, microwave, utensils, CATV, clocks, coffee/tea, cots, cribs, hair dryers, ice, housekeeping service, auto-mart, playground, rollaways, snack vending, washer/dryer. Rates: $48 per room. All categories can make reservations.

TML: BOQ. Building 423, officers, all ranks, leave or official duty. Check in 24 hours daily. Check out 1200 hours. Handicapped accessible. Bedroom rooms and suites, private and semi-private baths (71). Refrigerator, food vending, ice vending, housekeeping service, color TV, washer/dryer. Older structure. New phone system and CATV. Rates: $8 (room), $12 (suite). Maximum one person. Duty can make reservations, others Space-A.

TML: BEQ. Building 422, 423, 297, enlisted, all ranks. Bedroom, private and semi-private baths (600). Refrigerator, food vending, housekeeping service, CATV, washer/dryer. Modern structure. Rates: sponsor $4. Maximum 3 per unit. Duty can make reservations, others Space-A.

TML Availability: Extremely limited. Best Nov-Jan. Difficult May-Jul.

CREDIT CARDS ACCEPTED: Visa, MasterCard, American Express and Discover at the Navy Lodge.

The Marina has boat rentals, sailing lessons and a clubhouse, "Gull Park" is on the tip of the Mole, and "Marine Park" is used for picnics and has a great view of Los Angeles Harbor.

Locator 547-6002   Medical 547-7979   Police 547-7731

Los Alamitos Armed Forces Reserve Center (CA39R4)
Bldg 19, 11200 Lexington Drive
Los Alamitos, CA 90720-5001

TELEPHONE NUMBER INFORMATION: Main installation numbers: C-310-795-2000 D-312-972-2000. Police 795-2100.

Location: Off I-605 east of Long Beach. Clearly marked. *USMRA: Page 117 (E-6,7).* NMC: Los Angeles, 35 miles northwest.

Billeting Office: Bldg 19, Armed Forces Reserve Center. **C-310-795-2124**, FAX & Voice 310-795-2125, D-312-972-2124. Check in facility Sat-Thur 0800-1630, Fri 0800-2000, check out 1200 hours daily. After duty hours pick up key at Security, Bldg 57.

TML: TLF. All ranks, leave or official duty. Two bedroom shared, shared bath (female) (10); Two bedroom shared bath (enlisted) (198); two bedroom shared, hall bath (officers) (37); bedroom, private bath (O6+) (10); suites, private bath (O7+) (5). Amenities: After 1300 on Sunday, any authorized soldier/retiree/Federal or Civil employee may reserve a VIP &/or O6 quarters for their use until Friday. E1-O5 share quarters. Duty can make reservations, others Space-A.

TML Availability: Limited, particularly on weekends, call ahead.

Temporary Military Lodging Around the World - 35

CALIFORNIA
Los Alamitos Armed Forces Reserve Center, continued

CREDIT CARDS ACCEPTED: Visa, MasterCard, American Express, and Diners'.

Los Alamitos is used extensively for reserve training, but Anaheim (Disneyland!) and Orange County, including great beach cities are nearby.

Los Angeles/Long Beach Coast Guard
Eleventh Coast Guard District (CA25R4)
USCG LHA LA/LB P.O. Box 3127
Terminal Island Station
San Pedro, CA 90731-0208

TELEPHONE NUMBER INFORMATION: Main installation numbers: C-310-514-6450/6451.

Location: Take Gaffey St. exit off Hwy 110. Take Gaffey till road ends. Co-located with PT Fermin Lighthouse on Coast Guard Base, Terminal Island, San Pedro, CA, 13 miles west of Long Beach. *USMRA: Page 117 (C-7).* NMC: Long Beach, 11 miles east.

Lodging Office: Local Housing Office, LA/LB, P.O. Box 3127, Terminal Island Station, San Pedro, CA 90731-0208, **C-310-514-6450/6451**, FAX 310-514-6459, 0730-1600 M-F, check in lodging office 1400, check out 1100 hours daily. Government civilian employee billeting on Space-A basis only.

TML: Guest House. **Point Fermin.** All ranks, leave or official duty. Two bedroom, private bath (2). Kitchen, complete utensils, color TV, washer/dryer. Outstanding View. Rates: vary by rank. Active Duty, Reservists and retirees can make reservations on a priority basis.

TML Availability: Good year round, but very busy Jun-Sep & holiday weekends.

Close to beach cities, Los Angeles harbor, and all that Southern California has to offer.

March Air Force Base (CA08R4)
The March Inn
655 M Street, Ste 4
March AFB, CA 92518-2113
Scheduled to close 3/3/96

TELEPHONE NUMBER INFORMATION: Main installation numbers: C-909-655-1110, D-312-947-1110.

Location: Off CA-60 and on I-215 which bisects AFB. *USMRA: Page 111 (G-14).* NMC: Riverside, 11 miles southwest.

Lodging Office: 655 M Street, Ste 4, **The March Inn**, **C-909-655-5241**, FAX 909-655-4574, DSN FAX 312-947-4574, 24 hours daily. Check in lodging office, check out 1100 hours daily.

TML: VOQ/VAQ/TLF. Buildings 100, 102, 125, 501, 2418, 2419, 2420, 2421, all ranks, leave or official duty. Rooms, apartments, & suites (500+ beds). Refrigerator, kitchen or kitchenette (except for bldg. 2418), A/C, color TV room & lounge, housekeeping service, cots & washer/dryer, ice vending. Modern structures. "McBride Suites" (VOQ). TLF refurbishing includes new TVs, dishware, cookware and blinds. Recent VAQ refurbishment. Rates: VOQ, sponsor $8; VAQ, sponsor $8; TLF, sponsor, $23; suites $12-$14. Duty can make reservations, others Space-A.

CALIFORNIA
March Air Force Base, continued

DV/VIP: HQ 15th Air Force, Protocol, March AFB, D-909-655-4764, O6+ duty or on leave. DVQ rate: $12-$14. Lower ranks Space-A.

TML Availability: Good, Oct-Feb. More difficult, May-Sep.

CREDIT CARDS ACCEPTED: Visa, MasterCard and American Express.

This Inn has more than 500 bedspaces, serving 40,000 visitors a year with a staff of about 65, lots of recent improvements, a good place to stay. See nearby Riverside, the Mission Inn, Castle Park, Riverside Raceway.

Locator 655-3192   Medical 7-911   Police 7-911

Mare Island Naval Shipyard (CA56R4)
Mare Island Naval Shipyard, CA 94592-5000
Scheduled to close 4/30/96.

CLOSED - 1996

Marines' Memorial Club (CA20R4)
609 Sutter Street
San Francisco, CA 94102-5000

TELEPHONE NUMBER INFORMATION: Main installation numbers: C-415-673-6672, FAX 415-441-3649. Reservations, **1-800-5-MARINE** or **415-673-6604 (direct).**

CALIFORNIA
Marines' Memorial Club, continued

Location: Use CA-101 or CA-580. Take CA-580 north to SF, cross the Bay Bridge. Take 5th St exit, up 5th St to O'Farrell. Turn right and go to Powell St. Turn left, go to Sutter St, turn left. Corner of Sutter and Mason. *USMRA: Page 119 (C-5).* **Author's Note:** This is NOT "military lodging" in the sense that we list other military installations in this book. The Marines' Memorial Club is a club/hotel exclusively for uniformed services personnel, active duty & retirees and their guests. Any former member of the Armed Forces of the United States with an Honorable discharge may join the club. Call 1-800-5-MARINE for information. The club is not a part of the government but is a private, non-profit organization and is completely self-supporting. This club/hotel is a living memorial to Marines who lost their lives in the Pacific during WWII. It opened on the Marine Corps' Birthday, 10 Nov 1946, and chose as its motto "A tribute to those Marines who have gone before; and a service to those who carry on."

Office: Check in and out at lobby desk. Check out 1200 hours daily. Occupancy limited to two weeks except when vacancies exist, 24 hours daily. For brochure or more info write to the above ATTN: Club Secretary, or call 415-673-6672.

TML: Hotel, all ranks, leave or official duty. Guest rooms (137); deluxe suites (11); family suites (3). Reservations required. Courtesy coffee/tea in room, ice, soft drinks vending, room service, large closets. Rates: average room $65-70, average suite $150. Rates higher for guests of members. All active duty military services, PHS and NOOA considered as members. Retirees membership fee tax deductible. Club facilities include theater, library/museum, swimming pool, gym, coin-operated launderette, valet, exchange store, package store, rooms for private parties, and a dining room and lounge in the Skyroom on the 12th floor, overlooking San Francisco. Convenience store/news stand and coffee shop outside hotel adjacent to entrance. Hotel discount parking on Sutter St. Ask at desk.

TML Availability: Best, winter months. Make reservations well in advance.

CREDIT CARDS ACCEPTED: Visa, MasterCard, American Express and Diners.

In the heart of San Francisco, within walking distance of Cable Cars, many major attractions.

Medical 911   Police 553-0123

McClellan Air Force Base (CA35R4)
77 SPTG/SVML
5405 O'Malley Ave
McClellan AFB, CA 95652-1003

TELEPHONE NUMBER INFORMATION: Main installation numbers: C-916-643-4113, D-312-633-1110.

Location: Off I-80 North. From I-80 take Madison Ave exit. Clearly marked. *USMRA: Page 110 (C-6).* NMC: Sacramento, 10 miles southwest.

Lodging Office: Building 89, 5405 O'Malley Ave, Palm Gate, **C-916-643-3267,** 916-643-6223, D-312-633-6223, FAX 916-643-6222. Check in billeting 24 hours daily, check out 1200 hours daily. Government civilian billeting.

TML: Guest House. Building 1430, all ranks, leave or official duty. One & two bedroom available, private bath (20). Kitchen, utensils, A/C, color TV, cribs/cots, washer/dryer. Modern structure. Rates: $24 per unit. Duty can make reservations, others Space-A. Also, VOQ/VAQ available for single occupancy only $8.

38 - Temporary Military Lodging Around the World

CALIFORNIA
McCellan Air Force Base, continued

DV/VIP: Protocol, building 200, C-916-643-4311. O6+. Retirees/lower ranks Space-A.

TML Availability: Good, winter months. Difficult, summer through fall months.

CREDIT CARDS ACCEPTED: Visa, MasterCard, American Express and Diners.

Northern Californian skiing, water sports, and Sacramento cosmopolitan activities make McClellan a good choice for a stopover.

Locator 643-4113   Medical 643-4733   Police 643-6160

Miramar Naval Air Station (CA14R4)
BQ MGR, Code 193A/Bldg M312
19920 Polaris Ave
San Diego, CA 92145-5399

TELEPHONE NUMBER INFORMATION: Main installation numbers: C-619-537-1011, D-312-577-1011.

Location: Fifteen miles north of San Diego, off I-15. Take Miramar Way exit or Miramar Rd exit. *USMRA: Page 118 (C,D-2,3,4; E,F-2,3).* NMC: San Diego, 15 miles southwest.

Lodging Office: Building M-312. Check in facility, check out 1200 hours daily. **C-619-537-4235,** D-312-577-4235, FAX 619-537-4243, DSN FAX 312-577-4243. Desk 619-537-4233, D-312-577-4233.

TML: Navy Lodge. Building 516, all ranks, leave, official duty or retirees. Reservations: **1-800-NAVY-INN**. Lodge number is C-619-271-7111, D-312-577-4855, FAX 619-695-7371, 24 hours daily. Check in 1500-1800, check out 1200. Units, two double beds (40), queen (4), king (16), double w/sofa bed (28), handicapped rooms (2), all w/private bath. Seventy non smoking. Kitchenette, microwave, stovetop, refrigerator, toaster, complete utensils, A/C, CATV, coffee/tea, phones, cribs, rollaways, coin washer/dryer, housekeeping service, mini-mart. Modern structure. Rates: $41 per unit. All categories can make reservations. Kennels near lodge on base.

TML: BEQ. Building 639, 640, enlisted, leave or official duty only, 24 hours daily. Shared room, private bath (104). CATV, washer/dryer. Older structure. Rates: $6.50 per person. Duty on orders can make reservations, others Space-A.

TML: BOQ. Building M-312, M-325, all officer ranks, leave or official duty, 24 hours daily. Rooms & suites, private and shared baths. Color TV, housekeeping service, washer/dryer. Older structure. Rates: $12 per person. Duty on orders can make reservations, others Space-A.

DV/VIP: C-619-537-1221, O6+. Retirees Space-A.

TML Availability: Good Nov-Dec, summer difficult.

CREDIT CARDS ACCEPTED: Visa, MasterCard and Navy Travel Card. Navy Lodge accepts Visa, MasterCard, American Express and Discover.

CALIFORNIA
Miramar Naval Air Station, continued

San Diego's Old Town, Shelter and Harbor Islands, Sea World, and Balboa Park downtown, are all not to be missed. Water sports, golf, tennis, and nearby Mexico will keep visitors from ever being bored in this lovely city.

Locator 537-1011   Medical 537-4655   Police 537-1213

Moffett Federal Air Field (CA15R4)
Moffett, CA 94035-5000
This installation has been converted to a NASA & Federal agency base.

TELEPHONE NUMBER INFORMATION: Main installation numbers: C-415-604-5000, D-312-359-5000.

Location: On Bayshore Freeway, US-101, 35 miles south of San Francisco, CA. *USMRA: Page 119 (F-9).* NMC: San Jose, 7 miles south.

Lodging Office: C-415-603-9503, D-312-359-9503, 24 hours daily. Reservations C-415-603-9805.

TML: Navy Lodge, Bldg 593, Vernon Ave., Mountain View CA 94013. All ranks, leave or official duty, reservists, retirees. For reservations call **1-800-NAVY-INN**, Lodge number is 415-962-1542, FAX 415-694-7538, 0700-2300 hours daily. Bedroom, 2 double beds, kitchenette, microwave, private bath (50). Housekeeping service, washer/dryer, ice vending. Modern structure. Rates: $43 per unit. All categories can make reservations.

TML Availability: Limited.

CREDIT CARDS ACCEPTED: Visa, MasterCard, and American Express are accepted at the Navy Lodge.

Visit historic Hangar One for a trip into Naval Aviation. Carmel by the sea and Pebble Beach are nearby.

Locator 604-5000   Medical 603-8251   Police 604-5461

Monterey Naval Postgraduate School (CA16R4)
Combined Bachelor Quarters
1 University Circle, Room 118a
Monterey, CA 93943-5007

TELEPHONE NUMBER INFORMATION: Main installation numbers: C-408-656-2441/2/3. D-312-878-2441/2/3.

Location: Take CA-1 North to central Monterey exit, right at light onto Camino Aguajito. Immediate, very sharp, right onto Tenth Street, left onto Sloat Ave and into Main Gate. Or South on CA-1, take Aguajito Rd exit to Mark Thomas Dr, left on Sloat Ave, turn right into Main Gate. *USMRA: Page 111 (B-9).* NMC: Monterey, in city limits.

Billeting Office: Building 220, **Herrmann Hall**, 1 University Circle, **C-408-656-2060/69**, FAX 408-656-3024, D-312-878-2060/69, DSN FAX 312-878-3024, 24 hours daily. Check in billeting 1500

CALIFORNIA
Monterey Naval Postgraduate School, continued

hours with reservation, 1600 hours for Space-A, check out 1100 hours daily. Write to: CBQ, Monterey, CA 93943. Government Civilian employee billeting (BOQ). Duty billets available during school vacations.

TML: BOQ. Buildings 220, 221, 222, officers all ranks, official duty and Space-A. Bedroom, private bath (139); two room suites (VIP) (4); single room suites (VIP) (4). Microwave, refrigerator, TV, VCR, telephone, housekeeping service, cots/cribs washer/dryer, food/ice vending, pool table. Older, structure. Rates: standard room $10 per day per person, $2.50 each additional guest; single VIP suite $20, $5 each additional guest, two room suite ($25), each additional guest $6 per day. Duty can make reservations. No children under 12. No pets.

TML: BEQ. Buildings 259, 205 enlisted E1-E9, on official duty. Check out 1100 hours. Three (3) Bedrooms, (6 spaces for males, 3 spaces for females). Refrigerator (in room), TV, washer/dryer, vending machine, fooseball and exercise equipment in lounge. Unaccompanied personnel only. No pets.

DV/VIP: Building 220, officers O6+, official duty, and Space-A can make reservations at C-408-656-2511/2/3/4.

TML Availability: Best, Christmas during school vacation. Other times, extremely limited. Call for availability.

In the heart of one of the most prestigious areas of California, The BOQ (Herrmann Hall) began life as the Hotel Del Monte. Nearby are Pebble Beach, 17 mile drive, Steinbeck's Cannery Row, Fisherman's Wharf and Carmel Mission.

Locator 656-2441   **Medical 656-2333**   **Police 656-2555**

North Island Naval Air Station (CA43R4)
Lodging Office, Bldg I
North Island NAS, CA 92135-0001

TELEPHONE NUMBER INFORMATION: Main installation numbers: C-619-545-1011, D-312-735-0444.

Location: From I-5 north or south exit at Coronado Bridge (toll). Also, from CA-75 north to CA-282 to base. In Coronado. *USMRA: Page 118 (B,C-6,7)*. NMC: San Diego, 4 miles northeast.

Lodging Office: Building I for officers, **C-619-545-7545**, FAX 619-545-9220. Building 773 for enlisted, C-619-545-9551, 24 hours daily. Check in facility (between 1500-1800 for confirmed reservations), check out 1200 hours daily. Government civilian employee billeting available at BOQ.

TML: Navy Lodge. Building 1402, all ranks, leave, official duty, retirees. Reservations call **1-800-NAVY-INN**. Lodge number is 619-545-6940. Bedroom, 2 queen beds, private bath (90). Kitchen, limited utensils, A/C, color TV, housekeeping service, cribs, coin washer/dryer, ice vending. Modern structure on ocean front, all rooms renovated in '93. Rates: $50. Maximum 5 per room. All categories can make reservations. *New 100 room addition scheduled to open November 1996.*

DV/VIP: PAO. C-619-545-8167, O6+, retirees and lower ranks if approved by commander.

CALIFORNIA
North Island Naval Air Station, continued

TML Availability: Good, except Apr-Oct.

CREDIT CARDS ACCEPTED: Visa, MasterCard, American Express and Discover accepted at Navy Lodge.

North Island is the birthplace of Naval aviation. The San Diego Trolley connects to downtown and bus routes. See Mission Valley, the zoo, Balboa Park. 100 additional Navy Lodge units available November 1996.

Locator 545-1011   Medical 545-4306   Police 545-7423

Oakland Army Base (CA18R4)
Jacobs Hall Guest Facility
Bldg 650, Oakland Army Base
Oakland, CA 94626-5000

TELEPHONE NUMBER INFORMATION: Main installation numbers: C-510-466-9111, D-312-859-9111.

Location: Near junction of I-80, I-580, and CA-880, south of the San Francisco Oakland Bay Bridge. *USMRA: Page 119 (D-5)*. NMC: Oakland, 2 miles southeast.

Lodging Office: Jacobs Hall, building 650, **C-510-466-3205**, FAX 510-466-2997, D-312-859-3113, DSN FAX 312-859-2997, 24 hours daily. Check in front desk, check out 1100 hours daily. Government civilian employee billeting.

TML: Guest House, Building 650, all ranks, leave or official duty. Bedroom, double beds, private bath (23); two room suites, queen-size bed, living room, sofa bed, private bath (25); three room suites with bedroom, living room, den with sofa bed, private bath (4). All have refrigerator, cable color TV w/HBO. Video movie rentals, ice vending, housekeeping service, irons and ironing boards, complimentary coffee, some non-smoking rooms. Modern structure. Rates: Standard $35-$45, two room suite $45-$55, three room suites $55-$65. All categories can make reservations.

TML Availability: Good.

CREDIT CARDS ACCEPTED: Visa, MasterCard, American Express, Diners and Discover.

Lake Merritt, Lakeside Park, the Oakland Museum, Jack London Square in Oakland are of interest to visitors. Across the bay is San Francisco itself; just north is the wine country and the Redwoods, both treasures.

Locator 466-9111   Medical 466-2918   Police 466-2424

Petaluma Coast Guard Training Center (CA23R4)
Bldg T-134, Nevada Avenue
Petaluma, CA 94952-5000

TELEPHONE NUMBER INFORMATION: Main installation numbers: C & FTS-707-765-7211.

Location: Exit US-101 north to East Washington Ave West. Follow Washington Ave 9 miles west to Coast Guard Training Center. *USMRA: Page 110 (B-6,7)*. NMC: San Francisco, 49 miles south.

CALIFORNIA
Petaluma Coast Guard Training Center, continued

Lodging Office: Building T-134, Nevada Avenue, **C-707-765-7248**, 0900-1700 hours daily. Check in at facility, check out time discussed with manager. Government civilian employee billeting, maximum stay 2 weeks. Reservations accepted Mon-Fri from 0800-1800.

TML: TLQ. Building 134, all ranks, leave or official duty. Bedroom, private bath (8); Four person unit, semi-private bath (1). Refrigerator, color TV, cribs, washer/dryer, ice vending, microwave. Older structure. Rates: $20 per room, semi-private rooms $10. All categories can make reservations. PCS have priority.

DV/VIP: One VIP suite in Harrison Hall (O6+), leave or official duty. Private bath, refrigerator, color TV, housekeeping service. Rate: $25 per night. Retirees Space-A. Call CO's office for reservations, C-707-765-7248.

TML Availability: Generally good. Difficult, summer months.

The Petaluma area is saturated with historical lore and legend. Early California missions, a Russian fort (Fort Ross), Sonoma County wineries, and Russian River swimming, fishing and canoeing will all draw visitors.

Locator 554-4020   Medical 765-7200   Police 765-7215

Point Mugu Naval Air Weapons Station (CA40R4)
The Missile Inn, CBQ
Point Mugu NAWC, CA 93042-5000

TELEPHONE NUMBER INFORMATION: Main installation numbers: C-805-989-1110, D-312-351-1110.

Location: Eight miles south of Oxnard and 40 miles north of Santa Monica, on Coast Highway, CA-1. *USMRA: Page 111 (E-13).* NMC: Los Angeles, 50 miles southeast.

Lodging Office: The Missile Inn, CBQ, building 27, D Street, between Sixth and Seventh Streets. **C-805-989-8255/8235**, D-312-351-8255, FAX 805-989-7470, DSN FAX 312-351-7470, 24 hours daily. Check in facility, check out 1000 hours daily. Government civilian employee billeting.

TML: BOQ. Various buildings, some cottages. Officers all ranks, leave or official duty. Bedroom, two beds, private bath, (46). Refrigerator, color TV, VCR, housekeeping service, roll-away cots, washer/dryer, essentials, food and ice vending. Older structure, renovated. Rates: $10 per person per room; suites $15. Duty and civilians on orders can make reservations, all others Space-A.

TML: BEQ. Enlisted E1-E6, leave or official duty. Bedrooms, common bath. Refrigerator, color TV, VCR, housekeeping service, essentials, food vending, washer/dryer. Older structure, renovated. Rates: E1-E4 $6 per person, E5-E6 $8, E7-E9 $12, O1-O5 $10 room and $12 suite. Duty only can make reservations, unaccompanied retirees Space-A. No dependents.

TML: TVEQ. Enlisted E7-E9, leave or official duty. Suites, private bath (9). Refrigerator, color TV, VCR, housekeeping service, essentials, food and ice vending, washer/dryer. Older structure, renovated. Rates: Suites $15 per person. Eligibility same as BEQ.

TML: DV/VIP. Building 170, officers O6+, leave or official duty. Bedroom suites, private bath (8). Kitchenette, above amenities. Older structure, renovated. Rates: $15 room and $25 suite. Duty can make reservations, others Space-A.

Temporary Military Lodging Around the World - 43

CALIFORNIA
Point Mugu Naval Air Weapons Station, continued

TML: Recreational Motel: **The Mugu Lagoon Beach Motel. C-805-989-8407,** D-312-351-8407. All ranks, leave or official duty. Check in at facility, 24 hours daily. Check out 1100 hours. Late check out call front desk. Bedroom, 2 beds, private bath (22); suites, 2 beds, private bath (2). Kitchenette, limited utensils, color TV, housekeeping service, essentials, cribs/cots, coin washer/dryer, handicapped accessible, ice vending. Rates: $40, each additional person $4; suites $57, each additional person $4. All categories may make reservations. Snack/convenience store. New facility 1993, in wildlife refuge area. Availability very good year round, most difficult in June, July, and August.

TML: Beach Cabins, on one of the finest surfing and swimming beaches in California. All ranks, retired, DoD civilians, base contractors, family members and guests. **C-805-989-8407.** D-312-351-8407. Bedrooms, two rooms, one double bed, one hideaway, private bath (6); Kitchen, utensils, CATV, fenced in porch, housekeeping, barbecue, pets at an additional fee. Rates: $33, each additional person $4. All categories may make reservations.

DV/VIP: Command Protocol, building 36, C-805-989-8672, O6+.

TML: Availability: Fair. Difficult, Mar-Sep.

CREDIT CARDS ACCEPTED: Visa, MasterCard and American Express.

This facility is on the Pacific Ocean, close to the great shopping in Santa Monica, and within reach of coastal range recreation as well as the famous beaches of Southern California. Full range of support facilities on base.

Locator 989-7209   Medical 989-8875   Police 989-7670

Port Hueneme Naval Construction Battalion Center (CA32R4)
Bldg 1435, Pacific Road
Port Hueneme NCBC, CA 93043-5000

TELEPHONE NUMBER INFORMATION: Main installation numbers: C-805-982-4711, D-312-360-4711.

Location: Seven miles west of US-101. Take Victoria Ave exit in Ventura to Channel Islands Blvd, left to Ventura Road, right to Pleasant Valley Road, turn right and enter at Pleasant Valley Gate. *USMRA: Page 111 (D,E-13).* NMC: Los Angeles, 40 miles southeast.

Lodging Office: Building 1435, Pacific Road. **C-805-982-4497**, 24 hours daily. Check in at facility. Government civilian employee no billeting.

TML: Navy Lodge. Building 1172, all ranks, leave or official duty. Reservations required. For reservations call 1-800-NAVY-INN. Lodge number is 805-985-2624, FAX 805-984-7364. Check in 1500-1800, check out 1200. Two double beds, private bath, kitchenette, (22);. Queen size bed, private bath (26). 11 non-smoking rooms. Microwave, coffee/tea, color TV, housekeeping service, cots, phones, cribs, coin washer/dryer, mini-mart, picnic grounds, playground, ice vending, Western Union. Modern structure, remodeled. Rates: Single $46; double $50. Maximum 4 persons. Duty and retirees can make reservations, others Space-A.

CALIFORNIA
Port Hueneme Naval Construction Battalion Center, continued

TML: BEQ: Duty only, C-805-982-4497, FAX 805-982-4948. BOQ: Duty only, C-805-982-5785, FAX 805-982-5622. Female enlisted quarters: Duty only, C-805-982-4497. May have TML Space-A.

TML: DV/VIP. Guest House, buildings 39, 1435, officers O6+, leave or official duty. Reservations required, call protocol C-802-985-4741, check in Building 1164. Building 39, 1 cottage (Doll House), private bath. Kitchen, utensils, color TV, housekeeping service. Older structure (1925), patio. Active Duty can make reservations, others Space-A.

DV/VIP: Planning & Mobilization Office. Building 14, Room 204, C-805-982-4401, O7/GS-16+.

TML Availability: Good, winter months. Difficult, summer months.

CREDIT CARDS ACCEPTED: Visa, MasterCard and American Express. Visa, MasterCard, American Express, Diners and Discover are accepted at the Navy Lodge.

In easy access of metropolitan Los Angeles, coastal Ventura County boasts wonderful weather. This is the home of the famous Seabees, a bustling complex of 10,000 military and civilians, and more than 1600 acres.

Locator 982-4711   Medical 982-6301   Police 982-4591

San Diego Marine Corps Recruit Depot (CA57R4)
MCRD Billeting
Bldg 625, 3800 Chosin Ave
San Diego, CA 92140-5196

TELEPHONE NUMBER INFORMATION: Main installation numbers: C-619-524-1011, D-312-524-1720.

Location: From airport, Pacific Coast Highway to MCRD exit. From Interstate 5 S and 8 W take Rosecrans exit, turn left on Midway, and right on Barnett Ave. *USMRA: Page 118 (C-6)*. In the city.

Lodging Office: Building 625, **C-619-524-4401**, FAX 619-524-0617, 24 hours, daily. Lodging available for DoD civilians on official duty.

TML: Transient Officers' Quarters. Building 312, officers, all ranks, leave or official duty. Check in billeting 24 hours daily. Check out 1200 hours. Suites with separate bedroom, private bath (10). Kitchenettes in suites, others common kitchen, refrigerators, coffee pots and essentials, color TV, telephones, housekeeping service, washer/dryer, cribs, new carpeting, recently remodeled modern structure. Handicapped accessible. Rates: sponsor $20, additional adult $2. Maximum $22 per family. Maximum 3 persons per room. Military on orders have priority, others Space-A. No pets.

TML: Transient Enlisted Quarters. Buildings 619, 625, enlisted all ranks, leave or official duty. Check in billeting 2400 hours daily, check out 1200 hours. Room with two beds, private bath (39); suites, separate bedroom, private bath (2); units with shared bath (178). Refrigerator, coffee pots, essentials, housekeeping service, color TV, washer/dryer, cribs. Modern structure, new carpeting, satellite service, telephones, new furniture in each room. Handicapped accessible. No pets. Rates: sponsor $8, additional adult $7. Maximum $15 per family. Maximum 2 per room. Military on orders have priority, others Space-A.

TML: DV/VIP. Building 31, room 238. Protocol officer, D-619-524-1275, O6+. Active duty and retirees, DoD civilians: TOQ & TEQ available. Others Space-A.

Temporary Military Lodging Around the World - 45

CALIFORNIA
San Diego Marine Corps Recruit Depot, continued

TML Availability: Good to very good. Best Jan-May, Sep-Dec. Difficult Jun-Aug.

CREDIT CARDS ACCEPTED: Visa, MasterCard, American Express and Discover.

This is the Marine Corps' oldest operating installation on the West coast, and is a short distance from downtown San Diego. Check out San Diego Zoo, Seaworld, beaches, fishing, and bargain shopping in nearby Tijuana, Mexico.

Locator 524-1728   Medical 524-4079   Police 524-4202

San Diego Naval Station (CA26R4)
Combined Bachelor's Quarters
Naval Station Box 368145, Code 84
2450 McHugh St., Suite 1
San Diego, CA 92136-5395

TELEPHONE NUMBER INFORMATION: Main installation numbers: C-619-556-1011, D-312-526-1011.

Location: Off I-5, 7 miles south of San Diego Airport. Take 28th St exit. NS is at 28th & Main Sts. *USMRA: Page 118 (D-7,8)*. NMC: San Diego, 7 miles south.

Lodging Office: Bldg 3362 (BEQ), Building 3144 (BOQ). **C-619-556-8672 (BEQ)**, FAX 619-556-9325, **C-619-556-8156 (BOQ)**, FAX 619-556-9325, 0730-1630 hours daily. Other hours, Watch Section/Central Assignments, Building 3362. Check in facility, check out 1200 hours daily. Government civilian employees billeting.

TML: Navy Lodge. Building 3191, 3526, all ranks, leave or official duty. For reservations call **1-800-NAVY-INN.** Lodge number is 619-234-6142, FAX 619-238-2704, 24 hours daily. Check in 1500, check out 1200 hours. 143 total units, 2 double beds, private bath (82); King size bed, private bath (8); One double bed, private bath (48). Five handicapped accessible, 105 non-smoking. Each room sleeps 5. Kitchenette, utensils, microwave, coffee, A/C, CATV, clocks, phones, cribs, rollaways, coin washer/dryer, ice vending, vending machine, playground, heated swimming pool, housekeeping service. Rates: $44-$50. Government civilian employees billeting if O2+ equivalent with ID and orders. All categories can make reservations.

TML: BEQ. Building 3362, enlisted all ranks, official duty only. Beds, semi-private bath (E7+ private bath) (3500). Telephone, TV lounge, housekeeping service, washer/dryer, ice vending. Rates: E1-E6 $8 per person, E7-E9 $10-$12 per person, (4) DoD civilian VIP rooms available at $12. Dependents not authorized. Reservations required.

TML: BOQ. Building 3203, officers all ranks, official duty only. Bedroom, private bath (75); separate bedrooms, private bath (57). Telephones, refrigerator, color TV, housekeeping service, washer/ dryer, ice vending. Rates: $8 per person. Maximum 2 per room. Children not authorized. Duty can make reservations, others Space-A.

TML: BOQ. Building 3144, officers all ranks, official duty only. Bedroom, private bath (77), two room suite with kitchenette (8). All rooms have telephones, CATV, microwave, refrigerator, coffee, housekeeping service, washer/dryer, ice vending. Rates: $10-$18 per person. Children not authorized. Duty can make reservations, others Space-A.

CALIFORNIA
San Diego Naval Station, continued

TML: Fisher House. San Diego Naval Medical Center. Note: Appendix C has the definition of this facility. **C-619-532-9055.**

TML Availability: Good except PCS rotations, summer months.

CREDIT CARDS ACCEPTED: Visa, MasterCard, American Express and Discover. The Navy Lodge accepts Visa, MasterCard, American Express, Diners and Discover.

America's Finest City welcomes you to vacation paradise! Visit the world famous San Diego Zoo, Wild Animal Park, Sea World, Seaport Village, Old Town, Balboa Park and much more. Enjoy the best year-round climate in the U.S.

Locator 556-1011   Medical 556-1801   Police 556-1526

San Diego Naval Submarine Base (CA79R4)
Dolphin Lodge & Inn
140 Sylvester Rd., Bldg 601
San Diego NSB, CA 92106-3521

TELEPHONE NUMBER INFORMATION: Main installation numbers: C-619-553-1011, D-312-933-1011.

Location: From I-5 take Rosecrans west onto base. *USMRA: Page 118 (B-6).* NMC: San Diego, in the city.

Lodging Office: Dolphin Lodge and Inn. BOQ. Building 601, Sylvester Road, **C-619-553-9381**, FAX 619-553-0613, BEQ Building 300, **C-619-553-7533.** Check in facility. Check out 1200 hours.

TML: BOQ. Building 601. Officers, all ranks, official duty or leave. Bedroom, private bath (75); separate bedrooms, kitchenette, private bath (55). Roll-away beds, food/ice vending, utensils, housekeeping service, refrigerator, telephones, voice-mail, CATV, washer/dryer, weight room, billiard room, jacuzzi, two catering facilities. Modern structure. Rates: sponsor $15, VIP suites $25, additional person $3. Duty can make reservations, others Space-A.

TML: BEQ. Building 300, enlisted, E1-E6, official duty or leave. Rooms with various bath combinations; MCPO suites (2). Food/ice vending, housekeeping service, refrigerator, telephones, voice-mail, CATV, washer/dryer. Modern structure. Rates: sponsor $6; MCPO suites $20. Duty can make reservations, others Space-A.

TML Availability: Fairly good. Best Oct-Dec. Difficult May-Aug.

CREDIT CARDS ACCEPTED: Visa, MasterCard and American Express.

Located on beautiful Point Loma, with a spectacular view of San Diego Harbor, and the city, this facility is on the bus line close to beaches, Old Town, Sea World, the San Diego Zoo, and many other recreational delights.

Locator 553-1011   Police 553-7070   Medical 532-6400

Temporary Military Lodging Around the World - 47

CALIFORNIA

San Diego Naval Training Center (CA54R4)
Lodging Office, Bldg 584
San Diego, CA 92133-5000
Scheduled to close 12/31/98.

TELEPHONE NUMBER INFORMATION: Main installation numbers: C-619-524-1011, D-312-524-1011.

Location: From I-8 W take Rosecrans exit to Lytton St, left on Lytton to NTC gate #1. From I-5 N take Rosecrans exit, left on Lytton to gate. From I-5 S take Pacific Highway exit to Barnett Ave which becomes Lytton St, turn left to Gate #1. *USMRA: Page 118 (B,C-6)*. NMC: San Diego, 4 mi E.

Lodging Office: Bldg 584, **C-619-524-4788,** D-312-524-4788, 0630-1530 hours M-F.

TML: BEQ. Building 584. Rates: Single $4, others $2 each.

TML: BOQ. **Admiral Kidd Inn,** building 82, officers all ranks, leave or official duty, **C-619-524-5382,** Fax 619-524-0754. Separate bedroom, shared bath. Refrigerator, microwave, CATV. Rates: $18.

TML: DV/VIP. Officers, **C-619-524-0558.** Rates: $20, $5 additional person. Enlisted, **C-619-524-4788.** Rates: $15.

See Mission Valley, the zoo, and Balboa Park.

Locator 524-1935   **Medical 524-4929**   **Police 524-5796**

San Diego YMCA Inns (CX01R4)
500 West Broadway
San Diego, CA 92101-5000

TELEPHONE NUMBER INFORMATION: Main installation numbers: Reservations: **C-619-234-5252,** FAX 619-234-5272.

Location: Take CA-5 South to CA-8 East to 163 South; 163 turns into 10th Ave. Turn right on Broadway, to 500 West Broadway. *USMRA: Page 118 (C-6)*.

Author's Note: This is NOT "military lodging" in the sense that we list other military installations in this book. The Downtown Armed Services YMCA reopened this hotel under new management as "The Inn at the YMCA" February 1, 1993. It will continue to offer quality accommodations for budget travelers, students and the military. It is accessible to the harbor, the Greyhound Bus station, Amtrak, and trolley stations as well as being minutes from the airport. Also, Horton Plaza, The Gaslamp Quarter, Seaport Village, Little Italy, the San Diego Convention Center, Coronado Island, and the Santa Fe Train depot are close by. Services include a full-service restaurant, fitness facilities, indoor pool and hot tub, a large military lounge and recreation area, laundry and dry cleaning and a barber shop and 24 hour desk service. It is available to all military personnel, whether on duty or on leave, retirees and their guests at reduced rates. as well as budget travelers and students.

Office: Check in and out at lobby desk, 24 hours daily. Check out 1100 hours daily. For a brochure or more info write to: The Inn at the YMCA, 500 West Broadway, San Diego, CA 92101, or call the above number.

CALIFORNIA
San Diego YMCA Inns, continued

TML: Hotel, all ranks, leave or official duty. Guest rooms, private bath (224). Reservations required. Refrigerator, microwave, color TV in lounge and in room, housekeeping service, coin operated washer/dryer, handicapped accessible units, food vending (restaurant on premises). Rates: $15 per person, per night, $80/week, $290/month ($55 deposit for weekly/monthly guests). Cash, travelers checks, money orders and government issued checks. No pets.

TML: La Pensione Hotel. 1546 Second Ave, San Diego, CA 92101. **C-619-236-9292,** FAX-619-236-9988, 24 hours daily. Free airport limousine transportation, Highway 5 South, exit Civic Center, right on Second Ave. This non-military hotel is owned by the same company that owns the Inn at the YMCA. It caters to military personnel, with special programs and rates. Bedrooms, private bath, each equipped with a refrigerator and microwave, color TV, housekeeping service, coin washer/dryer, handicapped accessible units, and has a Deli on the premises. Rates: $29.95 per person, per night, $140 per week. All categories may make reservations. No pets.

TML Availability: Good, best in winter months. Make reservations well in advance.

In the heart of San Diego, and within walking distance of a trolley system that can take you to famous Southern California beaches, a world class zoo, and Mexico!

Sierra Army Depot (CA44R4)
Lodging Office, Bldg P144
Herlong, CA 96113-9999

TELEPHONE NUMBER INFORMATION: Main installation numbers: C-916-827-2111, D-312-855-4910.

Location: 55 miles north of Reno, NV, off US-395. Right on CA-A26 from Reno. When traveling south on US-395, left on CA-A25. *USMRA: Page 110 (E-4).* NMC: Reno, 55 miles southeast.

Lodging Office: Building P144, **C-916-827-4544,** D-312-855-4544, FAX 916-827-5360, DSN FAX 312-855-5360, duty hours. Other hours, Sec Radio Room, Building P-100, C-916-827-4345. Check in facility, check out 1100 hours daily.

TML: Guest House, building P144, (Club), all ranks, leave or official duty. Bedroom, private bath (15). Microwaves (in 5 apartments), refrigerator, limited utensils, housekeeping service, cribs/cots, TV, VCR, washer/dryer. New structure. Rates: $38-$53. PCS/TDY can make reservations, all others Space-A.

DV/VIP: PAO, C-916-827-4544. Determined by Commander.

TML Availability: Good, winter. Difficult, summer.

CREDIT CARDS ACCEPTED: American Express.

Water sports, hiking, skiing, and most outdoor activities are popular in this Northern California paradise. Lassen Volcanic National Park, the Eagle Lake Marina, and the Reno/Tahoe areas have rich recreational opportunities.

Locator 827-4328   Medical 827-4141/4575   Police 827-4345

The Armed Services Committee has approved MWR funds for a guest house for this facility. Keep updated with Military Living's travel newsletter, *R&R Space-A Report.*

CALIFORNIA

Stockton Naval Communications Station (CA51R4)
Lodging Office, Bldg 128
Stockton, CA 95203-5000

TELEPHONE NUMBER INFORMATION: Main installation numbers: C-209-944-0284/0343, D-312-466-7284/7343.

Location: From I-5 north exit at Rough & Ready Island, right at Fresno St to Washington St to Station. *USMRA: Page 110 (C-7)*. NMC: Stockton, in the city.

Lodging Office: Building 128, Hooper Dr & McCloy Ave, **C-209-944-0284/0343**, 0730-1600 M-F. Other hours. DMAA Office, building 128. Check in facility, check out 1200 hours daily.

TML: TLQ/BOQ/BEQ. Buildings 24, 128, 129, all ranks, leave or official duty. E7+ and civilian equivalents, suites (2). Rates: $8 per person. E5, E6 unaccompanied males, two persons per room. E4 and below male, four man rooms. E6 and below female, 2 women per room (1). Rates $4. For O3+ VIP suite (1). Rate: $25, each additional guest $15. Refrigerator, A/C, CATV, housekeeping service (M-F), washer/dryer. Under 12 free. Maximum 4 per room. Active Duty can make reservations, others Space-A.

TML Availability: Fairly good, winter months and holidays. Difficult, summer.

Situated between San Francisco, Sacramento and near Yosemite, Stockton is within reach of many California landmarks.

Locator 944-0284/0343   Medical 944-0445   Police 944-0451

Travis Air Force Base (CA50R4)
Westwind Lodge, Bldg 404
Travis AFB, CA 94535-2216

TELEPHONE NUMBER INFORMATION: Main installation numbers: C-707-424-1110/5000, D-312-837-1110.

Location: Off I-80 North, take Travis AFB Parkway exit. *USMRA: Page 110 (C-7)*. NMC: San Francisco, 45 miles southwest.

Lodging Office: Building 404, Sevedge Dr. **C-707-424-2987**, D-312-837-2987, FAX 707-424-5489, 24 hours daily. Check in facility, check out 1200 hours daily. Government civilian employee billeting.

TML: TLQ. Building 404, all ranks, leave or official duty. Studio apartments and two bedroom apartments, private bath (79). Kitchen, color TV, A/C, housekeeping service, telephone. Modern structure. Rates: $24 per unit. Duty can make reservations, others Space-A.

TML: VOQ. Building 404, officers all ranks, leave or official duty. Bedroom, semi-private bath (201). Refrigerator, A/C, TV, housekeeping service. Older structure. Rates: $8 per person. Duty can make reservations, others Space-A.

TML: VAQ. Building 404, enlisted all ranks, leave or official duty. Reservations accepted. Rooms with various bath combinations (645). Same as VOQ above.

CALIFORNIA
Travis Air Force Base, continued

TML: DV/VIP. Building 404, officer O6+, leave or official duty. D-312-837-3185. Suites, private bath (23). A/C, color TV, housekeeping service. Older structure. Rates: $14 per person. Duty can make reservations, others Space-A.

TML: Fisher House. Note: Appendix C has the definition of this facility. **C-707-423-7947.**

DV/VIP: DV lounge at Air Term, D-312-837-3185, O6+. Retirees Space-A.

TML Availability: Very limited, summer. Good, other times.

CREDIT CARDS ACCEPTED: Visa, MasterCard and American Express.

San Francisco, almost unlimited cultural and recreational opportunities. California beach towns and wine country, the capital city of Sacramento, and the Sierra Nevada mountains are all within reach of Travis.

Locator 424-2026   Medical 423-3462   Police 438-2011

Treasure Island Naval Station (CA21R4)
Bldg 369, California Avenue
Treasure Island NS, CA 94130-5004
Scheduled to close 9/30/97.

TELEPHONE NUMBER INFORMATION: Main installation number: C-415-395-1000, D-312-475-1000.

Location: On Treasure Island in San Francisco Bay off Hwy I-80 (Oakland Bay Bridge), take exit from left lane. *USMRA: Page 119 (C,D-5)*. NMC: San Francisco, 3 miles southwest.

Lodging Office: BOQ. Building 369, California Avenue, C-415-395-5274, D-312-475-5274, 24 hours. Reservations: **C-415-395-5273 (BOQ)**, D-312-475-5273; **C-415-395-5412 (BEQ)**, D-312-475-5412. Check in facility, check out 1100 hours daily. Space-A call after 1600 hours.

TML: BOQ/BEQ. All ranks, leave or official duty. BOQ rooms, private and semi-private baths (244). Refrigerator, color TV, housekeeping service, washer/dryer, hot tub, sauna, mini weight room. Older structure, renovated. Rates: sponsor $25, each additional person $8. Duty can make reservations, others Space-A.

DV/VIP: Protocol Office, Code 122, building 369, C-415-395-5001. O7+, retirees Space-A.

TML Availability: Good, Dec. Other times, limited.

Boat rentals at the base marina, miniature golf, theater, bowling and a fitness center are available on base; Golden Gate bridge, Fisherman's Wharf, Coit Tower, China Town and wonderful dining and entertainment in San Francisco.

Medical 395-3649   Police 395-5490

Temporary Military Lodging Around the World - 51

CALIFORNIA

Tustin Marine Corps Air Station (CA86R4)
Tustin MCAS, CA 92710-5001
Scheduled to close 12/31/97.

TELEPHONE NUMBER INFORMATION: Main installation numbers: C-714-726-3011, D-312-977-3011.

Location: Near the I-5 and 55 interchange, take Red Hill Ave exit. West 1.5 miles to main gate (Valencia is the cross street). *USMRA: Page 117 (G-7).* NMC: Irvine/Tustin, Los Angeles, 45 miles NW.

Lodging Office: Billeting Office, building 20A, Moffett/Cross Sts, **C-714-726-7984/7336,** D-312-997-7984/7336, 0700-1530 daily. After duty hours SDO, building 4, C-714-726-7324. Check in, check out at billeting.

TML: DV/VIP "Quarters C" (**Hideaway**). O6+, leave or official duty. Commanding Officer, MCAS Tustin. C-714-726-7301.

TML Availability: Difficult to extremely limited.

Located near Disneyland, Newport Beach, and Laguna, there is no shortage of entertainment nearby, if you can stay here.

Locator 726-3736   Medical 726-9911   Police 726-9911

Twentynine Palms Marine Corps Air/Ground Combat Center (CA27R4)
Billeting Fund
P.O. Box X-15
MCAGCC
Twentynine Palms, CA 92278-5006

TELEPHONE NUMBER INFORMATION: Main installation numbers: C-619-830-6000, D-312-957-6000.

Location: From west on I-10 exit on CA-62 NE to base. From east on I-40 exit south at Amboy. *USMRA: Page 111 (H,I-13,14).* NMC: Palm Springs, 60 miles southwest.

Lodging Office: Building 1565, 5th St near Desert View, Conference Center, **C-619-830-6573**, D-312-957-5980, FAX 619-830-5980, DSN FAX 312-957-5980, 24 hours daily. Check in facility 1400, check out 1100 hours daily. Government civilian employee billeting.

TML: BOQ/BEQ, all ranks, leave or official duty. VIP Quarters O4/GS-10+ (5); three CG guest house rooms; 16 rooms (O4+); 69 rooms (O1-O3); 40 SNCO rooms. Community kitchen, A/C, color TV, microwave in room & lounge, housekeeping service, washer/dryer, ice vending. Older structure. Rates: Adults $12, $15, $23. Duty can make reservations, except in guest house, others Space-A. No pets. No smoking rooms are available.

TML: TLF. Building 690, two miles from main gate. C-619-830-6583. One bedroom family units, trundle beds, private bath (24). Kitchen, washer/dryer, BBQ, playground. Walking distance to commissary, 7 day store, Burger King and Child Development Center. Rec equipment check out

CALIFORNIA
Twentynine Palms, continued

center available. Rates: $28 per unit. Maximum 6 persons per room. All ranks may make reservations. No pets.

DV/VIP: Protocol Office, C-619-830-6109, O4+. Retirees and lower ranks Space-A.

TML Availability: Good, winter months. Difficult, summer months.

CREDIT CARDS ACCEPTED: Visa, MasterCard, American Express and Diners.

Five miles from Joshua Tree national monument where the low Colorado and the high Mojave deserts come together. Many come from miles around to see the desert blooming with wild flowers.

Locator 830-6853   Medical 830-7254   Police 830-6800

Vandenberg Air Force Base (CA29R4)
Vandenberg Lodge
P.O. Box 5579
Vandenberg AFB, CA 93437-5079

TELEPHONE NUMBER INFORMATION: Main installation numbers: C-805-734- 8232, D-312-276-8232.

Location: From south on US-101, west on CA-246, north on CA-S20 to AFB. From north on US-101, west on US-1 from Gaviota, north on CA-S20 to AFB. *USMRA: Page 111 (C-12).* NMC: Santa Maria, 22 miles north.

Lodging Office: ATTN: **Vandenberg Lodge**, Building 13005, Oregon at L St. **C-805-734-8232, EX-6-2245**, FAX 805-275-0167, DSN FAX 312-276-0720, 24 hours daily. Check in billeting 1500, check out 1200 hours daily. Government civilian employee billeting.

TML: TLF. all ranks, leave or official duty. Handicapped accessible. One or four bedroom, private bath (26). Kitchen, complete utensils, CATV, housekeeping service, cribs/cots, washer/dryer, essentials. Modern structure. Rates: $16-$21 per room. Maximum 5 per room. Duty can make reservations. Retirees can make reservations for medical appointments only, others Space-A.

TML: VAQ. Building 13140A, enlisted all ranks, leave or official duty. Private bedroom/shared bath (61); Senior NCO quarters, E7+ (10), bedroom/private bath, living room with sofa bed. Vending machines, essentials. Rates: $7 per person; SNCO $10 per person. Also have (4) E9+ quarters at $14 per person. Duty can make reservations, others Space-A.

TML: VOQ. 11000 area. Officers all ranks, leave or official duty. Handicapped accessible. Bedroom, private bath (77); Essentials, ice vending. Modern structure. Rates: $10 per person. Maximum 2 persons per unit. Duty can make reservations, others Space-A.

TML: VOQ. Building 13800 area. Officers all ranks, leave or official duty. Private bedroom, private bath (96). Rooms arranged in quads, where full kitchen, living room and washer/dryer are shared. Rates: $10 per person. Duty can make reservations, others Space-A.

TML: DV/VIP. **Marshallia Ranch**, building 1338, officers O7/GS-16+, leave or official duty, C-805-734-3711. Four bedroom, private and semi-private bath, suites (4). Kitchen, utensils, A/C, color

CALIFORNIA
Vandenberg Air Force Base, continued

satellite TV, housekeeping service, washer/dryer, ice vending. Historic structure. Rates: $14 per person. All categories can make reservations.

DV/VIP: For reservations 30 SPW/CCP. C-805-734-3711. O6+.

TML Availability: Best, Nov-Jan. Difficult Apr-Oct.

CREDIT CARDS ACCEPTED: Visa, MasterCard and American Express.

Central Coastal California is a treasure trove for visitors. Visitors should see Solvang ("little Denmark"), Gaviota Beach, Santa Barbara and the Hearst Castle (San Simeon), to name only a few attractions within reach of Vandenberg.

Locator 6-1841   Medical 6-1847   Police 6-3911

The Navy Lodge at San Diego Naval Station. Photo courtesy of the Navy Lodge.

Too Late To Copy
Alameda Coast Guard Support Center, Housing Office, Bldg. 21, McCullough Dr. 0730-1530 daily. **C-510-437-3180**; other hours OOD, Bldg. 3, C-510-437-3304. Limited facilities. DV/VIP C-510-437-3303. Duty personnel only.
Camp Roberts, San Roberts, CA 93451-5000. Lodging Office, **C-805-238-8312**.

California, Too Late To Copy, continued on page 346

COLORADO

Fitzsimons Army Medical Center (CO10R3)
Fitzsimons Billeting
P.O. Box 6388
Aurora, CO 80045-6388
Scheduled to close. No closure date has been established.

TELEPHONE NUMBER INFORMATION: Main installation numbers: C-303-361-8241, D-312-943-8241.

Location: From I-70 take Peoria Ave (281), exit south on Peoria Ave, about 1 mile to Colfax Ave, Turn left (east) to first traffic light. Left again to enter main gate. From I-25 take I-225 north to Colfax Ave, west on Colfax Ave to third traffic light. Right at light to enter main gate. *USMRA: Page 116 (C-3)*. NMC: Denver 8 miles west.

Lodging Office: Building 400, Charlie Kelly Blvd, **C-303-361-8903**, D-312-943-8903, 24 hrs daily. Reservations accepted Mon-Fri 0800-1500. Check in/out at facility.

TML: VOQ/VEQ: Building 400, all ranks, leave or official duty. Check out 1100 hours daily. Rooms, private bath, 1 person (115); rooms, private bath, 2 persons (75). CATV, refrigerator, telephone w/wake-up service/private voice mail, coffee makers, cribs, rollaways, housekeeping service, washer/dryer, ice machine. No pets, kennels near installation. Rates: $18-$24. TDY military and DoD civilian, PCS military, reservists on individual orders, military family members on medical TDY orders and attendants to patients in hospital can make confirmed reservations, others Space-A.

TML: Fisher House. Note: Please see Appendix C for a definition of this facility. **C-303-361-4659**.

DV/VIP: Cmdr's office, C-303-361-8824, D-312-942-8824, O6+. Retirees Space-A.

TML Availability: Good, Oct-Dec. More difficult, other times.

CREDIT CARDS ACCEPTED: Visa, MasterCard and American Express.

Outdoor activities abound in two national parks, four national monuments, and eleven national forests. Denver visitors must see the state capital complex, US Mint, Larimer Square, and the Denver Museum of Art.

| Locator 361-8802 | Medical 361-3754 | Police 361-3791 |

Fort Carson (CO02R3)
Colorado Inn
Bldg 7301, Woodfill Road
Colorado Springs, CO 80913-5023

TELEPHONE NUMBER INFORMATION: Main installation numbers: C-719-526-3431, D-312-691-3431.

Location: From Colorado Springs, take I-25 or CO-115 south. Clearly marked. *USMRA: Page 109 (F,G-5,6) & Page 115 (C,D-6,7)*. NMC: Colorado Springs, 6 miles north.

Lodging Office: Colorado Inn, building 7301, Woodfill Road, **C-719-526-4832**, FAX 719-526-5239, 24 hours daily. Check in facility 1400 hours, check out 1100 hours daily. Government civilian

COLORADO
Fort Carson, continued

employee billeting. Phones in all rooms. **Reservations 60 days in advance.** No pets. Smoking and non-smoking rooms available.

TML: DV/VIP. Building 7305, officers O5+, enlisted E9, leave or official duty. One & two bedroom, private bath (8). A/C, kitchen, housekeeping service, CATV, washer/dryer. Older structure, renovated in 1993. Rates: sponsor, $28, adult $13, child under 16 free. Reservations through Protocol Office.

TML: VOQ/VEQ. Buildings 7302, 7304, all ranks, leave or official duty. Bedroom, private baths (156). Shared kitchenette, A/C, CATV, washer/dryer. Rates: sponsor $23.00, adult $10.00, child under 16 free.

TML: VEQ. Buildings 7301, all ranks, leave or official duty. Bedroom, shared bath (19). Shared kitchenette, A/C, CATV, washer/dryer. Rates: sponsor $20.00, adult $5.00.

DV/VIP: Protocol Office, building 1430, C-719-526-5811, O5+. Retirees, lower ranks Space-A.

TML Availability: Difficult. Best Nov-Apr.

CREDIT CARDS ACCEPTED: Visa, MasterCard and American Express.

Don't miss a visit to historic Pikes Peak, see the Royal Gorge and early mining towns, gambling casinos, and Cripple Creek, which lured thousands to the "golden west".

Locator 526-0227   Medical 526-7000   Police 526-2333

Peterson Air Force Base (CO06R3)
Bldg 1042, Stewart Avenue
Peterson AFB, CO 80914-5000

TELEPHONE NUMBER INFORMATION: Main installation numbers: C-719-556-7321, D-312-834-7321.

Location: Off US-24 (Platte Ave) east of Colorado Springs. Clearly marked. *USMRA: Page 109 (G-5) & Page 115 (D,E-5,6).* NMC: Colorado Springs, 4 miles west.

Lodging Office: Building 1042, Stewart Avenue, C-719-556-7851, D-312-834-7851. Reservations: **719-597-2010**, FAX 719-556-7852, 24 hours daily. Check in facility, check out 1100 hours daily. Government civilian employee lodging.

TML: TLQ. Buildings 1091-1094, all ranks, leave or official duty. Handicapped accessible. Bedroom, private bath (40). Refrigerator, kitchen, complete utensils, color TV, A/C, housekeeping service, cribs, washer/dryer, ice vending. Older structure, redecorated. Rates: $24 per unit, sleeps 4 persons. Duty can make reservations, others Space-A. Space-A policies same as VOQ below.

TML: VOQ. Buildings 1026, 1030. Officers all ranks, leave or official duty. Handicapped accessible. Bedroom, private bath (32); bedroom suites, private bath (DV/VIP) (33). Kitchen, cots, essentials, ice vending, refrigerator, A/C, color TV, housekeeping service, washer/dryer. Modern structures. Rates: sponsor/adult, building 1026 $8 per person, building 1030 $14 per person. Maximum 2 persons per unit. Maximum charge $16 (building 1026), $28 (building 1030). No children, no infants. Duty can make reservations, others Space-A. Space-A released when rooms clean and available. First come, first served. Unaccompanied dependents may be Space-A with active duty or retired sign in.

COLORADO
Peterson Air Force Base, continued

TML: VAQ. Building 1143, enlisted E1 to E6, leave or official duty. Bedroom, double occupancy, semi-private bath, (64); bedroom, double occupancy, private bath (18); senior NCO suites, private bath (7). A/C, color TV in room & lounge, refrigerator, housekeeping service, washer/dryer, ice/food vending, essentials. Modern structure. Rates: VAQ, sponsor/adult, $7 per person. No children, no infants. Maximum 2 persons per unit. Maximum charge $14. Rates: SNCO suites, sponsor/adult, $14 per person. Maximum 2 persons per unit. Maximum charge $28. No children, no infants. Duty can make reservations, others Space-A. Space-A policies same as VOQ above.

TML: DV/VIP. Buildings 999, 1026, 1030, officer O7+. Bedroom, private bath (10). A/C, cots, essentials, ice vending, kitchen w/complete utensils, housekeeping service, refrigerator, color TV, washer/dryer. Buildings 999 and 1030 upgraded. Rates: sponsor/adult, $14 per person. Maximum 2 persons per unit. Maximum charge $28 on leave, $14 active duty. No children, no infants. Rooms for protocol reservations. Lower ranks Space-A except 999.

DV/VIP: Protocol, building 1, 719-556-5007, O7+. Retirees Space-A. VOQ Space-A policies.

TML Availability: Difficult. Best Dec-Feb.

CREDIT CARDS ACCEPTED: Visa, MasterCard and American Express.

Area skiing and camping are some of the finest in the US; this is the home of NORAD, Space Command HQ. Visit historic Pikes Peak and USAF Academy.

Locator 556-4020   **Medical 556-4333**   **Police 556-4000**

United States Air Force Academy (CO07R3)
10 Service Squadron/SVML Bldg 3130
Academy Dr., Ste 100
Colorado Springs, CO 80840-4980

TELEPHONE NUMBER INFORMATION: Main installation numbers: C-719-472-1818, D-312-259-3110.

Location: West of I-25 north from Colorado Springs. Two gates, about 5 miles apart, provide access from I-25 and are clearly marked. *USMRA: Page 109 (F-4,5) & Page 115 (A,B,C-1,2,3).* NMC: Colorado Springs, 5 miles south.

Lodging Office: Building 3130, Academy Dr., **C-719-472-3060**, FAX 719-472-4936, 24 hours daily. Check in facility, check out 1100 hours daily. Government civilian employee lodging.

TML: DVQ. Building 3130, officers O7+, leave or official duty. Bedroom, private bath (8). Kitchen, study, living room, refrigerator, utensils, color TV, housekeeping service, washer/dryer, cribs/cots, ice vending, handicapped accessible. Modern structure, renovated. Rates: sponsor $14, adult $14. Maximum 2 per family. Most reservations handled through protocol office for O7+ and equivalent.

TML: VOQ. Building 3130/3134, officers all ranks, leave or official duty. Bedroom, private bath (10); separate bedrooms, semi-private bath (14); two bedroom, semi-private bath (16). Refrigerator, color TV in lounge, housekeeping service, cribs/cots, washer/dryer, ice vending, handicapped accessible. Modern structures. Rates: sponsor $8, adult $8, child $8, infant up to 2 years free. Maximum capacity depends on type of room. Duty can make reservations, others Space-A, will accept 3 days prior to arrival for non-confirmed space-A reservation.

COLORADO
United States Air Force Academy, continued

TML: TLF. Building 4700/02, all ranks, official duty or leave. Three bedroom houses (26). Kitchen, complete utensils, color TV, housekeeping service, cribs/cots, washer/dryer. Modern structures. Rates: $24 per night. Family quarters intended primarily for use by PCS personnel in/out. Others Space-A on day-to-day basis.

TML: Fisher House. Note: Appendix C has the definition of this facility. **C-719-472-3445.**

DV/VIP: Protocol Office, Harmon Hall, building 2304, room 328, C-719-472-3540, O7+.

TML Availability: Best, Jan-Apr. Difficult, other times.

CREDIT CARDS ACCEPTED: Visa, MasterCard and American Express.

At the foot of the Rocky Mountains, near skiing and mountain resorts. New visitor's center, gift shop and exhibits. Guided tours, 18 hole golf courses. Cadet Wing holds 1300 hrs formation, visitors watch from the chapel wall.

Locator 472-4262   Medical 472-5000   Police 472-2000

CONNECTICUT

New London Naval Submarine Base (CT01R1)
ATTN: CO/Lodging
Groton, CT 06349-5000

TELEPHONE NUMBER INFORMATION: Main installation numbers: C & FTS-203-449-3011, D-312-241-3011.

Location: From I-95 north take exit 86 to CT-12. Go left on Crystal Lane, right on to main gate. Base clearly marked. *USMRA: Page 16 (H-8) & Page 25 (C,D-1).* NMC: Hartford, 50 miles northwest.

Lodging Office: None. Call BOQ & BEQ for reservations and Space-A information (listed below).

TML: Navy Lodge, **off main base, from CT-12 South, left on Pleasant Valley Rd., left on Lestertown Rd, right on Dewey Ave.** 77 Dewey Ave, Groton, CT 06340, bldg CT-380, all ranks, leave or official duty. Check in 1500-1800 daily, check out 1200. For reservations call **1-800-NAVY-INN**. Lodge number is 203-446-1160 Fax 203-446-0808. Bedroom, 2 double beds, private bath (49), bedroom, queen bed and studio couch, private bath (18). Twenty four interconnecting, 2 handicapped accessible, 34 non-smoking. Kitchenette, microwave, utensils, A/C, CATV, clocks, coffee/tea, cribs, phones, housekeeping service, coin washer/dryer, picnic grounds, playgrounds, snack vending. Modern structure, renovated. Rates: $41 per unit. Maximum 4 persons. All categories can make reservations.

TML: BOQ. Buildings 379 D,M officers, all ranks, enlisted E7+, leave or official duty. **C-203-449-3416.** Check in 24 hours daily, check out 1100 hours daily. Bedroom, private bath (105); DVQ bedroom, private bath (7). A/C, kitchen, in room phones, CATV, housekeeping service, ice machine, coffee machines, essentials, washer/dryer. Newly renovated '93. Bar/night club in BOQ '93. Rates: $10 per person. DVQ bedroom $23.

TML: BEQ. Ten buildings. E1-E8, leave or official duty. **C-203-449-3117**, FAX 203-449-2673. Check in 1500, check out 1100 hours daily. Bedroom, 2 persons per room, shared bath (75); bedroom, shared bath (30) (new facility Aug.'93). A/C, color TV, telephones, housekeeping service, washer/dryer, microwave in lounge. Rates $8-$15 per night depending upon rank.

TML: TQ. **Chalet Susse International Hotel.** E6+ hotel on New London NSB. Check in 24 hours daily, check out 1100 hours. C-above number. Bedroom, private bath (150). A/C, refrigerator, CATV, telephones, laundry area, housekeeping service. Rates: $57.77 per night.

DV/VIP: Suites in BOQ and Swiss Chalet. Call above number.

TML Availability: Fairly good, Navy Lodge, all year.

CREDIT CARDS ACCEPTED: Visa, MasterCard and American Express. Visa, MasterCard, American Express and Discover are accepted at the Navy Lodge.

Visit Mystic seaport for history, USCG Academy, USS Nautilus Memorial/Submarine Force Library and Museum for a view of the modern Navy. Try a game of chance at Foxwood Casino.

Locator 449-3082   Medical 449-3666   Police 445-9721

Too Late To Copy
United States Coast Guard Academy, Bldg. 3130, New London, CT 06320. **C-203-446-1160.**

DELAWARE

Dover Air Force Base (DE01R1)
Lodging Manager
Bldg 805, 14th Street
Dover AFB, DE 19902-5000

TELEPHONE NUMBER INFORMATION: Main installation numbers: C-302-677-3000, D-312-445-3000.

Location: Off US-113. Clearly marked. *USMRA: Page 42 (I-3)*. Dover, 5 miles northwest.

Lodging Office: Building 805, 14th St (across from O'Club), **C-302-677-2841**, D-312-445-2841, FAX 302-677-2963, DSN FAX 312-445-2963, 24 hours daily. Check out 1200 hours daily.

TML: VOQ/TLF. Building 803, all ranks, leave or official duty. TLF: bedroom family suites, private bath (14); VOQ: bedroom, double beds, shared bath (27). Kitchenette, sofa sleeper (TLF) refrigerator, A/C, color TV, housekeeping service, cribs/cots, washer/dryer, ice vending. Older structure. Rates:$20. PCS/TDY can make reservations, others Space-A.

TML: VOQ/DV. Building 806, officers O4+, enlisted SNCOs, leave or official duty. Suites, private bath (DV) (10); suites, private bath (SNCO) (5). Refrigerator, A/C, color TV, housekeeping service, washer/dryer. Modern structure. Rates: $14 per person. Maximum 2 per room. (Arnold Suite by Protocol 677-4366).

TML: VAQ. Buildings 481, 482, enlisted E1-E4, leave or official duty. Bedrooms, single beds, common bath (92). A/C, color TV, refrigerator, housekeeping service, clock radio, coffee makers. Rates: $8. No children.

TML: VAQ. Building 801, all ranks, leave or official duty. Bedrooms, single beds, shared bath (55). A/C, refrigerator, color TV, housekeeping service, telephones, clock radio, coffee maker. Rates: $8.

TML: VAQ. Building 802, enlisted aircrew members, TDY, SNCOs. Bedrooms, single beds, shared bath (55). A/C, refrigerator, color TV, housekeeping service, telephones, clock radio, coffee maker. Rates $8. No children.

TML: VOQ. Buildings 804, 803 (Note: Bldg 803 will be renovated in late '95 into early '96) all ranks, leave or official duty. Building 805, official aircrew members. Bedrooms, double bed, shared bath (27); bedrooms, double beds, kitchenette, private bath (14). 805 bedrooms, double beds, shared bath (54). Rates: $8.

TML Availability: Very good, Oct-Apr. Very limited, other times.

Dover is the jumping off point for many Space-A flights to Europe and beyond. See *Military Space-A Air Opportunities Around the World*, and *Military Space-A Air Basic Training* for information on this money saver for the military.

Locator 677-3000   Medical 735-2600   Police 677-6664

DISTRICT OF COLUMBIA

Bolling Air Force Base (DC01R1)
11th Wing
Bolling AFB, DC 20332-5000

TELEPHONE NUMBER INFORMATION: Main installation numbers: C-202-767- 6700, D-312-297-0101.

Location: Take I-95 (east portion of Capital Beltway, I-495) north or south, exit to I-295 north, exit 1, right onto Overlook Ave at the light, and continue to South Gate. I-295 south, exit 1 to first light. Right at the light to the South Gate. From South Capitol St, south past Main Gate and bear right onto Overlook Ave to South Gate. Clearly marked. *USMRA: Page 55 (F-6)*. NMC: Washington, in southeast section of the city.

Lodging Office: Bolling Inn. Building 602, 52 Thiesen St, 1100 MWRS/MWMH. **C-202-767-5316**, FAX 202-767-5878, 24 hours daily. Check in billeting 1400, check out 1200 daily.

TML: TLF. Apartments, all ranks, leave or official duty. Separate bedrooms, private bath (49). Kitchen, A/C, color TV in room & lounge, housekeeping service, washer/dryer, ice vending. Older structure. Rates: $24 per room. Maximum 4 persons. Unaccompanied dependents not authorized. Reservations TDY, others Space-A.

TML: VOQ. Officer O1-O6, leave or official duty. Suites, private bath (55); Refrigerator, A/C, color TV in room & lounge, housekeeping service, washer/dryer, ice vending. Rates: $14 per person. Reservations TDY personnel only, others Space-A.

TML: VAQ. Enlisted E1-E6. Bedroom, shared bath (44); Refrigerator, CATV, housekeeping service, washer/dryer. Older structure. Rates: $8 per person. Reservations TDY, others Space-A.

TML: VIP. O7+. Suites, private bath (23). Refrigerator, A/C, color TV, housekeeping service, washer/dryer. Older structure. Rates: $14 per person. Duty can make reservations. Also senior noncommissioned officers' quarters, $14 per person, reservations via Protocol. Others Space-A.

DV/VIP: Protocol Office, building P-20, C-202-767-5584, O7+. Retirees Space-A.

TML Availability: Difficult. Better during winter months.

CREDIT CARDS ACCEPTED: Visa, MasterCard and American Express.

On the Potomac, across from historic Alexandria, and in sight of the Capitol, and famous monuments, Bolling is headquarters for the Air Force District of Washington.

Locator 767-4522   Medical 767-5233   Police 767-5000

Fort Lesley J. McNair (DC05R1)
Bldg 50, Johnson Lane
Washington, D.C. 20593-5050

TELEPHONE NUMBER INFORMATION: Main installation numbers: C-202-433-4073, D-312-288-4073.

Temporary Military Lodging Around the World - 61

DISTRICT OF COLUMBIA
Fort Lesley J. McNair, continued

Location: At confluence of Anacostia River and Washington Channel, SW. Enter on P. St, SW. Take Maine Ave, SW, to right on 4th St, SW, to dead end at P St. Left then immediate right to main gate. *USMRA: Page 55 (F-5).* NMC: Washington DC in SW section of city.

Lodging Office: Building 50, Johnson Lane, **Fort Myer, VA**, 24 hours daily, **C-703-696-3576/77**, D-312-226-3576/77. Check in 1400 hours, check out 1200 hours daily. Late check out 697-7051.

TML: VOQ/VEQ. Building 54, Fort McNair (historic building), all ranks, leave or official duty. Reservation, check in & out at building 50, Fort Myer, VA. Suites, two beds, private bath (2); bedroom, private bath (25). Refrigerator, A/C, color TV in room & lounge, housekeeping service, washer/dryer. Rates: $25 sponsor, $5 each additional person, suites $30 sponsor, $5 each additional person. Maximum 2 per unit. TDY, PCS can make reservations, field grade Space-A. No pets.

TML Availability: Very Good. Difficult Apr-Nov.

CREDIT CARDS ACCEPTED: Visa, MasterCard and American Express.

Included in the original plans for the District of Columbia, Ft. McNair is nearly 200 years old. Site of the trial and execution of President Lincoln's conspirators, and where Walter Reed did his research work. Home of the National Defense University, National War College, Industrial college of the Armed Forces and the Inter-American Defense College. See the Washington waterfront, restaurants, seafood markets, monuments and the scenic Potomac River nearby.

Locator 545-6700   Medical 475-1829   Police 475-2004

Walter Reed Army Medical Center (DC03R1)
6900 Georgia Avenue
Washington, DC 20307-5000

TELEPHONE NUMBER INFORMATION: Main installation numbers: C-202-782-3501/02, D-312-662-3501/02.

Location: 6900 Georgia Avenue, NW. From I-495 (Capital Beltway) take Georgia Ave/Silver Spring exit south to Center, enter first or second gate. To reach the Forest Glen support facilities from Georgia Ave, south, right turn on to Linden Lane, cross over B&O railroad bridge, support facility on left (.75 miles from Georgia Ave). *USMRA: Page 55 (F-2).* NMC: Washington, DC, in the city.

Lodging Office: Building 6825, Georgia Ave (at Butternut St), **C-202-782-2096/2076**, 0800-1530 daily. Check in facility, check out 1100 hours daily. No government civilian employee billeting.

TML: Guest House. Building 17, all ranks, leave or official duty, **C-202-782-3044**, D-312-291-3044. Rooms, common baths, semi-private bath, private bath (62). A/C, CATV, housekeeping service, cribs/cots, coin washer/dryer, ice vending, facilities for DAVs. Older structure. Rates: $28-$32/night. Maximum 3 per unit. Priority to PCS, members of immediate family of seriously ill patients and MEDEVAC/AIRVAC personnel. Out-patients may make reservations, others Space-A.

TML: VOQ. Building 18, all ranks, leave or official duty, C-782-2076/2096. Check out 1100 hours daily. Bedroom, private bath (54) (3 with kitchen); separate bedrooms, private bath (5). Kitchen, complete utensils, A/C, CATV, housekeeping service, cots, coin washer/dryer, ice vending. Modern structure, remodeled '92. Rates: $34, $40 suites w/kitchen (O6+TDY). Maximum 3 per room. Duty can make reservations, others Space-A.

DISTRICT OF COLUMBIA
Walter Reed Army Medical Center, continued

TML: Fisher House. Located at Forest Glen Annex. Note: Appendix C has the definition of this facility. **C-301-427-6542/3.**

DV/VIP: Chief of Staff, C-202-782-3117, 3 units available.

TML Availability: Best, Mar-Apr & Sep-Oct. Difficult, others times.

Walter Reed is in D.C. near the National Zoo and National Cathedral, both star attractions for visitors. Other monuments are within 1/2 hour's drive.

Locator 782-3501/02   Medical 782-3317   Police-782-2511

Washington Navy Yard (DC04R1)
Billeting, Bldg 74
2701 S. Capitol St. SW
Anacostia Naval Station
Washington, DC 20374-5061

TELEPHONE NUMBER INFORMATION: Main installation numbers: C-202-545- 6700, D-312- 222-6700.

Location: The HQ is in the Washington Navy Yard, 9th & M Sts SE. From I-95 (beltway) take I-295 north, exit at Naval Research Laboratory onto Overlook Ave. Left at first light into Bellevue Housing, building 12, Bowling Green S.W. *USMRA: Page 55 (F,G-5).* NMC: Washington, DC, in the city.

Lodging Office: Building 72, **C-202-433-8796/0806**, 0730-1600 hours daily, other hours, 433-2193. Check in 1500-1800, check out 1200 hours daily. Write to BLDG 72/CMAA, 2701 S Capitol St SW, Naval Station Anacostia, Washington, D.C. 20374-5061. No government civilian employees billeting. This office is for permanent party only.

TML: Navy Lodge. All ranks, leave or official duty. For reservations call **1-800-NAVY-INN** (1-800-628-9466). Lodge number is 202-563-6950. Bedroom, private bath (50). Kitchen, utensils, A/C, color TV, cribs, high chairs, ironing boards, dining/living room areas, sleeps up to 4 persons (2 double beds). Two rooms available for the physically challenged. Modern structure. Rates: $50 per unit. PCS on orders may make reservations anytime, active duty may make reservations 60 days in advance, others 30 days in advance.

TML: VFQ. Building 2, officers, O7+ official duty or leave. Reservations: C-202-433-4052. Bedroom suites, private bath (9). Kitchenette (some), microwave, A/C, color TV, housekeeping service. Rates: $30, $5 family members. No pets. Reservations, 30 days in advance. PCS, TDY have priority, others Space-A.

TML: BOQ. **At Anacostia.** Exit from I-295 North, take Naval Station Exit, (1 exit past Bolling AFB). Turn right at traffic light to gate. From Defense Blvd. on left, past Reserve Center, turn right to BOQ. Building 93. Officers, official duty or leave. C-202-433-2006/7. Check in 0700, check out 2100 M-F, check in 0900 check out 2100 weekends & holidays. Government civilian employees G7+. Bedroom (twin beds), private bath (4 shared). A/C, CATV, housekeeping service, microwave, washer/dryer. Active duty on orders and government civilian employees, GS7+ may make reservations, others are Space-A.

DISTRICT OF COLUMBIA
Washington Navy Yard, continued

TML: BEQ. At Anacostia. Above directions. Enlisted billeting, active duty, on orders only, 1 week stay only. Bedroom, private bath (2) (One male, one female), in the barracks. C-202-767-4455 for reservations.

TML Availability: Good, Dec-Apr. Difficult, other times.

CREDIT CARDS ACCEPTED: Visa, MasterCard, American Express and Discover are accepted at the Navy Lodge.

For military history buffs, visit the Navy Memorial Museum, the Display Ship Barry (DD-933), the Marine Corps Museum (with famous flags raised over Mt. Suribachi and Iwo Jima), and the Combat Art Gallery.

Locator 703-545-6700   Medical 433-3757   Police 433-2411

Too Late To Copy
Washington Naval Security Station, 3801 Nebraska Avenue, NW, Washington, DC 20393-5440.
BEQ C-202-282-0254, D-312-292-0254.

New 200 Room Hotel in Washington, DC
(Walter Reed Army Medical Center)

The Mologne House is a 200 room hotel under construction at the Army's major medical center at Walter Reed. The foundation is now complete, with work on the second level being done as we go to press.

The $16 million complex is being built in front of the Walter Reed Army Institute of Research building and faces the main drive on the main campus of Walter Reed.

The four floor Georgian Revival-style building matches Building 1 and will have 95,000 square feet with 75 parking spaces. In addition to rooms, the hotel will have a 150 seating capacity restaurant on the first floor.

Security is a big concern and the front lobby area will include a resident computerized check-in service and a security monitoring system.

The hotel will offer three types of rooms: a standard room, with two double beds; an efficiency, with two double beds and a kitchen; and a suite with two rooms and a kitchen. Fifty percent of the hotel will be equipped for handicap use. Inside corridors will allow for ample wheelchair space.

Reservations are expected to be taken about 90 days before the hotel is completed which is projected to be in May 1997. The Mologne House is named for the beloved former commander of Walter Reed, Major General Lewis A. Mologne who passed away there in 1988.

This hotel is a non-appropriated funds project. Rates will be based on keeping the hotel self-sufficient.

FLORIDA

Camp Blanding Training Site (FL42R1)
Billeting Office
Route 1, Box 465
Starke, FL 32091-9703

TELEPHONE NUMBER INFORMATION: Main installation numbers: C-904-533-2268, D-312-960-2268.

Location: From Jacksonville, take SR21 (Blanding Blvd) 15 miles south to SR 215. Take SR 215 until you reach SR16. Turn west and proceed 1 mile to main gate. *USMRA: Page 38 (F,G-4)*. NMC: Jacksonville, 30 mi N.

Lodging Office: Bldg 2392, Finegan Lodge. **C-904-533-3381**, D-312-960-3381, Mon-Sa 0800-1700. After duty hours report to MP at Main Gate. Check in facility, check out 1100 hours. Government civilian employee billeting.

TML: TLF. Bldg 2392, Finegan Lodge. All ranks, leave or official duty. Bedroom, semi-private bath (50). Color/cable TV, housekeeping service, coin washer/dryer, ice vending. Rates: Active duty PCS/TDY$10, all others $10.81. Reservations can be made by Active duty, retirees, etc.

DV/VIP: Contact Training Site Manager at 904-533-3357, D-312-960-3357. O6+, retirees and lower ranks Space-A.

TML Availability: Good, May-Aug.

Under 1 hour drives to Gainesville, Jacksonville and St. Augustine. 3 hours to Walt Disney World and the Orlando area.

Locator 533-2268 **Medical 533-3105** **Police 533-3462**

Cecil Field Naval Air Station (FL06R1)
Combined Bachelor's Quarters
P.O. Box 117, Bldg 331
NAS Cecil Field, FL 32215-0117
Scheduled to close 9/30/98.

TELEPHONE NUMBER INFORMATION: Main installation numbers: C-904-778-5626, D-312-860-5626.

Location: Take Normandy exit west off I-295 and follow Normandy (FL-228) to main gate. *USMRA: Page 38 (G-3)*. NMC: Jacksonville, 20 miles east.

Lodging Office: Building 331, D Ave & 4th St. **C-904-778-5255**, FAX 904-778-6730, D-860-5255/5258, 24 hours daily. Check in facility, check out 1100 hours daily.

TML: BOQ. Building 331, officers all ranks, leave or official duty. Bedroom, private bath (50); separate bedroom, private bath (61); bedroom, shared bath (20). Refrigerator, A/C, essentials, color TV, housekeeping service, cribs/cots, washer/dryer, food/ice vending. Modern structure. Rates: sponsor on leave $8, sponsor on duty $4, adult $4, child $4. Duty can make reservations, others Space-A.

FLORIDA
Cecil Field Naval Air Station, continued

TML: BEQ. Building 92, enlisted, all ranks, leave or official duty. Check out 1200 hours. C-904-778-6191/2, D-312-860-6191/2. Bedroom, private bath (6). Two (or more) beds in room (78). A/C, essentials, food vending, housekeeping service, color TV in lounge, washer/dryer. Older structure, renovated. Rates: sponsor $4. Adult guests $2. Duty can make reservations, others Space-A.

DV/VIP: BOQ, Building 331. C-904-778-0641, D-312-860-5255/8. O6+. Retirees and lower ranks Space-A. Rates: sponsor $16, guest $5. BEQ, building 92. E8-E9 sponsor $12, guest $6.

TML Availability: Good, Nov-Jan. More difficult at other times.

CREDIT CARDS ACCEPTED: Visa, MasterCard and American Express.

St Augustine is 45 miles south. Check out the beaches and the Jacksonville seaport.

Locator 778-5240   Medical 778-5508/5378   Police 778-5381

Eglin Air Force Base (FL27R1)
96 SVS/SVML
Eglin AFB, FL 32542-5000

TELEPHONE NUMBER INFORMATION: Main installation numbers: C-904-882-1110, D-312-872-1110.

Location: Exit I-10 at Crestview, & follow posted signs to Niceville and Valparaiso, (Eglin AFB). *USMRA: Page 39 (B,C,D-13) & Page 53 (E,F,G,H-1,2,3,4).* NMC: Fort Walton Beach, 14 miles west.

Lodging Office: Eglin Inn, building 11001, Boatner Rd, **C-904-882-8761**, D-312-872-8761, FAX 904-882-2708, DSN FAX 312-872-2708, 24 hours daily. Check in billeting 1400, check out 1100 hours daily.

TML: VAQ. All ranks, leave or official duty. Suite (SNCOQ) (18); bedroom, private bath (89); bedroom, shared bath (54). Rates: $8-$12 per person. TLF. Bedroom, private bath (33); two bedroom, private bath (32); three bedroom, private bath (1); separate bedroom, private bath (1). Rates: $20-$24. VOQ. Bedrooms, private bath (112); suites (several). Rates: $8, $12, $14 per person. Refrigerator, microwave, A/C, color TV, housekeeping service, ice and food vending. Duty can make reservations, others Space-A.

DV/VIP: HQ AFDTC/CCP, building 1 (Command Section). C-904-882-3011/3238.

TML Availability: Very good, Nov-Jan. Difficult, other times.

CREDIT CARDS ACCEPTED: Visa, MasterCard and American Express.

Eglin Inn recently won the 1996 Air Force Innkeeper Award in the large base category. Their exemplary customer service, facilities, equipment, and procedures won Eglin Inn the award for the second year in a row. Phone Natural Resources on Eglin for information on the wonderful outdoor activities on Eglin Reserve. Don't miss Fort Walton Beach's Miracle Strip, deep sea fishing off Destin, and visit historic Pensacola, 50 miles west.

Locator 882-1113   Medical 882-7227   Police 882-2502

FLORIDA

Hurlburt Field (FL18R1)
16 SVS/SVML
301 Tully Street
Hurlburt Field, FL 32544-5844

TELEPHONE NUMBER INFORMATION: Main installation numbers: C-904-884-1110, D-312-579-1110.

Location: Off US-98, 5 miles west of Fort Walton Beach. Clearly marked. *USMRA: Page 39 (C-13) & Page 53 (H-4)*. NMC: Pensacola, 40 miles west.

Lodging Office: Building 90509, Simpson Street, **C-904-884-6245 & 581-1627**, D-312-579-6245, FAX 904-884-5043, 24 hours daily. Check in billeting, check out 1200 hours daily. Government civilian employee billeting.

TML: VAQ/VOQ. Buildings 90344-90346, 90507, 90508, all ranks, leave or official duty. Handicapped accessible. Bedroom, private and semi-private bath (179); separate bedrooms, private bath (29). Kitchen, limited utensils, A/C, color TV, housekeeping service, cribs/cots, essentials, washer/dryer, ice vending, VOQ stocked wet bar. Older structure. Rates: sponsor, $8; DVs, $14. Maximum 2 persons per unit. Duty can make reservations, others Space-A. See Eglin AFB listing for other TML.

TML: TLF. Units (24). $20 per night.

DV/VIP: Protocol Office, building 1, C-904-884-2308. O6+. Retirees and lower ranks Space-A.

TML Availability: Difficult. Best, Dec-Feb.

CREDIT CARDS ACCEPTED: Visa, MasterCard and American Express.

The catching and eating of fish is a big deal here! "The World's Luckiest Fishing Village" caters to all fishing needs. Numerous fine restaurants. Various facilities will be under renovation from 1995 to 1997.

Locator 884-6333   Medical 884-7882   Police 884-6423

Jacksonville Naval Air Station (FL08R1)
CBQ, Box 11
Jacksonville, FL 32212-5000

TELEPHONE NUMBER INFORMATION: Main installation numbers: C-904-772-2345, D-312-942-2345.

Location: Access from US-17 south (Roosevelt Blvd). On the St Johns River. *USMRA: Page 38 (G-3) & Page 50 (B,C-6,7)*. NMC: Jacksonville, 9 miles northeast.

Lodging Office: Building 11, **C-904-772-3138/3139** enlisted, **C-904-772-3537/4052**, officer, FAX 904-772-5002, 24 hours daily. Check in facility, check out 1200 hours daily. Government civilian employee billeting.

FLORIDA
Jacksonville Naval Air Station, continued

TML: Navy Lodge. All ranks, leave or official duty. For reservations call **1-800-NAVY-INN**. Lodge number is 904-772-6000, 24 hours daily, check in 1500-1800, check out 1200. Bedroom, 2 double beds, private bath (50). Six interconnecting, 2 handicapped accessible, 25 non-smoking. Kitchenette, microwave, utensils, A/C, CATV w/HBO, clocks, coffee/tea, cots, cribs, phones, irons/boards, housekeeping service, coin washer/dryer, food/ice vending, picnic grounds, playground, rollaways. Modern structure. Rates: $38 per unit. Active duty can make reservations 60 days in advance, retired, 30 days.

TML: BOQ. Buildings 11, 845, officers all ranks, leave or official duty. Bedroom, private bath (110); bedroom, shared bath (8); separate bedroom, private bath (96). Refrigerator, telephones, TV in room & lobby, one large, two small conference rooms, housekeeping service, washer/dryer, food/ice vending, sauna, fishing dock. Building 11, older structure. Rates: TAD $12 per person, dependents 12 years+ $3 (one charge). Reservations taken 45 days in advance for transient personnel. No pets. Call billeting for more information. Geographical bachelors on Space-A basis in inadequate quarters only.

DV/VIP: PAO, C-904-772-3147/3138, O6/GS-15+. Retirees & Space-A only after 1800.

TML Availability: Fair. Difficult, summer months.

CREDIT CARDS ACCEPTED: Visa and MasterCard.

Don't miss boating and water sports on over 74 square miles of inland waters, golf courses, wonderful beaches that are among Florida's finest. Also visit museums, symphony, St Augustine, and Cypress Gardens.

Locator 772-2340   Medical 777-7300   Police 772-2661/2662

Key West Naval Air Station (FL15R1)
Trumbo Point Annex
Key West, FL 33040-5000

TELEPHONE NUMBER INFORMATION: Main installation numbers: C-305-293-3700, D-312-483-3700.

Location: For Trumbo Point Annex, take Florida Turnpike, US-1 south, turn right at Key West. At intersection of Palm turn right. Next traffic light, look for six story white building. Boca Chica Key is seven miles north of Key West. *USMRA: Page 39 (G-16)*. NMC: Miami, 150 miles north.

Lodging Office: No central billeting office. BOQ at Trumbo Point Annex, building C2076. **C-305-293-4100**, 24 hours daily. Check in facility, check out 1200 hours daily. Government civilian employee billeting, GS 1+ (on orders only).

TML: BOQ. Officers, all ranks, leave or official duty. Handicapped accessible. Reservations required for personnel on orders. BOQ: bedroom, private bath (217); DVOQ Suites, separate bedroom, private bath (18); DVOQ single (24). Community kitchen, ice/food vending, housekeeping service, refrigerator, color TV in rooms and lounge, washer/dryer. Rates: single rooms $14-$16, $3-$4 each additional person, and $14, $3 each additional person. DVOQ Suites $28, $7 each additional person, DVOQ single $16, $4 each additional person. Maximum 3 persons per unit.

FLORIDA
Key West Naval Air Station, continued

TML: BEQ Boca Chica, E1-E9, **C-305-293-2488**. Substandard rooms, barracks type, common bath (600); VIP suite, private bath (2). Community kitchen, ice/food vending, washer/dryer. Rates: barracks $6, VIP $20. **(Note: Closed for renovation, see BOQ (all hands))**

TML: Navy Lodge. Bldg 4114, Sigsbee Park, 6 miles south of NAS in Key West, on the bay. Reservations call **1-800-NAVY-INN.** Lodge number is 305-292-7556. All ranks, leave or official duty. Check in 1500-1800, check out 1200 hours. Bedrooms, 2 double beds, private bath (26). Two units handicapped accessible. Kitchenette, microwave, utensils, hair dryer, ice, iron/board, A/C, cribs/cots, phones, coin operated washer/dryer, ice vending. Rates: $58 per day, October to May; $48 per day June to September; $45 PCS all year round w/proof of orders. MWR Sunset Lounge, community center with tickets, commissary and exchange across the road. MWR marina boat and snorkel rental gear. Modern structure. All categories may make reservations.

TML: MWR Trailers. Near Old Town Key West. **C-305-293-4431**, D-312-483-3144. Office closed Sun, Mon & Holidays (arrivals for these days will be arranged). Mail one night deposit to: MWR Dept., Box 9027, NAS Key West 33040. Duty or retired, DoD civilians, dependents. Two bedroom, double beds, private bath (12). A/C, kitchen, complete utensils, dining room, microwave, linens provided, limited housekeeping service, within walking distance of Old Key West. Rates: per night $48 (May-Dec), $55 (Jun-Apr). All categories can make reservations 3-4 months in advance.

TML: DV/VIP. Quarters FF Guest house, Truman Annex, O6+. Three bedroom beach house (1). A/C, kitchen, all amenities. Rates: $36, guests $9. Call CO Secretary, NAS Key West, Fl 33040. Reservations required, others Space-A.

TML Availability: Extremely limited. Best in summer.

Here is the place to kick back and relax by the ocean.

Locator 292-2256   Medical 292-4444   Police-292-2531

MacDill Air Force Base (FL02R1)
MacDill Inn
56 SG/MWMH/Lodging
P.O. Box 6826
MacDill AFB, FL 33621-5000

TELEPHONE NUMBER INFORMATION: Main installation numbers: C-813-828-1110, D-312-968-1110.

Location: Take I-75 south to I-275 south. Exit at Dale Mabry west, 5 miles south to MacDill AFB main gate. *USMRA: Page 38 (E,F-8) & Page 54 (E,F-3,4)*. NMC: Tampa, 5 miles north.

Lodging Office: MacDill Inn, Building 411, corner Hangar Loop Rd & Tampa Blvd, **C-813-828-2661**, FAX 813-828-2660, 24 hours daily. Check in lodging, check out 1100 hours daily. Government civilian employee billeting.

TML: TLF. Buildings 893, 905, 906, all ranks, PCS families are Priority 1, all others are Priority 2. Handicapped accessible. Bedroom, private bath (24). Kitchen, refrigerator, utensils, A/C, color TV, VCR, cots/cribs, housekeeping service, essentials, washer/dryer, food/ice vending. Rates: $23 per family. Maximum 5 persons. Duty can make reservations, others Space-A.

FLORIDA
MacDill Air Force Base, continued

TML: VAQ. Building 372, enlisted E1-E6, leave or official duty. Bedroom, shared bath (62). Refrigerator, A/C, color TV, housekeeping service, washer/dryer. Older structure. Rates: $8 per person. Maximum 2 persons. Duty can make reservations, others Space-A.

TML: VOQ. Buildings 312, 366, 390, 411, officers all ranks, leave or official duty. Bedroom, private bath (117); bedroom, semi-private bath (44). A/C, color TV, housekeeping service, washer/dryer, ice vending. Modern structure. Rates: sponsor $8 per person. Maximum 2 persons. No children. Duty can make reservations, others Space-A.

DV/VIP: 56th FW/CCP, C-813-828-2056. O6+.

TML Availability: Extremely limited Jan-Mar. Limited Apr-Sep. Best Oct-Dec.

CREDIT CARDS ACCEPTED: Visa, MasterCard and American Express.

Local attractions include Busch Gardens, Tampa Aquarium, Epcot Center, Disney World, Sea World - this is an area with lots of interesting things to see.

Locator 828-2444   Medical 828-2334   Police 828-3322

Mayport Naval Station (FL13R1)
Lodging Office
Bldg 425, P.O. Box 20098
Mayport, FL 32228-0098

TELEPHONE NUMBER INFORMATION: Main installation numbers: C-904-270-5011, D-312-960-5011.

Location: From Jacksonville, FL on Atlantic Blvd (FL-10) east to Mayport Rd (FL-A1A) left (north) to Naval Station. *USMRA: Page 38 (H-3) & Page 50 (G-3,4).* NMC: Jacksonville, 10 miles west.

Lodging Office: No central billeting office. Check in facility, check out 1200 daily. Government civilian employee billeting.

TML: BOQ. Building 425, officers all ranks, leave or non-Navy personnel on orders, C-904-247-1376, official Navy duty (SATO) 1-800-576-9327. Kitchenette, CATV, refrigerator, A/C, housekeeping service, washer/dryer, ice vending. Modern structure. Rates: VIP $15, DV $18. Duty on orders to Mayport can make reservations, others Space-A.

TML: BEQ. Building 1586, enlisted all ranks, leave or non-Navy personnel on orders, C-904-270-5575, official Navy duty (SATO) 1-800-576-9327. Bedroom, hall and private baths (244); separate bedroom (1). DV/VIP with kitchen. Rates: $4 per person. Duty on orders to Mayport can make reservations, others Space-A.

TML: Navy Lodge. All ranks, leave or official duty. For reservations call **1-800-NAVY-INN**. Lodge number is 904-247-3964, fax 904-270-6153. Check in between 1400-1600. Check out 1200 hours daily. Two bedroom mobile homes, private bath (19), kitchen, complete utensils, A/C, color TV, cribs, housekeeping service, coin washer/dryer. Rates: $50. All categories can make reservations. **New 71 unit lodge opening April 1996. Rates: $46-$50.**

DV/VIP: Cmdr/DO, C-904-270-4501, E9, O7+.

FLORIDA
Mayport Naval Station, continued

TML Availability: Very good, Nov-Mar. Difficult, other times.

CREDIT CARDS ACCEPTED: Visa, MasterCard and American Express. The Navy Lodge accepts Visa, MasterCard, American Express and Discover.

Near Jacksonville, historic St. Augustine. Deep sea fishing, and famous Florida beaches - shark's teeth are picked up on local beaches.

Locator 270-5401   Medical 270-5303   Police 270-5583

Oak Grove Park (FL09R1)
MWR Dept.
Pensacola, FL 32508-5000

TELEPHONE NUMBER INFORMATION: Main installation numbers: C-904-452-0111, D-312-922-0111.

Location: From I-10, south on I-110, Garden Street Exit to Navy Blvd to front gate. *USMRA: Page 39 (A,B-13) & Page 53 (E-4,5).* NMC: Pensacola, 2 miles northeast.

Lodging Office: None.

TML: Recreational Cabins, officer and enlisted, all ranks, leave or official duty. **C-904-452-2535**, check in 1200-1630 hours, check out 0730-1000 hours. Handicapped accessible. Bedroom cabins, private bath (12). A/C, kitchen, complete utensils, refrigerator. Modern structures. All categories can make reservations up to 3 months in advance.

DV/VIP: No Protocol Office.

TML Availability: Best, Oct-Apr. Difficult other times.

CREDIT CARDS ACCEPTED: Visa, MasterCard and American Express.

Coastal Florida, near Pensacola is known for water recreation, fishing.

Locator 452-0111   Medical 452-4256   Police 452-2353

Orlando Naval Training Center (FL11R1)
Navy Orlando Inn
1200 Leahy St., Bldg 375
Orlando NTC, FL 32813-5005
Scheduled to close 12/31/98.

TELEPHONE NUMBER INFORMATION: Main installation numbers: C-407-646- 4111, D-312-791-4111.

Location: On Bennet Rd, .5 mile north of FL-50 (Colonial Dr). Bennet Rd is about 3 miles from I-4 on FL-50. *USMRA: Page 38 (H-7), Page 53 (D-3).* NMC: Orlando, in the city.

Lodging Office: Building 375, 1200 Leahy St, **C-407-646-5614**, FAX 407-646-4855, 0730-1600 hours duty days. Other hours, SDO, building 2702, C-407-646-4501. Check in facility. Government civilian employee billeting (GS7+).

FLORIDA
Orlando Naval Training Center, continued

TML: BEQ/BOQ. Building 375, officer, enlisted all ranks, official duty. C-407-646-5614. Check out 1000 daily. Bedroom, 3 beds, private bath (130). A/C, color TV lounge, washer/dryer. Modern structure. Rates: $5 per person. Official orders Space-A. Bedroom, semi-private bath (28); bedroom, private bath (22); two bedroom cottage, private bath (VIPs/Flag Officers). Refrigerator (12) units, A/C, color TV, housekeeping service, cots, washer/dryer. Older structure, renovated. Rates $8-$25. Duty can make reservations, others Space-A.

TML Availability: Best, Aug-Nov, Jan-Apr.

CREDIT CARDS ACCEPTED: Visa, MasterCard and American Express.

Don't miss Disney World, Cypress Gardens, Universal Studios, Sea World.

Locator 646-5340   **Medical 646-5322**   **Police 646-4340**

Panama City Naval Coastal Systems Station
Naval Surface Warfare Center (FL35R1)
Bldg 126, Crag Road
Panama City, FL 32407-5000

TELEPHONE NUMBER INFORMATION: Main installation numbers: C-904-234-4011, D-312-436-4011.

Location: In the Northwest section of Florida. Exit I-10 (N&S) to Hwy 231 (N&S) to Florida Hwy 98 (N&S). The facility is located off Hwy 98. *USMRA: Page 39 (E-14)*. NMC: Pensacola 100 miles west and Tallahassee, 100 miles east.

Lodging Office: Housing, Bldg 126, Crag Road. **C-904-234-4425/4248**, D-312-436-4425/4248. 0800-1600 M-F.

TML: BOQ. Seashore Inn. Building 349, officers, W1+, leave or official duty. Suites (30); senior suites (12); VIP suites (5). Some handicapped accessible. All rooms have private bath, kitchenette, A/C, phones, limited utensils, color/cable TV. Washer/dryers, jacuzzi, food and ice vending machines. Fully remodeled facility. Rates: DV suites $20 (member), $5 (guest); Senior suites $14 (member) $3.75 (guest); suite $10 (member), $2.50 (guest). Limit 2 to 3 persons per room. Reservations required for official duty, all others Space-A. **C-904-234-4217/4556**, FAX 904-234-4991, D-312-436-4217/4556. Check in 1600, check out 1100 hours. No children under 16. No pets allowed.

TML: All ranks. BEQ Building 304. Bedrooms, private bath (40). A/C, food and ice vending, refrigerators, CATV, washer and dryer. Modern building with recent remodeling, and more anticipated. All rooms $10, $2.50 per guest. Limit 4 persons per room. Very limited family lodging.

DV/VIP: BOQ. Bedrooms, private bath (2). O6+, GM/GS 15 & above, others Space-A. Call PAO, building 110, C-904-234-5464, D-312-436-5464.

TML Availability: Good, Oct-Feb. Difficult Mar-Sep.

CREDIT CARDS ACCEPTED: American Express.

Visit the Armament Museum, beautiful sandy white beaches, and enjoy Florida sport fishing.

Locator 234-4011   **Medical 234-4316**   **Police 234-4332**

FLORIDA

Patrick Air Force Base (FL03R1)
Space Coast Inn
45 SVS/SVML
P.O. Box 5005
Patrick AFB, FL 32925-3223

TELEPHONE NUMBER INFORMATION: Main installation numbers: C-407-494-1110, D-312-854-1110.

Location: Take I-95 south to exit 73 (Wickham Rd), 3 miles to State Road 404 (Pineda Causeway), 6 miles, left on A1A, 3 miles to Patrick AFB. *USMRA: Page 38 (I-8)*. NMC: Cocoa Beach, 2 miles north.

Lodging Office: Space Coast Inn, Buildings 720, 820 Falcon Ave, **C-407-494-6570**, D-312-854-2075, 24 hours. Check in lodging 1500, check out 1100 hours daily. Government/Military civilian employee lodging.

TML: TLF. Buildings 1030, 1034, 1036, 1038, 1042, 1046, 1048, 1050, 1056, 1058, 1060, 1061, all ranks, leave or official duty. Two bedroom, private bath (31); three bedroom, private bath (20). Kitchen, living room, utensils, A/C, color TV, housekeeping service, cribs, washer/dryer. Older structure, renovated. Rates: $24.50 per unit. PCS duty families can make reservations, others Space-A.

TML: VAQ. Buildings 501, 556, 727, enlisted E1-E8, leave or official duty. Bedroom, living room, private bath (28); bedroom, private bath (16); bedroom shared bath (132). A/C color TV, refrigerator, microwave, housekeeping service, washer/dryer, ice vending. Older structure, renovated. Rates: $8, $12.50, $14, per person. Duty can make reservations, others Space-A.

TML: VOQ. Buildings 264, 265, 404, officers all ranks, leave or official duty. Two bedroom, shared bath, living room (94); suites, private baths (11). A/C, color TV, refrigerator, microwave, housekeeping service, washer/ dryer, ice vending. Renovated. Rates: $12.50 and $14 per person. Duty can make reservations, others Space-A.

TML: DV/VIP. Buildings 250, 251, 253, officers O6+, leave or official duty. Bedroom suite, private bath (2); two bedroom suite, private bath (1); four bedroom house (1). AC, color TV, refrigerator, full kitchen with utensils, washer/dryer, housekeeping service. Older structure, renovated. Rates $14 per person. Building 255, enlisted E9, leave or official duty. Bedroom suite, private bath (3). AC, color TV, kitchen with utensils, washer/dryer, housekeeping service. Older structure, renovated. Rates $14 per person. Reservations: PROTOCOL 407-494-4506. Duty can make reservations, others Space-A.

TML Availability: Good, Nov-Jan. Limited, other times.

Florida's "Space Coast" includes US Air Force Space Museum, Kennedy Center, Disney World, Sea World, Epcot Center, Cypress Gardens.

Locator 494-4542   Medical 494-8133   Police 494-2008

Pensacola Naval Air Station (FL14R1)
Billeting Office, Bldg 3472
Pensacola NAS, FL 32508-5000

TELEPHONE NUMBER INFORMATION: Main installation numbers: C-904-452-0111, D-312-922-0111.

FLORIDA
Pensacola Naval Air Station, continued

Location: Off US-98, 4 miles south of I-10. Take Navy Blvd from US-98 or US-29 directly to NAS. USMRA: Page 39 (A,B-13) & Page 53 (A,B-4,5). NMC: Pensacola, 8 miles north.

Lodging Office: Billeting office, building 3472, **C-904-452-3438/4609**, FAX 904-4523-6483, 24 hours daily.

TML: Navy Lodge. Building 3875, all ranks, leave or official duty. For reservations call **1-800-NAVY-INN**. Lodge number is 904-456-8676. Check in 1500-1800, check out 1200 daily. Bedroom, two queen beds, kitchenette (22) Rates: $36 per night. Two-bedroom, living room, kitchen, private bath mobile home (12). Rates: $54 per night. A new 52 unit beachside lodge has opened at Lighthouse Point, bldg. 3875. Rates $43-54. Kitchen, microwave, utensils, A/C, color TV, coffee/tea, housekeeping service, cribs/cots, phones, coin washer/dryer, ice/snack vending, picnic grounds, playground. Modern structure. No maximum per unit. All categories can make reservations.

TML: BOQ. Building 600, officers all ranks, leave or official duty, C-904-452-2755, Fax 904-452-3188, 24 hours daily. Check in 24 hours, out 1100. Bedrooms, private bath (52); VIP rooms, private bath (O6+) (38); flag officer suites, private bath (5). CATV, microwave, coffee pots etc. Renovated. Rates: $10; VIP $15, Flag $25. Duty, authorized civilians, can make reservations.

TML: BEQ. Bayshores. Building 3472, enlisted E1-E9. C-904-452-3438/4609, D-312-922-3438/4609, 24 hours daily. E5-E9, bedroom, private bath (1 man) (48); VIP suites, E7-E9, private bath (2); E1-E4, shared room, shared bath (112). CATV, coffee pots, microwave, refrigerator. Rates: E5-E9 $9.60; VIP $16.60, E1-E4 $5.60, $2 guest, personnel assigned to NAS/no family check w/BEQ on space-A. Duty, TAD, reservists (orders) make reservations, retired and leave personnel Space-A.

TML Availability: Limited due to ongoing renovations for the next two years.

CREDIT CARDS ACCEPTED: Visa, MasterCard and American Express.

See miles of sugar-white sand beaches, fishing etc.; Saenger Theater of performing arts in Pensacola; the Blue Angels; the USS Lexington.

Locator 452-4693   Medical 452-4138   Police 452-2653

Shades of Green
on WALT DISNEY WORLD® Resort
(FL49R1)
P.O. Box 22789
Lake Buena Vista, FL 32830-2789

TELEPHONE NUMBER INFORMATION: Main installation numbers: C-407-824-3400, FAX 407-824-3460.

Location: From Orlando take I-4 W, exit 26B, Walt Disney World, follow Magic Kingdom Resort signs, go through Magic Kingdom toll booth, stay in far right lane following signs to Resort and hotels, at first light turn left, Seven Seas Dr past Polynesian Resort, come to three way stop, turn right on Floridian Way, driveway is first road to the left, Magnolia Palm Dr. USMRA: Page 39 (G-7), Page 53 (A-2,3). NMC: Orlando, 15 mi NE.

FLORIDA
Shades of Green, continued

Description of Area: The Army leased the Disney Inn at Walt Disney World in Lake Buena Vista, Florida, to serve as an Armed Forces Recreation Center (AFRC). The Disney Inn which had 287 rooms was renamed *"Shades of Green on Walt Disney World Resort."* Shades of Green has been very popular with families because of its large rooms and easy access to transportation to various parts of Disney World.

Shades of Green was built in 1973 and was one of the older and smaller hotels, but it has been impeccably maintained and has had recent renovations. It is across from the Grand Floridian and adjacent to the Magnolia and Palm golf courses.

Season of Operation: Year round.

Reservations: Required. Military personnel, active, retired, Guard & Reserve, family members **and** DoD employees may make reservations by calling **407-824-3600** or FAX 407-824-3460. Write for reservations and information packet: Shades of Green on Walt Disney World Resort, P.O. Box 22789, Lake Buena Vista, FL 32830-2789.

The inn has 287 large rooms each appointed with two queen-size beds, sofa-bed, private bath. There are 2 outdoor pools & a kiddy pool, tennis courts, and easy access to Walt Disney World transportation. *RATES: E1-5, $55. E6-E9, O1-O3, WO1-CW3, GS 1-10, $79. O4-O6, CW4-5, GS 11-15, $89, O7-10, $95. Rates are for double occupancy. Single room subtract $2. There will be an added charge of $10 per additional adult above two per room. * These rates go into effect 1 October 1995.

A vacation dream come true, a visit to Walt Disney World, Epcot Center, Disney MGM Studios Theme Park, and Blizzard Beach. Other attractions within an hour's drive are Busch Gardens, Cypress Gardens, hot air balloon rides, deep sea fishing Daytona and Cocoa Beach and Cape Canaveral where you can visit the Space Museum and if you're lucky, watch the space shuttle launch. If this is not enough to keep you busy, there is golf, swimming, and tennis all without leaving the resort.

Tyndall Air Force Base (FL04R1)
325 SVS/SVML/Lodging
Bldg 1332
Tyndall AFB, FL 32403-5000

TELEPHONE NUMBER INFORMATION: Main installation numbers: C-904-283-1110, D-312-523-1110.

Location: Take I-10, exit US-231 south to US-98 east, signs mark the AFB. *USMRA: Page 39 (E-14).* NMC: Panama City, 10 miles northwest.

Lodging Office: PO Box 40040, building 1332, Suwannee & Oak Dr, **C-904-283-4210 ext 0**, D-312-523-4210, FAX 904-283-4800, DSN FAX 312-523-4800, 24 hours daily. Check in billeting 1400, check out 1200 hours daily. Government civilian employee lodging.

TML: VAQ/VOQ/DV/TLF. **Sand Dollar Inn**, all ranks, leave or official duty. VOQ: separate bedrooms, kitchen, private bath (200); VAQ: shared bedroom and shared bath(144); DV Suites: Private bedroom & bath (19); SRNCOQ: bedroom, private bath (24); NCO: efficiency apartments, private bath (40), sleeps 4, cribs/roll-away available (TLF). A/C, color/cable TV in room and lounge, housekeeping service, washer/dryer, ice vending. Modern structure. Rates: E1-E6 $16 per unit, E7 & Officer $20 per unit. TLF, $6 per person VOQ $6 per person, VAQ $5 per person, DV & SRNCOQ $10 per person. Official duty should make reservations, others Space-A.

FLORIDA
Tyndall Air Force Base, continued

Note: Tyndall Fam-Camp has two bedroom cottages (3). Rates: $32 sponsor & spouse/guest, $2 each additional person. Call 904-283-2798 for more information and reservations.

DV/VIP: Hq, Building 647. C-904-283-2232. O6+. Retirees and lower ranks Space-A.

TML Availability: Very good, Jan-Feb. Fair, other times.

CREDIT CARDS ACCEPTED: Visa, MasterCard and American Express.

Beautiful white sand beaches, water sports, fishing, and small friendly communities.

Locator 283-2138   Medical 283-7523   Police 283-4124

Whiting Field Naval Air Station (FL05R1)
Consolidated Bachelor Quarters
7426 USS Lexington Circle
Milton, FL 32570-5000

TELEPHONE NUMBER INFORMATION: Main installation numbers: C-904-623-7011, D-312-868-7011.

Location: From US-90 east exit, FL-87 north 7 miles to NAS. *USMRA: Page 39 (B-13)*. NMC: Pensacola, 25 miles southwest.

Lodging Office: Building 2942, Lexington Circle, **C-904-623-7606**, FAX 904-623-7238, D-312-868-7606, 24 hours daily. Check in 1500, check out 1200 hours daily. Government civilian employee billeting.

TML: BOQ. Building 2957. Two-bedroom suites (123). Officers assigned bedrooms and share living room/lounge with one other person. BOQ houses barber shop, pool table, lounge w/large screen TV, physical fitness, sauna and laundry facilities. O'Club, swimming pool and academic training buildings within walking distance of BOQ.

TML: BEQ. Building 2958, all ranks, leave or official duty. Rooms suites, private bath (52). Refrigerator, A/C, color TV in lounge, housekeeping service, cribs, washer/dryer, ice vending. Rates: $8 per room single, $10 per room double, $16 suite. Active Duty can make reservations, others Space-A.

DV/VIP: Admiral's Office, building 1401. C-904-623-7201. O6+. Retirees Space-A. Rates: $14 single, $20 double, $28 suite.

TML Availability: Under renovation, availability limited through 1996.

CREDIT CARDS ACCEPTED: Visa, MasterCard and American Express.

Small growing community, 25 miles northeast of Pensacola, 18 hole golf course, newly built commissary. Stop in and see the new Whiting Field.

Locator 623-7011   Medical 623-7584   Police 623-7387

76 - *Temporary Military Lodging Around the World*

GEORGIA

Albany Marine Corps Logistics Base (GA17R1)
Live Oak Lodge Billeting
9201-A Williams Blvd.
Marine Corps Logistics Base
Albany, GA 31705-1003

TELEPHONE NUMBER INFORMATION: Main installation numbers: C-912-439-5000, D-312-567-5000.

Location: Approximately 3 miles SE of Albany. Accessible from US-82, US-300, and US-19. Follow the signs. *USMRA: Page 37 (C-8).* NMC: Albany, 3 mi W.

Lodging Office: Live Oak Lodge, building 9201, **C-912-439-5614,** D-312-567-5614, FAX 912-439-5690, DSN FAX 312-567-5690, 0730-1700 M-F. After hours, contact DO, building 3500. Check out time 1130.

TML: Family Transient Quarters. Buildings 9251, 9253, 9255. Separate houses, 3 bedrooms, 1 1/2 baths, recently upgraded. All facilities and amenities. All ranks, primarily for active duty military on PCS. Rates: $20 per night. Maximum 6 adults or children per unit. Housekeeping service not available during occupancy. Military on leave, retirees, Space-A.

TML: TEQ. Building 7966. One bedroom, private bath units for E6 and above, equivalent graded government employees on official orders. Rate: $9 per night. Maximum 2 adults, 2 children per unit. Retired military, Space-A.

TML: Enlisted quarters available for E5 and below. No charge, call for information. No housekeeping service.

TML: TOQ. Buildings 10201, 10202, officers all ranks on leave/official duty. Equivalent government employees on official duty. One, three, and four-bedroom suites with kitchenettes. Handicapped suite available. Renovated. Rates: $12 to $24 per unit. Retired military, Space-A.

TML: DV/VIP. Building 10300, officer O6+, leave or official duty. Two bedroom, completely furnished detached house, private bath. All facilities and amenities. Housekeeping service, color TV, washer/dryer. Modern structure. Rates: $25. Official duty, leave/retirees, Space-A.

DV/VIP: Contact Live Oak Billeting Office, O5+. Retirees & lower ranks Space-A.

TML Availability: Fairly good. Best Nov-Mar.

CREDIT CARDS ACCEPTED: American Express and Diners.

Swimming at beautiful Radium Springs, south of Albany, outdoor sports, local Concert Association, Little Theater. Albany is a trade and distribution center for Southwest Georgia.

Locator 439-5000/5103   Medical 435-0806   Police 439-5181

GEORGIA

Athens Navy Supply Corps School (GA12R1)
The Oaks
1425 Prince Avenue
Athens NSCS, GA 30606-2205

TELEPHONE NUMBER INFORMATION: Main installation numbers: C-706-354-1500, D-312-588-1500.

Location: From Athens take bypass, exit on Prince Ave, continue 1 mile to base at intersection of Prince & Oglethorpe Avenues. *USMRA: Page 37 (D-3)*. NMC: Atlanta, 70 miles west.

Lodging Office: The Oaks. 1425 Prince Avenue, **C-706-354-7360**, D-312-588-7360, 0800-0100 daily, Fax 706-354-7370, DSN Fax 312-588-7370. Check in (Brown Hall between 0730-0100), check out 1300 hours daily. Reservations 45 days in advance for those on orders to NSCS. All others Space-A (2 day limit), reservations may be made 48 hours in advance. No pets.

TML: Brown Hall. All ranks, leave or official duty. Two room suites, private bath (35). Micro-refrigerator, A/C, color TV, VCR, coffee pot, iron/ironing board, washer/dryer, housekeeping service, ice/food vending. Rates: $25 per person. No pets

TML: Wright Hall. All ranks, leave or official duty. One room suites, private bath (72). Micro-refrigerator (in some rooms), A/C, color TV, VCR, coffee pot, iron/ironing board, washer/dryer, housekeeping service, ice/food vending. Rates: $10 sponsor, $5 guest. Maximum of 2 persons per room. No pets.

TML Availability: Dependent on student/class loading. **Lodging in Wright Hall will be extremely limited until September 1996 due to planned renovation and the 1996 Olympics in Atlanta.**

The Oaks is the recipient of Chief Naval Education and Training "Innkeeper of the Year" for 1993, 1994, 1995, and the 1994 Admiral Elmo R. Zumwait Award for Excellence in BQ Management. Athens has museums, restaurants, shopping, and the University of Georgia; the state botanical garden, and the Chattahoochee National Forest nearby. Atlanta 70 miles away...lots to do and see.

Locator 354-1500   Medical 354-7321   Police 354-1500

Atlanta Naval Air Station (GA16R1)
Combined Bachelor's Quarters
Bldg 54, Room 120
Marietta, GA 30060-5099

TELEPHONE NUMBER INFORMATION: Main installation numbers: C-770-421-5392, D-312-925-5392.

Location: From I-75, exit to GA-280, W to GA-3, S to main gate, adjacent to Dobbins AFB on the W. *USMRA: Page 37 (B-3) & Page 49 (A-1)*. NMC: Atlanta, 15 miles SE.

Lodging Office: Building 54. **C-770-919-5393**, D-312-925-5393, FAX 770-919-5276, 24 hours daily. Check in billeting 1400, check out 1200 hours daily. government civilian employees billeting (orders).

GEORGIA
Atlanta Naval Air Station, continued

TML: BOQ. Building 53, officers, all ranks, official duty or leave. Suites, private bath (5). A/C, microwave, housekeeping service, washer/dryer, telephones, CATV. Modern structure. No pets. Rates: $6 per night. Reservations required for those on orders, others Space-A.

TML: BEQ. Building 54, 63, enlisted, all ranks, official duty or leave. Bedroom, shared bath (23). Bedroom, private bath (1). A/C, microwave, housekeeping service, CATV, washer/dryer. Modern structure. No pets. Rates: $6 per night. Reservations required, others Space-A.

TML Availability: Very good during the week, weekends very difficult.

CREDIT CARDS ACCEPTED: Visa, MasterCard and American Express.

Stone Mountain State Park, with hiking, fishing and other outdoor activities, Six Flags over Georgia. Note: Lake Altoona Navy Rec Site has cabins for rent. Call 770-421-5502, and read *Military RV, Camping & Rec Areas Around the World.*

Locator 919-5392   Medical 919-5300   Police 919-5394

Dobbins Air Reserve Base (GA13R1)
Dobbins Inn
1295 Barracks Ct., Bldg 800
Dobbins ARB, GA 30069

TELEPHONE NUMBER INFORMATION: Main installation numbers: C-770-919-5000, D-312-925-5000.

Location: From I-75 north exit to GA-280 (exit 111) west to ARB. Clearly marked. *USMRA: Page 37 (B-3) & Page 49 (A-1).* NMC: Atlanta, 17 miles southeast.

Lodging Office: Dobbins Inn. Building 800, 1295 Barracks Ct., **C-770-919-4745,** FAX 770-919-5185, D-312-925-4745, 24 hours daily. Check in facility, check out 1200 hours daily. Government civilian employee lodging.

TML: VAQ. Building 801, enlisted, E1-E6, leave or official duty. Bedroom, semi-private bath (75). Refrigerator, A/C, cribs, essentials, color TV, washer/dryer, ice vending. Older structure, renovated '90. Rates: $6 per person. Maximum 2 persons. Duty can make reservations, others Space-A.

TML: DV/VIP. Building 401, officer O6+, available to lower ranks Space-A. Leave or official duty. Bedroom suites, private bath and sitting room (5). Bedrooms (44). Refrigerator, A/C, cribs, essentials, ice vending, housekeeping service, color TV, washer/dryer. VOQ renovated '92. Rates: DV rooms $10 per person, maximum charge $20 per night; other rooms $6 per person, maximum $12 per night. Maximum 2 persons. Duty can reserve rooms, others Space-A.

TML: Senior NCO Quarters. Building 800, E7-E9. Two room suites (4). Rate: $10 per person per night. Other SNCO rooms (40) single occupancy, share bath. SNCO rooms renovated '92. Rate: $6 per person per night.

DV/VIP: PAO, C-770-919-4520. O6+. Retirees and lower ranks Space-A.

GEORGIA
Dobbins Air Reserve Base, continued

TML Availability: Good, Nov-Mar. More difficult, Apr-Oct.

CREDIT CARDS ACCEPTED: Visa, MasterCard and American Express.

Excellent fishing and boating in the Metro Atlanta area at Lake Altoona and Lake Lanier. Visit underground Atlanta, the Cyclorama, Stone Mountain Park and the Jimmy Carter Presidential Library.

Locator 919-5000   **Medical 919-5305**   **Police 919-4907**

Fort Benning (GA11R1)
Lodging Office, Bldg 399
Fort Benning, GA 31905-5122

TELEPHONE NUMBER INFORMATION: Main installation numbers: C-706-545-0110, D-312-835-0110.

Location: 12 miles South of Columbus off I-185. Can be reached from US-80 and US-280. *USMRA: Page 37 (B-6).* NMC: Columbus, 5 mi NW.

Lodging Office: Building 399, **C-706-689-0067** (Auto Attendant), D-312-835-3146/47, FAX 706-682-9842, 24 hours. Check in facility, check out 1200 hours. All ranks, dependents (Space-A), reservists, and government civilian employees on TDY orders. Fee charged for late checkouts. No pets. No children.

TML: Guest House. Buildings 36-38, and 96. C-706-689-1142, all ranks. Priority PCS personnel, all others Space-A. Bedrooms, private bath, refrigerator, A/C, color TV, housekeeping service (M-F), living room sofa bed. Older structures, New Structure (Bldg 96), includes kitchenettes. Call for rates. Check out time: 1100. (Fee equal to room).

TML: VOQ/VEQ. Buildings 73, 75, 83, 399, all ranks, primarily for TDY students, may have Space-A for transients. C-706-689-2505. Children not authorized. Check out time 1200. Call for rates. (Fee equal to room).

TML: MWR Destin Army Recreation Area, 557 Calhoun Ave, Destin, Fl 32541, **C-1-800-642-0466, 904-837-2725.** All ranks, leave or official duty, retirees, Fort Benning personnel. Motel: bedrooms, two double beds, private bath (34); cottages, two bedroom, private bath (20); three bedroom, private bath (4). Refrigerator, CATV, coffee pot, towels/linens, recreation rental equipment (large fishing and party vessels), close to Hurlburt field support. Rates: based on rank, motel $30-36 daily; cottages $37-$47 daily. Additional fee for non ID card holders. Cabin #1 O6+, call SGS 404-1545-3946/4411 for reservations. No pets. **Note:** see *Military RV, Camping & Rec Areas Around the World* for additional information.

TML: MWR, Uchee Creek Army Campground and Marina. Located south of Columbus, easy access from US-80, I-185, US-280, US-431 and AL165. Building 0007. Reservations: **C-706-545-7238/4055,** D-312-835-7238/4053. Write: Community Recreation Division, PO Box 53323, ATTN: Uchee Creek Army campground/marina, Fort Benning, GA 31905-5226. VISA & Mastercard. Check in at facility, check out 1100 hours. All ranks, family members, government civilian employees. Secluded cabins, largest sleeps 6, private bath (4); medium, sleeps 4, private bath (10); small, sleeps

GEORGIA
Fort Benning, continued

4, no bath or kitchen facilities (comfort station on site). Large and medium cabins have: microwave, stove, refrigerator, utensils, TV/VCR, A/C, heat. Guests furnish linen and towels, blankets and pillows provided. No pets. Recreation and rental equipment, country store, RV pads, marina, playground, fishing, and pool on campground. Availability: best weekdays, worst weekends and holidays, in summer. Winter, good all season.

TML: DV/VIP. McIver St. Officer O6+. Protocol RSVP C-706-545-5724, D-312-835-5724, private bath suite. Refrigerator, A/C, color TV, housekeeping service (M-F). Older structure. Rates $23, $10 for additional occupant. Retired and lower ranks Space-A. Check out 1100 (fee of $15 for late check out).

TML Availability: Best: Dec, worst: Jun-Sep.

CREDIT CARDS ACCEPTED: Visa, MasterCard, American Express, Diners and Discover.

For those interested in military history, visit the Infantry museum, the Infantry Hall of Fame and a number of other Fort Benning points of interest. See more about Camp Uchee in Military Living's *Military RV, Camping and Rec Areas Around the World*.

Locator 545-5216   Medical 544-2041   Police 544-3911

Fort Gillem (GA21R1)
Billeting
AFZK-PWH
Bldg 816 Fort Gillem
Forest Park, GA 30050-5000

TELEPHONE NUMBER INFORMATION: Main installation numbers: C-404-363-5000, D-312-797-1001.

Location: From I-75, east on I-285 to US-54 (Jonesboro Road), S for 3 miles to the main gate. Fort is 5 miles from Hartsfield IAP. *USMRA: Page 37 (C-4) & Page 49 (C-4)*. NMC: Atlanta, 10 miles northwest.

Lodging Office: Building 816, Hood Ave, **C-404-363-5810,** 0730-1600 hours duty days. Check in facility, check out 1000 hours daily. No government civilian employee billeting. This is a sub-post of Fort McPherson.

TML: VOQ/VEQ. Buildings 131, 134, all ranks, leave or official duty. Bedrooms, private bath (7); bedroom, private bath, (7). Kitchen, utensils, A/C, color TV, housekeeping service, washer/dryer, ice vending. Older structure. Rates: $23/$25 per apartment. Duty can make reservations, others Space-A.

DV/VIP: Billeting Office, C-404-363-5431, O6/GS-15+. Retirees & lower ranks Space-A.

TML Availability: Extremely limited.

CREDIT CARDS ACCEPTED: Visa, MasterCard and American Express.

GEORGIA
Fort Gillem, continued

"Gone with the Wind" country, and historic Atlanta attractions, combine with seashore, flatlands and mountains to make this area a joy to visit.

Locator 363-5000   Police 363-5982   Medical 752-3711

Fort Gordon (GA09R1)
HQDA, USASC&FC (ATZH-DIH-B)
Fort Gordon Billeting NAFI
Bldg 250, Griffith Hall
Fort Gordon, GA 30905-5040

TELEPHONE NUMBER INFORMATION: Main installation numbers: C-706-791-0110, D-312-780-0110.

Location: Between US-78/278 and US-1. Gates are on both US-78 & US-1. *USMRA: Page 37 (F-4).* NMC: Augusta, 12 miles northeast.

Lodging Office: Griffith Hall, building 250, Chamberlain Ave, 24 hours daily. Reservations: **C-706-791-2277,** FAX 706-796-6595, check in facility, check out 1100 hours daily. Government civilian employee billeting.

TML: Stinson Guest House. building 37300, all ranks, leave or official duty, **C-706-793-7160,** D-312-780-7183, 24 hours daily. Check in 1300 to 1800 hours, check out 1100 hours daily, one hour additional on request. Bedrooms, private bath (103); handicapped accessible rooms, private bath (3); kitchenettes (12). Refrigerator, microwave, A/C, color TV, cribs/rollaways ($2), washer/dryer, fitness center, spa, playground, BBQ grills, park area, video rental service, free breakfast, coffee service twice daily. Modern structure. Rates: $27/$29/$31 per room. PCS/hospital visitors can make reservations 60 days in advance, all others 7 days in advance. Reservations held until 6 p.m. unless prepaid with credit card. Pets must be boarded off post prior to check-in. Boarding information available at front desk.

TML: Guest House. Building 34602, enlisted E1-E4, check in billeting. Bedroom, common bath (4); separate bedroom, private bath (15). Microfridge, A/C, color TV in room & lounge, housekeeping service, washer/dryer. Older structure. Rates: $5 single, $8 family. Maximum 2-3 per room. PCS and hospital visitors can make reservations, others Space-A. Payment is due in advance. Pets must be boarded off post prior to check-in.

TML: Guest House. Building 18404, enlisted E7-E9, check in billeting. Two bedroom apartments, private bath (2). Kitchen, utensils, A/C, color TV, housekeeping service. Modern structure. Rates: $20.50 single, $22.50 family. PCS and hospital visitors can make reservations, others Space-A. Pets must be boarded off post prior to check-in.

TML: VOQ/VEQ. Buildings 250, 36700, Military TDY all ranks, leave or official duty. Check in billeting. Bedroom, private bath (444). Refrigerator, microwave, A/C, color TV in room & lounge, housekeeping service, washer/dryer, ice vending. Modern structure. Rates: $22.50 single, $2 each additional person. Maximum 2 per room. Children authorized in Guest Housing only. Duty can make reservations, others Space-A. Pets must be boarded off post prior to check-in.

82 - Temporary Military Lodging Around the World

GEORGIA
Fort Gordon, continued

TML: DVQ. Buildings 250, 36700, 34503/04/06, 34601/05, and quarters 6, officers O3+. Separate bedrooms, private bath (19). Kitchen, complete utensils, A/C, color TV, housekeeping service, cots. Bldg. 250 and 36700 modern structures, others older structures. Rates: $25 single, $2 each additional person. Duty can make reservations, others, including lesser ranks, Space-A. Pets must be boarded off post prior to check-in.

TML: Fisher House. Note: See appendix C for a definition of this facility. **C-706-787-3319.**

DV/VIP: Protocol Office, 10th floor, Signal Towers, C-706-791-5376/0022, O6+. Retirees and lower ranks (O3+) Space-A.

TML Availability: Good.

CREDIT CARDS ACCEPTED: Visa, MasterCard, American Express and Discover.

Locator 791-4675   **Medical 787-6686**   **Police 791-4537/2681**

Fort McPherson (GA08R1)
Billeting Office
Bldg T-22
Fort McPherson, GA 30330-5000

TELEPHONE NUMBER INFORMATION: Main installation numbers: C-404-752-3113, D-312-572-1110.

Location: Off I-75 take Lakewood Freeway (GA-166), exit to US-29 (Main St exit). Main gate is at Main St exit. *USMRA: Page 49 (B-3)*. NMC: Atlanta, in city limits.

Lodging Office: Building T-22. **C-404-752-3833/2253**, FAX 404-752-3376, DSN FAX 312-572-3376, 0600-2330 hours daily. Other hours, SDO, building 65, 404-752-2980. Check in facility 1400 hours, check out 1000 hours daily. Government civilian employee billeting.

TML: Transient Quarters. Building T-109 (**Chalet**), all ranks, leave or official duty. One bedroom, semi-private bath (8). Refrigerator, microwave, community kitchen, utensils, individual telephone, A/C, color TV, lounge, housekeeping service, washer/dryer. Older structure. Rates: $20. Duty can make reservations, others Space-A.

TML: VOQ/VEQ. Building T-22 (**Chateau**), all ranks, leave or official duty. One bedroom, private bath (20). Refrigerator, microwave, community kitchen, individual telephone, A/C, color TV, lounge, housekeeping service, washer/dryer, ice vending. Older structure. Same rates as above.

TML: VOQ/VEQ. Building 168 (**Hardee Hall**). All ranks, leave or official duty. Eight suites, nine single rooms, private bath, refrigerator/microwave, color TV, individual telephones, common area kitchen. Modern structure. Duty can make reservations.

TML: DV/VIP. Lee Hall, officer O6+, leave or official duty, C-404-752-5388. Various size suites, private bath (8). Refrigerator, community kitchen, A/C, color TV in room & lounge, housekeeping service, ice vending. Historic structure. Rates: $30.00. Duty can make reservations, others Space-A.

GEORGIA
Fort McPherson

DV/VIP: Protocol Office, building 200, C-404-752-4145, O6+. Retirees and lower ranks Space-A.

TML Availability: Good. Best Dec-Feb.

CREDIT CARDS ACCEPTED: Visa, MasterCard and American Express.

Fort McPherson is steeped in history, and surrounded by the vibrant city of Atlanta. Note: Lake Altoona Army Rec Area has cabins and apartments. Call 706-974-3413/9420 and read *Military RV, Camping and Rec Areas around the World*.

Locator 752-2743/4174   Medical 752-3711   Police 752-2281

Fort Stewart (GA15R1)
Fort Stewart Guest House
4951 Coe Ave
Fort Stewart, GA 31331-5000

TELEPHONE NUMBER INFORMATION: Main installation numbers: C-912-767-1110, D-312-870-1110.

Location: Accessible from US-17 or I-95. Also GA-119 or GA-144 crosses the Post. *USMRA: Page 37 (G,H-7)*. NMC: Savannah, 35 miles northeast.

Lodging Office: ATTN: AFZP-DPW-B. Building 4951. **C-912-767-8384,** D-312-870-8384, FAX 912-876-7469, 0730-2345 hours daily. Other hours, SDO, building 01, C-912-767-8666. Check in billeting 1400, check out 1100 hours daily. Government civilian employees billeting TDY, PCS.

TML: Guest House. Building 4951, all ranks, leave or official duty, C-912-767-8384/368-4184. Bedroom, dining room, private bath (sleeps 6) (70). Kitchen, A/C, CATV, housekeeping service, cribs/cots, essentials, handicapped accessible, washer/dryer, ice vending. Modern structure. Rates: $22 per room per night. Duty and DAVs can make reservations, others Space-A.

TML: BOQ/VOQ. Building 4950, C-912-767-8384, officers all ranks, official duty only. Reservations accepted (VOQ), not taken (BOQ). Bedroom, private bath (45). Kitchen, A/C, color TV, housekeeping service, washer/dryer, ice vending. Modern structure. Rates: $20 per room per night. BOQ rooms, rates not available. Inquire at above number. Maximum 1 per room.

TML: DVQ. Officer O6+, leave or official duty, C-912-767-8610. Two bedroom cottages, private bath (2). A/C, cots/cribs, essentials, ice vending, kitchen, complete utensils, housekeeping service, handicapped accessible, color TV, washer/dryer. Rate: $20-TDY, $22-PCS. Active and retirees can make reservations, others Space-A.

DV/VIP: Protocol, building 01, C-912-767-8610. O6+. Retirees and lower ranks Space-A.

TML Availability: Fairly good. Best Nov-Apr. More difficult, other times.

CREDIT CARDS ACCEPTED: Visa, MasterCard, American Express, Discover and Espirit.

GEORGIA
Fort Stewart, continued

Local recreational activities are hunting, fishing, tennis and golf. Ocean beaches are within driving distance, and historic Savannah is 40 miles northeast with many attractions.

Locator 767-2862   Medical 767-6666   Police 767-2822

Hunter Army Airfield (GA10R1)
Hunter Billeting Office
Bldg 6010
Hunter Army Airfield, GA 31409-5206

TELEPHONE NUMBER INFORMATION: Main installation numbers: C-912-352-6521, D-312-971-1110.

Location: From I-95 to GA-204 east for 13 miles to Savannah. Turn left onto Stephenson Ave, proceed straight into Wilson Ave Gate to Installation. *USMRA: Page 37 (H-7).* NMC: Savannah, in southwest part of city.

Lodging Office: Building 6010, Duncan and Leonard Sts. C-912-352-5910/5834 or 355-1060, FAX 912-352-6864, DSN FAX 312-971-6864, 0700-2400 hours M-F, 0800-1700 hours Sa-Su, holidays. After hours, SDO, building 1201, C-912-352-5140. Check in time 1400, check out 1100 hours daily. Government civilian employee billeting.

TML: Guest House/VOQ/VEQ. Buildings 6005, 6010, all ranks, leave or official duty. Two bedroom suites, private bath (32); bedroom, semi-private bath (9). Kitchen, complete utensils, essentials, A/C, color TV in room & lounge, housekeeping service, cribs/cots, washer/dryer, food/ice vending, handicapped accessible. Older structures. Renovated and remodeled. Rates: $20-$34 per family. All categories can make reservations. PCS have priority.

DV/VIP: Cmdr, 24th Inf Div, ATTN: AFZP-CS-P, building 1. C-912-767-7742, D-312-971-8610. O5+. Retirees Space-A.

TML Availability: Very good, all times.

CREDIT CARDS ACCEPTED: Visa, MasterCard, American Express and Diners.

Near historic Savannah. Hunting, fishing, coastal Georgian beaches.

Locator 767-2862   Medical 352-5551   Police 352-6133

Kings Bay Naval Submarine Base (GA03R1)
Bachelor Housing Office, Bldg 1056
952 James Madison Rd
Kings Bay, GA 31547-5015

TELEPHONE NUMBER INFORMATION: Main installation numbers: C-912-673-2165, D-312-860-2111.

GEORGIA
Kings Bay Naval Submarine Base, continued

Location: Off I-95 north of GA/FL border. Take exit 1 which leads right into base, or exits 2A or 2B, east to Kings Bay and follow road north to base. *USMRA: Page 37 (G-9).* NMC: Jacksonville, 40 miles south.

Lodging Office: ATTN: Housing Office QL31, building 1056, 952 James Madison Rd, **C-912-673-2165,** 0800-1630 hours M-F. Check in billeting, check out 1200 daily.

TML: Navy Lodge. Building 0158, all ranks, leave or official duty. For reservations call **1-800-NAVY-INN**, lodge number is 882-6868. Check in 1500-1800, check out 1200 hours daily. Bedroom, 2 double beds, private bath (26). Four sets interconnecting, two handicapped accessible, 13 non-smoking. Kitchenette, microwave, utensils, A/C, CATV, housekeeping service, playground, cribs, coin washer/dryer, ice/snack vending. Modern structure. Rates: $35 per room. Maximum 5 per room. Duty and retirees can make reservations.

TML: BEQ. Building 1041, enlisted all ranks, leave or official duty, C-912-673-2163/2164. Bedroom, private bath (142). Refrigerator, A/C, color TV, cots, essentials, food/ice vending, housekeeping service, washer/dryer, microwave, coffee pot. Modern structure. Rates: VIP $12 for one person, $15 for two, $18 for 3 or more; all others $6 for one person, $12 for two, $9 for 3 or more. Maximum charge VIP & family suite $18, maximum charge for rooms $9. Maximum 4 persons. Duty can make reservations, others Space-A.

TML: BOQ. Building 1056, officers, all ranks, leave or official duty, C-912-673-2165/2169. Handicapped accessible. Bedroom, private bath (38); separate bedroom, private bath (98). A/C, cots, essentials, food/ice vending, housekeeping service, color TV in room, washer/dryer. Modern structure. Rates: $7-$15 per person, maximum charge $16-$20. Maximum 4 persons. Duty can make reservations, others Space-A.

TML Availability: Good. Best Oct-Dec. Difficult Jun-Sep.

CREDIT CARDS ACCEPTED: Visa, MasterCard and American Express.

From the beauty and history of old Savannah to the beaches of the Golden Isles near Brunswick and the Cumberland Island National Seashore, coastal Georgia offers everything from sightseeing to fishing and hunting.

Locator 673-2000   Medical 882-5109   Police 882-2265

Moody Air Force Base (GA02R1)
347 SVS/SVML
3131 Cooney St
Moody AFB, GA 31699-1511

TELEPHONE NUMBER INFORMATION: Main installation numbers: C-912-257-4211, D-312-460-4211.

Location: On GA 125, 12 miles north of Valdosta. Also, can be reached from I-75 Exit 6 via US-41 and Inner Perimeter road as well as I-75 via GA-122. *USMRA: Page 37 (D,E-9).* NMC: Valdosta, 10 miles south.

GEORGIA
Moody Air Force Base, continued

Lodging Office: Building 3131, Cooney St, **C-912-257-3893**, FAX 912-257-4971, DSN FAX 312-460-4971, 24 hours daily. Check in lodging at 1400, check out 1200 hours. Government employee off base contract quarters.

TML: TLF. Building 3080, all ranks, leave or official duty. Two bedroom, private bath (12). Kitchen, A/C, color TV, housekeeping service, cribs/cots, washer/dryer. Community motel design. Rates: E1, E2 & O1, $11; E3-E6, $17; E7 & up, $24. PCS in/out, permissive TDY w/ family or PCS, retirement, separation, out patients, friends, relatives of patients, all others Space-A.

TML: VAQ. Building 3080, enlisted all ranks, leave or official duty. Units, private bath (29). Refrigerator, A/C, color TV, housekeeping service, washer/dryer. Community motel design. Rates: $7 per person. PCS in/out, TDY can make reservations, others Space-A.

TML: VOQ. Building 3132, officers all ranks, leave or official duty. Bedroom, private bath (23). Kitchen, refrigerator, A/C, color TV, housekeeping service, washer/dryer. Community motel design. Rates: $7 per person. PCS in/out, TDY can make reservations, others Space-A.

TML: DV. Buildings 3132/3080, officers O6+, E8-E9, leave or official duty. Bedroom suites, private bath (officer) (5), $10 per person; two bedroom suite, private bath (Officer) (1), $14 per person; one bedroom suite, private bath (Officer) (1), $14 per person; bedroom suites, private bath (E8-E9) (2). Kitchen, A/C, color TV, housekeeping service, washer/dryer. Community motel design. Rates: $10 per person. PCS in/out, TDY can make reservations, others Space-A.

DV/VIP: Protocol Office, 347 WG/CCP, building 5113, C-912-257-3480, O6+, E9, retirees and lower ranks Space-A.

TML Availability: Good, May, Sep, Dec. Difficult, Jun-Aug.

CREDIT CARDS ACCEPTED: Visa, MasterCard and American Express.

Visit the mansion Crescent, in Valdosta, for tours, particularly during Azalea season. There are many freshwater lakes for fishing and water sports. Dove, quail, turkey and other wild game hunting in season is also popular.

Locator 257-3585   Medical 257-3232   Police 257-3108

Robins Air Force Base (GA14R1)
78 SPTG/SVML
755 Warner Robbins St
Robins AFB, GA 31098-1469

TELEPHONE NUMBER INFORMATION: Main installation numbers: C-912-926-1113, D-312-468-1001.

Location: Off US-129 on GA-247 at Warner Robins. Access from I-75 south. *USMRA: Page 37 (D-6)*. NMC: Macon, 18 miles northwest.

Lodging Office: Pine Oaks Lodge, building 557, Club Dr, **C-912-926-2100**, FAX 912-926-0977, DSN 312-468-2100, 24 hours daily. Check in facility.

GEORGIA
Robins Air Force Base, continued

TML: TLF. Building 1180-1183, all ranks, leave or official duty. Check out 1000 hours. Bedroom, private bath (40). Kitchen, complete utensils, A/C, color TVs, housekeeping service, cots/cribs, ice vending, washer/dryer. Older structure. Rates: $18. Maximum 5 per unit. Duty may make reservations, others Space-A.

TML: VOQ. Buildings 551, 553, 557, officers all ranks, leave or official duty. Handicapped accessible. Check out 1200 hours. DV Suites (5); Sr Officer suites (5). Bedroom, private bath (40); Private bedroom, semi-private bath (4); two bedroom, semi-private bath (40). Kitchen, complete utensils, A/C, refrigerator, color TV, housekeeping service, cribs/cots, washer/dryer. Older structure. Rates: DV Suites $14; other rooms $8 per person, maximum family rate $16. Maximum 4 per unit. Duty may make reservations, others Space-A.

TML: VAQ. Building 755, enlisted all ranks, leave or official duty. Check out 1200 hours. Private bedroom, shared bath (24); shared bedroom, shared bath (2); two bedroom, shared bath (40); E9 suites, private bath (7). Refrigerator, A/C, color TV, housekeeping service, washer/dryer, ice vending. Older structure. Rates: $8 per person. Duty may make reservations, others Space-A. Chief suites $14.

DV/VIP: Building 215, C-912-926-2761, O6+.

TML Availability: Good, Oct-May. Difficult, other times.

CREDIT CARDS ACCEPTED: Visa, MasterCard and American Express.

Macon, 18 miles northwest, is the geographic center of Georgia, where shopping, parks (this is the Cherry Blossom Capital of the World) welcome visitors with true Southern hospitality. Also visit the Museum of Aviation, home of the Georgia Aviation Hall of Fame.

Locator 926-6027   **Medical 926-3845**   **Police 926-2187**

Too Late To Copy
Camp Frank D. Merrill, Wahsega Road, Dahlonega, GA 30533-9499. Small lodging facility (two units), **C-706-864-3327 EX-187.** All ranks. (Can be bumped by incoming assigned duty status personnel).

HAWAII

Barbers Point Naval Air Station (HI10R6)
CBQ, Bldg 77
Barbers Point, HI 96862-5050
Scheduled to close 7/31/99.

TELEPHONE NUMBER INFORMATION: Main installation numbers: C-808-684-6266, D-315-484-6266.

Location: Take HI-1 West (toward Waianee) to NAS/Makakilo exit, south for 2.5 miles to main gate. *USMRA: Page 129 (C-7).* NMC: Honolulu, 12 miles east.

Lodging Office: Combined Bachelor Quarters, building 77, BEQ **C-808-684-9146,** D-315-484-9146, FAX 808-684-0704, DSN FAX 315-484-0704, 24 hours daily. Active duty check in 0700, check out 1200, Space-A check in 1600, check out 1000 hours.

TML: BOQ. Building 77, Hornet St., officers all ranks, leave or official duty. Bedroom, living room private bath (77). Refrigerator, microwave, coffee makers, A/C, color TV in room & lounge, VCR, hair dryers, housekeeping service, washer/dryer, ice vending. VHS movies available for no charge - sign out at front desk. Rates: Adult $8. No children. Maximum 2 persons per room. Senior officer suites (12), $12 per person. Duty can make reservations, others Space-A.

TML: BEQ. Building 48, enlisted all ranks, leave or official duty. E1-E4 shared room, shared bath (53); E7-E9 bedroom, shared bath (32); E5-E9 private room, private bath (14); E7-E9 senior enlisted suites, private room, private bath (4). Refrigerator, microwave, coffee makers, A/C, color TV in room & lounge, telephone system, housekeeping service, washer/dryer, vending machine. Modern structure, renovated '92. Rates: $4-$8 per person. No children. Duty can make reservations, others Space-A.

DV/VIP: O5+. Rates: $12. E7-E9, rates $8. Renovated '93.

TML Availability: Good, winter months. Difficult, summer months.

CREDIT CARDS ACCEPTED: Visa, MasterCard, American Express and Diners.

Easy access to commissary and exchange facilities. The southwestern coast of Oahu, known for its beautiful beaches. Check Barbers Point Rec Area listing for more lodging.

Locator 684-1005/6266   Medical 684-8245   Police 684-6222/7114

Barbers Point Recreation Area (HI01R6)
Morale Welfare Rec Dept
Naval Air Station
Barbers Point, HI 96862-5050
Scheduled to close 9/30/97.

TELEPHONE NUMBER INFORMATION: Main installation numbers: C-808-684-6266, D-315-484-6266.

HAWAII
Barbers Point Recreation Area, continued

Location: Take HI-1 West to Barbers Point/Makakilo exit. Left at sign then go through main gate. Turn right on Saratoga, 2nd bldg on left, Bldg 1924. *USMRA: Page 129 (C-7)*. NMC: Pearl Harbor, 10 miles northeast.

Lodging Office: Morale, Welfare, Recreation Dept, Beach Cottages, Barbers Point NAS, HI 96862-5050, **C-808-682-2019**, D-315-430-0111/2019, FAX 808-682-4235, 0800-1700 hours M-F. Reservations 60 days in advance. Priority system in effect. Call for information. Confirmation four weeks in advance. Mail applications to MWR Cottage Reservations, Naval Air Station, Barbers Point, HI 96862-5050. Reservations for 3 days F-M, 4 days M-F, 7 days M-M or F-F. Check in at area 1400 hours daily, check out 0900 hours daily. Cottages cannot be used as party facility. Operates year round.

TML: Rec Cottages, all ranks, leave only. Handicapped accessible. Two bedroom enlisted cottages (14); two bedroom officer cottages (6), VIP cottages (O6+) (2). Kitchen, complete utensils, color TV (VIP only), cribs/cots, BBQ grills. Rates: enlisted $40 per unit; officer/VIP $40 per unit. Maximum 6 persons. All categories can make reservations by written application, see information above.

DV/VIP: Administration Office, building 1, C-808-474-4103, O7/GS-16+. Retirees and lower ranks Space-A. Flag Officer Cottages 1760 and 1775 (Space-A to O-6+), Reservations: **C-808-474-2101**, D-315-430-0111, 315-474/1181, FAX 808-474-8751.

TML Availability: Good, Jan-Apr & Oct-Nov. Difficult, other times.

CREDIT CARDS ACCEPTED: Visa, MasterCard and American Express.

Complete beach rec area. Check with Special Services, Ticket Office for tourist/island activities. Complete support facility at NAS. For full details see Military Living's Military RV, Camping & Rec Areas Around The World.

Barking Sands Pacific Missile Range Facility (HI04R6)
MWR, PO Box 128
Kehaha, Kauai, HI 96752-0128

TELEPHONE NUMBER INFORMATION: Main installation numbers: C-808-335-4111, D-315-471-6111.

Location: From the airport, take Highway 50 west about 30 miles. *USMRA: Page 129 (B-2)*. NMC: Waimea, 8 miles south.

Lodging Office: Bldg 1261, C-808-335-4383, D-315-471-6383, FAX 808-335-4679, DSN FAX 315-471-6769, 24 hours daily. Information, on MWR Beach Cottages, **C-808-335-4752,** D-315-471-6752, from 0600-1430. Reservations are made by application only. You may call or write to: MWR Department, Beach Cottage Reservations PMRF, Barking Sands, PO Box 128, Kekaha, HI 96752-0128. Reservations can be made up to 60 days in advance. Check in at Rec Center (Bldg 1264), 1400-2100, after 2100 check in at BEQ office (Bldg 1261), check out 1000. A late checkout will be charged one (1) days rental fee, unless prior notice is made to reservationist.

HAWAII
Barking Sands Pacific Missile Range Facility, continued

TML: MWR Beach Cottages. All ranks, leave or official duty. Two bedrooms, private bath, sofabed, sleeps 6 (9). Accessible to handicapped. Kitchen, utensils, microwave, refrigerator, color TV, washer/dryer, iron and board, outdoor BBQ, balcony, ceiling fans. Rates: $50/2 persons, $4 each additional person. All categories can make reservations. All Hands Club, Shenanigans, Fatty's galley/mess hall Menehune Inn. Indoor/Outdoor gear rentals, fitness gym, craft center, pool, theater.

DV/VIP: Two cottages set aside for O6+. Write to: Commanding Officer, PMRF Barking Sands, Kekaha, HI 96752. C-808-335-4255, D-315-471-6255.

TML Availability: Very good, Sep through Feb. Difficult, Mar through Aug.

This is truly the Navy's "Best Kept Secret In Paradise!!" Captain Cook's historic landing place, and Waimea Canyon, "the Grand Canyon of Hawaii" and a seven mile strip of white sandy beach are nearby.

Locator 335-4111   **Medical 335-4203**   **Police 335-4523**

Bellows Recreation Area (HI02R6)
Reservation Office
P.O. Box 220
Bellows AFS, HI 96853-5000

TELEPHONE NUMBER INFORMATION: Main installation numbers: C-1-800-437-2607, D-315-259-8841.

Location: From Honolulu Airport or Hickam AFB, take H1 east to exit 21A (Pali Highway). Go north on Pali Hwy (Hwy 61). Turn right onto Kalanlanaole Hwy (Hwy 72). Clearly marked. *USMRA: Page 129 (E-7).* NMC: Kailua, 9 miles northwest.

Lodging Office: Write to: Bellows Reservation Office, PO Box 220, Tinker Rd., Waimanalo, HI 96795-5000. C- (From US Mainland) **1-800-437-2607, All Others C-808-259-8841.** Priorities: active duty 90 days in advance, in summer and December holiday time frames, others 75 days in advance. Other times reservations taken up to 1 year in advance. Maximum 14 day occupancy, sponsor or family member may register. Deposit (1 night's rent) required 10 days after reservations made, (MC, Visa, checks, and cash accepted) cancellations 14 days prior to occupancy. Note: When reservation period includes a Friday, Saturday or Federal Holiday - the beginning date of a reservation may not be canceled without canceling the entire reservation. Reservation office open 24 hours daily. Check in 1400 hours, check out 1200 hours.

TML: Two bedroom cottages. All ranks, leave only. See above. Cottages, private bath, two bedroom configurations (105) (single & duplex units), 50 for officers, 55 for enlisted. Kitchen, complete utensils, CATV, ceiling fans, cribs, dishes, linens, towels, bedding all furniture. Rates: Back row $47, ocean view $52.

TML Availability: Good, Oct-Apr. Difficult, other times.

CREDIT CARDS ACCEPTED: Visa and MasterCard.

HAWAII
Bellows Recreation Area, continued

On Oahu's northwest coast, about 16 miles from downtown Waikiki, turquoise waters and gorgeous beaches await your arrival! Beach front rec center. For camping see *Military RV, Camping & Rec Areas Around The World*.

Locator (Mgr) 259-5428   Medical 257-3133   Police-259-5955

Fort Shafter (HI09R6)
453B Burr Road
Fort Shafter, HI 96858-5000

TELEPHONE NUMBER INFORMATION: Main installation numbers: C-808-471-7110, D-315-430-0111.

Location: Take HI-1 West exit at Fort Shafter, clearly marked. USMRA: Page 129 (D-7) & Page *131 (D-2; E-1, 2)*. NMC: Honolulu, 7 miles east.

Lodging: 453B, Burr Road, **C-808-839-2336**, 0745-1545 hours daily. Write to: TAMC Billeting Fund, Tripler Army Medical Center, Tripler AMC, HI 96859-5000. Check in billeting or facility, check out 1100 hours daily.

TML: Guest House. Building 453B, Burr Rd, all ranks, leave or official duty. Two bedroom (4 units no kitchen) private bath (8); Three bedroom, private bath (4). Kitchen, complete utensils, color TV, housekeeping service, cribs/cots, washer/dryer. Older structure. Rates: 2 bedroom cottage, no kitchen $25, with kitchen $30; 3 Bedroom cottage, with kitchen $35, $5 each additional person. Children under 1, free. Maximum 7 per unit. PCS can make reservations and have priority; PCS out 7 days maximum, reservation in advance, PCS in 10 days. Others Space-A.

TML: Cottages. All ranks, leave or official duty, family members, retirees, DoD employees on official duty. Bedroom, with twin or double beds (12). Kitchen (some), utensils, color TV, iron/board, phones, cribs, playground, housekeeping service. Rates: not available. Call above number. Reservations 2 months in advance. All categories can make reservations.

TML Availability: Fair, most of the year.

The oldest army post in Hawaii, part of the post is a National Historic Place. Visit the Bishop Museum in Honolulu, the Honolulu Academy of Arts, Mission Houses Museum, and don't miss the beach!

Locator 438-1904   Medical 433-6620   Police 438-2885

Hale Koa Hotel AFRC (HI08R6)
2055 Kalia Road
Honolulu, HI 96815-1998

TELEPHONE NUMBER INFORMATION: Main installation numbers: **C-808-955-0555** (24 hours), reservations: **1-800-367-6027**; D-315-438-6739 (official travel), FAX 1-800-425-3329, (24 hrs, except holidays).

HAWAII
Hale Koa, continued

Location: At 2055 Kalia Road, Waikiki Beach, Honolulu, HI. Fort DeRussy, is on Waikiki Beach, between the Ala Moana Blvd, Kalakaua Ave and Saratoga Road, about 9 miles east of Honolulu International Airport. *USMRA: Page 131 (F-4)*. NMC: Honolulu, in the city.

Description of Area: This morale-boosting, all ranks hotel, was opened in October 1975. Fourteen stories with 814 guest rooms with views of the Pacific Ocean and Koolau Mountains. All rooms identical in size, with private bath, lanai, color TVs, room-controlled air-conditioning, refrigerators. Some rooms handicapped accessible. Coin-operated washers & dryers available. Beautifully landscaped gardens, famous Waikiki Beach, swimming pool, and recreational activities: tennis, snorkeling, swimming, volleyball and racquet ball. Casual or fine dining: Pool side Snack Bar, Happy's Self-Service Snack Bar, Snack Shack, Koko Cafe, Bibas Restaurant, or the Hale Koa Room, the hotel's signature restaurant. Private banquets, meetings, and conferences arranged through the hotel's catering services. Live entertainment and dancing in the Warriors Lounge, Pool side drinks at the Barefoot Bar. Fitness center with sauna and locker rooms, Post Exchange, jewelry store, barber & beauty shops, car rental desk and tour and travel desk. Three dinner shows each week: Hale Koa Luau, Tama's Polynesian Revue, and Tuesday Night Magic. The **Hale Koa** is a complete resort. Dress: aloha-wear at all times. The 1996 double rates quoted below.

1996 double rates (**rates will change 1 October 1996**):

	I	II	III
Categories For Both Active & Retired	PVT-SGT	SSG-CSM O1 - CWO3 LT-CAPT Widows/ DAV*	CW4-CW5 MAJ-GEN CAPT (USN) TDY, TLA Foreign
Standard	$48	$60	$73
Moderate	$56	$70	$85
Superior	$59	$74	$90
Partial Ocean View	$64	$80	$97
Ocean View	$70	$87	$106
Deluxe Ocean View	$74	$92	$112
Ocean Front	$78	$98	$119
Deluxe Ocean Front	$86	$108	$132

Rates are subject to change on or before October 1, 1996.

* Must have DD-1173. Note: Widows(ers) may sponsor guest. Write or call Hotel for more information.

Season of Operation: Year round.

Reservations: Required. Write for reservation and information packet: 2055 Kalia Road, Honolulu, HI 96815-1998. Call **1-800-367-6027** 0800-1600 daily HI time, D-315-438-6739 (official travel) or FAX 808-425-3329.

Eligibility*: Active duty, retired, DoD civilians, Reserve and National Guard. Ocean front rooms have king beds only. Daily rates based on room location (generally the higher floors reflect increased rates) and the number of occupants (maximum of 4 persons permitted. Over 2 persons, add $10 for each additional person over age 12. On family plan, children under 12 free in parent's room (no

HAWAII
Hale Koa, continued

additional beds required). Most rooms have two double beds. Cribs available at $4 per night. Reservations may be made for a maximum stay of 30 days. Extensions permitted on a Space-A basis.

* Active and Retired (DD form 2 Retired-Gray or Blue) and dependents (DD1173), all services, all ranks, family & guests meeting eligibility requirements.

Hale Koa Luau on Monday and Thursday, $27.95 for adults, $17.95 children under 12. Tama's Polynesian Revue Dinner Show Wednesday night in the Banyan Tree Showroom, $17.95 for adults and $9.50 for children under 12. The Tuesday Night Magic Show Mexican/Italian dinner buffet $18.95 for adults and $9.50 for children under 12. ID cardholders may sponsor guests.

Check out the Army Museum, Diamond Head, Honolulu Zoo, Waikiki Aquarium, and Ala Moana Center, not to mention Downtown Honolulu.

Hickam Air Force Base (HI11R6)
Hickam Lodging
15 SVS/SVML
15 G Street, Bldg 1153
Hickam AFB, HI 96853-5000

TELEPHONE NUMBER INFORMATION: Main installation numbers: C-808-471-7110, D-315-471-7110.

Location: Adjacent to the Honolulu IAP. Accessible from HI-1 or HI-92. Clearly marked. *USMRA: Page 129 (D-7) & Page 131 (B,C-3,4)*. NMC: Honolulu, 6 miles east.

Lodging Office: ATTN: 15 SVS/SVML, building 1153, **C-808-449-2603,** D-315-449-2603, FAX 808-449-3572, 24 hours daily. Check in facility, check out 1200 hours daily. Government civilian employee billeting.

TML: VOQ. Nine buildings adjacent to O'Club. Officers all ranks, leave or official duty. Bedroom, private bath (34); two bedroom apartments, living room, private bath (88). Kitchen, microwave TV, housekeeping service. Older structure. Rates: $9.50 per person, maximum $19 per family. Duty can make reservations, others Space-A.

TML: VAQ. Buildings 470, 471, senior enlisted E7+, leave or official duty. Two bedroom apartments, private bath (16) (kitchen, microwave, TV); single rooms, private bath (24). Housekeeping service. Older structure. Rates: $9.50 per person. Maximum $46 per family. Duty can make reservations, others Space-A.

TML: VAQ. Building 1153 (female); Buildings 1166, 1168 (male), enlisted E1-E6, leave or official duty. Bedroom, 2 persons per room, communal bath (33). Housekeeping service. Older structure. Rates: $9.50 per person. Duty can make reservations, others Space-A.

TML: DV/VIP. Building 728, officers O9+, leave or official duty. Buildings 725, 922, 934, one and two bedroom apartments, living room, private bath (26). Kitchen, microwave, TV, housekeeping service. Older structure. Rates: $14.00 per person, maximum $28 per family. Duty can make reservations, others Space-A.

HAWAII
Hickam Air Force Base, continued

DV/VIP: PACAF Protocol Office, O7+, C-808-449-1781. Building 1153, C-808-449-2603.

TML Availability: Difficult, most of the year.

CREDIT CARDS ACCEPTED: Visa, MasterCard and American Express.

Waikiki, Pearl Harbor's historic war memorial, shopping and sightseeing in Honolulu, hikes in local parks that put you in touch with Oahu's natural wonders. Whether you want relaxation or excitement, it's all here.

Locator 449-0165   Medical 449-9907   Police 449-7114

Kaneohe Bay Beach Cottages (HI12R6)
Morale, Welfare & Recreation
P.O. Box 63073
Kaneohe Bay MCBH, HI 96863-3062

TELEPHONE NUMBER INFORMATION: Main installation numbers: C-808-471-7110, D-315-430-0111.

Location: Take H-3 to MCAS. Cottages are across from the airstrip along the coast line, near Pyramid Rock overlooking Kaneohe Bay. *USMRA: Page 129 (E-6)*. NMC: Honolulu, 14 miles southwest.

Lodging Office: TLF. Building 3038. Reservation priority list available on request. Waiting list. For reservations for cottages call **C-808-254-2716/2806**, FAX 808-254-2716. Check in after 1400, before 1800. Check out no later than 1000. After hours check in call 808-254-2663 or 808-261-5196. Closed Thanksgiving, Christmas and New Years Day.

TML: Beach Cottages, all ranks. Two bedroom, living room, dining areas, private bath (12); CB cottage, private bath (1). Kitchen, complete utensils, color TV, lanai, 19th Puka Community Center. Completely furnished. Rates: $50 per day. All categories can make reservations. No pets.

TML Availability: Fairly good.

CREDIT CARDS ACCEPTED: Visa, MasterCard and Discover.

MCB full support facilities. (For details see Military Living's *Military RV, Camping & Rec Areas Around The World*). Beaches, boating, or just plain relaxing. You won't regret your stay at Kaneohe.

Locator 257-1294   Medical 257-3133   Police 257-2123

Kaneohe Marine Corps Base (HI12R6)
Custodian Billeting Fund/Facilities Department
P.O. Box 63062, MCBH
Kaneohe MCB, HI 96863-5001

TELEPHONE NUMBER INFORMATION: Main installation numbers: C-808-471-7110, D-315-

HAWAII
Kaneohe Marine Corps Base, continued

430-0110.

Location: At end of H-3 on the windward side of Oahu. Off Makapu Blvd and Kaneohe Bay Dr. Clearly marked. *USMRA: Page 129 (E-6)*. NMC: Honolulu, 14 miles southwest.

Lodging Office: Building 503, C-808-257-2409, 0700-2330 daily, holidays 0800-2030. Check in facility 1400 hours, check out 1000 hours daily. Closed Christmas and Easter.

TML: Hostess House, building 3038, 1/4 mile from main gate. Leave or official duty. C-808-254-2716, all ranks, leave or official duty. Bedrooms, private bath, kitchens (24). One mile from Subway, Cajun Chicken, package store and enlisted club. One mile from commissary exchange and 7 day store. Rates: $40 per day. $65 with temporary living allowance. Maximum 6 persons per unit. Older structure. Duty can make reservations, others Space-A.

TML: BOQ. Building 503, officers all ranks, leave or official duty, C-808-257-2409, D-315-457-2409. Suites, private bath (37). Refrigerator, community kitchen, utensils, color TV in room & lounge, housekeeping service, washer/dryer, ice vending, spa/jacuzzi. Older structure. Rates: sponsor $19.50, maximum $6 each dependent. Maximum 4 per suite. Duty can make reservations, others Space-A.

TML: Building 386. SNCO bedroom shared bath (12), 1 VIP suite.

DV/VIP: FMF PAC Protocol, Kaneohe MCB, HI 96863-5001. C-808-257-2378, O6+, retirees Space-A.

TML Availability: Good. Best, Nov-Jan. More difficult, May-Jun.

See Kaneohe Bay Beach Cottages listing.

Locator 257-2008   Medical 257-2505   Police 257-2123

Kilauea Military Camp AFRC (HI17R6)
ATTN: Reservations Office
Hawaii National Park, HI 96718-5000

TELEPHONE NUMBER INFORMATION: Main installation numbers: C-808-967-8321.

Location: On island of Hawaii, 216 air miles southeast of Honolulu, 32 miles from Hilo IAP. Scheduled bus transport to Camp, reservations required Hilo to KMC. *USMRA: Page 129 (I,J-6,7)*. NMC: Hilo, 32 miles northwest.

Lodging Office: ATTN: Reservations Office, Hawaii Volcanoes National Park, HI 96718-5000. C-808-967-8333/8343, FAX 808-967-8343, Oahu 808-438-6707 reservations required. First come, first served basis regardless of rank one year prior to the requested arrival date during non-peak periods. Include name, rank, service, status & list children & guest(s) when applying for reservation. Priority I, AD, call 90 days in advance; or write 120 days in advance; priority II, retirees, 60 days in advance; priority III, DoD civilian and other authorized personnel, 45 days. Reservations Office, 0800-1600 daily. Check in 1500, check out 1100 hours daily. From Oahu, call toll free above number (0800-1600 daily). Others call direct.

HAWAII
Kilauea Military Camp, continued

TML: Apartments & Cabins (all with fireplaces). One bedroom, private bath (37); two bedroom w/kitchen, private bath (12); two bedroom, private bath (10); three bedroom, private bath (1); four bedroom cabin, private bath (1); two dormitories w/common baths and showers for large groups. Refrigerator or kitchen, CATV, housekeeping service, cribs ($1/night), rollaways ($1), coin laundry. Rec lodge, 18 hole golf course, deep sea fishing and helicopter charters, bus tours. Rates: E1-E5, $25-$50; E6-E9, W1-O3, O1-3 $35-$60; W4, O4, DoD Civilian, $45-$70, up to two person occupancy, $5 each additional person. No charge under age 5. Dormitories $5-$7.50 per night.

TML Availability: Good, fall, winter, spring. More difficult, summer.

CREDIT CARDS ACCEPTED: Visa, MasterCard, American Express and Carte Blanche.

On the rim of Kilauea Crater at 4,000 feet, temperature 50-65 degrees, quiet guest cottages, hiking, lectures, movies, support facilities, this is the place to get away from it all. For more details see Military Living's *Military RV, Camping & Rec Areas Around the World.*

Locator 967-7315   Medical 967-8367   Police 967-8378

Lualualei Naval Magazine (HI23R6)
3 Constellation Street
Waianae, HI 96782-4301

TELEPHONE NUMBER INFORMATION: Main installation numbers: C-808-474-4340, D-312-474-4340.

Location: Follow H-1 Freeway W towards Waianaeto Ewa exit. Follow for Weaver Rd S to Iroqouis Point Rd. Turn left and travel to West Loch Branch gate. USMRA: Page 129 (B,C-7). NMC: Honolulu, 20 mi southeast.

Lodging Office: Building 600, **C-808-474-7908**, D-312-474-7908, FAX 808-474-7922, DSN FAX 312-474-7922, 0600-2200 (after hours call 808-474-4341).

TML: BEQ. Buildings 601, 602, enlisted E1-E6 Active duty on orders to Lualualei Naval Magazine and its tenants only. Two person bedroom, shared bath (91). Refrigerator, A/C, TV in lounge, washer/dryer, ice/food vending.

TML Availability: Extremely limited. **No Space-A.**

Locator 474-4330   Police 668-3261

Pearl Harbor Naval Station (HI20R6)
Bldg 1623, Barracks Road
Pearl Harbor NS, HI 96860-6000

TELEPHONE NUMBER INFORMATION: Main installation numbers: C-808-471-8053, D-315-474-5210.

Location: Off H-1 adjacent to Honolulu International Airport. Clearly marked. *USMRA: Page 129 (C-7).* NMC: Honolulu, 5 miles east.

HAWAII
Pearl Harbor Naval Station, continued

Lodging Office: Building 1723 (Arizona Hall), Barracks Road, **C-808-471-9188**, 24 hours daily. Check in at facility, check out 1300 hours daily. Government civilian employee billeting BOQ.

TML: BOQ. Building 662, officers all ranks, leave or official duty. Bedroom, private bath (192); Makalapa VIP suites (6). A/C, refrigerator, color TV, housekeeping service, washer/dryer, food/ice vending, room telephones. Modern structure. Rates: sponsor $20, adult $4. Maximum 2 persons. Duty can make reservations, others Space-A. No children.

TML: BEQ. Building 1723, enlisted all ranks, leave or official duty. Singles only. Bedroom (84). Refrigerator, color TV, housekeeping service, washer/dryer, food/ice vending. Modern structure. Rates: $10 per person. Duty can make reservations, others Space-A. No dependents. Building 1507, E7-E9 only. Bedroom, private bath (15), rates $20.

DV/VIP: CINCPACFLT Protocol, C-808-474-7256, O7+. Only O6 Space-A. Rates: $50.

TML Availability: Difficult. Best Nov-Feb.

Visit the Bishop Museum and Planetarium to see what old Hawaii was like, Pier 9 at the foot of Fort Street Mall has spectacular views of Honolulu and the harbor from the Aloha Tower. Don't forget the Arizona Memorial and USS Bowfin.

Locator 474-6249   Medical 471-9541   Police 474-1237

Schofield Barracks (HI13R6)
Inn at Schofield Barracks
563 Kolekole Avenue
Wahiawa, HI 96786-5000

TELEPHONE NUMBER INFORMATION: Main installation numbers: C-808-655-4930, D-315-455-4930.

Location: From the airport take H-1 west until you see exit for H-2, Wahiawa/Mililani exit (right side). Stay on H-2 until it ends at a divided highway. At first light turn left on Kunia Rd. Turn right through Foote Gate, left on Road A until it merges right onto Lyman Rd. On Lyman take right onto Humphrey's. At stop sign turn left onto Kolekole Ave, inn is the next right. *USMRA: Page 129 (C-6)*. NMC: Honolulu, 20 miles southeast.

Lodging Office: Inn at Schofield Barracks, 563 Kolekole Ave. **C-808-624-9650, 1-800-490-9638**, FAX 808-624-5606. Check in 1500, check out 1200 hours.

TML: Inn at Schofield Barracks. All ranks, leave or official duty. The inn has 192 rooms with private bath. A/C, color TV, VCR, microwave, refrigerator, coin washer/dryer, ice vending. Rates: 1 bed or 2 bed per room, single $52, double $66. 1 bed w/sleeper sofa, $84. Reservations, PCS 1 year prior, all others 45 days in advance. No pets.

DV/VIP: Protocol Office, Fort Shafter, building T-100, C-808-438-1577, O6+. Retirees and lower ranks Space-A. Primarily for TDY personnel.

TML Availability: Good, most difficult summer.

HAWAII
Schofield Barracks, continued

CREDIT CARDS ACCEPTED: Visa, MasterCard, American Express, Diners and Discover.

In winter don't miss Major surfing meets held in Haleiwa on the north shore, just nine miles away, golf at Kalakaua, the post museum, and recreation equipment rental.

Locator 471-7110   Medical 655-4747   Police 655-5555

Tripler Army Medical Center (HI03R6)
Billeting
Bldg 228B, Jarrett White Road
Tripler AMC, HI 96859-5000

TELEPHONE NUMBER INFORMATION: Main installation numbers: C-808-433-6661, D-315-433-6661.

Location: Take H-1 West from Honolulu to Tripler exit. Turn right on Jarrett White Rd to Tripler AMC. *USMRA: Page 129 (D-7) & Page 131 (D-1,2).* NMC: Honolulu, 3 miles southeast.

Lodging Office: TAMC Billeting, building 228B, Jarrett White Road, **C-808-433-2336**, (TDY-433-6905) 0630-2200 M-F, 0800-1600 Sa-Su. Other hours, info desk in hospital lobby, EX-6661. Check in billeting 1300, check out 1100 hours daily. Government civilian employee billeting.

TML: Guest House. Building 228B, 226E, 222C, 220D, all ranks, leave or official duty. Bedroom, 2 beds, shared bath (53); suites, 2 beds, living room, private bath (42). Refrigerator, community kitchen, microwave, color TV, housekeeping service, cribs/cots, washer/dryer, food/ice vending. Older structure, renovated. Rates: $27 with private bath, $19 without private bath, $6 each additional person. Child under 1 no charge. No pets. Reservations accepted for TDY only. All others Space-A on day of arrival.

TML: Fisher House. Note: Appendix C has the definition of this facility. **C-808-839-2336.**

TML Availability: Difficult. Best, winter.

Hawaii's rare and endangered plant life may be better appreciated at: Haiku Gardens, Kaneohe, Foster Garden botanical park, and Paradise Park in Manoa Valley. Don't forget the Honolulu Zoo, in Kapiolani Park.

Locator 433-6661   Medical 433-6620   Police 438-7116

Waianae Army Recreation Center (HI05R6)
Waianae, HI 96858-5000

TELEPHONE NUMBER INFORMATION: Main installation numbers: C-808-668-3636.

Location: Located on west coast of Oahu. Take I-H1 West to HI-93 (Farrington Hwy) West to Waianae. Look for Aloha Gas Station on your left, turn left on Army St. *USMRA: Page 129 (B-6).* NMC: Honolulu, 35 miles southeast.

HAWAII
Waianae Army Recreation Center, continued

Lodging Office: Rest Camp, Building 4070, 85-010 Army St, **C-1-800-333-4158 (mainland) 1-800-847-6771 (outer island) 696-4158 (Oahu),** 0900-1600 M-F. AD Army 90 days in advance. Other military personnel/retirees 80 days in advance. Reservist/DoD civilian 60 days in advance. Deposit required. Twenty-one (21) day occupancy limit in a 60 day period. Year round operation. Check in 1630-1930, check out 1200 hours.

TML: Cabins. Leave, official duty, retirees. Two bedroom cabins with kitchen (25); studio cabins with kitchen (5); deluxe cabins (9). A/C, ceiling fans, refrigerator, color TV, deck, BBQ and picnic facilities, housekeeping service. Deluxe rooms have carpeting and VCR's. Utensils, dishes, bedding, tableware all furnished. Bring personal items and beach towels. Cribs (one time $5 charge), rollaways ($10 per night). No pets. Rates: deluxe 2 bedroom $60-$75 daily, 3 bedroom $70-$80 daily; standard 2 bedroom, with kitchen $45-$60 daily, studio with kitchen $35-$45. Reservations in advance. Active duty Army 90 days, other duty and retired 80 days, reservists and DoD employees 60 days.

TML Availability: Good all year.

CREDIT CARDS ACCEPTED: Visa and MasterCard.

On the "Leeward", western side of Oahu, with the look of old Hawaii, and Waianae Mountain Range at 4,000 feet. The heart of "Pokai Bay" has one of the best beaches. Rentals, catering and meeting facilities. See Military Living's *Military RV, Camping and Rec Areas Around the World* for more information.

Locator 696-4158   **Police 696-2811**   **Medical 911**

Too Late To Copy
Pearl Harbor Naval Submarine Base, Pearl Harbor, HI 96860-6500. BEQ/BOQ **C-808-474-1144.** DV C-808-422-9494.
Wahiawa Naval Computer and Telecommunications Area Master Station, Eastern Pacific, 500 Center Street, Wahiawa, HI 96786-3050. BEQ **C-808-653-5367,** D-315-453-5367, Fax 808-653-4600.

IDAHO

Mountain Home Air Force Base (ID01R4)
Sagebrush Hotel
445 Falcon St
Mountain Home AFB, ID 83648-5000

TELEPHONE NUMBER INFORMATION: Main installation numbers: C-208-828-2111, D-312-728-1110.

Location: From Boise, take I-84 southeast, 40 miles to Mountain Home exit, follow road through town to Airbase Rd, 10 miles to main gate. *USMRA: Page 98 (B,C-9).* NMC: Boise, 51 miles northwest.

Lodging Office: Sagebrush Hotel. 455 Falcon St, **C-208-832-4661**, D-312-728-6451, FAX 208-828-4797, DSN FAX 312-278-4797, 24 hours daily. Check in facility, check out 1200 hours daily. DoD civilians on orders are eligible.

TML: Motel. Building 2604, all ranks, leave or official duty. Bedroom, semi-private bath (105); two bedroom, private bath (11); three bedroom, private bath (4); four bedroom, private bath (1). Units designated DV/VIP (15). Rates: E1-E5, O1 $10; E6/O2 $17; E7+ $22. Refrigerator, community kitchen, limited utensils, A/C, color TV in room & lounge, housekeeping service, cribs/cots, washer/dryer, ice vending, CATV. Older structure. Duty can make reservations, others Space-A.

TML: VOQ/VAQ. All ranks leave or official duty. Bedroom with semi-private bath (84); Bedroom with private bath (9). DV/VIP, suites (6). Rates: VOQ $8, VAQ $8, DV/VIP $14.

DV/VIP: 366 WG/CCP, building 1506, 208-828-4536, 06+. Retirees Space-A. Active duty can make reservations, Space-A can reserve **non-confirmed** 72 hrs prior to arrival.

TML Availability: Very good, winter. Difficult, Jun-Aug.

CREDIT CARDS ACCEPTED: Visa, MasterCard, American Express and Optima.

Locator 828-2111   **Medical 828-2319**   **Police 828-2256**

Too Late To Copy
Gowen Field, Lodging office, Bldg. 669. 0800-1700 daily, **C-208-422-6023**, D-312-941-6023.

ILLINOIS

Charles Melvin Price Support Center (IL04R2)
SATAS-JH-C
Housing Dept, Bldg 102
Granite City, IL 62040-1801

TELEPHONE NUMBER INFORMATION: Main installation numbers: C-618-452-4211, D-312-892-4211.

Location: From I-70 take McKinley Bridge exit, cross Mississippi River, follow signs to Center. From I-270, cross river bridges and take first Granite City exit (IL-3) south to Center. *USMRA: Page 64 (C,D-7).* NMC: St. Louis, 7 miles west.

Billeting Office: Building 102, Niedringhaus Ave, **C-618-452-4287**, 0730-1615 hours daily. Other hours, Security Office, building 221, C-618-452-4224. Check in facility 1400, check out 1000 hours daily. No government civilian employee billeting.

TML: Guest House. Buildings 101, 116, all ranks, leave or official duty, C-618-452-4287. Separate bedrooms, private bath (5); two bedroom, private bath, kitchen (2). Microwave, refrigerator, limited utensils, toaster, coffee pot, A/C, color TV, housekeeping service M-F, cots, washer/dryer. Older structure. Rates: sponsor $15, maximum $20 per family. PCS reservations 90 days in advance, 30 day in advance.

TML Availability: Good, Nov-Mar. Difficult, May-Aug.

Nearby St Louis, with its cultural offerings, provides the excitement while small middle American communities make visitors feel right at home.

Locator 452-4211   Police 452-4224   Medical 331-4851

Great Lakes Naval Training Center (IL07R2)
Bldg 62
2701 Sheridan Road
Great Lakes NTC, IL 60088-5000

TELEPHONE NUMBER INFORMATION: Main installation numbers: C-708-688-3500, D-312-792-2002.

Location: From I-94 north or US-41 north of Chicago, exit to IL-137 (Buckley Rd) east to IL-137 (Sheridan Ln) north to NTC. Clearly marked. *USMRA: Page 64 (G-1).* NMC: Chicago, 30 miles south.

Lodging Office: BOQ. Building 62, **C-708-688-3777**, D-312-792-3777. BEQ. Building 834, **C-688-2170**, D-312-792-2170, 24 hours, daily. Check in facility, check out 1300 hours. Government civilian employee billeting (If on official duty).

TML: Navy Lodge. Building 2500, **C-1-800-NAVY-INN.** Lodge number is 708-689-1485, FAX 708-689-1489, all ranks, leave or official duty. Check in 1500-1800, check out 1200 hours. Bedroom, 2 double beds, private bath (50). Four

ILLINOIS
Great Lakes Naval Training Center, continued

sets interconnecting, 2 handicapped accessible, 25 non-smoking. Kitchenette, utensils, A/C, color TV, phones, housekeeping service, coin washer/dryer, food/ice vending. Modern structure. Rates: $46.50 per room. Maximum 5 per room. No pets. All categories can make reservations.

TML: BOQ. Building 62, ATTN: BQ, Bldg. 62, NTC, Great Lakes, IL 60088-5121, FAX 847-688-5815. Officers all ranks, leave or official duty. Government civilians, all grades, official duty. Bedroom, sitting room, shared private bath (54); bedroom, private bath (1); suites, separate bedroom/sitting room, private bath (112); DV/VIP cottage, private bath (1). Refrigerator (kitchenette in cottage), microwave, VCR, iron, ironing board, color TV in room & lounge, game room, exercise room, washers/dryers, cribs/cots, snack/drink/ice vending, A/C, housekeeping service, essentials. Brick barracks structure. No pets. Rates: single bedroom/sitting room, sponsor $17; suite bedroom, sponsor $25. Additional occupants over age 6 $7. Maximum 5 per unit. Duty, Reservists, National Guard on orders and Medal of Honor recipients can make reservations, others Space-A. No pets.

TML: BEQ. Building 833, 834, FAX 847-688-4736, enlisted all ranks, leave or official duty. Building 833: E5-E9, bedroom, private bath (62); bedroom, private bath (76). Building 834, E6 and below, bedroom, private bath (214). Refrigerator, microwave, A/C, color TV in room and lounge, housekeeping service, essentials, coffee/tea, washer/dryer, food vending. Brick barracks structure, renovated. Rates: sponsor $8, additional adult $8, child over six $8. Maximum 2 per unit. Duty, Reservists and National Guard on orders can make reservations, others Space-A. DVEQ's E7-E9. Retirees and lower ranks Space-A. Reservations required, call the Command Master Chief at 847-688-3569. Rates $15 single, maximum charge for additional occupant(s) $25. No pets.

DV/VIP: Cmdr, building 1. C-847-688-3400. O6+. DVEQ Space-A E9+. Retirees and lower ranks Space-A. Check with commander, building 1. Rates: sponsor $37, additional occupants over age 6, $9. Maximum 5.

TML Availability: Good Sept-Feb, difficult Jun-Aug.

CREDIT CARDS ACCEPTED: Visa, MasterCard and American Express.

Boating, swimming and all water sports are available through the marina Beach House. An 18 hole golf course, bowling center, and extensive other support facilities are available on base.

Locator 688-3777   Medical 688-3333   Police 688-3430

Rock Island Arsenal (IL08R2)
SIOAI-PW (Housing)
Bldg 102
Rock Island, IL 61299-5000

TELEPHONE NUMBER INFORMATION: Main installation numbers: C-309-782-6001, D-312-793-6001.

Location: From I-74 N in Moline exit to 3rd Avenue W and follow signs to Arsenal Island located in middle of Mississippi River. *USMRA: Page 64 (C-2).* NMC: Quad cities of Rock Island and Molne IL and Davenport and Bettendorf in IA.

ILLINOIS
Rock Island Arsenal, continued

Housing Office: Building 102, **C-309-782-2376**, D-312-793-2376, FAX 309-782-0133, DSN FAX 312-793-0133. 0715-1545 daily, after hours report to police (Bldg 225). Check in housing office, check out 0900 hours daily.

TML: Building 60, all ranks, leave or official duty. (1) Fully equipped apartment ; bedroom (2 beds), bath, kitchen, refrigerator, microwave, dinning area, TV, A/C, housekeeping service, washer/dryer.

While here visit the Rock Island Arsenal Museum, national Cemetery, Confederate Cemetery, and the Colonel Davenport House.

Locator 782-6002   Medical 782-0801   Police 782-5507

Scott Air Force Base (IL02R2)
The Scott Inn
375 SVS/SVML
Scott AFB, IL 62225-5000

TELEPHONE NUMBER INFORMATION: Main installation numbers: C-618-256-1110, D-312-576-1110.

Location: Off I-64 east or west, exit 19A west to IL-158 south, 2 miles and watch for signs to AFB entry. *USMRA: Page 64 (D-8)*. NMC: St Louis, 25 miles west.

Lodging Office: The Scott Inn, Building 1510, "F" St., **C-618-744-1200**, D-312-576-1844 (front desk), DSN FAX 312-576-6638 (For duty reservations only, no Space-A reservations), 24 hours daily. Check in lodging office, check out 1200 hours daily. Government civilian employee billeting in VOQ/VAQ.

TML: TLF. Buildings 1550-1551, all ranks, leave or official duty. Separate bedroom, private bath, sleeps 5, (36). A/C, Microwave, refrigerator, color TV, housekeeping service, washer/dryer, ice vending, beverages, snacks, stocked bar. Rates: $24. PCS to Scott can make reservations, others Space-A. No pets.

TML: DVQ. Building 150. **Essex House.** O6+, leave or official duty. Suites, private bath (10). A/C, refrigerator, microwave, color TV, housekeeping service, washer/dryer, ice vending, beverages, snacks, stocked bar. Rates: $14 per person per night, maximum $28. TDY can make reservations, other O6+ Space-A. Reservations made through Protocol, below number. No pets.

TML: VOQ. Building 1508. Officers, all ranks, leave or official duty. Bedroom, private bath (32); separate bedroom suites (2). Same amenities as above. Rates: $14, $28 maximum. Building 1509 A,B. Bedroom, private bath (39); separate bedroom suites, private bath (8). Amenities as above. Rates: $12, maximum $24; suites $14 maximum $28. Building 1510 A. Bedroom, private bath (41); suites, private bath (7). Amenities as above. Rates: $8, maximum $16; suites $14, maximum $28. Building 1510B. Bedroom, private bath (37); bedroom, shared bath (14). Amenities as above, no stocked bar. Rates: $8, maximum $16. TDY can make reservations, others Space-A. No children under 18, no pets.

ILLINOIS
Scott Air Force Base, continued

TML: VAQ. Building 1512. Enlisted, all ranks, leave or official duty. Bedroom, private bath, sleeps 2 (47); suites, private bath (9). Amenities as above, except for stocked bar and snacks. Suites have officer amenities. Building 1513. Bedroom, private bath, sleeps 2 (44); bedroom, shared bath (4). Rates: $8, maximum $16. Amenities as above, no stocked bar, snacks. TDY can make reservations, others Space-A. No children under 18, no pets.

DV/VIP: AMC protocol, C-618-256-5555, D-312-576-5555. O6+. Retirees Space-A.

TML Availability: Fairly Good, Nov-Jan. Difficult, other times.

Near the "Gateway to the West", visitors enjoy the cultural, sporting, and outdoor activities St Louis affords. Nearby small communities reflect the stability and warmth of middle America.

Locator 256-1841   **Medical 256-1847**   **Police 256-2223**

INDIANA

Crane Division Naval Surface Warfare Center (IN03R2)
Combined Bachelor Quarters
Crane NSWC, IN 47522-5000

TELEPHONE NUMBER INFORMATION: Main installation numbers: C-812-854-1225, D-312-482-1225.

Location: From US-231 north or south exit to IN-45 or IN-645 to enter the center from the west. *USMRA: Page 65 (D-8)*. NMC: Bloomington, 22 miles northeast.

Lodging Office: Building 2682, **C-812-854-1176**, D-312-482-1176, FAX 812-854-4416, 0730-1500. After duty hours, C-812-854-1225/1222, building 1. Check in billeting.

TML: BOQ/VIP. Building 2681, officers, all ranks, leave or official duty. Bedroom, private bath (14); separate bedrooms, private bath, kitchen, living room (VIP) (2). A/C, food vending, refrigerator, microwave, housekeeping service, CATV in room & lounge. Older structure, remodeled. Rates: $11 per night, VIP suites $25 per night. Maximum 2 persons. All categories can make reservations.

TML: BEQ. Building 2682, enlisted, all ranks, leave or official duty. Bedrooms, semi-private bath. A/C, essentials, food vending, housekeeping service, refrigerator, CATV in room/lounge, washer/dryer. Modern structure, renovated. All categories can make reservations. Rates: $11 single, $6 per person for multiple occupancy.

DV/VIP: Building 1, C-812-854-1210, O6+. Retirees Space-A.

TML Availability: Very good, all year.

CREDIT CARDS ACCEPTED: Diners.

Sportsman's paradise, 22,500 acres for hunting, fishing, boating. Camping available through the Marina. Nine (9) hole golf course. Approximately 1 mile of nature trails.

| Locator 854-2511 | Medical 854-1220 | Police 854-3300 |

Fort Benjamin Harrison (IN02R2)
Bldg T-609, Green Avenue
Fort Benjamin Harrison, IN 46216-5450
Scheduled to close 8/31/96.

TELEPHONE NUMBER INFORMATION: Main installation numbers: C-317-546-9211, D-312-699-1110.

Location: Take I-465 east to Fort Harrison exit 40, east on 56th St, or take Pendleton Pike (IN-67/US-36) exit 42 to Post Rd and North Fort Harrison. *USMRA: Page 65 (E-5)*. NMC: Indianapolis, 8 miles southwest.

Lodging Office: Building T-609, Green Avenue (Post Rd), **C-317-549-5455**, 24 hours daily. Check in facility, check out 1200 hours daily. Government civilian employee billeting. Motels available through billeting.

INDIANA
Fort Benjamin Harrison, continued

TML: Guest House. Building T-51, all ranks, leave or official duty. Bedroom, 2 full-size beds, private bath (14); bedroom, 1 bed, private bath (2). Handicapped accessible facilities. All have sleeper sofas. Kitchen, complete utensils, A/C, color TV, housekeeping service, cribs/cots, washer/dryer, ice vending. Modern structure. Rates: $25-$30 per room per night. PCS in/out have priority, others Space-A.

DV/VIP: Protocol Office. Building 600, D-312-542-4186, O6/GS-15+. Retirees Space-A with approval of Protocol Office.

TML Availability: Extremely limited. Best, end of Dec.

See Indianapolis sports events, including the Indianapolis 500; also a world class symphony. Parks, museums and a zoo to keep you busy here.

Locator 542-4537   Medical 549-5194/5   Police 549-5350

Grissom Air Reserve Base (IN01R2)
Grissom Inn, Bldg 550
434 SVML
Grissom ARB, IN 46971-5000

TELEPHONE NUMBER INFORMATION: Main installation numbers: C-317-688-5211, D-317-928-5211.

Location: Off US-31, 7 miles southwest of Peru, 65 miles north of Indianapolis. *USMRA: Page 65 (E-3)*. NMC: Indianapolis, 65 miles south.

Lodging Office: Grissom Inn, building 550, Lancer St, **C-317-688-2596**, FAX 317-688-8751, DSN FAX 312-928-8751, 24 hours daily. Check in facility, check out 1200 hours daily.

TML: VAQ. Buildings 328, 329, 331, 332, enlisted all ranks, leave or official duty. Bed spaces (300). Refrigerator, A/C, color TV in room, housekeeping service, washer/dryer, ice/food vending. Modern structure. Rates: $7. Duty can make reservations, others Space-A. No pets.

TML: VOQ. Buildings 327-333, officers all ranks, 76 rooms. Rate: $8-$14. No pets.

DV/VIP: CSG/ESO, building 551, C-317-688-2844. O6+. Retirees Space-A. VOQ suites (4) VAQ suites (2). Rates: $14. No pets.

TML Availability: Good, Aug-April. Difficult, May-July.

CREDIT CARDS ACCEPTED: Visa, MasterCard and American Express.

If the Indianapolis 500 isn't excitement enough, try the historic Union Railroad Station, the Indianan Repertory Theater, the Bluegrass Music Festival, walking tours of Victorian Mansions, and Independence Day in Evansville.

Medical 688-3335   Police 688-3385

Temporary Military Lodging Around the World - 107

IOWA

Camp Dodge (IA02R2)
Combined Bachelor Quarters
7700 Northwest Beaver Drive
Johnston, IA 50131-1902

TELEPHONE NUMBER INFORMATION: Main installation numbers: C-515-252-4000 or 1-800-294-6607, D-312-946-2000.

Location: From I-35/I-80, take Merle Hay/Camp Dodge exit (exit 131); N on Iowa 401 approximately 4 mi to camp. *USMRA: Page 77 (E-5).* NMC: Des Moines, 5 mi SE.

Lodging Office: Building A-8, 7th St & Des Moines Avenue, **C-515-252-4238 or 1-800-336-9142**, D-312-946-2238, FAX-515-252-4092, DSN FAX 312-946-2092, 0730-1700 daily. Check in Billeting Office, check out 0800 hours daily (late checkout call 252-4238).

TML: TLF. Building A-5, all ranks, leave or official duty. Bedrooms, private bath (6), bedrooms, semi-private bath (4). Refrigerator, TV, housekeeping service, washer/dryer. Rates: Active duty $8, others $14. Active duty/reservists on orders can make reservations, others Space-A. No pets.

TML: BEQ. Building B-30, E7-E9, leave or official duty. Bedroom, hallway bath (6). Refrigerator, TV, A/C, housekeeping service. Renovated structure. Rates: $8 active duty, others $14. Active duty/reservists on orders can make reservations, others Space-A. No pets.

TML: BOQ. Building M-1, O1-O3 (male only), leave or official duty. Bedroom, hallway bath (13). Refrigerator, TV, housekeeping service. Rates: $8 active duty, others $14. Active duty/reservists on orders can make reservations, others Space-A. No pets.

TML: BOQ. Building M-3, O4-O5, leave or official duty. Bedroom, hallway bath (13), bedrooms, semi-private bath (4). Refrigerator, TV, housekeeping service. Rates: $8 active duty, others $14. Active duty/reservists on orders can make reservations, others Space-A. No pets.

DV/VIP: Buildings A-2, A-4, A-7, A-18, A-62; O6+, leave or official duty. Bedroom, private bath (5). Refrigerator, microwave, TV, housekeeping service. Rates: $8 active duty, others $14. Active duty/reservists on orders can make reservations, others Space-A. No pets.

TML Availability: Good.

While here visit Adventureland Theme Park, White Water University Park, aquarium, zoo, and State Fairgrounds.

Medical 252-4235   Police 911

KANSAS

Fort Leavenworth (KS04R3)
Lodging Operations, Hoge Barracks
DCA USACAC
115 Grant Ave
Fort Leavenworth, KS 66027-1201

TELEPHONE NUMBER INFORMATION: Main installation numbers: C-913-684-4021, D-312-552-4021.

Location: From I-70 take US-73 north to Leavenworth. Fort is adjacent to city of Leavenworth. *USMRA: Page 78 (J-3).* NMC: Kansas City, 30 miles southeast.

Lodging Office: Building 695, 115 Grant Ave, **C-913-684-4091 or 1-800-854-8627**, FAX-913-684-4397, 24 hours daily. Check in lodging after 1400 hours, check out 1000 hours daily. No pets.

TML: Guest House. Building 427, all ranks, leave or official duty, C-684-4091. D-312-552-4091. Two and three bedroom, private bath (12). Kitchen, complete utensils, A/C, color TV, housekeeping service, cribs/cots, room telephones, ice vending, washer/dryer. Older structure, renovated. Rates: E1-E6, $25; E7+, $35. PCS can make reservations 30 days in advance, others Space-A.

TML: VOQ. **Hoge Barracks**, Truesdell Hall, Root & Schofield Hall. Officers/enlisted, all ranks, leave or official duty. Units (704), private and semi-private bath. Kitchen (some), A/C, color TV, housekeeping service, room telephones, ice vending, washer/dryer. Rates: $16 (semi-private bath), $20 (private bath), additional persons $5. TDY can make reservations, others Space-A.

TML: DV/VIP: Building 22 (**Cooke Hall**), building 3 (**Thomas Custer House**), building 213 (**Otis Hall**). Officers O6+, leave or official duty. Bedroom, private bath (8); Kitchen (some), refrigerator, utensils, A/C, TV, housekeeping service, room telephones, ice vending, washer/dryer. Older structure. Rates: sponsor $20, each additional person $5. TDY can make reservations, others Space-A.

DV/VIP: Executive Services, C-913-684-4064, O6+. Retirees and others Space-A.

TML Availability: Difficult. Best Dec. Limited, other times.

CREDIT CARDS ACCEPTED: Visa, MasterCard and American Express.

Sample Leavenworth's Frontier Crossroads Club and local performing arts, Buffalo Bill Days, and Kansas City, where everything is "up to date". Visit the Crown Center, and The Plaza for wall to wall shopping.

Locator 684-3651/4021   Medical 684-6000   Police 684-2111

Fort Riley (KS02R3)
Lodging Office
45 Barry Avenue
Fort Riley, KS 66442-5921

TELEPHONE NUMBER INFORMATION: Main installation numbers: C-913-239-3911, D-312-856-1110.

KANSAS
Fort Riley, continued

Location: On KS-18 and off I-70 in the central part of the state. Junction City, 5 miles southwest and Manhattan, 10 miles northeast. *USMRA: Page 78 (G,H-3,4).* NMC: Topeka, 64 miles east.

Lodging Office: Billeting office, building 45, Barry Ave, **C-913-239-2830/8073, 1-800-643-8991,** FAX 913-239-8882, 24 hours daily. Check in billeting office, check out 1100 hours daily. Government civilian employee billeting on official duty.

TML: Guest House. Building 170, all ranks, leave or official duty. Bedroom, living room, kitchen, private bath (6); two bedroom, living room, kitchen, private bath (2). Older structure. Rates: $30-$35 per unit. Duty on PCS orders can make reservations, others Space-A.

TML: Guest House. Building 5309, all ranks, leave or official duty. Two room suites, private bath (27); single rooms, private bath (3). Community kitchen, cribs, washer/dryer. Older structure. Rates: suites $25; rooms $15. PCS can make reservations, others Space-A.

TML: VOQ/VEQ. **Carr Hall**, buildings 470, 471, 541, 542, 620, 621, all ranks, leave or official duty. Two room suites, private bath, kitchenette (16); two bedroom, private bath, living room, kitchen (20); one bedroom, private bath, living room, kitchen (8); single rooms, kitchenette (63). Color TV, VCR, cribs, washer/dryer. Older structures. Rates: $18-$35 per unit. Pet fee (building 620 only), $5 per night. Duty on PCS/TDY can make reservations, others Space-A.

TML: DV/VIP. **Grimes Hall**, building 510. **Bacon Hall**, building 28. Officer O4+. Leave or official duty. Bacon Hall is a 3-bedroom house for $40 per night; Grimes Hall offers Custer Suite for $30 per night; Stuart Suite for $25 per night; one bedroom suites for $20 per night (5). Kitchen, washer/dryer. Older structure, all categories can make reservations.

TML Availability: Limited.

CREDIT CARDS ACCEPTED: Visa, MasterCard, American Express, Discover and Espirit.

Don't miss the US Cavalry Museum, in building 30, which traces the history of this illustrious post, the battle of the Little Big Horn, Wounded Knee, and then tour the Custer House.

Locator 239-9867   **Medical** 239-7777   **Police** 239-3053/MPMP

McConnell Air Force Base (KS03R3)
22 SVS/SVML
53050 Glen Elder, Suite 1
McConnell AFB, KS 67221-5000

TELEPHONE NUMBER INFORMATION: Main installation numbers: C-316-652-3840, D-312-743-3840.

Location: From the north, take I-35 (the Kansas Turnpike, which is a toll road) south to Wichita, exit at Kellogg St (US-54) west to Rock Road, south to McConnell AFB. From the south, take I-35 (the Kansas Turnpike, which is a toll road) north to 47th Street, east to Rock Road, north to McConnell AFB. *USMRA: Page 78 (G-6).* NMC: Wichita, 6 miles northwest.

Lodging Office: Bldg 193, 53050 Glen Elder, Suite 1, **C-316-683-7711,** D-312-743-6500, 24 hours daily, Fax 316-652-4190, DSN Fax 312-743-4190. Check in 1500 hours, check out 1200 hours daily.

KANSAS
McConnell Air Force Base, continued

TML: TLF. Twenty-one leased apartments at 2200 S. Rock Road, (1 mile north of McConnell AFB) building 17 & 18. One bedroom (6). Two bedrooms (15). Fully furnished, equipped kitchen, A/C CATV, telephones - No long distance service - credit card and collect calls only. Housekeeping, coin operated washer/dryer, vending in building 18. Rates: $24.00 PCS IN/OUT may make reservations, others Space-A.

TML: VOQ. Buildings 202, civilians and officers, leave or official duty. Suites, private bath (10). Kitchenette with refrigerator, microwave, A/C, CATV, telephones, housekeeping, washer/dryer, ice vending, sundries on sale in room. Rates: $8 per person, not to exceed $16. Official duty may make reservations, others Space-A.

TML: VOQ. Building 196. Civilians and officers, leave or official duty. Single rooms, private bath (20); suites (8). Kitchenette with refrigerator, microwave, A/C, CATV, telephones, housekeeping, washer/dryer, ice vending, sundries on sale at desk. Rates: singles $8 per person, not to exceed $16; suites $8 per person, not to exceed $16. Official duty may make reservations, others Space-A.

TML: VAQ. Building 317. Enlisted personnel, leave or official duty. Single room, shared bath (20); SNCO suites, private bath (6). Game room with pool tables, (vending, pinball, video games), A/C, CATV, telephones, ice, washer/dryer, housekeeping, refrigerators, microwaves. Rates: $8 per person, maximum $16. Note: cannot put couples in single room. Duty can make reservations, others Space-A.

TML: VAQ. Buildings 202, Chief Suites (4). SNCO's, leave or official duty. A/C, CATV, telephones, housekeeping, washer/dryer, refrigerator, microwave, ice vending, sundries on sale in room. Rates: $8 per person, not to exceed $16. Official duty may make reservations, others Space-A.

TML: DV/VIP. Building 202, officer O6+, leave or official duty. One bedroom suites, private bath (4). Two bedroom suites, private bath (2). A/C, CATV, telephones, housekeeping, washer/dryer, refrigerator, microwave, ice vending, sundries on sale in suites. Rates: $14 per person. Maximum $28. Duty can make reservations, others Space-A through Protocol C-316-652-3110, D-312-743-3110.

TML: DV/VIP. Building 185, officers O7+, leave or official duty. Two bedroom house, fully furnished, two private baths, kitchen (and utensils), washer/dryer, garage, refrigerator, microwave, CATV, A/C, housekeeping, telephones, sundries on sale in room. Rates $12.25 per person. Maximum $24.50. Official duty may make reservations, others Space-A through Protocol C-316-652-3110, D-312-743-3110.

DV/VIP: HQ, C-316-693-6500, O6+. Retirees & lower ranks Space-A.

TML Availability: Good, Nov-Feb. Difficult, other times.

CREDIT CARDS ACCEPTED: Visa, MasterCard and American Express.

Visit Charles Russell, and others in the Wichita Art Museum, and Wyatt Earp in the Old Cowtown Museum. Stroll through one of the 80 municipal parks available to you, still restless? There are more than 600 nightclubs in Wichita.

Locator 652-3555   **Medical 652-3555**   **Police 652-3975**

KENTUCKY

Fort Campbell (KY02R2)
Billeting Office
Bldg 1581, Lee Road
Fort Campbell, KY 42223-5130

TELEPHONE NUMBER INFORMATION: Main installation numbers: C-502-798-2151, D-312-635-2151.

Location: In the southwest part of KY, 4 miles south of intersection of US-41A and I-24. 10 miles northwest of Clarksville, TN. *USMRA: Page 40 (E,F-7)*. NMC: Hopkinsville, 15 miles north.

Lodging Office: Building 1581, Lee Rd, **C-502-798-5618, D-312-635-2865**, 0730-2100 hours daily. Check in facility 1400, check out 1000 hours daily. Government civilian employee billeting. **NOTE:** ask about TDY/PCS/visitor billeting in this building.

TML: Guest House. **Clifford C. Sims Guest House,** 28th & Indiana, building 2601, C-502-798-2865, D-635-2865, all ranks, leave or official duty. Handicapped accessible. Bedroom, 2 double beds, private bath (74). Community kitchen, refrigerator, A/C, color TV in room & lounge, housekeeping service, cribs/cots, washer/dryer, food/ice vending. Modern structure. Rates: double occupancy $30. All categories can make reservations.

DV/VIP: Protocol Office, building T-39, C-502-431-8924, O6+.

TML Availability: Difficult.

CREDIT CARDS ACCEPTED: Visa, MasterCard and American Express.

Stroll Clarksville's Public Square and architectural district for turn-of-the-century buildings. Visit local watershed lakes for fishing and picnicking.

Locator 798-7196   Medical 798-8401   Police 798-2677

Fort Knox (KY01R2)
P.O Box 1171
Fort Knox, KY 40121-5000

TELEPHONE NUMBER INFORMATION: Main installation numbers: C-502-624-1151, D-312-464-0111.

Location: From I-65 north in Louisville, exit Jefferson Freeway, 841W to 31W. Go south to Fort Knox. From I-64, exit I-264 west (Waterson) to I-65 south, to Jefferson Fort Knox to US-31W south to Fort Knox. From I-71, exit I-65 south to exit Jefferson Freeway 841, west to 31W then south to Fort Knox. Four entrances, look for main gate. *USMRA: Page 40,41 (H,I-3,4)*. NMC: Louisville, 25 miles north.

KENTUCKY
Fort Knox, continued

Lodging Office: ATTN: ATZK-PWH, building 4770 (**Newgarden Tower**), Dixie Highway 31W, **C-502-942-1000**, D-312-464-3491, FAX 502-942-8752, 24 hours daily. Check in/out as indicated. Government civilian employee billeting.

TML: Wickam Guest House. Building 6597, all ranks, leave or official duty, qualified family members and DoD civilians. **C-502-942-0490,** 24 hours daily. Check out 1200 hours. Bedroom, 2 beds, (50); bedroom, 3 beds, (24). Private bath, A/C, telephones, refrigerator, TV, cribs and microwaves available, washer/dryer, ice vending machines. Modern structure. Rates: from $15.50 single, $35.50 double occupancy, $3 each additional guest. All categories can make reservations.

TML: Guest House. **Loriann Annex I,** buildings 6625. All ranks, PCS only. C-502-942-0490. Check out 1200. Two-bed rooms (16); 5 have private bath, others shared bedroom (1). Refrigerator, TV, pay phone in lounge, A/C in lounge, housekeeping service, washer/dryer, vending machines, cribs, community kitchen. Older structure. Rates: $10, no charge for additional occupant. PCS may make reservations, others Space-A.

TML: Guest House. **Loriann Annex II,** building 6631. All ranks. PCS only. C-502-942-0490, 24 hours daily. Check out 1200. Bedroom, 2 beds, shared bath (15); bedroom, 1 bed, shared bath (1). Refrigerator, TV, pay phone/AC in lounge, Community kitchen. housekeeping service, washer/dryer, ice vending. Modern structure. Rates: sponsor $10, no charge additional person. PCS may make reservations, others Space-A.

TML: DVQ. Building 1120, **Henry House**, officers O7+, leave or official duty. C-502-624-6951, D-312-464-6951. Check out 1200 hours. Four bedroom house (1). Kitchen, color TV, housekeeping service, washer/dryer. Older structure. Rates: $27.50, additional person $5. Duty can make reservations, others Space-A.

TML: DVQ. Building 1117, **Yeomans Hall**, officers O6+, leave or official duty, C-502-624-6951. D-312-464-6951. Check out 1200 hours daily. Bedroom suites, private bath (10). A/C, color TV, refreshment center, housekeeping service. Older structure. Rates: $27.50, $5 each additional person. Duty can make reservations, others Space-A.

TML Availability: Good. Best, Nov-Mar. More difficult, other times.

CREDIT CARDS ACCEPTED: Visa, MasterCard, and American Express.

Visit the Patton Museum of Calvary and Armor, the US Bullion Depository, and Louisville, home of the Kentucky Derby and historic points of interest.

Locator 624-1141   Medical 624-0911   Police 624-0911

LOUISIANA

Barksdale Air Force Base (LA01R2)
Bldg 5155, Hangarline Road
Barksdale AFB, LA 71110-5000

TELEPHONE NUMBER INFORMATION: Main installation numbers: C-318-456-2252, D-312-781-1000.

Location: Exit I-20 at Airline Dr, go south to Old Minden Rd (.24 mile), left on Old Minden Rd (1 block), then right on North Gate Dr (1 mile) to North Gate of AFB. *USMRA: Page 79 (B-2).* NMC: Shreveport, 1 mile west. Co-located with Bossier City and Shreveport.

Lodging Office: Building 5155, Hangarline Road, second building on left after entering North Gate on Davis Ave. **C-318-747-4708/3091**, D-312-781-3091, 24 hours daily, Fax 318-456-2267, DSN Fax 312-781-2267. Check in facility, check out 1200 hours daily. Government civilian employee billeting.

TML: VAQ. Barksdale Inn, building 5155, 4359, enlisted, leave or official duty. Handicapped accessible. Separate bedroom, private bath (SNCO)(27); separate bedroom shared bath (E1-E6) (76). Refrigerator, A/C, color TV in lounge, housekeeping service, cribs, washer/dryer, ice vending. Older structure, renovated. Rates: $6-$8 per person. Maximum $12-$16 per day. Duty can make reservations, others Space-A.

TML: VOQ. Buildings 5123, 5167, 5224, officers all ranks, leave or official duty. Separate bedroom private bath (72); building 5224, separate bedroom, private bath (O4+)(8); Refrigerator, A/C, color TV in room and lounge, housekeeping service, washer/dryer, ice vending. Older structure, renovated. Rates: building 5167, $7 per person, maximum $14 per day; Bldg 5123 $7-$8 per person, maximum $14-$16 per day; Bldg 5224 $12 per person. Maximum $24 per day. Duty can make reservations, others Space-A. Space-A can make reservations for 1 day if available.

TML: TLF. Building 5243, all ranks, leave or official duty. Large family units (sleeps 5) (16); small units (sleeps 4) (8). Kitchen, complete utensils, refrigerator, A/C, color TV, cribs, housekeeping service, washer/dryer, ice vending. Older structure, renovated. Rates: $24 per day maximum. Duty can make reservations, others Space-A.

TML: DV/VIP. Officer O6+, leave or official duty. Three bedroom house, fully furnished, duty O7+ only, no retirees; bedroom suites, private bath (12); two bedroom, private bath (4). Refrigerator, kitchen, complete utensils, A/C, color TV, housekeeping service, washer/dryer, ice vending. Older structure, renovated. Rates: $12 per person, maximum $24 per day; house: $12 per person, maximum $24 per day. Duty can make reservations, others Space-A.

DV/VIP: PAO, 2nd Wing, C-318-456-4228, O6+. Retirees Space-A.

TML Availability: Good, all year.

Visit Barnwell Garden and Art Center, and the Shreveport-Bossier City American Rose Center, located in a 118 acre wooded park. Hunting and fishing in season on Barksdale, call Base Forestry C-318-456-2231/3353.

Locator 456-2252   Medical 456-4051   Police 456-2551

LOUISIANA

Fort Polk (LA07R2)
Magnolia House
Bldg 522, Utah Avenue
Fort Polk, LA 71459-5000

TELEPHONE NUMBER INFORMATION: Main installation numbers: C-318-531-2911, D-312-863-1110.

Location: Off US-171 9 miles south Leesville. *USMRA: Page 79 (C-4)*. NMC: Alexandria, 45 miles west.

Lodging Office: Magnolia House, building 522, Utah Avenue, **C-318-531-2941** or 318-537-9591, D-312-863-2941/4822, 24 hours daily. Check in Magnolia House, check out 1100 hours daily. Government civilian employee billeting.

TML: Guest House. Building 522, Magnolia House. All ranks, leave or official duty. Bedroom, sleep sofa, private bath (70). Kitchen, microwave, color TV, housekeeping service, washer/dryer, vending machine. Rates: $25 all units. Active duty on PCS, visiting relatives and guests of patients in the hospital, and active and retired military receiving outpatient care can make reservations, others Space-A. No pets in rooms, pet kennels Space-A.

TML: VOQ. Building 350, Woodfill Hall. Rooms (22); building 331, 332, Cypress Inn Complex (2 conference rooms with fax & computer ($10)). Rooms (58). Rates: $20 first person, $5 each additional person; cottages $20 first person, $5 each additional person. Inquire about reservations. No pets.

TML: DV/VIP. Buildings 8-12, 15, 17, 18, 426, 5674, officers O6+, DoD civilian GS-15+, and Sergeant Major of the Army. Official duty only. One, two. three and four bedrooms, private bath. Kitchen, complete utensils, A/C, color TV, housekeeping service. Older structure, renovated. Rates: $20 first person, $5 each additional person. Bldgs 11, 12 & 246 are $20 per bedroom and $5 each additional occupant. Upon request, personnel in grades O5+, on PCS in/out, may be given tentative, unconfirmed reservations. No pets.

TML Availability: Good, Oct-Mar. More difficult, other times.

CREDIT CARDS ACCEPTED: Visa, MasterCard and American Express.

Best known for its outdoor recreation, the area is a paradise for hunters, and fishermen. Early Indian sites, a history that reads like a who's who of American legendary characters, and Lake Charles festivals are all of interest.

Locator 531-6622   Medical 531-3368/9   Police 531-2677

Jackson Barracks (LA13R2)
Military Dept., State of Louisiana
Bldg 58, Jackson Barracks
New Orleans, LA 70146-0330

TELEPHONE NUMBER INFORMATION: Main installation numbers: C-504-278-6207, D-312-485-8207.

Temporary Military Lodging Around the World - 115

LOUISIANA
Jackson Barracks, continued

Location: From I-10 E to Claiborne exit to Jackson Barracks. USMRA: Page 90 (F-3,4). NMC: New Orleans, in city limits.

Lodging Office: Building 58, **C-504-278-6207**, D-312-485-6207, FAX 504-278-7325, Mon-Fri 0730-1600, Sa 0800-1600, Su 0800-1100, after duty hours report to Security (Bldg 34). Check in at Billeting Office, check out 1100 hours.

TML: BOQ. Building 27, O1-O4, leave or official duty. Bedrooms, private bath (4), bedrooms, hall bath (12). Kitchenette, utensils, TV, housekeeping service (if requested), cots available, washer/dryer. Rates: $10-$15 per person, maximum $20. Reservations required. No pets.

TML: BEQ. Building 209, E6-E9, leave or official duty. Apartments, bedroom (1 bed), private bath (1), bedroom (2 beds), private bath (2). Handicapped accessible. Kitchenette, utensils, TV, housekeeping service (if requested), cots available, washer/dryer. Rates: $20 per person, maximum $25. Reservations. No pets.

TML: BEQ. Building 214, E1-E5, leave or official duty. Bedroom, hall bath (1), bedrooms, hall bath (11). Refrigerator, TV, housekeeping service (if requested), cots available, washer/dryer. Building 301, E1-E4, open bay barracks, male & female separate sides, 70 beds, TV in lounge, washer/dryer. Rates: Bldg 214, $8 per person, maximum $15; bldg 301, $5. Reservations are required.

DV/VIP: Building 24, 30, 49, 50, O5+, leave or official duty. Bldg 24, bedroom, private bath (2); bldg 30, bedroom, private bath (1); bldg 49, apartment (1); bldg 50, apartment (2). Kitchenette, utensils, TV, housekeeping service (if requested), cots available, washer/dryer. Rates: bldgs 24 & 30, $30 per person, maximum $40; bldgs 49 & 50, $25 per person, maximum $35. Reservations are required. No pets.

TML Availability: Fairly good Jan-May and Sept-Dec. Most difficult June-August.

Locator 278-6364   **Medical 278-8011**   **Police 278-6460**

New Orleans Naval Air Station/Joint Reserve Base (LA11R2)
Bldg 40, 4th Street
Bell Chase, LA 70143-1001

TELEPHONE NUMBER INFORMATION: Main installation numbers: C-504-678-3011, D-312-363-3011.

Location: Off LA-23 in Belle Chase. Clearly marked. *USMRA: Page 79 (H-7) & Page 90 (F-6)*. NMC: New Orleans, 13 miles north.

Lodging Office: BOQ, building 40, 4th Street, **C-504-678-3842**. BEQ, building 22, 2nd St, **C-504-678-3419**, FAX 504-392-1959 (BOQ/BEQ), 24 hours daily. Check in facility 1400, check out 1300 hours daily. Government civilian employee billeting.

TML: BOQ. Building 40, all ranks, leave or official duty. Bedrooms, 2 beds, hall bath (42); separate bedroom suites, queen bed, fold out couch, private bath (8). Handicapped accessible (2). Refrigerator, A/C, color TV in room & lounge, housekeeping service, cots, washer/dryer, ice vending. Older structures, renovated '92. Rates: $8 per person, guests $5. Military widows and unaccompanied

LOUISIANA
New Orleans Naval Air Station, continued

dependents of active duty on leave Space-A. Others can make reservations. **Note:** no reservations on drill weekends except command officers and O5+.

TML: BEQ. Building 22, all ranks, leave or official duty. Bedrooms, (2, 3, 4 man rooms), common bath (73). Refrigerator, A/C, color TV in room & lounge, housekeeping service, cots, washer/dryer, ice vending. Older structures, renovated. Rates: $4. Duty may make reservations, others Space-A. No dependents.

DV/VIP: CO, building 46, C-504-678-3202, O6+. Retirees Space-A.

TML Availability: Good, except on drill weekends.

CREDIT CARDS ACCEPTED: American Express.

Should you be unable to get lodging here, don't forget there is a Navy Lodge at the Naval Support Activity nearby, call 1-800-NAVY-INN.

Locator 678-3253   Medical 678-3663   Police-678-3265

New Orleans Naval Support Activity (LA06R2)
BEQ, Bldg 703 / BOQ Bldg 700
New Orleans, LA 70142-5000

TELEPHONE NUMBER INFORMATION: Main installation numbers: C-504-678-2655/6, D-312-485-2655/6.

Location: On the west bank of Mississippi River. From east, from I-10 east, take exit 235 B (right) to Cleveland Ave, to Claiborne Ave, right to Claiborne Center Lane ahead 3 stop lights to I-10, follow Business District/Westbank, Gretna signs (90W) across Mississippi River, take first exit (right) off bridge and follow Gen DeGaulle signs to left. Left turn on Shirley Drive and follow to end. Base is on Gen Meyer Ave at foot of Shirley Drive. Take Gen DeGaulle east exit after passing over bridge and turn left at Shirley Dr which leads to NSA. *USMRA: Page 90 (E,F-3,4)*. NMC: New Orleans, 5 miles east.

Lodging Office: none.

TML: BOQ/BEQ. Buildings 700, 703, 705, 710. All ranks, leave or official duty. BOQ **C-504-485-2264/5**; BEQ **C-504-678-2252/2220**, FAX 504-678-2318, D-312-485-2252/2220, 24 hours daily. Check in at facility, check out 1200 hours. Government civilian employee lodging. Bedroom, private bath (255); suites, private bath (12). A/C, color TV, housekeeping service, essentials, washer/dryer, ice vending. Barracks structure, renovated. Rates: BEQ $4; BOQ $8; suite $12. Duty, Reservists and National Guard on orders may make reservations, leave and retirees Space-A. No pets. Jan-Mar difficult.

DV/VIP: BOQ C-504-678-2104; BEQ **504-678-2208**. O6+; E7+, lower ranks Space-A. No retirees.

TML: Navy Lodge. Building 702, Gen. Meyer Ave., 0700-2000 hours daily. Check in 1500-1800, check out 1200 hours. All ranks, leave or official duty. For reservations call **1-800-NAVY-INN**. Lodge number is 504-366-3266.

LOUISIANA
New Orleans Naval Support Activity, continued

Bedroom, 2 double beds, private bath (22) (recently remodeled)). Six sets interconnecting, 11 non-smoking. Kitchen, microwave, utensils, A/C, CATV, clocks, coffee/tea, housekeeping service, cribs, high chairs, irons/boards, playground, ice/snack vending, coin washer/dryer, ramps for DAVs. Modern structure, remodeled. Smoking and non-smoking rooms available. Rates: $41 per unit. Maximum 4 persons. All categories can make reservations.

TML Availability: Good, Nov-Jan. Difficult, Apr-Sep.

CREDIT CARDS ACCEPTED: American Express. The Navy Lodge accepts Visa, MasterCard, American Express and Discover.

Visit stately old homes, take a paddle-wheel boat dinner cruise, visit the new zoo, and the Aquarium of the Americas. Take in the Garden District and Bourbon Street. The French Quarter is made for strolling. One half block to Special Services and tickets!

Locator 393-3011   **Medical 911**   **Police 678-2570**

Too Late To Copy
Camp Beauregard, Pineville, LA 71360-5000. Lodging Office, **C-318-640-2080 EX 269/302.**

MAINE

Bangor Air National Guard Base (ME10R1)
Pine Tree Inn, Bldg 346
22 Cleveland Ave.
Bangor ANGB, ME 04401-3099

TELEPHONE NUMBER INFORMATION: Main installation numbers: C-207-990-7700, D-312-698-7700.

Location: Located in Bangor city limits. Northbound on I-95 take exit 45B (West on Route 2). Turn right at Odlin Road (first set traffic lights). One mile, Cleveland St on the right. Up the hill, Pine Tree Inn is located in building 346, 22 Cleveland Ave. *USMRA: Page 18 (E-6,7).* NMC: Bangor, in city limits.

Lodging Office: Pine Tree Inn, building 346, 22 Cleveland Avenue, **C-207-942-2081**.

TML: The Army National Guard operates Pine Tree Inn for military members, retirees, and their families, C-207-942-2081. Check out 1200 hours. Bedroom, semi-private bath (46). Community kitchen, essentials, housekeeping service, refrigerator, color TV lounge, washer/dryer. Rates: official users $7 per night, non-official $12. Duty can make reservations, others Space-A.

DV/VIP: No Protocol Office.

TML Availability: Fairly good any time.

Medical 911   **Police 911**

Freeport Maine, home of millions of outlet shoppers, is an easy drive from Bangor ANGB. Don't miss this opportunity to go broke saving money!

Brunswick Naval Air Station (ME07R1)
CBQ Officer, Box 49
Brunswick, ME 04011-5000

TELEPHONE NUMBER INFORMATION: Main installation numbers: C-207-921-1110, D-312-476-1110.

Location: From I-95 north exit US-1 north to Brunswick, Old Bath Rd (Route 24) to main gate of NAS. *USMRA: Page 18 (C-9).* NMC: Portland, 30 miles southwest.

Lodging Office: Building 220, **C-207-921-2245**, FAX (BEQ) 207-729-0232, (BOQ) 207-921-2492, 24 hours daily. Check in facility (Space-A check in at 1800), check out 1100 hours. No government civilian employee billeting.

TML: Navy Lodge. Building 364. **Topsham Annex, off base, call lodge for directions.** All ranks, leave or official duty. Reservations call **1-800-NAVY-INN**. Lodge C-207-921-2206, 0800-2000 hours. Check in 1500-1800, check out 1200 hours. Other hours OD, C-207-921-2214. Bedroom, 2 beds, private bath (12); bedroom, double bed, private bath (2). Kitchenette, microwave, utensils, CATV, clocks, cots, cribs, ice/snack vending,

MAINE
Brunswick Naval Air Station, continued

iron/ironing boards, mini-mart, playground, rollaways, housekeeping service, coin washer/dryer. Older structure. Rates: $32-$35 per unit. All categories can make reservations.

TML: BOQ/BEQ. All ranks, leave or official duty. Bedroom, private bath (10); separate bedroom, private bath (24). Refrigerator, community kitchen, limited utensils, color TV in room & lounge, housekeeping service, cots, washer/dryer, ice vending, picnic tables, tennis courts, sauna, gym. Older structure. Rates: BEQ, PCS $5, VIP suites $12 per night, additional person, $5, Space-A surcharge $10. Maximum 3 per room. Duty can make reservations, others Space-A. Kennels in town.

TML: Transient BOQ/BEQ. Buildings 220, 512, official duty only, officers O6+, enlisted E8-E9. Rooms, private bath (5); two bedroom, private bath (3); three bedroom, private bath (28). Essentials, food vending, housekeeping service, refrigerator, color TV, washer/dryer. VIP suites have VCR, water beds, bar, hair dryers, clock radios. Older and modern structures. Older structure, renovated and remodeled. Rates: BOQ, PCS $8 per night, $2 additional person, VIP suites $20 per night, $5 additional person, Space-A surcharge $10. Families not authorized. Maximum 3 persons. Duty can make reservations.

DV/VIP: Brunswick NAS, building 512, C-207-921-2214, O5+, retirees Space-A.

TML Availability: Good, Sep-Jan. Difficult, Apr-Aug.

CREDIT CARDS ACCEPTED: Visa, MasterCard and American Express. The Navy Lodge accepts Visa, MasterCard, American Express and Discover.

Fishing and hunting are considered "tops" here, 60 ski areas, including Sugarloaf (it has a 9,000 foot gondola line) make winter skiing here a favorite. But if you've never tasted shrimp and lobster, do it here! Freeport (home of L.L. Bean) is just 15 minutes south.

Locator 921-1110   Medical 921-2610   Police 921-2585

Cutler Naval Computer and Telecommunications Station (ME08R1)
Morale Welfare & Recreation
East Machias, ME 04630-1000

TELEPHONE NUMBER INFORMATION: Main installation numbers: C-207-259-8203, D-312-476-7203.

Location: Take Hwy 95 to Bangor; 395 around Bangor; Routes 1A and 1 to East Machias; 191 to base (7 miles off route 1). *USMRA: Page 18 (G,H-7)*. NMC: Bangor, 90 miles west.

Lodging Office: None. **C-207-259-8284/8201.** Check in MWR Hobby Shop, 0730-1600 hours daily. Check out 1200. After duty hours, Quarterdeck, building 500.

TML: Rustic cabins (1), at Sprague's Neck, all ranks, leave or official duty. No electricity. Gas lights, wood stove, running water and indoor toilet. Kitchenette and utensils. Pets allowed. Call for further information and rates. All categories can make reservations.

TML Availability: Extremely limited, best Apr to Sep.

MAINE
Cutler Naval Computer and Telecommunications Station, continued

A real rustic get away for hunting, fishing, swimming, skiing, snow mobiling, or enjoying friendly "down east folks".

Locator 259-8229   Medical 259-8209   Police 259-8226

Winter Harbor Naval Security Group Activity (ME09R1)
10 Fabbri Green, Suite 84
Winter Harbor, ME 04693

TELEPHONE NUMBER INFORMATION: Main installation numbers: C-207-963-5534, D-312-476-9011.

Location: From Ellsworth, take US-1 north to ME-186 east to Acadia National Park. Naval Security Station is on Schoodic Point in the park. *USMRA: Page 18 (F-7,8)*. NMC: Bangor, 45 miles northwest.

Lodging Office: Combined billeting office in building 84, **C-207-963-5534-EX-223/203**, D-312-476-9223-EX-223/203, 24 hrs daily. Check in billeting, check out 1300 hours daily. Government civilian employee billeting.

TML: BEQ. Building 84, enlisted, leave or official duty. Bedroom, shared bath (E1-E6) (12); bedroom, shared bath (24); bedroom, shared bath (E7-E9) (6). Refrigerator, community kitchen, CATV/VCR in room & lounge, housekeeping service washer/dryer. Modern structure, new '91. Rates: $4.

TML: BOQ. Building 192, officers all ranks, leave or official duty. Bedroom, private bath (4). Kitchen, limited utensils, CATV, housekeeping service, washer/dryer. Modern structure. Rates: $8 per person. Maximum 2 per room. Duty can make reservations, others Space-A.

TML: MWR cabins and mobile homes, **Winter Harbor Recreation Area**. All ranks, leave or official duty, retirees, family members, **C-207-963-5537**. Cabins, 3 bedroom, private bath, fully furnished, sleep 5 (5); mobile homes, 2 bedroom, private bath, fully furnished, sleep 5 (5). Fully equipped kitchen, all linens, TV, 1 cabin handicapped accessible, pets allowed in trailers for additional $10 fee. Full range of recreational opportunities, both summer and winter available. Close to base support activities. Rates: May-Sept $50, mobile homes $35; Oct-Apr $40 & $30. All categories may make reservations 90 days in advance.

TML Availability: Good, Nov-Mar. Difficult, May-Sep.

CREDIT CARDS ACCEPTED: American Express.

Located in Schoodic Point section of Acadia National Park, this is a favorite with hunters, fishermen, snow and water skiers. For additional information on the rec area, read *Military RV, Camping & Rec Areas Around the World*.

Locator 963-5534/5535   Medical EX-297/298   Police EX-202

MARYLAND

Aberdeen Proving Ground (MD11R1)
UPH Management Br.
STEAP-FE-HU, Bldg 2207
Aberdeen PG, MD 21005-5001

TELEPHONE NUMBER INFORMATION: Main installation numbers: (Aberdeen Area) C-410-278-5201,(Aberdeen Area) D-312-298-1110, (Edgewood Area) C-410-671-5201, (Edgewood Area) D-312-584-1110.

Location: Aberdeen Area: take exit 85 east from I-95 north on MD-22 east for 2 miles to main gate. Also, from US-40 north to right on Maryland Blvd, entrance to main gate. NMC: Baltimore, 23 miles southwest. Edgewood Area: take exit 77 from I-95 north on MD-24 east for 2 miles to main gate. Also, from US-40 right on MD-24 to main gate. *USMRA: Page 42 (G-2,3)*. NMC: Baltimore, 13 miles southwest.

Lodging Office: Building 2207, Bel Air St, 24 hours daily. **C-410-278-5148/5149**, D-312-298-4373/5148, FAX 410-273-6500 ext 7740. Check in billeting (except TLF), check out 1100 hours. Government civilian employee billeting.

TML: Guest House, check in at front desk, building 3322, all ranks, leave or official duty, **C-410-278-3856**, D-312-298-3856. Bedroom, 2 double beds, private bath (37); one to four bedroom apartments, private bath (18). Refrigerator, microwave, A/C, color TV in room & lounge, housekeeping service, cribs, cots, washer/dryer, ice vending. Modern structure. Rates: E1-E6 $21, E7-E9 $26.50, O1+ $31.50. Maximum persons per unit: 5 in rooms, 8 in apartments. TDY and active duty, reservists, national guard can make reservations, others Space-A.

TML: VOQ/VEQ. Several buildings, officers all ranks, enlisted E6+, official duty, **C-410-278-5148/49**. Check out 1300 hours. Bedroom, private bath (214); separate bedroom, semi-private bath (120). Essentials, kitchenette, A/C, color TV in room & lounge, housekeeping service, washer/dryer. Older structure, recently remodeled. Rates: $31 per night. Maximum 1 per room. No pets allowed. Active duty, reservists and national guard can make reservations.

TML: DV/VIP. **Ryan Building**, officers O6+, GS-15 and above, leave or official duty, **C-410-278-5156/57**. Two separate bedrooms, private bath (2); two bedroom, private bath (4); three bedrooms, private bath (2). Kitchen, complete utensils, A/C, color TV, housekeeping service, cribs/cots. Check out 1300 hours daily. Older structure. Rates: $45 per night. Duty can make reservations, others Space-A.

DV/VIP: TECOM Protocol, Ryan Building, C-410-278-1038. Or USAOC&S Protocol, building 3071, C-410-278-5595, O6+, retirees Space-A.

TML Availability: Good, Nov-Jan. Difficult, other times.

CREDIT CARDS ACCEPTED: Visa, MasterCard and American Express.

On the Chesapeake Bay. Hunting, fishing, boating, 3 golf courses, 5 swimming pools, theater, bowling alley, fitness center, Marylander restaurant. Baltimore is 30 miles south, DC 75 miles south, and Philadelphia 92 miles north. Lots to do here.

Locator 278-5201   Medical 272-2557   Police 278-5291

MARYLAND

Andrews Air Force Base (MD02R1)
Gateway Inn
86th SVS/SVML
1375 Arkansas Rd
Andrews AFB, MD 20331-7002

TELEPHONE NUMBER INFORMATION: Main installation numbers: C-301-981-1110, D-312-858-1110.

Location: From I-95 (east portion of Capital Beltway, I-495) north or south, exit 9, first traffic light after leaving exit ramp turn left, go to main gate of AFB. Clearly marked. USMRA: Page *42 (E-5) & Page 55 (I,J-6,7)*. NMC: Washington, DC 6 miles northwest.

Lodging Office: Gateway Inn, 1375, Arkansas Rd, **C-301-423-1412**, D-312-858-4614, FAX 301-981-7997, DSN FAX 312-858-7997, 24 hours daily. Check in lodging, check out 1200 hours daily. Government civilian employee billeting.

TML: TLF. Buildings 1801-1804, 1328, 1330, all ranks, leave or official duty. Separate bedrooms, private bath (68). Kitchen, utensils, A/C, color TV, housekeeping service, cribs, washer/dryer, ice vending, iron/ironing board. Modern structure. Rates: $24. Maximum 5 per room. PCS to Andrews can make reservations, others Space-A.

TML: VAQ. Buildings 1373, 1376, 1580, 1629. Suites, private bath (5); Chief suites (2); rooms, shared bath (65). Refrigerator, microwave, A/C, color TV, VCR, iron/ironing board. Rates: Suites $14, rooms $8 per person. Reservations required.

TML: VOQ. Buildings 1349, 1360-1371. Officers, all ranks, leave or official duty. Bedrooms, private bath (30); suites, private bath (60). Refrigerator, microwave, A/C, color TV, VCR, iron/ironing board. Rates: Suites $14, rooms $8 per person. Reservations required.

TML: DV/VIP. Building 1349. Officers O6+, leave or official duty. DV rooms, private bath (31), DV suites, private bath (8). Kitchen, A/C, color TV, housekeeping service, washer/dryer, iron & board. Older structure. Rates: $8 rooms, $14 suites, per person, per night. Official travellers can make reservations, others Space-A.

DV/VIP: Protocol, 89 AW/CCP, C-301-981-4525, O7+. Retirees Space-A.

TML Availability: Best, Dec-Feb. Difficult, Mar-Nov.

CREDIT CARDS ACCEPTED: Visa, MasterCard and American Express.

Andrews is the military aerial gateway to Washington, DC for most overseas VIP's, and the home of "Air Force One", the President's aircraft. If you're lucky you can witness "important people" coming and going here.

Locator 981-1110   **Medical 981-6250**   **Police-981-2500**

MARYLAND

Curtis Bay Coast Guard Yard (MD01R1)
Coast Guard Exchange System
Bldg 33, Curtis Bay
Baltimore, MD 21226-1797

TELEPHONE NUMBER INFORMATION: Main installation numbers: C-410-636-4194/4188.

Location: Take I-695 to exit 1, bear to your right, right on Hawkins Point Rd, left into Coast Guard Yard. *USMRA: Page 42 (F-3) & Page 49 (C-4).* NMC: Baltimore, 5 miles northwest.

Lodging Office: No central billeting office. BQ Manager, building 28A (BOQ), C-410-636-7373, 0830-1500 M-F. Family Transient Lodging, building 84, **C-410-636-4187,** 0730-1500 M-F. Reservations required. After duty hours, JOOD, building 33, C-410-636-7493 (if reservations made). Check in facility after 1400 hours, check out 1000 hours daily. No government civilian employee billeting.

TML: TLF. Building 84. All ranks, leave or official duty. Three bedroom suites, private bath (5). Kitchen, complete utensils, A/C, color TV, cribs, washer/dryer, playground. Handicapped accessible. Older structure. Rates: 1 bedroom $20, 2 bedroom $25, 3 bedroom $30 per night. Sofa bed available. Maximum 8 per family. All categories except widows and unaccompanied dependents can make reservations. PCS in/out have priority.

TML: BOQ. Building 28A, officer all ranks, official duty only. Reservations required. C-410-636-7373, 0830-1500. After duty hours, OD, building 33, C-410-636-4147. Bedroom, 2 beds, private bath (5). A/C, color in TV lounge, microwave, refrigerator, pool table and VCR in lounge, washer/dryer. Modern structure. Rates: sponsor $5. Maximum 2 persons per unit.

TML Availability: Good, Oct-Apr. More difficult, other times.

Southeast of Baltimore, a city rich in history and entertainment, where the Inner Harbor buzzes with shopping, dining and recreational opportunities.

Locator 636-4147   Medical 636-3144   Police 636-7476

Fort Detrick (MD07R1)
Billeting Office Manger/MCHD-EHH
Bldg 810, Suite 133
Frederick, MD 21702-5000

TELEPHONE NUMBER INFORMATION: Main installation numbers: C-301-619-8000, D-312-343-1110.

Location: From Washington, DC, take I-270 north to US-15 north. From Baltimore, take I-70 west to US-15 north. From US-15 north, in Frederick, exit Seventh St. Clearly marked to post. *USMRA: Page 42 (D-2).* NMC: Baltimore, 50 miles east and Washington, DC, 50 miles southeast.

Lodging Office: 810 Schreider Street, Suite 133. **C-301-619-2154,** 0745-1630 hours M-F. Check out 1000 hours daily. Government civilian employee billeting.

MARYLAND
Fort Detrick, Continued

TML: Guest House. Buildings 800-801, all ranks, leave or official duty. Two bedroom, private bath (1); three bedroom, private bath (3). Kitchen, utensils, microwave, dishwashers, telephones, housekeeping service, CATV, iron/boards, sofa bed, A/C, color TV, washer/dryer. Completely modernized. Rates: $24 per unit. PCS can make reservations, others Space-A. No pets.

TML: VOQ. Building 660, all ranks, leave or official duty. Bedroom suites, double beds, private bath (16). Kitchen, microwave, limited utensils, A/C, sofa bed, iron/boards, color TV, CATV, housekeeper service, washer/dryer, soda/snack machine, phone. Older structure, remodeled. Rates: $10 per room. TDY can make reservations, others Space-A. No pets.

TML: DVQ. Building 715, officers, leave or official duty. Suite, queen bed, private bath (1). Kitchen, microwave, limited utensils, A/C, CATV, color TV, iron/board, telephone, housekeeping service. Older structure, remodeled. Rates: $18 per night. TDY can make reservations, others Space-A. No Pets.

DV/VIP: HQ Ft Detrick. C-301-619-7114. O6+. Retirees and lower ranks Space-A.

TML Availability: Good, Oct-Mar. Difficult, Jun-Aug.

Historic Frederick County offers visitors a variety of cultural, sports and recreational options. Both Baltimore and Washington DC are nearby.

Locator 619-2233   Medical 619-7175   Police 619-7114

Fort George G. Meade (MD08R1)
Post Lodging
P.O. Box 1069
Fort George G. Meade, MD 20755-5115

TELEPHONE NUMBER INFORMATION: Main installation numbers: C-410-677-6261, D-312-923-6261.

Location: Off Baltimore-Washington Parkway, I-295, exit MD-198 east which is Fort Meade Road. Clearly marked. *USMRA: Page 42 (E,F-4).* NMC: Baltimore and Washington, DC, 30 miles from each city.

Lodging Office: Brett Hall, Post Billeting Fund, Building 4707, Ruffner Rd, **C-410-677-6529/5884,** D-312-923-5884, 24 hours daily. Check in billeting, check out 1200 hours daily. Government civilian employee billeting.

TML: Guest House. Building 2793, **Abrams Hall**, all ranks, leave or official duty. Handicapped accessible, C-410-677-2045. Check in 24 hours daily. Bedrooms with 2 beds, private bath (54). Refrigerator, community kitchen, A/C, essentials, color TV room & lounge, housekeeping service, cribs, washer/dryer, food/ice vending, CATV, in-room telephone, microwaves. Older structure, completely renovated 1993-1994. Has a new $50,000 playground. Rates: PCS in/out $22.50-$26.50 per room. Priorities: PCS, hospital visitors, visitors of active duty assigned, TDY may stay 30 days. Reservations 30 days in advance, 1 night confirmed stay. (This does not pertain to personnel who are PCS, hospital visitors, active duty assigned, TDY, etc.)

MARYLAND
Fort George G. Meade, continued

TML: VOQ. Buildings 4703, 4704, 4707, 4709, officers all ranks, leave or official duty. Bedroom, semi-private bath (142); one bedroom, private bath (4); separate bedroom suites, private bath (16). Kitchen (14 units), refrigerator, A/C, CATV, housekeeping service, washer/dryer, ice vending. Older structures, bathrooms renovated. Rates: $28.00 per room. TDY room confirmation duration of stay, confirmed 60 days in advance.

TML: SEBQ. Building 4705, enlisted E7-E9, official duty. Separate bedroom, private bath (30). Modern structure. Rates: No charge. For SNCO on PCS to Ft Meade only.

TML: BOQ. Bldg 4717, 4720, 4721, officers all ranks, official duty. Separate bedrooms, private bath (62). Rates: No charge. PCS to Ft Meade only.

TML: DVQ. Building 4415, officer O5+, TDY, PCS, leave or official duty. Separate bedrooms, private bath (5); two bedroom, private bath (2). Kitchen, limited utensils, A/C, color TV, housekeeping service, washer/dryer. Older structure, renovated. Rates: $28.00-$45.00 per room. Duty can make reservations, Protocol Office, others Space-A. Reservations 60 days in advance, 1 night confirmed stay for "others".

TML Availability: Good. Best months, Oct-Mar.

CREDIT CARDS ACCEPTED: Visa, MasterCard, American Express and Diners.

Visit Baltimore's Fort McHenry National Monument, and new Inner Harbor, or see Annapolis' quaint shopping areas. Washington DC is also a short drive from Fort Meade.

Locator 677-6261   Medical 677-2570   Police 677-6622

Fort Ritchie (MD13R1)
Fort Ritchie Guest House
Bldg 520, Cushman Ave.
Fort Ritchie, MD 21719-5010
Scheduled to close. No closure date has been established.

TELEPHONE NUMBER INFORMATION: Main installation numbers: C-301-878-1300, D-312-277-1300.

Location: From US-15 north exit at Thurmont, to MD-550 north for 7 miles to Cascade and main gate. From Hagerstown, take MD-64 east to MD-491, north to MD-550 and north to Cascade and main gate. *USMRA: Page 42 (C,D-1).* **NMC:** Hagerstown, 16 miles southwest, Baltimore, 50 miles southeast, Washington, DC, 55 miles southeast.

Lodging Office: Guesthouse, Building 520, Cushman Ave., **C-301-878-5171**, D-312-277-5171, FAX-301-241-4585, 0800-1845 M-F, 0800-1645 Sa-Su, holidays. Other hours, MP Desk, building 123. Check in facility, check out before 1130 hours daily. Government civilian employee billeting.

TML: Guest House. Building 520, all ranks, leave or official duty. Bedroom, private bath (21). Kitchen (9 units), refrigerator (12 units), complete utensils, VCR, CATV with HBO, housekeeping

MARYLAND
Fort Ritchie, continued

service, cribs/cots, coin washer/dryer, ice vending. Modern structure. Rates: PCS without kitchen $24, with kitchen $26. Maximum 5 per room. PCS can make reservations, others Space-A.

TML: VOQ/VEQ. Building 800, officers all ranks, enlisted E7-E9, leave or official duty. Bedroom, private bath (11); bedroom suite (DV)(1). (VQ) refrigerator, community kitchen, VCR, CATV with HBO in room & lounge, housekeeping service, washer/dryer. Rates: VQ $17.50, DVQ $24, $6 each additional person. TDY can make reservations, others Space-A.

TML: Lakeside Hall. Building 11, C-301-878-4361, all ranks, leave or official duty. Bedroom, private bath, small living area w/pull-out couch (6); apartments with kitchenettes (2); Ritchie Suite (VIP)(1). Rates: non-members: rooms $35, apartments $40. Military Club members take off $5. Refrigerator, microwave, coffee pot, color TV, in room phones, FAX machine, laundry service available, meal service in dining room, disco on weekends. T-F lunch 11-1, T-F dinner, Sunday brunch. Activities for guests. Overlooking lake, lakeside activities include swimming, paddle boating, fishing, newly renovated, color TV, telephones in room, FAX machine. Laundry service available.

DV/VIP: HQ 7th SIG, building 307, C-301-878-5754, O6+. Retirees, Space-A.

TML Availability: Good, most of the year. Best, Mar-Jun.

CREDIT CARDS ACCEPTED: Visa, MasterCard and American Express.

Beautiful scenic small post. Great location for ski resorts in the area, swimming, fishing, golf and Gettysburg National Park.

Locator 878-5685   **Medical 878-4132**   **Police 878-4228**

Indian Head Naval Surface Warfare Center (MD04R1)
CBQ (Code 115), Indian Head Division
Indian Head, MD 20640-5000

TELEPHONE NUMBER INFORMATION: Main installation numbers: C-301-743-4000, D-312-354-4000.

Location: Take I-495 (Capital Beltway) east, exit to MD-210 south for 25 miles to station. *USMRA: Page 42 (D-5,6).* NMC: Washington, DC 25 miles north.

Lodging Office: Building 902, **C-301-743-4845**, D-312-354-4845, FAX 301-743-4838, 24 hours daily. Reservations are highly recommended.

TML: BOQ. Building 969, all ranks, leave or official duty, 24 hours daily. Officer/enlisted rooms, semi-private baths, most 2 bedroom. Kitchen, complete set of cooking & eating utensils, A/C, color TV lounge, VCR, housekeeping service, washer/dryer, food vending. Older structure, renovated. Rates: $6 permanent/students (longer 21 weeks), $8 transient. Duty can make reservations, others Space-A. No Space-A for families or dependents.

TML: BEQ. Building 1752, 902, all ranks, leave or official duty, C-301-743-4845, 24 hours. Bedroom with 1 bed, semi-private bath (108). A/C, color TV, housekeeping service, washer/dryer, food vending. Rates: $4 per day. Duty can make reservations, others Space-A. No Space-A for families or dependents. All Hands dinning facility located in building 902.

MARYLAND
Indian Head Naval Surface Warfare Center, continued

DV/VIP: PAO. Building 20, C-301-743-4627. Inquire about qualifying rank. Lodging considered substandard by Navy standards. Retirees Space-A.

TML Availability: Fair, Jan-May, Sept-Dec. Difficult, other times.

CREDIT CARDS ACCEPTED: Diners.

Only 25 miles from Washington D.C. makes this place within "shouting distance" of the many cultural and sporting events available to the area. The nearby Potomac River also provides recreational opportunities.

Locator 743-4303   Medical 743-4601   Police 743-4381

National Naval Medical Center (MD06R1)
Lodging Office, Bldg 60
Bethesda, MD 20889-5000

TELEPHONE NUMBER INFORMATION: Main installation numbers: C-301-295-5385, D-312-295-4611 (Hospital Information).

Location: From I-495 (Capital Beltway) take exit 34, Wisconsin Ave (Md-355, Rockville Pike) south for 1 mile to Naval Medical Center on left. Enter first gate, Wood Rd S, for support facility. Also, can enter the center from Jones Bridge Rd, off Wisconsin Ave. *USMRA: Page 55 (D,E-1).* NMC: Washington, DC 1 mile southeast.

Lodging Office: Billeting Office for BOQ/BEQ, building 60. Check in facility, check out 1200 hours daily. Government civilian employee lodging. **C-301-295-5855/56,** FAX 301-295-0172. No government employee billeting. Duty Office - main hospital (central figure for problems) **C-301-295-4611.**

TML: Navy Lodge, building 52, 8901 Wisconsin Ave., all ranks, medical and PCS have priority. For reservations call **1-800-NAVY-INN** (1-800-628-9466). Lodge number is 301-654-1795, 24 hours daily, Fax 301-654-9373. Check in 1500-1800, check out 1200. There are 72 units. Bedroom, 2 double beds, private bath. Single rooms w/queen bed (does not include entire kitchenette facility). Four sets interconnecting units, 14 non-smoking rooms. Kitchenette, microwave, A/C, color CATV with Showtime, housekeeping service, cribs, phones,fax service, high chairs, rollaways, ice/snack vending, coin washer/dryer, irons/boards, lounge, playground. Modern structure. Rates: $51.50-$61.50 per unit. Active duty may make reservations 60 days in advance, retirees/reservists 30 days in advance, PCS/patients anytime in advance.

TML: BOQ. Building 11, officers, all ranks, official duty. Reservations required, C-301-295-1110/1. Bedroom, common bath (89); separate bedrooms, private bath, kitchen (4) (DV/VIP); family rooms, kitchen, private bath (2) maximum 2 persons, rates: $8, $12 and $15. Refrigerator, community kitchen, utensils, A/C, color TV in lounge, housekeeping service, cots, washer/dryer, ice vending. Older structure. Quarters are inadequate & substandard.

TML: Fisher House. Note: Appendix C has the definition of this facility. **C-301-295-5334.** A second Fisher House opened in December 1993.

MARYLAND
National Naval Medical Center, continued

DV/VIP: Cmdr, NATNAVMEDCEN, building 1, room 5156A, C-301-295-5800, O6+. Retirees Space-A.

TML Availability: Very limited.

CREDIT CARDS ACCEPTED: The Navy Lodge accepts Visa, MasterCard, American Express and Discover.

Bethesda is located just north of Washington DC, shopping, and the Metro are close by.

Locator 295-5385   Medical 295-0999   Police 295-0999

Patuxent River Naval Air Warfare Center (MD09R1)
Lodging Office, Bldg 406
Patuxent River NAWC, MD 20670-5199

TELEPHONE NUMBER INFORMATION: Main installation numbers: C-301-342-3000, D-312-342-3000.

Location: From I-95 (east portion of Capital Beltway, I-495) exit 7A to Branch Ave (MD-5) south. Follow MD-5 until it turns into MD-235 near Oraville, on to Lexington Park, and the NAS. Main gate is on MD-235 and MD-246 (Cedar Point Rd). *USMRA: Page 42 (F-7; G-6,7)*. NMC: Washington, DC, 65 miles west.

Lodging Office: Building 406. C-301-342-3601, D-312-342-3601. FAX 301-342-1015, check in facility, check out 1200 hours daily.

TML: Navy Lodge. Building 2119, **1-800-NAVY-INN**. Lodge number is C-301-342-2400, FAX 301-342-7866. All ranks leave or official duty, civilian employees on orders, retirees. Bedroom, 2 double beds, private bath (50). Six sets interconnecting, 2 handicapped accessible, 41 non-smoking. Kitchenette, microwave, utensils, A/C, cribs, rollaways, high chairs, irons/boards, phones, ice/snack vending, kitchen, housekeeping service, CATV w/HBO, playground, mini-mart, washer/dryer. Rates: $43 per unit. Maximum 5 persons per room. All categories can make reservations.

TML: BOQ. Building 406, officers all ranks, leave or official duty, C-301-342-3895. Rooms/suites, private baths (76). Kitchen, refrigerator, A/C, color TV, housekeeping service, cots, washer/dryer, ice vending, telephone. Two rooms handicapped accessible. Rates: $8 per person, child up to 12 free. Reservations only from persons on TAD orders, retirees Space-A.

TML: DV/VIP. C-301-342-3895, one bedroom, king-size bed suites, dining room, living room, private bath, kitchen (2).

TML: DV/VIP. **Crowe's Nest** (located at Officers' Club). 1 suite, private bath. Ask about Gull Cottage. For reservations contact C-301-342-3601, O6+.

DV/VIP: PAO. C-301-342-7503, O7+, retirees Space-A.

TML Availability: Fairly good, winter. More difficult, Jun-Aug.

MARYLAND
Patuxent River Naval Air Warfare Center, continued

CREDIT CARDS ACCEPTED: Visa, MasterCard, American Express and Discover at the Navy Lodge.

The Special Interest Coordinator's office in building 423 (863-3510) has discount tickets to Kings Dominion, Wild World, Busch Gardens, Hershey Park, local ski resorts, Colonial Williamsburg, sporting events.

Locator 342-3000   Medical 342-1422   Police 342-3911

Solomons Navy Recreation Center (MD05R1)
Lodging Office, Bldg 411
Solomons, MD 20688-0147

TELEPHONE NUMBER INFORMATION: Main installation numbers: 410-326-4216 or 301-863-9074, DC Area 800-NAVY-230.

Location: Off base, on Patuxent River. From US-301, take MD-4 southeast to Solomons; or take MD-5 southeast to MD-235, then MD-4 northeast to Solomons. *USMRA: Page 42 (F-6).* NMC: Washington, DC, 65 miles northwest.

Lodging Office: Building 411, **C-410-326-4216**, FAX (410) 326-4280, DC Area 800-628-9230, 0800-2200 Sa-Th, 0800-2400 F. Late check-in if arranged in advance. All ranks, leave or official duty. Check in billeting, check out 1100 hours daily.

TML: Units are apartments, bungalows, & cottages. Two bedroom, private bath (1); three bedroom, private bath (25); four and five bedroom, private bath (2 & 9). Kitchen, limited utensils, rental linens, A/C, cribs (fee), coin washer/dryer, food/ice vending. Older structures, some renovated. Rates: cottages E1-E5 $34-$47; E6-E9 $43-$55; Officers $51-$63; DoD civilians $64-$79; bungalows E1-E5 $33-$34; E6-E9 $41-$44; Officers $50-$53; DoD civilians $63-$66. All rates per night. Maximum 3 persons per bedroom. All categories except unaccompanied dependents can make reservations. Call for information about lottery reservation system.

TML Availability: Good, Oct-Apr. Difficult, other times.

Complete river recreational/camping area. Full support facility available at nearby Patuxent River NAWC. St Maries City, Calvert Cliffs, Calvert Marine Museum, Farmers' Market, charter fishing, Point Lookout State Park. For complete details see *Military RV, Camping & Rec Areas Around The World.*

Locator 326-3566   Medical 911   Police 826-3563

United States Naval Academy/ Annapolis Naval Station (MD10R1)
BOQ
2 Truxton Road
Annapolis, MD 21402-5000

TELEPHONE NUMBER INFORMATION: Main installation numbers: C-410-293-1000, D-312-281-0111.

MARYLAND
United States Naval Academy, continued

Location: Two miles off US-50/301. Two exits to the Academy, clearly marked. Main gate is on King George St, in Annapolis. Naval Station is across Severn River off US-50/301 east, first exit. Clearly marked. *USMRA: Page 42 (F-4) & Page 48 (D,E,F,G-1,2,3).* NMC: Annapolis, in city.

Lodging Office: Billeting Office, 2nd floor, **Officers' and Faculty Club, C-410-293-3906**, D-312-281-3906, FAX 410-293-2444, DSN FAX 312-281-2444, Mon-Fri 0730-1530 hours Tu-Th, 0730-1800, Sat-Sun & holidays 0900-1400. Check in 1300 at billeting, check out 1100 at billeting. Government civilian employee billeting.

TML: O & F Club, second & third deck, officers all ranks, equivalent government employees, leave or official duty. Suites, private bath, sleeps to 5 persons (14). A/C, color TV, washer/dryer, housekeeping service. Older historic structure, remodeled. Rates: $10; $2 each additional person. PCS, TAD/TDY have priority, others Space-A.

DV/VIP: O & F Club, third deck, reservations through Superintendent's Protocol Office: C-410-293-2403, O6+. VIP suites, private bath, coffee bar, honor bar with kitchenette (2). Rates: suites w/ kitchenette $20, plus $5 each additional person, guest suite $15, $3 each additional person. Retirees Space-A.

TML Availability: Best, Oct-Apr. Difficult, summer months.

CREDIT CARDS ACCEPTED: American Express.

Don't miss a visit to the waterfront shopping and restaurant area, where dreaming over yachts is "SOP". Visit the Naval Academy Chapel and historic buildings, and walk around historic Maryland's capital.

Locator 293-1000   **Medical 293-3333**   **Police 293-4444**

MASSACHUSETTS

Armed Services YMCA of Boston (MA16R1)
150 Second Avenue
Charlestown Navy Yard, Charleston MA 02129
(This is not U.S. Government/Military Lodging).

TELEPHONE NUMBER INFORMATION: Main installation numbers: C-617-241-8400, FAX-617-241-2856.

Location: From the Massachusetts Turnpike to Boston; JFK Expressway exit #25 and follow signs to USS Constitution; from North I-93 to Sullivan Square Exit, follow signs to USS Constitution. *USMRA: page 24 (E,F-5)*. NMC: Boston, in the city.

Lodging Office: C-617-241-8400, FAX 617-241-2856, 24 hours daily. Check in facility, check out 1130 hours daily. Government civilian employee billeting.

TML: All ranks, leave or official duty. Single and family accommodations. Write to: 150 Second Ave., Charlestown, MA 02129. Bedroom, two beds, private bath; adjoining rooms; suites, private bath (DV/VIP). A/C, kitchenette (must provide own cooking and eating utensils). DV/VIP, CATV, housekeeping service, coin washer/dryer, YMCA space rentals (meetings, gym, pool, function room) available. Rates: Military $40 and up, Civilian $60 and up. All categories may make reservations. Rates subject to change.

TML Availability: Very good.

CREDIT CARDS ACCEPTED: Visa, MasterCard and American Express.

Boston is one of America's most "walkable" cities - see bustling Faneuil Hall Marketplace and waterfront areas, the shops of Back Bay and picturesque squares of Beacon Hill. The Hub's many athletic and cultural events are only a few minutes away by car or Boston's rapid transit system, the "T".

Locator none   Medical 911   Police 911

Boston Coast Guard Support Center (MA07R1)
ATTN: MAA
427 Commercial St
Boston, MA 02109-1027

TELEPHONE NUMBER INFORMATION: Main installation number: C-617-223-3313.

Location: Take Atlantic Avenue exit off of I-93, turn onto Commercial St. Located at corner of Commercial and Hanover. *USMRA: Page 24 (E,F-4,5)*. NMC: In heart of downtown Boston.

Lodging Office: 427 Commercial St, Building 1. **C-617-223-3171**, FAX 617-723-3166, 0600-1730 hours, Mon-Fri. Check in billeting, check out 1100.

TML: BOQ/BEQ. All ranks, leave or official duty. Handicapped accessible units. Shared rooms, shared bath (15). TV in lounge area, washer/dryer, ice/food vending. Rates: Were not furnished, please call for rates.

MASSACHUSETTS
Boston Coast Guard Support Center, continued

TML Availability: Fairly good. Best, Oct-Feb, difficult, Mar-Sep.

Boston is one of America's most "walkable" cities - see bustling Faneuil Hall Marketplace and waterfront areas, the shops of Back Bay and picturesque squares of Beacon Hill. The Hub's many athletic and cultural events are only a few minutes away by car or Boston's rapid transit system, the "T".

Cape Cod Coast Guard Air Station (MA10R1)
ATTN: Temporary Quarters, Bldg 5204
USCG Air Station - Cape Cod
Otis ANGB, MA 02542-5024

TELEPHONE NUMBER INFORMATION: Main installation numbers: C-508-968-1000, D-312-557-4401, National Guard Base. Coast Guard Air Station, C & FTS-508-968-6300, D-312-557-6300.

Location: Take MA Military Reservation exit off MA-28, south on Connley Ave approximately 2 miles to Bourne Gate. *USMRA: Page 17 (M-7)*. NMC: Boston, 50 miles northwest.

Lodging Office: ATTN: Temporary Quarters, building 5204, **C-508-968-6461,** 0800-1600 hours M-F. 1200-1600 hours Sa & Su. Check in billeting. Check out 1100 hours.

TML: TLF/BOQ. All ranks. Leave or official duty. Accessible to handicapped. Advance payment required. Bedrooms with kitchen, private bath (4); two bedroom town houses, private bath (9); bedroom, private bath (BOQ) (3); bedroom efficiency apartments, private bath (16). Cots/cribs, essentials, food vending, housekeeping service, refrigerator, color TV in lounge & room, utensils, coin washer/dryer, small child's playroom. Older structure, remodeled. Rates: moderate, determined by rank. Reservations: PCS 90 days in advance, others 30 days. In summer vacationers, TDY 2 weeks in advance.

TML Availability: Good. Best Oct-Apr.

Otis has 9-hole golf course and driving range. Newport mansions, beaches, Martha's Vineyard, and Nantucket Islands nearby make this a special place to visit.

Locator 968-1000   Medical 968-6570   Police 968-4010

Fort Devens (MA09R1)
Billeting/AFZD-DEH-B
Bldg P-22, Sherman Ave.
Fort Devens, MA 01433-5000

Scheduled to close. At press time, Fort Devens was in the process of closing. Please call the Public Affairs Office for more information: C-508-796-3307.

TELEPHONE NUMBER INFORMATION: Main installation numbers: C-508-796-3911, D-312-256-3911.

Location: From Boston follow MA-2 west and exit at Fort Devens, about 5 miles west of I-495. In Ayer. *USMRA: Page 17 (I-2,3)*. NMC: Boston, 35 miles southeast.

MASSACHUSETTS
Fort Devens, continued

Lodging Office: ATTN: AFZD-DEH-B, building 2002, 10th Mtn Div Rd, **C-508-772-1600**, D-312-256-3774, FAX 508-796-3916, 24 hours daily. Check in MaGrath Guest House, check out 1100 hours daily. Government civilian employee billeting.

TML: Guest House. Building 2002, (located behind Burger King), **McGrath Guest House**, all ranks, official duty. Separate bedrooms, private bath (58). Full kitchen facilities, refrigerator, color TV, housekeeping service, cribs. New facility. Rates: E1-E3 $12; E4 $14; E5 $16; E6 $20; E7-E8, WO1-W2, O1-O2 $25; E9, WO3-WO4, O3-O4 $31; O5-O10 $35. Additional person $3, maximum $6. **Note: McGrath Guest House will remain open until Jan 1996.**

TML: VOQ. Building P-22, **Washington Hall**, soldiers on official orders. Suites, private bath (29). Some amenities. Building P-19, **Rogers Hall**, WO1+, soldiers on official orders and DV guests through Protocol. Bedrooms (14); suites (6). Kitchen (12), some other amenities. Rates: $15. Additional occupant fee: Washington Hall and regular rooms in Rogers Hall $3; suites $5.

TML: DVL. Building 314, **Prescott House**, O6+, leave or official duty. Suites, private bath (6). Rates: sponsor $25, each additional person $5, maximum $35 per family.

DV/VIP: Protocol Office, building P-1, C-508-796-3711, O5+. Retirees Space-A. Hours 0700-1600 M-F, except holidays.

TML Availability: Good, Dec-Mar. Very difficult, summer.

CREDIT CARDS ACCEPTED: Visa, MasterCard and (Government) American Express.

Locator 796-2748   Medical 796-6816   Police 796-3333

Fourth Cliff Family Recreation Area (MA02R1)
P.O. Box 479
Humarock, MA 01731-5001

TELEPHONE NUMBER INFORMATION: Main installation numbers: C-617-377-4441, D-312-478-4441.

LOCATION: Off base. I-95 or I-93 to MA-3, approximately 30 miles south of Boston; south to exit 12; MA-139 east to Marshfield. 1.5 miles to Furnace St; turn left. Continue to "T" intersection; turn left on Ferry St. Stay on Ferry St to Sea St; right over South River Bridge; left on Central Ave and proceed to gate. Check in at Building 7. NMC: South Weymouth NAS, 15 miles northwest. *USMRA: Page 17 (M-4).* NMC: Boston, 30 miles north.

Lodging Office: None. Reservations required. Confirmation w/credit card/cash/check within 5 days. Ask for map. **C-617-837-9269 (0800-1630 M-F)** or **1-800-468-9547**. Rec area open Memorial Day through Columbus Day. Cabins open year round.

TML: One to three bedroom cottages (16), all ranks, leave or official duty. Rates: $45-$75 daily. All categories can make reservations. Pets not allowed in cabins but may be leashed in other areas. RV Camping available *(Check out Military Living's RV Camping & Rec Areas Around the World for more info)*.

TML Availability: Limited. Book early.

MASSACHUSETTS
Fourth Cliff Family Recreation Area, continued

Easy access to Boston, Cape Cod, Martha's Vineyard and Nantucket Islands, and located high on a cliff overlooking the Atlantic and scenic North River, this is a superb location for a summer or winter vacation.

Hanscom Air Force Base (MA06R1)
Hanscom Inn
66 SVS/SVML
1427 Kirtland St.
Hanscom AFB, MA 01731-5000

TELEPHONE NUMBER INFORMATION: Main installation numbers: C-617-377-4441, D-312-478-4441.

Location: From I-95 north take exit 31A, MA-2A west for 2 miles to right on Hartwell Rd which bisects the AFB. *USMRA: Page 17 (J-3) & Page 24 (A-2).* NMC: Boston, 17 miles southeast.

Lodging Office: Hanscom Inn. Bldg 1427, **C-617-377-2112**, FAX 617-377-4961, DSN FAX 312-478-4961, 24 hours daily. Check in 1400 hours, check out 1100 hours.

TML: TLF. Buildings 1412, 1423, all ranks, official duty. C-617-377-2044. Handicapped accessible. Building 1423, single bedroom, sofa bed, private bath, full kitchen, A/C, housekeeping service, cribs, washer/dryer in building. Rates for TLF $24 per night. TLF is used for PCS in/out. 30 days PCS in, 7 days PCS out. Space-A guests first come first served. Call for details.

TML: VOQ. Building 1412, 1426, all ranks, official duty. Bldg 1426, bedroom, semi-private bath, A/C, housekeeping service, washer/dryer in building. Rates: $11.75 per person per night. TDY personnel have priority. Space-A guests first come first served. Building 1412, all ranks, single bedroom, private bath, washer/dryer in building. Rates: $11.75 per person per night. Renovated in '94. Call for details.

DV/VIP: Protocol Office, building 1606, C-617-377-5151. O7+, retirees Space-A.

TML Availability: Fair. Best in Nov-Mar.

CREDIT CARDS ACCEPTED: Visa, MasterCard and American Express.

Delve into U.S. history by visiting Minute Man National Historical Park, Battle Road near Fiske Hill in Lexington, the Wayside Unit, home of the Alcotts, Nathaniel Hawthorne and others, and Lexington Green.

Locator 377-5111   Medical 377-2333   Police 377-7100

South Weymouth Naval Air Station (MA05R1)
CBQ, Bldg 31
South Weymouth, MA 02190-5000
Scheduled to close 9/30/96

TELEPHONE NUMBER INFORMATION: Main installation numbers: C-617-682-2500, D-312-478-5980.

MASSACHUSETTS
South Weymouth Naval Air Station

Location: From MA-3 (Pilgrims Highway) exit 16B to MA-18 S (Main St). Base is approximately two miles ahead. Main gate is on left side of MA-18. *USMRA: Page 17 (L-4,5) & Page 24 (G,H-10).* NMC: Boston, 15 miles northwest.

Lodging Office: Building 31, Shea Memorial Dr, **C-617-682-2738, 1-800-248-8805,** FAX 617-331-2594, D-312-955-2738, 24 hours daily. Check in facility, check out 1000 hours daily. Confirmation numbers given out 24 hours daily.

TML: TLQ. Building 31 and O'Club, all ranks, leave or official duty for officers. Double rooms (2 people), common bath (42); family suites, living room, bedroom, private bath (9); single rooms, private bath (8); single rooms, shared bath (6). Refrigerator (suites), color TV, housekeeping service, microwaves, cribs, washer/dryer, ice vending. Rates: $6, doubles; $8, suites and singles, under 6 free. Older structures, renovated. All categories can make reservations.

DV/VIP: Executive Officer Secretary, Administration Building, C-617-682-2600.

TML Availability: Space limited F-Sa. Available Su-Th.

CREDIT CARDS ACCEPTED: American Express.

Twenty minutes from historic Boston, Cape Cod, Plymouth Rock, beaches, coastal recreation, and many other exciting attractions.

Locator 682-2800   **Medical 682-2674**   **Police 682-2610**

Westover Air Reserve Base (MA03R1)
650 Airlift Dr., Bldg 2201
Chicopee, MA 01022-1309

TELEPHONE NUMBER INFORMATION: Main installation numbers: C-413-557-1110, D-312-589-1110, 1-800-367-1110 ask for ext 2700 (base lodging).

Location: Take exit 5 off I-90 (MA Turnpike) in Chicopee. Westover is on MA-33. Signs mark way to base. *USMRA: Page 16 (F-4).* NMC: Springfield, 8 miles south.

Lodging Office: Flyers Inn, building 2201, 650 Airlift Drive. VOQ/VAQ: **C-413-557-2700,** D-312-589-2700, FAX 413-557-2835, DSN FAX 312-589-2835, weekends only. Space Available check in 1700, check out 1100 hours daily. Government civilian employee billeting.

TML: VOQ. Buildings 2200, 2201. Officers, all ranks, leave or official duty. Bedroom, semi-private bath (10); two bedroom suites, semi-private bath (29). A/C, essentials, color TV, VCR rental, housekeeping service, ice vending. Older structure, remodeled. Rates: $6 per person. DV Suites $8 per person. Maximum 4 persons. Maximum depends on number per family. Duty can make reservations, others Space-A.

TML: VAQ. Buildings 5101-5105, enlisted, E1-E8, leave or official duty. Rooms, shared bath (250); SNCO suites, private bath (32). Food/ice vending, housekeeping service, refrigerator, color TV, washer/dryer. Older structures, 5101, 2 renovated. Rates: $6 per person, SNCO suites $8. Maximum 2 persons. Duty can make reservations.

MASSACHUSETTS
Westover Air Reserve Base, continued

DV/VIP: Building 2200. C-413-557-5421, O5+ or unit commander. Rates: $8 per person, maximum 2 persons. Retirees and lower ranks Space-A.

TML Availability: Good, except Jun-Sep.

Museums, parks, ski areas, Basketball Hall of Fame, professional stage and Symphony Hall in Springfield, are of interest to visitors. Several golf courses. Visit Forest Park Zoo, and the Naismith Memorial Hall of Fame.

Locator 557-3874   Medical 557-3565   Police 557-3557

MICHIGAN

Camp Grayling (MI10R2)
Lodging Office, Bldg 560
Grayling, MI 49739-0001

TELEPHONE NUMBER INFORMATION: Main installation numbers: C-517-348-7621, D-312-623-7621.

Location: On I-75 take Grayling exit. Camp Grayling is 4 miles west of Grayling. *USMRA: Page 66 (D,E-5)*. NMC: Traverse City, 60 miles west.

Lodging Office: Housing - bldg. 560, **C-517-348-3661**, D-312-623-3661, Fax 517-348-3844, DSN Fax 312-623-3844. Check in by 1600 on a duty day, check out 1000. O'Club - bldg. 311, **C-517-348-9033**. Check out 1000.

TML: Run by Housing: Billeting for those on official duty. Individual rooms with centrally located restroom..Most buildings are unheated.

TML: Run by Housing: CTQ - all ranks, official duty and retirees. Reservations are a first come basis. Housekeeping service, microwave, kitchenettes, TVs, some with VCRs, radio alarm clocks. Rates: $12 official duty, $20 unofficial duty.

TML: Run by O'Club: Lake front cottages (4) and lake front mobile homes (2) available for officers. Fully furnished and equipped, can accommodate up to six people. Rates: $35 (minimum two night stay), $200 weekly.

TML: Run by O'Club: Rooms (10) available with two to four beds in each for officers. Rates: $7.

TML: Run by O'Club: Campground space available to all active and retired National Guard Soldiers. Reservations required. Rates: $9. See Military Living's *Military RV, Camping & Rec Areas Around the World* for detailed information.

TML Availability: Limited, especially during colder months.

CREDIT CARDS ACCEPTED: O'Club accepts Visa, MasterCard and Discover.

Hunting, camping, fishing and winter sports are available on this Limited on post support facilities, but Wurtsmith AFB is 80 miles east. Commercial airlines available in Traverse City.

Selfridge Air National Guard Base (MI01R2)
ATTN: AMSTA-CYACH
Bldg 410, George Avenue
Selfridge ANGB, MI 48045-5004

TELEPHONE NUMBER INFORMATION: Main installation numbers: C-810-307-4011, D-312-273-4011.

Location: Take I-94 north from Detroit, to Selfridge exit, then east on MI-59 to main gate of base. *USMRA: Page 66 (G-9) & Page 70 (G-1)*. NMC: Detroit, 25 miles southwest.

MICHIGAN
Selfridge Air National Guard, continued

Lodging Office: Building 410, ATTN: AMSTA-CYACH, George Ave. Operated by U.S. Army MWR, **C-810-307-4062**, 24 hours, 7 days. Check in billeting, check out 1200 hours daily. Government civilian employee billeting.

TML: Guest House. Building 916, all ranks, leave or official duty. Two bedroom, living room, dining room, private bath (7); bedroom, living room, dining room, private bath (8). Kitchen, utensils, color TV, cribs, washer/dryer. Older structure. Rates: $16, 1 bedroom; 2 bedroom $19. Maximum 3 in 1 bedroom, 5 in 2 bedroom. Duty can make reservations, others Space-A. Pets $3 per day.

TML: VOQ/VEQ. Building 410, all ranks, leave or official duty. Separate bedrooms, private bath (27). Microfridges, color TV, housekeeping service, food/beverage vending, washer/dryer. Older structure, renovated. Rates: $21.50. VIP Suites $23 TDY, others $32. DV on TDY can make reservations, others call 1 day in advance Space-A.

TML Availability: Fairly good.

Camping, hunting, fishing, boating, golfing and water sports are available in the many parks and recreational areas. Visit Museums, the Detroit Zoo, and don't forget Canada across Lake St. Clair or cross the border at Port Huron.

Locator 307-4011   **Medical 307-4650**   **Police 307-4673**

MINNESOTA

Minneapolis-St. Paul Air Reserve Station (MN01R2)
North Country Inn
934 SPTG/SVML - Bldg 711
760 Military Highway
Minneapolis, MN 55450-2000

TELEPHONE NUMBER INFORMATION: Main installation numbers: C-612-725-5011, D-312-825-5110.

Location: From I-35 west to crosstown MN-62 to 34th Ave entrance. Follow signs to AFB. *USMRA: Page 89 (C-3).* NMC: Minneapolis-St Paul, in the city.

Lodging Office: The North Country Inn. 934 SPTG/SVML, building 711, **C-612-725-5320**, FAX 612-725-8158, D-312-825-5320, DSN FAX 312-825-8158, 0700-2400 hours. Check in billeting 1430, check out 1000 hours. Active duty, reservist, retired military, authorized dependents and duty government civilian employee billeting.

TML: VOQ. Building 711, officers, civilians, females (regardless of rank), SNCO (E7+), leave or official duty. Bedroom, private and semi-private baths. Officers (95); SNCO suites (3); DV suites (7). Refrigerator, A/C, color TV in room, housekeeping service, washer/dryer, ice vending. Older structure. Rates: $6 per person, suites $8. Maximum 2 per room. Duty can make reservations, others Space-A.

TML: VAQ. Building 716, enlisted males (E6 & below). Bedrooms, private baths & central latrines (83). Refrigerator, A/C, color TV, housekeeping service, washer/dryer, ice/vending. Older structure, to be renovated '94. Rates: $6. Duty can make reservations, others Space-A.

TML Availability: Good. Difficult during Air Force (934th & 133AW) UTA drill weekends each month.

CREDIT CARDS ACCEPTED: American Express.

While you're here check out the Mall of America, the Minnesota Zoo, various art museums and theaters. Also stop by the Metrodome to see either the Twins or Vikings play.

Locator 725-5011   **Medical 725-5402**   **Police 725-5402**

MISSISSIPPI

Columbus Air Force Base (MS01R2)
Magnolia Inn, Bldg 956
14 SVS/SVML
179 F Street, Suite 6107
Columbus AFB, MS 39710-5000

TELEPHONE NUMBER INFORMATION: Main installation numbers: C-601-434-7322, D-312-742-7322.

Location: Off US-45 north, 60 miles west of Tuscaloosa, via US-82. *USMRA: Page 43 (G-3).* NMC: Columbus, 10 miles south.

Lodging Office: Magnolia Inn, ATTN: 14th SVS/SVML, building 956, F St, **C-601-434-2548**, FAX 601-434-2777, D-312-742-2548, DSN FAX 312-742-2777, 24 hours daily. Check in billeting, check out 1200 hours daily. Government civilian employee billeting.

TML: TLF. Building 955, all ranks, leave or official duty. Bedrooms, private bath (20). Kitchen, utensils, A/C, color TV, housekeeping service, cribs/rollaway, washer/dryer, ice/food vending, facilities for DAVs. Modern structure. Rate: $14 per unit E1-E6; $18, E7+. Duty can make reservations, others Space-A.

TML: VOQ. Building 954, 956, officers all ranks, leave or official duty. Bedroom private bath (73); bedroom, private bath, kitchenette (58). Color TV, housekeeping service, washer/dryer, ice/food vending. Older structure. Rates: $6 per person per night. Duty can make reservations, others Space-A.

TML: VAQ. Building 956, enlisted all ranks, leave or official duty. Spaces, semi-private bath (40); SNCO suites, private bath (3). Color TV, housekeeping service, washer/dryer, ice/food vending. Older structure. Rates: $5 per person per night. Duty can make reservations, others Space-A.

DV/VIP: WG Exec, building 724, C-601-434-7002 (active duty O6+ only). SNCO contact WG SEA at C-601-434-7005.

TML Availability: Good, Nov-Feb. More difficult, other times.

CREDIT CARDS ACCEPTED: American Express.

Columbus, with many antebellum structures never destroyed during the Civil War, is of interest to visitors. The area also hosts excellent fishing, boating and hunting along the Tennessee Tombigbee Waterway.

Locator 434-2841   Medical 434-2244   Police 434-7129

MISSISSIPPI

Gulfport Naval Construction Battalion Center (MS03R2)
BQ Director/Code 540
5200 CBC 2nd St.
Gulfport NCBC, MS 39501-5000

TELEPHONE NUMBER INFORMATION: Main installation numbers: C-601-871-2121, D-312-868-2121.

Location: Take US-49 south to Gulfport, follow signs to Center, from US-90 exit to US-49 (Broad Ave), from I-10 exit to US-49. *USMRA: Page 43 (F-10).* NMC: New Orleans, LA, 70 miles west.

Lodging Office: ATTN: Commanding Officer, Code 540 BQ Director, 5200 CBC 2nd St, Gulfport, MS 39501-5001. Reservations BEQ/BOQ: **C-601-871-2505**. Check in facility, check out 1200 hours daily. Government civilian employee billeting.

TML: Navy Lodge. Building 331. All ranks, leave, retired or official duty. Reservations call **1-800-NAVY-INN** (1-800-628-9466). Lodge number is 601-864-3101, Fax 601-868-7392, check in 0700-1830 hours, check out 1200 hours daily. Bedroom, private bath (15). Two interconnecting units, 1 handicapped accessible, 8 non-smoking. Kitchenette, microwave, utensils, A/C, CATV, VCR, clocks, coffee/tea (in office), cribs, rollaways, phones, hair dryers, high chairs, ice, vending, irons/boards, housekeeping service, coin washer/dryer & playground. Modern structure. Rates: $46 per unit. Maximum 5 per room. All categories can make reservations.

TML: BOQ. Building 300, officers all ranks, leave or official duty, C-601-871-2226. Bedroom, private bath (36), (2 VIP rooms). Kitchen, A/C, color TV in room & lounge, housekeeping service, cribs/cots, washer/dryer, ice vending. Modern structure. Rates: $12 per person. Max 3 persons. Duty can make reservations C-601-871-2505.

TML: BEQ. Building 314, enlisted all ranks, leave, retired or official duty, C-601-871-2506. Bedroom, shared bath (90). A/C, color TV in room & lounge, telephone, housekeeping service, washer/dryer. Modern structure. Rates: $6-$8 per person. Duty can make reservations, others Space-A.

DV/VIP: CO's Guest House. Building 102, C-601-871-2202, O6+. Rates: $22-$28. Retirees and lower ranks Space-A.

TML Availability: Good, Sep-Mar. Difficult, other times.

CREDIT CARDS ACCEPTED: Visa, MasterCard, American Express and Discover.

Swimming, fishing, sailing, windsurfing, sunning and beach combing in summer are popular. Visit Beauvoir (Confederate President Jefferson Davis' home), Gulf Islands National Seashore, Shearwater Pottery showroom.

Locator 871-2286   Medical 871-2809   Police 871-2361

MISSISSIPPI

Keesler Air Force Base (MS02R2)
81 SVS/SVML
509 Larcher Blvd
Keesler AFB, MS 39534-2346

TELEPHONE NUMBER INFORMATION: Main installation numbers: C-601-377-1110, D-312-597-1110.

Location: From I-10 exit 46, follow signs to base. From US-90, north on White Ave to main gate. *USMRA: Page 43 (F-10)*. NMC: Biloxi, in the city.

Lodging Office: Consolidated Front Desk for the **Inns of Keesler**: building 2101, **Muse Manor** (C-601-377-2420), **C-601-377-2631/3663** D-312-597-2631/3663, FAX 601-597-3588, M-F. Check in facility, check out 1200 hours. Government civilian employee billeting.

TML: Guest House. Building 0470, all ranks, leave or official duty. Two bedroom, living room, dining room, semi-private bath (21). Refrigerator, housekeeping service, cribs, washer/dryer, ice vending. Rates: $20 per two bedroom unit or $10 per bedroom. Primarily for hospital patients and families of patients.

TML: VAQ. Buildings 2101, 2002, 5025, enlisted all ranks, leave or official duty, C-601-377-2631. Bedroom, 2 beds, semi-private bath (638); separate bedrooms, semi-private bath for E7+ (8); bedroom, 1 bed, semi-private bath for E7+ (112). Refrigerator, A/C, color TV, housekeeping service, washer/dryer, food/ice vending. Modern structure, renovated. Rates: $5 per person. Maximum 3 per room. Duty can make reservations, others Space-A.

TML: TLF. 0300 block, all ranks, leave or official duty. Separate bedrooms, private bath (40). Kitchen, utensils, A/C, color TV in room & lounge, housekeeping service, essentials, washer/dryer, food/ice vending, playground rear of facility. Modern structure, renovated. Rates: $16, E1-E6; $20 E7+. Maximum 5 persons. Duty can make reservations, others Space-A.

TML: VOQ. Building 3821, 3823, 0470, 2004, officers all ranks, leave or official duty. Bedroom, private bath (224); bedroom, semi-private bath (328); two bedroom, semi-private bath (12); DV suites, private bath (6). Kitchen (98 rooms), A/C, color TV, housekeeping service, washer/dryer, ice vending. Modern structure. Rates: $6 per person rooms; maximum $18 per room; $10 per person suites, maximum $20 per suite. Duty can make reservations, others Space-A.

TML: Fisher House. Note: Appendix C has the definition of this facility. **C-601-377-8265.**

DV/VIP: KTTC/CCP, C-601-377-3359, E9+ & O6+, retirees and lower ranks Space-A.

TML Availability: Fairly good, all year. Best, Dec-Jan.

CREDIT CARDS ACCEPTED: Visa, MasterCard and American Express.

Biloxi is rich in history: eight flags have flown over the city. Visit the Old French House off Hwy 90, Ship Island, 12 miles offshore, the Jefferson Davis Shrine. White sand beaches, golf, fishing, boating and sailing are available.

Locator 377-2798   Medical 377-6555   Police 377-3720

MISSISSIPPI

Meridian Naval Air Station (MS04R2)
Billeting Manager
Bldg 218 (CBQ), Fuller Rd.
Meridian NAS, MS 39309-5000

TELEPHONE NUMBER INFORMATION: Main installation numbers: C-601-679- 2211, D-312-367-2211.

Location: Take Hwy 39 north from Meridian for 12 miles to 4-lane access road, clearly marked. Right for 3 miles to NAS main gate. *USMRA: Page 43 (G-6)*. NMC: Meridian, 15 miles southwest.

Lodging Office: Building 218 (CBQ), Fuller Rd, **C-601-679-2186/2386,** FAX 601-679-2745, 24 hours daily. Check in facility, check out 1300 hours daily. Government civilian employee billeting.

TML: Family Quarters. Building 208, enlisted all ranks, leave or official duty. Separate bedrooms, private bath (25). Refrigerator, community kitchen, A/C, color TV, movie rental, housekeeping service, cribs/rollaways $1, washer/dryer. Older structure, renovated in '88. Rates: $13 per room per night first 3 persons, $1 each additional person. Maximum 5 per room. Duty can make reservations, others Space-A.

TML: BEQ. Buildings 218, enlisted all ranks, leave or official duty, handicapped accessible. Bedroom, semi-private bath (12); bedroom, private bath (17). Refrigerator, community kitchen, A/C, color TV, movie rental, housekeeping service, washer/dryer, food/ice vending. Older structure, remodeled. Rates: E1-E9 $6. Maximum 2 per room. Duty can make reservations, others Space-A.

TML: VOQ. Building 218, officers all ranks, leave or official duty. Handicapped accessible. Separate bedrooms, private bath (40). Community kitchen, A/C, color TV, movie rental, housekeeping service, cribs/rollaways $1, washer/dryer, ice vending. Older structure, remodeled. Rates: $10 per night single, $15 per night up to three persons, $1 each additional occupant. Maximum 5 per room.

TML: DV/VIP. Building 218, officer O6+, leave or official duty, handicapped accessible. Two bedroom, private bath (6). Two units have kitchen, all have refrigerators. Community kitchen, limited utensils, A/C, color TV & VCR, movie rental, housekeeping service, cribs/rollaways $1, washer/dryer, ice vending. Older structure, remodeled. Rates: $18 per room. Maximum charge $18. Maximum 3 per room. Duty can make reservations, others Space-A.

TML Availability: Good, Sep-Feb. Difficult, other times.

CREDIT CARDS ACCEPTED: Visa, MasterCard and American Express.

Take a driving tour of the historic Natchez Trace, a local flea market, nearby Flora's Petrified Forest, and the Choctaw Fair for American Indian life and lore. ITT (in MWR) has information on theatrical, sports, special events tickets.

Locator 679-2528 **Medical 679-1829** **Police 679-2958**

MISSISSIPPI

Pascagoula Naval Station (MS04R2)
100 Singing River Island, Bldg 63
Pascagoula, MS 39567-5000

TELEPHONE NUMBER INFORMATION: Main installation numbers: C-601-761-2181, D-312-358-2181.

Location: From I-10 E, exit 69, 4 mi south to Hwy 90, 4 mi west to Ingalls Access Road, 1 mi to Naval Station Causeway, 3 mi to gate. *USMRA: Page 43 (G-10).* NMC: Pascagoula 2 mi East.

Lodging Office: Building 63, Singing River Island, **C-601-761-2182,** D-312-358-2182, FAX 601-761-2179, DSN FAX 312-358-2179, 24 hours daily. Check in, check out 1200 hours daily, for late check out call 761-2179. Government civilian employee billeting.

TML: TLF. Building 63, all ranks, leave or official duty. Handicapped accessible. Separate bedrooms, semi-private bath (3), bedrooms, semi-private bath (12). Refrigerator, A/C, color TV, housekeeping service, washer/dryer, food/ice vending. Older structure, remodeled. Rates: $5-$17 depending upon rank. Active duty/reservists may make reservations, other Space-A.

TML Availability: Very Good.

CREDIT CARDS ACCEPTED: Visa, MasterCard and American Express.

Take a driving tour of the historic Natchez Trace, a local flea market, nearby Flora's Petrified Forest, and the Choctaw Fair for American Indian life and lore. ITT (in MWR) has information on theatrical, sports, special events tickets.

Medical 761-2363   Police 761-3333

Too Late To Copy
Camp Shelby Training Site, Camp Shelby, MS 39407-5500. BEQ/BOQ **C-601-679-5955.**

MISSOURI

Fort Leonard Wood (MO03R2)
Billeting Manager
Bldg 315, Room 126, MO Ave.
Fort Leonard Wood, MO 65473-5000

TELEPHONE NUMBER INFORMATION: Main installation numbers: C-314-596-0131, D-312-581-0110.

Location: Two miles south of I-44, adjacent to St Robert & Waynesville, at Ft Leonard Wood exit. *USMRA: Page 81 (E-6,7)*. NMC: Springfield, 85 miles southwest.

Lodging Office: Building 315, room 126, MO Ave, **C-1-800-677-8356**, 24 hours daily. Check in billeting, check out 1200 hours daily. Government civilian employee billeting.

TML: Guest House. Many buildings, all ranks, leave or official duty. Handicapped accessible (4). Separate bedroom, private bath (79). Refrigerator, microwave, stove top burners, utensils, iron/ironing board, A/C, color TV, housekeeping service, cribs/cots, washer/dryers, playroom. Rates: active duty by grade, all others $35 plus $1 for each additional person. Pets allowed in 4 units at $3 per day. Reservations accepted for PCS in/out, persons with hospital appointments, and families of graduating soldiers, others Space-A.

TML: TDY. Eleven buildings, all ranks, official duty only. Bedroom, private bath (500). A/C, essentials, food/ice vending, kitchen, limited utensils, housekeeping service, refrigerator, color TV, washer/dryer. Modern structure. Rates: sponsor $20, each additional person $3.50. Maximum 2 persons. Duty can make reservations, others Space-A.

TML: VOQ. Buildings 4102, 4104, officers all ranks. TDY only. Bedroom, private bath (74); separate bedroom suites, private bath (8). Kitchen (47 units), refrigerator (74 units), A/C, color TV, housekeeping service, washer/dryer, ice vending, coffee makers, irons/ironing boards. Modern structure, remodeled. Rates: sponsor $20, each additional person $3.50. Maximum 2 per room. Duty can make reservations, others Space-A.

TML: DV/VIP. Building 315, officer O6+, official duty. Separate bedroom suites, private bath (8); three bedroom suite, private bath (1). Kitchen, utensils, A/C, color TV, housekeeping service. Modern structure. Rates: sponsor $24, each additional person $3.50. Maximum 2 per room. Duty can make reservations, others Space-A.

DV/VIP: Protocol Office, C-314-596-6183, O6/GS-15+. Retirees and lower ranks Space-A.

TML Availability: Good. Best Dec. Difficult May-Oct.

CREDIT CARDS ACCEPTED: Visa, MasterCard, American Express and Discover.

Crystal clear rivers and streams provide fishing, float trips, canoeing. Campers, hikers, hunters and horseback riders find the Ozarks a paradise. Guided tours through caves, and all levels of spelunking are available.

Locator 596-0677　　　　Medical 596-0496　　　　Police 596-6141

MISSOURI

Lake of the Ozarks Recreation Area (MO01R2)
Rt 1, Box 380
Linn Creek, MO 65052

TELEPHONE NUMBER INFORMATION: Main installation numbers: C-314-596-0131, D-312-581-0110.

Location: From I-70 at Columbia, take Hwy 63 to Jefferson City, then take US-54 southwest to Linn Creek area, left at County Rd A for 6 miles. Left on Lake Rd (county sign A33) for 4.7 miles to travel camp. From I-44 northeast of Springfield, MO-7 northwest to Richland, right on County Rd A and travel 19.8 miles to Freedom, right on Lake Road A-5 4.7 miles to travel camp. *USMRA: Page 81 (D-6)*. NMC: Jefferson City, 40 miles northeast.

Lodging Office: Building 528, Fort Leonard Wood, MO. Reservations required (by phone only) **C-314-346-5640**, Mon-Tue 0900-1300, Wed-Fri 0900-1700. Call 30-45 days in advance. Full service Memorial Day weekend-Labor Day weekend. Fri-Sun operations, Apr/May & Sep/Oct. Check in facility 1500 hours, check out 1100 hours day of departure. Active/Retiree/Reserve/National Guard/DoD Civilians are eligible.

TML: Mobile Homes, cabins, duplexes. Two and three bedroom, fully equipped, A/C. Rates: $28-$56, E1-E4; $41-$68, E5-E6; $47-$74, E7+ and civilians. A/C, kitchen, dishes and utensils, some cleaning supplies, color TV, no linens provided (except lake view mobile homes, duplexes). Rates applicable for active and retired personnel.

TML Availability: Fairly good, in season. Very good, off season.

CREDIT CARDS ACCEPTED: Visa, MasterCard, American Express and Discover.

New Lake front trailers, cabins, duplexes, rustic & hookup campsites, rental office, and a 20 bay berthing dock for private boat storage. This is a large and fully equipped recreational area, see Military Living's *Military RV, Camping and Rec Areas Around the World*.

Locator 596-0131   Medical 596-9331   Police 346-3693

Whiteman Air Force Base (MO04R2)
Whiteman Inn
P.O. Box 5032
Whiteman AFB, MO 65305-5000

TELEPHONE NUMBER INFORMATION: Main installation numbers: C-816-687-1110, D-312-975-1110.

Location: From I-70 south exit to US-13 to US-50 east for 10 miles, then right on MO-132 which leads to AFB. *USMRA: Page 81 (C-5)*. NMC: Kansas City, MO 60 miles west.

Lodging Office: The Whiteman Inn. Building 325, Mitchell Ave, **C-816-687-1844**, FAX 816-687-3052, DSN FAX 312-975-3052, 24 hours daily. Check in lodging 1600-1800, check out 1200 hours daily.

Temporary Military Lodging Around the World - 147

MISSOURI
Whiteman Air Force Base, continued

TML: TLF. Buildings 3003, 3201/3/5 & 6 all ranks, leave or official duty. Three bedroom apartments, private bath (2); Bedroom, private bath (29). Kitchen, complete utensils, A/C, essentials, refrigerator, color TV, housekeeping service, cribs/cots, washer/dryer, ice vending. Handicapped accessible (1). New and older structure, renovated. Rates: $10, E1-E2; $17, E3-E6; $22, E7+ and Space-A. PCS in/out can make reservations (60 days in advance recommended), others Space-A.

TML: Military Hospital. All ranks, leave or official duty, check in facility. Bedroom, semi-private bath (25). A/C, black/white TV, facilities for DAVs. Modern structure. Rates: $6.50 per person. Duty can make reservations, others Space-A.

TML: VOQ. Building 3200, officers all ranks, leave or official duty. Bedroom, living room, private bath (52), DV Suites (9). Refrigerator, microwave, A/C, essentials, color TV, housekeeping service, cribs/cots, washer/dryer. Modern structure. Rates: 1 person $8, 2 or more persons $16; DV Suites, $14 and $28. Maximum 2 per room. Duty can make reservations, others Space-A.

TML: TAQ/VAQ. Building 1551, enlisted all ranks, leave or official duty. Separate bedrooms, semi-private bath (50); suites, semi-private bath (6). Refrigerator, A/C, essentials, CATV in room & lounge, housekeeping service, cots/cribs, ice vending, washer/dryer. Handicapped accessible. Modern structure. Rates: sponsor $8 for suites, adult maximum charge $16. Maximum 2 persons in suites. Duty can make reservations, others Space-A.

TML: DV/VIP. Buildings 3001 (Truman House), 119 Travis Lane (Century House), 115 Travis Lane (Travis House) officers O6+, leave or official duty. Three bedroom house, 2 baths, (2); two bedroom house, private bath (1). Kitchen, all amenities. Rates: 1 person $14, 2 persons $28. Duty can make reservations, others Space-A.

DV/VIP: Protocol: 351 SMW/CCP, C-816-687-6543, O6+. Retirees and lower ranks if other quarters are full.

TML Availability: Good all year except late July because of State Fair. Best, winter.

CREDIT CARDS ACCEPTED: Visa, MasterCard and American Express.

Locator 687-1841   **Medical 687-3733**   **Police 687-3700**

Too Late To Copy
Marine Corps Activities at Richards-Gebaur Airport, Lodging office, Bldg. 250, Kensington St, 0730-2330 daily, **C-816-843-3855/3850-2125**, D-312-894-3855/3850.

MONTANA

Malmstrom Air Force Base (MT03R3)
Malmstrom Inns
341 SVS/SVML
7028 4th Avenue North
Malmstrom AFB, MT 59402-6835

TELEPHONE NUMBER INFORMATION: Main installation numbers: C-406-731-1110, D-312-632-1110.

Location: From I-15 north or south take 10th Ave south exit to AFB. From east take Malmstrom exit off US-87/89 to AFB. Clearly marked. *USMRA: Page 99 (D,E-3,4)*. NMC: Great Falls, 1 mile west.

Lodging Office: Malmstrom Inns. 7028 Fourth Ave, North, Bldg 1680, **C-406-727-8600/731-3895**, D-312-632-3394, FAX C-406-731-3848, DSN FAX 312-632-3848, 24 hours daily. Check in lodging, check out 1200 hours daily. Government civilian employee lodging.

TML: TLF. Buildings 1210, 1212, 1214, 1216. One mile from billeting office. All ranks, leave or official duty. Separate bedrooms, private bath (39). Kitchen, utensils, A/C, color TV, housekeeping service, cribs/cots, washer/dryer, ice vending. Older structure, renovated. Rates: E1-E2 $10; O1 $14; all others & Space-A $23.50 per unit. Maximum 5 per unit. Duty can make reservations, others Space-A.

TML: VOQ. Building 1620, officers all ranks, leave or official duty. Bedroom, private bath (22); separate bedroom suites, private bath (4); separate bedroom suites, private bath (DV/VIP) (4). Refrigerator, wet bar, microwave, color TV, housekeeping service, washer/dryer, ice vending. Older structure, renovated 1994. Rates for leave/duty status: $8 per room, $8 additional person; suites $14, double occupancy $28. Children not authorized. Duty can make reservations, others Space-A.

TML: VAQ. Building 1680, enlisted all ranks, leave or official duty. Bedroom, semi-private bath (27). Private rooms (2), separate bedroom suites (4). Refrigerator, microwave, color TV, ice vending, washer/dryer. Rates: $8 single, $16 double, $14 suite, $28 double suite. Maximum 2 persons. No children. Duty can make reservations, others Space-A.

DV/VIP: Protocol Office. 341 MW/CCP, building 500, C-406-731-3086, O6+. Retirees Space-A.

TML Availability: Good, winter. Difficult, Jul-Sep.

CREDIT CARDS ACCEPTED: Visa, MasterCard and Discover.

This facility won the Air Force Innkeeper Award for 1996. It is one of AMC's certified (four star) facilities in the command. Visit the Malmstrom Museum on base.

Locator 731-4121   Medical 731-3483   Police 731-3042

NEBRASKA

Offutt Air Force Base (NE02R3)
Offutt Inns
105 Grants Pass Street
Offutt AFB, NE 68113-2084

TELEPHONE NUMBER INFORMATION: Main installation numbers: C-402-294-1110, D-312-271-1110.

Location: From south-bound I-29/east or west-bound I-80, exit to US-75, then south 6/5 miles to AFB entrance. From north-bound I-29, exit to US-370, west 5 1/2 miles to Lincoln St, then south .25 miles to AFB gate. *USMRA: Page 82 (I,J-5)*. NMC: Omaha, north 8 miles.

Lodging Office: Guest Reception Center, building 44, Grants Pass St, **C-402-294-9000**, FAX 402-294-3199, D-312-271-3671, 24 hours daily. Check in 1400 hours, check out 1200 hours daily. Government civilian employee lodging. Reservations accepted on first-call, first-served basis. Duty personnel encouraged to re-confirm 3 days prior to arrival. Space-A confirmed/non-confirmed 3 duty days prior to arrival.

TML: DVQ. **Fort Crook House**, quarters 13 (non-smoking), officers O6+, official duty or leave. Two bedroom, private bath (2). Full kitchen, microwave, A/C, color TV, housekeeping service, essentials. Historic building - 1900, renovated. Rates: $14 single, $28 double. Maximum 2 persons per unit.

TML: VOQ. **Fort Crook House,** quarters 13 (non-smoking), officers/senior enlisted, official duty or leave. Separate bedroom suite, private bath (6); separate bedroom suite, shared bath (2). Kitchen, refrigerator, microwave, utensils, A/C, color TV, washer/dryer, housekeeping service, essentials. Historic building -1900, renovated. Rates: $8 single, $16 double. Maximum 4 persons per unit.

TML: VOQ/SNCOQ. **Malmstrom Inn**, building 432 (non-smoking), officers all ranks, SNCO (E7+), official duty or leave. Separate bedroom suite, private bath (28) SNCOQ (8). Refrigerator, microwave, A/C, color TV, housekeeping service, washer/dryer, ice vending, essentials. Older structure, renovated. Rates: SNCOQ $14 single, $28 double; VOQ $8 single, $16 double. Maximum 2 per unit.

TML: VOQ/VAQ. **O'Malley Inn**, building 436 (non-smoking). Officer/enlisted, all ranks, official duty or leave. Bedroom, private bath (79). One handicapped accessible unit. Refrigerator, microwave, A/C, color TV, housekeeping service, washer/dryer, ice vending. Modern structure. Rates: $10 single, $20 double. Maximum 2 per unit.

TML: DVQ. **Offutt Inn**, building 479 (smoking), officer O6+, official duty or leave. Separate bedroom suites, private bath (5). Refrigerator, microwave, A/C, color TV, housekeeping service, washer/dryer, ice vending, essentials. Older structure, renovated. Rates: $14 single, $28 double. Maximum 2 per suite.

TML: VOQ/VAQ. **Offutt Inn**, building 479, (smoking), officer/enlisted all ranks, official duty or leave. Bedroom, private bath (39). Older structure, renovated; two units handicapped accessible. Refrigerator, microwave, A/C, color TV, washer/dryer, ice vending, housekeeping service, essentials. Older Structure - Renovated. Rates: VOQ $8 single, $16 double, VAQ $7 single, $14 double; maximum 2 persons per room.

NEBRASKA
Offutt Air Force Base, continued

TML: VOQ. **Bellevue/Papillion Lodges**, buildings 5791/2. Officer/enlisted; large family; official duty or leave. Three bedroom, private bath (2). Complete kitchen, microwave, A/C, color TV, washer/dryer, housekeeping service, essentials. Older Structure - Renovated. Rates. $14 single, $28 double; maximum 6 persons per unit.

TML: TLF. **Platte River Lodge**, buildings 5089-5093, all ranks, official duty or leave. Two room, private bath cottage (60). Complete kitchen, microwave, A/C, color TV, VCR, crib, highchair, washer/dryer, ice machines, housekeeping service. Older structure, renovated. Rates: E1, O1 $12, E3-E6; $18, E7+, $24; maximum 6 persons per unit.

DV/VIP: USSTRATCOM Protocol, Bldg: 500, C-402-294-4212, O7+. Retirees, Space-A.

TML Availability: Good. Best, Dec-Jan. More difficult, other times.

CREDIT CARDS ACCEPTED: Visa, MasterCard and American Express.

Try nearby Omaha's Old Town for shopping and dining, Fontenelle Park for hiking and the historic Southern Railroad Depot for getting in touch with this interesting area. Don't miss the Joslyn Art Museum. The Henry Dooly Zoo is located next to Rosenblatt Stadium, which hosts the College World Series in June.

Locator 294-5125   **Medical 294-7332**   **Police 294-5677**

Temporary Military Lodging Around the World - 151

NEVADA

Fallon Naval Air Station (NV02R4)
CBQ, Bldg 304
Fallon NAS, NV 89486-5000

TELEPHONE NUMBER INFORMATION: Main installation numbers: C-702-426-5161, D-312-830-2110.

Location: From US-50 exit to US-95 south at Fallon, for 5 miles to left on Union St to NAS. *USMRA: Page 113 (C-4).* NMC: Reno, 61 miles west.

Lodging Office: BEQ, **C-702-426-2521/15** D-312-830-2521/15, BOQ **C-702-423-6671**, FAX 702-426-2908, DSN FAX 312-830-2908, open 24 hours daily. BOQ check in facility, check out 1000 hours. Government civilian employee billeting.

TML: BEQ. Barracks 3, 5, 6, 7, 10, 11, 12, enlisted all ranks, leave or official duty. Total 587 units. Bedroom, shared bath; bedroom, 2 beds, shared bath; bedroom, 2 beds, hall bath; VIP rooms (10). Refrigerator, A/C, color TV w/VCR, housekeeping service, washer/dryer, ice vending. Modern structure. Rates: $4 transient, $6-$15 VIP. Duty can make reservations, retired and leave, Space-A.

TML: BOQ. Building 468, officers all ranks, leave or official duty. Total 324 units. Bedroom, semi-private bath; separate bedrooms, private bath; DV/VIP suites, private bath (8). DVQ Suites w/fullsize kitchen (2). Kitchen (114 units), refrigerator, A/C, color TV, housekeeping service, washer/dryer, ice vending. Modern structure. Rates: sponsor $8 or $10 (depending on rank), each additional person $3. DV/VIP $25. Duty can make reservations, others Space-A.

TML: Navy Lodge. Near Exchange Mall. C-702-426-2489. Check in at Mini-Mart. Large Double rooms, private bath, Kitchen (6). Rates: $38 per unit per night. Call 702-426-2489 which is the mini-mart located just inside the front gate. The mini-mart is the place to check in and out.

DV/VIP: BOQ billeting C-702-423-6671.

TML Availability: Impossible during CVW deployments - excellent rest of the time.

The Carson River and Lake Lahontan fishing, boating, swimming, water skiing and local rock collecting are of interest. Call MWR for special rates to Reno, ghost towns, Virginia City, and other points of interest.

Locator 426-5161   **Medical 426-3100**   **Police 426-2803**

Nellis Air Force Base (NV01R4)
554 SVS/SVML
5990 Fitzgerald Blvd.
Nellis AFB, NV 89191-6514

TELEPHONE NUMBER INFORMATION: Main installation numbers: C-702-652-1110, D-312-682-1110.

NEVADA
Nellis Air Force Base, continued

Location: Off I-15 north of Las Vegas. Also accessible from US-91/93. Clearly marked. *USMRA: Page 113 (G-9)*. NMC: Las Vegas, 8 miles southwest.

Lodging Office: Building 780, 5990 Fitzgerald Blvd, **C-702-643-2710**, D-312-682-2711, FAX 702-652-9172, DSN FAX 312-682-9172 (**FAX numbers for those on official orders only**), 24 hours daily. Check in billeting, check out 1200 hours daily. Government civilian employee billeting. Note: there is additional lodging at Indian Springs, call (702) 652-0401 for information.

TML: TLF. 2900's (9 buildings). All ranks, leave or official duty. Handicapped accessible. Bedroom, private bath (60). Queen Sofa couch in living room. A/C, refrigerator, kitchen, complete utensils, color TV, housekeeping service, cribs/cots, playground for children, washer/dryer, food/ice vending. Modern structure, remodeled. Rates: $18-24. Maximum 5 persons per unit. Duty can make reservations, others Space-A.

TML: VAQ. Buildings 536 and 552, enlisted, all ranks. Bedroom, semi-private bath (258). SNCO rooms, private bath (5). Chief's suite, private bath (1). Single rooms (1 double bed), shared bath (8). Refrigerator, A/C, color TV, housekeeping service, washer/dryer, essentials, food/ice vending, microwave, room telephone, clock radio. Modern structure, remodeled. Rates: $8 per person. Chief's suite $9. Maximum 2 persons per unit. Children not allowed during deployments. Duty can make reservations, others Space-A.

TML: VOQ. Buildings 523, 538, 540, 545, officers all ranks, leave or official duty. Bedroom, private bath (153). VIP suites, private bath (5). Kitchen, utensils only in suites, essentials, refrigerator, A/C, color TV, housekeeping service, washer/dryer, microwave, room telephone, clock radio, iron/ironing boards. Modern structures. Rates: $10 per person, $11 per person VIP suites, all other VOQ rooms, $8. Maximum 2 persons per unit. No children. Duty can make reservations, others Space-A.

DV/VIP: Protocol Office, building 620, room 112, C-702-643-2987, D-312-682-2987.

TML Availability: Extremely limited. Best, spring & Nov-Dec. Difficult other times.

CREDIT CARDS ACCEPTED: Visa, MasterCard and American Express.

The Las Vegas area offers Lake Mead for boating and swimming, Mt Charleston for snow skiing, Red Rock Canyon for scenic hiking, and Hoover Dam for sheer wonderment. Of course, Las Vegas is noted for night life and gaming!

Locator 652-1841   Medical 652-2343   Police 652-2311

Indian Springs Air Force Auxiliary Field (NV03R4)
Lodging Office, Bldg 65
Indian Springs, NV 89018

TELEPHONE NUMBER INFORMATION: Main installation numbers: C-702-652-0401, D-312-682-0401.

Location: On US 95, 45 miles North of Las Vegas. Clearly marked. *USMRA: Page 113 (F-8)*. NMC: Las Vegas, 4 miles south.

NEVADA
Indian Springs Air Force Auxiliary Field, continued

Lodging Office: Building 65, **C-702-652-0401,** D-312-682-0401, 0730-1630 hours daily. Check in billeting, check out 1100 hours daily. Late checkout call 20401 or DSN: 682-0401. Write to: P.O. Box 489, Indian Springs, NV, 89018.

TML: VOQ. Building 37, officers, O6+. Bedroom, 2 beds, hall bath (1); separate bedroom suite, private bath (1). Kitchen, utensils, color TV, VCR, housekeeping service, essentials, washer/dryer.

TML: VAQ/VOQ. Buildings 4-8, 24,127. All ranks, leave or official duty. Bedroom, 2 beds, private bath (107). Kitchenette (bldg 127), utensils on request, refrigerator, color TV in lounge & room, housekeeping service, toiletries, washer/dryer, ice machine (bldg 24), snack vending. Rates: enlisted $4.50; officer $6.50. All categories may make reservations. No pets.

TML Availability: Fairly good. Best winter months, more difficult, summer.

There is a casino off base with gaming available here, and the Las Vegas area offers many other activities. But the desert also attracts rock hounds, and would-be archeologist who look at Indian drawings among the red rock formations.

Medical 118   **Police 116**   **Fire 117**

NEW HAMPSHIRE

Portsmouth Naval Shipyard (NH02R1)
CBQ/H-23
Portsmouth, NH 03801-5000

TELEPHONE NUMBER INFORMATION: Main installation numbers: C-207-438-1000, D-312-684-0111.

Location: From I-95 north take Maine exit #2 to Route 236, approx 1.5 mi to gate #2. Located on an island on Piscataqua River between Portsmouth and Kittery, ME. *USMRA: Page 23 (H-9)*. NMC: Boston, 60 miles south.

Lodging Office: Building H-23, **C-207-438-1513/2015**, FAX-207-438-3580, 24 hours. Check in after 1400, check out 1200 hours. Government civilian employee billeting.

TML: BOQ/BEQ/CPOQ. All ranks, leave (space available) or official duty (may make reservations 30 days in advance), handicapped accessible. Hot tub with sauna, VCR in rooms. Housekeeping service daily. Hairdryer, amenities basket, USA Newspaper, refrigerator/microwave, color TV, large screen TV in lounge, washer/dryer. Rates: officer $8/$4 spouse, $4 additional person. Enlisted E7+ $5 per person. No pets. Duty can make reservations, others Space-A. DV/VIP: Officers: $15-$25, $15 additional person, enlisted $10-$20.

TML: Enlisted family suites. Six rooms with the above amenities. Rates: $10 per couple and $5 for each additional person. Maximum charge $20 per day. No Pets.

TML Availability: Fairly good. Depends on number of ships in overhaul.

CREDIT CARDS ACCEPTED: Diners.

Local skiing at White Mountain, outlet shopping in nearby Kittery, and trips to Boston are some of the favorite pursuits in this area.

Locator 438-1000   **Medical 438-2555**   **Police 438-2351**

Temporary Military Lodging Around the World - 155

NEW JERSEY

Armament Research, Development and Engineering Center (NJ01R1)
US Army ARDEC
ATTN: AMSTA-AR-PWH, Bldg 3359
Picatinny Arsenal, NJ 07806-5000

TELEPHONE NUMBER INFORMATION: Main installation numbers: C-201-724-4021, D-312-880-4021.

Location: Take I-80 west, exit 34B, follow signs to Center, 1 mile N. From I-80 east, exit 33 follow signs to Center. *USMRA: Page 19 (E-2)*. NMC: Newark, 30 miles east.

Lodging Office: ATTN: AMSTA-AR-PWH, building 3359, Belt Rd, **C-201-724-3506/2633**, FAX 201-724-6801, DSN FAX 880-6801, 0800-1630 M-F. Check in billeting, check out 1100 hours daily. After hours, persons with reservations may check in with Desk Sgt, building 173, C-201-724-6666. Government civilian employee billeting.

TML: Guest House/DVQ. Bldg 110, all ranks, leave or official duty. Four room, 3 bed DVQ suite, kitchen, living room, dining area, private bath (1); two room apartments, private bath (2); one room apartment, private bath (1). Community kitchen, refrigerator, A/C, color TV in room & lounge, housekeeping service, cribs/cots, washer/dryer. Older structure, renovated. Rates: Guest House, single $15, double $20; child, 2-12 $1, 13+ $5, no children under 2; DVQ, single $25, double $32, children 2-12 $2, 12+ $7, no children under 2. Duty can make reservations, others Space-A.

DV/VIP: Protocol Office, AMSTA-AR-GSP, building 1, 4th fl, C-201-724-7026/27, O6+. Retirees and lower ranks Space-A.

TML Availability: Fairly good, Oct-Apr. More difficult, other times.

CREDIT CARDS ACCEPTED: Diners.

Visit the Village Green in Morristown for shopping, enjoy local restaurants specializing in German, French, Italian, Spanish and Greek food. Don't miss the New Jersey Shakespeare Festival at Drew University.

Locator 724-2852   **Medical 724-2113**   **Police 724-6666**

Bayonne Military Ocean Terminal (NJ10R1)
Liberty Lodge
Bldg 51A, Military Ocean Terminal
Bayonne, NJ 07002-5302

TELEPHONE NUMBER INFORMATION: Main installation numbers: C-201-823-5111, D-312-247-0111.

Location: From New Jersey Turnpike, exit 14A to NJ-169 east to main gate. Follow green and white signs. *USMRA: Page 26 (C-5,6)*. NMC New York City, 10 miles northeast.

156 - Temporary Military Lodging Around the World

NEW JERSEY
Bayonne Military Ocean Terminal, continued

Lodging Office: None.

Guest House: Liberty Lodge. C-201-823-8700, D-312-247-5666, FAX 201-823-5664 for reservations and information. Bedrooms, with two double beds, private bath (40). TV, telephone, individually controlled heating and A/C. Rates: room $50 per night, with kitchenette $55. All ranks, retirees, DoD Civilians, family & friends Space-A basis.

TML Availability: Fair.

CREDIT CARDS ACCEPTED: Visa, MasterCard, American Express and Diners.

Inexpensive day: take the ferry from Staten Island to Battery Park. From there you can visit the Statue of Liberty, (by taking another ferry), or walk to the World Trade Center, Wall Street, or Chinatown, (Canal St, from the Park subway).

Locator 823-5111   Medical 823-7371   Police 823-6666/6000

Cape May Coast Guard Training Center (NJ13R1)
MWR Office
1 Munroe Ave.
Cape May, NJ, 08204-5000

TELEPHONE NUMBER INFORMATION: Main installation numbers: C-609-898-6900, D-312-898-6900.

Location: From the Garden State Parkway south, Parkway turns into Lafayette. Go over 2 bridges and turn left onto Sidney Ave., left on Washington, then take the first right and follow to Pittsburgh. Follow sign to Training Center entrance. *USMRA: Page 19 (D-10).* NMC: Wildwood, 8 miles north.

Lodging Office: MWR Office, Building 269. 0800 to 1630 M-F. No after hours, Sat, Sun or holiday. **C-609-898-6922,** Check in, out at MWR Office. Government civilian employee billeting.

TML: TLQ. Officers and enlisted all ranks. Cottages, 2 bedrooms, private bath (6). Refrigerator, kitchenette, utensils, CATV, cribs/cots. Wood frame buildings. PCS and TDY have priority, others Space-A. Rates equivalent to BAQ and VHA per day.

DV/VIP: MWR Office. C-609-898-6922. O6+. Retirees & lower ranks Space-A.

TML Availability: Lodging in the TLQ on a Space-A basis is quite rare year round, according to officials at Cape May.

Resort Area. Fishing Boating, beaches. Museums, and parks abound.

Locator 898-6900   Medical 898-6959   Police 911

NEW JERSEY

Earle Naval Weapons Station (NJ11R1)
Morale Welfare & Recreation
201 Hwy 34 S
Dept. 15 Bldg. C-29
Colts Neck, NJ 07722-5020

TELEPHONE NUMBER INFORMATION: Main installation numbers: C-908-866-2000, D-312-449-2000.

Location: From Garden State Parkway, south, exit 100-B, Rt 33 West to Rt 34 North. *USMRA: Page 19 (F,G-5).* NMC: Newark, 50 miles north.

Lodging Office: ITT Office, NWS Earle, 201 Hwy 34 S. C-29, **C-908-866-2167**, D-312-449-2167, 0830-1600 M-F. Check in facility. No civilian employee billeting, primarily for PCS use.

TML: BEQ, BOQ, TLQ. Active duty, PCS or active assigned at Earle only. Mobile homes, private bath (4). Maximum 6 per unit. No pets. Refrigerator, color TV, kitchen with utensils. Rates $19.50-$30 per night, depending on rank.

TML Availability: Difficult. Best winter.

Seven miles from the New Jersey shore, where sport fishing, swimming and boating are available. One hour from New York City.

Locator 724-2345   Medical 866-2300   Police 866-2291

Fort Dix Army Training Center (NJ03R1)
AFZT-EH-H, Billeting Branch
P.O. Box 419
Fort Dix, NJ 08640-5523

TELEPHONE NUMBER INFORMATION: Main installation numbers: C-609-562-1011, D-312-944-1110.

Location: From NJ Turnpike (I-95), exit 7, right onto NJ-206, short distance left on NJ-68 and continue to General Circle and main gate. *USMRA: Page 19 (E,F-6).* NMC: Trenton, 17 miles northwest.

Lodging Office: ATTN: ATZD-EH-H, building 5255, Maryland Ave & First St, **C-609-562-4849**, 24 hours daily. Check in facility, check out 1100 hours daily.

TML: Doughboy Inn. Guest House, building 5997, all ranks, leave or official duty, C-609-562-6663. Bedroom, 2 double beds, private bath (76). Community kitchen, A/C, color TV, telephone, housekeeping service, cribs/cots ($2.50 per night), coin washer/dryer, ice vending. Modern structure. Rates: TDY $35, double, $40, three persons, $45 four or more. All categories can make reservations.

TML: VOQ/VEQ. Building 5255, all ranks, leave or official duty. Bedroom, semi-private bath (VEQ) (65); separate bedrooms, private bath (VOQ) (10). Refrigerator, A/C, color TV in room & lounge,

NEW JERSEY
Fort Dix Army Training Center, continued

housekeeping service, cribs/cots, washer/dryer, ice vending. Older structure, renovated. Rates: TDY $21 per night, $5 each additional person. All categories can make reservations.

TML: DVQ. Building 5256, officers O6+, leave or official duty. Bedroom suites, private bath (4); two bedroom apartments, private bath (4). Kitchen (apartments), refrigerator (suites), utensils, A/C, color TV in room & lounge, housekeeping service, cribs/cots, washer/dryer, ice vending. Modern structure. Rates: $21, $5 each additional person. All categories can make reservations.

DV/VIP: HQ USATC & Ft Dix, ATTN: Office of The Secretary General Staff, C-609-562-5059/6293, O6+/civilian equivalent. Retirees Space-A.

TML Availability: Good, Oct-Mar. Difficult, other times.

CREDIT CARDS ACCEPTED: Visa, MasterCard and American Express.

Nearby Brindle Lake, a 30 acre lake surrounded by about 2,000 acres of pine forest provides rental boats (no power boats), camping, picnic and barbecue facilities. Visit Trenton and its historic sites 17 miles northwest.

Locator 562-1011   Medical 562-2695   Police 562-6001

Fort Monmouth (NJ05R1)
Lodging Office
Bldg. 270, Allen Ave.
Fort Monmouth, NJ 07703-5108

TELEPHONE NUMBER INFORMATION: Main installation numbers: C-908-532-9000, D-312-992-9000.

Location: Take NJ Turnpike to I-95, exit 7A (Shore Points); east to Garden State Parkway; north to exit 105 for Eatontown and Fort Monmouth. *USMRA: Page 19 (G-5)*. NMC: New Brunswick, 23 miles northwest.

Lodging Office: Building 270, Allen Ave, **C-908-532-1635/1092**, FAX 908-532-8996, 0745-2345 hours daily. Other hours, Work Center Office, building 166, C-908-532-1122. Check in lodging office, check out 1100 hours daily. Government civilian employee billeting on official business.

TML: Guest House. Bldg 360, 365, all ranks, leave, or official duty. Suites bedroom/sitting room, private bath (90). All have kitchen, microwave, color TV, housekeeping service, sleeper couch, cots, washer/dryer and ice vending. Five units handicapped accessible. Rates: E1-E7, O1, $21 single, 2 or more persons $27; E8+, O2+; $30 single, 2 or more persons $35; unofficial business; $40 single, 2 or more persons $45. All categories can make reservations Space-A. No pets.

TML: VOQ. Buildings 270, 363, 364, 1202, officers, TDY civilians, enlisted, senior NCO's on official duty. Inquire about rooms and services. $25 per night, $37 for 2 or more persons. No children. Duty can make reservations, others Space-A. No pets.

NEW JERSEY
Fort Monmouth, continued

TML: DVQ. Building 259, **Blair Hall**, officers O6+, leave or official duty. Inquire about rooms and services available. Modern structure, renovated. Rates: $25 per night, 2 or more persons $27. Duty can make reservations, others Space-A. No pets.

TML Availability: Good.

CREDIT CARDS ACCEPTED: Visa, MasterCard and American Express.

Within 5 miles of the ocean, the area also has two race tracks for thoroughbreds and trotters. Atlantic City 1 1/2 hours south, New York City, 1 hour north. Nearby Garden State Art Center for ballet has concerts year round.

Locator 532-1492/2540   Medical 532-2789   Police 532-1112

Lakehurst Naval Air Warfare Center (NJ08R1)
Combined Bachelor's Quarters
NAWC Bldg 481
Lakehurst, NJ 08733-5000

TELEPHONE NUMBER INFORMATION: Main installation numbers: C-908-323-2011, D-312-624-1110.

Location: Take Garden State Parkway south to NJ-70 west to junction of NJ-547 right and proceed 1 mile to base. *USMRA: Page 19 (F-6)*. NMC: Trenton, 30 miles northwest.

Lodging Office: Building 481, **C-908-323-2266**, D-312-624-2266, FAX 908-323-2269, DSN FAX 312-624-2269, 24 hours daily. Check in facility, check out 1100 hours daily. Government civilian employee billeting.

TML: BOQ. Building 33, officers, O3 & below, official duty. Bedroom suites, private bath (16). A/C, microfridge, essentials, ice vending, housekeeping service, color TV, washer/dryer. Rates: $8/night. Older structure. Active duty, retirees may make reservations at above number, or write to: CBQ, NAWC Lakehurst, NJ, 08733.

TML: BEQ. Building 480, **Casey Hall**, enlisted, E-4 & below, official duty. Building 481, 481, **Maloney Hall**, enlisted, all ranks, official duty. Bedrooms, hall bath (62); VIP bedrooms (E-7+), private bath (3). Essentials, ice vending, housekeeping service, color TV, washer/dryer, sauna, jacuzzi, exercise room. Rates $4 and $15/night. Older structure. Active duty, retirees may make reservations at above number, or write to: CBQ, NAWC Lakehurst, NJ, 08733.

TML: DV Quarters. Cottages, private bath (6). Kitchenette, complete utensils, essentials, housekeeping service, color TV, washer/dryer (available in building 481). Older structure, renovated '91. Rates $25/night. Maximum 4 per unit. No pets. All categories may make reservations at above number and address.

TML: DV/VIP: Guest House, O6+. Contact Exec's Office, C-908-323-2369.

TML Availability: Very good, all year.

NEW JERSEY
Lakehurst Naval Air Warfare Center, continued

CREDIT CARDS ACCEPTED: Visa, MasterCard and American Express.

This is the site of the crash of the Airship Hindenburg. On base golf course and driving range and club house, biking, boating, fishing and hunting in season. There is a nearby Lakehurst conservation area.

Locator 323-2582　　　　　Medical 323-2231　　　　　Police 323-2332

McGuire Air Force Base (NJ09R1)
All American Inn, Bldg 2717
SVS/SVML
McGuire AFB, NJ 08641-5012

TELEPHONE NUMBER INFORMATION: Main installation numbers: C-609-724-1100, D-312-440-0111.

Location: From New Jersey Turnpike, exit 7 to 206 south to NJ-68 southeast to AFB. Adjacent to Fort Dix. Clearly marked. *USMRA: Page 19 (E-6)*. NMC: Trenton, 18 miles northwest.

Lodging Office: All-American Inn SVS/SVML, building 2717, **C-609-724-2954**, D-312-440-2954, FAX 609-724-2035, 24 hours daily. Check in facility by 1700, check out 1100 hours daily. Government civilian employee billeting.

TML: TLQ. Buildings 2418/19, all ranks, leave or official duty, C-609-724-3336/7 0745-1600 hours M-F. Other hours, C-609-724-2340. One bedroom with foldout couch, private bath (30). Kitchen, A/C, housekeeping service, washer/dryer. Older structure. Rates: O1, $21.50; E1-E2, $16.50; all others $24 per unit. PCS have priority, others Space-A.

TML: VOQ/VAQ. Buildings 1902, 1903, 1912, 2704 (VAQ), 2707 (VOQ), all ranks, leave or official duty. Bedroom, semi-private bath (VOQ) (100); bedroom, semi-private bath (VAQ) (359). A/C, color TV, housekeeping service. Older structure. Rates: $8 officers and enlisted. Duty can make reservations, others Space-A.

TML: DV/VIP. Building 2706, officers O6+, leave or official duty, C-609-724-2954. Bedroom suites, private bath (13). Kitchen in 1 unit. A/C, color TV, housekeeping service. Rates: $14 per person. Duty can make reservations, others Space-A.

DV/VIP: Protocol Office, C-609-724-2405, O6+.

TML Availability: Good, Oct-Apr. Difficult, other times.

CREDIT CARDS ACCEPTED: Visa, MasterCard and American Express.

New Jersey coastal fishing is popular here. Trenton, the state capital, has many historic sites and an excellent Cultural Center. Miles of roads and trails show off a number of well kept state forests. Atlantic City, New York and Philadelphia are nearby.

Locator 724-1100　　　　　Medical 562-4061　　　　　Police 911

NEW MEXICO

Cannon Air Force Base (NM02R3)
Caprock Inn
401 S. Olympic Blvd.
Cannon AFB, NM 88103

TELEPHONE NUMBER INFORMATION: Main installation numbers: C-505-784-3311, D-312-681-1110.

Location: From Clovis west on US-60/84 to AFB. From NM-467 enter the Portales Gate. *USMRA: Page 114 (H-5)*. NMC: Clovis, 7 miles east.

Lodging Office: Caprock Inn. 401 S. Olympic Blvd, **C-505-784-2918/2919**, D-312-681-2918/2919, FAX 505-784-4833, DSN FAX 312-681-4833, 24 hours daily. Check in billeting, check out 1200 hours daily. Government civilian employee billeting.

TML: TLF. Buildings 1812, 1818, 1819. All ranks. Leave or official duty. Family units (44); Kitchen, utensils, A/C, color TV, housekeeping service, washer/dryer, ice vending. Older structure. Rates: $22 per room. PCS in/out can make reservations, others Space-A. List of kennels available.

TML: VOQ, VAQ. Building 1800B. Officer all ranks, DoD civilians. Leave or official duty. VOQ units (20); VAQ units (32). Rooms share community living area & kitchen. A/C, color TV in room and lounge, housekeeping service, washer/dryer, ice vending. Older structure. Rates: $7. Duty can make reservations, others Space-A.

TML: DV/VIP. Buildings 1800A and 1812. C-505-784-2727. E-9 and officer O6+. Leave or official duty. Separate bedroom suites, private bath (6). Kitchen, utensils, color TV, housekeeping service, washer/dryer, ice vending. Older structure. Rates: $10 per person, maximum charge $20. Duty can make reservations, others Space-A.

DV/VIP: Protocol Office, 27TFW/CCEP, Bldg 1, C-505-784-2727, O6+. Retirees Space-A.

TML Availability: Good, Nov-Feb. Difficult, other times.

CREDIT CARDS ACCEPTED: Visa, MasterCard and American Express.

Visit the Blackwater Draw Museum, Roosevelt County Museum, or the Oasis State Park outside Portales for fishing, hiking, picnics and camping. Local lakes offer good fishing.

Locator 784-2424   Medical 784-4033   Police 784-4111

Holloman Air Force Base (NM05R3)
1040 New Mexico Avenue
Holloman AFB, NM 88310-8159

TELEPHONE NUMBER INFORMATION: Main installation numbers: C-505-475-6511, D-312-867-1110.

Location: Exit US-70/82, 8 miles southwest of Alamogordo NM. Clearly marked. *USMRA: Page 114 (D,E-7)*. NMC: La Cruces NM, 50 miles southwest, El Paso, TX 65 miles southeast.

NEW MEXICO
Holloman Air Force Base, continued

Lodging Office: Building 583, 1040 New Mexico Ave, **C-505-475-6123**, D-312-867-6123, FAX 505-479-6131 x1302, DSN FAX 312-867-7753, 24 hours daily. Check in facility, check out 1200 hours daily. Government civilian employee billeting.

TML: TLF. Buildings 590, 591, 592, 593, 594, all ranks, leave or official duty. Bedroom, private bath, sofa and chair sleepers (50). Kitchen, complete utensils, A/C, color TV, housekeeping service, cribs/cots/hi-chairs, washer/dryer, ice vending. Rates: $10-$24. PCS in/out can make reservation, others Space-A. No pets.

TML: VAQ. Building 342, enlisted all ranks, leave or official duty. Bedroom, semi-private bath (128); Refrigerator, microwave, coffee makers, A/C, color TV, housekeeping service, washer/dryer, ice and vending machines. New facility '93. Rates: $8 per person. Maximum 2 per room. TDY, PCS in/out can make reservations, others Space-A. No pets.

TML: VOQ. Buildings 582, 583, 584-587, officers all ranks, leave or official duty. Bedroom, private bath (30); separate bedrooms, private bath (130); two bedroom, semi-private bath (24). Kitchen, microwave, coffee makers, A/C, color TV, housekeeping service, cots. Modern structure. Rates: $8 per person. DVOQ: $14. TDY, PCS in/out can make reservations, others Space-A. No pets.

DV/VIP: 49 FW/CC, Building 29, D-312-867-5573/74, E9/O6+/GS-15+.

TML Availability: Good, Nov-Jan. Difficult, other times.

CREDIT CARDS ACCEPTED: Visa, MasterCard and American Express.

Locator 475-7510   Medical 475-7768   Police 475-7171

Kirtland Air Force Base (NM03R3)
377th Service Squadron/SVML
2000 Wyoming Blvd SE, Suite 5661
Kirtland AFB, NM 87117-5661

TELEPHONE NUMBER INFORMATION: Main installation numbers: C-505-846-0011, D-312-246-0011.

Location: From I-40 east, exit on Wyoming Blvd, south for 2 miles to Wyoming Blvd. gate to AFB. *USMRA: Page 114 (D-4)*. NMC: Albuquerque, NM, 1 mile southeast.

Lodging Office: Kirtland Inn, Box 5418, Kirtland AFB, NM 87185, building 22016, Club Dr, **C-505-846-9653**, D-312-246-9653, 24 hours daily, Fax 505-846-4142, DSN Fax 312-246-4142. Check in billeting, check out 1200 hours daily. Government civilian employee billeting.

TML: TLF. Building 23227, all ranks, leave or official duty. Separate bedroom suites, private bath (24). Kitchen, A/C, color TV, housekeeping service, cots, ice vending, washer/dryer. Renovated '92. Rates: $24 per suite, per day. PCS in/out can make reservations, others Space-A. No pets.

TML: Cottages. All ranks, leave or official duty. Two bedroom, private bath (16); Kitchen, A/C, color TV, housekeeping service, cots, washer/dryer. Older structure, renovated. Rates: $24 per cottage, per day. PCS in/out can make reservations, others Space-A. No pets.

NEW MEXICO
Kirtland Air Force Base, continued

TML: VOQ. Buildings 1911, 22001, 22003, 22010, 22011, 22012, 23225, officers all ranks, official duty & Space-A. Suites, living room, bedroom, private bath (140). Refrigerator, A/C, color TV, housekeeping service, washer/dryer, ice vending. Older structure. Rates: $8 per person, per night. Duty on orders can make reservations, others Space-A. No pets.

TML: VAQ. Buildings 22002, 20101, 23226. Enlisted all ranks, official duty, Space-A. SNCO suites, living room, bedroom, kitchenettes, private bath (22). Super Chief Suites (2) (reserve through Protocol); bedrooms, semi private bath and private bath (144). All buildings have washer/dryers, color TV, A/C, housekeeping service, ice vending. Rates: $8 per person per night. Chief Suites $14. Duty makes reservations, others Space-A. No pets.

TML: DV/VIP. Buildings 22000, 22011. Suites "top of the line" (25). Rates: $14 per person, per night, leave or official duty. No pets.

DV/VIP: 377 ABW/Protocol Office, reservations C-505-846-4119, D-312-246-4119, O6+, civilian equivalents.

TML Availability: Best, late fall and winter. Fri & Sat nights always better than during the week. Worst, June-Oct.

Take the tram to the Sandia Mountains, investigate the National Atomic Museum, and Old Town Albuquerque, founded in 1706. Enjoy local skiing, the State Fair in September, the International Hot Air Balloon Fiesta each October.

Locator 846-0011   Medical 846-3730   Police 846-7926

White Sands Missile Range (NM04R3)
WSMR Billeting Office
P.O. Box 37
White Sands Missile Range, NM 88002-0037

TELEPHONE NUMBER INFORMATION: Main installation numbers: C-505-678-2121, D-312-258-2121.

Location: From Las Cruces, east on US-70, 30 miles to WSMR. From Alamogordo west on US-70, 45 miles to WSMR. *USMRA: Page 114 (D-6,7,8)*. NMC: El Paso, TX 45 miles south.

Lodging Office: ATTN: WSMR Billeting Office, P.O. Box 37, **C-505-678-4559**, FAX 505-678-8969, 745-1545 hours daily. Other hours SDO, building 100, C-505-678-2031. Check out 1200 hours daily. Charge for late checkouts.

TML: VOQ/DVQ. Buildings 501, 502. All military and DoD civilians on official duty. Bedroom, private bath (3); suites, private bath (43); three bedroom houses, private bath (8). Refrigerator, microwave, community kitchen, complete utensils, A/C, color TV, housekeeping service, cribs, washer/dryer. Rates: TDY $25, spouse $2 additional. Reservations confirmed only for TDY or PCS military families in/out. No pets. Three bedroom houses at $30-$45 per night depending upon number of beds used are also available.

NEW MEXICO
White Sands Missile Range, continued

TML: Guest House. Building 506. All ranks, PCS/TDY, official duty, leave and retired military. Reservations confirmed only for military in PCS/TDY status. Bedroom, 2 double beds, sofa bed, private bath, kitchen units, complete utensils, A/C, color TV, cribs, washer/dryer. Modern structure. Rates: $24.

DV/VIP: CG, WSMR, ATTN: STEWS-PC, building 100, room 227, C-505-678-1028, O6/GS-15+.

TML Availability: Very good.

CREDIT CARDS ACCEPTED: Visa, MasterCard, American Express and Discover.

Las Cruces' blending of three cultures, and New Mexico State University supply much entertainment locally. Visit the International Space Hall of Fame in Alamogordo, White Sands National Monument, and El Paso, gateway to the Southwest and Mexico.

Locator 678-1630   **Medical 678-2882**   **Police 678-1234**

Temporary Military Lodging Around the World - 165

NEW YORK

Fort Drum (NY06R1)
Lodging Office
Bldg T-2227, Officers' Loop
Fort Drum, NY 13602-5097

TELEPHONE NUMBER INFORMATION: Main installation numbers: C-315-772-6900, D-312-341-6011.

Location: From Syracuse, take I-81 north to exit 48, past Watertown, and follow signs to Fort Drum. *USMRA: Page 21 (J-3,4).* NMC: Watertown, 8 miles southwest.

Lodging Office: Building T-2327, Officers' Loop, 24 hours daily, **C-315-772-5435**. Check in billeting, check out 1100 hours daily. Government civilian employee billeting.

TML: Guest House. Building 2340, all ranks, leave or official duty. Fax 315-773-2566. Separate bedrooms, private bath (9); two bedroom, private bath (5). Kitchen, complete utensils, color TV, housekeeping service, cribs/cots, washer/dryer. Older structure. Rates: based on BAQ/VHA ranging from $12-$28. All categories may make reservations.

TML: VOQ. Cottages (9), 1 and 2 bedroom (2), private bath. Fax 315-772-9647. All ranks, leave or official duty. Kitchens, complete utensils, color TV, housekeeping service, cribs/cots, washer/dryer. Rates $15, $5 for additional person.

TML: TLF. **The Inn.** Civilian funded motel operated by the Army, all ranks, leave or official duty, C-315-773-7777. Rooms (111), 64 with kitchenettes and microwaves. Queen size beds, remote control CATV, room telephones, individual A/C & heating. Rates: This facility is included under Guest House rates, as above.

DV/VIP: Protocol Office, building P-10000, C-315-772-5010, Fax 315-772-9647 O6+. Retirees and lower ranks Space-A.

TML Availability: Good, Oct-Apr. Difficult, other times.

CREDIT CARDS ACCEPTED: Visa, MasterCard, American Express, Diners' and Discover.

Sackets Harbor Battle Ground, site of war of 1812 battle. Nearby is the fascinating area called 1,000 Islands, rich in water recreation. Canada is 45 minutes away.

Locator 772-5869   Medical 772-5236   Police 772-5156

Fort Hamilton (NY02R1)
Adams Guest House
109 Schum Avenue
Brooklyn, NY 11252-5330

TELEPHONE NUMBER INFORMATION: Main installation numbers: C-718-630-4101, D-312-232-1110.

Location: From Belt Parkway, exit 2 (Fort Hamilton Parkway) to 100th St, right to Fort Hamilton

NEW YORK
Fort Hamilton, continued

Parkway, right to main gate. *USMRA: Page 26 (D-7)*. NMC: New York, in the city.

Lodging Office: Building 109, Schum Ave, **C-718-630-4564**, D-312-232-4564, 24 hours daily. Check in facility after 1400 hours daily. Check out 1000 hours daily. Government civilian employee billeting (on orders).

TML: Adams Guest House. Building 109. All ranks, leave or official duty. Bedroom, private bath (39). Kitchen, A/C, color/cable TV in room & lounge, coin washer/dryer, ice vending. Older structure, renovated '91. Rates: $44 single, $47 two, maximum $53. Special rates for PCS military personnel. All can make reservations.

TML: Transient quarters. Building 110. All ranks, leave or official duty. Bedrooms, shared bath (48). Above amenities. Rates: 1 person, $35, two person, $40. TDY has priority, others Space-A.

TML: DV/VIP. Building 109, officers O6+, leave or official duty, C-718-630-4324. Separate bedrooms, private bath (2). Refrigerator, color /cable TV, coffee/bar set up, A/C, housekeeping service. Rates: $45 single, $50 two or more, maximum $55. Duty and retirees can make reservations.

DV/VIP: Liaison & Protocol Office, bldg 302, room 13, C-718-630-4324, O6+. Retirees Space-A.

TML Availability: Good, winter months. Difficult, summer months.

Locator 630-4958   **Medical 630-4615**   **Police 630-4456**

Gateway National Park (NY07R1)
Bldg 408
North Platt Rd
Staten Island, NY 10305-5000

TELEPHONE NUMBER INFORMATION: Main installation numbers: C-718-442-0413. Police 718-816-1709.

Location: I-95 N to Elizabeth, NJ, I-278 to Staten Island. Last exit before Verrazano bridge, Bay St exit, follow signs. *USMRA: Page 26 (C-7)*. NMC: New York.

Lodging Office: Navy Lodge. Call **1-800-NAVY-INN**, 24 hours daily, or **C-718-442-0413**, FAX 718-816-0830. Check in 1500 (after hours guaranteed reservations pick up room key at front gate pass office), check out 1200. Notify Lodge of late check in, out. Eligibility: check Appendix D.

TML: Navy Lodge. All ranks. Bedrooms, 2 double beds, private bath, dining area (50). Three sets interconnecting, two handicapped accessible, 25 non-smoking. Kitchenette, microwave, utensils, A/C, CATV, phone, irons/boards, cribs, washer/dryer, housekeeping service, food/ice vending, parking, playground. No pets (nearby kennel). Rates: $53. All categories can make reservations.

TML Availability: Good all year, weekends difficult.

CREDIT CARDS ACCEPTED: Visa, MasterCard, American Express and Discover.

Temporary Military Lodging Around the World - 167

NEW YORK

New York Coast Guard Support Center (NY01R1)
Lodging Office, Bldg S-293
Governors Island, NY 10004-5000

TELEPHONE NUMBER INFORMATION: Main installation numbers: C & FTS-212-668-7000.

Location: Take free Governors Island Ferry from Battery Park area of Manhattan. *USMRA: Page 26 (D-5)*. NMC: New York, 1 mile northwest.

Lodging Office: Building 293, opposite O'Club, **C-212-668-3452**, check in facility after 1300, check out 1100 hours daily. Reservations required. No government civilian employee billeting.

TML: Super 8 Motel. Building 293, all ranks, leave or official duty, **C-212-269-8878**. Bedroom, 1 double bed, private bath (11); bedroom, 2 double beds, private bath (38); apartments, efficiency (PCS to Governor's Island) (8). Two handicapped accessible rooms. A/C, color TV, housekeeping service, cribs, ice vending. Modern structure. Rates: single and double rooms $50 first person, $5 each additional person over 12, holidays slightly higher; efficiency apartments PCS rates. Special weekend and holiday rates (higher). All major credit cards. All categories can make reservations at above number.

TML: BOQ. Officers all ranks (occasionally enlisted personnel may use if special circumstances warrant), leave or official duty. Rooms, private bath (80+), 10 rooms ground floor are efficiency. Single persons only. No families. Be prepared to share room. Rates: $7 per person on orders, $15 on leave. All categories may make reservations.

DV/VIP: CO, C-212-668-7251, O7+, building 12, suites, reservations required.

TML Availability: Good, Oct-May. Difficult, other times.

A favorite with New York city visitors who would rather spend their $ on theater, restaurants and shopping than on lodging. Comfortable, safe, and convenient. Ferry runs 24 hours, 7 days. Free on base parking.

Locator 668-7000   **Medical** 668-7167   **Police** 668-7474

Niagara Falls Air Reserve Base (NY12R1)
914th AW/SVML
10780 Kinross St.
Niagara Falls IAP/ARB, NY 14304-5058

TELEPHONE NUMBER INFORMATION: Main installation numbers: C-716-236-2000, D-312-238-3011.

Location: Take I-190 to Niagara Falls, exit #23 Packard Rd and turn right - straight through to Lockport Road. Approximately 4 miles from the exit. From US-62 West to Walmore Road, North to AFB. *USMRA: Page 20 (D-6)*. NMC: City Niagara Falls 6 miles west of AFB.

NEW YORK
Niagara Falls Air Reserve Base, continued

Lodging Office: Building 312, 10780, Kinross St. Reservations **1-800-456-4990**, **C-716-236-2014**, D-312-238-2014, FAX 716-236-6348, DSN FAX 312-238-6348, hours of operation 0700-2300. Checkout 1200 hours daily. Government civilian employee billeting.

TML: VOQ. Building 312, officers all ranks, leave or official duty. Bedroom, private bath (43), telephone, refrigerator, AC, color TV and other essentials. Housekeeping service, washer/dryers, ice vending, crib and cots. Lounge with microwave. Rates: $6 per person. Duty can make reservations, others Space-A.

TML: VOQ/VIP. Building 312, officers O5+, GS/GM 13+, leave or duty. Living room/bedroom suites, private bath (6). A/C, telephone, color TV, refrigerator microwave and other essentials. Housekeeping service. Rates: $8 per person. Duty can make reservations, others Space-A.

TML: VAQ. Buildings 502 and 504, enlisted, all ranks, leave or official duty. Bedroom, 2 beds per room each building, common bath (34), TV, A/C refrigerator, essentials, housekeeping service, washer/dryer and ice vending. Rates: $6 per person. Duty can make reservations, others Space-A.

TML: VAQ. Building 508, enlisted all ranks. Bedroom, semi-private bath (36). Housekeeping service, washer/dryer and ice vending. Rates: $6 per person. SNCO: living/bedroom suites, private bath (2). TV, A/C refrigerator telephone and other essentials. Rates: $8 per person.

TML: VOQ/VIP. DV Suites (4). Buildings 304E, 304W, 306E, 306W. Three bedrooms, queen size bed, private bath, shared living room. A/C, telephones, color TV, refrigerators, microwave, washer/dryers, housekeeping service. Rates: $6 per person.

TML: VOQ/VIP. Building 308. Bedrooms, king size bed, private bath (2). A/C, telephone, color TV, refrigerator. Shared living room, and dining area. Washer/Dryer, housekeeping service. Rates: $8 per person.

TML Availability: Good, Oct-Mar. Difficult, Apr-Sep. Avoid weekends!

CREDIT CARDS ACCEPTED: Diners.

Niagara Falls, Winter Gardens, Niagara Power Vista, Old Fort Niagara, Our Lady of Fatima Shrine, Native American Center for the Living Arts, Art Park, and the Aquarium are all attractions in this area. Also visit the amusement parks and scenic area surrounding the Niagara frontier.

Locator 236-2002   Medical 236-2086/7   Police 236-2278

Seneca Army Depot (NY03R1)
Lake Shore Travel Park
Romulus, NY 14541-5001

TELEPHONE NUMBER INFORMATION: Main installation numbers: C-607-869-1110, D-312-489-5110.

Location: On post. Twelve miles south of intersection of US-20/NY-96A near Geneva. Take New York State Thruway (I-90) to exit 42, and Hwy 96 south to main gate. *USMRA: Page 20 (H-7)*. NMC: Rochester, NY, 55 miles SE.

NEW YORK
Seneca Army Depot, continued

Lodging Office: Building 2485, **C-607-869-1211**, D-312-489-5211, FAX 607-869-1507, open 0700-1630 M-F. Check in at facility, 1400-1600 hours daily. Check out 0830-1030 hours. No government civilian employee billeting.

TML: Lake Shore Travel Camp. Mobile homes (21). All ranks, PCS personnel have priority. Three bedrooms private bath (15); two bedrooms (6). Kitchenette, refrigerator, TV, utensils, washer/dryer available. No Pets. Rates: $40/day. BAQ rate in winter only, (all year for E1-E4). Active duty, accompanied, unaccompanied family members, all categories can make reservations. Active duty, Reservists and National Guard on orders accommodated on a space available basis. Write to: Lake Shore Travel Park, Seneca Army Depot, Romulus, NY 14541-5001.

TML Availability: Good. Difficult in summer.

CREDIT CARDS ACCEPTED: American Express and Diners'.

Located in the center of the Finger Lakes Region. Seneca Lake is the "lake trout capital of the world", the largest of the Finger Lakes.

Locator 869-1110   Medical 869-1242   Police 869-1448

Soldiers', Sailors' and Airmen's Club (NY17R1)
283 Lexington Avenue
New York, NY 10016-3540

TELEPHONE NUMBER INFORMATION: Main installation numbers: C-212-683-4353, FAX 212-683-4374. In US toll free **1-800-678-TGIF**.

Location: From Lincoln Tunnel, E. on 34th St, to 3rd Ave., left to 37th st. (1 block), left on Lexington Ave, club on left mid-block. *USMRA: Page 26 (O,E-4)*. NMC: New York, in the city.

Author's Note: The **Soldiers', Sailors' and Airmen's Club** is a tax exempt, not-for-profit organization founded in 1919 to serve the needs of service personnel while visiting New York. It is the only club of its kind in the city.

Office: Check in and out at the lobby desk, 24 hours daily. Check out 1230 hours.

TML: Hotel. Open to all ranks, active duty, reserve, national guard, service academy/ROTC students, retirees and former service personnel with honorable discharge, and allied member forces and their dependents. Note: unaccompanied spouses and widows with ID may use facilities on a Space-A basis. Bedrooms, most having 2 beds, hall baths (29). Facilities include lounges, library, TV rooms, pool room, and canteen. Older structure, renovations on-going. **No elevator.** Rates: Enlisted, $25; Officers $30 Sun-Thur, $35 Fri-Sat; Children age 3 and under free when occupying a bed w/parent; Children age 3-12, $15. Inquire about group rates. Reservations for weekends suggested. Continental breakfast Saturday, Sunday and holidays. Friday night wine & cheese upon arrival (1900-2100).

CREDIT CARDS ACCEPTED: Visa, MasterCard, American Express and Discover.

170 - Temporary Military Lodging Around the World

NEW YORK
Soldiers', Sailors', and Airmen's Club, continued

The SS&A has been in this location since 1926. Here's your chance to visit the Big Apple to shop and see the sights. There is controlled access, a helpful staff, and the building has a new fire alarm and communication systems. Definitely one of New York's best kept secrets!

Stewart Army Sub-Post (NY09R1)
Five Star Inn, Bldg 2605
P.O. Box 9000
New Windsor, NY 12553-9000

TELEPHONE NUMBER INFORMATION: Main installation numbers: C-914-564-6309, D-312-247-3524.

Location: From I-87 take Newburgh exit to Union Ave, south to NY-207. Stewart is approximately 15-20 minutes north of West Point. Follow signs to Stewart Airport. *USMRA: Page 21 (M-10)*. NMC: Newburgh, 4 miles northeast.

Lodging Office: Five Star Inn. The West Point and STAS Guest House, building 2605, New Windsor, NY, **C-914-563-3311**, FAX 914-564-6328, D-312-688-3009, 24 hours daily. Check out 1000 hours daily. Active duty and family, PCS, visiting relatives and guests of hospital patients, active, reservist and retired military personnel, civilians sponsored by military personnel; military and DoD civilians on TDY. Reservation taken daily 0800-2200.

TML: Guest House. Building 2605, **Five Star Inn**, all ranks, leave or official duty. Bedroom, private bath (18); bedrooms, semi-private bath (34); apartments (8). A/C, vending, laundry, CATV, direct dial telephones, auto wake-up service, complimentary coffee, lounge, refrigerator, cribs, food and ice vending. Older structure, redecorated '92. Rates: range from $29 to $45, additional person $5. PCS rates charged by BAQ/VHA. Maximum 3 per room. Children under 2 free. Reservations 30 days prior for Space-A, 60 days PCS. Reservations confirmed with credit card or advance deposit.

TML Availability: Fairly good, Oct-Mar. Difficult, other times.

Visit the Crawford House in Newburgh, try antique shopping near Millbrook, tour a local winery, or try a balloon tour near Port Jervis. Visit Sugar Loaf Crafts Village - the Hudson River Valley is full of interesting things to do.

Locator 564-6309   Medical 563-3430   Police 564-0580

United States Military Academy, West Point (NY16R1)
Housing Division
Bldg 620, Thomas Hall
ATTN: MAEN-H (CHRRS)
West Point, NY 10996-5000

TELEPHONE NUMBER INFORMATION: Main installation numbers: C-914-938-4011, D-312-688-1110, FAX 914-564-6328.

NEW YORK
United States Military Academy, West Point, continued

Location: Off I-87 or US-9 west. Clearly marked. *USMRA: Page 21 (M,N-10) & Page 28 (D-3).* NMC: New York City, NY 36 miles south.

Lodging Office: Building 674, **C-914-446-4731**, or toll free **1-800-247-5047,** 24 hours daily. Check in facility, check out 1200 hours daily. No government civilian employee billeting.

TML: Hotel Thayer. C-914-446-4731, or toll free 1-800-247-5047, D-312-688-2632. Bedroom, private bath (200). A/C, color TV in room & lounge, housekeeping service, cribs/cots $10 each, ice vending. Older structure, renovated. Government rates (with ID): single room $64, double room $69 valid Sunday-Thursday, government rates include continental breakfast. TDY rates available on request. Open to public. Reservations accepted 1 year in advance.

DV/VIP: Protocol Office, Bldg 600, C-914-938-4315/4316, O7/GS-16+. Retirees Space-A.

TML Availability: Good, except during special holiday events at USMA.

CREDIT CARDS ACCEPTED: Visa, MasterCard and American Express.

Part of the US Armed Forces Recreation System, the history of the Military Academy, sporting events, and special vacation packages are available at this castle-like hotel rising above the Hudson River.

Locator 938-4412   **Medical 938-3637**   **Police 938-3333**

NORTH CAROLINA

Camp Lejeune Marine Corps Base (NC10R1)
ATTN: AC/S Facilities, Bachelor Housing
PSC Box 20004
Camp Lejeune, NC 28542-0004

TELEPHONE NUMBER INFORMATION: Main installation numbers: C-910-451-1113, D-312-484-1113.

Location: Main gate is 6 miles east of junction of US-17 and NC-24. *USMRA: Page 45 (M-5)*. NMC: Jacksonville, 3 miles northwest.

Lodging Office: Building 2617, **Seth-Williams**. **C-910-451-1385/2146**, FAX 910-451-1755, 24 hours daily. Check in 1400, check out 1100 hours daily. Government civilian employee billeting.

TML: Hostess House. Building 896, off Holcomb Ave near MCX, four miles from main gate. C-919-451-3041. Check in after 1400 hours daily, 24 hour desk. All ranks. Leave or official duty. Bedroom, 2 double beds, semi-private bath, fold-out couch, sleeps 5 persons (90). Kitchen, utensils, A/C, color TV, housekeeping service, porta cribs, cots ($1), coin washer/dryer, video players, many extras. Modern structure, motel type. Across street from Burger King and Dominos Pizza. Rates: $24 per unit. Duty can make reservations, others Space-A.

TML: BOQ/BEQ. Building 2617 (BOQ), C-910-451-1385/2146. Officer all ranks. Building HP-53 (BEQ), C-910-451-5262. Enlisted E6-E9. Leave or official duty. Efficiencies, private bath, kitchenette (18); Suites, living room, bedroom, private bath, kitchenette, refrigerator w/ice maker (53); bedroom SNCO transient billeting (21). Utensils, AC, color TV in room & lounge, housekeeping service, cribs/cots, washer/dryer, facilities for DAVs, coffee & coffee maker. Older structure, renovated. Rates: $10-$20. Duty can make reservations, others Space-A.

TML: DG/VIP. Building 2601: two bedroom suite, private bath, kitchen (1); bedroom suites, private bath, kitchen (2). Building 2607: separate bedroom suites, private bath, kitchenettes (6). All have A/C, housekeeping service, washer/dryer, cribs. Rates: DV $15-$26 per unit. Building HP53, C-910-451-5262: SNCO bedroom, private bath (2). All categories can make reservations.

DG/VIP: Protocol Office, C-910-451-2523. O6+. Retirees and lower ranks Space-A.

TML Availability: Limited, year round.

CREDIT CARDS ACCEPTED: Visa, MasterCard and American Express.

Nearby Onslow Beach offers swimming, surfing and picnicking, and local marinas offer boat rentals. Two 18 hole golf courses are also nearby.

Locator-451-3074   Medical-451-4372   Police-451-2555

NORTH CAROLINA

Cape Hatteras Coast Guard
Recreational Quarters (NC09R1)
Lodging Office, P.O. Box 604
Buxton, NC 27920-0604

TELEPHONE NUMBER INFORMATION: Main installation numbers: C-919-995-6435.

Location: From the North. Follow Route 12 from Nags Head about 50 miles to Buxton. In Buxton, turn left at Red Drum Texaco (Old Lighthouse Rd). Road leads to Group Office and Recreation Quarters. From the South. Follow Route 70 East from Morehead City 45 miles to Cedar Island. Board Ocracoke Ferry (1.5 hr. ride w/toll charge). Follow Route 12 to Hatteras Island Ferry (no charge). On Hatteras proceed North Route 12 to Buxton. Turn right at Red Drum Texaco (Old Lighthouse Rd.) Road leads to Group Office and Recreation Quarters. *USMRA: Page 45 (P-3)*. NMC: Elizabeth City, 110 miles northwest.

Billeting Office: None. Reservations required with advance payment 30-90 days by mail. Summer months **C-919-995-6435.** Address: Cape Hatteras Recreational Quarters, Group Cape Hatteras, P.O. Box 604, Buxton, NC 27920-0604.

TML: Rooms that sleep 4 (6), rollaway available. Private bath, portable refrigerator, TV. Rates: $25-$32. Room 2 sleeps 6, private bath, kitchen area, TV. Rate: $37-$52. Room 8 (VIP suite) O4+, sleeps 6, private bath, kitchen area, TV. Rates: $55. Winter rates available. All categories can make reservations.

TML Availability: Limited. Book early.

Within walking distance of historic Cape Hatteras Lighthouse. Famous for fishing, a mecca for wind surfers - "the best surfing on the east coast". For those with less strenuous interest, peaceful, clean beaches, and solitude (off season).

Cherry Point Marine Corps Air Station (NC02R1)
Billeting Fund
Bldg 487, BOQ 1 Madison Dr.
Cherry Point MCAS, NC 28533-5079

TELEPHONE NUMBER INFORMATION: Main installation numbers: C-919-466-2811, D-312-582-1110.

Location: On NC-101 between New Bern and Morehead City, NC. US-70 south connects with NC-101 at Havelock, NC. *USMRA: Page 45 (M,N-4)*. NMC: Morehead City, 18 miles southeast.

Lodging Office: Building 487 (Officer) **C-919-466-5169**; building 3673 (enlisted ranks E1-E9). **C-919-466-3060**, FAX 919-466-5221, 24 hours daily. Check in facility, check out 1200 hours daily. Government civilian employee billeting.

TML: Guest House (DGQ). Building 487, O6+ leave or official duty. Commander, C-919-466-2848, D-312-582-2848. Four bedroom, private bath (1). One bedroom suites, private bath (4). Kitchenette, microwave, complete utensils, A/C, color TV, VCR, housekeeping service, washer/dryer. Rates: $30 (four bedroom); $20 suites. O6+ may make reservations, others Space-A.

NORTH CAROLINA
Cherry Point Marine Corps Air Station, continued

TML: BOQ. Buildings 487, 496, officers all ranks. Leave or official duty. C-919-466-5169. D-312-582-5169. Check out 1200 hours. Bedroom, private bath (47); separate bedroom suites, private bath (29). Refrigerator, A/C, color TV, housekeeping service, washer/dryer, ice vending. Older structure, renovated. Rates: single $14, suite $17. Duty, leave, retired can make reservations, others Space-A.

TML: BEQ. Building 3673. Enlisted, leave or official duty. 104 total spaces, E1-E5 two man rooms, private bath. SNCO bedroom, private bath (40). A/C, color TV (E5+/SNCO), housekeeping service, washer/dryer, ice vending. Older structure, renovated. Rates: $7 per person. TAD/PCS have priority, others Space-A.

DV/VIP: Commander's Office. C-919-466-5169, D-312-582-5169.

TML Availability: Limited, book early.

CREDIT CARDS ACCEPTED: Visa, MasterCard and American Express.

New Bern museums, shopping and dining, area historical attractions, the sailing center at Oriental, where you can catch Neuse River blue crabs, the nearby Outer Banks, and Cape Lookout National Seashore - don't miss them!

Locator 466-2109   Medical 466-4410   Police 466-3615

Elizabeth City Coast Guard Support Center (NC03R1)
Lodging Office, Bldg 7
Elizabeth City CGSC, NC 27909-5006

TELEPHONE NUMBER INFORMATION: Main installation numbers: C & FTS-919-338-3941.

Location: Take I-64 east to VA-104S to US-17 south to Elizabeth City, left on Halstead Blvd, 3 miles to main gate of Center. *USMRA: Page 45 (O-1)*. NMC: Elizabeth City, in the city.

Lodging Office: Building 7, **C-919-335-6548**, 0800-1630 hours daily. Reservations accepted up to two months in advance. Check in facility, check out 0800-1000 hours daily. No government civilian employee billeting.

TML: Mobile homes. 16A-F, all ranks, leave or official duty. Two bedroom, private bath (6). Kitchen, limited utensils, A/C, color TV, coin washer/dryer. Modern structure. Rates: $20 per night, sleeps 6. All categories may make reservations.

TML Availability: Good, Oct-Apr. Difficult, other times.

Visit Kitty Hawk and the Outer Banks. Read *Military RV, Camping & Rec Areas Around the World* for more information on this area.

Locator 335-6397   Medical 335-6460   Police 335-6398

NORTH CAROLINA

Fort Bragg (NC05R1)
Lodging Office
Bldg D-3601, Room 101
Fort Bragg, NC 28307-5000

TELEPHONE NUMBER INFORMATION: Main installation numbers: C-910-396-0011, D-312-236-0011.

Location: From I-95 exit to NC-24 west which runs through post as Bragg Blvd. From US-401 (Fayetteville Bypass) exit to All American Expressway, 5 miles to Fort. *USMRA: Page 45 (I,J-4)*. NMC: Fayetteville, 15 miles southeast.

Lodging Office: Building D-3601 (**Moon Hall**), room 101, off Bastogne Dr, **C-910-396-6334**, FAX 910-396-2025, DSN FAX 312-236-2025, 24 hours daily. Check in facility, check out 1100 hours daily. Government civilian employee billeting.

TML: Guest Houses. All ranks, leave or official duty. **Delmont House**, Bastogne Dr, building D-4215, C-910-436-2211, D-312-236-4496. **Normandy House**, Totten & Armistead St, building 1-4228, C-910-436-2250, D-312-236-1970. **Leal House**, Reilly Rd, behind NCO Club. C-910-436-3033, D-312-236-8770. Bedroom/private bath (111), separate bedroom suites, private bath (7). Kitchen (some), refrigerator, A/C, color TV in room & lounge, housekeeping service, cribs/cots, washer/dryer, ice vending, facilities for DAVs (**Delmont House**). Modern structures. Rates: E1-E6 $22, E6+ $28. PCS can make reservations, others Space-A.

TML: VOQ/VEQ. Buildings D-3601, D-3705, M-1939. All ranks, leave or official duty. C-910-396-7700. Bedroom, private bath (520); separate bedroom suites; private bath (27). Kitchen (suites), refrigerator, A/C, color TV, housekeeping service, washer/dryer, ice vending, facilities for DAVs. Modern structures. Rates: $19 all ranks, $21 suites. Maximum 2 per unit. Duty can make reservations, others Space-A.

TML: DV/VIP. Building 1-4425. Officer O7+, leave or official duty. C-910-396-2804. Three-bedroom suite, private bath (1). Kitchen, complete utensils, A/C, color TV, housekeeping service, cribs/cots, washer/dryer. Modern structure. Rate: $21. All categories can make reservations.

TML: Fisher House. Note: Appendix C has the definition of this facility. **C-919-432-1486.**

DV/VIP: Protocol Office. C-910-396-2804. O7+. Retirees Space-A.

TML Availability: Good, Sep-Apr. Difficult, other times.

CREDIT CARDS ACCEPTED: Visa, MasterCard and American Express.

The 82nd Airborne Division War Memorial Museum has over 3,000 objects on view. The Historic Fayetteville Foundation gives walking tours of historical sites, and Sandhills area golf resorts are world famous.

Locator 396-1461   Medical 432-0301   Police 396-0391

NORTH CAROLINA

Fort Fisher Air Force Recreation Area (NC13R1)
P.O. Box 380
Kure Beach, NC 28449-3321

TELEPHONE NUMBER INFORMATION: Main installation numbers: C-910-458-6549.

Location: From the north, take I-40 south to Wilmington. Follow Hwy 132 south to Hwy 421 to Kure Beach. From I-95 travelling north from SC, take Hwy 75/76 into Wilmington, then south on Hwy 421 to Kure Beach. *USMRA: Page 45 (L-6)*. NMC: Wilmington NC.

Lodging Office: Building 118, Reception Center. **C-910-458-6549**, 0800 to 1900 daily. Check in reception center, 1600 to 1900 daily. Check out 1100. Late check outs call reservations. Rooms may not be ready before 1600, but use of resort facilities allowed until check in.

TML: One of the Air Force's beachside resorts. Operated by Seymour Johnson Air Force Base MWRSS Division, year round. All ranks. Total units - 141. Lodge rooms (21), lodge suites, (16) common bath; executive rooms (6), executive suites, private bath (2); four bedroom cottages, private bath (4); three bedroom cottages, private bath (22); mobile homes, private bath (6). A/C in rooms, suites, cottages, some kitchenettes, refrigerators, housekeeping service, CATV, complete utensils, linens, washer/dryer (cottages only), coin washer/dryer other facilities. Convenience store, gift and beach shop, restaurant, basketball and tennis courts, dock, boat ramp, petting zoo. Access to beach, sailing, boating, fishing, swimming. Bicycle, pontoon boat and sail boat rentals. Pets allowed in cottages ($25 fee). Pets must be on leash, kennel service available $5/night.

Rates: Winter (1 November-31 March), summer (1 April-31 October). Cottages (sleeps 6-12) $40-$80/day, $55-$95/weekend, $230-$500 standard week, $280-550 premium week; executive suite (sleeps 4) $30-$45/day, $40-$55/weekend, $175-$275 standard week, $200-$300 premium week; executive room (sleeps 2), $20-$35/day, $30-$45/weekend, $125-$200 standard week, $150-$225 premium week. Lodge suite (sleeps 4-6) $25-$40/day, $35-$50 weekend, $125-$225 standard week, $150-$250 premium week; lodge rooms (sleep 2) $15-$20/day, $20-25/weekend, $100-$125/standard week, $125-$150/premium week. Additional persons in all units charged extra. Weekdays are Sun through Thurs, weekends are Fri, Sat, and nights prior to a holiday. Standard weeks are Sat to Sat, Mon to Mon or Wed to Wed. Premium weeks are Fri to Fri or Sun to Sun. Rollaway beds available (linens and towels furnished, $5 per person).

Reservations: All categories. Active duty Air Force 90 days ahead. All other active duty 85 days ahead. Retirees 75 days ahead. All others, 60 days ahead. Confirmed with Visa, MasterCard, American Express, Seymour Johnson AFB Club Card, or advance payment. Limits to number of rooms reserved during Memorial Day to Labor Day. Cancellations 15 days prior, or one night fee.

TML Availability: Very good. Best, 1 November-31 March.

CREDIT CARDS ACCEPTED: Visa, MasterCard, Seymour Johnson AFB Club Card and American Express.

Aside from all the recreational activities at this resort, the North Carolina Aquarium at Fort Fisher, the Fort Fisher State Historic Site Civil War Museum, and USS NC Battleship Memorial, Orton and Poplar Grove Plantations are worth visiting.

NORTH CAROLINA

New River Marine Corps Air Station (NC06R1)
Lodging Office
Bldg 705, Flounder Road
Jacksonville, NC 28545-5079

TELEPHONE NUMBER INFORMATION: Main installation numbers: C-910-451-1113, D-312-484-1113.

Location: Off US-17, 2 miles south of Jacksonville. Clearly marked. *USMRA: Page 45 (L,M-5).* NMC: Jacksonville, 2 miles northeast.

Lodging Office: Building 705, Flounder Road. **C-910-451-6621/6903,** FAX 910-455-0997, 24 hours. Check in at facility, check out 1200 hours daily. Government civilian employee billeting.

TML: BOQ. Building 705. Officers, all ranks; E6+, leave or official duty. Bedroom, private bath (50). Refrigerator, A/C, VCR, color TV in room & lounge, housekeeping service, cribs/cots $2, essentials, washer/dryer, food/ice vending, coffee makers, microwave, telephones. Modern structure, remodeled. Rates leave status: $8 single room, $12 two room suite, $2 each additional person. Maximum 4 persons per unit. Duty can make reservations, others Space-A.

TML Availability: Difficult. Best Sep-Mar.

CREDIT CARDS ACCEPTED: American Express and Diners.

Some area interests include Fort Macon, Hammocks Beach, Hanging Rock, Jones Lake, and Cape Hatteras National Seashore. North Carolina National forests and local festivals are all drawing cards for visitors.

Locator-451-6568   Medical-451-6532   Police-451-6111

Pope Air Force Base (NC01R1)
Carolina Inn
23 SVS/SVML
302 Ethridge St.
Pope AFB, NC 28308-2310

TELEPHONE NUMBER INFORMATION: Main installation numbers: C-910-394-0001, D-312-486-1110.

Location: Take I-95, exit to NC-87/24 W. Signs point the direction to AFB and Ft Bragg. *USMRA: Page 45 (J-4).* NMC: Fayetteville, 12 miles southeast.

Lodging Office: Carolina Inn, 302 Ethridge St, **C-910-394-4131,** D-312-486-4131, FAX 910-394-2572, DSN FAX 312-486-2572, 24 hours daily. Check in billeting, check out 1200 hours daily. Government civilian employee billeting with reservations.

TML: VOQ. Buildings 229-247, all ranks, leave or official duty. Bedroom, private bath (96); separate bedroom, private bath (12); eight bedroom units (8). Community kitchen, refrigerator, A/C, color TV,

NORTH CAROLINA
Pope Air Force Base, continued

housekeeping service, cribs, washer/dryer, ice vending. Older structure. Rates: $8. TDY can make reservations, others Space-A.

TML: VAQ. Building 287, enlisted all ranks, leave or official duty. Bedroom, shared bath (68); separate bedroom, private bath (4). Refrigerator, A/C, color TV, housekeeping service, washer/dryer, ice vending. Older structure, renovated '91. Rates: $7. TDY can make reservations, others Space-A.

TML: DV/VIP. Building 295, officer O6+, leave or official duty. C-910-394-4739. Bedroom, private bath (4). Kitchen, utensils, A/C, color TV, housekeeping service, washer/dryer, ice vending. Older structure. Rates: $14 per person. All categories can make reservations.

TML: TLF. Building 229, all ranks, PCS in/out. Bedroom, private bath (8), kitchenette, utensils, A/C, color TV, housekeeping service, washer/dryer. Rates: E1-E2 & O1, $13; E3-E6, $20; E7+, $24. PCS can make reservations, all others Space-A.

DV/VIP: Protocol Office. 259 Maynard St, Suite C, C 910-394-2374. O6+. Retirees Space-A.

TML Availability: Good, winter. Difficult, other times.

CREDIT CARDS ACCEPTED: Visa, MasterCard and American Express.

Near Goldsboro, Cliffs of the Neuse River, picnicking, refreshments, fishing swimming and rental rowboats, museum. Also visit historic Fort Macon, the Cape Hatteras National Seashore, and Fayetteville.

Locator 394-4822   **Medical 394-2232**   **Police 394-2800**

Seymour Johnson Air Force Base (NC11R1)
Southern Pines Inn
4 SVS/SVML
1235 Wright Avenue
Seymour Johnson AFB, NC 27531-5000

TELEPHONE NUMBER INFORMATION: Main installation numbers: C-919-736-5400, D-312-488-1110.

Location: From US-70 in Goldsboro take Seymour Johnson exit onto Berkeley Blvd to main gate. Clearly marked. *USMRA: Page 45 (L-3).* NMC: Raleigh, 50 miles northwest.

Lodging Office: Southern Pines Inn. ATTN: 4 SVS/SVML. Building 3804, 1235 Wright Ave. C-919-736-6705, D-312-488-6705, FAX 919-736-5643, 24 hours daily. Check in billeting 1500, check out 1200 daily. Government civilian employee billeting VOQ.

TML: TLF. Building 3802. All ranks. Leave or official duty. Bedroom, private bath (3); separate bedrooms, private bath (22); two bedroom, private bath (2). Kitchen, limited utensils, A/C, color TV, housekeeping service, washer/dryer, ice vending. Older structure. Rates: (For PCS) E1-E2 & O1, $13; E3-E6, $18; E7+, $24; all Space-A $24 per unit. Maximum based on size of unit. Duty can make reservations, others Space-A. No pets.

NORTH CAROLINA
Seymour Johnson Air Force Base, continued

TML: VOQ. Building 3804. Officers all ranks, leave or official duty. Bedroom, private baths (39). A/C, color TV, conference room, housekeeping service, washer/dryer, ice vending. Modern structure, renovated. Rates: $7 per person. Maximum 2 persons. Duty can make reservations, others Space-A. No pets.

TML: VAQ. Building 3803. Enlisted all ranks. Leave or official duty. Bedroom, private and semi-private baths (21); SNCO suite, private bath (5); bedroom, private bath (3). Chief suite, private bath (1). Color TV, housekeeping service, washer/dryer, ice vending. Modern structure. Rates: $6 per person, SNCO, Chief suites $12. Max 2 persons. Duty can make reservations, others Space-A. No pets.

TML: DV/VIP. Building 3804. Officer O6+. Leave or official duty. Separate bedrooms suites, private bath (2). Kitchen, color TV, housekeeping service, washer/dryer. Older structure. Rates: $12 per person. Duty can make reservations, others Space-A. Call protocol 919-736-6483.

TML Availability: Good, Nov-Apr. Difficult, other times.

CREDIT CARDS ACCEPTED: Visa, MasterCard and American Express.

Nearby Ashville is good for rafting, hiking and skiing, while Carowinds, in Charlotte, is a large family entertainment center. Ashboro's zoological park, and Raleigh, the state capital, are well worth visits.

Locator 736-5584   **Medical 736-5577**   **Police 736-6413**

180 - Temporary Military Lodging Around the World

NORTH DAKOTA

Camp Gilbert C. Grafton (ND03R3)
A.T.S. Supply Office
Route 5, Box 278A
Devils Lake, ND 58301-9235

TELEPHONE NUMBER INFORMATION: Main installation numbers: C-701-662-0200, D-312-344-5226.

Location: On US-57 and 20, 5 miles south of Devils Lake. *USMRA: Page 83 (G-3)*. NMC: Devils Lake, 5 miles north.

Lodging Office: ATTN: Billeting, Camp Grafton, Route 5, Box 278A, Devils Lake, ND 58301-9235, **C-701-662-0239**, D-312-344-5226, EXT 239, FAX 701-662-04448, 0700 to 1600 hours daily. After hours use phone in information center, building 6010. Check in at billeting, check out 1000 hours. Late checkout pays extra day.

TML: BOQ/BEQ. Building 6010, all ranks, leave or official duty, C-701-662-2184. Bedroom, 2 beds, shared bath (80); separate bedroom, 1 bed, shared bath (30). Refrigerator (40), kitchenette (19), limited utensils, color TV (59), housekeeping service, washer/dryer in separate building, food vending. Modern structure, renovated. Rates: adult $6, child/infant $4 per unit. Maximum charge $20. Maximum per unit 6 persons. Reservations required for National Guard and reservists on orders, others Space-A. No pets.

TML: Guesthouse. Double wide trailers, 2 bedrooms, private baths (19). Kitchen, utensils, color TV, housekeeping service, washer/dryer. Rates: sponsor $6, family members $6 each. $20/day maximum. Reservations required for National Guard and reservists on orders, others Space-A. No pets.

TML: DV/VIP. Houses, 2 bedrooms, private bath (2), fully equipped kitchen, A/C, housekeeping service, color TV. Rates: sponsor $6, family members $6 each; $20/day maximum. Reservations required for National Guard and reservists on orders, others Space-A. No pets.

TML Availability: Good. Best Sept. to May, difficult May to Sept.

This area is known for its fishing, and at certain times of the year the skies are black with migrating ducks and geese. Only 90 miles from the Canadian border, an outdoor paradise.

Locator 662-0200   Medical 662-5323   Police 662-5323

Grand Forks Air Force Base (ND04R3)
ATTN: 319 SVS/SVML
Lodging Office, Warrior Inn (Bldg 117)
Grand Forks AFB, ND 58205-0001

TELEPHONE NUMBER INFORMATION: Main installation numbers: C-701-747-3000, D-312-362-3000.

Location: From I-29 take US-2 west exit for 14 miles to Grand Forks, County Rd B-3 (Emerado/Air Base) 1 mile to AFB. *USMRA: Page 83 (I-3)*. NMC: Grand Forks, 15 miles east.

NORTH DAKOTA
Grand Forks Air Force Base, continued

Lodging Office: Warrior Inn, Building 117, Holzapple & 6th Ave, **C-701-747-3070/6188**, FAX 701-747-3069, DSN FAX 312-362-3069, 24 hours daily. Check in 1400, check out 1200 hours daily. Government civilian employee lodging.

TML: TLF. Across street from billeting, all ranks, leave or official duty. Efficiency apartments, private bath (40). Kitchen, limited utensils, A/C, color TV, housekeeping service, washer/dryer, ice vending. Modern structure. Rates: $20 per unit. PCS in/out reservations required. Duty can make reservations, others Space-A.

TML: VOQ. Building 117, officers all ranks, leave or official duty. Two bedroom suites, private bath (12); bedroom, semi-private bath (6). Refrigerator, A/C, color TV, housekeeping service, washer/dryer, ice vending. Rates: $8 per person. PCS in/out reservations required, duty can make reservations, others Space-A.

TML: VAQ. Building 117, enlisted all ranks, leave or official duty. Bedroom, semi-private bath (12); two bedroom suites, private bath (10). Refrigerator, color TV, housekeeping service, washer/dryer, ice. Rates: $8 per person. PCS in/out reservations required. Duty can make reservations, others Space-A.

TML: DV/VIP. Building 132, officers O6+, leave or official duty. Four bedroom house, private bath, kitchen, living room, dining room, washer/dryer (1). Rates: $14 per person. For reservations contact Protocol (see below).

TML: DV/VIP. Building 117, enlisted E8-E9, leave or official duty. Two bedroom suites, private bath (2). Living room, refrigerator, color TV, A/C, housekeeping service, washer/dryer, ice vending. Rates: $14 per person. For reservations contact Protocol.

DV/VIP: 319 AD Protocol Office, building 305, C-701-747-4513, E9. C-312-362-5055, O6+. Retirees and lower ranks Space-A.

TML Availability: Good, winter. Difficult, spring and summer.

CREDIT CARDS ACCEPTED: Visa, MasterCard and American Express.

Locator 747-3344   Medical 747-5600   Police 747-5351

Minot Air Force Base (ND02R3)
Sakakawea Inn
5 SVS/SVML
201 Summit Dr., Unit 5
Minot AFB, ND 58705-5049

TELEPHONE NUMBER INFORMATION: Main installation numbers: C-701-723-1110, D-312-453-1110.

Location: On US-83, north of Minot. *USMRA: Page 83 (D-2).* NMC: Minot, 12 miles south.

Lodging Office: Sakakawea Inn. 201 Summit Drive, **C-701-723-3108**, D-312-453-2184, FAX 701-723-1844, DSN FAX 312-453-1844, 24 hours daily. Check in 1400, check out 1200 hours.

NORTH DAKOTA
Minot Air Force Base, continued

TML: TLF. Buildings 221, 223, 227, 229, all ranks, leave or official duty, C-701-723-2184. Separate bedroom apartments, private bath (39). Kitchen, complete utensils, A/C, microwave, color TV, housekeeping, washer/dryer, ice vending. All non-smoking units available. One unit meeting all ADA (Americans with Disabilities Act) requirements. Modern structure. Rates: $23 per unit. Space-A reservations accepted; confirmation based on availability.

TML: VOQ. Building 16, officers all ranks, leave or official duty, C-701-723-2184. Bedrooms, private and semi-private bath (40). Refrigerator and/or complete kitchen, A/C, microwave, color TV, VCR, housekeeping, washer/dryer, ice vending, all non-smoking rooms. Modern structure. Rates: $8-$14 per person. Space-A reservations accepted, confirmation based on availability.

TML: VAQ. Building 14, enlisted all ranks, leave or official duty, C-701-723-2184. Bedroom, private and semi-private bath (32). Refrigerator and/or complete kitchen, A/C, microwave, color TV, housekeeping, washer/dryer, ice vending, all non-smoking rooms. Chief suites. Modern structure. Rates: $8-$14 per person. Space-A reservations accepted, confirmation based on availability.

TML: DVQ. Building 12 Summit Dr (Rough Rider Suite & Magic City Suite), officers O6+, C-701-723-2184. Suites, private bath (5,), bedroom suite w/office (3). Kitchen, A/C, microwave, color TV, VCR, housekeeping, washer/dryer. Rates: $13 per person. Space-A reservations accepted, confirmation based on availability.

DV/VIP: Protocol Office, building 167, 201 Summit Dr. C-701-723-3474, D-312-453-3474. Rates: $10-$25.

TML Availability: Generally good. Difficult Jul and Oct.

CREDIT CARDS ACCEPTED: Visa, MasterCard and American Express.

Swimming pools, tennis courts, city zoo are in Roosevelt Park. Visit General Custer's command post at Fort Lincoln State Park, and the International Peace Garden on the Manitoba/North Dakota border. Lake fishing, abundant hunting for deer and fowl.

Locator 723-1841   **Medical 723-3474**   **Police 723-3096**

OHIO

Camp Perry Clubhouse (OH06R2)
Building 600
Port Clinton, OH 43452-9578

TELEPHONE NUMBER INFORMATION: Main installation numbers: C-419-635-4114, D-312-346-4114.

LOCATION: On post. On OH-2, 5 mi W of Port Clinton. Check in 1400-2200. *USMRA: Page 67 (D-3)*. NMC: Sandusky, 25 mi SE.

RESERVATIONS: Preferred, up to 1 year in advance, Address: Clubhouse Manager, Bldg 600, Camp Perry Military Training Site, Port Clinton, OH 43452-9578. **C-419-635-4114**, D-312-346-4114. Open to the public. Military discount.

TML: Cottages, Buildings 501-527, 1 & 2 bedroom, private bath, A/C (27), sofa-bed, telephone upon request, utensils, dishes, toaster, coffeepot, vending,. Rates: $27-$80 daily.

TML: Motel, buildings 120, 150, 160, 170, 529, 530, units w/kitchen, one double bed, sofa bed, private bath, A/C (20), utensils, dishes, toaster, coffeepot, Rates: $27-$40 daily. Motel units w/o kitchen, private bath, A/C (207) Rates: $16-$35 daily. Vending, coin-op laundry.

Note: Daily housekeeping service is not provided. Cleaning and trash removal is a personal responsibility. Cleaning materials provided upon request. Linen exchange: towels exchange daily, Bed linens exchange bi-weekly. No pets allowed.

TML Availability: Good, Jan-Mar. Difficult other times.

CREDIT CARDS ACCEPTED: Visa, MasterCard and American Express.

Situated along Lake Erie approx 30 mi from the Canadian border. Limited support facilities available on post. Fishing/license, swimming, fishing pier, grills, picnic area.

Locator 635-4114   Medical 9-911   Police 9-911

Defense Construction Supply Center(OH05R2)
Bldg. 1/1, 2nd floor
3990 E. Broad St.
Columbus, OH 43216-5000

TELEPHONE NUMBER INFORMATION: Main installation numbers C-614-692-3131, D-312-850-3131.

Location: From I-270 (Beltway) take exit 39 to Broad Street W, main gate at 4990 Broad Street. *USMRA: Page 67 (D-6)*, NMC: Columbus, in city limits.

Lodging Office: Bldg. 1/1, 3990 E. Broad Street. **C-614-692-4758**, 312-850-4758, FAX 614-692-3656, DSN FAX 312-850-3656, 0730-1600 Mon-Fri. Check in billeting 1400, check out 1100 hours daily.

Kilauea Military Camp AFRC Hawaii Volcanoes National Park. Photo by Major & Mrs. Robert S. Furrer, USAF (Ret.).

Living room of a cabin at Kilauea Military Camp AFRC Hawaii Volcanoes National Park. Photo by Major & Mrs. Robert S. Furrer, USAF (Ret.).

Osprey Inn I, Bachelor Officers Quarters, Marine Corps Recruit Depot, Parris Island, South Carolina. Photo courtesy of Bachelor Officers Quarters.

Osprey Inn II, Bachelor Enlisted Quarters, Marine Corps Recruit Depot, Parris Island, South Carolina. Photo courtesy of Bachelor Enlisted Quarters.

OHIO
Defense Construction Supply Center, continued

TML: TLQ. Building 201, C-614-692-4758, bedroom, private bath (6); suite, private bath (2); apartment (2), all have kitchenette, refrigerator, utensils, color TV, housekeeping service, washer/dryer. Reservations are required. Rates: $17-$35.

DV/VIP: Protocol, C-614-692-2167, D-312-850-2167, O6+. Retirees and lower ranks Space-A. Rates: PCS $20, all others $30.

Locator 692-3131   **Medical 692-2227**   **Police 692-3722**

Wright-Patterson Air Force Base (OH01R2)
88 SPTG/SVML
2439 Schlatter Drive
Wright-Patterson AFB, OH 45433-5519

TELEPHONE NUMBER INFORMATION: Main installation numbers: C-513-257-1110, D-312-787-1110.

Location: South of I-70, off I-675 at Fairborn. Also, access from OH-4, AFB clearly marked. *USMRA: Page 67 (B-7).* NMC: Dayton, 10 miles northwest.

Lodging Office: Building 825, 2439 Schlatter Dr, **C-513-257-3451**, D-312-787-3451, FAX 513-257-2787, DSN FAX 312-787-2787, 24 hours daily. Check in billeting, check out 1200 hours daily. Government civilian employee billeting.

TML: TLQ. Building 825, all ranks, leave or official duty, C-513-257-3810. Bedroom, bath (40) Kitchen, complete utensils, microwaves, A/C, color TV, housekeeping service, cribs, washer/dryer, ice vending. Modern structure, renovated. Rates: $17 per unit. Sleeps 5. Duty can make reservations, others Space-A.

TML: VOQ. Building 825, all ranks, leave or official duty. Bedroom, private bath (108); Bedroom, semi-private bath (492). Refrigerator, microwave, beverage, snacks, microwavable dinners, coffee maker, A/C, color TV, housekeeping service, washer/dryer, ice vending. FAX service available at no charge for VOQ/VAQ quests. Rates: $8 per person. Maximum $16 per family. Maximum 3 per room. Duty can make reservations, others Space-A.

TML: DV/VIP. Buildings 825/826, call about eligibility, C-513-257-3810. Leave or official duty. Two bedroom suites, private bath (22), Top three suites, private bath (11). Refrigerator, A/C, color TV, housekeeping service, cribs/cots, washer/dryer, ice vending, microwaves, microwave dinners, beverage, snacks. Rates: $14 per person. Maximum 5 per suite. Duty can make reservations.

TML: Hope Hotel and Conference Center, the Air Force's first private sector financed hotel. Building 823, all ranks, leave or official duty. DoD Civilian lodging. One and two bed rooms (doubles), private bath (260). A/C, CATV, ice vending, irons and boards available, handicapped accessible. Seven full service conference rooms available, catering available from on site restaurant. Call for rates. Official duty reservations call billeting at **C-513-257-3810**, D-312-787-3810. Others, **C-513-257-1285**, D-213-787-1285. Major credit cards accepted.

TML: Fisher House. Note: Appendix C has the definition of this facility. **C-513-257-4239.**

OHIO
Wright-Patterson Air Force Base, continued

DV/VIP: Protocol, 645 ABW/CCP, building 10, C-513-257-3110, O7/GS-16+. Retirees and lower ranks Space-A.

TML Availability: Good, late Nov, early Jan. Difficult other times.

The Air Force museum on base, and the city of Dayton with its art and natural history museums, local arts and the Nutter Sports Center all make this area an interesting place to visit.

Locator 257-3231 **Medical 257-2968** **Police 257-6841**

Too Late To Copy
Youngstown Air Reserve Base, 910 AW, 3976 King Graves Road, Vienna, OH 44473-0910. C-216-392-1268.

OKLAHOMA

Altus Air Force Base (OK02R3)
Red River Inn Lodging
97 SVS/SVML
209 South 6th Street
Altus AFB, OK 73523-5146

TELEPHONE NUMBER INFORMATION: Main installation numbers: C-405-481/482-8100, D-312-866-1110.

Location: Off US-62 south of I-40 and west of I-44. From US-62 traveling west from Lawton, turn right at 1st traffic light in Altus and follow road to main gate northeast of Falcon Rd. *USMRA: Page 84 (E-5).* NMC: Lawton, 56 miles east.

Lodging Office: Building 82, **C-405-481-7356**, D-312-866-7356, FAX 405-481-5704, DSN FAX 312-866-5704, 24 hours daily. Check in billeting, check out 1400 hours daily, except TLF - 1200 hours daily. Government civilian employee billeting.

TML: VOQ. Buildings 81-85, officers all ranks. Bedroom, private bath (96); separate bedrooms, private bath (30). Kitchen, A/C, color TV, housekeeping service, washer/dryer. Modern structure, hotel type lodging. Rates: $6 per person. Duty can make reservations, others Space-A.

TML: VAQ. Building 82, enlisted all ranks. Bedroom, common bath (198). A/C, color TV in room & lounge, housekeeping service. Modern structure. Rates: $5 per person. Duty can make reservations, others Space-A.

TML: DV/VIP. Building 84, officer O4+, leave or official duty. Separate bedrooms private bath (6). Kitchen, A/C, color TV, housekeeping service, washer/dryer. Modern structure, hotel type lodging. Rates: $10 per person. Duty can make reservations, others Space-A.

DV/VIP: Wing EXO, building 1, C-405-481-7044, O6+. Retirees & lower ranks Space-A.

TML Availability: Good, Dec. Difficult, other times.

CREDIT CARDS ACCEPTED: American Express.

Visit the Museum of the Western Prairie for the saga of the area's wild west roots. Quartz Mountain State Park hosts the county fairs, rodeos and roundups that are part of life here.

Locator 481-7250   Medical 481-5213   Police 481-7444

Camp Gruber Training Site (OK03R3)
ATTN: OKCG-L-H
P.O. Box 29
Braggs, OK 74423-0029

TELEPHONE NUMBER INFORMATION: Main installation numbers: C-918-487-6001, D-312-487-6057.

OKLAHOMA
Camp Gruber, continued

Location: Exit I-40 at Webber Falls (exit 287), take Hwy 64 to Gore, OK, take state Hwy 10 to Braggs. First entrance to camp after passing through Braggs. USMRA: Page 84 (I-4). NMC: Muskogee, 20 mi northwest.

Lodging Office: Building 155, 4th St & Anzio Drive. **C-918-487-6067**, FAX 918-487-6009, 0730-1600. Check in, check out 1000. Late arrivals OK w/reservation.

TML: BOQ/BEQ. All ranks, leave or official duty. Two bedroom mobile home (11). Kitchen, refrigerator, A/C, color TV, housekeeping service. Rates: Active duty $8; all others (includes AD on leave) $12. No pets.

TML: BOQ/BEQ. E9, WO3, O3+, leave or official duty. Three bedroom mobile home (1); two bedroom mobile home (6). Kitchen, refrigerator, microwave, A/C, color TV, housekeeping service. Rates: Active duty $8; all others (includes AD on leave) $12. No pets.

TML: BOQ/BEQ. Building 232. E9, WO3, O3+, leave or official duty. Refrigerator, microwave, A/C, color TV, housekeeping service. Rates: Active duty $7; all others (includes AD on leave) $10. No pets.

TML: BOQ/BEQ. Buildings 226, 227, 228. All ranks, leave or official duty. Semi-private bedroom, shared bath (30). Refrigerator, microwave, color TV, housekeeping service. Rates: Active duty $7; all others (includes AD on leave) $10. No pets.

DV/VIP: General officer. Three bedroom, double-wide mobile home. Refrigerator, microwave, A/C, color TV, housekeeping service. Rates: Active Duty $10; all others (includes AD on leave) $15. No pets.

TML: RV Park. All ranks. Modern sites, full hookups (12). Rates: $7 per day. *(For more info consult Military Living's Military Camping & Rec Areas Around the World).*

TML Availability: Best, Sep-Apr. Difficult, May-Aug.

Located in the heart of Green Country, next to Greenleaf Lake, Arkansas River, twenty minutes from lake Tenkiller, twenty minutes from lake Fort Gibson.

Locator 487-6001   Security 487-6021

Fort Sill (OK01R3)
ATTN; ATZR-EHB
P.O. Box 33334
Fort Sill, OK 73503

TELEPHONE NUMBER INFORMATION: Main installation numbers: C-405-442-8111, D-312-639-7090.

Location: From I-44 at Lawton take US-62/277, 4 miles northwest to post. Clearly marked. *USMRA: Page 84 (E,F-5)*. NMC: Lawton, adjacent to city.

Lodging Office: Building 5676, Fergusson Rd, **C-405-442-5007/442-5000**, D-312-639-5000, FAX 405-442-6908, 24 hours daily. Check in billeting, check out 1200 hours daily. Government civilian employee billeting DV/VOQ.

190 - Temporary Military Lodging Around the World

OKLAHOMA
Fort Sill, continued

TML: Guest House. Office in building 5690, Geronimo Rd, C-405-442-3214, D-312-639-3214, 24 hours daily. Check in building 5690, all ranks, leave or official duty. Rooms (75). Refrigerator, microwave, kitchen, A/C, color TV in room & lounge, housekeeping service, cribs/cots, washer/dryer, ice vending. Rates: E1-E4, $16 per room; E5- E6, W1, & O1, $21.50 per room; E7-E9, WO2-WO4, O2-O3, $27 per room. O4-O5, guests, $36 per room. PCS can make reservations, others Space-A.

TML: BOQ/BEQ. E7+. Official duty only, reservations not taken - waiting list maintained. Must be signed into unit to get on waiting list. Spaces in BOQ (97); spaces in BEQ (8). Modern structure, renovated. Rates: no charge for room; maid fee $3/$4 per day. Maximum 1 per room. Dependents not authorized.

TML: VOQ/VEQ. Both take overflow from Guest House. All ranks, official duty only. Spaces in VOQ (690); spaces in VEQ (130) and VIP suites (25). Modern structure, renovated. Rates: sponsor $16, adult $7; VIP suites $20.50-$25. No children. Billeting recommends that children stay in guest house with spouse. Duty can make reservations, others Space-A.

TML: DVQ. Building 460. Officer O6/GS-15+, leave or official duty, C-405-442-5511. Kitchen, complete utensils. Modern structure, renovated. Rates: sponsor $25 at Comanche House (building 460); all other DVQs $20.50-$25, additional adult $7. Duty can make reservations, others Space-A.

DV/VIP: Protocol Office, building 460, C-405-442-4825, O6/GS-15+. Retirees Space-A.

TML Availability: Fairly good, fall, winter, spring. Difficult, summer.

CREDIT CARDS ACCEPTED: Visa, MasterCard, American Express and Discover.

Don't miss the original stone buildings constructed by the "Buffalo Soldiers" of the 10th Calvary, the Guardhouse where Geronimo was confined, the large museum on post, and the Museum of the Great Plains in Lawton.

Locator 442-3924   Medical 458-2500   Police 442-2101

McAlester Army Ammunition Plant (OK09R3)
ATTN: SMCMC-DEH
McAlester, OK 74501-5000

TELEPHONE NUMBER INFORMATION: Main installation numbers: C-918-421-2642, D-312-956-6642.

Location: Take I-244 west (loops around Tulsa). Exit toward Broken Arrow, and continue on I-244 to exit 75 south to Henryetta. Follow 75 south to I-40 (Indian Nation Turnpike). South on turnpike to 2nd exit to McAlester on Hwy 69 south. Gate 2 miles south on right hand off ramp. *USMRA: Page 84 (I-5).* NMC: Tulsa 95 mi. NW.

Lodging Office: Commander, MCAAP, ATTN: SMCMC-DEH. **C-918-421-2480,** D-312-956-6480, FAX 918-421-2489, DSN FAX 312-956-6489, 0630-1700 M-Th. After hours, weekends, Dispatch, building 31, C-918-421-2642. Check in billeting or Dispatch by 1300, check out 1200 hours. Call ahead if arriving other than duty hours. Government civilian employee billeting.

OKLAHOMA
McAlester Army Ammunition Plant, continued

TML: BOQ/BEQ. Building 2. All ranks, leave or official duty. BOQ: separate bedroom, queen bed, private bath (9). BEQ: bedroom, twin beds, private bath (9). A/C, refrigerator, microwave (BOQ), utensils, CATV, housekeeping service, washer/dryer, essentials (BOQ). Modern structure, recently renovated. Rates: BOQ $10 per unit (TDY); BEQ $8 (TDY). Duty, Reservists and National guard on orders can make reservations, others Space-A. No pets.

TML: VOQ. Buildings 83, 84. Officers, all ranks, leave or official duty. Bedroom, full bed, private bath (2). A/C, refrigerator, microwave, utensils, CATV, housekeeping service, washer/dryer, essentials. Modern structure, renovated. Rates: $10 TDY. Duty, Reservists and National guard on orders can make reservations, others Space-A. No pets.

DV/VIP: Apartment, two bedroom (2). Rates: $10 per night, additional occupant charge. Also used for PCS, retirees and Space-A.

TML Availability: Good. Best Sept-Feb, difficult Mar-Aug.

CREDIT CARDS ACCEPTED: American Express.

Fishing on post or at Lake Eufaula (700 acre lake!) 15 miles away has a marina and amusement park. Rec Services has boats. A small commissary/PX, the Lake view O'Club, bowling and swimming are available on post.

Locator 421-2642   **Medical 2911**   **Police 2911**

Tinker Air Force Base (OK04R3)
Indian Hills Inn
ATTN: 72 SPTG/SVML
Tinker AFB, OK 73145-5000

TELEPHONE NUMBER INFORMATION: Main installation numbers: C-405-732-7321, D-312-884-1110.

Location: Southeast Oklahoma City, off I-40. Use gate 1 off Air Depot Blvd. Clearly marked. *USMRA: Page 84 (G-4)*. NMC: Oklahoma City, 12 miles northwest.

Lodging Office: Indian Hills Inn. 4002 Mitchell Street, **C-405-734-2822**, FAX 405-734-7426, 24 hours daily. Check in billeting, check out 1100 hours daily for DV, VOQ, VAQ, and TLQ. Government civilian employee billeting.

TML: TLF. Buildings 5824, 5826, 5828, 5830, 5832, all ranks, leave or official duty. Rooms (39). Refrigerator, A/C, color TV, housekeeping service, washer/dryer. Rates: $21 per unit. Duty can make reservations, others Space-A.

TML: VOQ. Buildings 5604, 5605, 5606, officers, all ranks, leave or official duty. Rooms, private and semi-private baths (100). Refrigerator, A/C, color/cable TV, VCR, housekeeping service, washer/dryer. Rates: $8 per person. Duty can make reservations, others Space-A.

TML: VAQ. Building 5915, enlisted, leave or official duty. Rooms, private and semi-private (45). Refrigerator, A/C, color/cable TV, VCR housekeeping service, washer/dryer. Rates: $8 per person. Duty can make reservations, others Space-A.

OKLAHOMA
Tinker Air Force Base, continued

DV/VIP: OC-ALC/CCP, building 3001, C-405-734-5511, O6/GS-15+. Retirees and lower ranks Space-A.

TML Availability: Good all year.

CREDIT CARDS ACCEPTED: Visa, MasterCard and American Express.

In Oklahoma City visit Remington Park, the National Cowboy Hall of Fame and Western Heritage Center, the city Zoo, tour the mansions of Heritage Hills. Five municipal golf courses, four lakes, and many sports events are available.

Locator 734-2456   Medical 734-8249   Police 734-2151

Vance Air Force Base (OK05R3)
71 FTW/NW-SL
426 Goad St., Suite 131
Vance AFB, OK 73705-5116

TELEPHONE NUMBER INFORMATION: Main installation numbers: C-405-237-2121, D-312-940-7110.

Location: Off US-81 south of Enid. Clearly marked. *USMRA: Page 84 (F-3)*. NMC: Oklahoma City, 90 miles southeast.

Lodging Office: Building 714, Goad St, **C-405-249-7358,** D-312-940-7358, FAX 405-249-6278, 24 hours daily. Check in billeting, check out 1200 hours daily. Government civilian employee billeting.

TML: TLF. Building 790, all ranks, leave or official duty. Separate bedrooms, private bath (10). Kitchen, utensils, A/C, color TV, housekeeping service, cribs, washer/dryer, ice vending. Rates: E6, $14 per unit; E7+, $18 per unit. Duty can make reservations, others Space-A.

TML: VOQ/TAQ. Buildings 713, 714, all ranks, leave or official duty. Bedroom, private bath (48); separate bedroom suite, private bath (DV/VIP) (1); two bedroom suites, private bath (DV/VIP) (2). Kitchen, microwave, A/C, color TV in room & lounge, housekeeping service, washer/dryer, ice vending, facilities for DAV's. Modern structure. Rates: $6 per person ($10 DV/VIP). Maximum $12 per family ($30 DV/VIP). Duty can make reservations, others Space-A.

DV/VIP: Retirees Space-A, duty reservations as above.

TML Availability: Difficult. Best, Dec, Jan.

CREDIT CARDS ACCEPTED: Diners.

In Enid visit Government Springs Park where cowboys watered cattle 75 years ago - swimming pool, waterfall and lake for boating; and Meadowlake Park has an 18 hole golf course, amusement park, and a 14 acre lake.

Locator 249-7791   Medical 249-7416   Police 249-7200

OREGON

Kingsley Field (OR03R4)
Kingsley Lodge
Bldg 208, McConnell Circle
Klamath Falls, OR 97603-0949

TELEPHONE NUMBER INFORMATION: Main installation numbers: C-541-885-6365, D-312-830-6365.

Location: On Highway 140. *USMRA: Page 100 (D-8)*. NMC: Klamath Falls, 3 miles west.

Lodging Office: Kingsley Lodge. Building 208, McConnell Circle., **C-541-885-6365**, 0800-1600 hours M-F (closed 1200-1300). After hours extra keys at Security Gate.

TML: VOQ. All ranks, leave or official duty. Suites, private bath (16); bedrooms, 2 beds, semi-private bath (40). Wood frame structure. Rates: suites $10 one person, $18 for dbl., single rooms $8 per person. All categories may make reservations.

TML Availability: Very good. (NOTE: Due to lack of funding lodging available to personnel on official business only.)

There is a clinic and small BX on base. Experience top notch fishing, bald eagles that winter nearby, world class skiing, golf, horseback riding, camping, hunting. Then there's Crater Lake and Mt. Shasta within an hour's drive.

NOTE: Both VOQ and restaurant (Trapper's Inn w/full bar) operated under contract to Commission for the Blind.

Too Late To Copy
Camp Rilea, For more information, write Rt 2 Box 497E, Warrenton, OR 97146, or call C-503-861-4018. Limited facilities. Rates: $7 per person per night.

194 - Temporary Military Lodging Around the World

PENNSYLVANIA

Carlisle Barracks (PA08R1)
ATZE-DPW-GH
Bldg 7 Washington Hall
Ashburn St., Carlisle Barracks
Carlisle, PA 17013-5002

TELEPHONE NUMBER INFORMATION: Main installation numbers: C-717-245-3131, D-312-242-4141.

Location: From I-81 exit 17 to US-11, 2 miles southwest to Carlisle, signs clearly marked to Barracks and Army War College. *USMRA: Page 22 (F-6).* NMC: Harrisburg, 18 miles north.

Lodging Office: Building 7, Ashburn St, **C-717-245-4245,** FAX 717-245-3757, 0700-1800 hours weekdays, 0800-1600 hours weekends. Other hours building 400, pick up key at MP desk. Check in 1400-1800 hours daily, check out 1100 hours daily. Government civilian employee billeting. Note: only family members with valid ID card can stay at this facility.

TML: Guest House. Buildings 7, 37, all ranks, leave or official duty. Bedrooms, private bath (14); bedrooms, shared bath (4); bedrooms, community bath (6); VIP suites, private bath (1 night only) (4). Community kitchen, A/C, color TV in room & lounge, housekeeping service, cribs/cots ($2), ice vending. Rates: $20 single, $25 double with private bath, $15-$20 with shared bath, $10-$15 with community bath, $25-$30 suites. PCS and guests of USAWC have priority. All categories can make reservations.

TML Availability: Good, Jan-May. Difficult, other times.

CREDIT CARDS ACCEPTED: Visa, MasterCard and American Express.

An arsenal during the Revolutionary War; near the Gettysburg Battlefields; site of the Military History Institute, home of the Army War College, Carlisle Barracks has an illustrious history worth tracing.

Locator 245-3131   Medical 245-3915/3400   Police 245-4315

Defense Distribution Region East (PA06R1)
ATTN: WIH
Bldg 268, J Avenue
New Cumberland, PA 17070-5001

TELEPHONE NUMBER INFORMATION: Main installation numbers: C & FTS-717-770-6011, D-312-977-6011.

Location: From I-83 take exit 18 to PA 114. East for 1 mile to Old York Rd, left .75 mile to Ross Ave, right for 1 mile to main gate. *USMRA: Page 22 (G-6).* NMC: Harrisburg, 7 miles northeast.

Lodging Office: ATTN: WIH, building 268, J Avenue, **C-717-770-7035,** 0700-1700 hours daily. Government civilian employee billeting in VOQ.

PENNSYLVANIA
Defense Distribution Region East, continued

TML: VOQ/DV/VIP. Building 268, all ranks, leave or official duty. Bedroom, shared bath (18); separate bedroom, private bath (1); two bedroom, private bath (1). Refrigerator, community kitchen, A/C, color TV, housekeeping service, cribs, cots, washer/dryer. Older structure, renovated. Rates: VOQ $25, DVQ $26. Duty with TDY, PCS orders can make reservations, others Space-A. Maximum 2 adults and 1 child per unit.

DV/VIP: Protocol Office, building 81, C-717-770-7192, O6/GS-15+, retirees and lower ranks Space-A.

TML Availability: Good, Oct-Dec and Feb-Mar. Difficult, other times.

Visit Hershey Park, famous Pennsylvania Dutch Country, Gettysburg National Military Park, and General Lee's Headquarters and Museum.

Locator 770-6011   **Medical 770-7281**   **Police 770-6222**

Fort Indiantown Gap (PA04Rl)
Housing Division
1 Garrsison Rd, Room 28
Annville, PA 17003-5033
Scheduled to close 10/31/98

TELEPHONE NUMBER INFORMATION: Main installation numbers: C-717-861-2000, D-312-491-2000.

Location: From I-81 take exit 29 west, north on PA-934 to facility. *USMRA: Page 22 (G-6).* NMC: Harrisburg, 20 miles southwest.

Lodging Office: 1 Garrison Road, Room 28. **C-717-861-2512/2540**, D-312-491-2512/2540, FAX 717-861-2821, DSN FAX 312-491-2821, 0800-2330 hours daily. Check in billeting 1500, check out 1100 hours daily.

TML: Reserve/National Guard post. VOQ/BEQ. All ranks, leave or official duty. Room, common bath (26); separate bedroom, private bath (5); Cottages (13). A/C, CATV, housekeeping service, washer/dryer, facilities for DAVs. Older structure, renovated. Rates: Rooms $7-$10 per room; Cottages $20, $4 additional in suites/cottages for extra persons over age 8. Dependents allowed.

TML Availability: Difficult, most of the time. Best, Nov-Mar.

CREDIT CARDS ACCEPTED: American Express.

Hershey Park, Museum and Chocolate World, guided tours at the local Tulpehocken Manor Inn and Plantation, Indian Echo Caverns, with a spectacular underground display, and local Pennsylvania German farm and village festivals and crafts demonstrations are "must sees."

Locator 861-2000   **Medical 861-2091**   **Police 861-2727**

PENNSYLVANIA

Letterkenny Army Depot (PA03R1)
Lodging Office
ATTN: SDSLE-EH
Chambersburg, PA 17201-4150

TELEPHONE NUMBER INFORMATION: Main installation numbers: C-717-267-8111, D-312-570-5110.

Location: From I-81 exit 8 west on PA-997 to PA-433 on left and enter depot at Gate 6. *USMRA: Page 22 (E-7)*. NMC: Harrisburg, 45 miles northeast.

Lodging Office: ATTN: SDSLE-EH, building 663, **C-717-267-8890,** 0730-1600 hours M-F. Other hours call security C-717-267-8800. Check in billeting 1300 hours, check out 1100 hours daily. Government civilian employee billeting.

TML: Guest House. Building 539, all ranks, leave or official duty. One bedroom, private bath (1); one bedroom, private bath, kitchen (1); two bedroom, private bath, kitchen (1). Limited utensils, A/C, color TV, housekeeping service, cribs/cots, washer/dryer. Older structure, renovated. Rates: 1 bedroom $12, separate bedroom, kitchen $14, 2 bedroom $17. Reservations required, others Space-A.

TML: VOQ. Bldg 503, officers and government service ranks, leave, PCS or official duty. Two bdrm, private bath, kitchen (1); one bdrm, private bath (1). A/C, color TV, housekeeping service, washer/dryer. Rates: 1 bdrm $8, two bdrm, $15. Reservations required, others Space-A.

DV/VIP: ATTN: SDSLE-CA, bldg 500, C-717-267-8659, DV/VIP determined by CO. Retirees Space-A.

TML Availability: Best, Sep-Mar.

Tour famous Gettysburg Battlefield, try local bass and trout fishing in Rocky Springs Reservoir, local hunting is very good.

Locator 264-1413   Medical 267-8416   Police 267-8800

Tobyhanna Army Depot (PA05R1)
Community Recreation Division
P.O. Box 5044
Tobyhanna, PA 18466-5044

TELEPHONE NUMBER INFORMATION: Main installation numbers: C-717-895-7000, D-312-795-7110.

Location: I-80 East or West to I-380 North, exit 7 to depot. *USMRA: Page 22 (I-4)*. NMC: Scranton, 24 miles northwest.

Lodging Office: Building 1001, **C-717-895-7970,** FAX 717-895-7419, DSN FAX 312 795-7419, 0730-1600 hours M-F. Other hours Security, building 20, C-717-895-7550. Check in billeting 1400, check out 1000 hours daily.

PENNSYLVANIA
Tobyhanna Army Depot, continued

TML: Guest House, buildings 1013,1014, all ranks, leave or official duty. Two bedroom, private bath (3); three bedroom, private bath (1). Kitchen, limited utensils, color TV, housekeeping service, cribs, washer/dryer. One older structure, two newly renovated. Rates: $30 per day, $5 each additional person over 3 years old. Reservations can be made 90 days in advance.

DV/VIP: ATTN: Protocol Office, building 11-2, C-717-895-6223, O6+. No DV/VIP quarters.

TML Availability: Good, Apr-Nov. More difficult, other times.

In the Pocono Mountains Resort Area. Nearby lakes and streams provide fishing and water sports. Skiing and winter sports Jan thru Mar. State parks and forest picnic areas in the immediate area will lure visitors.

Locator 895-7000   Medical 895-7121   Police 895-7550

Willow Grove Naval Air Station/ Joint Reserve Base (PA01R1)
CBQ Bldg 609
NAS/JRB Willow Grove
Willow Grove, PA 19090

TELEPHONE NUMBER INFORMATION: Main installation numbers: C-215-443-1000, D-312-991-1000.

Location: Take PA Turnpike (I-276), exit 27 north on PA 611, 5 miles to NAS. *USMRA: Page 22 (I,J-6)*. NMC: Philadelphia, 21 miles south.

Lodging Office: Building 609, **C-215-442-5800/5801**, FAX 215-442-5817, 24 hours daily. Check in facility 1500, check out 1100 daily.

TML: BOQ. Building 5, officers all ranks. Leave or official duty. Single bedroom, common bath (20). A/C, refrigerator, microwave, color TV, housekeeping service, washer/dryer. Inadequate older structure, renovated. Rates: $8 per person. PCS, TDY, active duty can make reservations, retirees, others Space-A.

TML: BEQ. Building 609, enlisted E6 and below, leave or official duty. Bedroom, shared bath (40); two bedroom suites, private bath (8). A/C, housekeeping service, refrigerator, microwave, color TV, washer/dryer. Rates: $4 per person. Suites $12. Duty can make reservations, retirees, others Space-A.

TML: MWR Chalets, sleeps 6, two bedrooms + loft (2). C-215-443-6085 for information.

DV/VIP: Contact the PAO at C-215-443-1776/1777.

TML Availability: Fair except weekends when extremely limited due to Reserve Unit training.

See Philadelphia's Liberty Bell, Society Hill, New Market, summer open air concerts along the Parkway and at Robin Hood Dell. Visit the 9th Street Market in little Italy (Rocky Balboa made his famous run here).

Locator 443-1000   Medical 443-1600   Police 443-6067

RHODE ISLAND

Newport Naval Education & Training Center (RI01R1)
Newport, RI 02841-0001

TELEPHONE NUMBER INFORMATION: Main installation numbers: C-401-841-2311, D-312-948-1110.

Location: From I-95 south take the East Greenwich/Rt 4 exit, continue for approximately 20 minutes. Take exit for 138 East/Newport. Continue on 138 East over Newport Bridge. Once past bridge, continue until stoplight (Jai Alai will be directly in front of you). Turn right, you will approach a rotary, go half way around and continue straight. NETC Gate One will be directly in front of you. From US-1 exit to 138 East over Newport bridge. Once past bridge, continue until stoplight (Jai Alai will be directly in front of you). Turn right, you will approach a rotary, go half way around and continue straight. NETC Gate One will be directly in front of you. *USMRA: Page 17 (J-8); Page 25 (B,C-1,2,3)*. NMC: Newport, 2 miles south.

Lodging Office: No central billeting office. Officers, building 684, **C-401-841-3156,** FAX 401-841-3906. Enlisted, building 447, **C-401-841-4410**, both 24 hours daily. Check in facility 1300 hours. Check out 1100 hours daily. Government civilian employee billeting in BOQ.

TML: BOQ/BEQ. Bedroom, private/shared bath (575); separate bedrooms, private bath (4). Full facility. Rates: moderate, no families. Duty can make reservations, others space-A.

TML: Navy Lodge. Building 685, all ranks, leave or official duty. For reservations call **1-800-NAVY-INN**. Lodge number is 401-849-4500, 0700-2300 hours daily. Check in 1500-1800, check out 1200 hours. Bedroom, 2 double beds, private bath (39); bedroom, 2 double beds, studio couch (28). Kitchenette, utensils, coffee/tea, A/C, clocks, color TV, housekeeping service, cribs, phones, high chairs, game room, ice/snack vending, irons/boards, lounge, coin washer/dryer. Modern structure. Rates: November - April, $50 apartment, $30 room; May - October, $62 apartment, $50 room. All categories can make reservations.

DV/VIP: Contact CO, C-401-841-3715.

TML Availability: Good, winter months. Difficult, summer months.

CREDIT CARDS ACCEPTED: Visa, MasterCard and American Express.

Stroll along cobblestone streets, or ocean front walks; admire turn-of-the-Century mansions; visit many national historic landmarks, and the Naval War College Museum. Admire the wonderful sailing vessels - this is Newport!

Medical 841-3111/2222   Police 841-3241

Temporary Military Lodging Around the World - 199

SOUTH CAROLINA

Beaufort Marine Corps Air Station (SC01R1)
BOQ, Bldg 431
Beaufort MCAS, SC 29904-5000

TELEPHONE NUMBER INFORMATION: Main installation numbers: C-803-522-7100, D-312-832-7100.

Location: From I-95 exit at Pocataligo to SC-21, 4 miles to MCAS. Clearly marked. *USMRA: Page 44 (G-9).* NMC: Savannah, 40 miles south.

Lodging Office: BOQ, building 431, **C-803-522-7676**, 24 hours daily. Check in facility, check out 1200 hours daily. Government civilian employee billeting.

TML: de Treville House, building 1108, **C-803-522-1663**. All ranks, leave or official duty. Bedroom, private bath (21); separate bedroom, private bath (21). Kitchen (in separate bedroom), A/C, cots ($5), cribs, ice vending. housekeeping service, special facilities for DAVs, color TV, complete utensils, washer/dryer, playground, picnic area with grills. Handicapped accessible. Staff NCO Club adjacent. Modern structure. Rates: $35, $45 with kitchenette. Maximum 5 adults per unit. Make reservations. Non-military personnel visiting relatives stationed at Beaufort may stay on a Space-A basis.

TML: BOQ. Building 431, all ranks, leave or official duty. Bedrooms (officers) (39); suites, private bath (officers) (5); bedroom, private/shared bath (enlisted) (17). Refrigerator, community kitchen, limited utensils, A/C, color TV room & lounge, housekeeping service, washer/dryer, ice vending. Modern structure, renovated. Room and suite rates: duty $6 rooms, $10 suites; others $11 rooms, $17 suite, $2 each adult family member, no children. No pets. Duty can make reservations, others Space-A.

DV/VIP: Contact CO, building 601, C-803-522-7158. Retirees and lower ranks Space-A.

TML Availability: Very good, most of the year. Best, Sep-Apr.

CREDIT CARDS ACCEPTED: Visa, MasterCard, American Express, Diners and Discover.

Locator 522-7188   **Medical 522-7311**   **Police 522-7373**

Charleston Air Force Base (SC06R1)
The Charleston House
102 N. Davis Dr.
Charleston AFB, SC 29404-4825

TELEPHONE NUMBER INFORMATION: Main installation numbers: C-803-566-6000, D-312-673-2100.

Location: From I-26 East exit to West Aviation Ave to traffic light, continue through light to 2nd light on right, follow Rd around end of runway to Gate 2 (River Gate). *USMRA: Page 44 (H-8,9).* NMC: Charleston, 5 miles southeast.

SOUTH CAROLINA
Charleston Air Force Base, continued

Lodging Office: The Charleston House, 102 N. Davis Dr, C-803-552-9900, D-312-673-2100 EX-860. Reservations: M-F 0800-1700, **C-803-566-3806**, D-312-673-3806, FAX 803-566-3394. Check in facility, check out 1200 hours daily. Government civilian employee billeting in contract quarters.

TML: VOQ/DV/VIP. Buildings 343, 344, 362, officers, all ranks, leave or official duty. Bedroom, shared bath (102); bedroom suites, private bath (O6+) (4). Kitchen (suites only), micro-refrigerator, A/C, housekeeping service, cribs/cots, washer/dryer, ice vending. Modern structure. Rates: DV/VIP (suites) $14 per person, maximum $28; DV Mini-Suites & VOQ $8 per person, maximum $16. Maximum 5 per room. Duty can make reservations, others Space-A. No pets allowed.

TML: VAQ. Senior enlisted (E7+), building 346, leave or official duty. Bedroom, private bath (4); bedroom, shared bath (40). A/C, color TV, housekeeping service, washer/dryer, ice vending. Rates: suites: $14 per person, maximum $28 per room; rooms: $8 per person, maximum $16 per room. Duty can make reservations, others space A. No pets.

TML: Junior enlisted (E1-E6), building 346, leave or official duty. Bedroom, shared bath (395). A/C, color TV, housekeeping service, washer/dryer, ice vending. Rates: $8 per person. Duty can make reservations, others Space-A. No dependents, no pets.

TML: TLF. Building 330, all ranks. Bedroom suites, private bath, kitchen, sleeps 5 (18). A/C color TV, housekeeping service, washer/dryer, ice vending. Rates: $20 per family. Duty can make reservations, others Space-A.

DV/VIP: Office of the Wing CP, building 103, room 1, C-803-566-5644, O6+. Retirees Space-A. No pets.

TML Availability: Good, Nov-Dec. Difficult, other times because of duty traffic.

CREDIT CARDS ACCEPTED: Visa, MasterCard and American Express.

Visit stately mansions along the Battery, and Boone Hall, where scenes from "Gone With the Wind" and "North and South" were filmed. Take a water tour, and visit historic Fort Sumter and Charleston Harbor.

Locator 566-3282   Medical 566-2775   Police 566-3600

Fort Jackson (SC09R1)
Fort Jackson, SC 29207-5000

TELEPHONE NUMBER INFORMATION: Main installation number: C-803-751-7511, D-312-734-1110.

Location: Exit from I-20 north of the fort or from US-76/378 south of the fort or US-601 east of the fort. From I-20 take Ft Jackson or Two Notch Rd exit, left on Decker Blvd, right on Percival Rd to fort entrance. *USMRA: Page 44 (G-6).* NMC: Columbia, SC 12 miles southwest.

Lodging Office: Building 2785, corner Semmes Rd & Lee Rd, **C-803-751-6223**, D-312-734-6223. Toll free reservations for government official duty personnel (on post) and local hotels **1-800-751-7081 (subject to change)**, 24 hours daily. Check in billeting, check out 1000 hours daily. Government civilian employee billeting.

SOUTH CAROLINA
Fort Jackson, continued

TML: Guest House, **Palmetto Lodge**, building 6000, all ranks, leave or official duty, C-803-751-4779. Bedroom, private bath, sleeps 6 persons (70). Kitchen, limited utensils, A/C, telephone, color TV in room & lounge, housekeeping service, washer/dryer, ice vending. Rates: $35 per day per room. No pets. Duty can make reservations, others Space-A.

TML: Kennedy Hall, building 2785, all ranks, leave or official duty. Bedroom, 1 bed, private bath (transient units) (92); BOQ units (30). Refrigerator, A/C, color TV, housekeeping service, washer/dryer. Modern structure, remodeled. Rates: $22 per couple, PCS $12 per couple. Maximum 2 per unit. No pets. Duty can make reservations, others Space-A.

TML: VEQ. Building 2464, enlisted all ranks, official duty. Bedroom, 1 bed, private bath (12). Refrigerator, color TV, housekeeping service. Rates: sponsor $22 per couple, PCS $12 per couple. No pets. Duty can make reservations, others Space-A.

TML: DV/VIP. Cottages, buildings 3640-3645, 4410, Legion Landing & Dozier House. Officers O5+, official duty. Check out 1100 hours. Bedroom, private bath (2), two bedroom, private bath (4), three bedroom, private bath suite (1). Kitchen, utensils, A/C, color TV, telephone, housekeeping service. Remodeled. Rates: $22 per couple, $5 additional guests. No children, no pets. Duty can make reservations, others Space-A.

DV/VIP: Protocol Office, HQ Building, C-803-751-6618, D-312-734-5218, O6+.

TML Availability: Very good, Oct-May.

Riverbanks Zoological Park, Town Theater amateur productions, and a carriage ride along historic Broad Street compete with local golf courses, Lake Murray and numerous public recreation areas as local popular pastimes.

Locator 751-7671   Medical 911   Police 751-3113

Parris Island Marine Corps Recruit Depot (SC08R1)
Billeting Office, Bldg 330
Parris Island MCRD, SC 29905-5000

TELEPHONE NUMBER INFORMATION: Main installation numbers: C-803-525-2111, D-312-832-1110.

Location: From I-95 South take exit 5 to Beaufort via SC-170; from I-95 North take exit 33 via US 17 t r US-21, east to SC-280 to SC-802 which leads to main gate of depot. *USMRA: Page 44 (G-10).* NMC: Savannah, 45 miles southwest.

Lodging Office: Billeting office, building 330, for information/reservations call **C-803-525-2976/3460**, D-312-832-2976/3460, FAX 803-525-3815, DSN FAX 312-832-3815. Check in facility after 1400, check out no later than 1100 hours. Government civilian employee billeting in Hostess House. Reservations accepted 90 days in advance. **All Space-A required to confirm 72 hours in advance.**

TML: Hostess House. Building 200, two miles from main gate. All ranks, leave or official duty C-803-525-2976/3460. Bedroom, 2 beds, sleep sofa, private bath (30). Kitchen, limited utensils, A/C, color TV in room & lounge, housekeeping service, cribs, washer/dryer, ice vending, facilities for

SOUTH CAROLINA
Parris Island Marine Corps Recruit Depot, continued

DAVs. Modern structure, renovated. Rates: officer/enlisted $25, $35 with kitchen. All categories can make reservations.

TML: VOQ. Beaufort River Inn. Building 254, officers all ranks, leave or official duty, retired, DAV's, military widows, accompanied dependents, government civilians GS7+ on official duty. Bedroom, private bath, kitchen, complete utensils(4). Bedroom, private bath (2). Refrigerator, A/C, color TV in room & lounge, housekeeping service, cots, washer/dryer, ice vending. Older structure, renovated. Rates: $8-$15 per room, $3 extra per person; civilian $20-$25, $3 extra per person. Maximum 4 persons. All categories can make reservations.

TML: BOQ. Osprey Inn I. Building 289, officers all ranks leave or official duty, civilian government employees, retired, DAV's, military widows, C-803-525-2744. Bedroom, private bath (19); bedrooms, common bath (4). A/C, color TV, washer/dryer, ice vending. Older structure. Rates: O1-O3, $8-$12 per room; O4+, $12-$15 per room, $3 extra per person; GS7-GS10, $12-$16 per room; GS11+, $17-$20 per room, $3 extra per person. Maximum 4 per room. All categories can make reservations.

TML: BEQ. Osprey Inn II. Building 330, enlisted all ranks leave or official duty, civilian government employees, retired, DAV's, military widows. Bedroom, hotel style with all amenities (1); bedroom, hotel style w/private bath (5); bedroom, college style, shared bath (64). Refrigerator, microwave, A/C, color/cable TV, housekeeping service, washer/dryer, ice vending. Modern structure. Rates: E7-E9 (Hotel style w/amenities) $8-$12, $3 extra per person; all other rooms $6-$10 for military, $8-$12 for civilians, $3 extra per person.

DV/VIP: VOQ. Beaufort River Inn. Building 254, contact staff secretary for reservation at C-803-525-2567/2594 active & retired officers O6+, leave or official duty, distinguished guests. Two bedroom suite, sitting room, & dining area, kitchen and private bath, completely furnished with all amenities. Older structure, renovated. Rates: Active duty, $15-$20 per room, $3 extra per person; civilian $20-$25, $3 extra per person. Maximum 4 persons.

TML Availability: Good except graduation days.

CREDIT CARDS ACCEPTED: Visa, MasterCard and (Government) American Express.

Locator 525-3358   Medical 525-3315   Police 525-3444

Shaw Air Force Base (SC10R1)
Carolina Pines Inn
471 Myers St.
Shaw AFB, SC 29152-5000

TELEPHONE NUMBER INFORMATION: Main installation numbers: C-803-668-8110, D-312-965-1110.

Location: Off US-76/378 8 mi west of Sumter, SC. Clearly marked. *USMRA: Page 44 (H-6).* NMC: Columbia, 35 miles west.

Lodging Office: Carolina Pines Inn, building 471, Myers St, **C-803-668-3210, 1-800-769-7429,** D-312-965-5125/5124, FAX 803-668-5756, DSN FAX 312-965-5756, 24 hours daily. Check in facility,

SOUTH CAROLINA
Shaw Air Force Base, continued

check out 1200 hours daily. Government civilian employee billeting. Advanced Space-A reservations accepted. Space-A, can request availability 72 hours in advance.

TML: TLF. Buildings 931-934, all ranks, leave or official duty. Handicapped accessible. Separate bedrooms, sleeper sofa, private bath (40). Kitchenette, A/C, color TV (HBO), housekeeping service, cribs/cots, washer/dryer. Modern structure. Rates: $24 per unit. Maximum 5 per apartment. Duty can make reservations, others Space-A.

TML: VAQ. Building 900, enlisted all ranks, leave or official duty. Bedroom, 1 bed, shared bath (SNCO rooms have private bath)(44). A/C, color TV (HBO), housekeeping service, cots, washer/dryer, ice vending. Modern structure. Rates: $8 per person, $14 chief suites. Duty can make reservations, others Space-A.

TML: VOQ. Buildings 911, 924, 927, officers all ranks, leave or official duty. Bedroom, private bath (68); separate bedroom suites, private bath (14). Kitchen, limited utensils, A/C, color TV (HBO), housekeeping service, cots, washer/dryer, ice vending. Modern structure. Rates: $8 per person. Maximum 2 per room. Duty can make reservations, others Space-A.

TML: DV/VIP. Bldg 924, officer O6+, leave or official duty. Bedroom, private bath (6). Kitchen, complete utensils, A/C, color TV (HBO), housekeeping service, cots, washer/dryer, ice vending. Older structure, remodeled. Rates: $14 per person. Maximum $28 per room. Duty can make reservations, others Space-A.

DV/VIP: Protocol Office. C-803-668-2156/2311, D-312-965-2156/2311, O6+. Retirees Space-A.

TML Availability: Good. Best, Dec-Mar.

CREDIT CARDS ACCEPTED: Visa, MasterCard and American Express.

An 18 hole golf course, 3 swimming pools, tennis courts and fitness center on base, and Columbia, the state capital, and Charleston, not to mention Myrtle Beach, the Blue Ridge and Smokey Mountains.

Locator 668-2811   Medical 668-2778   Police 668-2493

Short Stay Navy Recreation Area (SC02R1)
211 Short Stay Road
Moncks Corner, SC 29461

TELEPHONE NUMBER INFORMATION: Main installation numbers: C-803-761-8353.

Location: Take I-26 to US 17-A toward Moncks Corner (15 miles). Left on US 52 for 3 miles. Follow signs to Navy Recreation Area. *USMRA:* Page 44 (H-8). NMC: Charleston, 35 miles South.

Lodging Office: 211 Short Stay Road,, SC 29461, **C-803-761-8353/743-5608,** 24 hours daily. Office hours Su-Th 0715-1830 hours, F-Sa 0715-1930 hours. Check in at facility 1500 hours. Check out 1100 hours. Late checkout call C-803-761-8353. Security at front gate when office is closed.

TML: Six cabins, 24 two bedroom villas, 12 three bedroom villas. Cabins sleep and two bedroom villas sleep 4, three bedroom villa sleeps 6. Three units handicapped equipped. All units include

SOUTH CAROLINA
Short Stay Navy Recreation Area, continued

kitchenette, private bath, deck, cable color TV, picnic tables, grills. 4 reservable pavilions. Recreation center, convenience store, snack bar, boat rental, bait & tackle, swimming beach, miniature golf, game room, laundry, gas. Rates: villas $30-50 (low, mid, high seasons, military, civilian rates); cabins $33-$44. Write for brochure. Cancellations OK 3 days prior to check-in date (later, $15 fee). One unit per ID per time period. Minimum age to reserve 21. Pets permitted in campground only. Restrictions apply.

DV/VIP: None.

TML Availability: Good. Best Sep-May, difficult June-Aug.

CREDIT CARDS ACCEPTED: Visa, MasterCard and American Express.

Located on Lake Moultrie (60,000 acres), fishing, watersports, Charleston offers beaches, golf, historic sites. Read Military Living's *Military RV, Camping and Rec Areas Around the World* for more information.

Locator 761-8353   **Medical 911**   **Police 911**

<u>Too Late To Copy</u>
Charleston Naval Weapons Station, 1 Mayhan Circle, Goose Creek, SC 29445-8601. BEQ **C-803-764-7646.**

SOUTH DAKOTA

Ellsworth Air Force Base (SD01R3)
Pine Tree Inn
2349 Risner Dr.
Ellsworth AFB, SD 57706-4708

TELEPHONE NUMBER INFORMATION: Main installation numbers: C-605-385-1000, D-312-625-1110.

Location: Off I-90 (exit 66), 10 miles east of Rapid City. Clearly marked. *USMRA: Page 85 (B-5).* NMC: Rapid City, 10 miles west.

Lodging Office: Pine Tree Inn, 2349 Risner Dr., **C-605-385-2844**, FAX 605-385-2718, D-312-675-2844, 24 hours daily. Check in facility 1500, check out 1000 hours daily (TLF 1000 hours). No government civilian employee billeting.

TML: TLF. Building 4101, all ranks, leave or official duty, C-605-385-1362. Bedroom, shared bath (4); double rooms, shared bath (21). Refrigerator, microwave, A/C color/cable TV, housekeeping service, washer/dryer, ice vending. Older structure. Rates: enlisted $7, officer $8, $23 per family unit. Duty can make reservations, others Space-A (1 Oct -30 Apr).

TML: VOQ/VAQ. Building 1103, all ranks, leave or official duty. Two bedroom, private bath (VOQ) (51); bedroom, 1 bed each room, shared bath (VAQ) (70). Refrigerator, A/C, color TV in room & lounge, housekeeping service, washer/dryer, ice vending. Older structure. Rates: $8 per person VOQ, $6 per person VAQ, maximum $16 per room. Maximum 3 per room. Duty can make reservations, others Space-A (1 Oct -30 Apr).

TML: DV/VIP. Building 4100, officers O6+, leave or official duty. Separate bedroom suites, private bath (6). Color TV, housekeeping service. Older structure. Rates: $8 per person. Duty can make reservations, others Space-A (1 Oct -30 Apr).

DV/VIP: Executive Support, C-605-385-1205, O6+. Retirees and lower ranks Space-A (1 Oct-30 Apr) with approval.

TML Availability: Good, Oct-Apr (Only time Space-A reservations are accepted). More difficult, other times.

CREDIT CARDS ACCEPTED: Visa, MasterCard and American Express.

While you're here visit the Air & Space Museum, Mount Rushmore, the Badlands, Crazy Horse Monument, Deadwood and the Black Hills.

Locator 385-1379   **Medical 385-3534**   **Police 399-4001**

206 - Temporary Military Lodging Around the World

TENNESSEE

Arnold Air Force Base (TN02R2)
Forest Inn
P.O. Box 4176
Tullahoma, TN 37388

TELEPHONE NUMBER INFORMATION: Main installation numbers: C-615-454-3000, D-312-340-3000.

Location: From Tullahoma, take Arnold Engineering Development Center access highway. From I-24 take AEDC exit 117, 4 miles south of Manchester. Clearly marked. *USMRA: Page 41 (I-9,10).* NMC: Chattanooga, 65 miles southeast; Nashville, 65 miles northwest.

Lodging Office: Forest Inn, P.O. Box 4176, **C-615-454-3099,** D-312-340-3099, M-F 0600-2200, Sa 1000-2000, Su 1200-2200. After hours, SDO C-615-454-7752. Check in billeting, check out 1200 hours. No government civilian employee billeting.

TML: VOQ. Building 3027, all ranks, leave or official duty. Bedroom, shared bath (40); separate bedroom (DV/VIP) (5). Refrigerator, microwave, coffee maker, community kitchen, limited utensils, A/C, color TV in room & lounge, housekeeping service, cribs, washer/dryer, ice vending. Older structure. Rates: $8 per person, $14 DV/VIP. Duty can make reservations, others Space-A.

DV/VIP: Billeting Office. O6+, retirees, Space-A.

TML Availability: Good, all year.

CREDIT CARDS ACCEPTED: Visa, MasterCard, American Express.

On this 44,000 acre installation, Woods Reservoir has a 75 miles shoreline for fishing and all water sports. Visit the Grand Ole Opry, Music Row, the Parthenon, the Hermitage in Nashville, Jack Daniels Distillery, Rock City, Look-out Mountain, and NASA Space Center in Huntsville, AL. Civil War buffs: lots to see.

Locator 454-3000   **Medical 454-5351**   **Police 454-5662**

Memphis Naval Support Activity (TN01R2)
Bachelor Quarters Dept.
Millington, TN 38054-6024

TELEPHONE NUMBER INFORMATION: Main installation numbers: C-901-873- 5111, D-312-966-5111.

Location: From US-51 North at Millington, exit to Navy Rd, right to first gate on right, main gate. *USMRA: Page 40 (B-9,10).* NMC: Memphis, 20 miles southwest.

Lodging Office: Bachelor Quarters Dept, C-901-873-7082, D-312-966-7082. BOQ reservations **C-901-873-5348,** BEQ **C-901-873-5459,** 24 hours daily. Check in facility, check out 1200 hours daily.

TENNESSEE
Memphis Naval Air Station, continued

TML: Navy Lodge. Buildings N-762, N-931, all ranks, leave or official duty, and NEX associates. For reservations call **1-800-NAVY-INN,** lodge number is C-901-872-0121, FAX 901-873-1695. Check in 1500-1800, check out 1200 hours. Bedroom, 2 X-long double beds, private bath (49). Four interconnecting units, 23 non-smoking. Kitchenette, microwave, utensils, A/C, CATV, BBQ, clock radio, coffee, vending mart, cribs, phones, high chairs, ice vending, iron/boards, picnic grounds, playground, rollaways, housekeeping service, coin washer/dryer. Rates: $39. All categories can make reservations. No Pets, kennel nearby. Tennis, golf, gym, pool, Navy Lake, stables nearby.

TML: BOQ/BEQ. All ranks, leave or official duty. Check in at facility. Officers: bedroom, private bath (82); enlisted: bedroom, private bath (some shared bath) (163). Refrigerator, A/C, TV in lounge, housekeeping service, washer/dryer, ice vending, special facilities for DAV's. Modern structure.

Rates: BOQ $9-$21 per person, BEQ $5-$17 per person. Dependents must use Navy Lodge. Duty can make reservations, others Space-A.

DV/VIP: Cmdr, C-901-873-5101/2, O6+. Retirees Space-A.

TML Availability: Good, Dec. Difficult, other times.

CREDIT CARDS ACCEPTED: Visa, MasterCard, American Express and Discover are accepted at the Navy Lodge.

Check out the nearby attractions of Graceland, Beale Street (Home of the Blues), Shelby Forest State Park provides thousands of acres of native woodlands for walking, riding, picnicking and boating. The Memphis area is famous for bird and duck hunting.

Locator 873-5111   **Medical 911**   **Police 873-5533**

Too Late To Copy
McGhee Tyson Air National Guard Base, Knoxville, TN 37950-5000. **C-423-985-3300,** D-312-266-3300. Rates: $4 per person. No reservations, 39 units.

208 - Temporary Military Lodging Around the World

TEXAS

Armed Services YMCA (TX50R3)
7060 Comington Street
El Paso, TX 79930-4239

TELEPHONE NUMBER INFORMATION: Main installation numbers: C-915-562-8461.

Location: From I-10 take Alamagordo exit to left at Fred Wilson exit, turn left. At Dyer St turn left, right on Hayes St, to Fort Bliss gate. Residence center straight ahead. *USMRA: Page 86 (B-6)*. NMC: El Paso, within city limits.

Lodging Office: Building 7060, Comington Street, **C-915-562-8461**, FAX 915-565-0203, 24 hours daily. Check in front desk, check out 1100 hours daily. **Note: This facility is on Fort Bliss. For additional TML see Fort Bliss listing.**

TML: Motel style ASYMCA, residence. All ranks, leave, retirees or official duty. King-size room, private bath (16); doubles, private bath (36). Cable color TV, refrigerator (all), kitchenette (30 units), lounge area with food service and cable color TV, housekeeping service, essentials, cots, coin washer/dryer, handicapped accessible units, ice/food vending. Rates: Active Duty $28, Retired $29, Civilian Personnel $31, per room, per night, maximum 4 persons per room, arrangements can be made to adjust. All categories may make reservations. Pets allowed.

TML Availability: Good. Best Sept-May, difficult Jul-Aug, and Jan.

CREDIT CARDS ACCEPTED: Visa, MasterCard, American Express and Diners.

Visit old Juarez and the Tiqua Indian Reservation. There are numerous military museums on post.

Locator 568-1113   Medical 569-2331   Police 568-2115

Belton Lake Recreation Area (TX07R3)
Reservations Office
ATTN: AFZF-CA-CRD-OR-BLORA
Fort Hood, TX 76544-5056

TELEPHONE NUMBER INFORMATION: Main installation numbers: C-817-287/ 288-1110, D-312-737/738-1110.

Location: From I-35 take Loop 121 N to Sparta Rd. Stay on Sparta, turn right on Cottage road, area marked. *USMRA: Page 87 (K-4,5)*. NMC: Austin, 60 miles south.

Lodging Office: Reservations Office, **C-817-287-2523**, D-312-737-8303. Check in cottages after 1500 hours, check out 0730-1200 hours.

TML: Cottages. All ranks, leave or official duty. Bedroom, private bath, sleeps 4 persons (10). Kitchen, kitchen appliances, dishwasher, A/C, color TV, fully equipped. Rates: E1-E4, $25 daily, all other authorized users $30 daily. One day deposit required within 72 hours of reservation. All categories can make reservations. No Pets.

TEXAS
Belton Lake Recreation Area, continued

TML Availability: Good, winter months. Difficult, May-Sep.

CREDIT CARDS ACCEPTED: Visa, MasterCard, American Express and Espirit.

A full round of recreational opportunities is offered here: jet skiing, sailing, windsurfing, deck boats, fishing, paddle and ski boats can be rented; the picnic ares, RV camp sites, tent camping sites and party pavilions are fun, fun, fun.

Locator 287-2137   Medical 288-8000   Police 287-2176

Bergstrom Air Reserve Base (TX27R3)
924th Lodging
924 SVF/SVML
3601 Bergstrom Drive
Austin, TX 78719-2558
Scheduled to close 6/1/96

TELEPHONE NUMBER INFORMATION: Main installation numbers: C-512-369-2207, D-312-685-1110.

Location: From US-183 or TX-71. Clearly marked. *USMRA: Page 87 (K-6).* NMC: Austin, 7 miles northwest.

Lodging Office: Building 3710, Consolidated Club, **C-512-369-2207**, FAX 512-369-3224, D-312-685-2207, 0600-23(' hours daily. Check in facilities, check out 1200 hours daily. Government civilian employe͵   g.

TML: VOQ/VAQ. Bʮ   3708-3709 (VOQ). All ranks, leave or official duty. VOQ: single suite, private bath, kitchenettͼ ⱽing room (22); SNCO suites, private bath (6); enlisted rooms, 2 beds, shared bath (55). A/C, color TV, washer/dryer, lounge, housekeeping service. Older structure, remodeled. Rates: $10 per person. Duty can make reservations.

TML: DV/VIP. Building 3708, officer O6+, leave or official duty. Suites, private bath (6). Kitchen, living room, A/C, color TV, housekeeping service, cots/cribs, washer/dryer. Rates: $10 per person. Duty can make reservations.

DV/VIP: Protocol, C-512-369-3815. O6+. Retirees and lower ranks Space-A.

TML Availability: Good, Jan, Feb, Mar. Difficult other times.

CREDIT CARDS ACCEPTED: Visa, MasterCard and American Express.

Old Pecan St/Sixth St is a seven block strip of renovated Victorian buildings, and a favorite place to shop and eat. Check out Austin, the capitol of Texas.

Police 369-2604

TEXAS

Brooks Air Force Base (TX26R3)
Brooks Inn
2804 5th Street
Brooks AFB, TX 78235-5000

TELEPHONE NUMBER INFORMATION: Main installation numbers: C-210-536-1110, D-312-240-1110.

Location: At intersection of I-37 and Loop 13 (Military Drive). *Page 91 (C-4)*. NMC: San Antonio, 5 miles northwest.

Lodging Office: Brooks Inn, building 214, 2804 5th St, **C-210-536-1844**, D-312-240-1844, FAX 210-536-2327, DSN FAX 312-240-2327, 24 hours daily. Check in facility, check out 1200 hours daily. Government civilian employee billeting.

TML: TLF. Building 211, all ranks, leave or official duty. Handicapped accessible. Bedroom, private bath (8). Kitchen, living room, cribs, A/C, utensils, linen, housekeeping service, washer/dryer. Rates: $22. Duty can make reservations. PCS in 30 day limit. PCS out 7 day limit. PCS have priority, others Space-A.

TML: VAQ. Building 718, C-210-536-3031, enlisted all ranks, leave or official duty. Separate bedrooms, private bath (2); two bedroom, shared bath (52). A/C, ice vending, housekeeping service, refrigerator, color TV, washer/dryer. Modern structure. Rates: $8-$14, person. Duty can make reservations, others Space-A.

TML: VOQ. Buildings 212, 214, 218, 220, officers all ranks, leave or official duty. Separate bedrooms, private bath (109); two bedroom, shared bath (50). A/C, cribs/cots, ice vending, housekeeping service, refrigerator, color TV, washer/dryer. Modern structure. Rates: sponsor $8-$14, maximum $16-$28 per family. Duty can make reservations, others Space-A.

TML: DV/VIP. Officer O6+, leave or official duty, C-210-536-3238. Separate bedrooms, living room, private bath (6). Housekeeping service, washer/dryer. Rates: $14 per person. Duty can make reservations, others Space-A.

DV/VIP: PAO Office, C-210-536-3238. O6+. Retirees Space-A.

TML Availability: Limited. Base has contract hotel/motel billeting. Contact Billeting Office, C-210-536-1844.

CREDIT CARDS ACCEPTED: Visa, MasterCard and American Express.

Popular with Brooks' people are the recreation areas at Canyon Lake, on the Guadalupe River northwest of New Braunfels.

Locator 536-1841   Police 536-2851   Medical 536-3278

TEXAS

Corpus Christi Naval Air Station (TX10R3)
Combined Bachelor Quarters
Corpus Christi, TX 78419-9999

TELEPHONE NUMBER INFORMATION: Main installation numbers: C-512-939-2811, D-312-861-2811.

Location: On TX-358, on southeast side of Corpus Christi. The south gate is on NAS Dr. *USMRA: Page 87 (K-8,9).* NMC: Corpus Christi, 10 miles northwest.

Lodging Office: Building 1281, Ocean Dr, **C-512-939-2388/89**, D-312-861-2388/39, FAX 512-939-3275, DSN Fax 312-861-3275. CBQ 24 hours, Navy Lodge 0800-1800 hours M-F, 0900-1800 hours Sa-Su, holidays.

TML: CBQ. Building 1281, all ranks, leave or official duty. Bedroom, private bath (205). Refrigerator, microwave, A/C, color TV/VCR in room & lounge, housekeeping service, washer/dryer. Modern structure, renovated. Rates: E1-E9, $11.00;$2.75 each additional person, W1-O5 Suite, $16, $4 each additional person; O6, GS15 and above DV Suite, $24, $6 each additional person. Maximum 3 persons. Duty can make reservations, others Space-A.

TML: Navy Lodge. Building 1281, all ranks, leave or official duty. Call **1-800-NAVY-INN**. Lodge number is C-512-937-6361. 0800-1800 hours M-F, 0900-1800 hours Sa-Su, holidays. Suites, one double bed, sofa sleeper, private bath (10); bedroom, double bed, private bath (11). One handicapped accessible unit, 12 non-smoking. Kitchenette, microwave, utensils, A/C (seasonal), CATV, clocks, coffee/tea, cribs highchairs, hair dryers, irons/boards, housekeeping service, rollaways, coin washer/dryer, ice/snack vending. Modern structure. Rates: $31-$39 per unit. All categories can make reservations. PCS on orders can make reservations anytime.

DV/VIP: Protocol Office. Building 1281, Admin Office, C-512-939-2388/2389, D-312-861-2388/2389. Commander's discretion. Retirees and lower ranks Space-A.

TML Availability: Very Good, Jan-Mar & Jun-Dec. Difficult, Apr-May.

CREDIT CARDS ACCEPTED: The Navy Lodge accepts Visa, MasterCard, American Express, Diners and Discover.

The Padre Island National Seashore, the famous King Ranch, the Confederate Air Force Flying Museum, and the Texas State Aquarium are all local sights worth seeing.

Locator 939-2383   Medical 939-3735/3839   Police 939-3460

TEXAS

Dallas Naval Air Station (TX12R3)
Combined Bachelors Quarters
8100 West Jefferson Blvd
Dallas, TX 75211-5000

Scheduled to move to Fort Worth NAS/Joint Reserve Base in 1996. Dallas NAS will close after the move is complete. Call ahead in ensure TML is still available.

TELEPHONE NUMBER INFORMATION: Main installation numbers: C-214-266-6111, D-312-874-6111.

Location: Exit from I-30 at loop 12 west of Dallas, go south on loop 12 to Jefferson Ave exit. NAS on left, south side, of ave. Near Grand Prairie. *USMRA: Page 88 (E-3)*. NMC: Dallas, 15 miles northeast.

Lodging Office: Building 209, 8100 West Jefferson Blvd, **C-214-266-6155**, 24 hours daily. Check in facility, check out 1100 hours daily. Government civilian employee billeting.

TML: BOQ. Building 8, officers all ranks, leave or official duty, C-214-266-6134/5. Bedroom, hall bath (80); suites (VIP); family room (1). Washer/dryer. Older structure. Rates: $8 per person, $2 each additional person; Suites, $15 per person, $3 each additional person; VIP $20, $5 each additional person. Duty can make reservations, others Space-A.

TML: BEQ. Buildings 209, 231, enlisted all ranks, leave or official duty. Beds, hall bath (564). Rates: $5 per day, private room, E5+, $8, guests $2 additional; VIP E7+, $15, guests $3 additional. Duty can make reservations, others Space-A.

DV/VIP: Administrative Officer, C-214-266-6103/6104. Commander's discretion.

TML Availability: Difficult & unpredictable.

CREDIT CARDS ACCEPTED: Visa, MasterCard and American Express.

Texas is "another country" and Dallas is big city Texas. Don't miss the museums, the shopping and especially Texas Barbecue! Also, checkout Wet n' Wild Water Park and Six Flags Over Texas.

Locator 266-6111   Medical 266-6283   Police 266-6139

Dyess Air Force Base (TX14R3)
Dyess Inn
441 5th Street
Dyess AFB, TX 79607-1244

TELEPHONE NUMBER INFORMATION: Main installation numbers: C-915-696-3113, D-312-461-1110.

Location: Six miles southwest of Abilene. Main gate is 3 miles east of I-20. Accessible from I-20 & US-277. *USMRA: Page 87 (I-3)*. NMC: Abilene, 6 miles northeast.

TEXAS
Dyess Air Force Base, continued

Lodging Office: Dyess Inn, building 441, 5th St, **C-915-696-8610**, D-312-461-2681, FAX D-312-461-2836, 24 hours daily. Check in facility, check out 1200 hours daily. Government civilian employee lodging.

TML: TLF. Bldg 325 Fourth St, all ranks, leave or official duty, handicapped accessible. Separate bedroom, private bath (sleeps 5)(340). Kitchen (w/utensils), A/C, color TV, cribs/cots, washer/dryer, ice vending. Modern structure. Rates: $11-$24. Duty can make reservations, others Space-A.

TML: VAQ. Building 313 Fifth St, enlisted all ranks, leave or official duty. Single rooms, shared bath (52). Refrigerator, A/C, color TV, housekeeping service, washer/dryer, ice vending. Rates: $8-$14. Duty can make reservations, others Space-A.

TML: VOQ. Buildings 225, 233, 241, 249, 441, officers all ranks, senior enlisted only. Handicapped accessible, leave or official duty. One bedroom, private bath (42), separate bedroom DV/VIP suites (8), private bath. Kitchen (suites only), refrigerator, A/C, color TV, housekeeping service, washer/dryer, ice vending. Older structure, remodeled. Rates: $8-$14 per person. Maximum 2 per room. Duty can make reservations, others Space-A.

DV/VIP: 7 WG. Protocol Office, C-915-696-5610, O6+. Retirees & lower ranks Space-A.

TML Availability: Very good all year.

CREDIT CARDS ACCEPTED: Visa, MasterCard and American Express.

Abilene has an award winning Zoo, a collection of vintage aircraft on display at the base Air Park, boating, fishing and sailing at Lake Fort Phantom Hill, and a visit to Buffalo Gap Historic Village a "must".

Locator 696-3098   **Medical** 696-4677   **Police** 696-2131

Fort Bliss (TX06R3)
Fort Bliss Billeting
P.O. Box 16150
Fort Bliss, TX 79906-1150

TELEPHONE NUMBER INFORMATION: Main installation numbers: C-915-568-2121, D-312-978-0831.

Location: From I-10 take airport exit to Robert E Lee gate. From US-54 take Pershing Road to Ft Bliss. *USMRA: Page 86 (B,C-5,6).* NMC: El Paso, within city limits.

Lodging Office: Building 251, Club Rd, **C-915-568-4888**, D-312-978-4888, FAX 915-568-7078, DSN FAX 312-978-7078, 24 hours daily. Check in billeting, check out 1100 hours daily. **Note: see Armed Services YMCA for additional TML on Fort Bliss.**

TML: Guest House. The Inn at Fort Bliss, **C-915-565-7777**, all ranks, leave or official duty. Deluxe kitchenette units with microwave and coffee maker and additional standard units. CATV, A/C, cribs ($2), housekeeping service, ice vending. Rates: For standard rooms, $31.75 single, $37.50 double, $5 each additional person; for deluxe rooms, $34.25 single, $41 double, $5 each additional person. Call

TEXAS
Fort Bliss, continued

for reservation information.

TML: Transient Facilities. Officer and senior enlisted, leave or official duty, C-915-568-4888/2703. Building 251 for check-in. Shared bath, private bath, refrigerator, A/C, color TV, housekeeping service. Private suites. Rates: $22, TDY to Fort Bliss can make reservations, others Space-A.

TML: DV/VIP. Three houses, 4 suites, officers O7+, leave or official duty, C-915-568-5319. Completely furnished DV/VIP facility. Rates: $24 daily. All categories can make reservations.

TML: Fisher House, (William Beaumont Army Medical Center). **C-915-568-6600, ext 6433.** Note: Appendix C has the definition of this facility.

DV/VIP: Protocol Office, C-915-568-5319/5225, O7+, retirees and lower ranks Space-A.

TML Availability: Good, Nov-Jan. Difficult, other times.

CREDIT CARDS ACCEPTED: Visa, MasterCard and American Express.

Visit old Juarez and the Tiqua Indian Reservation, check out the Scenic Drive that gives you a view of all of El Paso and old Mexico. There are numerous military museums on post.

Locator 568-1113   Medical 569-2331   Police 568-2115

Fort Hood (TX02R3)
Transient Billeting, Bldg 108
Fort Hood, TX 76544-5057

TELEPHONE NUMBER INFORMATION: Main installation numbers: C-817-288-1110, 287-1110, D-312-738-1110.

Location: From I-35 North exit to US-190 West, 9 miles to Killeen. Main gate is clearly marked. *USMRA: Page 87 (K-4,5).* NMC: Killeen, at main entrance.

Lodging Office: Building 36006, Wratten Dr, **C-817-287-0422**, FAX 817-288-7604, 24 hours daily. Check in facility, check out 1100 hours daily. Reservations, call 817-287-3815/2700, 0730-1630 Mon-Fri. Government civilian employee billeting.

TML: Poxon Guest House. Building 111, all ranks, leave or official duty, C-817-288-3067. Bedroom, private bath (75). Refrigerator, community kitchen, A/C, color TV room & lounge, housekeeping service, cribs/cots, washer/dryer, ice vending, handicapped accessible. Older structure, renovated. Rates: $16 single, $22 double, maximum $25 per large family (2 rooms). Duty can make reservations, others Space-A. Kennels available.

TML: VQ. Building 36006, all ranks, leave or official duty. Bedroom, private bath (225). Refrigerator, A/C, color TV, housekeeping service, washer/dryer, ice vending. Older structure renovated. Rates: $20 TDY/PCS. Duty can make reservations, others Space-A.

TML: VQ. Buildings 5786/88/90/92, all ranks, leave or official duty. Bedroom, (113). Refrigerator, community kitchen, A/C, color TV, housekeeping service, washer/dryer, ice vending. Older structure, renovated. Rates: $24.50 TDY, $29.50 PCS. Duty can make reservations, others Space-A.

TEXAS
Fort Hood, continued

TML: Junior Guest Quarters. Buildings 2305/06/07, enlisted E1-E4, leave or official duty, C-817-288-3067. Bedroom, shared bath (48). Refrigerator, community kitchen, A/C, color TV in room & lounge, housekeeping service, cribs/cots, washer/dryer. Older structure. Rates: $10. Duty can make reservations, others Space-A.

TML: DV/VIP. Building 36006, officers O6+, leave or official duty, C-817-288-5001. Two bedroom, private bath (10). Kitchen, utensils, A/C, color TV, housekeeping service, cribs/cots, washer/dryer, ice vending. Older structure, remodeled. Rates: $25 TDY/PCS. Duty can make reservations, others Space-A.

DV/VIP: Executive Service. Building 1, C-817-288-5001, O6/GS-15+, retirees Space-A.

TML Availability: Good, winter months. Difficult, May-Sep.

CREDIT CARDS ACCEPTED: Visa, MasterCard and American Express.

Visitors should tour Lake Belton, and other lakes in the regions where boating, fishing, swimming and camping are main pursuits for residents.

Locator 287-2137   Medical 288-8133   Police 287-2176

Fort Sam Houston (TX18R3)
Billeting Office
Bldg 592, Dickman Road
Fort Sam Houston, TX 78234-5000

TELEPHONE NUMBER INFORMATION: Main installation numbers: C-210-221-1110, D-312-471-1110.

Location: Take the Fort Sam Houston exit off of I-35. *USMRA: Page 91 (C,D- 2,3).* NMC: San Antonio, northeast section of city.

Billeting Office: Building 592, Dickman Rd, **C-210-221-6125/6262**, D-312-471-6125/6262, FAX 210-221-6275, DSN FAX 312-471-6275, 24 hours daily. Check in facility 1300, check out 1100 hours daily. Government civilian employee billeting.

TML: Guest House. Building 1002, Gorgas Circle, all ranks, leave or official duty, C-210-221-2744. Rooms, private bath (115). Two room suites, refrigerator, microwave, A/C, color TV, housekeeping service, cribs, coin washer/dryer, rollaway $4. Rates: $22, $26 suites. Duty can make reservations, others Space-A.

TML: VOQ. Buildings 592 & 1384, officers all ranks, leave or official duty. Rooms, private bath (500). Kitchen, refrigerator, A/C, color TV, housekeeping service, washer/dryer. Rates: $23, second guest $11.75. Duty can make reservations, others Space-A.

TML: VEQ. Buildings 590/591. TDY enlisted students only. Units, shared bath (228). Refrigerator, microwave, A/C, color TV, housekeeping service, washer/dryer. Rates $23.50.

TML: DV/VIP. Buildings 48 (Staff Post Rd), 107 (Artillery Post), officers O6+ and comparable grade DoD civilian, leave or official duty. Two bedroom suite, private bath (3), one bedroom suite, private

TEXAS
Fort Sam Houston, continued

bath (21). Breakfast served (M-F) both buildings. Refrigerator, A/C, color TV, honor bar, housekeeping service. Recently renovated. Rates: $29.50, second guest $14.75. All categories can make reservations. All except TDY subject to bump.

TML: Fisher House, Brook Army Medical Center. Note: Appendix C has the definition of this facility. **C-210-228-4855-EX-101.**

DV/VIP: PROTOCOL. C-210-221-2231, O6+, retirees & lower ranks Space-A.

TML Availability: Good. Best Oct-Mar.

CREDIT CARDS ACCEPTED: Visa, MasterCard, and American Express.

Surrounded by San Antonio, this historic post has seen much colorful military history, from its namesake to the "Rough Riders" and Teddy Roosevelt, and key roles in WWI and WWII, to today's role as a medical training center. While you're here why not visit The Alamo, Retama Horse Racing Park and Sea World. Also visit the Quadrangle Military Museum.

Locator 221-2302   Medical 221-6141/6142   Police 221-2222

Fort Worth NAS/Joint Reserve Base (TX21R3)
CBQ, Building 1565
Fort Worth NAS/Joint Reserve Base, TX 76127

TELEPHONE NUMBER INFORMATION: Main installation numbers: C-817-782-5000, D-312-739-1110.

Location: On TX-183. From Fort Worth, west on I-30, exit at Camp Bowie Blvd., then turn right onto Horne St. Follow signs to main gate. *USMRA: Page 87 (K-3) & Page 88 (A-3)*. NMC: Fort Worth, 7 miles east.

Lodging Office: Building 1565, D Street, **C-817-782-5449**, FAX 817-782-7606, 24 hours daily. Check in facility, check out 1200 hours daily. Government civilian employee billeting.

TML: VAQ/VOQ. Buildings 1565/6, officers all ranks, leave or official duty. Bedroom, shared bath. All rooms have a shared bath, refrigerator, microwave, A/C, color TV, housekeeping service, laundry room in building, ice. Modern structure. Rates: $8, each additional person $8. Maximum 2 per unit. TDY can make reservations, others Space-A.

TML: DV. Building 1565, officer O6+, leave or official duty. Chief suites (5), Officer suites (5). One bedroom suites, shared bath. Sitting room, Refrigerator, microwave and limited utensils, A/C, color TV, housekeeping service, washer/dryer, ice. Modern structure. Rates: $12, each additional person, $12. Duty can make reservations, others Space-A.

DV/VIP: Protocol, C-817-782-7614.

TML Availability: Limited space due to rehabilitation of many buildings. It's best to make reservations 30-45 days in advance.

CREDIT CARDS ACCEPTED: Visa, MasterCard, and American Express.

TEXAS
Fort Worth NAS/Joint Reserve Base, continued

Visit the historic Stockyard District, and then world renowned art museums. How about Southfork? Or the Water Gardens? Or Six Flags Over Texas, and the Opera? Fort Worth has come a long way since 1841!

Locator 782-5000   Police 782-5200

Goodfellow Air Force Base (TX24R3)
Angelo Inn, Bldg 3305
313 E. Kearney Blvd E.
Goodfellow AFB, TX 76908

TELEPHONE NUMBER INFORMATION: Main installation numbers: C-915-654-3231, D-312-477-3217.

Location: Off US-87 or US-277, clearly marked, *USMRA: Page 86 (H-6,7)*. NMC: San Angelo, 2 miles northwest.

Lodging Office: Angelo Inn, building 3305, Kearney Blvd, **C-915-654-3332,** D-312-477-3332, FAX 915-654-5177, DSN FAX 312-477-5177, 24 hours daily. Check in facility, check out 1200 hours daily. Government civilian employee billeting.

TML: TLF. Buildings 910, 920, 922, 924, all ranks, leave or official duty. Handicapped accessible. Separate bedrooms, private bath (29). Kitchen, complete utensils, color TV, housekeeping service, cribs, washer/dryer, ice vending. Modern structure. Rates: E6, $14; E7+, $18. PCS can make reservations, others Space-A.

TML: VAQ. Buildings 3307,3311, enlisted all ranks, leave or official duty, handicapped accessible. Room with bed, shared bath (100); room with 2 beds, shared bath (270). Building 239 - NCO Academy, bedroom, shared bath (60). Refrigerator, microwave, A/C, color TV, housekeeping service, washer/dryer. Modern structure. Rates: $4 per person. Duty can make reservations, others Space-A.

TML: VOQ. Buildings 702, 711, officers all ranks, leave or official duty. Separate bedrooms, private bath (115). Kitchenette, microwave, A/C, color TV, housekeeping service, washer/dryer, microwave. Modern structure. Rates: $5-$10 per person. TDY can make reservations, others Space-A.

TML: DV/EV. Building 910 (DV), building 3307 (EV), officers O6+, enlisted E7, leave or official duty. Separate bedrooms, private bath (10). Kitchen, complete utensils, A/C, color TV, housekeeping service, washer/dryer, ice vending. Modern structure. Rates: $10 per person. Duty can make reservations, others Space-A.

TML Availability: Fairly good all year.

CREDIT CARDS ACCEPTED: Diners.

Visit historic Fort Concho, a preserved Indian fort, and home of the "Buffalo Soldiers", the Concho River Walk and Plaza, and three lakes within 20 minutes of downtown feature camping, boating and fishing.

Locator 654-3410   Medical 654-3135   Police 654-3304

218 - Temporary Military Lodging Around the World

TEXAS

Kelly Air Force Base (TX03R3)
Bldg 1650 Goodrich Road
Kelly AFB, TX 78241-5000

TELEPHONE NUMBER INFORMATION: Main installation numbers: C-210-925-1110, D-312-945-1110.

Location: All of the following, I-10, I-35, I-37, I-410 intersect with US-90. From US-90 take either the Gen Hudnell or Gen McMullen exit and go south to Kelly AFB. *USMRA: Page 91 (B-3,4).* NMC: San Antonio, 7 miles northeast.

Lodging Office: Building 1650, Goodrich Road, **C-210-925-1844/924-7201**, D-312-945-1844, 24 hours daily. Check in billeting, check out 1200 hours daily. Government civilian employee billeting.

TML: VOQ. Building 1676, officers all ranks, leave or official duty. Bedroom, private bath (12 private, 32 shared). Kitchen (shared), microwave, A/C, CATV, housekeeping service, washer/dryer, ice vending. Older structure. Rates: $5.75 per person. Maximum 2 persons. Duty can make reservations, others Space-A.

TML: VAQ. Building 1650, enlisted all ranks, leave or official duty. Bedroom, shared bath (E7-E8) (2); separate bedroom, private bath (E9) (2); bedroom, 2 beds, common bath (E1-E6) (22). Refrigerator, microwave, A/C, CATV, housekeeping service, washer/dryer, ice vending. Older structure. Rates $5.75 per person. Maximum 2 persons. Duty can make reservations, others Space-A.

TML: DV/VIP. Building 1676, officers O9+, leave or official duty. Separate bedrooms, private bath (6). Kitchen, A/C, CATV, housekeeping service, cribs/cots, washer/dryer, ice vending. Older structure. Rates: $14 per person. Maximum 4 persons. Duty can make reservations, others Space-A.

DV/VIP: Protocol Office, building 1680, C-210-925-7678, O7/GS-16+. Retirees and lower ranks Space-A.

TML Availability: Poor all year.

Your trip to San Antonio will be well remembered if you visit Sea World, Fiesta Texas, the Alamo and the historic mission sites.

Locator 925-1841   Medical 925-4544   Police 925-6811

Kingsville Naval Air Station (TX22R3)
CBQ, Bldg 2700
1140 Moffett Ave.
Kingsville NAS, TX 78363-5000

TELEPHONE NUMBER INFORMATION: Main installation numbers: C-512-595-6121, D-312-861-6121.

Location: Off US-77 South, exit to TX-425 Southeast to main gate. *USMRA: Page 87 (K-8).* NMC: Corpus Christi, 40 miles northeast.

TEXAS
Kingsville Naval Air Station, continued

Lodging Office: Building 2700, 1140 Moffett Avenue, **C-512-595-6321**, FAX 512-595-6428, 24 hours daily. Check in facility after 0800, check out by 1200 hours daily. Government civilian employee billeting.

TML: BOQ/BEQ. Buildings 2700, 3729, 3730, 3730A, 3730W, all ranks. Bedrooms, private bath, shared lounge (36); bedrooms, private bath, shared lounge (16). CATV, refrigerator, amenities, microwaves, A/C, laundry facilities, vending machines, housekeeping service. Thirty-five upgraded rooms, new carpet, furniture. Rates: officer $8, accompanied by rank; enlisted $4, accompanied by rank; DoD civilian $18, accompanied $24. PCS-in, PCS-out personnel should make reservations, others Space-A.

DV/VIP: Protocol Office, building 3730W, C-512-595-6481, O6+. VIP three room suites (6). Retirees Space-A.

TML Availability: Excellent Dec-Jan.

CREDIT CARDS ACCEPTED: Visa, MasterCard and American Express.

Home of the King Ranch, for Santa Gertrudis cattle, beautiful thoroughbred and quarter horses, the historic ranch house, and other interesting sites. Texas A&I University is located here.

Locator 595-6136   **Medical 595-6455**   **Police 595-6217**

Lackland Air Force Base (TX25R3)
37 SVS/SVML
1750 Femoyer Street
Lackland AFB, TX 78236-5431

TELEPHONE NUMBER INFORMATION: Main installation numbers: C-210-671-1110, D-312-473-1110.

Location: Off US-90 South. Loop 13 (Military Drive) bisects Lackland AFB. *USMRA: Page 87 (J-6,7); Page 91 (A,B-3,4).* NMC: San Antonio, 6 miles northeast.

Lodging Office: Building 10203, 1750 Femoyer Street, **C-210-671-2523/4277**, D-312-473-2556, FAX 210-671-4822, DSN FAX 312-473-4822 0730-1630 M-F. Mailing address: 1750 Femoyer St, Lackland AFB, TX 78236-5431.

TML: TLQ/VAQ. All ranks, building 10203, west side of base, Femoyer Street, 24 hours daily, C-EX-4270/4277. Check in facility, check out 1200 hours daily. Separate bedrooms, private bath (160); Two person rooms, semi-private baths (770) and 78 SNCO rooms, semi-private baths. A/C, color TV, housekeeping service, cribs, washer/dryer, ice vending. Handicapped accessible. Modern structure. Rates: TLQ $16-$22 per unit, VAQ $4-$10 per unit. Duty can request reservations, all others Space-A.

TML: VOQ/DV/VIP: Building 2604, 24 hours daily, C-210-671-3622, officers all ranks, leave or official duty. Separate bedrooms, shared bath (32); separate bedrooms, private bath (96). Microwave, refrigerator, A/C, color TV, housekeeping service, washer/dryer, ice/snack vending. Bedroom suites, private bath (DV/VIP) (13) Two bedroom suites, private bath (DV/VIP) (4). Refrigerator, A/C, color

TEXAS
Lackland Air Force Base, continued

TV, housekeeping service, washer/dryer, ice vending. Older structure, remodeled. Rates: $5-$10 per person. Duty can make reservations, others Space-A.

TML: Fisher House. Note: Appendix C has the definition of this facility. **C-210-678-3000.**

DV/VIP: Protocol Office, C-210-671-2423. O6+.

TML Availability: Difficult, Feb-Oct.

San Antonio takes its name from Mission San Antonio de Valero or, the Alamo. Visiting the local Missions, and brushing up on the long history of this gracious city, is only one of a number of activities for visitors here.

Locator 671-1110   Medical 670-7100   Police 671-2018

Laughlin Air Force Base (TX05R3)
Laughlin Manor
47 SVS/SVML
416 Liberty Drive
Laughlin AFB, TX 78843-5000

TELEPHONE NUMBER INFORMATION: Main installation numbers: C-210-298-3511, D-312-732-1110.

Location: Take US-90 west from San Antonio, 150 miles or US-277 south from San Angelo, 150 miles to Del Rio area. The AFB is clearly marked off US-90. *USMRA: Page 86 (H-9)*. NMC: Del Rio, 8 miles northwest.

Lodging Office: Laughlin Manor. 416 Liberty Drive, **C-210-298-5731**, D-312-732-5731, FAX 210-298-5272, DSN FAX 312-732-5272, 24 hours. Check in billeting, check out 1200 hours daily. No government civilian employee billeting.

TML: TLF. Buildings 460-463, all ranks, leave or official duty. Separate bedroom, private bath (20). Kitchen, utensils, A/C, color TV, limited housekeeping service, cribs, washer/dryer (building 463), ice vending. Modern structure. Rates: E1-E6, $16 per unit; E7+, $20 per unit. Duty can make reservations, others Space-A.

TML: VOQ/VAQ. Building 470, all ranks, leave or official duty. Bedroom, shared bath (officers all ranks) (16); bedroom, shared bath (enlisted all ranks) (14). Refrigerator, A/C, color TV in room & lounge, housekeeping service, cribs/cots, washer/dryer, ice vending. Older structure, renovated. Rates: $6 per person VOQ, $5 per person VAQ. Duty can make reservations, others Space-A.

TML: DV/VIP. Building 470, officers O6+, leave or official duty. Separate bedroom, private bath (2); three bedroom, private bath (4). Kitchen, utensils, color TV, housekeeping service, washer/dryer, ice vending. Older structure, renovated. Rates: $10 per person. Duty can make reservations, others Space-A.

DV/VIP: 47 FTW/CCP, building 338, room 1, C-210-298-5041, O6+.

TEXAS
Laughlin Air Force Base, continued

TML Availability: Good, Nov-Jan. Difficult, other times.

CREDIT CARDS ACCEPTED: American Express.

Visit the historical district in Brown Plaza, particularly for Cinco de Mayo and Diez Y Seis de Septiembre celebrations. The Brinkley Mansion, Valverde Winery, and the visitor's center at Lake Amistad, are all worthwhile to visit.

Locator 298-3511   Medical 911   Police 911

Randolph Air Force Base (TX19R3)
12 SVS/SVML
415 B Street East
Randolph AFB, TX 78150-4424

TELEPHONE NUMBER INFORMATION: Main installation numbers: C-210-652-1110, D-312-487-1110.

Location: From I-35 take exit 172, Pat Booker Rd. From I-10 take exit 587, TX FM-1604. *USMRA: Page 91 (E-2)*. NMC: San Antonio, 6 miles south.

Lodging Office: Building 118, **C-210-652-1844**, FAX 210-652-2616, 24 hours daily. Check in billeting, check out 1200 hours daily. Government civilian employee billeting in TDY status.

TML: TLF. Buildings 152-155, all ranks, PCS in/out, leave or official duty. Handicapped accessible (1). Bedroom, private bath (30). Living room, full kitchen, utensils, A/C, color TV, housekeeping service, iron & board, hair dryer, cribs/cots, washer/dryer, ice vending. Older structure, renovated. Rates $16-$20 per person, depending on rank. PCS in/out can make reservations, others Space-A.

TML: VOQ. Buildings 110, 111, 120, 121, 161, 162, 381, officers all ranks, leave or official duty. Bedroom, living room, private bath (100), 76 with stocked bar & snacks; bedroom, private bath (256), 160 with stocked bar & snacks; two bedroom, two private bath, living room, kitchen with stocked bar & snacks (2). A/C, refrigerator, microwave, color TV, utensils for two, iron & board, hair dryer, housekeeping service, washer/dryer, cribs/cots, ice vending. Some modern, some older structures. Rates: $6-$10 per person. Duty can make reservations, others Space-A.

TML: VAQ. Buildings 861, 862, enlisted all ranks, leave or official duty. Bedroom, living room, kitchen, stocked bar & snacks, private bath (3); bedroom, queen bed, private bath, stocked bar & snacks (68); bedroom, queen bed, shared bath (54). Bedroom, single bed, shared bath (48). A/C, color TV, housekeeping service, refrigerator, microwave, utensils for two, iron & board, hair dryer, cribs/cots, ice vending, washer/dryer. Modern structure. Rates: $5-$10 per person. TDY can make reservations, others Space-A.

DV/VIP: Protocol. Bldg 900, room 306, C-210-652-4126, O7+/SES. All retirees Space-A.

TML Availability: Good, Nov-Feb. Fair, other times.

CREDIT CARDS ACCEPTED: Visa, MasterCard and American Express.

TEXAS
Randolph Air Force Base, continued

San Antonio is nestled between the Texas Hill Country and the coast, and there are a wealth of local things to do. Visit New Braunfels, to the north for a fascinating look at Texas' German past, and Sequin to the East.

Locator 652-1841   Medical 652-2734   Police 652-5700

Red River Army Depot (TX09R3)
Housing Office
ATTN; SDSRR-O
100 Main Drive
Texarkana, TX 75507-5000

TELEPHONE NUMBER INFORMATION: Main installation numbers: C-903-334-2141, D-312-829-4110.

Location: From I-30 East or West, take Red River Army Depot exit #206 south 1/2 mi. Route clearly marked. *USMRA: Page 87 (N-2)*. NMC: Texarkana, 20 miles east.

Lodging Office: Building 228, 100 Main Dr., **C-903-334-3976/3227**, FAX-903-334-2494, D-312-829-3976, 0700-1700 M-Th. Check in billeting, check out 1100 hours. No government civilian employee billeting. Red River Army Depot has won Army Community of Excellence Awards three years in a row! Red River also won a Presidential Quality Improvement Prototype Award for 1995, having been a runner-up in 1994.

TML: BOQ. Building 40, all ranks, leave or official duty, retired. Bedroom, private bath (1), refrigerator, microwave, coffee service, A/C, CATV w/HBO; separate living room/bedrooms, private bath (5), kitchenette, microwave, coffee service, A/C, CATV w/HBO. TV room, housekeeping service (Mon-Fri), washer/dryer, roll-away beds, cribs. New building and furnishings. Rates: sponsor $11.50, additional adult, child, infant $4, maximum per family $19.50. Maximum five per room. Reservations for after hours check-in. Small pets if leashed outside OK.

TML: DV/VIP. Building 40, officers O6+, leave or official duty. Report to Protocol Office, C-903-334-2316. Separate rooms, private bath (2), one with bedroom, refrigerator/microwave, coffee service; one with living room, bedroom, kitchenette/microwave, limited utensils (2). Rooms adjoin and may be used as a single, 2-bedroom unit. A/C, CATV w/HBO & TV room, housekeeping service, laundry and TV room, roll-away beds, cribs. New building and furnishings. Rates: same. Duty can make reservations, others Space-A. DV/VIP are designated non-smoking rooms.

DV/VIP: Protocol Office, ATTN: SDSRR-AP, building 15, C-903-334-2316, O6+, GS-14+. Retirees, lower ranks DoD civilians Space-A.

TML Availability: Extremely limited, best, Nov-Mar, worst, Apr-Oct.

CREDIT CARDS ACCEPTED: Diners.

Lake Texarkana, nine miles southwest of the city, offers all water sports. Many local golf courses, and September's Four States Fair and Rodeo are the pride of local residents. There's a 9-hole golf course, tennis courts, and a swimming pool all within walking distance of BOQ.

Locator 334-2141   Medical 911   Police 334-2911

TEXAS

Reese Air Force Base (TX20R3)
Reese Inn
64th SVS/SVML
377 D Street, Suite 1
Reese AFB, TX 79489-5011

TELEPHONE NUMBER INFORMATION: Main installation numbers: C-806-885-4511, D-312-838-1110.

Location: From west side of Loop 289 at Lubbock take 4th St West, 6 miles. Road terminates at AFB, main gate is one block north. *USMRA: Page 86 (F-4)*. NMC: Lubbock, 6 miles east.

Lodging Office: The Reese Inn, building 1142, K St, **C-806-885-3155/3185,** D-312-838-3155, FAX 806-885-6510, DSN Fax 312-838-6510 24 hours daily. Check in billeting, check out 1200 hours daily. No government civilian employee billeting.

TML: TLF. Building 1150, all ranks, leave or official duty. Bedroom, private bath (25). Units 1 & 2 dedicated for DAVs. Kitchen, microwave, limited utensils, color TV, housekeeping service, cribs/cots, washer/dryer, ice vending. Modern structure. Rates: E6, $15 per unit; E7+, $19 per unit. PCS can make reservations, others Space-A.

TML: VAQ. Building 1030, enlisted E1-E7, leave or official duty. Efficiency rooms, private bath (16). Kitchen, microwave, limited utensils, A/C, color TV, housekeeping service, washer/dryer, ice vending. Modern structure. Rates: $6 per person. TDY/PCS can make reservations, others Space-A.

TML: VAQ. Building 1030, E8-E9, leave or official duty. Bedroom/living room SNCO suites, private bath, (4). Kitchen, microwave, limited utensils, A/C, color TV, housekeeping service, cots, washer/dryer, ice vending. Modern structure. Rates: $10 per person. TDY/PCS can make reservations, others Space-A.

TML: VOQ. Building 1030, O1+. Leave, or official duty. Efficiency rooms, private bath (14). Kitchen, microwave, limited utensils, A/C, color TV, housekeeping service, washer/dryer, cots, ice vending. Modern structure. Rates $7 per person. TDY/PCS can make reservations, others Space-A.

TML: DV. Building 1030, O5+, leave or official duty. Bedroom/living room suites (2). Kitchen, microwave, limited utensils, A/C, color TV, VCR, housekeeping service, cots, washer/dryer, ice vending. Modern structure. Rates: $10 per person. TDY/PCS can make reservations, others Space-A.

TML: VIP. Building 1030, O5+, leave or official duty. Bedroom/living room suites (2). Kitchen, microwave, limited utensils, A/C, color TV, housekeeping service, cots, washer/ dryer, ice vending. Modern structure. Rates: $7 per person. TDY/PCS can make reservations, others Space-A.

DV/VIP: Wing Protocol, building 800, C-806-885-6187, D-312-838-6187.

TML Availability: Good, winter months. Difficult, summer months.

CREDIT CARDS ACCEPTED: American Express.

TEXAS
Reese Air Force Base, continued

Visit the Museum complex of Texas Tech, Moody Planetarium, Ranching Heritage Center and the Prairie Dog Town in Mackenzie State Park.

Locator 885-3276 **Medical 885-3285** **Police 885-3333**

Sheppard Air Force Base (TX37R3)
SVS/SVML
400 J Avenue
Sheppard AFB, TX 76311-5000

TELEPHONE NUMBER INFORMATION: Main installation numbers: C-817-676-2511, D-312-736-1001.

Location: Take US-281 North from Wichita Falls, exit to TX-325 which leads to main gate, clearly marked. *USMRA: Page 87 (J-1)*. NMC: Wichita Falls, 5 miles southwest.

Lodging Office: Sheppard Inn, 400 J Avenue, **C-817-855-7370**, D-312-736-2631/2632, FAX 817-676-7434, DSN FAX 312-736-743424 hours daily. Check in billeting, check out 1200 hours daily. Government civilian employee billeting.

TML: TLF. Buildings 160-165, all ranks, leave or official duty, C-817-855-2707. Separate bedrooms, private bath (50). Kitchen, utensils, A/C, color TV, housekeeping service, cribs/cots, washer/dryer, ice vending. Modern structure. Rates: E1-E6, $14; E7+, $18. Maximum 4 per unit. Duty can make reservations, others Space-A.

TML: VAQ. Buildings 693, 791, 792, 793,, 1601, 1602, 1603, 1604, enlisted all ranks, leave or official duty, C-817-855-2707. D-312-736-1844. Bedroom, two beds, shared bath (736); separate bedrooms, private bath (7); bedroom, 1 bed, private bath (348). A/C, ice vending, housekeeping service, refrigerator, color TV, washer/dryer, microwaves in lounges. Modern structure. Rates: $4 per person standard room, $10 per person suites. Maximum 2 per room. Duty can make reservations, others Space-A.

TML: VOQ. Buildings 260, 331, 332, 333, 370, Ave G, building 1511, Ream Ave, building 370, Ave I, officer all ranks, leave or official duty, C-817-855-2707, D-312-736-1844. Bedroom, private bath (300); separate bedrooms, private bath (14); bedroom, shared bath (47). Bedroom, private bath, kitchenette (120). Refrigerator, A/C, color TV, washer/dryer. Rates: $5 per person standard room, $10 per person suite. Max 2 per room. Duty can make reservations, others Space-A.

TML: DV/VIP. Building 332, officer O6+, leave or official duty, C-817-855-2123. D-312-736-2123. Separate bedroom suites (6), private bath. A/C, kitchenette, housekeeping service color TV, utensils, washer/dryer. Modern structure. Rates: $10 per person. Maximum 2 per room. Duty can make reservations, others Space-A.

DV/VIP: ATTN: STTC/CCEX, Stop 1, building 400, C-817-855-2123, D-312-736-2123. O6+. Retirees and lower ranks Space-A.

TML Availability: Good during winter months, difficult Apr-Sep.

CREDIT CARDS ACCEPTED: Visa, MasterCard and American Express.

TEXAS
Sheppard Air Force Base, continued

Visit the Wichita Falls Museum and Art Center, Lucy Park, and the 3 1/2 mile drive to Wichita Falls' waterfall (the original washed away 100 years ago, and this one is man made!).

Locator 676-1841   **Medical 676-2333**   **Police 676-6302**

Too Late To Copy
Ingleside Naval Station, 1455 Ticonderoga, Suite W123, Ingleside, TX 73862-5001. BEQ, **C-512-776-4420**, D-312-776-4420, FAX 512-776-4620.

UTAH

CAMP W.G. WILLIAMS
Camp Williams Billeting
17800 S. Camp Williams Road
Riverton, UT 84065

TELEPHONE NUMBER INFORMATION: Main installation numbers: C-801-524-3669, D-312-924-3669.

Location: From I-15 take exit 296 (Draper./Riverton), turn W onto Hwy 111. Turn left at second traffic light, drive approximately 7 mi, Camp Williams is on the left. *USMRA: Page 112 (D-4)*. NMC: Salt Lake City, 25 mi N.

Lodging Office: Building 802, 17800 S. Camp Williams Rd, **C-801-576-3674**, D-312-766-3674, FAX 801-576-3672, 1000-1600 daily. Check in at Billeting Office, check out 1200.

TML: TLF. Building 820, officers, all ranks, enlisted E7-E9. Rooms, semi-private bath (60); Bedroom, private bath (5). Refrigerator, color TV, housekeeping service, washer/dryer. Rates: $4-$8. Active duty/reserve may make reservations, others Space-A.

TML Availability: Difficult. Best, fall and winter.

While you're here visit Salt Lake City's Temple Square, planetarium, Hogle Zoo, Trolley Square for shopping, Salt Palace for pro sports. Close to skiing and hiking.

Locator 524-3669   **Police 524-3669**

Dugway Proving Ground (UT04R4)
Billeting Office, 5228 Valdez Circle
Dugway, UT 84022

TELEPHONE NUMBER INFORMATION: Main installation numbers: C-801-831-2151, D-312-789-2151.

Location: Isolated but can be reached from I-80. Take Skull Valley Rd (exit 77) for 40 miles south. *USMRA: Page 112 (B,C-4,5)*. NMC: Salt Lake City, 80 miles northeast.

Lodging Office: Building 5228, Valdez Circle, **C-801-831-2333/2334**, FAX 801-831-2669, DSN FAX 312-789-2669, M-Th 0630-1845, F 0630-1445, closed weekends and holidays. After hours, Main Gate, 801-831-2718. Check in billeting 1800, check out 1100 hours daily. Government civilian employee billeting.

TML: VOQ/Houses. Buildings 5226, 5228, officer and enlisted, all ranks, leave or official duty. Bedroom, semi-private bath (19); separate bedroom suites (23); two bedroom houses (dual occupancy) (9). Refrigerator, A/C, color TV/VCR in room & lounge, housekeeping service (weekdays only), essentials, cribs/cots, washer/dryer, ice vending, microwave in lobby. Handicapped accessible. Older structures, remodeled. Rates: $8 per room, $20 per house, each additional occupant over 12, $3. Duty can make reservations, others including contractors and social guests Space-A.

DV/VIP: C-801-831-2020.

UTAH
Dugway Proving Ground, continued

TML Availability: Good. Best, fall and winter.

CREDIT CARDS ACCEPTED: Visa, MasterCard and American Express.

Pristine alpine mountains, vast deserts, the mysterious Great Salt Lake - this area offers a full round of outdoor activities without entry fees or hype, and is only minutes away from metropolitan Salt Lake City!

Locator 831-2151   **Medical 831-2222**   **Police 831-2933**

Hill Air Force Base (UT02R4)
5847 D Avenue
Hill AFB, UT 84056-5206

TELEPHONE NUMBER INFORMATION: Main installation numbers: C-801-777-7221, D-312-777-1100.

Location: Adjacent to I-15 between Ogden and Salt Lake City. Take exit 336, east on UT-193 to south gate. *USMRA: Page 112 (D-3)*. NMC: Ogden, 8 miles north.

Lodging Office: Mountain View Inn, building 146, D Ave, **C-801-777-1844**, FAX 801-775-2014, 24 hours daily. Check in lodging office, check out 1200 hours daily. Government civilian employee billeting.

TML: DV/VIP. Building 1118, officers O6+, official duty, leave or space-A. Separate bedroom suites, private bath (6). Kitchen (no stove), microwave, refrigerator, coffee pot, limited utensils, A/C, essentials, two color TVs, VCR, housekeeping service, washer/dryer, ice vending. Older structure, renovated. Rates: $14 single, $28 double. Duty can make reservations, others Space-A.

TML: DV-VOQ. Building 134. Three bedroom, dining, living, complete kitchen, 1 1/2 private baths (5). Laundry room, small yard. Two color TVs, A/C, VCR, essentials, ice machine, housekeeping service. Older structure, renovated. Rates: $14 single; $28 family. Official duty, leave or Space-A.

TML: DV-VOQ. Building 150. Separate bedroom suites, private bath (8); bedroom, private bath (1). Two color TV/s (suites), A/C, microwave, refrigerator, coffee pot, essentials, housekeeping service. Older structure, renovated. Rates: $14 single, $28 double. Official duty or Space-A.

TML: VOQ. Buildings 141, 142, officers all ranks, leave or official duty. Bedroom, private bath (40). Microwave, A/C, refrigerator, coffee pot, color TV, washer/dryer, ice machine, housekeeping service, essentials. Older structure, renovated. Rates: $8 single, $14 double. Duty can make reservations, others Space-A.

TML: VAQ. Buildings 350, 351, enlisted all ranks, leave or official duty. Building 351. Separate bedroom suites, private bath (76); building 350 (Prime Knight quarters) separate bedroom suites (25) (38 enlisted, 6 SNCO). Microfridge, A/C, TV, coffee pot. Older structures, renovated. Rates: $8, Chief suites $14. No families. Official duty may make reservations, others Space-A.

TML: VOQ-Chief Suites. Building 480. Separate bedroom suites, kitchen, bath; bedroom, shared living, kitchen and bath (16); bedroom, shared kitchen and bath (8). Two color TVs, A/C, complete utensils, ice machine, laundry room. Rates $8 single, $14 double. Official duty or Space-A.

UTAH
Hill Air Force Base, continued

TML: Building 472, all ranks. Separate bedroom, private bath, kitchen (40). A/C, complete utensils, two color TVs, cribs, rollaways. Washer/dryer, ice machine, limited housekeeping service. Older structure, renovated. Rate $22 per night. PCS/TDY can make reservations, others Space-A.

TML: Hillhaus Lodge, 5501 E. Snow Basin Road, P.O. Box 320, Huntsville, Utah, 84317. **C-801-777-2102,** D-312-458-3525, FAX 801-394-1416. **This lodge is now open to the public, reservations are highly recommended.** Bedrooms, private bath (3); suites, private bath (4); loft, sleeps 7 (1). Lounge, sun deck, gas fireplace, snack bar, kitchen, dining area. A-frame, renovated. Sleep and Ski packages. Rates: range from $45-$87.50. Entire lodge rental $450 per day. Breakfast, lunch and dinner offered. **Note:** check Military RV, Camping & Rec Areas Around the World for more information.

DV/VIP: Protocol ALC/CCP, building 1118, C-801-777-5565, O6+. Retirees Space-A.

TML Availability: Good.

CREDIT CARDS ACCEPTED: Visa and MasterCard. Hillhaus Lodge accepts Visa, MasterCard and American Express.

Locator 777-1844   Medical 777-1100   Police 777-3056

Tooele Army Depot (UT05R4)
ATTN; SDSTE-PWH
Tooele, UT 84074-5008

TELEPHONE NUMBER INFORMATION: Main installation numbers: C-801-833-3211, D-312-790-1110.

Location: From west I-80, exit 99 to UT-36 south for 15 miles to main entrance. *USMRA: Page 112 (C-4).* NMC: Salt Lake City, 40 miles northeast.

Lodging Office: Building 1, HQ Loop, **C-801-833-2124,** 0630-1700 hours M-Th, closed on Friday. Other hours, SDO, building 8, C-801-833-2304. Check in billeting, check out 1100 hours daily. Government civilian employee billeting.

TML: VOQ/DVQ. Building 35, all ranks, leave or official duty. Two bedroom apartments, private bath (9). One bedroom apartments, private bath (3). Kitchen w/utensils, A/C, CATV, housekeeping service, building washer/dryers. Rates: sponsor $8, additional adults $2. No charge for children, All categories may make reservations. No pets.

Military Discount Lodging: Comfort Inn, 491 S Main, Tooele, **C-801-882-6100. Best Western Inn,** 365 N Main, Tooele, **C-801-882-5010.**

TML Availability: Good. Best, Dec-Mar.

Some special sights in Salt Lake City: the Mormon Temple and Temple Square, the Pioneer Memorial museum. There are several local ski resorts within reach of Tooele.

Locator 833-2094   Medical 833-2572   Police 833-2314/2559

VIRGINIA

Camp Pendleton
Virginia National Guard (VA50R1)
Virginia Beach, VA 23461

TELEPHONE NUMBER INFORMATION: Main installation numbers: C-804-491-5140.

Location: Camp Pendleton is north of Dam Neck Fleet Combat Training Center, and south of Virginia Beach. Going south across the bridge from Virginia Beach on General Booth Blvd, watch for gate on the left. *USMRA: Page 52 (J-7)*. NMC: Virginia Beach, VA

Lodging Office: C-804-775-9101, FAX-804-775-9338. Write to: Adjutant Gen. Office, Dept. Military Affairs, 600 E. Broad St., Richmond, VA, 23219-1832. Government civilian employee lodging.

TML: Cottages and trailers. All ranks, leave or official duty. Two and three bedroom cottages, private bath (5); two bedroom trailers (5). A/C, color TV, screened porch, full kitchen, utensils, no housekeeping service (renters leave quarters clean), linens provided except for towels (bath and kitchen) cribs must be brought by renters. Rates: cottages $45-$60; trailers $30. One mile from beach. Write to above address for reservations. Reservations open 15 Mar. Cottages rent year round, trailers close 1 Nov. $100 deposit required. Two week notice for cancellation. After 1 April one week stay mandatory. National Guard has priority, others Space-A.

TML Availability: Difficult in summer. Best, Sept-Mar.

Its closeness to the eastern shore makes this place a find for visitors lucky enough to be able to rent one of the cottages or trailers.

Cheatham Annex Fleet and Industrial Supply Center (VA02R1)
Morale, Welfare & Recreation
108 Sanda Ave.
Williamsburg, VA 23185

TELEPHONE NUMBER INFORMATION: Main installation numbers: C-804-887-4000, D-312-953-4000.

Location: From I-64 take exit 242-B on US-199 east to main gate of Cheatham Annex. *USMRA: Page 47 (N-8)*. NMC: Williamsburg, 6 miles west.

Lodging Office: MWR, building 284, 108 Sanda St, **C-804-887-7224/7101/7102**, 0800-1530 hours week days, after duty hours, building 295, C-804-887-7418. No government civilian employee billeting.

TML: Recreation Cabins. Cabins 161, 163-165, 167-170, 261, 262, active duty, retirees and reservists, handicapped accessible. Reservations required 90 days advance. Minimum 2 night stay in cabins. Twelve cottages, private bath, kitchen, complete utensils, refrigerator, cribs ($1), color TV, central heat and air, woodburning stove, boat, electric motor, battery charger, paddles, cushions. No woodburning stove in mobile homes. Rates: winter 1 Nov thru 31 Mar - cabins, $33-$48 daily/$198-

VIRGINIA
Cheatham Annex Fleet & Industrial Supply Center, continued

$288 week. Summer 1 Apr thru 31 Oct - cabins, $35-$51 daily/$210-$306 week. First call first serve basis.

DV/VIP: Cabins 261, 161, reserved O6+. Commander's Office, C-804-887-7108.

TML Availability: Good, Nov-Mar. Good Mon-Fri., Difficult, other months, Fri-Sun.

CREDIT CARDS ACCEPTED: Visa, MasterCard and American Express.

Near Colonial Williamsburg/Jamestown, many museums. Busch Gardens. Great deer hunting, contact Special Services. Fitness Center, pool, racquetball, tennis courts, bowling alley, Snack Bar.

Locator 887-4000   **Medical 887-7222**   **Police 887-7222**

Dahlgren Naval Surface Warfare Center (VA06R1)
Lodging Office, Bldg 960
Dahlgren, VA 22448-5000

TELEPHONE NUMBER INFORMATION: Main installation numbers: C-540-653-8531, D-312-249-1110.

Location: From I-95 in Fredericksburg, VA, east on VA-3 to VA-206 (17 miles), left at VA-206, east to Dahlgren (11 miles). Also, US-301 south to VA-206, east to main gate. *USMRA: Page 47 (M-6)*. NMC: Washington, DC, 38 miles north.

Lodging Office: Building 960, **C-540-653-7671/72,** D-312-249-7671/72, FAX 540-653-4272, 24 hours daily. Check in billeting, check out 1100 hours daily. Government civilian employee billeting.

TML: BOQ. Buildings 215, 217, officers, all ranks, leave or official duty. Bedroom, private bath (12); separate bedrooms, private bath (20); two bedroom, private bath suite (DV/VIP) (1). Community kitchen, limited utensils, refrigerator, A/C, essentials, ice vending, color TV in room & lounge, housekeeping service, washer/dryer. Older structures, renovated. Rates: $16 for officer transients, slightly higher for DV/VIP. Duty can make reservations, others Space-A.

TML: BEQ. Building 959, E5-E9, leave or official duty. Bedroom, private bath (4). A/C, essentials, ice vending, housekeeping service, refrigerator, color TV in room & lounge, washer/dryer. Rates: $10, E5-E6; $16, E7-E9. Duty can make reservations, others Space-A.

TML: TLQ. Building 909, all ranks, leave or official duty, PCS IN/OUT have priority. Two bedroom, private bath (4). Kitchen with utensils, housekeeping service, color TV. Older structure, renovated. Rates: $10, E4 and below, $12, E5-E6, $15, E7+. Duty can make reservations, others Space-A.

DV/VIP: Public Affairs Office, C-540-653-8153, O6+/SES equivalent. Retirees Space-A.

TML Availability: Difficult. Best Nov-Feb.

CREDIT CARDS ACCEPTED: Visa, MasterCard and American Express.

Temporary Military Lodging Around the World - 231

VIRGINIA
Dahlgren Naval Surface Warfare Center, continued

Take a walk through Dahlgren's Beaver Pond Nature Trail, and then savor the history of Washington's and Lee's birthplace, in historic Fredericksburg. The area is full of interesting historic sites.

Locator 653-8216/8701   Medical 911   Police 653-8500

Dam Neck Fleet Combat Training Center Atlantic (VA25R1)
CBQ Billeting
FCTCLANT
1912 Regulas Avenue
Virginia Beach, VA 23461-2098

TELEPHONE NUMBER INFORMATION: Main installation numbers: C-804-433-2000, D-312-433-2000.

Location: On the ocean front, "Dam Neck at the Dunes" is 2 miles southeast of Oceana NAS, off Dam Neck Road. *USMRA: Page 47 (O-9,10); Page 52 (J-7,8).* NMC: Virginia Beach, 3 miles south of the resort strip.

Lodging Office: "Dam Neck at the Dunes". Enlisted building 566C, **C-804-491-2449.** Check in facility 1400, check out 1000 hours daily. Officers building 241, **C-804-433-6366.** FAX 804-433-6228. Check in/ check out same. Government civilian employee billeting. Note: This facility won 2nd place in the Admiral Elmo R. Zumwalt Award for excellence in management, quality of service and facilities for FY '94.

TML: BOQ. Buildings 225, 241, officers all, leave or official duty. Bedroom, private bath (96); bedroom, living room, private bath (53); DV rooms, kitchenette, private bath (4); VIP suites, private bath, living room (13). Refrigerators, coffee makers, A/C, CATV and VCR, housekeeping service, cots, washer/dryer, ice vending. Sun deck, hot tub and sauna. Modern structures. Rates: $10 per person standard room; $15 per person per suite; $25 per person DV rooms. Under five no charge. Duty on orders can make reservations, others Space-A.

TML: BEQ. Buildings 550, 532, 566, enlisted all ranks. Total 1,336 rooms including 56 Chief's rooms. Refrigerator, A/C, color TV and VCR, housekeeping service, washer/dryer, lounges. Modern structures. Others: Sun deck, BBQ, phone, CATV, washer/dryer and housekeeping service. Rates: CPO $10; duty $5.50; others $5.50. Reservations accepted for official orders, others Space-A.

DV/VIP: Protocol Office, Taylor Hall, C-804-433-6542. For O7+/civilian equivalent. Reservations: C-804-433-7718, D-312-433-7718, retirees space A.

TML Availability: Because this is a training command, availability is usually poor and only fair at best.

CREDIT CARDS ACCEPTED: Visa, MasterCard and American Express.

Some rooms have ocean views. Building 241 and 225 are on the beach. Lake with boat rentals and fishing. Dam Neck is 2 miles from Ocean Breeze Water Park and the Marine Science Museum.

Locator 433-6211   Medical 677-7200   Police 433-6929

VIRGINIA

Fort A.P. Hill (VA17R1)
Housing Division
Bldg TT0114
Bowling Green, VA 22427-5000

TELEPHONE NUMBER INFORMATION: Main installation numbers: C-804-633-8760, D-312-578-8760.

Location: From I-95 southbound, take Fort A.P. Hill exit, US-17 (bypass) east to VA-2 south to Bowling Green, take VA-301 northeast to main gate. Also, exit I-95 northbound to VA-207 north to VA-301 north and to main gate. *USMRA: Page 47 (L,M-6,7).* NMC: Fredericksburg, 14 miles northwest.

Lodging Office: Building TT0142, corner 2nd & Burke St, **C-804-633-8335**, D-312-633-83350800-1630 hours daily, 0800-2300 hours Fri, SDO, building TT-0101, C-804-633-8201. Check in 1500, check out 1200 hours. Government civilian employee billeting.

TML: Guest House. **Dolly's House.** All ranks, leave or official duty. Bedroom, private bath (2 rooms make a suite), (6); handicapped accessible (1). Same amenities as DV/VIP. New structure '90. Rates: $20 per person, additional person $4. Reservations at 804-633-8219. Rates subject to change.

TML: VOQ/VEQ. Buildings TT-0117, TT-119, TT-0146, all ranks, leave or official duty. Bedroom, semi-private bath (23). Community kitchen, limited utensils, A/C, color TV (some), housekeeping service, ice vending. Older structures. TT0118, Four suites with bedroom, private bath, and livingroom. Rates: $25 per person. TDY can make reservations, others Space-A.

TML: VOQ/VEQ. Cottages, 5 each, all ranks, leave or official duty. Bedroom, private bath (2); two bedroom, private bath (2); three bedroom, private bath (1). Kitchen, complete utensils, A/C, color TV, housekeeping service. Older structures. Rates: $25-$30 per person. TDY can make reservations, others Space-A. Rates subject to change.

TML: DV/VIP. Recreation buildings SS-0252-0254, PO-0290, officer O6+, C-804-633-8367. Separate bedrooms, private bath (2); two bedroom, private bath (2); three bedroom, private bath (1). Kitchen, complete utensils, A/C, color TV, housekeeping service. Rates: $20 per person, family rates available. TDY can make reservations, others Space-A.

TML: Recreation Lodge. Building SS-0251, all ranks, leave or official duty, **C-804-633-8219**. Nine bedroom, (sleeps 18) semi-private bath (1). Kitchen, complete utensils, freezer, ice maker, color TV, 2 woodburning fireplaces, lounge chairs. Rates: $120 per day for groups of 6 (minimum) or $20 per person, All categories can make reservations.

TML: Recreation Cabins. Buildings PO-0292/93/94, all ranks. Report to building TT-0106, C-804-633-8219. Check out 1100 hours. Three bedroom, private bath (3). Kitchen, complete utensils, A/C, color TV, washer/dryer. Modern structures. Rates: $20 per person, family rates available. Maximum 6 persons per family. All categories can make reservations.

DV/VIP: Commander's Office, building TT-0101, C-804-633-8205, O6+.

TML Availability: Good, Oct-Mar. Difficult, other times.

VIRGINIA
Fort A.P. Hill, continued

CREDIT CARDS ACCEPTED: Visa, MasterCard and American Express.

This is a <u>very</u> rustic area, with good hunting and fishing in season. Dolly's House is named for Kitty "Dolly" Hill, wife of Gen. A.P. Hill, for whom the Fort is named. Support facilities: snack bar, exchange and theater on base. Limited facilities off base. Good variety in Fredericksburg, 30 minutes NE.

Locator 633-8324   Medical 833-8216   Police 633-8239

Fort Belvoir (VA12R1)
Transient Billeting Branch
9775 Gaillard Road, Suite 144
Fort Belvoir, VA 22060-5905

TELEPHONE NUMBER INFORMATION: Main installation numbers: C-540-545-6700, D-312-227-0101.

Location: From I-95 south or US-1 south take Fort Belvoir exits. Clearly marked. *USMRA: Page 47 (L,M-5); Page 55 (B,C-8).* NMC: Washington, DC, 10 miles northeast.

Lodging Office: Building 470, 9775 Gaillard Road, **C-800-295-9750 or 540-805-2333**, D-312-277-9750, FAX 540-805-3566, DSN FAX 312-655-3566, 24 hours daily. Billeting Manager, C-540-805-2005. Check in 1700, check out 1200 hours daily. Government civilian employee billeting VOQ.

TML: VOQ/VEQ. Various buildings, officers all ranks, leave or official duty. Bedroom, private bath (VOQ) (321); bedroom, semi-private bath (VOQ) (122); separate bedroom, private bath (VOQ)(50); two bedroom, private bath (VEQ) (13); double rooms for E1-E6, shared bath (VEQ) (8); single rooms for E7-E9, private bath (VEQ) (8). Color TV, housekeeping service, telephones, microwave/refrigerator, utensils, washer/dryer, cribs/rollaways. Modern structure. Rates: sponsor $30 standard room, $36 two room suite, spouse $5, child $3. Maximum $34.50 per family. TDY and PCS can make reservations. No pets.

DV/VIP: C-703-805-2640. Buildings 20 (O'Club), 470, officers O6+, leave or official duty. Separate bedroom suites, private bath (4); (470) bedroom, double bed, private bath (7). Kitchen, complete utensils, A/C, color TV, housekeeping service, cribs/cots, ice vending. Modern structure, renovated '92. Rates: sponsor $39.50, spouse $5, child $3; maximum $47.50 per family. Duty can make reservations. No pets.

TML Availability: Good, Dec. Difficult, May-Sep.

CREDIT CARDS ACCEPTED: Visa, MasterCard and American Express.

Exit Walker Gate to see George Washington's Mill, and visit nearby Woodlawn Plantation, Gunston Hall. See Capitol Hill in downtown Washington DC; northern Virginia is rich in colonial and Civil War history.

Locator 805-2043   Medical 805-1106   Police 805-1104

VIRGINIA

Fort Eustis (VA10R1)
P.O. Box 4278
Fort Eustis, VA 23604-5200

TELEPHONE NUMBER INFORMATION: Main installation numbers: C-804-878-1110, 312-927-1110.

Location: From I-64, exit 60A to VA-105, west to fort. *USMRA: Page 47 (N-9); Page 52 (B,C-2,3).* NMC: Newport News, 13 miles southwest.

Lodging Office: 2110 Pershing Ave, **C-804-878-5807**, D-312-927-5807, Fax 804-878-3251, DSN Fax 312-927-3251, 24 hours daily. Check in 1600, check out 1100 hours daily. Government civilian employee billeting.

TML: VOQ/VEQ/DVQ/TLQ. Building 2110, all ranks, leave or official duty. Suites (29) & 4 cottages for transient persons; VOQ: bedrooms (236); VEQ: bedrooms (302); DVQ suites (9). Refrigerator, community kitchen, kitchen (cottages and DVQ only), A/C, essentials, color TV in room & lounge, housekeeping service, cribs/cots, washer/ dryer, food/ice vending, handicapped accessible. Rates: DVQ $34, VOQ $28-$30, VOQ/VEQ $28, VEQ $10-$30, $7 each additional person. Priority for VOQ: officers attending Transportation Office Basic Course. Priority for VEQ: enlisted personnel attending Advanced Non-commissioned Officer Course and Basic Non-commissioned Officer Course. Duty can make reservations, others Space-A. Space-A check in 1800 hours. Pets allowed in cottages, $5/day.

DV/VIP: Protocol Office. Building 210, Room 207, C-804-878-6010/30. O6+. Retirees and lower ranks Space-A.

TML Availability: Good. Best Oct-May.

CREDIT CARDS ACCEPTED: Visa, MasterCard and American Express.

Visit Busch Gardens, the Army Transportation Museum, tour historic Yorktown Battlefield, and Colonial Williamsburg for a crash course in United States' early history.

Locator 878-5215   Medical 878-7765   Police 878-4555

Fort Lee (VA15R1)
Fort Lee Lodging Operation
P.O. Box 5019
Fort Lee, VA 23801-5000

TELEPHONE NUMBER INFORMATION: Main installation numbers: C-804-734-1011, D-312-765-3000.

Location: From I-95 take Fort Lee/Hopewell exit, and follow VA-36 to main gate. *USMRA: Page 47 (L-8).* NMC: Petersburg, 3 miles west.

VIRGINIA
Fort Lee, continued

Lodging Office: Building 8025, Mahone Ave, C-1-800-403-8533 or 804-734-6699, D-312-687-6698/6694, FAX 804-733-6873, 24 hours daily. Check in lodging 1530-2300, check out 1200 Mon-Sat, 1000 Sun and holidays. Government civilian employee lodging VOQ.

TML: Guest House. Building 9056, all ranks, leave or official duty. Bedroom, 2 beds, sofa bed, living room, private bath (40). Refrigerator, A/C, color TV, housekeeping service, cribs/cots, washer/dryer. Modern structure. Rates: sponsor $18-$24, 2nd person free, child no charge. Maximum $18-$24 per family. Duty can make reservations, others Space-A. Note: primarily for PCS in/out. No pets.

TML: VOQ. Buildings P-8025/26, P-9051-55, P-4229, officers all ranks, E7-E9, leave or official duty. Bedroom, private bath (482). Kitchen, A/C, color TV, housekeeping service, washer/dryer, ice vending, handicapped accessible (2). Modern structures. Rates: sponsor $22, 2nd person $5. Maximum 2 per room. Duty can make reservations, others Space-A. Note: primarily for TDY personnel. No pets.

TML: DV/VIP. Davis House, building P-8042, officers O6+, enlisted E9. Official duty only. Two story, 4 bedroom house (1), living room, dining room, kitchen, complete utensils, microwave, seating room, two private bathrooms, AC, color TV, housekeeping service, handicapped accessible. Modern structure. Rates: sponsor $22, 2nd person $5. Maximum 2 per room. Duty can make reservations, others Space-A. Primarily for TDY personnel. No pets.

DV/VIP: Protocol Office, building P-5000, room 221, C-804-733-4293, O6/GS-15+. Retirees and lower ranks Space-A. No pets.

TML Availability: Difficult. Best Dec, also on weekends and holidays.

CREDIT CARDS ACCEPTED: Visa, MasterCard and American Express.

Visit the Quartermaster Museum, and Battlefield Park, which is rich in Civil War history. Wonderful bass and crappie fishing is on the Chickahominy River. Virginia Beach swimming, fishing and boating is 85 miles east.

Locator 734-6855   Medical 734-9000   Police 765-0988

Fort Monroe (VA13R1)
ATTN: ATZB-WH
Bldg. T179, Pratt St.
Fort Monroe, VA 23651-6000

TELEPHONE NUMBER INFORMATION: Main installation numbers: C-804-727-2111, D-312-680-2111.

Location: From I-64 exit Hampton and follow tour signs through Phoebus to Fort Monroe. *USMRA: Page 47 (N-9); Page 52 (F-4)*. NMC: Hampton, 1 mile southeast.

Lodging Office: Building T179, Pratt St, **C-804-727-2128**, D-312-680-2128, 0800-1645 hours M-F. Check in billeting. Check in 1400, check out 1000 hours. No government civilian employee billeting.

VIRGINIA
Fort Monroe, continued

TML: VQ. Buildings 61, 80, 136, 137, all ranks, leave or official duty. Two bedroom suites, private bath (2); bedroom suites, private bath, kitchen w/utensils, A/C, color TV, housekeeping service, cribs/cots, washer/dryer. Older Victorian, renovated. Rates: $30 single, maximum $37.50 per family. All categories can make reservations.

TML: DVQ. Building 147, 80, officer O6+, leave or official duty, C-804-727-3596, D-680-3596. Check in 0700-1645, check out 1100 hours daily. Two bedroom suites, private bath (4). Kitchen, complete utensils, A/C, color TV, housekeeping service, washer/dryer. Older Victorian, remodeled. Rates: $37.50 and maximum $45 per family. All categories can make reservations, others Space-A.

DVQ: ATTN: Protocol Office, building 133, C-804-727-4401, O6+.

TML Availability: Fairly good, Oct-Apr. More difficult, May-Sep.

CREDIT CARDS ACCEPTED: American Express (Government)

A National Historic Landmark, touring Fort Monroe is a US history lesson. Historic Hampton is also nearby, as well as Williamsburg. This area is a treasure trove for history buffs.

Locator 727-3175   Medical 727-2840   Police 727-2238

Fort Myer (VA24R1)
UPH Branch
Fort Myer, VA 22211-5050

TELEPHONE NUMBER INFORMATION: Main installation numbers: C-202-545-6700, D-312-227-0101.

Location: Adjacent to Arlington National Cemetery. Take Fort Myer exit from Washington Blvd, at 2nd St, or enter From US-50 (Arlington Blvd) first gate. Also, exit from Boundary Drive to 12th St north entrance near the Iwo Jima Memorial. *USMRA: Page 55 (E-5).* NMC: Washington, DC, 6 miles northeast.

Lodging Office: Building 50, Johnson Lane, Mon-Thu 24 hours daily, Fri 0600-2200, Sat 0800-1600, Sun 0600-2200, **C-703-696-3576/77**, D-312-226-3576/77. Check in 1400 hours, check out 1200 hours daily. Late checkout 697-7051. Government civilian employee billeting. No pets. **This facility is in charge of Fort Lesley J. McNair billeting in Washington, D.C.**

TML: DV/VIP. Building 50, officers O7+, leave or official duty. Bedroom suites, living room, private bath (18). Refrigerator, bar, A/C, color TV in room & lounge, telephone, housekeeping service, cribs/cots, washer/dryer, ice & food vending. Older structure, remodeled. Max 3 per unit. Rates: $50 sponsor, $5 each additional person, child/infant up to 10 free. Duty, Reserve and National Guard can make reservations, others Space-A.

DV/VIP: Write to: DA Protocol, Pentagon, building 50, C-703-697-7051, D-312-297-7051, O7+. Retirees & lower ranks Space-A.

TML Availability: Very Good. Difficult Apr-Nov.

CREDIT CARDS ACCEPTED: Visa, MasterCard and American Express.

VIRGINIA
Fort Myer, continued

Tour Arlington National Cemetery for a fascinating look at military history and traditions. Don't miss the stables of ceremonial horses used in military funerals, the Old Guard Museum. Fort Myer is home to the US Army Band.

Locator 545-6700   **Medical** 696-3628   **Police** 696-3525

Fort Pickett (VA16R1)
ATTN: AFRC-FMP-PW-H
Blackstone, VA 23824-5000
Scheduled to close 9/31/96

TELEPHONE NUMBER INFORMATION: Main installation numbers: C-804-292-8621, D-312-438-8621.

Location: On US-460, 1 mile from Blackstone. Clearly marked. *USMRA: Page 47 (K-9)*. NMC: Richmond, 60 miles northeast.

Lodging Office: Building T-469, Military Road, **C-804-292-2443**, 0730-1600 duty days, other hours, PMO, building T-471, C-804-292-8344, D-312-438-8444, FAX 804-292-8617, DSN FAX 312-438-8617. Check in billeting, check out 1000 hours daily. Government civilian employee billeting. Note: confirm all reservations by phone at least 24 hours in advance.

TML: VOQ. Cottages. Officers all ranks, E6-E9, leave or official duty. Bedroom, 2 beds private bath (13). Kitchen, complete utensils, A/C, color TV, housekeeping service, cribs, cots $5 per extra person. Older structures. Rates: $20 per unit. Maximum 4 persons. Maximum 3 guests per sponsor. Duty can make reservations, others Space-A. Pets allowed outside.

TML: VOQ. Officers all ranks, leave or official duty. Bedroom, common bath (28); Bedroom suites, 2 beds, private bath (4). Community kitchen, complete utensils, A/C, color TV in lounge, housekeeping service, cribs, cots $5 per extra person, washer/dryer. Older structures. Rates: $8-$20 per adult. Maximum 3 guests per sponsor. Duty can make reservations, others Space-A. Pets allowed outside.

TML: VEQ. Enlisted all ranks, leave or official duty. Bedroom, common bath (28); Bedroom suites, 2 beds, private bath (4). Community kitchen, complete utensils, A/C, color TV in lounge, housekeeping service, cribs, cots ($5 extra), washer/dryer. Older structure. Rates: $8-$20 per adult. Maximum 3 guests per sponsor. Duty can make reservations, others Space-A. Pets allowed outside.

DV/VIP: C-804-292-2454.

TML Availability: Good, Sep-Mar. Difficult, other times.

CREDIT CARDS ACCEPTED: Visa, MasterCard, American Express, Diners and Discover.

Some of the best hunting and fishing in the state of Virginia. Charlottesville, Richmond, Williamsburg, the James River Plantations and Washington DC are within easy reach of this facility.

Locator 292-2266   **Medical** 292-2528   **Police** 292-8444

VIRGINIA

Fort Story (VA08R1)
Billeting Office
Bldg 582, Atlantic Ave
Fort Story, VA 23459-5010

TELEPHONE NUMBER INFORMATION: Main installation numbers: C-804-422-7305, D-312-438-7305.

Location: From Interstate 64: take exit 79, Northampton Blvd (US-13) for 4.3 miles, take Shore Drive (Route 60) exit. (Sign = East-West Shore Drive, Beaches). Turn right to Shore Drive and after 5 miles turn left to West Gate, Fort Story (Route 305 North) just after the entrance to Seashore State Park). *USMRA: Page 47 (O-9); Page 52 (I,J-5,6).* NMC: Virginia Beach, 7 miles south.

Lodging Office: Bldg 582, Atlantic, **C-804-422-7321/2**, D-312-927-9321, 0730-2330 hours daily. Check in billeting 1400 hours, check out 1000 hours daily. Government civilian employee billeting.

TML: TLQ. Buildings 511, 526, 537, all ranks, leave or official duty. Bedroom, private bath (1); Two separate bedrooms, private bath. Kitchen, refrigerator, community kitchen, limited utensils, A/C, color TV in room & lounge, housekeeping service, essentials, cribs/cots, washer/dryer, accessible to handicapped (1). Older structures, redecorated. Rates: sponsor $26-$28, each additional person $7. Duty can make reservations, others Space-A.

TML: Cape Henry Inn. This is a brand new hotel with 50 rooms. See page 348 for more information.

TML: DV/VIP. Cottages for O4, E9 and W4+, Memorial Day-Labor Day. Contact office of the Commanding General, USATCFE, Ft. Eustis, VA 23604-5000, **C-804-878-4804**, D-312-927-4804. Requests for reservations accepted first working day in January. O3 and below **C-804-422-7028**, D-312-438-7028, first working day of the month for the following month, beginning 0730, during the off-season, day after Labor Day through Thursday before Memorial Day weekend. Summer reservations, Memorial Day weekend through Labor Day, are reserved by "lottery." Cottages are 2 bedroom (12) and 3 bedroom (6). All have kitchens, stove, refrigerator, A/C/heat, CATV, housekeeping service, cribs (upon request), on-post telephone, BBQ and picnic tables available. Sponsor or spouse must accompany group. Inventories taken. Reservations held to 2000. No shows (failure to cancel) counts against future reservations. One reservation per service member, summer season. One reservation per service member per month for winter season. Rates: DVQ, $35 per day, sponsor, $7 per additional person (12+), all other cottages, $31 per day, sponsor, $7 per additional person (12+), $5 pet fee, per pet, two pet limit. Leave only, all categories can make reservations. Cottages on Chesapeake Bay/Atlantic Ocean. Swimming, Recreation Center, Gym, Bowling, Fishing/equipment available, golf.

DV/VIP: Handled by Fort Story/Ft Eustis as indicated above, C-804-878-5206.

TML Availability: Good, Oct-Mar. Difficult, other times.

CREDIT CARDS ACCEPTED: Visa, MasterCard and American Express.

See the Old Cape Henry Lighthouse, Douglas MacArthur Memorial, Virginia Beach Science Museum, Williamsburg Pottery Factory. Busch Gardens, Ocean Breeze Park and Norfolk Naval Base nearby.

Locator 422-7682   Medical 422-7802   Police 422-7141

VIRGINIA

Judge Advocate General's School (VA01R1)
ATTN: SSL-H
600 Massie Road
Charlottesville, VA 22903-1781

TELEPHONE NUMBER INFORMATION: Main installation numbers: C-804-972-6300, D-312-934-7115, ask for 3 digit extension.

Location: On the North grounds of the University of Virginia at Charlottesville. Take the 250 bypass off I-64 to the Barracks Road exit, then turn right at light, then right onto Millmont, then right onto Arlington Blvd, then right at the top of the hill to the school. *USMRA: Page 47 (J-7).* NMC: Charlottesville, within city limits.

Lodging Office: 600 Massie Road, **C-804-972-6450**, FAX 804-972-6328, 0750-1650 M-F. Other hours, SDO front desk. Check in 1500, check out 1200 hours. Government civilian employee billeting only on orders to TJAGS.

TML: VEQ/VOQ. All ranks, leave or official duty. Handicapped accessible. Bedroom, one bed, private bath (72). A/C, community kitchen, cots ($2), ice vending, housekeeping service, refrigerator, color TV, washer/dryer. Modern structure. Rates: TDY, sponsor $8, family member $5; active duty on leave and retirees $20, family members $5. Most space reserved for TJAGS students.

DV/VIP: ATTN: JAGS-ZA, C-804-972-6301, O6+. Retirees and leave Space-A. Sponsor $25, family member, $5.

TML Availability: Very limited, last two weeks in June. Difficult, other times.

CREDIT CARDS ACCEPTED: American Express.

Visit historic Monticello, Ash Lawn and the Michie Tavern. For outdoor activities, try Wintergreen, Shenandoah National Park, Barboursville Vineyard, Montfair Camp Grounds, Lake Albemarle.

Langley Air Force Base (VA07R1)
Langley Inns
1 SVS/SVML
66 Nealy Avenue
Langley AFB, VA 23665-5528

TELEPHONE NUMBER INFORMATION: Main installation numbers: C-804-764-9990, D-312-574-9990.

Location: From I-64 east in Hampton take Armistead Ave exit, go right to stop light; right onto La Salle Ave and enter AFB. *USMRA: Page 47 (N-9); Page 52 (E-3).* NMC: Hampton, 1 mile west.

Lodging Office: 66 Nealy Avenue, **C-804-764-4667** FAX 804-764-3038, D-312-574-4667, DSN FAX 312-574-3038, 24 hours daily. Check in facility, check out 1200 hours daily. Government civilian employee billeting.

VIRGINIA
Langley Air Force Base, continued

TML: TLQ. North and South. All ranks, leave or official duty. Separate bedrooms, private bath (39). Kitchen, utensils, A/C, color TV, housekeeping service, cribs/cots, washer/dryer, ice vending. Modern structures, renovated. Rates: $24 per unit, sleeps 5. Duty can make reservations, others Space-A.

TML: VOQ. Buildings 14, 16, officers, leave or official duty. Bedroom, private bath (78). Kitchen, A/C, color TV, housekeeping service, cots, washer/dryer, ice vending. Modern structures. Rates: $8 per person. Duty can make reservations, others Space-A.

TML: VAQ. Building 66, 45 enlisted all ranks, leave or official duty. Bedroom, 1 & 2 bed units, common bath (92); separate bedrooms, private bath for SNCOs (5). Refrigerator, A/C, color TV, housekeeping service, washer/dryer, ice vending. Modern structure, renovated. Rates: $8 per person, maximum 2 per room. SNCO suites $14. Duty can make reservations, others Space-A.

TML: VAQ. Boots Hall, building 45, enlisted, E4+ leave or official duty. Bedroom, shared bath (123). Refrigerator, A/C, color TV, housekeeping service, washer/dryer, ice vending. Modern structure. Renovated. Rates: $8 per person (1 person per room). Duty can make reservations, all others Space-A.

TML: DV/VIP. Buildings 132 (Lawson Hall), 141 (Dodd Hall), officers O6+/GS-15+, leave or official duty. Lawson: separate bedroom suites, private bath (11). Dodd: separate bedroom suites, private bath (10). Kitchen, limited utensils, A/C, color TV, housekeeping service, cribs/cots, washer/dryer, ice vending. Older structures, renovated. Rates: $14 per person. Duty can make reservations, others Space-A.

DV/VIP: Protocol Office, building 205, C-804-764-5044, O6+. Retirees and lower ranks Space-A.

TML Availability: Good, winter months. Difficult, summer months.

CREDIT CARDS ACCEPTED: Visa, MasterCard and American Express.

Historic Colonial Williamsburg, Busch Gardens, beautiful Virginia beach, and the Mariner's Museum are all close by and worth a visit.

Locator 764-5615   Medical 764-6833   Police 764-5092

Little Creek Naval Amphibious Base (VA19R1)
Combined Bachelor Quarters
Norfolk, VA 23521-2698

TELEPHONE NUMBER INFORMATION: Main installation numbers: C-804-464-7000, D-312-564-7000.

Location: From I-64 south through Hampton Roads Bridge Tunnel take Northampton Blvd exit, 5 miles to base, exit VA-225. From Chesapeake Bay Bridge Tunnel proceed west on US-60 to base. *USMRA: Page 47 (N,O-9); Page 52 (G,H-5,6).* NMC: Norfolk, 11 miles southwest.

Lodging Office: Officers: Drexler Manor, building 3408, 1120 A St, **C-804-464-1183**, FAX 804-464-8635, DSN FAX 312-680-8635. Enlisted: Shields Hall, building 3601, 1350 Gator Blvd, **C-804-464-**

VIRGINIA
Little Creek Naval Amphibious Base, continued

7577, FAX 804-464-7149, DSN FAX 312-680-7149. Check in facility, check out 1330. Government civilian employee billeting.

TML: Navy Lodge. Building 3531, all ranks, leave or official duty. For reservations call **1-800-NAVY-INN**, lodge number is C-804-464-6215, FAX 804-464-1194. Check in prior to 1800 to avoid cancellation. Check out 1200 hours daily. Bedroom, 2 beds, private bath (72); queen bed and sofa bed, private bath (18). Kitchen, complete utensils, A/C, color/cable TV, housekeeping service, coin washer/dryer, ice vending. Modern structure, renovated. Rates: $37 per room per night (Sep-May), $43 (May-Sep). Handicapped accessible rooms. All categories can make reservations. No pets except birds in cages, fish in tanks.

TML: BOQ. Drexler Manor, building 3408, 1120 A Street, NAB Little Creek, Norfolk, VA 23521-2230. Officers all ranks, leave or official duty, C-804-464-7522. Check out 1330 hours daily. Bedroom, private bath (230); separate bedroom suites, private bath (14). Microwaves, A/C, CATV, housekeeping service, washer/dryer, ice vending. Modern structure, renovated. Rates: $8 per person, suites $20. No accompanied members until Navy Lodge is full. Duty on orders can make reservations, others, 1 day basis, Space-A.

TML: BEQ. Shields Hall, building 3601, 1350 Gator Blvd., NAB, Little Creek, Norfolk, VA 23521-2698. Enlisted all ranks, on official duty, C-804-464-1183, D-312-680-7577. Check out 1300 hours daily. Bedroom, private bath (320); bedroom, 2 beds, private bath (140); single rooms, private bath (E7-E9) (75). Micro-frig, A/C, CATV, housekeeping service, washer/dryer, ice vending. Modern structure, renovated. Rates: E1-E9 $6 per person, VIP $10. Dependents not authorized. Duty can make reservations 90 days advance, others Space-A.

TML: DV/VIP. Building 3186, officer O6+, leave or official duty, **C-804-444-5901**, D-312-564-5901. Check out 1200 hours daily. Separate bedroom suites, private bath (4). Queen beds, refrigerator, community kitchen, limited utensils, A/C, CATV, housekeeping service, cots, ice vending. Older structure, remodeled. Rates: $15 per person active duty.

DV/VIP: SURFLANT-planetarium. C-804-444-5901, O6+. Retirees Space-A.

TML Availability: Good, Oct-Dec. Difficult, Jun-Aug.

CREDIT CARDS ACCEPTED: Visa, MasterCard and American Express. The Navy Lodge accepts Visa, MasterCard, American Express and Discover.

History is all around Little Creek, with Jamestown and Williamsburg 1 hour north. Nearby beautiful Virginia beaches beckon, and check out Norfolk.

Locator 444-0000   **Medical 363-4444**   **Police 363-4444**

Norfolk Naval Base (VA18R1)
Norfolk, VA 23511-2995

TELEPHONE NUMBER INFORMATION: Main installation numbers: C-804-444-0000, D-312-564-0000.

VIRGINIA
Norfolk Naval Base, continued

Location: From north or south I-64, take naval base exit, follow signs. *USMRA: Page 52 (F-5,6)*. NMC: Norfolk, in city limits.

Lodging Office: BEQ: Billeting Code N6, building I-A, Pocahontas & Bacon Sts, **C-804-444-4294**, 0730-1600 hours daily, other hours, Central Assignments, building A-48, C-804-444-4425. BOQ: BOQ Billeting Fund, building A-128, Powhattan Street off Maryland Ave, C-804-444-4151/3250, Fax 804-445-9888, 24 hours daily. Check in facility 1200, check out 1100 hours daily. Government civilian employee billeting.

TML: Navy Lodge. Building SDA-314 (Take I-64 to 564 exit to Terminal Blvd., right on Hampton Blvd. Lodge on left). All ranks, leave or official duty. For reservations call **1-800-NAVY-INN**, lodge number is C-804-489-2656, FAX 804-489-9621 (for large groups only!), 24 hours daily. Check in 1500-1800, check out 1200 hours. Bedroom, 2 double beds, private bath (226); bedroom, double bed, private bath (64). Kitchenette, microwave, utensils, A/C, CATV, clocks, coffeepot, housekeeping service, cribs, phones, FAX service, hair dryers, high chairs, ice/snack vending, minimart, picnic area, playground, coin washer/dryer, ice vending. Smoking or non-smoking rooms available. Modern structure. Rates: $45 per unit. All categories can make reservations. **This is the largest Navy Lodge in the world with 294 rooms!**

TML: BOQ. Buildings A-125, A-128, officers all ranks, leave or official duty. Bedroom, private bath (274); separate bedrooms, kitchen, private bath (3). Refrigerator, microwave, A/C, CATV room & lounge, housekeeping service, cots ($2), washer/dryer, ice vending, sauna/exercise room, jacuzzi, sun deck. Modern structures. Rates: $10 per unit, $14 double. Duty can make reservations, others Space-A.

TML: BEQ. Buildings A-48, room 102 (NAVSTA), U-16 (NAS), enlisted all ranks (no E7+ at NAS), leave or official duty. NAVSTA C-804-444-4425, NAS C-804-444-4983. Bedroom, hall bath (NAVSTA)(152); 5 buildings, hall bath (NAS). Check out NAVSTA 1100 hours daily, NAS 1000 hours daily. Both: Refrigerator, A/C, color TV room, housekeeping service, washer/ dryer, ice vending. Modern structures. Rates: $4 per person. Duty can make reservations, others Space-A.

DV/VIP: COMNAVBASE building KBB, C-804-444-2788. CINCLANTFLT **Camp Elmore**, C-804-444-6323, O7+, retirees Space-A. Suites used for O6+ with BOQ manager's permission (4). Rates: VIP suites $25, single $20.

TML Availability: Good, fall & winter. More difficult, other times.

CREDIT CARDS ACCEPTED: Visa, MasterCard and American Express. The Navy Lodge accepts Visa, MasterCard, American Express and Discover.

This is the largest naval base in the world. There is an interesting tour given daily. If you can see a ship launching, do so! Also, visit Hampton Roads Naval Museum, and the MacArthur Memorial. Nearby are Williamsburg, Yorktown and Jamestown.

Locator 444-0000   Medical 677-6291   Police 444-2324

VIRGINIA

Norfolk Naval Shipyard (VA26R1)
Combined Bachelor's Quarters
Bldg 1504A, Code 834
Norfolk Naval Shipyard
Portsmouth, VA 23709-5000

TELEPHONE NUMBER INFORMATION: Main installation numbers: C-804-396-3000.

Location: Take I-64 to I-264 through the tunnel. First exit turn left on Effington St. Follow signs to shipyard. *USMRA: Page 52 (F-7).* NMC: Virginia Beach, 15 miles northeast.

Lodging Office: Building 1504, **C-804-396-4449**, FAX 804-396-4968, D-312-961-4449. Check in at the facility, 24 hours daily, check out 1200 hours. Late checkout C-804-396-4562. Government civilian employee billeting.

TML: BEQ. Building 1531, 1503 enlisted (E1-E9), 1439 (ships in overhaul, official duty only), all ranks, leave or official duty. Reservations accepted. Check out 1200 hours daily. Rooms, semi-private bath (200); rooms, private bath (158); rooms for official ship overhaul duty only (building 1439)(242). Essentials, food vending, refrigerator, microwave, housekeeping service, color TV in room and in lounge, washer/dryer. Modern structure, remodeled 1994. Rates: sponsor $4. Family members not allowed to stay in facility, no guests of opposite sex in residents rooms. Active duty can make reservations, others Space-A. No pets. TAD personnel must make reservations through local SATO.

TML: The Landing. This new five-story BEQ has 202 rooms with private baths, microwaves, and refrigerators. Each floor has a kitchen and a lounge and there is also a fitness room and large laundry room.

TML: The Cheaspeake Inn, building 1530, **C-804-398-8500**, D-312-961-1030, all ranks, leave or official duty. Bedroom, private bath (78). Suites, VIP. Essentials, food vending, kitchenette, utensils, no stove, color TV/VCR in room & lounge, housekeeping service, cots, washer/dryer. Rates: sponsor $8, adult $4, VIP, $20. Maximum persons 3. No pets. All categories can make reservations, active duty, reserve and national guard on orders have priority, others Space-A. TAD personnel must make reservations through local SATO.

TML: DV/VIP. Code 800, building 1500, Portsmouth Naval Shipyard, Portsmouth, VA 23709, C-804-396-8605, D-312-961-8605. Building 1530, O7+. Suites are retiree eligible.

TML: Fisher House. Portsmouth Naval Hospital. Note: Appendix C has the definition of this facility. **C-804-399-5461.**

TML Availability: Good. Best in Dec, difficult Sep.

CREDIT CARDS ACCEPTED: American Express.

Virginia Beach's famed boardwalk and beaches will tempt summer visitors. See the Portsmouth Naval Shipyard museum, attend a play, dine on excellent seafood, or take in a ballgame at Harbor Park.

Locator 396-3000   Medical 396-3268   Police 396-7266

VIRGINIA

Oceana Naval Air Station (VA09R1)
Lodging Office
Bldg 460, G Street
Virginia Beach, VA 23460-5120

TELEPHONE NUMBER INFORMATION: Main installation numbers: C-804-433-2000, D-312-433-2000.

Location: From I-64 exit to Norfolk-Virginia Beach Expressway (VA-44 east), east on Virginia Beach Blvd. Bordered by Oceana Blvd (VA-615) and London Bridge Rd. Also, bordered by Potters and Harper Roads. *USMRA: Page 47 (O-9); Page 52 (I,J-7)*. NMC: Virginia Beach, in city limits.

Lodging Office: Building 460, G Street across from O'Club, **C-804-425-0500-EX-168/171/172**, D-312-433-3293, 24 hours daily. Check in billeting, check out 1100 hours daily. Government civilian employee billeting.

TML: BOQ. Building 460, officer all ranks, leave or official duty. VIP suites (9); suites, private bath (88); bedroom, private bath (105); essentials, ice/food vending, housekeeping service, refrigerator, color TV in room & lounge, HBO, washer/dryer. Hotel type telephone systems. Rates: single room $8; suite $15; VIP suite, $22; dependents additional charge. Reservations limited during summer months.

TML Availability: Good, winter months. Difficult, summer months.

Great beaches at Virginia Beach.

Locator 491-4260   Medical 433-2221/22   Police 433-9111

Quantico Marine Corps Base (VA11R1)
Bachelor Housing Branch
15 Liversedge Drive
Quantico, VA 22134-5013

TELEPHONE NUMBER INFORMATION: Main installation numbers: C-703-784-2121, D-312-278-2121.

Location: From I-95 north or south take Quantico/Triangle exit 150A. US-1 north/south is adjacent to base. Clearly marked. *USMRA: Page 47 (L-5,6)*. NMC: Washington, DC, 40 miles north.

Lodging Office: Building 15, Liversedge Hall (BOQ/SNCO) **C-703-784-3148**, FAX 703-784-5940, D-312-278-3148/9, 24 hours daily. Housing Office, 0800-1630 M-F. **C-703-784-2711**. Check in billeting, check out 1000 hours (1200 hours Hostess House). Government civilian employee billeting.

TML: Hostess House. Building 3072, three miles from main gate. All ranks, leave or official duty. Deposit required first day for guaranteed reservation. Maximum stay 15 days, **C-703-748-2983/7959**. Bedroom, semi-private bath (34). A/C, CATV in room and lounge, housekeeping service, cribs ($.50), rollaways ($1), washer/dryer ($.50), ice vending machine. Complimentary coffee A.M. No pets. Three blocks from Quantico town, and four miles from commissary and exchange. Older structure. Rates: $23 per person without orders, $18 with orders.

VIRGINIA
Quantico Marine Corps Base, continued

TML: BOQ. Bldg 15, Liversedge Hall, officers all ranks, official or non-official duty, C-703-748-3148/9, D-278-3148/9. Bedroom, semi-private bath (transient duty)(72); guest suites/visitor's suites, private bath (TAD/TDY) (18). Micro/fridge (6 units), limited utensils, A/C, CATV, in room & lounge, housekeeping service, cribs/cots, washer/dryer, ice vending. Older structure. Rates: TAD/TDY $14-$18; suites $20-$30. TAD/TDY Group reservations 90 days in advance. Names submitted 30 days prior to arrival. Non TAD/TDY 30 days in advance, others Space-A.

TML: SNCO Quarters. Building 3229, Shuck Hall, enlisted E6-E9, official duty (TAD/TDY) or non-official duty. C-703-748-3148/9. D-312-278-3148/9. Bedroom, semi-private bath (TAD/TDY) (22); separate bedroom suite, private bath, A/C, CATV, housekeeping service, washer/dryer. Older structure. Rates: $8-$12 per room, $18-$25 per suite. Duty on orders, may make reservations 30 days in advance, others Space-A.

DV/VIP. DGQ, Crossroads Cottage (Guest House). 3300 Russell Road, C-703-784-4477, D-312-278-4477. O7+. Rates: $23-$30. Duty on orders or leave, retirees, and dependents space-A.

TML Availability: Good, Oct-Apr. Difficult, summer months.

CREDIT CARDS ACCEPTED: Visa, MasterCard and American Express.

Located on the Potomac River, near Washington DC. Woodbridge is the major shopping and recreation district close by, but the battlefield of Manassas, Occoquan (craft shops and marinas) is also near.

Locator 748-2141   Medical 911   Police 911

Vint Hill Farms Station (VA03R1)
Post Billeting Office
Bldg 163, Bicher Rd
Warrenton, VA 22186-5010
Scheduled to close 12/31/97.

TELEPHONE NUMBER INFORMATION: Main installation numbers: C-703-349-6000, D-312-229-6000.

Location: From Washington, DC area take I-66 west to Exit 43 A, 29/211 south, go about 8 miles south to VA 215 east (Vint Hill Rd), for about 2 miles, bear to the right on 652 east to main gate. *USMRA: Page 47 (L-5).* NMC: Washington DC, 45 miles northeast.

Lodging Office: Building 163, Bicher Rd., **C-703-349-5139/6797/6796,** 0730-2300 hours M-F, 0800-1600 Sa, Su, holidays. After duty hours, building 158, C-703-349-6236. Check in after 1400 hours daily, check out 1100 hours. No Pets. Government civilian employee billeting.

TML: Guest House. Building 168, all ranks, leave or official duty. Bedroom, private bath (14), 3 can be converted to a suite. Kitchenettes, kitchen amenities available for check out, essentials, CATV, washer/dryer, lounge, ice machine, housekeeping. Modern structure. Rates: duty $25, each additional

VIRGINIA
Vint Hill Farms Station, continued

person $1; Space-A $25, additional person $5. PCS, TDY have priority, Space-A arrivals: M-F 1400-2300 hours, Sa-Su 1400-1600 hours check in.

TML: VOQ/VEQ. Building 163, all ranks, official duty. Bedroom, private bath (12); bedroom, semi-private bath (2). AC, refrigerator, microwaves, CATV, lounge, washer/dryer, ice machine. Modern structure. Rates: $26.50 per night, $5 each additional person. No families or children. Official duty may make reservations 30 days in advance.

TML: DVQ/VIP. **Inn at Vint Hill.** Building 247, officer O6+, leave or official duty. Second floor O'Club. Separate bedroom suite, private bath (1). Refrigerator, A/C, CATV, housekeeping. Historical structure, remodeled. Rates: sponsor $30 per night, each additional person $5. Duty on orders can make reservations, 30 days in advance.

TML Availability: Fairly good. Best Oct-May. Difficult, June-Sep and Dec.

CREDIT CARDS ACCEPTED: American Express.

Visit historic Bull Run Battlefield Park, the lovely Shenandoah Valley and Blue Ridge Mountains (Skyline Drive), fascinating Luray Caverns. Washington DC offers a full range of entertainment and shopping.

Locator 349-6000   Medical 349-6543   Police 349-6543

Wallops Island AEGIS Combat Systems Center (VA46R1)
Combined Bachelor Quarters
Wallops Island, VA 23337-5000

TELEPHONE NUMBER INFORMATION: Main installation numbers: C-804-824-2355.

Location: From S: Take Chesapeake Bay Bridge-Tunnel N. Stay on US Rt 13 to Rt 175 (a right at T's Corner) for 5 mi, a left at Rt 798 (Ocean Deli). BQ facilities will be on the right. From N: Take Rt 13 S, 5 mi over MD/VA line to Rt 175, same directions as above. *USMRA: Page 47 (P-7).* NMC: Salisbury, MD, 40 miles N.

Lodging Office: Building R-20. **C-804-824-2064**, FAX 804-824-1764, 24 hours daily. Write to: CBQ, ACSC Wallops Island, VA 23337-5000. Check in billeting, check out 11 a.m. Late check out call OD C-804-824-2068. Government civilian employee billeting.

TML: BOQ. Ospray Manor Bldg. Officers, all ranks, leave or official duty. Bedroom, private bath (16). Kitchenette, limited utensils, A/C, CATV in room and lounge, ice machine, housekeeping service, essentials, food vending, cribs, rollaways, washer/dryer, award winning modern stick-built structure. Handicapped accessible. Some non-smoking rooms. Outdoor screened gazebo. Rates: $8.50, $2 additional person. Duty, Reserves and National Guard on orders, military widows can make reservations, others Space-A. No pets.

TML: BEQ. Eagles Nest Bldg. Enlisted, all ranks, leave or official duty. Bedroom, private bath (25); bedroom shared bath (30); suites, private bath (7) (E7+). Kitchenette, limited utensils (suites), essentials, food vending, housekeeping service, refrigerator, microwave, cribs, rollaways, VCR,

VIRGINIA,
Wallops Island AEGIS Combat Systems Center, continued

CATV in room and lounge, washer/dryer, training trailer (weights etc.). Recreation room, pool table, ping pong and large screen TV. Screened in deck. Modern structure. Handicapped accessible. Some non-smoking rooms. Galley next door. Rates $5.50,$6.50, depending upon rank, $1.50 additional person. Duty, Reserves and National Guard on orders, military widows can make reservations, others Space-A. No pets.

TML Availability: Very Good. Best, Sept-Mar, more difficult Apr-Aug.

CREDIT CARDS ACCEPTED: American Express.

Close to Chincoteague National Wildlife Refuge and Assateague National Seashore Park, where wild ponies are auctioned each May. A variety of outdoor activities abound - boating, crabbing. This is the Eastern Shore!

Locator 384-0306   Medical 552-5555   Police 384-0823

Yorktown Naval Weapons Station (VA14R1)
Nelson House
Combined Bachelor Quarters
Yorktown, VA 23691-5000

TELEPHONE NUMBER INFORMATION: Main installation numbers: C-804-887-4545, D-312-953-4545.

Location: From I-64 exit to 249 west, .5 mile to gate 3, Skiffes Creek. *USMRA: Page 47 (N-8); Page 52 (B,C-1).* NMC: Newport News, 15 miles southeast.

Lodging Office: Nelson House, building 704, **C-804-887-7621**, 24 hrs. Check in facility, check out 1100 hours. Government civilian employee billeting if GS-7+ with advance reservations.

TML: BOQ. Building 704, officers all ranks, leave or official duty, C-804-887-7621. Bedroom, private bath, suite (DV/VIP) (2); separate bedroom suites, private bath (10). Community kitchen, A/C, color/cable TV in room & lounge, housekeeping service, cots, washer/dryer, ice vending, micro-fridge. Modern structure. Rates: sponsor $23 maximum per family, VIP $25 maximum per family. Duty can make reservations, others Space-A.

DV/VIP: MWR Director, Building 2011, C-804-887-4234, O6+/GS-15+.

TML Availability: Good, winter months. Limited, summer months.

CREDIT CARDS ACCEPTED: Visa, MasterCard and American Express.

The Battlefield at Yorktown, restored Colonial Williamsburg, and the first permanent English settlement in America, are all within a 20 mile radius of the station. Also check out Busch Gardens and WIlliamsburg Pottery. Stop by the MWR Department for special tickets to events and parks.

Locator 887-4000   Medical 887-7404   Police 887-4677

WASHINGTON

Bangor Naval Submarine Base (WA08R4)
Evergreen Lodge
Bldg 1101, Room 122
Bangor Submarine Base, WA 98315-5000

TELEPHONE NUMBER INFORMATION: Main installation numbers: C-360-396-1110, D-312-744-1110.

Location: From Bremerton, on WA-3, follow signs "Hood Canal", bypassing Bremerton and Silverdale. Follow SUBASE signs to main gate. *USMRA: Page 103 (A-1,2)*. NMC: Bremerton, 12 miles south.

Billeting Office: Evergreen Lodge, building 1101, **C-360-396-4399**, 0730-1600 hours daily. (BOQ & BEQ) **360-779-5514,** 24 hours daily. Check in facility, check out 1200 hours daily. Government civilian employee billeting.

TML: Navy Lodge. Building 2906, Trigger Ave., NSB Bangor, Silverdale, WA 98315. Reservations: **1-800-NAVY-INN**, lodge number is C-360-779-9100. Check in 1500-1800, check out 1200 hours. Bedroom, 2 queen beds, private bath (45); bedroom, 1 queen bed, sofa sleeper, private bath (5). Six sets interconnecting, 2 handicapped accessible, 34 non-smoking. Kitchenette, microwave, utensils, A/C, CATV, coffee/tea, hair dryers, cribs, high chairs, food/ice vending, housekeeping service, phones, irons/boards, coin washer/dryer, playground, rollaways. Rates: $44. Maximum 5 per room. Seeing eye dogs, fish, caged birds OK. *Winner of the Edward E. Carlson Award for Navy Lodge Excellence for 1993, 50 unit category.*

TML: BOQ. Bldg 2750, officers all ranks, leave/official duty. Bedroom, private bath, (66); suites, 2 with kitchen (VIP)(6). Micro refrigerator, color TV in room & lounge, cribs/cots, housekeeping service, washer/dryer, food/ice vending, computer, jacuzzi. Modern structure. Rates: sponsor $8, adult, $4 child under 12. Suites $16, $4 each additional person. PCS are confirmed, duty, reservists can make reservations, others Space-A.

TML: BEQ. Building 2200, enlisted all ranks, leave or official duty. Bedroom, semi-private bath, 1-3 beds depending on rank (600); bedroom, private bath (Chiefs)(8). Refrigerator, color TV in lounge, housekeeping service, cribs/cots, washer/dryer, food/ice vending, microwave. Modern structure. Rates: sponsor $4, adult, child $3 each. Duty can make reservations, others Space-A.

TML: VIP Cottage. Building 4189, officer O6+, leave or official duty. Bedroom cottage, private bath (1). Kitchen, complete utensils, housekeeping service, cribs/cots, color TV. Renovated and remodeled. Rates: sponsor $16, adult, child $4 each. Maximum 4 persons. Duty can make reservations, others Space-A.

DV/VIP: PAO, building 1100, room 213, C-360-396-5514, O6+. Civilians determined by commander, retirees Space-A.

TML Availability: Fairly good. Best Oct-Apr, difficult May-Sep.

CREDIT CARDS ACCEPTED: The Navy Lodge accepts Visa, MasterCard, American Express and Discover.

WASHINGTON
Bangor Naval Submarine Base, continued

Visit Poulsbo, known as "Little Norway", and stroll the boardwalk along Liberty Bay. Try Bremerton's Naval Shipyard Museum (Ferry Terminal on First St). For picnicking and boating visit Silverdale Waterfront Park.

Locator 396-6111   Medical 396-4222   Police 396-4444

Fairchild Air Force Base (WA02R4)
ATTN: 92 SVS/SVML
BLDG 2392, Short Street
Fairchild AFB, WA 99011-5000

TELEPHONE NUMBER INFORMATION: Main installation numbers: C-509-247-1212, D-312-657-1110.

Location: Take US-2 exit from I-90 west of Spokane. Follow US-2 through Airway Heights, after 2 miles left to base main gate and Visitors' Control Center. *USMRA: Page 101 (I-4).* NMC: Spokane, 12 miles east.

Lodging Office: Building 2392, Short St, **C-509-247-5519**, 24 hours daily. Check in billeting, check out 1200 hours daily. Government civilian employee billeting official duty only.

TML: VOQ. Buildings 2392, all ranks, leave or official duty. Bedroom, shared bath (27). Cots, washer/dryer, ice vending, ironing boards. Renovated structures. Rates: $8 per person, maximum $16 per family; DV/VIP $14 per person, $24 maximum per family. Duty can make reservations, others Space-A.

TML: VAQ. Building 2272, enlisted all ranks, leave or official duty. Bedroom, semi-private bath (29). Refrigerator, A/C, color TV, housekeeping service, washer/dryer. Modern structure. Rates: $8 per room. Maximum 2 per room. TDY can make reservations, others Space-A.

TML: TLF. Building 2399, all ranks, leave or official duty. one bedroom suites, private bath (18). Kitchen, complete utensils, color TV, housekeeping service, cribs/cots, washer/dryer, ice vending. New structure. Rates: E1-E2 $12, O1 $15, all others $22.

DV/VIP: Building 2393, C-509-247-2127. O6+. Retirees and lower ranks Space-A.

TML Availability: Good, Sep-Mar. More difficult, other times.

CREDIT CARDS ACCEPTED: Visa, MasterCard and American Express.

Visit Manito Park and Botanical Gardens, while there look at the local pottery, the Cheney Cowles Museum and historic Campbell House. Try Factory Outlet shopping in Post Falls, Greyhound racing in Coeur D'Alene.

Locator 247-5875   Medical 247-5661   Police 247-5493

WASHINGTON

Fort Lewis (WA09R4)
Fort Lewis Billeting
P.O. Box 33085
Fort Lewis, WA 98433-0085

TELEPHONE NUMBER INFORMATION: Main installation numbers: C-206-967-1110, D-312-357-1110.

Location: On I-5, exit 120 in Puget Sound area, 14 miles north of Olympia, 12 miles south of Tacoma. Clearly marked. *USMRA: Page 101 (C-5); Page 103 (A,B-7)*. NMC: Tacoma, 12 miles north.

Lodging Office: Building 2110, between Utah and Pendleton Avenues, Main Post: **C-206-967-2815/7862/6754**, D-312-357-2815/357-7862, FAX 206-967-2253, DSN FAX 312-357-2253, 24 hours daily. Check in facility, check out 1000. Government civilian employee billeting.

TML: Fort Lewis Lodge. Guest house, all ranks, leave or official duty. C-206-964-0211. Bedroom, private bath (74); bedroom, private bath cottages, fully furnished for enlisted PCS families (9). Community kitchen each floor, CATV, housekeeping service, recreation room, lounge, cribs/cots, coin washer/dryer, ice vending. Modern structure. Rates: based on rank of military member, $5 for each additional occupant. Maximum 5 per room. TDY can make reservations, others Space-A.

TML: VOQ/VEQ. Main Post, two buildings all ranks, leave or official duty. Bedroom, private bath suites (16); bedroom private bath suites (27); single rooms (3). At Madigan Army Medical Center (MAMC) two buildings with suites (40), and single rooms (3). Some suites and singles share bath. Community kitchen on each floor, limited utensils, CATV, housekeeping service, washer/dryer, cribs/cots available. Older structures. Rates: $26, each additional person $5. TDY can make reservations, others Space-A.

TML: DVQ. Building 1020, **Bronson Hall**, officer O4+, leave or official duty. VIP suites, private bath (3); main post cabins (2). Rates: $26 per night, $5 additional occupant. Cabins have kitchen. Refrigerator, in-room fee beverage service, CATV, housekeeping service, washer/dryer. Older structure. Rates: sponsor $26, each additional person $5. Duty can make reservations, others Space-A.

TML: Klatawa Village, officer cabins. Main Post, family units (6). Small kitchen, limited utensils, color TV, housekeeping service. Enlisted Cabins. PCS in/out families may make reservations, others Space-A. Family units (10). Rates: call.

DV/VIP: Protocol Office, building 2025, C-206-967-5834, D-312-357-5834, O7+.

TML Availability: Fair, Oct-Apr. Difficult, other times.

From majestic Mount Rainier, to the inland sea waters of Puget Sound, perfection for the outdoorsman. Tacoma, Olympia and Seattle are nearby.

Locator 385-2350   Medical 911   Police 911

Temporary Military Lodging Around the World - 251

WASHINGTON

Madigan Army Medical Center (WA15R4)
Lodging Office, Bldg 2110
Tacoma, WA 98431-0001

TELEPHONE NUMBER INFORMATION: Main installation numbers: C-206-967-5051, D-312-357-5151.

Location: From I-5 north or south take the Madigan exit. Clearly marked. *USMRA: Page 103 (A-7).* NMC: Tacoma, 12 miles north.

Lodging Office: Building 2110, **C-206-964-0211**, 24 hours daily. Check in billeting, check out 1000 hours daily. Government civilian employee billeting.

TML: Guest House. Bldg 9901, all ranks, leave or official duty. Bedroom, shared bath (6); separate bedrooms, semi-private bath (14). Community kitchen, refrig, limited utensils, housekeeping service, cribs/cots, washer/dryer. Older structure. Rates: sponsor $16-$26, additional person $5. Maximum 3 per unit. MEDEVAC priority.

TML: VOQ/VEQ. Building 9906, all ranks, leave or official duty. Bedroom, private bath (7). Bedroom, semi-private bath (16). Community kitchen, refrigerator, limited utensils, housekeeping service, washer/dryer. Older structure. Rates: $16-$26, additional person $5. TDY/med student reservations, others Space-A.

TML: Fisher House. Note: Appendix C has the definition of this facility. **C-206-964-0211.**

TML Availability: Fairly good. Best, Oct-May.

Locator 967-6221   Medical 968-1110   Police 967-3107

McChord Air Force Base (WA05R4)
Lodging Office
Bldg 166, Main Street
McChord AFB, WA 98438-5000

TELEPHONE NUMBER INFORMATION: Main installation numbers: C-206-984-1910, D-312-976-1110.

Location: From I-5 exit 125. Clearly marked. *USMRA: Page 101 (C-5); Page 103 (B-7).* NMC: Tacoma, 8 miles north.

Lodging Office: Building 166, Main Street, **C-206-584-1471**, 24 hours daily. Check in facility, check out 1100 hours daily. No government civilian employee billeting.

TML: VOQ/VAQ. Many buildings, all ranks, leave or official duty. Bedroom, private, semi-private, & common baths (172); separate bedrooms, private bath (18); two bedroom, private bath (19). Kitchen (VOQ), refrigerator, limited utensils, color TV, housekeeping service, cribs/cots, washer/dryer, ice vending, facilities for DAVs. Older structures. Rates: $8 per person. Maximum 2 room suite $16, 1 room $8. Duty can make reservations, others Space-A.

WASHINGTON
McChord Air Force Base, continued

TML: DV/VIP. Officer O6+, leave or official duty, **C-206-584-2621**. Bedroom suites, private bath (6); two bedroom suites, private bath (17); bedroom, private bath (48). Kitchen, complete utensils, honor bar, color TV, VCR, housekeeping service, cribs/cots, washer/dryer, ice vending. Older structure, redecorated. Rates: $14 per person. Duty can make reservations, others Space-A.

DV/VIP: EXO 62/MAW/CCE, building 100, C-206-584-2621, O6/GS-15+. Call billeting for reservations. Retirees and lower ranks Space-A.

TML Availability: Good, Nov-Feb. Difficult, Jun-Aug.

Locator 984-2474   Medical 984-5601   Police 984-5624

**Pacific Beach Resort
(WA16R4)**
P.O. Box 0
Pacific Beach, WA 98571-5000

TELEPHONE NUMBER INFORMATION: Main numbers: 1-800-626-4414.

Location: Located on the coast in Pacific Beach, WA, 150 miles southwest of Seattle. Accessible from US-101 (Coastal Highway) and US-12 from Yakima. *USMRA: Page 101 (A-4,5)*. NMC: Seattle, 150 miles northeast.

Lodging Office: Check in 1600, check out 1100 hours, **C-1-800-626-4414**, 0800-1600 hours. Reservations made over the phone are confirmed when made. Send information requests to: PACIFIC BEACH RESORT, P.O. Box 0, Pacific Beach, WA 98571. Make checks payable to: Pacific Beach. Cancellations must be received 10 days prior (A $15 cancellation fee will be assessed). Notices received less than 10 working days will be assessed one day's rental. Reservations not paid within 10 working days are subject to cancellation. Reservation Priority: (1 reservation per family) active duty, 90 days, other military personnel 60 days, all other authorized personnel 30 days. Note: A new Conference Center is now open.

TML: Cabin, suites, family (13) and studio units (13). Cabin, 3 and 4 bedrooms (28); suites, 1 bedroom, sitting room, private bath (adults only) (6); family and motel units. Each cabin sleeps two people per bedroom. The suite and the studios can accommodate two adults. The family units sleep two adults and two children. Oceanside cabin w/fireplace - add $10 per day, tent sites - add $5 per day. See Military Living's *Military RV, Camping and Rec Areas Around the World* for more information on camping and RV information. Crib linens not provided. Lodging can be reserved from 1 night in the suites, studios & family units and a minimum of 2 nights in the cabins. Maximum stay, except for the RV park, is two weeks. Extensions granted when space is available. Holiday weekends minimum of 3 nights (F-M). All other requests on a Space-A basis. Note: sponsor must accompany civilian guests during stay. All military ID card holders welcome. There are both pet and no-pet accommodations.

TML Availability: Fairly good. Best in winter months.

CREDIT CARDS ACCEPTED: Visa, MasterCard and American Express.

WASHINGTON
Pacific Beach Resort, continued

Seasonal Rates - (Off Peak Oct 1 - Mar 31/Peak Season Apr 1 - Sep 30)

Type of Lodging	E1-E5		E6-E9		O1-O9		DoD Civilians	
	Off Peak	Peak	Off Peak	Peak	Off Peak	Peak	Off Peak	Peak
RV****	$7	$9	$7	$9*	$7	$9	$9	$11
Motel	$20	$25	$25	$30	$30	$35	$35	$40
Family	$25	$30	$30	$35	$35	$40	$40	$45
Suites	$45	$50	$45	$50	$45	$50	$45	$50
*3 Bedroom Cabin	$45	$55	$50	$60	$55	$65	$60	$70
*4 Bedroom Cabin	$50	$60	$55	$65	$60	$70	$65	$75

RATES PER DAY PER UNIT
****Weekly & Monthly rates available. (RV only)
*Add $10 for oceanfront accommodations.

"May be the Navy's best kept vacation secret"! Social room with activities weekends off-season, and daily in spring, summer and fall. Bowling, exercise room, spa, restaurant and lounge, ball field, horseshoe pits, picnicking, and whale watching platform, for what else? Watching whales!

Puget Sound Naval Shipyard (WA11R4)
Lodging Office, Bldg 865
Bremerton, WA 98314-5000

TELEPHONE NUMBER INFORMATION: Main installation numbers: C-360-476-3711, D-312-439-3711.

Location: Take WA-16 West to end of freeway, NS clearly visible 3 miles north. *USMRA: Page 101 (C-4); Page 103 (A-3).* NMC: Seattle, 60 miles southeast.

Lodging Office: Building 865, C-360-476-7627, D-312-439-7627, 24 hours daily. Reservation desk 24 hours, **C-360-476-7627/7619,** D-312-439-7627, FAX-360-476-6895, check in facility, check out 1300 hours daily. Government civilian employee billeting.

TML: BEQ. Underwood Hall, Keppler Hall, Nibbe Hall, buildings 865, 885, 942. Enlisted all ranks, leave or official duty, C-360-476-7619, D-312-439-7627. Bedroom, shared bath (447); family rooms (6). Refrigerator in room, community kitchen 1st floor, color TV in room & lounge, housekeeping service, washer/dryer, ice, food vending, hot tub, mini gym, washer/dryer, microwave each floor, picnic facilities. Modern structure. Rates: $4 per person, family rooms $12. AD and retired can make reservations, others Space-A.

TML: BOQ. Building 847, officers all ranks & GS-7+, leave or official duty, C-360-476-2840, D-312-476-2840, FAX-360-476-0045. Bedroom, private bath (70); VIP/family suites, private bath (5). Refrigerators, cooking facility 1st floor, essentials, CATV in room & lounge, housekeeping service, washer/dryer, ice and food vending, complimentary coffee/doughnuts weekdays, telephones, sauna/spa, mini-gym, library and reading room, conference/meeting room, children's playground. Rates: $6 per person. Maximum 4 per room. Reservation services 24 hours.

DV/VIP: BOQ, Building 847, O6+, retirees Space-A, D-312-439-2840.

WASHINGTON
Puget Sound Naval Shipyard, continued

TML Availability: Fairly good, Nov-Mar. More difficult, Jun-Sep.

CREDIT CARDS ACCEPTED: Visa and American Express.

A beautiful Northwest location is supplemented by these lodging facilities.

Locator 476-3711　　　　**Medical 911**　　　　**Police 476-3393**

Whidbey Island Naval Air Station (WA06R4)
CBQ Billeting
Bldg 973, McCormick Center
5th Street
Oak Harbor, WA 98278-5200

TELEPHONE NUMBER INFORMATION: Main installation numbers: C-360-257-2211, D-312-820-0111.

Location: Take WA-20 to Whidbey Island, 3 miles west of WA-20 on Ault Field Road. *USMRA: Page 101 (C-2,3).* NMC: Seattle, 90 miles southeast.

Lodging Office: Building 973, McCormick Center, 5th Street, **C-360-257-2529**, officer/CPO. Building 2701, 8th Street, **C-209-257-5513**, FAX 360-257-5603, enlisted. Check in facility, check out 1200 hours daily. Government civilian employee billeting (on orders).

TML: BOQ. Building 973, officers, all ranks, leave or official duty. Bedroom, private bath (140). Refrigerator, housekeeping service, essentials, food/ice vending, color TV in room & lounge, washer/dryer. Older structure. Rates: $9.75 single occupancy, $12.25 double occupancy. Max 2 persons per unit. Duty can make reservations, others Space-A.

TML: BEQ. Building 2701, all ranks, leave or official duty. Beds, 3 per room, shared bath (36). Refrigerator, color TV in room & lounge, housekeeping service, ice/food vending, washer/dryer. Older structure. Rates: $4 per person. Duty can make reservations, others Space-A.

DV/VIP: CO Secretary, building 108, C-360-257-2345 or BQ manager, C-360-257-2076, O6+.

TML Availability: Difficult on weekends due to Reserve Training. Best during winter.

CREDIT CARDS ACCEPTED: Visa, MasterCard and American Express.

Whidbey Island can also be reached by ferry from Mukilteo (north of Seattle) to Clinton, in South Whidbey. Visit the hamlet of Langley then take a two hour drive north to Oak Harbor and beautiful Puget Sound scenery.

Locator 257-2211　　　　**Medical 679-4400**　　　　**Police 257-3122**

Too Late To Copy
The Navy Lodge at Whidbey Island opened in February of 1995. See page 348 for more information.

WISCONSIN

Fort McCoy (WI02R2)
Director of Logistics
ATTN: AFRC-FM-DLH-B
2101 South 8th Avenue
Sparta, WI 54656-5152

TELEPHONE NUMBER INFORMATION: Main installation numbers: C-608-388-2222, D-312-280-1110.

Location: From west on I-90 to north on WI-27 to northeast on WI-21 to fort. From east on I-90, to west on WI-21 to fort. *USMRA: Page 68 (C,D-7)*. NMC: La Crosse, 35 miles southwest.

Lodging Office: Building 2168, 8th St, **C-608-388-2107**, D-312-280-2107, FAX 608-388-3946, DSN FAX 312-280-3946, 24 hours daily. Check in billeting 1200, check out 1100 hours daily. Government civilian employee billeting.

TML: TLQ. All ranks, leave or official duty. Bedroom, shared bath (230); bedroom, private bath (70); bedroom (2) two bedroom (4) and three bedroom (1), private bath (4 units are trailers). Kitchen, utensils, A/C, color TV, cribs, cots ($3), essentials, washer/dryer. Older structure, new trailers. Rates: vary according to rank/grade of guest/type quarters occupied, call for details. All categories can make reservations.

DV/VIP: Protocol, building 100, C-608-388-3607, O6+, retirees and lower ranks Space-A.

TML Availability: Fairly good, Jan-May and Sep-Dec. Difficult, other times.

CREDIT CARDS ACCEPTED: Visa, MasterCard and American Express.

Mid December - February the installation ski hill has good cross country and downhill snow skiing. Visit the cheese factories, brewery, Amish shops and Cranberry Expo Museum. Equipment rental, C-EX-4498/3360. See *Military RV, Camping and Rec Areas Around the World* for more information.

Locator 388-2225   **Medical 338-2444**   **Police 115**

WYOMING

Francis E. Warren Air Force Base (WY01R4)
Crow Creek Inn
7103 Randall Street
Francis E. Warren AFB, WY 82005-2987

TELEPHONE NUMBER INFORMATION: Main installation numbers: C-307-775-1110, D-312-481-1110.

Location: Off I-25, 2 miles north of I-80, clearly marked. *USMRA: Page 102 (I-8)*. NMC: Cheyenne, adjacent to the city.

Lodging Office: Crow Creek Inn. 7103 Randall Street, 24 hours daily, **C-307-775-1844**,D-312-481-1844, Fax 307-775-4450, DSN Fax 312-481-4450. Check in facility, check out 1200 hours daily. Government civilian employee billeting.

TML: Guest Housing. Buildings 1454, 238, 241, all ranks, leave or official duty. One, two and three bedroom apartments. Kitchen, living room, housekeeping service, cribs and high chairs, washer/dryer, CATV, refrigerator in all units. Older structures, renovated. Rates: $26.50 per night. TDY and PCS can make reservations, others Space-A.

TML: VOQ. Buildings 21, 74, 79, 129, 275, officers and civilians, leave or official duty. Two houses, one bedroom apartments, private bath, some with kitchen. Refrigerator, CATV, housekeeping service, washer and dryer. Older structure, renovated. Rates $15.50 per person per night. TDY and PCS can make reservations, others Space-A.

TML: VAQ. Buildings 244, 274. DV/VIP units for E6-E9. Single rooms, shared bath. Refrigerator, microwave, CATV, housekeeping service, washer and dryer. Older structure, renovated. Rates: $11.50 per person per night.

DV/VIP: PAO. C-307-775-2137/3052, E8+/O6+. Historic houses. Rates $14-$25. Retirees Space-A.

TML Availability: Good, except last week of July for Cheyenne Frontier Day Rodeo.

CREDIT CARDS ACCEPTED: Visa, MasterCard, American Express and Diners'.

This base was once a frontier Army post, and many of its buildings are on the National Historic Register. Cowboy and Indian lore abound, and nearby Colorado skiing draws many visitors. Visit Fort Collins' Old Town nearer by.

Locator 775-1841   **Medical 775-3461**   **Police 775-3501**

UNITED STATES POSSESSIONS

GUAM

Andersen Air Force Base (GU01R8)
Lodging Office
Bldg 27006, 4th & Caroline Avenue
APO AP 96543-4004

TELEPHONE NUMBER INFORMATION: Main installation numbers: C-011-671-366-1110, D-315-366-1110.

Location: On the north end of the island, accessible from Marine Dr which extends entire length of the island of Guam. *USMRA: Page 130 (E,F-1,2)*. NMC: Agana, 15 miles south.

Lodging Office: Building 27006, 4th & Caroline Ave, **C-011-671-366-8201/8144**, D-315-366-8144, 24 hours daily. Check in billeting 1400 hours, check out 1200 hours daily. Government civilian employee billeting.

TML: VOQ. Buildings 25003, 27006, officers all ranks, leave or official duty. Bedroom (18), shared bath (100). Refrigerator, A/C, CATV, housekeeping service, washer/dryer, ice vending. Older structure. Rates: $10 per person. Duty can make reservations, others Space-A.

TML: VAQ. Building 25003, enlisted all ranks, leave or official duty. Two bedrooms, shared bath (60). Refrigerator, A/C, CATV, washer/dryer. Older structure. Rates: $10 per person. Duty can make reservations, others Space-A.

TML: TLF. Building 1656, officer, enlisted, all ranks, PCS move or leave. Bedrooms, private bath, (18). Kitchenette, A/C, CATV, housekeeping service, washer/dryer. Rates: $30 per unit. PCS can make reservations, others Space-A.

TML: DV/VIP. Building 27006, officer O6+, leave or official duty. Bedroom, private bath (6); separate bedroom, private bath suites (5). A/C, CATV, housekeeping service, washer/dryer. Rates: rooms $15, suites $20. Duty can make reservations, others Space-A.

DV/VIP: Protocol Office, 36 ABW, C-011-671-351-4228, O7+, retirees Space-A.

TML Availability: Good, year round.

Lots of sunshine, beaches, coral reefs, exciting WWII shipwrecks to explore for scuba enthusiasts. Hikers enjoy tropical mountains and jungles.

Locator 351-1110 **Medical-366-2978** **Police 366-2913**

GUAM

Guam Naval Station (GU02R8)
Combined Bachelor Quarters
PSC 455, Box 169
FPO AP 96540-1099

TELEPHONE NUMBER INFORMATION: Main installation numbers: C-011-671-351-1110. D-315-322-1110.
Location: South on Marine Drive, through main gate, clearly marked. *USMRA: Page 130 (C-3)*. NMC: Agana, 10 miles north.

Lodging Office: Centralized, contact CBQ Barracks 18 lower, on Chapel Road off Marine Drive, **C-011-671-339-5259**, D-315-339-6250, FAX-011-671-339-5139, 24 hours daily. Check in facility, check out 1300 hours daily. TLA approved. Government civilian employee billeting.

TML: CBQ. Barracks 7, 22, officers, enlisted, government civilian employees (stateside hire), all ranks, leave or official duty. Bedroom, private bath (12); suites, private bath (52). Refrigerator, CATV and VCR, A/C, housekeeping service, washer/dryer, ice, coffee maker. Rates: Barracks 7, $4 per person, Barracks 22, $10 per person. Duty can make reservations, others Space-A.

TML: BOQ. Buildings 2000, 179, officers and equivalent civilians, all ranks. Bedroom, private bath (58). Refrigerator, A/C, CATV and VCR, housekeeping service, washer/dryer, ice and coffee maker. Rates: $7 per person, $7 per family member over 8 years old. Duty can make reservations, others Space-A.

DV/VIP: Flag Lt, C-011-671-339-5202, O7+.

TML Availability: Fairly good. Best, December. Most difficult, Jul-Aug.

These quarters are within walking distance of all base support facilities. Scuba diving and other beach related activities are popular.

Locator 351-1110   **Medical 344-9369**   **Police 333-2989**

Watch for news of a new 100 room Navy Lodge at this location in late '96. Keep updated with Military Living's R&R Space-A Report.

PUERTO RICO

Borinquen Coast Guard Air Station (PR03R1)
La Plaza, Room 26
Aquadilla, PR 00604-5000

TELEPHONE NUMBER INFORMATION: Main installation numbers: C & FTS-809-882-3500.

Location: At old Ramey AFB, north of Aquadilla. Take PR-2 from San Juan or north from Mayaguez to PR-110 North to CGAS. *USMRA: Page 130 (B,C-2)*. NMC: San Juan, 65 miles east.

Lodging Office: La Plaza, room 26, **C-809-890-3127/2581**, 0800-1700 duty hours. Other hours, SDO, C-809-890-3501. Check in billeting, check out 1200 hours daily. Government civilian employee billeting at CGES office.

TML: Guest House. All ranks, leave or official duty. Bedroom, shared bath and private bath (5); three bedroom, private bath (4). Kitchen, complete utensils, A/C (2 units), color TV in lounge, housekeeping service, washer/dryer. Older structure. Rates: (3 bedroom), $20 - 1 person, $26, - 2 persons, $32 - 3 persons; (1 bedroom) $11 - 1 person, $16 - 2 persons, $20 - 3 persons. Duty and retirees can make reservations, others Space-A. PCS have priority. Personnel on leave/anyone on vacation should apply at least 15 days in advance. No pets.

TML: Lighthouse, Borinquen Recreation Area, opened July '91. Two bedroom apartment suites, private bath (2); queen, 2 single beds, living, dining, kitchen, microwave, utensils, A/C, CATV, housekeeping service, washer/dryer. No pets. Maximum capacity 4 persons. Rates: $35 active duty, $40 others. Duty may make reservations 45 days ahead, all others 30 days. Duty must make reservations (military widows make their own). Family members of legal age may use facilities unaccompanied, but duty who makes reservations assumes responsibility. Write to: Lighthouse Reservations, PO Box 520, Aquadilla, Puerto Rico 00604-5000.

TML Availability: Very limited. Best, Sep-May.

Recreation gear available for rent, theater (Fri-Sa) passes. Swimming pool on post, groceries 1 mile, picnic areas, Survival Beach belies its name - a lovely place to relax. Contact MWR for all information 809-890-6236.

Locator 882-3500   Medical 882-1500   Police 890-5201

Fort Buchanan (PR01R1)
Lodging Office, Bldg 119
Fort Buchanan, PR 00934-5042

TELEPHONE NUMBER INFORMATION: Main installation numbers: C-809-273-3401, D-313-740-1110.

Location: From Munoz Rivera International Airport take highway 26 west toward Bayamon to highway 22 to the Fort Buchanan sign. *USMRA: Page 130 (E-2)*. NMC: San Juan, 6 miles southwest.

Lodging Office: Building 119, **C-809-792-7877**, D-313-740-3821, FAX 809-273-3273, 0630-1800 hours daily. Other hours SDO, building 390, C-EX-3723. Check in facility 1300, check out 1100 hours daily. No government civilian employee billeting.

PUERTO RICO
Fort Buchanan, continued

TML: Su Casa Guest House, buildings 119 and 1315, all ranks, leave or official duty. Handicapped accessible. Bedroom, private bath (each with double bed and sleeper sofa) (29). Refrigerator, microwave, coffee pot, A/C, CATV, housekeeping service, cribs, cots, facilities for DAVs. Older structure, remodeled. Rates range from $18-$36, $5 each additional person. PCS may make reservations with orders. Other active duty fourteen days in advance, others Space-A.

DV/VIP: Headquarters Command, building 399, C-809-792-3340, O6+. Reservations through Protocol Officer.

TML Availability: Good, Nov-Apr. Difficult, June-Oct.

CREDIT CARDS ACCEPTED: Visa, MasterCard, and American Express.

This is the capital of Puerto Rico. Visit El Morro Castle, Plaza las Americas Shopping Center, Pawo la Princessa, El Condado, local Bacardi Rum Distillers, and beautiful beaches. Post facilities include a gym swimming pool, bowling alley and fitness center, PX and Commissary.

Locator 273-3400   Medical 793-5593   Police 273-3913

Roosevelt Roads Naval Station (PR02R1)
P.O. Box 3010
FPO AA 34051-5000

TELEPHONE NUMBER INFORMATION: Main installation numbers: C-809-865-2000, D-313-831-2000.

Location: From San Juan International Airport, turn left onto PR-26 for 20 minutes, turn left onto PR-3 (Carolina exit) for 30 minutes, then turn left after Puerto Del Rey Marina into NS. *USMRA: Page 130 (F-2,3)*. NMC: San Juan, 50 miles northwest.

Lodging Office: Building 729 (officers), building 1708 (enlisted). **C-809-865-2000-4334/3364 (officers), 809-865-2000-4145/4147 (enlisted),** 24 hours daily. Check in billeting, check out 1100 hours daily. Government civilian employee billeting.

TML: CBQ. Officers, all ranks, leave or official duty. Handicapped accessible. Two bedroom apartments, private bath (8); three bedroom apartments, private bath (4). Kitchen, refrigerator, limited utensils, A/C, color TV, VCR, movies, phones, FAX, housekeeping service, cots ($2), NEX mini mart. Modern structure. Rates: rooms (BEQ) $6, (VIP) $15; (BOQ) $10, (VIP) $20. Active duty on orders, PCS/TAD/TDY have priority for reservations, others Space-A.

TML: Guest House. Two bedroom houses (O6+)(2). Kitchen, complete utensils, microwave, A/C, CATV, phone, housekeeping service, washer/dryer. Rates: $25 + $10 ea. additional guest, per night. Duty can make reservations, others Space-A.

TML: Navy Lodge. All ranks, leave or official duty, **C-1-800-NAVY-INN,** the direct lodge number is 809-865-8281/8282, FAX 809-865-8283. Bedrooms, 2 double beds, private bath (72) (interconnecting units for large families, two handicapped accessible). Kitchenette, complete utensils, microwave, A/C, CATV, refrigerator,

PUERTO RICO
Roosevelt Roads Naval Station, continued

phone, hair dryers, housekeeping service, coin washer/dryer, mini mart, children's playground. Rates: $51 per night. All categories can make reservations. Check in 1500 to 1600 hours, check out by 1200.

TML: TVQ suites and apartments, Naval Reserve Station, downtown San Juan, stop 7 1/2. Naval Reserve buildings 441, 448. Enlisted E7+. Suites, private baths (2); guest house apartments, 2 bedrooms, private bath, full kitchen, patio (6). Rates: suites $20 per day, $10 additional guest, apartments $25 per day, $10 additional guest.

DV/VIP: C-809-865-3364, O7+, retirees Space-A.

TML Availability: Good, Oct-Mar. Difficult, Apr-Sep.

CREDIT CARDS ACCEPTED: Visa, MasterCard, American Express and Discover accepted at the Navy Lodge.

Don't miss El Yuunque (L-EE-UN-KEE) rain forest with its magnificent water falls, hiking trails, and restaurant.

Locator 865-2000   **Medical 865-5700**   **Police 865-4011**

The Navy Lodge at Roosevelt Roads in Puerto Rico. Photo courtesy of Navy Lodge, Roosevelt Roads.

062 - Temporary Military Lodging Around the World

FOREIGN COUNTRIES

BELGIUM

NATO/SHAPE Support Group (US) (BE01R7)
Hotel Raymond Billeting
80th ASG (NSSG), CMR #451
APO AE 09708-5000

TELEPHONE NUMBER INFORMATION: Main installation numbers: C-(USA) 011-32-65-32-75-11, ask operator to connect you; (BE) 065-31-1131/32, D-312-361-1110 (Chieveres Air Base - ask them to connect you).

Location: From Bruxelles Airport take E-10 toward Paris, exit at Mons, Belgium and follow signs to "GARE" (train station). Hotel is across from GARE. HE: p-35, E/3. NMC: Brussels, 50 miles north.

Lodging Office: Write to: Hotel Raymond, 80th ASG (NSSG), CMR #451, APO AE 09708-5000. Priority I - TDY military and civilians, PCS military personnel and their families. Priority II - Space-A personnel to include military/civilian personnel on leave, retirees and AAFES/DODDS personnel on PCS orders. Check in 1300 hours, check out 1000 hours daily, **C-(USA) 011-32-65-32-75-11,** (BE) 065-31-1131/32, FAX 011-32-65-32-75-01. Government civilian employee billeting. This hotel was renovated in 1993.

TML: Hotel Raymond, all ranks, leave or official duty. Bdrm, private bath (67). Refrigerator, color TV, full custodial service (except Sunday/holidays), cribs/cots, washer/dryer, buffet breakfast at nominal cost ($2.50), food/ice vending. Rates: $35 primary occupant, $5 each additional occupant. Space-A may check availability same day as arrival, above number.

TML Availability: Fairly good. Best Oct-Mid May.

CREDIT CARDS ACCEPTED: Visa, MasterCard, American Express, Diners and Discover.

In Mons visit the Church of St Waudru. "The Belfry" is accessible by elevator. Then visit the main square, town hall, and Van Gogh's house. To contact the Tourist Office, Grand-Place, 7000 Mons, call 065-33-55-80.

Locator 44-7111   Medical 44-3321   Police 27-5301

Tri-Mission Association (BE02R7)
c/o American Embassy
APO AE 09724-5000
(U.S. State Department Billeting)

TELEPHONE NUMBER INFORMATION: Main installation number: C-(USA) 011-32-2-502481.

Location: In Centrum Brussels, follow signs to "Centrum", a large avenue with tunnels. Look for #28 Boulevard Du Regent.

BELGIUM
Tri-Mission Association, continued

Lodging Office: 28 Blvd Du Regent, 0800-1600 Mon-Fri. C-(USA) **011-32-2-5082481**, FAX 011-32-25-11-1626, after duty hours report to American Embassy. Check in at facility (after hours at Embassy), check out 1000. No government civilian employee billeting.

TML: All ranks, leave or official duty. Ten (10) apartments, private bath, kitchenette, utensils, color TV weekly housekeeping service, cribs/cots, washer/dryer. Rates: $135 for AD, PCS/TDY; $85 for those on leave. Apartments are two and four bedroom that sleep up to seven. Active duty may make reservations, all others Space-A. Pets allowed ($20 cleaning fee).

TML Availability: Fairly good. Best Nov- May, difficult Jun-Oct.

CREDIT CARDS ACCEPTED: Visa, MasterCard, American Express, Diners and Discover.

Too Late To Copy
BAHRAIN
Bahrain Naval Support Unit, FPO AE 09834-2800. CBQ. C-011-973-727-762, 24 hours.

BELGIUM
SHAPE HQ, SHAPE Inn, Building 904, Room 108, B/7010, SHAPE, Belgium. C-011-32-65-44-4385, Fax 011-32-65-44-5323. BOQ units available - 93.

DENMARK
Thule Air Base (Greenland), Bldg 97, APO AE 09704-5000. C-011-299-50-636 ext 2022/3276/2270.

GREECE
Souda Bay Naval Support Activity/Air Facility (Crete), C-011-30-821-63388/63340, ask for lodging office.

ITALY
Gaeta Naval Support Activity, D-314-625-7677/7679.

UNITED KINGDOM
Brawdy Wales Naval Facility, BOQ/BEQ. C-011-44-1437-720654.

RAF Croughton, C-011-44-1280-708-394. D-314-263-4394, 0600-1800 hours.

CANADA

8th Wing Trenton (CN04R1)
Yukon Lodge
8th Wing, Trenton
Astra, Ontario CN, KOK 1BO
(Canadian Forces Billeting)

TELEPHONE NUMBER INFORMATION: Main installation numbers: C-613-392-2811 (recording, then press 1, then either 3793 or 3794), D-312-827-7011.

Location: From Toronto take Highway 401 east approximately 100 miles. May also be reached by crossing Canada/USA border at 1000 Islands, NY and proceeding west 70 miles on Highway 401. NMC: Toronto, 100 miles west.

Lodging Office: Bldg 76, **C-613-965-3793**, D-312-827-3793, FAX 613-965-3874, 24 hours daily. Reservations accepted for leave personnel and their family members. Write to: **Yukon Lodge**, 8th Wing Trenton, Astra, Ontario CN KOK 1BO. Check in at the facility 24 hours, check out 1200 hours, late checkout can be arranged.

TML: Yukon Lodge, all ranks, leave or official duty. Bedrooms, 1-5 beds each, private and semi private baths. Cribs, food vending, color TV in room and lounge, washer/dryer, telephones. Older structure. Rates: adult $6, child $5.50, active duty $5, (Canadian). Verification of military/family member status required. No pets. Space-A lodging only.

DV/VIP: Base Protocol, CFB Trenton, Astra, Ontario, CN KOK 1BO. Building 22, O6+. Limited number of accommodations. C-613-965-3379, D-312-827-3379.

TML Availability: Difficult. Best Oct-May, most difficult Jun-Sept.

CREDIT CARDS ACCEPTED: Diners.

The Bay of Quinte Region is filled with wonderful fishing, camping, sailing and historical landmarks. Write to Central Ontario Travel Association, PO Box 1566, Peterborough, Ontario K9J 7H7, or call 1-800-461-1912 for more info.

Locator 392-2811   Medical 392-3480   Police 392-3385

Royal Road Military College (CN08RI)
FMO, Victoria CN, VOS-1B&O
(Canadian Forces Billeting)

An R&R subscriber who recently visited Vancouver, British Columbia reports that there is temporary military lodging available at Royal Road Military College. Write to the above address for more information or telephone the Director of Administration at **C-604-363-4526.**

CUBA

Guantanamo Bay Naval Station (CU01R1)
PSC 1005, Box 53
FPO AE 09593-5000

TELEPHONE NUMBER INFORMATION: Main installation numbers: C-011-53-99-4063, D-313-723-3690/564-4063.

Location: In the southeast corner of the Republic of Cuba. Guantanamo Bay Naval Station is accessible only by air. NMC: Miami, FL, 525 air miles northwest. Note: All personnel not assigned must have the permission of the Commander to visit Guantanamo Bay Naval Station.

Lodging Office: ATTN: Billeting, PSC 1005, Box 53, **C-011-53-99-2400/01**, D-313-564-4063 ext 2400/01, FAX 011-53-99-2154, 24 hours daily. Check in facility, check out 1200 hours daily.

TML: Navy Lodge. PSC 1005, Box 38, FPO AE 09593-0003, all ranks, leave or official duty, reservations: **011-53-99-3103**, 0800-1830 M-F, 0800-1630 Sa, Su, Hol. Check out 1200 hours daily. Bedroom, 2 double beds, studio couch, private bath (26). Kitchen, A/C, color TV, in room telephones, coin washer/dryer. Rates: $39 per unit.

TML: BOQ/BEQ. Buildings 1660, 1661, 1670, 2146 all ranks, leave or official duty. Bedroom, private bath (officer) (20); bedroom, hall bath (enlisted) (18). Refrigerator, community kitchen (CPO), A/C, color TV in room & lounge, housekeeping service, washer/dryer, ice vending. Modern structure. Rates: Enlisted $5 per person; Officer $8 per person.

DV/VIP: BOQ. Building 1670, C-011-53-99-2400/01, D-313-564-2400/01, O6+. Rates: $25.

TML Availability: Good most of the year except holidays.

CREDIT CARDS ACCEPTED: American Express.

Locator 4453/4366   **Medical 72360**   **Police 4105/3813/4145**

266 - Temporary Military Lodging Around the World

GERMANY

Ansbach Base Support Battalion (GE60R7)
Katterbach BOQ Office
APO AE 09177-5000

TELEPHONE NUMBER INFORMATION: Main installation numbers: C-(USA) 011-49-981-83-1110 (Ansbach), 011-49-9802-832-1110 (Katterbach), (GE) 0981-83-1110, 09802-832-1110; ETS-468-7/8-1110 (Ansbach), 467-1110 (Katterbach); D-314-460-1110 Ask for ANS.

Location: Exit from A6 Autobahn east or west to B-14 or B-13 north 4 miles. Follow US Forces signs to Katterbach Kaserne. HE: p-40, E/2. NMC: Nürnberg, 26 miles northeast.

Lodging Office: Katterbach BOQ Office, **C-(USA) 011-49-9802-832-812,** (GE) 09802-83-1700, ETS-468-1700. Check in facility 0730-1600 M-Th, 0730-1500 F. Check out 1000 hours daily. Government civilian employee billeting.

TML: TLF, **Franconian Inn**, building 5908, all ranks, leave or official duty. Single rooms, private bath, shared kitchenette (28); family rooms, living room, private bath, private kitchenette (5). Kitchenettes have stove, refrigerator, microwave, toaster, coffee maker, utensils, color TV, VCR, cribs/cots available, housekeeping service, washer/dryer. Recently renovated. Leave status rates: $15 1st person, $10 2nd person, $5 each additional person; duty status rates: $21 1st person, $15 2nd person, $9 each additional person. PCS in/out can make reservations 30 days in advance, 2 weeks in advance for TDY, others Space-A.

DV/VIP: 235th BSB, ETS-468-1500, O6+, retirees Space-A.

TML Availability: Good. Best in Feb-Apr, and Sep-Oct.

Internationally famous for its yearly "Bach Week Ansbach", this Franconian capital also offers gourmet specialties, try "Schlotengeli", or "Pressack" with a cool Ansbach beer. Visit Orangerie Park at the "Hofgarten" afterwards.

Locator 4672-541/542   Medical 4672-717   Police 114

Augsburg Base Support Battalion (GE39R7)
Augsburg Guest House
6th ASG, AST Augsburg
Unit 25001
APO AE 09178-5000

TELEPHONE NUMBER INFORMATION: Main installation numbers: C-(USA) 011-49-821-448-1700, (GE) 0821-448-1700, ETS-434-1700, D-314-434-1700.

Location: From Munich-Stuttgart, Autobahn E-8, exit at "Augsburg West" and follow "US Military Facilities Augsburg" signs to Sheridan Kasernes. HE: p-40, F/4-5. NMC: Augsburg, in the city.

Lodging Office: Augsburg Guesthouse, building 184, Sheridan Kaserne, 86157 Augsburg. **C-(USA) 011-49-821-521540,** FAX, 011-49-821-52154105, (GE) 0821-448-1700, FAX-0821-441529, 24 hours daily. Check in 1300, check out 1000 hours. Government civilian employee billeting.

GERMANY
Augsburg Base Support Battalion, continued

TML: Guest House. Building 184, Sheridan Kaserne, all ranks, leave or official duty. VIP Suites, private bath(2); long term suites with private bath, queen size bed, living room, kitchenettes, color TV, VCR, coffee maker, housekeeping service Mon-Sat, cribs/cots ($6), washer/dryer. AAFES vending in building. Older structure, remodeled. Duty can make reservations, others Space-A.

TML: Buildings 180, 181, 182, Sheridan Kaserne, all ranks, leave or official duty. Bedroom, hall bath (17); VIP suites, private bath (3); building 181: Non Smoking Suites, queen beds, private bath, living room (16); building 182: suites, queen bed, private bath, living room (16). All rooms have refrigerator, microwave, color TV, VCR, housekeeping service Mon-Sat, washer/dryer. Older structure. Rates: single $35, $45 double, child $6; suites single $55, double $70, child $6; VIP suite, single $55, double $80, child $10. Older structure, remodeled. Duty can make reservations, others Space-A. **Bus line front of guest house. BX, Cafeteria, Burger King in walking distance.**

TML Availability: Good, Oct-Mar. Difficult, Apr-Sep.

German history is mirrored in the 2,000 year story of Augsburg. Visit imperial Maximilianstrasse, and the romantic alleys of the Lech area.

Locator 448-113   Medical 449-4132   Police 448-114

Babenhausen Kaserne (GE90R7)
Railgunner's Arms, Bldg 4502
APO AE 09089-5000

TELEPHONE NUMBER INFORMATION: Main installation numbers: C-(USA) 011-49-6073-38-655, (GE) 06073-38-655, D-314-348-3655.

Location: Located midway between Darmstadt and Aschaffenburg. Take route B26 east toward Babenhausen. The Kaserne is clearly marked and is on B26. HE: p-40, C/1. NMC Darmstadt, approximately 10 miles southwest.

Lodging Office: Railgunner's Arms, building 4502. **C-(USA) 011-49-6073-38-655**, (GE) 06073-38-655, D-314-348-3655, 0800-1700 M-F. Check in lodging office 0800-1700, check out 1100 hours. After hours SDO, building 4508. Government civilian employee billeting.

TML: Guest House. Building 4502, all ranks, leave or official duty. Bedroom, hall bath (17); suites, private bath (2). Refrigerator, utensils (loan closet kitchen packages), color TV, VCR, housekeeping service, essentials, cribs/cots, washer/dryer, ice vending, ironing board, iron, alarm clock radios. Modern building, renovated. Rates: sponsor $30, additional adult $10, children under 16, $5. PCS in/out have priority, all categories may make reservations.

DV/VIP: Protocol Office, C-011-49-6073-38-621. O1+, WO1. Retirees and lower ranks Space-A.

TML Availability: Good.

Babenhausen traces its history to year 1236, and possibly even earlier. A walled city with castle, it was largely destroyed during the 30 Years War and Plague. The late 19th century crossing of
two railway lines revitalized the town, and today it has a population of more than 15,000.

Locator 38-655   Medical 8376   Police 696233

GERMANY

Bad Aibling Station (GE91R7)
MWR Customer Service Center
APO AE 09098-5000

TELEPHONE NUMBER INFORMATION: Main installation numbers: C-(USA) 011-49-08061-38-5778/5779, (GE) 08061-38-5778/5779, ETS-441-3893.

Location: From Autobahn A-8 (Munich-Salzburg) take Bad Aibling exit and follow signs through Bad Aibling to Munich on secondary road. Station is one mile out of Bad Aibling. HE p-94, A-3. NMC: Munich, 30 miles west.

Lodging Office: WildBor Hof. MWR Customer Service Center, **C-(USA) 011-49-08061-38-5778/5779**, (GE) 08061-38-5778/5779.Check in 1400-2100, check out 1000 hours. Late checkout C-EX-5778/5779. Government civilian employee billeting.

TML: Visitors Quarters. Buildings 359, 361, all ranks, leave or official duty. Bedroom, living room, private bath (24); Family suites, living room, private bath (2); VIP suites (2). Refrigerator, color TV, alarm clock radio, housekeeping service. Community kitchen & washer/dryer located in each building. Older structure. Rates: standard room $42, family suite $54; VIP $60 per night, $12 per additional guest 18 years old and up, children under 18 free. Duty, reservists & national guard on orders can make reservations, others Space-A.

DV/VIP: Chief of Staff, building 302, O6+, GS15+, C-011-49-8061-38-5745. Duty may make reservations, others Space-A.

TML Availability: Very good. Best Dec-Jan, worst Feb-Nov.

Bad Aibling is a picturesque health resort near the Alpine mountains, excellent skiing opportunities are 20 minutes away in Austria. This location is only 50 miles from Salzburg on the crossroad to Italy and only 30 miles from historic Munich.

Medical 441-3781   **Police 441-3822**

Bad Kreuznach Community (GE01R7)
APO AE 09252-5000

TELEPHONE NUMBER INFORMATION: Main installation numbers: C-(USA) 011-49-671-1110, (GE) 0671-1110, ETS-490-1110, D-314-490-1110.

Location: Approximately 50 miles south from Frankfurt am Main, via Mainz to Bad Kreuznach Autobahn A-66 & A-60. Take B-41, at the east outskirts of the city, go south on Bosenheimer St, left on Alzyer St, to Nahe Club on the right, billeting next to club. HE: p-40, A/1. NMC: Bad Kreuznach, in city limits.

Lodging Office: ATTN: Family Housing Office, building 5649, Mannheimerstrasse, **C-(USA) 011-49-671-77122**, (GE) 0671-77122, 0730-1600 hours daily, D-314-490-1700, ETS-490-1700. Check in facility, check out 1100 hours daily. Government civilian employee billeting.

TML: Guest House/BOQ/BEQ/DV/VIP. Building 5649 (GH), 5648 (DV/VIP), all ranks, leave or official duty. Bedroom, shared bath (31); suites, private bath (DV/VIP) (3). Refrigerator, community

GERMANY
Bad Kreuznach Community, continued

kitchen, color TV, VCR, housekeeping service, cribs ($2), cots ($4), washer/dryer. Older structure. Rates: sponsor $22, additional occupant $10. Duty can make reservations, others Space-A. Pets OK for $5 per night.

DV/VIP: Protocol Office, **Rose Barracks**, C-011-49-671-6466, O6+. Retirees and lower ranks Space-A.

TML Availability: Good.

Visit the spa park on the slopes of the Hardt, the Oranienpark, Rose Island and the open air inhaling area with the Radon grading galleries for an interesting trip into German health care. Then take a sip of the local wine.

Locator 490-6274   Medical 490-116   Police 490-114

Bamberg Base Support Battalion (GE34R7)
ATTN: AETV-WG-BA
APO AE 09139-5000

TELEPHONE NUMBER INFORMATION: Main installation numbers: C-(USA) 011-49-951-300-1110, (GE) 0951-300-1110, ETS-469-1110, D-314-460-1110, ask for Bamberg.

Location: On GE 26/505. Warner Barracks, the main installation, is on the east side of the city between Zollner and Pödeldorter Strs. Follow signs. HE: p-40, E/1. NMC: Nürnberg, 30 miles southeast.

Lodging Office: Bamberg Inn. Guest House Office, building 7678, room 4, 1st floor, **C-(USA) 011-49-951-300-1700**, FAX 011-49-951-37957, (GE) 0951-300-1700, M-F: 0800-1730, Sa-Su: 1030-1430. Other hours, Military Police, building 7108, ETS-469-8700. Check in facility 1400, check out 1100 hours daily. Government civilian employee billeting.

TML: Bamberg Inn. Guest Houses, building 7678, annex building 7070, 1st floor, O'Club, Zollnerstrasse. All ranks, PCS, ETS, TDY. Bedrooms, shared baths (40); suite, private bath (VIP-O1+)(3); DV/VIP suite (O3+)(1). Refrigerator, color TV, alarm clock/radios in all rooms, vending rooms (2 microwaves, snack coffee and coke machines), laundry room, housekeeping M-F, cribs, irons, ironing boards available, hall phones. Older structure, renovated. Rates: $32 primary occupant, $5 each additional occupant. PCS, TDY & Space-A may make reservations. No pets.

DV/VIP: Deputy Community Cmdr. O5+. Call 011-49-951-300-1700. Retirees and lower ranks Space-A.

TML Availability: Limited.

CREDIT CARDS ACCEPTED: Visa, American Express and Diners.

Bamberg's streets are a Gothic tapestry, wander them and you'll find St Michaels Church, the Old Town Hall, and a Baroque castle-the Concordia. Don't miss "Little Venice".

Locator 469-7738   Medical 469-8741/97   Police 469-8700

GERMANY

Baumholder Annex (Bieuenfeld) (GE54R7)
Guest House, Bldg 9961
APO AE 09260-4675

TELEPHONE NUMBER INFORMATION: Main installation numbers: C-(USA) 011-49-6782-13-1110, (GE) 06782-13-1110, ETS-493-7-1110, D-314-485-1110, ask for NEU.

Location: On GE-41, about 90 miles SW from Rhein-Main Airport (Frankfurt), about 25 miles NW from Ramstein Air Base, near Baumholder. Follow signs to Neubruecke Hospital. HE: p-39, G/1. NMC: Baumholder, 9 miles east.

TML: Guest House. Building 9961, C-011-49-6782-13-287, ETS-493-7287, all ranks, leave or official duty. Handicapped accessible. Two bedroom, shared bath (30); two bedroom, private bath (2). Refrigerator, community kitchen, limited utensils, color TV, housekeeping service, cribs, washer/dryer. Older structure, remodeled. Rates for PCS/TDY on leave/vacation; sponsor $28, second person $15, additional person $10.

TML Availability: Best, Sep-Apr. Difficult, May-Aug.

CREDIT CARDS ACCEPTED: Visa, MasterCard, American Express, and EuroCard

The Rheinland Pflaz is full of colorful villages that preserve many German traditional customs.

Medical 116   Police 114

Baumholder Base Support Battalion (GE03R7)
Hotel Lagehof Inn
Ivy Street, Bldg 8076
APO AE 09034-5000

TELEPHONE NUMBER INFORMATION: Main installation numbers: C-(USA) 011-49-6783-6-1700, (GE) 06783-6-1700, ETS-485-113 ask for BHR+EX, D-314-485-113 ask for BHR+EX.

Location: From Kaiserslautern, take Autobahn 62 toward Trier, exit north at Freisen and follow signs to Baumholder and Smith Barracks. HE: p-39, F/G1. NMC: Kaiserslautern, 35 miles southeast.

Lodging Office: Hotel Lagerhof, Ivy Street, building 8076, **C-(USA) 011-49-6783-5182** or (GE) 06783-5182, D-314-485-1700., 0730-2000 M-F, C-EX-1700. Check in 1300-2000, check out 1100 hours daily. Government civilian employee billeting.

TML: Lagerhof Transient Billeting. Building 8076, all ranks, leave or official duty. Bedroom, private bath (10); two bedroom, private bath (8); Doll House, four bedroom, private bath (1); Chalet, two bedroom, bath (1). Community kitchen, limited utensils, refrigerator, color TV lounge, housekeeping service, cribs/cots, washer/dryer, color TVs. Older structure. Rates for PCS, TDY and Space-A: 1st person $28, 2nd person $15, 3rd person and each additional $10; DVQ $28, 3rd person $14. Doll House $30, 3rd person $15. Duty can make reservations, others Space-A.

DV/VIP: Commander, C-011-49-6783-6300, O6/GS-12+.

Temporary Military Lodging Around the World - 271

GERMANY
Baumholder Base Support Battalion, continued

TML Availability: Very good.

CREDIT CARDS ACCEPTED: Visa, MasterCard, American Express, Euro and Access.

Visit nearby Idar Oberstein for precious gems and stones, Trier's Roman ruins, the Mosel Valley's, castles and vineyards.

Locator 485-6446   **Medical-485-6647**   **Police-485-7547**

This area will be greatly reduced in the future. Keep posted on the latest developments with Military Living's *R&R Space-A Report*.

Chiemsee AFRC (GE08R7)
Reservations, Unit 24604
APO AE 09098-5000

TELEPHONE NUMBER INFORMATION: Main installation numbers: C-(USA) 011-49-8051-803172, (GE) 08051-803172, FAX-(USA) 011-49-8051-803158.

Location: Located directly off Munich-Salzburg Autobahn A-8 southeast of Munich. Buses use Felden exit; automobiles continue for 800 meters and exit when you see the sign for AFRC Chiemsee Campground. HE: p-94, B/3. NMC: Bad Aibling, 20 miles northwest.

TML: Two hotels; the Chiemsee Lake Hotel and the Park Hotel have accommodations for more than 300 guests.

Reservations: Accepted six months in advance. Write to: AFRC Chiemsee Reservations, Unit 24604, APO AE 09098-5000, or Rasthuas am Chiemsee, Felden 25, 83233, Bernau, C-(USA) 011-49-8051-803172, (GE) 080501-803172, FAX-(GE) 08051-803-158, 0800-1900 hours daily, closed American holidays.

Eligibility: AD/Retired/DoD civilian assigned overseas. See Garmisch listing for details.

Facilities: Cafeteria, laundromat, Lake Hotel restaurant & bar, AAFES, camp store, check cashing, sports equipment rental, boat rental, ESSO station nearby, ice, recreation room, campground.

Rates: (Park Hotel) E1-E5, single $48; E6-O3, $52, O4+ $56;(Lake Hotel) E1-E5 single $52, E6-O3, $56; O4+ $60. Group information rates and prices of larger rooms available on request.

AFRC Chiemsee is situated on the shores of Germany's largest lake - Chiemsee. Enjoy water sports such as canoeing, paddleboats, sailing and windsurfing. At the nearby Chiemgauer Alps you can hike, hang glide and take in the panoramic scenery.

Locator 440-355   **Medical 116**   **Police 114**

GERMANY

Darmstadt Base Support Battalion (GE37R7)
Patriot Inn Guest House
Cambrai Fritsch Kaserne
Bldg 4091
APO AE 09175-5000

TELEPHONE NUMBER INFORMATION: Main installation numbers: C-(USA) 011-49-6151-69-1700, (GE) 06151-69-1700, or 06151-96430, D-314-348-1700.

Location: Accessible from the E-5 and E-67 autobahns. One mile south of downtown Darmstadt (Cambrai Fritsch Kaserne). HE: p-40, B/1. NMC: Darmstadt, 1 mile north.

Lodging Office: Building 4091, Jefferson Village, **C-(USA) 011-49-6151-96430,** (GE) 06151-96430, D-348-1700, 0730-2100 M-F, Sa-Su 1200-2100, on American Holidays 1000-1800. Check in 1300, check out 1100. Call before 1800 for late check-in. Government civilian employee billeting.

TML: Patriot Inn. Building 4090, 4091, Jefferson Village, all ranks, leave or official duty. Single rooms, shared bath (20); suites, private bath (33). Refrigerator, community kitchen, utensils, color TV, housekeeping service, cribs/cots, lending closet, washer/dryer, ice vending. Older structure, remodeled. Rates: shared bath $30, suites $40 per night, $15 additional person, children under 16, $7. Duty and DAVs can make reservations, others Space-A.

TML Availability: Good, Sep. More difficult, Oct-Jun.

CREDIT CARDS ACCEPTED: Visa, MasterCard, American Express and Diners.

Downtown Darmstadt has a great "walkplatz" for shopping, hike to the Odenwald from the railroad station, or tour the Mathildenhöhe, and the Kranichstein hunting palace on the city's outskirts.

Locator 348-6229   Medical 116   Police 348-7777

Garmisch AFRC (GE10R7)
Reservations Office
Unit 24501
APO AE 09053-5000

TELEPHONE NUMBER INFORMATION: Main installation numbers: C-(USA) 011-49-8821-750575, (GE) 08821-750575, ETS-440-2575.

Location: South from Munich take Autobahn A-95 to Garmisch. From Austria take national roads numbered 2 or 187. HE: p-92, F/3. NMC: Munich, 60 miles north.

Description of Area: Garmisch has been Germany's leading winter recreation and sports area for over 50 years. Located 60 miles south of Munich, Garmisch sits at the foot of Germany's highest mountain, the Zugspitze. A $3 million renovation project was underway at press time at both the General Patton and General Von Steuben Hotels to increase room size and amenities, including new balconies, private baths, and entertainment systems. Kitchen, dining room, and lounge renovations will also upgrade guest services. Full range of ski programs, beginner to expert. Golf opportunities,

GERMANY
Garmisch AFRC, continued

tennis, kayaking, white-water rafting, windsurfing, mountaineering, arts and crafts. For more than 45 years AFRC Garmisch has provided the means for quality economy vacations.

TML: Two hotels: **General Patton, General Von Steuben and guest house Haus Flora.** Accommodations for about 540 guests per night. Off site apartments also available.

Reservations: Accepted up to six months in advance. One year for groups of 25 or more. Deposits required within 30 days after booking. Write to: AFRC Garmisch Reservations Office, Unit 24501, APO AE 09053 or Osterfelderstr. 2, 8100 Garmisch-Partenkirchen. **C-(USA) 011-49-8821-750575,** (GE) 08821-750575, ETS-440-2575, FAX-(USA) 49-8821-3942, (GE) 08821-3942. Office open 0800-1900 hours M-F, 0900-1700 Sa, 0900-1700 Su. **Note: Call early morning - 6 hours ahead of Eastern Standard Time.**

Season of Operation: Year round.

Eligibility: In general: US military forces and family members assigned in the USEUCOM area (permanently or temporarily); Reserve in training in Europe; US DoD civilian employees working full time in USEUCOM and family members residing with them (Red Cross, USO, certain US embassy personnel; US citizen consultant and technical representatives; personnel with USAREUR ID Card AE Form 600-700); retired US military personnel residing in or visiting Europe (Army, Navy, Marines and Air Force); PHS/NOAA not authorized; EUCOM Coast Guard; British Forces of the Rhein/Canadian Forces w/family members residing with them stationed in Germany; certain NATO forces/liaison personnel authorized to purchase in commissary/PX; those on official duty to AFRC or NATO/SHAPE School; unaccompanied widows/ers, and dependents retired with appropriate ID. Certain authorized guests, accompanied.

Facilities: APO, Merchants Bank, beauty/barber shop, commissary, chapel, Snack-O-Mat, library, sports shop, gym, Bavarian Shop, class VI (Package Store), Foodland, PX, Stars & Stripes AAFES Bookmark, child care center, hotel restaurants & bars, TV room and much more. (Note: No U.S. medical support in Garmisch). **AFRC Garmisch Room Rates:** Double w/ bath E1-E5-$49 (up to 4 persons in room, E6+ $53 (double occupancy). Single occupancy deduct $3 from double rate, more than two adult occupants, add $9 to double rate. Cribs $3/night, children under 16 free on available bed space - if cot or sofabed is needed, $6 per night. No pets. Recreation prices in May. Special rates may be available during non-peak seasons: April & November.

TML: Loisach Inn. *(Note: Loisach Inn belongs to Garmish Military Community and is not part of the AFRC).* From Munich, Autobahn 95 to Garmisch. Follow "Zugspitz" signs and turn right at last light in Garmisch. Building 718, Breitenau Housing. All ranks, leave or official duty. Bedrooms, private bath, twin beds (15). Refrigerator, microwave, color satellite TV, housekeeping service, cribs/cots ($6), washer/dryer. Rates: single $43; double $50-$58; $6 each additional person. Duty can make reservations, others Space-A. Shuttle bus in front of guest house runs to PX, AFRC Hausberg Ski Lodge. Tel: C-011-49-8821-750832.

TML Availability: Good except Jun-Aug and Christmas/New Year periods. Loisach Inn difficult Dec-Sept. Good Oct-Nov.

GERMANY

Giessen Base Support Battalion (GE23R7)
Guesthouse
414th BSB - North - Unit 20911
APO AE 09169-5000

TELEPHONE NUMBER INFORMATION: Main installation numbers: C-(USA) 011-49-641-402-1110, (GE) 0641-402-1110, ETS-343-1110, D-314-343-1110.

Location: Autobahn E-5 to Gambach Kreuz, take 485 to Giessen. Turn off Ursulun, follow signs to HHQ Giessen. HE: p-36, E/5. NMC: Giessen, in the city.

Lodging Office: Guest House, building 63, **C-(USA) 011-49-641-402.1700** (GE) 0641-402.1700, ETS-343-1700, 0800-2000 Mon-Fri, 0900-1700 weekends and holidays. Check in facility 1300, check out 1000 hours daily.

TML: Guest House. Building 63, Giessen General Depot, all ranks, leave or official duty. Bedroom suite, private bath (8); bedroom, private bath (6); bedroom, shared bath (8). In room cooking facilities, color TV, housekeeping service, cribs/cots, washer/dryer. Older structure, renovated. Rates: shared bath, 1 person $18, shared bath 2 person $30; suite with private bath, 1 person $31, 2 person $48. Pets $25 with non returnable deposit plus $2 per day. Duty can make reservations, others Space-A.

DV/VIP: Cmdr. ETS-343-8434. Determined by Cmdr.

TML Availability: Good.

CREDIT CARDS ACCEPTED: American Express.

Locator 343-8307   Medical 346-7701   Police 346-8601

Grafenwöhr Community (GE11R7)
Lodging Office
Bldg 213, Argonne Avenue
APO AE 09114-5000

TELEPHONE NUMBER INFORMATION: Main installation numbers: C-(USA) 011-49-9641-113, (GE) 09641-83-113, ETS-475-1110, D-314-475-1110.

Location: From Autobahn E-6 exit at Pegnitz/Grafenwöhr, follow signs to training area. HE: p-40, G/1. NMC: Nürnberg, 56 miles southwest.

Lodging Office: Building 213, Argonne Avenue, opposite O'Club, **C-(USA) 011-49-9641-83-6182/1700,** (GE) 09641-83-6182/1700, 0700-2000 M-F, weekdays 0700-1400. German holidays 0700-1400. After Duty hours see SDO 7th ATC Bldg. 621, C-011-49-9641-83-8302 for confirmed reservations or open rooms. Check out time 1100. Civilian employee billeting.

TML: VOQ. Buildings 209, 213, 214, 215, 228, officers and civilians, all ranks, leave or official duty. Shared bedroom, private bath (12); separate bedroom, private bath (10). Kitchen (9), refrigerator, color TV, housekeeping service, cribs, rollaways, sofa sleepers, washer/dryer. Older structure, renovated. Rates: $38 private bath and living room, additional person $6; separate bedroom, private bath $34, additional person $4. Reservations accepted no sooner than 3 days prior to arrival.

GERMANY
Grafenwöhr Community, continued

TML: VEQ. Buildings 211,225,226, enlisted and civilians, all ranks, leave or official duty. Single, double and family rooms with private or shared bath (hall bath). Community kitchen (bldg 211), color TV, housekeeping service, cribs, rollaway beds, washer/dryer. Rates: private bath/living room $34, additional person $4; shared bath $24, additional person $4. Reservations accepted no sooner than 3 days prior to arrival.

DV/VIP: Protocol Office, 7th Army Training Command, O6+, ETS-475-7145/6221, 3 DVQ suites. Rates $53, additional person $9. Retirees and lower ranks Space-A.

TML Availability: Best, Sept-Mar.

Interested in nutcrackers, stained glass crystal, and porcelain? Call Army Community Service for an exhaustive list of local castles, churches, clothing, restaurants and recreation.

Locator 475-1700　　　　Medical-116　　　　Police 475-8319

Hanau Community (GE13R7)
414th BSB CMR470
New Argonner Kaserne, Bldg 203
APO AE 09165-5000

TELEPHONE NUMBER INFORMATION: Main installation numbers: C-(USA) 011-49-6181-88-1700, (GE) 06181-88-1700, ETS-322-1700, D-314-322-1700.

Location: From Autobahn 66 to Highway 8 or 40 to Hanau, New Argonner and Pioneer Housing Area south of Highway 8. Clearly marked. HE: p-36, E/6. NMC: Frankfurt, 15 miles west.

Lodging Office: Building 203, New Argonner Kaserne, APO AE 09165, **C-(USA) 011-49-6181-88-1700 (ask for billeting)**, FAX 011-49-6181-955230(GE) 06181-88-1730 (ask for billeting), ETS-322-8947, 0730-2130 Mon-Fri; 0730-1600 Sa-SU. Check in billeting 1330, check out 0900 hours daily. Government civilian employee billeting.

TML: Guest House. Building 318, Pioneer Housing, all ranks, leave or official duty. Two bedroom, private bath (6); three bedroom, private bath (8); four bedroom, private bath (7). Cribs/cots, housekeeping service, refrigerator, microwave, color TV, VCR washer/dryer. Older structure. Rates: sponsor $31, second person $17, each additional $12. Duty can make reservations, others Space-A. Pets OK with $25 non-refundable fumigation fee + $2 per pet per night.

TML: Guest House. **New Argonner**, building 203, all ranks, leave or official duty. Bedroom, 2 beds, private bath (30). Cribs/cots, refrigerator, community microwaves, color TV, VCR, housekeeping service, washer/dryer. Older structure, renovated. Rates: same as Guest House above. Maximum 2 per room. Duty can make reservations, others Space-A. Pets OK with $25 non-refundable cleaning fee + $2 per night.

TML: VOQ. Building 204, O5+ and civilian equivalents. One bedroom suites, 2 beds, living room, private bath (2). Refrigerator, kitchenette with microwave, cribs/cots, color TV, VCR, housekeeping service, washer/dryer. Older structure, renovated '91. Rates: same as Guest House. Max 2 per room. Duty can make reservations, others Space-A.

GERMANY
Hanau Community, continued

TML: Copper Top Inn. Building 1617, Gelnhausen (30K from Hanau). Rooms with 2 beds, private bath, refrigerator, TV, VCR, microwave, laundry facilities (15). Reservations are made through Hanau Billeting.

DV/VIP: PAO, building 1202, C-011-49-6181-88-9001, O6+, retirees and lower ranks Space-A.

TML Availability: Difficult.

CREDIT CARDS ACCEPTED: Visa, MasterCard, American Express and Diners.

Remember Hansel and Gretel, Snow White and Little Red Riding Hood? Visit the monument to native sons, the Grimm Brothers on the Marktplatz in the center of town. Many other attractions are located in Hanau.

Locator 113   Medical 116   Police 110

Heidelberg Community (GE33R7)
US Army Guesthouse, Heidelberg
411th BSB-Hospitality Management Group
APO AE 09102-5000

TELEPHONE NUMBER INFORMATION: Main installation numbers: C-(USA) 011-49-6221-57-1700, (GE) 06221-57-1700, D-314-370-1700.

Location: South from Frankfurt Airport direction Karlsruhe/Basel, approximately 1 hour drive. Take Autobahn 5 to Schwetzingen (Patrick Henry Village) exit, At stop light turn left, follow road for 1/4 mile, turn right at 1st stoplight. At entrance of housing area, follow fork in road to the left. Continue straight until you reach building 4527 (hotel) on left side. HE: p-40, B/2. NMC: Heidelberg, in the city.

Lodging Office: Patrick Henry Village, building 4527, North Lexington Ave., 24 hours daily. Reservations 0730-1630 M-F. **C-(USA) 011-49-6221-795100,** FAX 011-49-6221-795600, (GE) 06221-795100, D-341-370-6941. Check in facility, check out 1100 hours daily. Government civilian employee billeting. **Note: This facility received the USAREUR Lodging Operation of the Year Award for medium-size billets for 1994.**

TML: Guest house. Building 4527, all ranks, leave or official duty. Bedroom, shared bath (30); bedroom, private bath (155), suites (32). Refrigerator, community kitchen, color TV/VCR, housekeeping service, cribs/cots, washer/dryer, international direct dial phone, handicapped accessible facilities, fitness room/sauna, non-smoking rooms available. Older structure, renovated. Rates: varies according to status and type of room, call for information. PCS reservations, 60 days ahead, TDY 21 days ahead, others Space-A. Firm reservation two weeks ahead for Weekend Getaway special w/credit card. $/DM conversion available for in-house guests. Pets allowed w/one day single room charge and $4 per day service charge. Cots and cribs available for $8 each, per night.

DV/VIP: SGS, HQ USAREUR, DSN: 314-370-8707/6502, O6/GS-15+. Suites, private bath (20). Retirees and lower ranks Space-A.

TML Availability: Good over Christmas holiday. Difficult all other times.

GERMANY
Heidelberg Community, continued

CREDIT CARDS ACCEPTED: Visa, MasterCard, American Express and Diners.

Visit famous University of Heidelberg, and its Students' Inns - Roten Ochsen (Red Ox) and Zum Sepp'l are adjacent on the Hauptstrasse. The Castle above the city, and bridge across the Neckar River also should not be missed.

Locator 370-7571   Medical 371-2891   Police 370-6400

Kaiserslautern Community (GE30R7)
86 SVS/SVMLH
Unit 3250 Box 500
APO AE 09094-0500

TELEPHONE NUMBER INFORMATION: Main installation numbers: C-(USA) 011-49-631-536-1110, (GE) 0631-536-1110, DSN-489-1110.

Location: Off the E-6 Mannheim-Saarbrucken Autobahn. Take Kaiserslautern exit for Vogelweh Housing Area. Follow signs to housing area or Kapun Barracks (AS). HE: p-40, A/2. NMC: Kaiserslautern, 3 miles northeast.

Lodging Office: Building 1002, **C-(USA) 011-49-6371-47-7345/7864/2445/2614**, FAX 011-49-6371-42589, (GE) 06371-47-7345/7864/2445/2614, DSN-480-7345/7864/2445/2614 (Vogelweh Office), 24 hours daily. Check out 1100 hours daily. Government civilian employee lodging. **Note:** see Ramstein & Landstuhl listing for more lodging. Building 305 on Ramstein AB manages all reservations for the Kaiserslautern Community which includes Ramstein AB, Sembach AB, Vogelweh and Landstuhl lodging facilities.

TML: Guest House, building 1002, 1003 and 1004, all ranks, leave or official duty. Suites (DV/VIP) (16). Bedrooms, shared bath (172); Family units, bedrooms, private bath (34). Washer/dryer, color TV, radio. Older structure. Rates: $8-$14 per person, Family units $32. Duty can make reservations, others Space-A.

DV/VIP: PAO. Ramstein AB, C-011-49-6371-47-6854, O6+, retirees Space-A.

TML Availability: Difficult. Best Dec-Jan.

The city hall (Rathaus), is the highest in Germany. There is an elegant restaurant in the penthouse. Visit the Pfalztheater for opera, operetta, plays and ballet. Harry's gift shop, known around the world by military families, is at 5-11 Manheimer Strasse (tel: 011-49-631-67081).

Locator 83-92   Medical 116   Police 114

GERMANY

Landstuhl Army Medical Center (GE40R7)
86 SVS/SVMLL
Unit 3250, Box 500
APO AE 09094-5000

TELEPHONE NUMBER INFORMATION: Main installation numbers: C-(USA) 011-49-6371-86-1110, (GE) 06371-86-1110, ETS-486-1110, D-314-486-1110.

Location: Take the Landstuhl exit from the A-6 Mannheim-Saarbrücken Autobahn. Follow signs for "2nd General Hospital". HE: p-40, A/2. NMC: Kaiserslautern, 10 miles northeast.

Lodging Office: 86 SVS/SVML, Unit 3250, Box 500, APO AE 09094-5000, **C-(USA) 011-49-6371-486-8342**, (GE) 06371-86-8342, D-314-486-8342, FAX 011-49-6371-486-7267, (GE) FAX 06371-42589, DSN FAX 314-486-7267. Ramstein AB, 24 hours daily. Check in facility 1400, check out 1200 hours daily. Government civilian employee billeting. Note: Building 305 on Ramstein AB manages all reservations for the Kaiserlautern Community which includes Ramstein AB, Sembach AB, Vogelweh and **Landstuhl lodging** facilities.

TML: VOQ/VAQ. Building 3752, all ranks, leave or official duty. Bedroom, shared bath (230). Refrigerator, color TV, housekeeping service, washer/dryer, microwave, VCR, video rental, irons, ceiling fan. Older structure, remodeled. Rates: $12 per person, maximum $24 per room. Duty can make reservations, others Space-A. **Note:** Check Ramstein, Kaiserslautern listings for more billeting.

DV/VIP: Community Cmdr, C-011-49-6371-486-7183, O6+.

TML Availability: Good, Nov-Feb. Difficult, summer months.

CREDIT CARDS ACCEPTED: Visa, MasterCard and American Express.

Visit the Marktplatz in Kaiserslautern for a traditional German farmer's market. Also, ask at USO Kaiserslautern for directions to local fests and sights -they have a wealth of information to share!

Locator 486-7183   Medical 486-8414   Police 486-8507

Mannheim Base Support Battalion (GE43R7)
HHD 293 BSB
Unit 29901, Box 3
APO AE 09086-5000

TELEPHONE NUMBER INFORMATION: Main installation numbers: C-(USA) 011-49-621-730-1110, (GE) 0621-730-1110, ETS-380-1110, D-314-380-1110.

Location: Accessible from the E12/A6 Autobahns. Take the Viernheim exit, follow B38 to Benjamin Franklin Village Housing Area on Fürther Strasse. HE: p-40, B/2. NMC: Mannheim, 8 miles southwest.

Lodging Office: Building 312, Benjamin Franklin Village Housing Area (BFHA), Fürtherstrasse, 0600-2400 daily. C-(USA) **011-49-621-730-8118/6547/1700**, (GE) 0621-730-8118/1700, ETS-

GERMANY
Mannheim Base Support Battalion, continued

380-8118/6547/1700, FAX-(GE) 0621-738607. Mon-Fri 0600-2400, Sat-Sun and holidays, 0800-2400. Check in 1200, check out 1000.

TML: Guest house. **Franklin House**, building 312, Benjamin Franklin Village Housing Area, Fuertherstrasse, all ranks, leave or official duty, **C-(USA) 011-49-621-730-1700/8118/6547**, (GE) 0621-730-1700/8118/6547. Two bedroom, private bath (39); suites, private bath (DV/VIP) (3). Housekeeping service, cribs/cots, ice vending, kitchenette, CATV, washer/dryer, VIP suites have honor bars. Older structure, renovated. No pets. Rates: $40 single room; $40 double room, $20 each additional person; VIP suites $50, $20 each additional person. Duty can make reservations, others Space-A. *Winner of the USAREUR Lodging of the Year Award for small lodging facilities and first runner-up in the Army worldwide lodging competition.*

DV/VIP: C-011-49-621-730-8118/6547/1700.

TML Availability: Good, Dec-Jun. Difficult, May-Sep,

CREDIT CARDS ACCEPTED: Visa, MasterCard, American Express and Diners.

Visit the National Theater, Observatory and Mannheim Castle. A good area for a Volksmarch.

Locator 730-1110   Medical 730-116   Police 730-114

Pirmasens Base Support Battalion (GE42R7)
415th Base Support Battalion
Grenadier Guest house, Bldg 4535
APO AE 09138-5000

TELEPHONE NUMBER INFORMATION: Main installation numbers: C-(USA) 011-49-6331-86-1110, (GE) 06331-86-1110, ETS-495-1110, D-314-495-1110 Ask for PMS.

Location: On the triangle of GE-10 from Zweibrücken and GE-270 from Kaiserslautern. HE: p-39, G/2. NMC: Pirmasens, 1 mile southeast.

Lodging Office: Building 4535, Bundestrasse 10, **C-(USA) 011-49-6331-5440**, (GE) 06331-87050, ETS-495-1700, 0730-1600 M-F. Other hours MP Station, building 4620, C-EX-7311, ETS-495-7311. Check in after 1300, check out 1000 hours daily. Government civilian employee billeting.

TML: Grenadier Guest House. Grenadier Guest house, building 4535, all ranks, leave or official duty. Handicapped accessible. Bedroom, private bath (29). Refrigerator, microwave, iron, ironing board, color TV, VCR, coffee maker, housekeeping service, cribs/cots, washer/dryer. Rates: sponsor $19, adult $8, child $8, infant $2. Maximum 3 per room. Duty can make reservations, others Space-A.

TML Availability: Good, all year round.

CREDIT CARDS ACCEPTED: Visa, MasterCard and American Express.

Pirmasens is known for its international trade fair and is also acknowledged as a tourist recreational center surrounded by mountains.

Locator 495-7117   Medical 116   Police 114

GERMANY

Ramstein Air Base (GE24R7)
86th SVS/SVH
Bldg 305, Washington Avenue
APO AE 09094-5000

TELEPHONE NUMBER INFORMATION: Main installation numbers: C-(USA) 011-49-6371-47-1110, (GE) 06371-47-1110, ETS-480-1110, D-314-480-1110.

Location: Two exits from Mannheim-Saarbrücken E-6 Autobahn, exit Landstuhl, turn left, follow signs to Ramstein. Also, west on B-40 to Landstuhl Str, turn right follow signs to Flugplatz Ramstein. HE: p-39, G/2. NMC: Kaiserslautern, 12 miles east.

Lodging Office: Kaiserslautern Community Lodging. 86th SVS/SVH, building 305, Washington Avenue. **C-(USA) 011-49-6371-47-7345/7864,** (GE) 06371-42589, 0730-1700 M-Th, 0730-1630 F. Check in facility, check out 1100 hours daily. Government civilian employee billeting. **Note:** see Kaiserslautern listing for more lodging.

TML: TLF. Buildings 303,908,1004, all ranks, leave or official duty. Bedroom, private bath (2); two bedroom, private bath (77). Kitchen (some), limited utensils, color TV in room & lounge, housekeeping service, washer/dryer, ice vending. Modern structure. Rates: $32.50 per unit. Maximum 6 per unit. Duty can make reservations, others Space-A.

TML: VAQ. Buildings 1003, 2408, 2409, 3752, 3756, enlisted all ranks, leave or official duty. Bedroom, shared bath (674); separate bedroom suites, private bath (2). Refrigerator, limited utensils, color TV in room & lounge, housekeeping service, cribs/cots, washer/dryer, ice vending. Modern structure. Rates: $8 per person. Duty can make reservations, others Space-A.

TML: VOQ. Buildings 304-306,1002,3751,3754. Officers all ranks. Bedroom, shared bath, private bath (533); separate bedrooms, private bath (27). Refrigerator, limited utensils, color TV in room & lounge, housekeeping service, washer/dryer, ice vending. Modern structure. Rates: $12 per person. Duty can make reservations, others Space-A.

TML: DV/VIP. Building 1018, officers O6+, leave or official duty. See numbers under Protocol below. Separate bedroom suites, private bath (11). Refrigerator, limited utensils, color TV, washer/dryer, ice vending. Modern structure, renovated. Rates: $22 per person. Duty can make reservations, others Space-A.

DV/VIP: Protocol, building 201. C-011-49-6371-47-4851. D-314-480-7558, O6+. Retirees Space-A.

TML Availability: Very good all year. Best, winter months.

Small villages surround Ramstein, it's fun to just drive through them. People here are friendly and helpful, and many speak English. Kaiserslautern, and Landstuhl are nearby.

Locator 480-6120/6989   Medical 486-82603   Police 480-2050

GERMANY

Rhein-Main Air Base (GE16R7)
Bldg 600
APO AE 09057-5000

TELEPHONE NUMBER INFORMATION: Main installation numbers: C-USA: 011-49-69-699-1110, (GE) 069-699-1110, ETS-330-1110, D-314-330-1110.

Location: Adjacent to Frankfurt International Airport off E-5 Autobahn to Darmstadt. HE: p-40, B/1. NMC: Frankfurt, 10 miles north.

Lodging Office: building 600, C-(USA) **011-49-69-699-6843**, (GE) 069-699-6843, D-314-330-6843, (for reservations) daily. Fax C-011-49-69-699-7440, D-314-330-7440. Check in at front desk, check out 1000 hours daily. Government civilian employee billeting on official duty.

TML: Rhein-Main Hotel, VQ, building 600, all ranks, leave or official duty. Bedroom with one double bed and shared bath (126), bedroom with one double bed equipped for handicapped with shared bath (2), bedroom with double bed, sitting room and private bath (15), DV bedroom with queen bed, sitting room and private bath (5). Refrigerator, microwave, color TV, housekeeping service, cribs, washer/dryer, ice vending, picnic area and playground. Rates: $10 per night per person, $15 per night per two persons; $34 per night per person, $51 per night per two persons. Duty can make reservations, others Space-A.

TML: TLF, building 634, all ranks, leave or official duty. Living/dining room, kitchen, bath, and two bedrooms (6), living/dining room, kitchen, bath, and three bedrooms (6). Refrigerator, microwave, color TV, housekeeping service, cribs, washer/dryer, ice vending, picnic area and playground. Rates: $33-$35 per night per family. Duty can make reservations, others Space-A.

TML Availability: Good, Dec-Jan. Difficult, other times.

CREDIT CARDS ACCEPTED: Visa, MasterCard, American Express.

Don't miss Frankfurt's famous Fairgrounds (Messa), for exhibits of all types, and the Frankfurt Zoo. The southern part of the city is a forest with deer, hiking and bicycling paths. Watch for special seasonal "fests".

Locator 7691/7348   Medical 7307   Police 114/7177

Schweinfurt Base Support Battalion (GE48R7)
Bradley Inn Guest house
280th Support Battalion
APO AE 09033-5000

TELEPHONE NUMBER INFORMATION: Main installation numbers: C-(USA) 011-49-9721-96-1700, (GE) 09721-96-1700, ETS-354-1700, D-314-350-1110, ask for Schweinfurt.

Location: 9 miles east of Kassel-Würzburg, E-70 autobahn. On GE-303, 2 miles past GE-B19. Follow US Forces signs. HE: p-40, D/1. NMC: Schweinfurt, in the city.

Lodging Office: Building 89, 0800-2300 hours daily, C-(USA) **011-49-9721-7940**, (GE) 09721-7940, ETS-354-1700. After hours contact SDO, building 1, Conn Barracks, C-09721-96-6288, D-

GERMANY
Schweinfurt Base Support Battalion, continued

314-354-6288. Check in facility between 1300-1800 hours M-F, check out 1000 hours daily. Government civilian employee billeting.

TML: Guest House. **Bradley Inn**, building 89, Conn Barracks. All ranks, leave or official duty. DV/VIP suites, private bath (2); large family room units, private bath (20); small family room units, private bath (14); single rooms, private bath (6); bedroom, double bed, private bath (2); bedroom, 2 single beds, private bath (8). Community kitchens, some utensils, housekeeping service, cribs/cots, washer/dryer, vending machine. Older structure, renovated. Rates: suites $55, 1 family member, $70, 2nd $85, 3rd $100; Lge. family room $35; 1 family member $50; 2nd $62, 3rd $72; Sm. family room $32, 1 family member $45, 2nd $56, 3rd $62; single room $29; bedroom, double and 2 single beds, $29, family member $39. Duty may make reservations, others Space-A. No pets. Schweinfurt is only 1 1/2 hours from Frankfurt International Airport. Travel to & from airport may be coordinated upon request.
DV/VIP: Chief, Community Operations, building 206, C-011-49-9721-803834, ETS-354-6715, O3/GS-13/14+. Retirees and lower ranks Space-A. VIP for **Bradley Inn**: C-011-49-9721-803834.

TML Availability: Good, all year.

CREDIT CARDS ACCEPTED: Visa, MasterCard and American Express.

Wednesday and Saturday morning, and Tuesday and Friday afternoon, the Schweinfurt Marktplatz hums with activity. Don't miss a colorful sight. Then stroll down to the Stadtpark and the Tiergehege near the Main River.

Locator 354-6748   Medical 09721-82397   Police 09721-802160

Sembach Air Base (GE18R7)
86 SVS/SVMLB
Unit 3250 Box 500
APO AE 09094-5000

TELEPHONE NUMBER INFORMATION: Main installation numbers: C-(USA) 011-49-6302-67-1110, (GE) 06302-67-1110, ETS-496-1110, D-314-496-1110.

Location: From the E-12 Autobahn exit A-6 marked Enkenbach-Alsenborn and follow B-48 in the direction of Bad Kruznach. Immediately past town of Munchweiller right to Sembach AB. Also, accessible from B-40 North. HE: p-40, A/2. NMC: Kaiserslautern 9 miles west.

Lodging Office: 86 SVS/SVMLB, building 216, Radar Ave, (known as Dorm Row), **C-(USA) 011-49-6302-67-7588/7149**, (GE) 06302-67-7588/7149, 24 hours daily. Check in billeting 1400 hours, check out 1200 hours daily. Government civilian employee billeting. Building 305 on Ramstein AB manages all reservations for the Kaiserslautern Community which includes Ramstein AB, **Sembach AB**, Vogelweh and Landstuhl lodging facilities.

TML: VOQ/DV/VIP. Building 110, 1st, 2nd and 3rd floors, C-011-49-6302-67-6194. Officers all ranks, leave or official duty. Handicapped accessible. Bedroom, shared bath (73); separate bedroom suites, (DV/VIP) (9). Refrigerator, community kitchen, limited utensils, color TV, housekeeping service, washer/dryer, ice vending. Older structure. Rates: rooms $8 per person, suites $14 per person. Duty can make reservations, others Space-A.

GERMANY
Sembach Air Base, continued

TML: VAQ. Buildings 210, 216, enlisted all ranks, leave or official duty. Building 210: new structure, bedroom, 2 beds, shared bath (221); separate bedroom suites, private bath (Chiefs) (4). Building 216: bedroom, 2 beds, hall bath (55). Housekeeping service, color TV, washer/dryer. Older structures, renovated. Rates: rooms $8 per person, suites $14. Duty can make reservations, others Space-A.

TML: TLF. All ranks, PCS families. Two bedroom, private bath (6); three bedroom, private bath (3); 4 bedroom, private bath (3). Cribs, housekeeping service, color TV, laundry.

DV/VIP: 601 SW/CCE, building 112, C-011-49-6302-67-7960, O6+, retirees Space-A.

TML Availability: Difficult. Best, Dec-Jan.

Sembach has been greatly reduced in size. The runway is closed and there is limited base support but Ramstein AB is within easy reach. Keep updated with Military Living's *R&R Space-A Report.*

Locator 496-7535   **Medical 116**   **Police 496-7171**

Spangdahlem Air Base (GE19R7)
52nd Services Squadron
Unit 3670, Box 170
APO AE 09126-5000

TELEPHONE NUMBER INFORMATION: Main installation numbers: C-(USA) 011-49-6565-61-1110, (GE) 06565-61-1110, ETS-452-1110, D-314-452-1110.

Location: From the Koblenz-Trier Autobahn E-1 exit at Wittlich, to B-50 west toward Bitburg. The AB is near Binsfeld 24 km west of Wittlich. Signs mark the AB entrance. HE: p-39, F/1. NMC: Trier, 21 miles southeast.

Lodging Office: Eifel Arms Inn, Building 38, C-(USA) **011-49-6565-61-6504**, (GE) 06565-61-6504, 24 hours daily. Check in facility 1800, check out 1100 hours daily. No government civilian employee billeting.

TML: VOQ/VAQ. Building 38, all ranks, leave or official duty. VOQ: bedrooms, private bath (60); suites, private bath (6); DV/VIP (12). Kitchenette, microwave, color TV, housekeeping service, washer/dryer, ice vending. Older structure, renovated. Rates: suites $14, maximum $28 for 2 persons. VOQ/VAQ: regular rooms $8, maximum $16 for two persons. Duty/official travel can make reservations, others Space-A.

TML: TLF. Facility is located 12 miles from the base. Check in at building 38, on main base. All ranks, PCS families, leave or official duty. Two bedroom, private bath (6); three bedroom, private bath (21); four bedroom, private bath (12). Kitchen, refrigerator, microwave, color/cable TV, housekeeping service. Modern structure. Rates $27 per unit. Duty can make reservations.

DV/VIP: Building 38 (6 suites). During duty hours reservations controlled by base protocol, C-011-49-6565-61-6434. After duty hours check with front desk at C-011-49-6565-61-6504.

TML Availability: Limited all year. Best, Nov-Dec.

GERMANY
Spangdahlem Air Base, continued

Trier lies where the Saar and Mosel rivers meet, and is Germany's oldest city, dating from the 2nd century. Don't miss lunch in the shadow of the Porta Nigra, and a stroll past renaissance half-timbered houses in the Hauptmarkt.

Locator 452-7227　　　　Medical 116　　　　Police 114

Stuttgart Community (GE20R7)
Hilltop Hotel, Bldg 169
APO AE 09154-5000

TELEPHONE NUMBER INFORMATION: Main installation numbers: C-(USA) 011-49-711-819-1110, (GE) 0711-819-1110, DSN-314-420-1110, D-420-1110.

Location: Can be reached from both E-11 and E-70 Autobahns. Look for signs to Robinson Barracks. HE: P-40, C/4. NMC: Stuttgart, within city limits.

Lodging Office: Hilltop Hotel, building 169, **C-(USA) 011-49-711-98140**, (GE) 0711-98140, DSN-314-420-1700, 24 hours daily. Check in facility, check out 1100 hours daily. Government civilian employee billeting.

TML: Hilltop Hotel. VOQ, building 169/at Robinson Barracks, all ranks, leave or official duty. Check in 1400 hours daily. Bedroom, private bath (50); separate bedroom suites, private bath (DV/VIP) (4). Refrigerator, microwave, color TV in room & lounge, housekeeping service, cribs/cots, laundry, sauna, fitness room. Older structure, renovated. Rates: $35, each additional person $4. All Ranks Community Club, D-420-6129. Maximum 2 adults/1 child per room. Duty can make reservations, others Space-A.

DV/VIP: Cmdr, DSN-314-420-7038, O6/GS-15+. Retirees Space-A.

TML Availability: Limited, all year.

Starting the end of April the Stuttgarter Frülingsfest, with carnival attractions and beer tents is a must for visitors. Also don't miss the Cannstatter Volksfest, at Bad Cannstatt at the end of September.

Locator 819-6036　　　　Medical 116　　　　Police 420-7317

Vilseck Base Support Battalion (GE85R7)
AST Vilseck
CMR 411, Box 917
APO AE 09112-5000

TELEPHONE NUMBER INFORMATION: Main installation numbers: C-(USA) 011-49-9662-83-4100, (GE) 09662-83-4100, ETS: 476-2555.

Location: From Nürnberg take Hwy 14 east to Hahnbach, turn north to Vilseck. Also E9 Autobahn north of Nürnburg to E85 south, Vilseck is east 3-5 miles. HE: p-40, G/1,2. NMC: Nürnberg, 38 miles southwest.

GERMANY
Vilseck Base Support Battalion, continued

Lodging Office: 100th ASG. Rose Barracks, building 275, C-(USA) **011-49-9662-83-2555/1700**, FAX 011-49-9662-83-4140, (GE) 09662-83-2555/1700, ETS-476-2555, 0700-2300. Check in at facility, check out 1100 hours. Government civilian employee lodging.

TML: TLQ. Kristall Inn. Buildings: 233, 241, 252, 253, 254, 255, 256. All ranks, leave or official duty. Rooms, private bath. color TV, refrigerator, housekeeping service, cribs/cots, washer/dryer. Modern structure, renovated. Rates: sponsor $34, additional occupant $4. Pets allowed (PCS), fee $3 per day (spray fee $20). All categories may make reservations.

DV/VIP: C-011-49-9662-414-100, O6+, GS12+.

TML Availability: Good. Best in winter, difficult Aug/Sep.

CREDIT CARDS ACCEPTED: Visa, MasterCard, American Express and Diners.

Vilseck is near Grafenwöehr. Army Community Service (VM 2650/2733) has a wonderful list of "points of interest" in the area put together by the Oberpfalz area women's clubs.

Locator 113   Medical 116   Police 287

Wiesbaden Base Support Battalion (GE27R7)
American Arms Hotel
221st Base Support Battalion (Wiesbaden)
APO AE 09096-5000

TELEPHONE NUMBER INFORMATION: Main installation numbers: C-(USA) 011-49-611-705-1110, (GE) 0611-705-1110, D-314-337/338-1110.

Location: Accessible from Autobahns E-3, E-5, connect to E-66. Take exit WI-Erbenheim (This will be B455). Stay straight on B455 (Do not take 2nd Erbenheim exit). Coming into Wiesbaden, you will come to an underpass. Stay in right lane, following signs to STADMITTE Kurhaus/Casino. When you come out of the underpass you will be on Frankfurter Strasse. Go through one traffic light. Hotel will be on the left. HE: p-40, A/1. NMC: Wiesbaden, in the city.

Lodging Office: American Arms Hotel, 17 Frankfurterstrasse, 24 hours daily, C- (USA) **011-49-611-343664**, FAX (USA) 011-49-611-304522, (GE) 0611-343664, D-314-338-7493. Check in at front desk, check out 1100 hours daily. Government civilian employee billeting.

TML: American Arms Hotel, 17 Frankfurterstrasse, all ranks, leave or official duty. Suites, private bath, living room bedroom, mini-bar refrigerator, coffee pot, TV and complementary bottle of wine (54); Bed-room, standard room, shared bath (160+). Refrigerator, phone, TV. Housekeeping service (all rooms), cribs/cots, washer/dryer, ice vending. Modern structure, renovated. Restaurant, bar, weinstube. Rates: Standard room, $49.50 single, $35(each person) double, each additional person (over age 11) $20, (age 5-11) $12, (under age 5) $8; Standard suite, $59.50, each additional person (over age 11) $25, (age 5-11) $15, (under age 5) $10; DV/VIP Suite, $69.50, each additional person (over age 11) $25, (age 5-11) $15, (under age 5) $10. Duty can make reservations, others Space-A.

TML: On Wiesbaden Air Base there are 92 Transient Officer billets, and 172 Enlisted billets, call ETS-339-6525 for information and accommodations.

GERMANY
Wiesbaden Base Support Battalion, continued

DV/VIP: Contact the Conference Sales Office of the American Arms Hotel at C- (USA) 011-49-611-343350, (GE) 0611-343350 D 314-338-7496, O5,+, GS14+. All other grades and retirees are Space-A.

TML Availability: Good.

The American Arms Hotel is conveniently located in historic downtown Wiesbaden. Hainerberg Shopping Center is 3 blocks away from lodging and is "shop till you drop" country! In the center of Wiesbaden, you are also within walking distance of wonderful architectural and cultural treasures (Wiesbaden had little damage during WWII).

Locator WBNC-705-5055   Medical 705-5237   Police 705-114

Wildflecken Community (GE86R7)
Bldg 3, Welcome Center
APO AE 09026-5000

TELEPHONE NUMBER INFORMATION: Main installation numbers: C-(USA) 011-49-9745-1239, (GE) 09745-1239, D-314-326-1700.

Location: Take the Autobahn toward Kassel and Fulda (A-66). Exit at Fulda and follow signs to Coburg. After coming over the Schwedenschanze, follow signs to Wildflecken. Then follow signs to the US Army Post. HE: p-36, F-G/6. NMC: Fulda, 25 miles north.

Lodging Office: Building 3, Welcome Center, C-(USA) **011-49-9745-1239**, (GE) 09745-1239, D-314-326-1700, 0730-1600 M-F, closed US and German holidays. Extra keys available with Staff Duty NCO, building 1. Check in billeting, check out 1100 hours. Government civilian employee billeting.

TML: Guest house. Building 2, all ranks. Bedroom, private and hall bath (9); separate bedroom, private bath (1); two bedroom, hall bath (3). Other accommodations available. Refrigerator, community kitchens, baths, laundry facilities, color TV. Rates: $20, additional occupant $4. All categories can make reservations. Duty personnel have priority. Pets OK for $3.50 per night.

TML: VOQ/VEQ. Buildings 25, 26, all ranks. Bedroom, hall bath (29). Bedroom, hall bath (27). Other accommodations available. Refrigerator, TV, common use kitchens, baths, laundry facilities. Rates: $20, additional person $4. All categories can make reservations. Duty personnel have priority.

TML: DVQ. Building 50, officers O6+, enlisted E-9. Separate bedroom suites, private bath (4). Kitchenette, complete utensils, color TV. Rates: $49, additional person $9. All categories can make reservations. Duty personnel have priority.

TML Availability: Good all year.

Excellent downhill and cross country skiing, volksmarching country. In warm, friendly villages where fresh trout is a specialty. Close to the former East zone, where guard towers still standing are a wall chipper's delight.

Locator 326-3471   Medical 326-3662   Police 114

Temporary Military Lodging Around the World - 287

GERMANY

Worms Community (GE31R7)
Thomas Jefferson Inn
Bldg 5032, Liebenauer Strasse
APO AE 09056-3879

TELEPHONE NUMBER INFORMATION: Main installation numbers: C-(USA) 011-49-6241-48-1110, (GE) 06241-48-1110, ETS-383-1110, D-314-383-1110.

Location: Take the Worms exit from the Mannheim-Saarbrücken E-6 Autobahn. Follow the signs to Thomas Jefferson Village. HE: p-40, B/2. NMC: Worms, in the city.

Lodging Office: Thomas Jefferson Inn, building 5032, Liebenauer Strasse, **C-(USA) 011-49-6241-48-7374/7763**, (GE) 06241-48-7374/7763, D-314-383-7763/7374, 0630-1830 M-F, 0800-1700 Sa-Su. Check out 1000 hours daily. Government civilian employee billeting.

TML: TLF. All ranks, leave or official duty. Bedroom, shared bath (16); VIP suites (4), family suites, separate bedroom, living room, private bath, bar (14). Refrigerator, color TV, VCR, cribs/cots ($2). Older structure. Rates: sponsor $25, each additional person $10 (rooms); sponsor $33, each additional person $10 (Family suites). TDY can make reservations, others Space-A.

TML Availability: Good.

Astonishing antiquity is everyday reality in Worms Cathedral, completed in 1184. Just outside the city visit Liebfrauen Kirche, from where the famous Liebfraunmilch wine was born.

Locator 383-92   Medical 116   Police 114

Würzburg Community (GE21R7)
American Guesthouse
Bldg 2, Leighton Barracks
APO AE 09244-5000

TELEPHONE NUMBER INFORMATION: Main installation numbers: C-(USA) 011-49-931-889-1110, (GE) 0931-889-1110, ETS-350-1110, D-314-350-1110.

Location: From west on Autobahn E-3 take Heidingsfeld exit to Rottendorfer Str north to Leighton Barracks. Take first right after Hq, building 6, proceed to building 2. HE: p-40, D/1. NMC: Würzburg, 1 mile south.

Lodging Office: American Guest house. Building 2, Leighton Barracks, **C-(USA) 011-49-931-700201**, (GE) 0931-700201, D-314-350-1700, 0730-1800 hours. Other hours DOC, building 6, C-EX-6223. Check in facility 1200 hours, check out 1000 hours daily. Government civilian employee billeting.

TML: American Guest House, building 2, all ranks, leave or official duty. Bedrooms, common bath (48); separate bedroom suite (VIP) (2). Kitchen (suites), refrigerator, color TV, VCR, housekeeping service (5 days/week), cribs, washer/dryer. Older structure. Rates: singles $40, $10 each additional person; suites $60, $15 each additional person. Duty can make reservations, others Space-A. **Note: when this facility is filled, guests are referred to the following officers' clubs, which have limited billeting, however, reservations may be made with them as well.**

GERMANY
Würzburg Community, continued

TML: Top of the Marne Officer's Club, Leighton Barracks (across from American Guest House), C-0931-709097/8. Bedrooms, doubles and singles, basin, hall shower (6); separate bedroom suite (VIP) (1). Color TV, housekeeping service, cribs ($5), washer/dryer. Older structure. Rates: bedrooms $38; suites $45 per day. Duty can make reservations, others Space-A.

TML: Kitzengen Officer's Club, Kitzengen, Harvey Barracks, **C-09321-31836.** Bedrooms, hall bath (10); separate bedroom suite, private bath (VIP) (1), two bedroom suite, private bath (VIP) (1). Refrigerator, housekeeping service, color TV, cribs ($5) washer/dryer. Duty can make reservations, others Space-A.

DV/VIP: SGS, Protocol, building 6, C-011-49-931-889-8308/8306, O6/GS-15+. Retirees Space-A.

TML Availability: Good, Oct-Mar. Difficult, other times.

The Annual Mozart Festival in summer, famous Franken wine in the light of a thousand candles at Würzburg Castle, the old walled city of Rothenburg on the Tauber, & the Marienberg Castle.

Locator 350-98   **Medical 116**   **Police 114**

Too Late To Copy
Friedberg Community, Bldg 3635, D-314-324-1700.

Geilenkirchen Air Base, Bldg 80, C-02451-63-4962. VOQ/VAQ, C-02451-4962.

Giebelstadt Community, Bldg 2, Leighton Barracks, C-0931-889-1700, 0931-700-201, D-314-350-1700.

Hohenfels Community, Guesthouse, Bldg 63, C-011-49-9472-950155/2 or C-011-49-9472-83-1700, D-314-466-1700/2219, Fax: C-011-49-9472-83-1543, Mon-Fri 0600-2200 hours, Sat & Sun 0730-1630 hours. Other accommodations are also available in Bldgs 70, 71, 6, 7, 1177, 1173, and 1172. Prices range from $24 to $53 per room per day. Reservations: C-0130-81-7065 (from Germany), C-1-800-462-7691 (from U.S.), Fax: C-09472-83-1534 (from Germany), C-011-49-9472-83-1534 (from U.S.).

Illesheim Community, BEQ, D-314-467-4650, BOQ, D-314-467-4550.

Kitzingen Community, 1-800-462-7691 (Worldwide Army Reservation Number), Leighton Barracks and Harvey Barracks (Woodland Inn).

Neubrücke Sub-Community, C (USA) **011-49-6782-13-287** (GE) 06782-13-287, D-314-483-7287.

Oberammergau Community, NATO School (SHAPE), 8103 Oberammergau, APO AE 09172-4251. C (USA) 011-49-8822-3385/330, (GE) 08822-3385/330, Fax 011-49-8822-7041.
TML: Guest house. **Haus Enzian,** double rooms (33), each with either a double bed or two single beds, bath, refrigerator, color TV, telephone, safe. Check out 1000 hours. Rates: $44.50-$49.50.
TML: Guest house. **Haus Edelweiss,** double rooms (32), each with either a double bed or two single beds, bath, refrigerator, color TV, telephone, safe. Check out 1000 hours. Rates: $44.50-$49.50.

ICELAND

Keflavik Naval Station (IC01R7)
Combined Bachelor's Quarters
U.S. Naval Air Station
PSC 1003 Box 34
FPO AE 09728-0334

TELEPHONE NUMBER INFORMATION: Main installation numbers: C-(USA) 011-354-25-0111 (IC) 425-0111, D-(USA) 312-450-0111 (Europe) D-314-228-0111.

Location: IAP shares landing facilities with Naval Station. From Reykjavik seaport take Hwy S follow signs to Keflavik. Well marked. Naval Station is 2.5 miles before town of Keflavik. HE: p-1, A/2. NMC: Reykjavik, 35 miles north.

Lodging Office: Building 761, C-(USA) **011-354-25-4333**, (IC) 425-4333, 24 hours daily. Check in at billeting, check out 1200 hours daily. Government civilian employee billeting.

TML: Navy Lodge. Naval Station, Box 10, building 786. All ranks, leave or official duty. C-(USA) 011-354-25--7595/2210, FAX 011-354-25-4524, (IC) 425-2000-EX-7594/2210. One and two bedroom units, private bath (27). Kitchens, color TV in room & lounge, housekeeping service, cribs/cots, coin washer/dryer, ice vending. Newly renovated structure. Rates: $51 - $86. Maximum 6 persons. All categories can make reservations. Trivia: Reykjavik McDonalds takes credit cards.

TML: CBQ. Buildings 761, 763, all ranks, leave or official duty. Bedroom, private bath (27). Refrigerator, color TV, housekeeping service, washer/dryer, food vending, community kitchen. Older structure. Rates: enlisted $8, officer and equivalent $9 per person. Sponsors for duty personnel can make reservations, others Space-A.

DV/VIP: Commander Iceland Defense Force, Box 1, FPO NY 09571-5000, C-011-354-25-4414. O5+, retirees Space-A. Note: All numbers are C- or D- extensions.

TML Availability: Lodge, good in winter months; billeting, fair. Lodge, difficult, Apr-Aug; billeting, poor.

CREDIT CARDS ACCEPTED: Visa, MasterCard and American Express at the Navy Lodge.

Into summer skiing? Visit the Kerlingarfjoll area. Fishing? July and August are best for brown trout, char and salmon. Also try sightseeing.

Locator 2100   Medical 3300   Police 2211

ITALY

Admiral Carney Park (IT03R7)
ATTN: MWR
PSC 810, Box 13
FPO AE 09619-1013

TELEPHONE NUMBER INFORMATION: Main installation numbers: C-(USA) 011-39-81-526-1579, (IT) 081-526-1579.

Location: On the west coast of Italy in Admiral Carney Park, 7 miles from Naples and 5 miles from US Naval Support Activity, Naples. HE: p-51, E/6. NMC: Naples, 7 miles south.

Lodging Office: Admiral Carney Park, Morale, Welfare and Recreation building, **C-(USA) 011-39-81-526-3396/1579**, (IT) 081-526-3396/1579, FAX-011-39-81-526-4813. Reservations required. Check in facility 1300, check out 1030 hours daily. No pets. Operates year round.

TML: The 54 acre recreational and sports complex is contained within the walls of a crater. All ranks. Bedroom cabins (13); two bedroom cabins (13). Bath house and laundromat separate, kitchenette, refrigerator, no utensils, grill and picnic area, linens, blankets, no towels. Rates: $30-$45 per night per cabin, weekly rates available. Maximum 4 per cabin. All categories can make reservations up to 90 days in advance.

TML Availability: Good, winter months. Difficult, summer months.

Visit historic Pompeii, Herculanum, the popular beaches on Capri, and Ischia. In Naples the National Museum, the Art Gallery of Capodimonte are nearby. This is a full rec park - for more details see *Military RV, Camping & Rec Areas Around The World*.

Locator 724-4367   Medical 724-4872   Police 724-4686

Aviano Air Base (IT04R7)
Aviano Lodging
31 SVS/SVML
Unit 6122, Box 45
APO AE 09601-2245

TELEPHONE NUMBER INFORMATION: Main installation numbers: C-(USA) 011-39-434-66-7111, (IT) 0434-66-7111.

Location: Adjacent to town of Aviano in Pordenone province. Thirty miles east of Udine, IT and 50 miles northeast of Venice. From A-28 North exit Pordenone to IT-159 for 8 miles to Aviano AB. HE: p-93, C/4. NMC: Pordenone, 8 miles south.

Lodging Office: Building 274, Pedemonte St, **C-(USA) 011-39-434-66-7262**, (IT) 0434-66-7262, D-314-632-7262/7722, FAX-011-39-434-660598, 24 hours daily. Check in facility, check out 1100 hours daily. Government civilian employee billeting.

TML: VOQ/VAQ. Buildings 230, 232, 255, 273, 274. All ranks, leave or official duty. Room, private bath (17); bedroom suites, private bath,(DV/VIP-Officer) (3); bedroom, private bath suites (DV/VIP Chiefs) (2). Family members OK. No TLF. Rates: VAQ $8 per night, VOQ $9 per night, DV suites $24 per night.

ITALY
Aviano Air Base, continued

DV/VIP: PAO, CCP, building 1360, room 4, D-314-632-7604, O6+.

TML Availability: Good, Dec-Jan. More difficult, other times.

CREDIT CARDS ACCEPTED: American Express.

Don't miss the Castello di Aviano, Aviano's castle ruins. Pordenone (eight miles south) for shopping, strolling and cappuccino. Many other sights are nearby.

Locator 66-7111   **Medical 66-116**   **Police 66-7200**

Camp Darby (IT10R7)
AESE BSL EH
Unit 31314, Box 60
APO AE 09613-5000

TELEPHONE NUMBER INFORMATION: Main installation numbers: C-(USA) 011-39-50-54-7111, (IT) 050-54-7111, ETS-633-7111.

Location: Located midway between Livorno & Pisa. From Autostrada A-12 take Pisa Central exit. Turn right and continue to end of road, right onto Via Aurelia (SS 1), right to S. Piero A Grado & follow Camp Darby signs. HE: p-50, A/3. NMC: Pisa, 6 miles north.

Lodging Office: Guest house, building 202, C-011-39-50-54-7448, 0800-1800 M-F, 0900-1500 Sa, Su, after duty hours, w/prior reservations, building 731, MP Desk. Check in billeting, check out 1000 hours daily. Rec area open year round.

TML: Sea Pines Lodge, outdoor recreation, building 836. **C-(USA) 011-39-50-54-7225**, (IT) 050-54-7225, ETS 633-7225 reservation desk, FAX C-(USA) 011-39-50-54-7758, (IT) 050-54-7758, ETS 633-7758, 0700-2100 hours daily (winter), 24 hours (summer). All ranks, leave or official duty. Bedroom (sleeps 4), private bath, refrigerator, TV, VCR (24); cabins, double bed, bunk beds, (sleeps 4), no linens, heated, close to showers (20). Community dining and microwave, housekeeping service, cribs ($3). Color TV, VCR, slot machines in recreation room (motel). Swimming pool in season. Modern structures. Rates: 1 person $35, 2 persons $45, 3 persons $50, 4 persons $55. Pets allowed, $3.50 per night + $50 damage deposit. Government civilian employee billeting (official duty). All categories may make reservations for summer beginning 1 Feb. Written requests mailed to: Sea Pines Lodge, 219 BSB CMR 426, MWR 31314, Box 20, APO AE 09613.

TML: Casa Toscana, Guest house, building 202, HQ Livorno AST, AESE-BSL-EH, Unit 31314, Box 20 MWR, APO AE 09613. E-mail: AESE-BSL-EH-O4 Livorno, EMH 1.-Army.MIL. Reservations: **C-(USA) 011-39-50-54-7448/7580**, (IT) 050-54-7448/7580, FAX C-011-39-50-54-7373. Check in Billeting, above building, hours. Rooms, suites and apartments. Bedroom, shared bath (3); separate bedroom, private bath (22); suite (1). Kitchenette, utensils (apartments only); refrigerator, essentials, cribs, housekeeping service (M-F), DAVs (ground floor), color TV/VCR. New A/C, carpeting, TV's, renovation '91. Rates: rooms $30, additional person $10; apartments $50 (1-2 persons), additional person $10, DVQ (1-2 persons) $60, additional person $10. Pets allowed $5 per pet/per day. Government civilian employee billeting. PCS in/out may make reservations. others Space-A.

ITALY
Camp Darby, continued

DV/VIP: Commander, 8th TASG, APO AE 09613, building 302, C-011-39-50-54-7505/7506, O6+/GS-13+, retirees Space-A.

TML Availability: Difficult, best Oct-Mar, worst Apr-Sep.

Located in the choice Tuscany region of Italy, one hour from Florence. Camp Darby even has its own stretch of Mediterranean beach at the resort town of Tirrenia. The famous Leaning Tower of Pisa is 6 miles north.

Locator 112   Medical 116   Police 114

La Maddalena Naval Support Activity (IT13R7)
Calabro Hall
FPO AE 09612-5000

TELEPHONE NUMBER INFORMATION: Main installation numbers: C-(USA) 011-39-789-798130, (IT) 0789-798130, D-314-623-8113.

Location: Located off the northern tip of the island of Sardinia. Take the main road (IT-125) north from Olbia to Palau (45 minute drive), then take a 20 minute ferry ride to La Maddalena and follow signs to the installation. HE: p-54, C/1. NMC: Olbia, 28 miles southeast.

Lodging Office: Calabro Hall, 0800-1700 daily. **C-(USA) 011-39-789-798249**, (IT) 0789-798249, D-314-623-8249. After hours contact NSO at C-011-39-789-798244. Check in facility, check out anytime. **Note: No TML available for personnel on leave or temporary duty. PCS facilities only. There is no BOQ.**

TML: Building 300, all ranks, PCS personnel only. Bedroom, 1 bed, shared bath (10); bedroom, 1 bed, shared bath (51); two bedrooms, private bath (5). A/C, ice vending, housekeeping service, refrigerator, washer/dryer. Modern structure. Rates: no charge. Maximum 2 per room.

DV/VIP: Write to: Supply Officer, NSA La Maddalena, FPO AE 09612. Building 13. Bedroom, 2 beds, private bath (1). Kitchenette, limited utensils, color TV, housekeeping service, washer/dryer, ice vending. Rates: N/A. Officers and GS on official orders. Reservations required. No pets.

TML Availability: Extremely difficult, especially in summer.

Locator 789-798-244   Medical 798-275   Police 798-244

Naples Naval Support Activity (IT05R7)
BEQ Office
PSC 817, Box 5
FPO AE 09622-1005

TELEPHONE NUMBER INFORMATION: Main installation numbers: C-(USA) 011-39-81-724-1110, (IT) 081-724-1110, D-314-625-1110.

Location: In Naples, a large port city south of Rome on the N-S Autostrada (toll road) and IT-1. HE: p-51, E/6. NMC: Naples, in the city.

ITALY
Naples Naval Support Activity, continued

Lodging Office: BEQ. Building 71, **C-(USA) 011-39-81-724-4842**, FAX 011-39-81-724-3512, DSN FAX 314-625-3512, (IT) 081-724-4842. Check in facility, check out 1200 hours daily. Enlisted military billeting only.

TML: BEQ. Building 71, enlisted all ranks, leave or official duty. Single rooms, hall and common bath. Refrigerator, color TV lounge, essentials, housekeeping service, washer/dryer, food/ice vending, microwaves in lounges. Older structure, upgraded '89. New quarters complex anticipated late '95. Rates: $6 per person, E7-E9 $12 (Note: awaiting authorization to change room rates from $6 to $12, and from $12 to $36). Dependents not authorized. Duty can make reservations, others Space-A.

TML: Navy Lodge. **Hotel Costa Bleu**, Pinetamare. All ranks, leave or official duty, **C-(USA) 011-39-81-509-7120/21/22/23**, (IT) 081-509-7120/21/22/23. Apartments: bedroom/sitting room, private bath (14); two bedroom, 2 bath (75); three bedroom, 2 bath (8); four bedroom, 3 bath (4). Full kitchen, utensils, Italian espresso maker, color TV w/military channel & satellite, washer/drying rack, bar/restaurant, weekend theater, game room, summer pool park for children, in housing area w/medical support, mini mart 1 mile, Naval Support Activity, 19 miles. No pets, kennel available. Rates: Based on number of occupants/fluctuating per diem. PCS have priority, others may make reservations. Availability: May-Sept difficult, other times good.

DV/VIP: Building 71, C-011-39-81-724-4721, NSA Protocol Office.

TML Availability: Extremely limited. Best, winter.

CREDIT CARDS ACCEPTED: American Express.

From the Navy Lodge, visit Caserta, which has a palace and gardens reminiscent of Versailles, and Pozzuoli for its volcanic activity and Roman ruins. Naples itself has wonderful possibilities. Contact MWR for tours of Pompeii, Capri, Ishia, etc.

Locator 4556   **Medical 300/301**   **Police 4686**

Sigonella Naval Air Station (IT01R7)
PSC 812, Code 192
FPO AE 09627-5000

TELEPHONE NUMBER INFORMATION: Main installation numbers: C-(USA) 011-39-95-86-1113 (NAS II), 86-1110 (NAS II) (IT) 095-56-1113, D-314-624-1113.

Location: On the east coast of the Island of Sicily. Accessible from A-19 or IT-417. HE: p-53, E/4. NMC: Catania, IT, 10 miles northeast.

Lodging Office: CBQ. Air Terminal Billeting Office **C-(USA) 011-39-95-86-5467/5575**, (IT) 095-86-5467/5575, Fax 011-39-95-86-6143, 24 hours daily. Check in facility, check out 1000 hours daily. Government civilian employee billeting.

TML: BOQ. Officers, all ranks, leave or official duty, C-011-39-95-86-2300. Bedroom, private bath (42); A/C, color TV, housekeeping service, washer/dryer, ice vending. Older structure. Rates: $10 per person. Maximum $25 per family. Maximum 3 per unit. Duty can make reservations, others Space-A.

ITALY
Sigonella Naval Air Station, continued

TML: BEQ. Enlisted, all ranks, leave or official duty, C-EX-5467. Bedroom, private bath (42); VIP suites, private bath (11). A/C, TV in lounge, washer/dryer, ice vending, housekeeping service. Older structure. Rates: $5 per day E1-E8; suites $15. Duty can make reservations, others Space-A.

DV/VIP: Protocol, building 632, C-011-39-95-86-2300, O6+. Separate bedroom suites, private bath (DV/VIP) (16). Rates: $25 per person. Retirees Space-A. No dependents under age 15.

TML Availability: Difficult.

CREDIT CARDS ACCEPTED: American Express.

Locator 113   Medical 624-3852   Police 114

The new Navy Lodge is open! For more information write PSC 824 Box 2620, FPO AE 09623-1010 or call C-(USA) 011-39-95-7130190, D-314-624-4082, Fax 011-39-95-7130190. Rates: $61.

Vicenza Community (IT06R7)
HQ 22nd ASG
Unit 31401, Box 15
Attn: Ederle Inn
APO AE 09630-5000

TELEPHONE NUMBER INFORMATION: Main installation numbers: C-(USA) 011-39-444-515190/518034, (IT) 0444-515109/518034, D-314-634-8034/8035/8036.

Location: Take the Vicenza (east) exit from the Number 4 Autostrada which runs from Trieste to Milano. Follow signs to Caserma Carlo Ederle or SETAF HQ's. HE: p-91, H/6. NMC: Vicenza, in the city.

Lodging Office: Building 345. **C-(USA) 011-39-444-518034**, (IT) 0444-515190, D-314-634-8034, 24 hours daily. Check in 1500 hours, check out 1100 hours daily. Government civilian employee billeting.

TML: Guest House/DVGH. Building 345, all ranks, official duty, PCS in/out and MTDY, TDY and leave Space-A. Handicapped accessible. Bedroom w/double beds, sofa sleeper, private bath, adjoining bedroom capability (25); three bedroom suites (subject to change) (4) (subject to change). A/C, color TV, microwave, mini-refrigerator, housekeeping service, cribs. Modern structure, remodeled. Rates: Guest House PCS/TDY $42, additional person $10. DV PCS/TDY $52, additional person $10, Space-A $42, additional person $10. Limited pet space.

DV/VIP: Protocol, HQ SETAF, Bldg 1, D-634-7712, O5/GS-15+, Retirees Space-A.

TML Availability: Good, Oct-Nov. Difficult, May-Sep.

Verona, the city of Romeo and Juliet, is rich in monuments of every period and a modern and hospitable city. Don't miss the Roman Arena, which is still an active entertainment site. Venice, Florence, Pisa, and many others are close.

Locator 634-1110   Medical 97 or 113   Police 634-7626

JAPAN

Atsugi Naval Air Facility (JA14R8)
BQ Housing Manager
NAF Atsugi, Japan
PSC 477, Box 19
FPO AP 96306-1219

TELEPHONE NUMBER INFORMATION: Main installation numbers: C-(USA) 011-81-3117-64-3334, D-315-264-3334, (JA) 0468-21-1944.

Location: In central Japan off Tokyo Bay. Yokohama is 15 miles east and Tokyo is 28 miles northeast. From Narita Airport, use bus or train service - information provided by the Northwest Military Counter at the airport. Camp Zama is 5 miles north. NMC: Tokyo, 28 miles northeast.

Lodging Office: BEQ, building 989, BOQ building 482, **C-(USA) BOQ-011-81-3117-64-3696**, **BEQ-011-81-3117-64-3698**, D-BOQ-315-264-3696, BEQ-315-264-3698, (JA) BOQ-0467-77-5321 BEQ-0467-70-4948, FAX: BOQ-011-81-467-77-5321, BEQ-011-81-3117-64-3256, BEQ-FAX: 011-81-3117-64-3256, BOQ-FAX: 011-81-467-77-5321. 24 hours daily. Write to: BOQ, PSC 477, Box 19, FPO AP 96306-1219. DoD Civilian employee billeting. Check in billeting. Check out 1200 hours (new front desk check in 1 August 95).

TML: Navy Lodge: Building 946, Navy Lodge, PSC 477, Box 10, FPO AP 96306-0003. All ranks, leave or official duty. Handicapped accessible. C-(USA) **011-81-311-764-6880**, FAX 011-81-311-764-6882, DSN FAX 312-264-6882, (JA) 0468-21-1950-EX-6880, D-315-264-6880, 0630-2230 hours daily. Check in 1500, check out 1200 hours. Bedroom, 2 double beds, private bath, no kitchen (30); Bedroom, 2 double beds, private bath, kitchen units w/ complete utensils (58). Refrigerator, color TV in lounge, cribs, essentials, ice vending, housekeeping service, washer/dryer. Modern structure. Rates: $44 - $46 per unit. Maximum 5 persons per unit. All categories can make reservations. No pets, kennels at Camp Zama.

TML: BOQ. Building 480. Officers, all ranks, leave or official duty and civilian employees on orders, others Space-A. Separate bedroom, double bed, private bath (124). Kitchenette, complete utensils, color TV, housekeeping service, essentials (toiletries), washer/dryer, ice vending, food vending, closed circuit movie channel, ping pong table. This new building opened July '93. Rates: $8, extra person $2. VIP rooms (0-6) $10, extra person $2. Guest Qtrs. (O7 & above) $20, extra person $5. Active duty, Reservists and National guard on orders may make reservations, others Space-A. No pets, kennels at Camp Zama (15 min by car).

TML: BOQ, building 482, officers, all ranks, leave or official duty. Separate bedroom, double bed, private bath (105). Kitchenette, limited utensils, color TV in lounge and room, housekeeping service, essentials, (toiletries), washer/dryer, ice and food vending, closed circuit movie channel, recently renovated. Active duty, Reservists and National Guard on orders may make reservations, others Space-A. Reservations required/accepted. Used to billet permanent party personnel, and transient officers and civilians, others Space-A.

TML: BOQ, building 483, officers, all ranks, leave or official duty. Separate bedroom, double bed, private bath (40). Kitchenette, complete utensils, TV, housekeeping service, essentials (toiletries), washer/dryer, ice and food vending, closed circuit movie channel, pool table. Active duty, Reservists

JAPAN
Atsugi Naval Air Facility, continued

and National Guard on orders may make reservations, others Space-A. Used for transient officers & civilians on orders.

TML: BEQ, building 484, enlisted E-7 to E-9, on leave or official duty. Separate bedroom, double bed, private bath (40). Kitchenette, complete utensils, color TV, housekeeping service, essentials (toiletries), washer/dryer, ice and food vending, closed circuit movie channel, pool table. BEQ Rates: E7+, $7, extra person $1. Active duty, Reservists and National Guard on orders may make reservations, others Space-A. Used to billet permanent party and transient enlisted on orders.

TML: BEQ, building 979, enlisted, all ranks, leave or official duty. (E1-E6) Separate bedroom, single bed, 3 beds per room, private bath (54). (E7-E9) Separate bedroom, double bed, private bath (51). Refrigerator, color TV in lounge and room, housekeeping service, essentials (toiletries), washer/dryer, ice and food vending, closed circuit movie channel, pool and ping pong tables. Central kitchen. Rates: E7+, $5, extra person $1; E1-E6, $3. Active duty, Reservists and National Guard on orders may make reservations, others Space-A.

TML: BEQ, building 985 & 986, enlisted, all ranks leave or official duty, Bedroom, 3 beds, shared bath (258). Refrigerator, color TV in lounge and room, closed circuit movie channel, pool and ping pong tables. Recently renovated. Active duty, Reservists and National Guard on orders may make reservations, others Space-A.

TML: BEQ, buildings 980, 981, 982, enlisted, all ranks, leave or official duty. Bedroom, 2 beds, shared bath (68). Refrigerator, color TV in room and lounge, housekeeping service, essentials (toiletries), washer/dryer, ice and food vending, closed circuit movie channel, recently renovated. Active duty, Reservists and National Guard may make reservations, others Space-A.

TML: BEQ, building 47, enlisted, E1-E3, leave or official duty. No female personnel. Bedrooms, 2 beds, communal bath (68). Refrigerator, color TV in room and lounge, housekeeping service, essentials (toiletries), washer/dryer, ice and food vending, VCR in rooms. Some renovation. Building built in 1942, General McArthur stayed here! Active duty, Reservists, National Guard may make reservations, others Space-A.

TML: BEQ, building 984, all ranks. PCS families into NAF Atsugi, limited space for Space-A families. Bedroom 2 beds, private bath (12). Refrigerator, color TV, housekeeping service, essentials (toiletries), cribs/cots, VCR, coffee pot, recently renovated. Reservations required.

TML: DV/VIP: Public Affairs Office, C-011-81-467-78-2664, D-315-264-3201. O6+, others Space-A. Off-base hotels located in front of main gate.

TML Availability: Difficult, best when CVW-5 is deployed, worst when in port or in the local area.

CREDIT CARDS ACCEPTED: American Express. The Navy Lodge accepts Visa, MasterCard and American Express.

Book a one day tour of Tokyo through MWR at Atsugi, or just ask the friendly Navy Lodge people to provide you with maps, directions and info, but don't miss seeing as much as you can of this marvelous city! Note: Expected to open BEQ 989 (266 rooms) 30 July 95.

Locator 228-3334   Medical 228-3311   Police 228-3200

Temporary Military Lodging Around the World - 297

JAPAN

Camp S. D. Butler Marine Corps Base (JA07R8)
Transient Billeting Fund
PSC 557, Box 935
FPO AP 96379-0935

TELEPHONE NUMBER INFORMATION: Main installation numbers: C-(USA) 011-81-98892-5111, (JA) 098892-5111, D-315-640-1110.

Location: Four miles south of Okinawa City on Hwy 330 at Camp Foster 2 miles north of Futenma. NMC: Naha, 7 miles south.

Lodging Office: ATTN: FACS, Billeting/Housing Director, **C-(USA) 011-81-98892-2459,** FAX 011-81-61175-7549, DSN FAX 315-645-7549, (JA) 098892-2191, D-315-635-2191, 0700-1630 daily. Other hours, building 1, OD, D-315-635-7218/2644. Check in facility, check out 1200 hours daily. Government civilian employee billeting.

TML: TLF. **Courtney Lodge,** building 2540, **Camp Courtney,** all ranks, leave or official duty, C-EX-9578, D-315-622-9578. Suites, private bath (16). Refrigerator, A/C, CATV in room & lounge, housekeeping service, cribs/cots, coin washer/dryer. 1/4 mile to 7 day store, 1 1/4 miles to commissary and exchange. Modern structure. Rates: $30 per unit, $5 each extra person. Maximum 3 per unit.

TML: TLF. **Hansen Lodge,** building 2540, **Camp Hansen,** all ranks, leave or official duty. C-EX 4511, D-315-623-4511. Same as Courtney except bedroom, shared bath (18). Older structure. Rates: $30 per room. Maximum 2 per room. Reservations accepted.

TML: Kuwae Lodge, building 400, **Camp Lester,** all ranks, leave or official duty. C-645-0214, D-645-9102/9106. Rooms with kitchen (165). Washer/dryer, playroom, rec rooms. Rates: $30, $5 extra person. Double adjoining rooms, $66-$70, 3 room suite. Reservations accepted 30 days in advance. Free shuttle bus service.

TML: WestPac Inn. Camp Foster, (TQ) all ranks, leave or official duty. Futenma, (VOQ) officers, all ranks, leave or official duty, C-EX-2191, D-315-635-2191. Separate bedroom, living room, private bath (20); (Futenma) bedroom, private bath (10); separate bedroom, private bath (2); suites, private bath (2). Maximum 2 per suite, 2 per room. Kitchen, A/C, color TV, housekeeping service, washer/dryer, video cassette reception in room. Older structure, renovated. Rates: $10, $12, $19 according to rank and status. Duty can make reservations, others Space-A.

TML: DV/VIP. **Day House, Awase House,** buildings 4205, 4515. Same as above. Rates: $30.

DV/VIP: Protocol Office, building 1, **Camp SD Butler MCB,** C-EX 7274, D-315-645-7274. Protocol Office, building 4225, III MEF, Camp Courtney, C-EX 7749, D-315-645-7749. Protocol Office, Building 1, 1st MAW, Camp SD Butler MCB, C-EX 2901, D-315-635-2901.

TML Availability: Good. Best, Aug-Mar. More difficult, other times.

CREDIT CARDS ACCEPTED: American Express (for TAD personnel only).

JAPAN
Camp S.D. Butler Marine Corps Base, continued

Don't miss seeing Nakagusuku Castle, left over from Okinawa's feudal period, and the Nakamura House, which displays Okinawan lifestyle of yesteryear. Check with the USO for locations and possible tours.

Locator 635-7456 Medical 634-1756 Police 635-7441

Camp Zama (JA06R8)
Commander
17th ASG-CM
ATTN: APAJ-GH-EH-HB (Billeting)
APO AP 96343-5000

TELEPHONE NUMBER INFORMATION: Main installation numbers: C-(USA) 011-81-3117-63-0000, (JA) 03117-63-0000, D-315-263-3830/4474.

Location: 25 miles south of Tokyo or north of Yokohama. Excellent rail service. NMC: Tokyo, 25 miles north.

Lodging Office: ATTN: APAJ-GH-EH-HB, building 563, Sand St, **C-(USA) 011-81-4062-51-1520 (ask for 263-3830/4474)**, FAX 011-81-3117-63-5890, DSN FAX 315-263-5890, (JA) 04062-51-5344 (ask for 263-3830/4474), D-315-263-4474/3830, 24 hours daily. Check in 1500 hours, check out 1200 hours daily. Government civilian employee billeting.

TML: VOQ/VEQ. Building 742, all ranks, official duty, or leave. Bedroom, private bath (38). Refrigerator, microwave, stocked bar, community kitchen, A/C, color TV and VCR, housekeeping service, washer/dryer, ice and food vending. Modern structure. Rates: sponsor $17, $3 each additional person. Duty can make reservations, others Space-A. Pets boarded at clinic for $4 per day.

TML: Guest House. Building 552, all ranks, PCS in and out, or official duty. Handicapped accessible 1st floor. Separate bedroom, private bath (56). Kitchenettes, complete utensils, housekeeping service, color TV and VCR, A/C, ice vending, washer/dryer. New structure, furnishings '92. Rates: sponsor $25, $5 each additional person. Duty can make reservations, others Space-A.

TML: Guest House. Building 780, all ranks, PCS in/out. Bedroom, hall bath (5); two bedroom, hall bath (14); three bedroom, private bath (2). A/C, refrigerator, microwave, complete utensils, community kitchen, color TV and VCR, housekeeping service, washer/dryer, ice vending. Older structure, refurbished '91. Rates: sponsor $14-$22, $4 each additional person. Duty can make reservations, others Space-A.

TML: DVQ. Building 550, officer O6+, official duty or leave. Separate bedroom, private bath (12). A/C, community kitchen, cots/cribs ($5), housekeeping service, refrigerator, stocked bar, microwaves, TV and VCR, ice vending, washer/dryer. Modern structure, refurbished '91. Rates: sponsor: $20, $5 each additional person. Duty can make reservations, others Space-A. Pets boarded at clinic for $4 per day.

DV/VIP: USARJ Protocol Office, building 101. C-011-81-263-4019, O7+, retirees Space-A.

TML Availability: Guest House: good, DVQ: good, Jan-Feb difficult. VOQ/VEQ: good, Jan-Feb difficult.

JAPAN
Camp Zama, continued

CREDIT CARDS ACCEPTED: Visa, MasterCard and American Express.

Check with the ITT office on base for local tours. A round trip shuttle bus to Tokyo (the New Sanno Hotel) is available, as are trips to Disneyland, Kamakura, Hakone, Mount Fuji, Kyoto, Nikko and Seto.

Locator 263-5344   Medical 263-4127   Police 263-3002

Iwakuni Marine Corps Air Station (JA12R8)
Morale, Welfare & Recreation
ATTN: Temporary Lodging Facility
PSC 561, P.O. Box 1867
FPO AP 96310-1867

TELEPHONE NUMBER INFORMATION: Main installation numbers: C-(USA) 011-81-827-21-4171, (JA) 0827-21-4171, D-315-253-5409. Direct dial from U.S. 011-81-6117-53-3181.

Location: Facing the Inland Sea on the south portion of the island of Honshu, 450 miles southwest of Tokyo, .5 miles off JA-188 on JA-189. NMC: Hiroshima, 25 miles north.

Lodging Office: Building 444, C-(USA) 011-81-6117-53-3221, (JA) 0827-21-4171-EX-3221, D-315-253-3221, 0800-2200 hours daily. Check in building 444, check out 1000 hours daily. Government civilian employee billeting.

TML: Transient Billeting. Buildings 603, 611, 1189, all ranks, leave or official duty, C-EX-3181. Some facilities handicapped accessible. Bedroom, common bath (enlisted) (19); separate bedroom, private bath (SNCOs and officers) (51); two bedroom, private bath (DV-Shogun House) (1); bedroom, two beds, common bath (enlisted) (17). Kitchenette (building 603), refrigerator, utensils, A/C, color TV, movie channel, housekeeping service, cribs/cots, ice vending. Essentials/souvenirs on sale front desk. Modern structure. Rates: sponsor/spouse and adult dependents over age 12, $7 officers, $7, SNCOs $6, E-5 and below $5, 12 and under $2. Duty can make reservations, others Space-A.

TML: Lodge Facility. Buildings 444 and 1188, 1/2 mile from gate. Single room, private bath, kitchenette (24); two room suites, private bath, kitchenette (24). 3/4 miles from commissary, exchange, 7 day store and clubs. Rates: $30-$40 for one or two persons, $2 each additional person. A priority system rather than a reservation system is used. PCS on station, command sponsored accompanied (Priority 1A); PCS off station, command sponsored (Priority 1B); all others Space-A.

DV/VIP: DGR, building 511, D-315-236-4211.

TML Availability: Good.

CREDIT CARDS ACCEPTED: Visa, MasterCard and American Express.

See the famous Kintai Bridge, and view the Iwakuni Castle Ropeway. Hiroshima is 50 minutes by train, and visitors should see the Peace Memorial Park, Atomic Bomb Memorial Dome, and reconstructed Hiroshima Castle. Don't miss the cherry blossoms in bloom, Mar-Apr.

Locator 113   Medical 253-5571   Police 253-3222

JAPAN

Kadena Air Base (JA08R8)
ATTN: 18 SVS/SVML
APO AP 96368-5000

TELEPHONE NUMBER INFORMATION: Main installation numbers: C-(USA) 011-81-611-938-1111, (JA) 061-938-41111, D-315-630-1110.

Location: Take Hwy 58 North from Naha to Kadena's Gate 1 on the right immediately north of USMC Camp Lester. NMC: Naha, 12 miles south.

Lodging Office: Building 332, Beeson Ave, C-(USA) 011-81-611-732-1000, D-315-632-1100, 24 hours daily. Check in 1500 at billeting, check out 1000 hours daily. Government civilian employee billeting.

TML: TLF. Family Quarters. Building 322, 437, 507, all ranks, leave or official duty. Handicapped accessible. Apartments (122). A/C, refrigerator, kitchen, complete utensils, color TV, VCR, housekeeping service, cribs, rollaway, washer/dryer. Modern structure. Rates: $25.50 per unit. Maximum 6 persons per unit. Duty can make reservations, others Space-A.

TML: VAQ. Buildings 317, 332, 504, 506, 509, 510, enlisted all ranks. Bedroom, private bath (124); shared bedrooms, semi-private bath (60). A/C, housekeeping service, refrigerator, color TV, VCR, washer/dryer. Rates: $9.50 per person per night. Maximum 2 persons. Duty can make reservations, others Space-A.

TML: VOQ. Buildings 306, 311, 314, 316, 318, 502, 508, officers all ranks. Bedroom, private bath (109); separate bedroom, semi-private bath (20). A/C, housekeeping service, refrigerator, color TV, VCR, washer/dryer. Rates: $9.50 per person. Maximum 2 persons. Duty can make reservations, others Space-A.

TML: DVQ. Buildings 78, 85, 315, 2024, officers O6+, leave or official duty. Bedroom, living area private bath (24); two bedroom, private bath, living area, dining area (2); bedroom, private bath, living area, dining area (1). A/C, essentials, kitchen, complete utensils, housekeeping service, color TV, VCR, washer/dryer. Rates: $14.00 per person. Duty can make reservations, others Space-A.

DV/VIP: Protocol Office, building 10, D-315-634-3548, O6+.

TML Availability: Good, Dec-Jan. Difficult, spring & summer.

CREDIT CARDS ACCEPTED: American Express.

This is the cross roads of the Pacific, and a great Space-A departure point, but don't miss seeing the Children's Park Zoo in Okinawa City, the Ryukyuan Village and Takoyama Habu Center. Near Nenoko see the Shell house, visited by shell collectors.

Locator 634-1110   Medical 634-1922   Police 634-2475

JAPAN

Misawa Air Base (JA03R8)
Misawa Inn
35 SVS/SVML
Unit 5019
APO AP 96319-5000

TELEPHONE NUMBER INFORMATION: Main installation numbers: C-(USA) 011-81-176-53-5181, (JA) 0176-53-5181, D-315-226-3526/4294.

Location: On the northeast portion of the Island of Honshu, 400 miles north of Tokyo. NMC: Hachinohe City, 17 miles southeast.

Lodging Office: Misawa Inn, 35 SVS/SVML, Unit 5019, APO AP 96319-5000, **C-(USA) 011-81-176-53-5181-EX-3526,** (JA) 0176-53-5181-EX-3526, D-315-226-3526, FAX 011-81-176-53-2165, DSN FAX 315-226-2165, 24 hours daily. Check in billeting, check out 1200 hours daily.

TML: TLF. Buildings 696-699, 109 A-D, all ranks, leave or official duty. Single family units (4). Two bedroom apartments, private bath (16). Shared living room, kitchen, refrigerator, utensils, color TV, VCR, housekeeping service, cribs/cots, washer/dryer. Older structure. Rates: $28 per unit. Duty can make reservations, others Space-A.

TML: TLF. Building 670, all ranks, leave or official duty. Single family units (40). Private bath, living room, kitchen, utensils. Rates: $25 per unit.

TML: VOQ. Buildings 662, 664, officers O1-O6, leave or official duty. Bedroom, private bath (56). Kitchen, utensils, refrigerator, color TV, VCR, housekeeping service, washer/dryer. Older structure. Rates: $9.50 per person. Duty can make reservations, others Space-A.

TML: VAQ. Building 669, enlisted all ranks, leave or official duty. Bedroom, private bath (28). Prime Knight Aircrew Quarters, (top three suites, 10); suites, private bath (E9) (2). Refrigerator, color TV, VCR, housekeeping service, washer/dryer, ice vending. Rates: $8 per person. Duty and civilians on official duty can make reservations, others Space-A.

TML: DV/VIP. Building 17, officer O6+ (M&F), leave or official duty. Bedroom, private bath, suites (4). Kitchen, utensils, refrigerator, A/C, color TV, VCR, housekeeping service. Modern structure. Rates: $9.50 per person. Duty can make reservations, others Space-A.

DV/VIP: 35th FW/CCP. C-011-81-176-53-5181-EX-4804, O6+. Retirees Space-A.

TML Availability: Good, Nov-Mar. Difficult, other times.

CREDIT CARDS ACCEPTED: American Express.

Enjoy the excellent eating establishments in downtown Misawa, and try a hot bath at Komakis. Explore the Komaki Onsen, Komaki Grand and the Second Grand Hotels. Get hints from MWR (building 1044) for trips farther afield.

Locator 0176-53-5181   Medical 226-2985   Police 226-4358

JAPAN

**The New Sanno
US Forces Center (JA01R8)**
Unit 45003
APO AP 96337-0110

TELEPHONE NUMBER INFORMATION: Main installation numbers: C-(USA) 011-81-3-3440-7871, (JA) 03-3440-7871.

Location: At 4-12-20 Minami Azabu, Minato-ku, Tokyo 106, a five minute walk from nearest subway station, Hiroo (Hibiya line). NMI: Tokyo Administrative Facility/Hardy Barracks, 1 mile. NMC: Tokyo, in city limits.

Description: Located in a quiet residential area not far from downtown Tokyo, only a five-minute walk from the nearest subway station, Hiroo. Offers guests commercial hotel quality, newly renovated accommodations and food service at affordable prices. Each of 149 guest rooms features private bath or shower, and central heating and air conditioning. Rental videos are available. Two traditional Japanese-style suites for guests to enjoy the full flavor of the Orient.

A family dining room, Japanese-style restaurant, fine dining restaurant, lounge and snack bar are available to guests of The New Sanno. Entertainment and special events are scheduled on a regular basis in The New Sanno's main ballroom which can seat up to 350 guests, and banquet and conference facilities are available.

There is a rooftop pool (seasonal), an exercise room and video game room, first and second floor arcades with a Navy Exchange, convenience store and concessionaires. An APO, military banking facility, pack & wrap service, barber shop, beauty salon, flower shop and laundry and dry cleaning, plus public rest rooms (handicapped accessible) on the lobby level, and other American-style conveniences make The New Sanno a meeting place for military personnel and their families touring Tokyo.

Tours, theater, concert and sporting event tickets are available through the Information and Tours Desk. They can also book airline reservations, C-03-3440-7871 EX 7200. If you are arriving at Narita International Airport, an economical airport express bus is available to The New Sanno's front door. Daily buses run to and from Yokota Air Base (schedule available at AMC terminal). The New Sanno is a Joint Services, all ranks facility managed by the US Navy as Executive Agent.

Room Rates for the New Sanno U S Forces Center

Room Type	No.	I*	II*	III*	IV*
Single (Queen bed)	43	$29	$38	$44	$63
Double (Queen + single bed)	78	$40	$47	$55	$77
King Suite (King + sofa)	50	$56	$61	$68	$95
Twin Suite (2 twins + sofa)	3	$56	$61	$68	$95
Family Suite (sgl room + bunk)	2	$56	$61	$76	$100
Japanese Suite	2	$70	$76	$84	$111

*I: E1-E5; II: E6-O3, WO1-WO4; III: O4-O10; IV: retired/non-DoD. I, II & III include comparable DoD Civilian grades. II includes DAVs, Unremarried Widows and Orphans (all with DD1173).

ALL RATES SUBJECT TO CHANGE.

JAPAN
The New Sanno, continued

Season of Operation: Year round.

Eligibility: Active/Retired/US Embassy Tokyo/UN Command(Rear), Active Reserves, DoD and other SOFA recognized Federal Civilian Employees on official orders to or through Japan.

Reservations: Recommended 45 days in advance with one nights deposit for each room reserved. Deposits by check, money order, American Express, Diners' Club, MasterCard, VISA. Address: The New Sanno Hotel, APO AP 96337-0110, Attn: Reservations. C-(USA) **011-81-3-3440-7871-EX-7121**, (JA) 03-3440-7871-EX-7121, D-315-229-7121, FAX-C-011-81-3-3440-7824, D-315-229-7102.

Restrictions: No pets.

Okuma Beach Resort - Okinawa (JA09R8)
Schilling Leisure Resource Center
Okuma Reservation
18th SVS/SVMR
Unit 5135, Box 10
APO AP 96368-5135

TELEPHONE NUMBER INFORMATION: Main installation numbers: C-(USA) 011-81-98-041-5164 (JA) 0980-41-5164, D-315-634-4601.

Location: On Hwy 58, 50 miles north of Kadena AB, Okinawa. Left off Hwy 58 before Hentona. NMC: Naha, JA 62 miles south.

Lodging Office: Schilling Leisure Resources Center. Duty, retired, DoD civilians assigned overseas. May make reservation up to 90 days in advance, C-(USA) **011-81-611-734-4322**, (JA) 098938-1110 EXT 634-4601, D-315-634-4322, 0700-2200 hours daily (summer), W-M (winter), building 116, check in 1500 hours, check out 1100 hours daily. Operates year round.

TML: Rec Cabana's. All ranks, leave or official duty. Bedroom, 2 double beds, shared bath, (30); bedroom, 2 double beds, private bath (10); bedrooms, double bed, private bath, dry bar, couples only (12); suites, 4 double beds, private bath (9); VIP suite (1). Refrigerator, microwave, A/C, color TV/VCR, housekeeping service, cribs/rollaways ($3), washer/dryer. Refurnished '92. Rates: shared bath $25-$45 daily. All categories can make reservations.

DV/VIP: 18th Wing/CCP, building 10, Kadena AB, Okinawa, D-315-634-0106, O6+. Retirees and lower ranks Space-A.

TML Availability: Good, Nov-Dec. Difficult, other times.

Great beach rec area. For full details and camping opportunities, see Military Living's *Military RV, Camping & Rec Areas Around The World.*

JAPAN

Sasebo Fleet Activities (JA15R8)
Combined Bachelor Quarters
U.S. Fleet Activities, Sasebo
PSC 476, Box 1
FPO AP 96322-1100

TELEPHONE NUMBER INFORMATION: Main installation numbers: C-(USA) 011-81-956-24-6111, (JA) 0956-24-6111, D-(USA) 315-252-1110.

Location: From either Nagasaki or Fukuoka. take the Nishi-Kyushu Expressway to SASEBO exit (both in Japanese and English). Follow Route 35 to downtown SASEBO, ask directions to naval base. Far southwestern Japan, on the Korean Strait, NMC: Fukuoka, 50 miles northeast.

Lodging Office: ATTN: CBQ Officer, U.S. Fleet Activities, Sasebo, PSC 476, Box 1, FPO AP 96322-1100. C-(USA) **011-81-956-24-6111 (BOQ ext 3794) (BEQ ext 3413)**, FAX (USA) 011-81-956-24-6111 (BOQ/BEQ ext 3530), (JA)095624-6111 (BOQ ext 3794) (BEQ ext 3413), D-315-252-3794 (BOQ), D-315-252-3413 (BEQ), above extensions, 24 hours daily. Check in BOQ/BEQ office, check out 1200 daily. Government Civilian Employee billeting.

TML: BOQ. Buildings 1455, 1603, all ranks leave or official duty. Bedrooms (145). Kitchenette, utensils, refrigerator, microwave, essentials, color TV /VCR in room and lounge, housekeeping service, food and ice vending, cribs, washer/dryer. Modern structure. Rates: $7 per person, per unit, $12 maximum for family, maximum 2 per unit. Active duty PCS and TAD/TDY (civilians GS7+) on orders to FLEACT Sasebo may make reservations up to 45 days in advance, all others Space-A. No pets.

TML: BEQ. Buildings 1604, 1663, all ranks leave or official duty. Shared bedrooms, private bath (140). Refrigerator, color TV/VCR in room/lounge, microwave, phone, food/ice vending machines, washer/dryer. Modern structure. Rates: $4 per person, per unit, $8 maximum (2 per unit). Active duty PCS and TAD/TDY (civilians GS7+) on orders to FLEACT Sasebo may make reservations up to 45 days in advance, all others Space-A. No pets.

TML: Navy Lodge, ATTN: Navy Fleet Activities Sasebo, PSC 476, Box 30, FPO AP 96322-0003. Reservations: C-**011-81-956-24-0173**, FAX 011-81-956-24-6111 to ext 252-3602, DSN FAX 312-252-3602, D-315-252-3608, or **1-800-NAVY-INN**, 0700-2300 hours daily. All ranks, leave or official duty. Bedroom, 2 double beds, private bath (26). A/C, color TV, housekeeping service, coin washer/dryer, ice vending. Near MWR, All Hands Club, Snack Bar, Swimming pool, Base Galley, NEX 10 minute walk. Modern structure. Rates: $46. All categories can make reservations.

TML: DV/VIP. Building 80, C-011-81-956-24-3401, leave or official duty. Duty can make reservations, others Space-A.

DV/VIP: Commander, Fleet Activities Sasebo, Attn: Protocol Officer, PSC 476, Box 1, FPO AP 96322-1100, BOQ O6+, BEQ E9+.

TML Availability: Fairly good, Apr-Aug. Difficult, Sep-Dec.

CREDIT CARDS ACCEPTED: American Express. The Navy Lodge accepts Discover.

JAPAN
Sasebo Fleet Activities, continued

Mount Yumihari has an excellent view. Take a 99 Islands boat cruise, from nearby Kashimae Pier (15 minutes from base by car). Hachiman Shrine is a 20 minute walk from base. Nagasaki and Fukuoka are one hour drives. Don't miss the Fukagawa/Noritake Chinaware Factory, the finest bone china in the world! Don't forget to see Huis Ten Bosch and Holland Village.

Locator 1110　　　　Medical 3624/3625　　　　Police 3446/3447

Tama Outdoor Recreation Area (JA10R8)
374 SPTG/SVBH
APO AP 96328-5000

TELEPHONE NUMBER INFORMATION: Main installation numbers: C-(USA) 011-81-423-77-7009, (JA) 0423-77-7009, D-315-224-3421/3422.

Location: Fifteen miles southeast of Yokota AB. NMC: Tokyo, 45 minute train ride.

Lodging Office: 374 SPTG/SVBH. Yokota AB, APO AP 96328-5000, C-(USA) **011-81-423-77-7009**, (JA) 0423-77-7009, D-315-224-3421/3422, 24 hours daily. Check in at facility 1400, check out 1100 hours daily. Operates year round. Reservations required with first days rent.

TML: Rec Lodge and cabins. All ranks, leave or official duty. Reservations required (60 days in advance for weekends, 90 days for weekdays). Suites, private bath (6); double rooms, private bath (14); executive and single cabins, private bath (18). Refrigerator, A/C, color TV, housekeeping service, washer/dryer, ice. Rates: $25 to $55. All categories can make reservations. Pets allowed in cabins.

TML Availability: Good, Oct-Mar. Difficult, other times.

This is a 500 acre retreat west of Tokyo. Its a quiet getaway offering many facilities. See Military Living's *Military RV, Camping & Rec Areas Around The World* for more details.

Locator 0423-77-7009　　　　Medical 225-9111　　　　Police 224-3421-EX-40

Tokyo Administration Facility (JA02R8)
Akasaka Press Center (Hardy Barracks)
Bldg 1, Room 413-A
APO AP 96337-0007

TELEPHONE NUMBER INFORMATION: Main installation numbers: C-(USA) 011-81-3117-29-3270 (JA) 03-3402-6024, touchtone 229-3270, D-315-229-3270/3345.

Location: At #7-23-17 Roppongi, Minato-ku, Tokyo. Near Imperial Palace and 2 miles by taxi from New Sanno Hotel. Nogizaka subway station, left out of exit #5. NMC: Tokyo, in the city.

Lodging Office: Hardy Barracks, building 1, Room 413-A, C-(USA) **011-81-3117-29-3270**, (JA) 03-3402-6024, 24 hours daily. Check in at facility 1600, check out 1200 hours daily. Government civilian employee billeting.

JAPAN
Tokyo Administration Facility, continued

TML: VOQ/VEQ. All ranks, leave or official duty. Bedroom, shared bath (19); separate bedroom suites, private bath (2). Refrigerator, community kitchen, A/C, color TV, VCR, micro-fridge, coffee, travel kit, housekeeping service, cribs, washer/dryer. Older structure. Remodeled March '90. Rates: sponsor $15-$20, each additional person $2-$5. Reservations may be made up to 15 days in advance by telephone or in person. Pets not allowed. **Note: Tokyo city bus 97 runs between the New Sanno Hotel and Hardy Barracks.**

DV/VIP: Call Camp Zama, building 101, room W-223, D-315-263-4474, for assistance.

TML Availability: Good. Best months Jan-Mar.

CREDIT CARDS ACCEPTED: Visa, MasterCard and American Express.

Check with the New Sanno Hotel for guided tours, or just pick up some city maps. Then visit the Ginza, Kabuki theater, Akasaka/Roppongi (the entertainment district), Ueno Park, Zoo, and shopping are musts.

Yokosuka Fleet Activities (JA05R8)
Combined Bachelor's Quarters
PSC 473, Box 40
FPO AP 96349-1110

TELEPHONE NUMBER INFORMATION: Main installation numbers: C-(USA) 011-81-0468-21-911, (JA) 0468-21-1911, D-315-243-1110.

Location: About 23 miles south of Tokyo and 25 miles north of Yokohama. NMC: Tokyo, 23 miles north. Excellent train service.

Lodging Office: Building G-27, Clements St, **C-(USA) 011-81-0468-21-911-EX 7777/5569**, (JA) 0468-21-1911-EX-7777/5569, D-315-243-7777, FAX-011-81-3117-43-EX-5088, DSN FAX 315-243-5088 (BEQ); DSN FAX 315-243-7317, D-315-234-7317 (BOQ), 24 hours daily. Check in facility, check out before 1200 hours daily. Government civilian employee billeting.

TML: Navy Lodge. Building J-4807, all ranks, leave or official duty, Reservations: C-(USA) 011-81-468-270080, FAX 011-81-3117-34-6759, (JA)0-468-270080, D-315-243-6708. Write to: Navy Lodge, PSC 473, Box 70, FPO AP 96349-0003. Bedroom, private bath (165) (90 connecting); 102 new rooms, queen size bed. Kitchen, refrigerator, TV, mini mart, all services. Rates: $44, kitchen units $48. Four handicapped accessible. Pets kept overnight in lounge until kennel opens.

TML: BEQ. Building 1492, enlisted, all ranks, leave or official duty. Bedroom, 3 beds, private bath (232). Refrigerator, A/C, color TV in room & lounge, housekeeping service, washer/dryer. Modern structure. Rates: $4 per person. Maximum 3 per room. Duty can make reservations, others Space-A.

TML: BOQ. Buildings 1556, 1723, officer all ranks, leave or official duty. Bedroom, private bath (95). Kitchen, A/C, color TV in room and lounge, housekeeping service, washer/dryer, barber shop. Modern structure. Rates: $8 per person; VIP $15; VIP Suite $20; Togo Room (O7+) $25. Duty can make reservations, others Space-A. Note: most rooms have only 1 single bed.

JAPAN
Yokosuka Fleet Activities, continued

TML: CPOQ. Building 1475, enlisted E7-E9, leave or official duty. Bedroom, private bath (26). Refrigerator, community kitchen, A/C, color TV in room & lounge, housekeeping service, washer/dryer, ice vending. Modern structure. Rates: $4 per person; VIP $5. Duty can make reservations, others Space-A. Note: all beds are singles.

TML: Other. **NASU Lodge.** 100 miles north of Tokyo. Rec Service Office. C-EX-5613/ 7306. Two-story wood-frame building accommodates up to 26 persons. Japanese style floor and bath. Kitchen and lodging requirements. Near many rec areas for skiing, fishing, hiking, horseback riding. Reservations taken 1 month in advance. Call for rates. Group rates available. All ranks.

DV/VIP: Protocol Office, C-011-81-468-21-1911-EX-5685, D-315-243-7317, O7+. Retirees Space-A.

TML Availability: Good. Somewhat difficult, Jun-Sep.

CREDIT CARDS ACCEPTED: American Express. The Navy Lodge accepts Visa, MasterCard and American Express.

Located close to Tokyo, near many historic Japanese shrines, beautiful beaches, a 10 minute walk to a shopping mall, and 2 hours from Disneyland Tokyo, Yokosuka boasts "the best MWR facility in the Pacific."

Locator 113   **Medical 116**   **Police 243-5000/5001**

Yokota Air Base (JA04R8)
Kanto Lodge
374 SPTG/SVML
APO AP 96328-5119

TELEPHONE NUMBER INFORMATION: Main installation numbers: C-(USA) 011-81-3117-55-1110 (JA) 03117-55-1110, D-315-248-1101.

Location: Take JA-16 South from Tokyo. AB is 1 mile west of Fussa JA. Clearly marked. NMC: Tokyo, 35 miles northeast.

Lodging Office: Building 10, Bobzien Ave & 1st St, **C-(USA) 011-81-425-52-2511-EX-5-7712,** FAX 011-81-425-52-3499, DSN FAX 315-225-3499(JA) 0425-52-2511-EX-5-7712, D-315-225-9270, 24 hours daily. Check in billeting, check out 1000 hours daily. Government civilian employee billeting.

TML: TLF. Building 10, all ranks, leave or official duty, C-EX-9270. Four bedroom, shared bath (31). Kitchen, utensils, A/C, color TV in room & lounge, housekeeping service, cribs, washer/dryer, handicapped accessible. Modern structure. Rates: $32 per room. Duty can make reservations, others Space-A. Limited pet care available on base.

TML: VOQ. Buildings 14, 120, 131-133, officers all ranks, leave or official duty, C-EX-9270. Bedroom, private bath (136); suites, separate bedroom, private bath, (15). Refrigerator, A/C, color TV, housekeeping service, washer/dryer. Older structure. Rates: $9.50 per person. Duty can make reservations, others Space-A.

JAPAN
Yokota Air Base, continued

TML: VAQ. Building 16, 690, 134, enlisted all ranks, leave or official duty, C-EX-9270. Bedroom, common bath (80); two bedroom (22). Refrigerator, A/C, color TV, housekeeping service, washer/dryer. Older structure. Rates: $9.50 per person. Maximum 4 per unit. Duty can make reservations, others Space-A.

TML: Kanto Lodge. Officers and enlisted. Family units have shared living space with kitchen. TDY personnel may make advance reservations, must present orders at registration, others Space-A. Leave personnel waiting list. Call for more information.

TML: DV/VIP. SNCO, Bldg 32, enlisted E7-E9, leave/official duty, C-EX-9270. Suites, bedroom, private bath, (3). Refrig, A/C, TV, housekeeping service, washer/dryer. Modern structure. Rates:$14/person. Duty can make reservations, others Space-A.

TML: DV/VIP. Buildings 13, 17, 32, officers O6+ (M&F), leave or official duty, C-EX-9270. Separate bedroom, private bath, suites (9); two bedroom, private bath, suites (4). Kitchen, utensils, A/C, color TV, housekeeping service, cribs, washer/dryer. Older structure. Rates: $14 per person. Duty can make reservations, others Space-A.

DV/VIP: 5th AF/CSP, C-011-81-425-52-2511-EX-5-4141, O6+. Retirees and lower ranks Space-A.

TML Availability: Good, Oct-Mar. Difficult, other times.

CREDIT CARDS ACCEPTED: American Express.

Locator 225-8390   Medical 225-9111   Police 116

Too Late To Copy
Torii Station, D-315-644-4294. DV/VOQ/VAQ: D-315-634-1371. TLF:D-315-632-1000/1100.

White Beach Recreation Services, C-011-81-634-6952/6954, 8 cabins (**Snuggler's Cove**), $30 daily. Getaway Special (for 2) includes cabin or room, dinner and breakfast for $60-$70 daily.

KOREA

Camp Henry (RK02R8)
Housing Division
DEH, 23rd Support Group
Unit #15228
APO AP 96271-0164

TELEPHONE NUMBER INFORMATION: Main installation numbers: C-(USA) 011-82-53-470-7440/59, D-315-768-7440/59.

Location: NMC: Taegu, in city limits.

Lodging Office: Building 1712. C-(USA) **011-82-53-470-7459**, FAX 011-82-053-470-8948, DSN FAX 315-768-8948, D-315-768-7459, 24 hours.

TML: BEQ/BOQ. Building 1712, all ranks, leave or official duty. Single bedroom, private bath (24). Kitchenette, refrigerator, color TV in room & lounge, housekeeping service, washer/dryer. Rates: $26; $5 each additional person.

TML: DV/VIP. Building 1712, all ranks, leave or official duty. Bedroom, private bath (5). Kitchenette, refrigerator, color TV in room & lounge, housekeeping service, washer/dryer. Rates: $35, maximum charge $45, for 2 persons per room.

TML Availability: Very good. Best, Nov-Dec. Difficult, May-Aug.

Camp Page (RK03R8)
DEH USAG
ATTN: Billeting
APO AP 96208-0210

TELEPHONE NUMBER INFORMATION: Main installation numbers: C-(USA) 011-82-279-13-1110.

Location: From Seoul, take MSR#46 northeast into Chunchon City. NMC: Chunchon City, in city limits.

Lodging Office: Building T-452. C-(USA) **011-82-361-59-5331**, D-315-768-77459, 24 hours.

TML: BEQ. Buildings S-1304, S-1306, S-1307, E1-E9, leave or official duty. Combination of single shared bedrooms, and single private bedrooms, private bath (48). Kitchenette, refrigerator, Rates: Primarily used by permanent party members, no rates furnished.

TML: BOQ. Buildings S-1416, S-1129, officers, leave or official duty. Bedroom, private bath (48). Kitchenette, refrigerator. Rates: Primarily used by permanent party members, no rates furnished.

TML Availability: Good. Best, December. Difficult, June.

Medical 721-5857   **Police 721-5410**

KOREA

Camp Humphreys (RK08R8)
Housing Division
DEH, 23rd Support Group
Unit #15228
APO AP 96271-0164

TELEPHONE NUMBER INFORMATION: Main installation numbers: C-(USA) 011-82-333-690-7356, D-315-753-7356.

Location: Fifty (50) miles south of Seoul via Highway I, take Pyongtaek exit. Camp Humphreys is located 8 miles south of Pyongtaek. NMC: Pyongtaek, 8 miles north.

Lodging Office: Building S-247. **C-(USA) 011-82-333-690-7355,** FAX 011-82-333-690-7357, DSN FAX 315-753-7357, D-315-753-7355, Mon-Fri 0800-1700, Sat 0800-1200. After hours report to EOC, Bldg 251. Check in billeting, check out 1200.

TML: BEQ. Buildings 727, 728, 738, all ranks, leave or official duty. Single bedroom, private bath (6); single bedroom, hall bath (46). Refrigerator, color TV, housekeeping service, washer/dryer. Rates: $13. Active duty can make reservations, all others Space-A.

TML: BOQ. Buildings 203, 206, 254, all ranks, leave or official duty. Bedroom, private bath (5). Kitchenette, refrigerator, color TV, housekeeping service, washer/dryer (in Bldg 206). Rates: $13.

TML Availability: Fairly good. Difficult, Dec-Feb.

Don't miss seeing the Secret Garden and Puyong Pavilion in Seoul.

Medical 116   Police 110

Chinhae Fleet Activities (RK06R8)
Combined Bachelor Quarters, PSC 479
FPO AP 96269-1100

TELEPHONE NUMBER INFORMATION: Main installation numbers: C-(USA) 011-82-553-40-5110, D-315-762-5110, Chinhae OOD (Officer of the Day).

Location: On the east coast of Korea, south of Pusan. Take the Seoul-Pusan expressway to Pusan, exit and continue along the coast for 25 miles south.

Lodging Office: Billeting Office, duty hours. **C-(USA) 011-82-553-40-5336,** D-315-762-5336. After hours, C-011-82-553-40-5110, D-315-762-5110. FAX 011-82-553-40-5526, D-315-762-5526. Check in facility, check out 1200 hours daily.

TML: BOQ/BEQ. Buildings 722, 783, all ranks, leave or official duty. BOQ: bedroom, private bath (2); BEQ: bedroom, hall bath, (8). A/C, telephone, housekeeping service. Older structure, renovated. Rates: $15 per night. Duty can make reservations, others Space-A.

TML: DV/VIP. Building 710, DV suite (2), A/C telephone, housekeeping service. Rates: $15.

TML Availability: Very limited.

KOREA
Chinhae Naval Facility, continued

If you are lucky enough to be in Chinhae in April (1-15) you will see the city covered in cherry blossoms, folk dances, and visit fascinating street markets, plus many other activities. This is a very interesting port city.

Locator 791-3110   Medical 762-5415   Police 791-3110

Dragon Hill Lodge (RK09R8)
Unit 15335
APO AP 96205-0427

TELEPHONE NUMBER INFORMATION: Main installation number: C-(USA) 011-82-2-790-0016, (RK) 2-790-0016.

Location: Located on South Post, Yongsan, in Seoul. From Kimpo International Airport, enter the Olympic Stadium Expressway 88 for approximately 15 miles, then take the Panpo Bridge exit and cross the bridge. Look for the Capital Hotel on the right side as you come off the bridge. Stay on the right side of the road and do not go under ground where the road splits. Go to the major intersection and turn left (one mile from bridge), enter the 2nd gate on the left side (gate 10) and proceed to the Lodge. NMC: Seoul, in the city.

Lodging Office: None. Check in at front desk. **C-(USA) 011-82-2-790-0016,** (RK) 790-0016, D-315-738-2222, FAX-011-822-790-1576 (FAX Korea 2-792-1576).

TML: Dragon Hill Lodge, all ranks, leave or official duty. Handicapped accessible. Bedroom, double bed, double sleeper sofa, private bath (289); 9th floor family rooms - bedroom, 2 double beds, living room w/sleeper sofa, private bath (10). Family rooms may be expanded as a three bedroom accommodation (additional charge). Non-smoking rooms on 7th and 8th floors. Five handicapped accessible rooms (partial ambulatory). Even numbered rooms face front of hotel, odd numbers face garden. A/C, kitchenette, microwave (in 277 of the 289 rooms), refrigerator, utensils, color TV, VCR, clock radio, phone, housekeeping service, cots ($10), cribs, ice vending, washer/dryer, recreation facilities, Oasis coffee shop/Mexican restaurant, Greenstreet restaurant, (breakfast, lunch, dinner, Sunday brunch) Sables fine dining restaurant, Bentleys Pub, Whispers Lounge, Anthony's pizza, deli/bakery. Other services: bank, ATM, hair care center, tailor shop, post exchange, bookstore, shopping arcade, fitness & health club. Rates: $90 per room for TDY, PCS personnel (Military, all ranks and grades, DoD civilians); $60 per room for leave/pass status (Chief Warrant 4, major-general, DoD civilians, foreign military, retirees, widows w/DD form 1173, DAV's); $50 per room for SSG-SGM, Warrant Officers 1-3, Lt-Capt); $40 Pvt-Sgt. Maximum 4 persons. All categories can make reservations. Pets can be boarded at vet clinic near Gate 17, South Post.

TML Availability: Good. Best, Oct-May.

CREDIT CARDS ACCEPTED: Visa, MasterCard and American Express.

See Myong-Dong (Seoul's Ginza), Korea House, Duksoo Palace. The National Museum and Folk Museum on Kyongbok Palace grounds acquaint visitors with Korean culture. Don't miss Walker Hill tourist complex twenty minutes away.

Locator 724-6830   Medical 737-5545   Police 724-8177

KOREA

Kunsan Air Base (RK05R8)
Kunsan Lodging
Bldg 392, Unit 2105
APO AP 96264-5000

TELEPHONE NUMBER INFORMATION: Main installation numbers: C-(USA) 011-82-654-470-1110, (RK) 0654-470-4604, D-315-782-1110.

Location: On the west central coast of RK. Exit from Seoul-Pusan expressway, directions to AB clearly marked. NMC: Kunsan City, 7 miles north.

Lodging Office: Building 392, **C-(USA) 011-82-654-470-4604**, FAX 011-82-654-472-5275, (ROK) 0654-470-4604, D-315-782-4604 24 hours daily. Check in billeting. Check out 1200 hours daily. Government civilian employee billeting.

TML: VOQ. Building 392, officers all ranks, leave or official duty, C-EX-4604. Bedroom, common bath (28). Refrigerator, A/C, color TV, housekeeping service, washer/dryer. Older structure. Rates: DVQ $14, VOQ/VAQ $9.50. Duty can make reservations, others Space-A.

TML Availability: Limited. **Ask about VAQ and DV quarters, above number.**

CREDIT CARDS ACCEPTED: Diners.

Kunsan is a deep water port on the Yellow Sea, and a major fishing port. The mountainous areas of Korea are dotted with temples and shrines of both Japanese and Korean influence and are set in magnificent natural scenery.

Locator 782-4351   Medical 782-4333   Police 782-4944

Osan Air Base (RK04R8)
51 SVS/SVML
Unit 2065, Bldg 771
APO AP 96278-2065

TELEPHONE NUMBER INFORMATION: Main installation numbers: C-(USA) 011-82-333-661-4110, (RK) 1-011-82-661-4110, D-315-784-4110.

Location: Exit the Seoul-Pusan expressway 38 miles south of Seoul. Directions to Osan AB clearly marked. Adjacent to Song Tan City. NMC: Seoul, 38 miles north.

Lodging Office: Building 771, **C-(USA) 011-82-331-661-1844/4597**, FAX 011-82-331-661-4872, DSN FAX 315-784-4872, D-315-784-1844/4597, 24 hours daily. Check in billeting 1200, check out 1200 hours daily. Government civilian employee billeting.

TML: TLF. Building 1007, all ranks, leave or official duty. Separate bedroom, sleeps 5, private bath (17). Kitchen, fully equipped, A/C, color TV, housekeeping service, cribs, washer/ dryer. Modern structure. Rates: $25.50 per unit. Maximum 5 per unit. Duty can make reservations, others Space-A.

KOREA
Osan Air Base, continued

TML: VOQ. Buildings 1001, 1093, 1094, officers, all ranks, leave or official duty. Bedroom, private bath (65). Kitchen, limited utensils, A/C, color TV, housekeeping service, cribs, washer/ dryer. Modern structure. Rates: $9.50 per person, maximum $18 per room. Maximum 2 persons. Duty can make reservations, others Space-A.

TML: VOQ/VAQ. Officers, building 745, 746, all ranks, leave or official duty. Bedroom with 2 beds, common bath (258). Refrigerator, community kitchen, limited utensils, A/C, color TV, housekeeping service, washer/dryer. Modern structure. Rates: $9.50 per person, maximum $12 per room. Duty can make reservations, others Space-A.

TML: DV/VIP. On Hill 180. Officer O6+, leave or official duty. Bedroom, private and semi-private baths (20); One separate bedroom suite, private bath. Refrigerator, A/C, color TV, housekeeping service, cribs/cots, washer/dryer. Modern structure. Rates: $10 per person. Maximum 2 persons. Duty can make reservations, others Space-A.

DV/VIP: Protocol Officer, 7th AF, C-011-82-333-661-6020, O6+. Rates: $10. Retirees & lower ranks Space-A.

TML Availability: Best, Nov-Feb. Difficult, other times.

CREDIT CARDS ACCEPTED: American Express.

Don't miss seeing Duksoo Palace (home of the National Museum), Kyonbok and Changduk Palaces, and the Secret Garden and Puyong Pavilion in Seoul. Onyang (a hot spring resort), and Walker Hill resort shouldn't be missed.

Locator 784-1841   **Medical 911**   **Police 911**

Yongsan Army Garrison (RK07R8)
Lodging Office, Bldg 1112
APO AP 96205-5000

TELEPHONE NUMBER INFORMATION: Main installation numbers: C-(USA) 011-82-2-7913-1110, (RK) 2-7914-8205/8184, D-315-724-8205/8184.

Location: In the Yongsan district of Seoul. NMC: Seoul, in the city.

Lodging Office: Billeting Office, building 1112, **C-(USA) 011-82-2-7918-3220,** (RK) 2-7918-3220 24 hours daily. Check in facility, check out 1200 hours daily. No government civilian employee billeting.

TML: VOQ. Buildings 8102, 8103, 8104, officers all ranks, enlisted E7-E9, C-(USA) 011-82-2-7918-4249, Official duty only. Separate bedroom suites, private bath (3); two bedroom, shared bath (1). Refrigerator, A/C, cribs, color TV, housekeeping service, washer/dryer. Modern structure. Rates: $15 per person, maximum $20 per family. Duty can make reservations, others Space-A.

TML: VEQ. Buildings 4110, enlisted E1-E6, leave or official duty, C-(USA) 011-82-2-7918-2222. Separate bedroom, common bath (29). Refrigerator, community kitchen, A/C, color TV, housekeeping service, washer/dryer. Modern structure. Rates: $4 per room. Duty can make reservations, others Space-A.

KOREA
Yongsan Army Garrison, continued

TML: DVQ. Buildings 3723, 4436, 4464, 4468, officer O7+ or civilian equivalent, leave or official duty. C-EX-7913-3315. Separate bedroom, private bath. Community kitchen, kitchenette, complete utensils, cribs, color TV, A/C, housekeeping service. Modern structure. Rates: sponsor $25, adults $12.50, children $5. Duty can make reservations, others Space-A.

DV/VIP: Sec Joint Staff, Protocol Branch, SJS-P, HHC, EUSA, building 2472. C-011-82-2--7913-3315, D-315-723-3315, O7+ or civilian equivalent. Lower ranks Space-A.

TML Availability: Good, but reserve early.

Locator 2-7912-8205   Medical 293-4581   Police 3666

Too Late To Copy
Camp Hialeah, Bldg 508, C-011-82-51-801-3668, D-315-763-3668/7562, 0700-2100 hours, Mon-Sun. BEQ: 35 three-bedroom units, 12 two-bedroom units, 14 one-bedroom units. BOQ: 4 four-bedroom units, 24 three-bedroom unirs, 24 two-bedroom units. Rates: $15-$18.

Temporary Military Lodging Around the World - 315

NETHERLANDS

Brunssum Officers' Club (NT02R7)
Lodging Office, Bldg H105
APO AE 09703-5000

TELEPHONE NUMBER INFORMATION: Main installation numbers: C-(USA) 011-31-45-26-2230, (NT) 045-26-2230.

Location: Take Autobahn A-2, A-76 or E-9. Also NE-39, exit at Nuth, follow signs to Brunssum. HE: p-35, G/2. NMC: Heerlen, NT, 10 miles southwest.

Lodging Office: Officers' Club, or US Protocol Office, building H105. **C-(USA) 011-31-45-26-2230 ext. 3188,** (NT) 045-26-2230, 0800-2230 hours duty days. Call C-045-26-3188 (Schinnen) after hours. Check in facility, check out 1200 hours daily. Government civilian employee billeting in local hotels.

TML: Officers' Club, above number for information. Officers all ranks, leave or official duty. Suites, private bath (20); bedroom suites, private bath suites (DV/VIP) (2). Rates: 50 guilders single, 82 guilders double, extra bed 17 guilders. No pets. Support facilities at Schinnen Community, 54th Area Support Group, 10 miles. This is NATO Allied and not U.S. government billeting. Brunssum AFCENT BX available to U.S. Forces.

DV/VIP: PAO, building T-8, room 204, C-04493-7-331, O6+.

TML Availability: Limited.

Locator 04493-7-199   **Medical-04526-3-177**   **Police 04493-7-323**

NEW ZEALAND

Christchurch Naval Antarctic Support Unit (NZ01R8)
MWR Director
PSC 467
FPO AP 96531-2000

TELEPHONE NUMBER INFORMATION: Main installation numbers: C-(USA) 011-64-3-358-1475, (NZ) 358-1475, FAX: 011-64-3-358-1448

Location: From Christchurch City Square, left into Columbo St., right to Salisbury St, left to Park Terrace, right on Harper Ave, and west on Fendalton Road and Memorial Ave. to front gate. NMC: Christchurch, 6 miles East.

Lodging Office: Building 7. Write to: MWR Director, NASU Christchurch, PSC 467, FPO AP 96531-2000, **C-011-64-3-358-1475, FAX: 011-64-3-358-1448** (NZ)358-1448, 24 hours daily. Check in at facility, check out 1200 hours.

TML: BEQ. Buildings 7 & 8, enlisted & officers all ranks, leave or official duty. Bedroom, hall and communal bath (separate facilities for females) (30). Refrigerator, lounge microwave, color TV in lounge, housekeeping service, Essentials, drinks, snacks, literature, washer/dryer (separate building) iron available, pool table. Wood frame barracks construction. Rates: Single $10-$15, double $15-$20, no charge for infants. No reservations. Active duty accommodations provided in local community.

TML Availability: Very good all year.

Locator none **Medical 111** **Police 111**

PANAMA

Fort Clayton (PN02R3)
Bldg 518, Hospital Road
APO AA 34004-5000

TELEPHONE NUMBER INFORMATION: Main installation numbers: C-(USA) 011-507-281-1212, (PN) 281-1212, D-313-281-1212/287-3105 (after hours).

Location: Near the Pacific Ocean entrance to the Panama Canal. Take Gaillard Hwy toward the Miraflores Locks. NMC: Panama City, 8 miles southwest.

Lodging Office: Building 518, Hospital Road, **C-(USA) 011-507-287-4451/3251,** D-313-287-4202, (PN) 287-4451-3251, FAX 011-507-287-5609, DSN FAX 313-287-5609, 0700-1530 M-F. Check in billeting 1400, check out 1100 hours daily.

TML: Clayton Guest House. Building 518, all ranks, leave or official duty. Bedroom, private bath (34); separate bedroom, private bath (5). Refrigerator, A/C, color cable TV, recreation room & lounge, housekeeping service, cribs, washer/dryer, ice vending, La Mola restaurant. Older structure. Rates: $29 per person, $34 maximum; suites, $33 per person, $38 maximum for family. Official duty and hospital visits can make reservations, others Space-A.

TML: Gold Coast Inns, Ft Sherman. All ranks, C-(USA) **011-507-287-4451/3251,** D-313-287-4202. Check in from the Clayton Guest house in building 518, 24 hours, Houses fully furnished with two separate bedrooms and private bath (2). Kitchenette, cooking utensils, A/C, refrigerator, color TV, housekeeping service, washer/dryer, outdoor picnic tables with grills. Rates: $36 per person, $41 maximum charge. Duty can make reservations, others Space-A.

TML: Quarry Heights VOQ, in Panama City, building 119, enlisted E7+/officers, all ranks, leave or official duty. C-(USA) **011-507-287-4202,** 24 hours. Separate bedroom, private bath (13). Refrig, A/C, CATV, housekeeping service, vending machine. Older structure. Rates: $27 per person, $32 maximum charge. Duty can make reservations, others Space-A.

TML: DV/VIP. Casa Caribe, building 77, **Ft Amador,** enlisted E9/O6+, leave or official duty. Protocol: C-(USA) **011-507-287-5057/5058,** (PN) 87-5057/5059. Bedroom, private bath (4)0; separate bedroom with private bath (2). Refrigerator, A/C, color cable TV, housekeeping service, washer/dryer. Breakfast served M-F, 0630-0900. Rates: regular $32, $37 maximum charge; suite $36, $41 maximum charge. Duty can make reservations, others Space-A.

TML: VEQ. Building 130, E6 and below, leave or official duty, **C-(USA) 011-507-287-4451/3251,** D-313-287-4202. Check in from the Clayton Guest house in building 518, 24 hours, Shared room, common bath (19); Refrigerator, A/C color cable TV, housekeeping service, washer/dryer, vending machines. Rates: regular $14 per person. Duty can make reservations, others Space-A.

DV/VIP: Protocol Office, building 95, room 171. C-011-507-287-5057/8, E9/O6+, retirees and lower ranks Space-A.

TML Availability: Good, Nov-Jan. Difficult, other times.

CREDIT CARDS ACCEPTED: Visa, MasterCard and American Express.

PANAMA
Fort Clayton, continued

Panama City is a shoppers paradise - see the Via Espaa - and if you have time don't miss San Bas for a pre-Columbian vision, and the forts of Portobelo.

Locator 285-3139   Medical 282-5400/5111   Police 287-4401

Howard Air Force Base (PN01R3)
24th SVS/SVMH
APO AA 34001-5000

TELEPHONE NUMBER INFORMATION: Main installation numbers: C-(USA) 011-507-284-9805, (PN) 284-84-9805, D-313-284-9805.

Location: Adjacent to Thatcher Hwy (K-2) on Pacific side of Panama. NMC: Panama City, 10 miles west.

Lodging Office: Building 708, **C-(USA) 011-507-284-6411/5306**, FAX 011-507-284-4589 (for those on official orders only), (PN) 284-284-4914/5305 24 hours daily. Check in billeting 1200, check out 1200 hours daily. No government civilian employee billeting.

TML: TLF. Building 1511, all ranks, official duty. C-EX-4914/4556. Two bedroom apartments (6). Kitchen, complete utensils, A/C, color TV, housekeeping service, cribs/cots, washer/dryer. Older structure, refurbished. Rates: $24 per room per night. Maximum 6 per room. Duty can make reservations, others Space-A.

TML: VAQ. Building 519, enlisted E7-E9, official duty only. Separate bedroom, private bath (22). Kitchen, A/C, washer/dryer. Older structure. Rates: No charge. Permanent party only. No dependents.

TML: BOQ. Buildings 19, 21, officers all ranks, official duty only. Separate bedroom, private bath (48). Kitchen, A/C, washer/dryer. Rates: No charge. Permanent party only. No dependents.

TML: VOQ. Buildings 13, 14, 117, 119, 174, officers all ranks, leave or official duty. Bedroom, private bath (2); separate bedroom, private bath (32). Refrigerator, A/C, color TV, housekeeping service, washer/dryer, ice vending. Older structure, remodeled. Rates: $8.50 per person, maximum $17 per family. Maximum 2 per room. Duty can make reservations, others Space-A.

TML: DV/VIP. Buildings 16, 118, 519, officers O6+, leave or official duty. Separate bedroom suite, private bedroom (1); two bedroom suite, private bath (1); three bedroom suite, private bedroom (1). Kitchen, utensils, A/C, color TV, housekeeping service, washer/dryer, ice vending. Rates: $8.50 per person. Maximum 2 per room. Duty can make reservations, others Space-A.

DV/VIP: USAFSO/CCP, Howard, C-011-507-284-4601, O6+, retirees and lower ranks Space-A.

TML Availability: Difficult at all times.

In Panama City visit the Avenida de los Martires and Avenida Central for shopping. Don't miss the church on Santa Ana Plaza, and San Jose church in Old Panama. Casco Viejo is quaint with Spanish and French architecture.

Locator 84-5306/6411   Medical 84-4100   Police 84-4711

PANAMA

Panama Canal (Rodman) Naval Station (PN09R3)
Lodging Office, Bldg 77
Unit 6262
APO AA 34061-1000

TELEPHONE NUMBER INFORMATION: Main installation numbers: C-(USA) 011-507-283-3859, (PN) 283-3859, D-313-221-3859.

Location: On the west bank of the Panama Canal, one mile left of Tatcher Ferry Bridge (Bridge of the Americas). Panama City, 18 miles northwest.

Lodging Office: Building 77, **C-(USA) 011-507-283-4440/4619**, (PN) 283-4440/4619, 0600-2400 daily. Check in billeting, check out 1100 hours daily. After hours CDO, Quarter Deck, building 51, C-EX-83-4166. Government Civilian Employee billeting.

TML: Guest House, BOQ, BEQ. All ranks, official duty. Bedroom, private bath; suites, private bath; apartments, private bath; rooms, 2 beds, kitchenette, shared bath (enlisted); bedroom, shared bath (enlisted) (30). Kitchenette, complete utensils, color TV, housekeeping service, washer/dryer, ice vending. No pets. Modern structure. Rates: officers, $12, enlisted $6, VIP $25. Duty can make reservations, others Space-A.

DV/VIP: Combined Bachelor Quarters, US NAVSTA Rodman, unit 6262, FPO AA 34061, C-011-507-83-4440/4619, O5+, reservations, Space-A.

TML Availability: Difficult. Best Dec-Feb, difficult Jul-Sep.

Duty free shopping at the International Airport, and Colon Free Zone, and Folklore nights at local hotels featuring Panamanian Cuisine are favorite pastimes here. Fishing, both lake and ocean, the canal itself and historic sites are also popular.

Locator 283-3300   **Medical 284-3014**   **Police 283-5611/12**

PORTUGAL

Lajes Field, Azores (PO01R7)
Mid-Atlantic Lodge
65 SVS/SVML
Unit 8010
APO AE 09720-8010

TELEPHONE NUMBER INFORMATION: Main installation numbers: C-(USA) 011-351-95-540100, EX-5178/6176, (PO) 95-52101, D-314-723-1410 (CONUS direct). Contact: 65th MWRS/MWMH, unit 8010, APO AE 09720.

Location: On Terceira Island (Azores PO) 20 miles long & 12 miles wide. Lajes Field is 2 miles west of Praia da Vitoria, PO, on Mason Hwy. NMC: Lisbon, 850 miles east.

Lodging Office: Mid-Atlantic Lodge, Bldg T-166, **C-(USA) 011-351-95-540100,** FAX 011-351-95-540100 EXT 3790, (PO)95-5178/7283, 24 hours daily for check in at facility, check out 1200 hours. Government civilian employee billeting. Note: Kennel available on base (fee).

TML: TLF. Building T-306, all ranks, leave or official duty. Handicapped accessible. Bedroom apartments, living room, private bath (30). Kitchenette, color TV, cribs/cots, washer/dryer. Modern structure. Rate: $32 per room, $12 for additional room. Maximum 5 per room. Active duty PCS out with family can make reservations, others Space-A.

TML: VOQ, VAQ: $8 per night, reservations TDY, PCS only, others Space-A.

DV/VIP: Contact billeting office, O6+. Retirees and lower ranks Space-A, $14 per night.

TML Availability: Best, Nov-Apr. Difficult, May-Oct.

CREDIT CARDS ACCEPTED: American Express.

Each island is unique, visit them all, if you can. Attend a formal bullfight, or a street bullfight (the bull is not killed here!), or listen to one of many village bands perform during a colorful religious holiday procession.

Locator 6130/4237   Medical 23233   Police 23222

****Late Breaking Entry****

SINGAPORE

Sembawang (SI01R1)
497th Combat Training Squadron/Lodging
PSC 470, BOX 3018
FPO AP 96534-5000

TML: TLQ. Lodging has approximately 100 rooms, Space-A. Rates: 1 person, $50; 2 persons, $70; family, $100. Rates may decrease in January 1996. For more information call **C-011-65-711-6848.** American Express cards are accepted.

Medical 824-2961   Police 999

SPAIN

Moron Air Base (SP01R7)
APO AE 09643-5000
(This is a contingency base)

TELEPHONE NUMBER INFORMATION: Main installation numbers: C-(USA) 011-34-55-848111, FAX 011-34-55-848009, (SP) 95-58-48111, D-314-722-1110.

Location: Sevilla, Spain to Alcala, Spain on N-334, pass Alcala to SE-333. At intersection of SE-342 and B-333 proceed on SE-342 to Moron AB. Base well marked. NMC: Sevilla, 40 miles northwest.

Lodging Office: Hotel Frontera. ATTN: 496 ABS, building P-303, 1st St, **C-(USA) 011-34-55-848089,** (SP) 95-5-848089, 24 hours daily. Check in facility, check out 1200 hours daily. Government civilian employee lodging. **ATTENTION: AD not assigned in Spain, retired personnel, widow(ers), government civilian employees not assigned in Spain, dependents of all groups, are not permitted to purchase any articles free of Spanish taxes on any military installation, i.e. Foodland. Military ID card holder visitors to Spain are permitted to make purchases in open messes, lodging and NEX Mart. Also, personnel arriving by military air at Rota NAS are advised to contact security or passenger service for immigration clearance. This notice applies to other Spanish listings.**

TML: VOQ/VAQ/DV/VIP. **Hotel Frontera**, building P-303, all ranks, leave or official duty. Separate bedroom, shared bath (55). Some DV suites, private bath. Refrigerator, community kitchen, A/C, color TV in lounge, housekeeping service, washer/dryer. Modern structure. Rates: $10 per person, $14 DV/VIP. Maximum 2 plus one crib per unit. Duty can make reservations, others Space-A.

DV/VIP: Lodging, C-and D-EX-2798. Determined by Commander, retirees Space-A.

TML Availability: Good Nov-Mar, fairly good Apr-Oct. Note: All numbers are C- or D- extensions.

CREDIT CARDS ACCEPTED: Diners.

Soak up the light and landscape of Sevilla along the Guadalquivir (Great River), and then visit the Cathedral (third largest in the world) and the Giralda Tower. Don't miss the gardens of the Alazar and the many others in the city.

Medical 8068   Police 8132

Rota Naval Air Station (SP02R7)
Box 2, FPO AE 09645-5000

TELEPHONE NUMBER INFORMATION: Main installation numbers: C-(USA) 011-34-56-82-2078, (From Spain but outside the province of Cadiz dial 956-822-078), D-314-727-0111.

Location: On Spain's South Atlantic Coast. Accessible from E-25 South and SP-342 West. HE: p-61, C-5. NMC: Cadiz, 22 miles south.

Lodging Office: No central billeting office. **C-(USA) 011-34-56-82-1750/51 (BOQ), 2460/2670/2680,** (SP) 821-750 (outside province of Cadiz) 956-82-2078, hours: 0730-1930 daily. Check in at facility, check out 1200. Government civilian employee billeting.

SPAIN
Rota Naval Air Station, continued

TML: Navy Lodge. Naval Station, Box 17, bldg 1674, check-in 1500-1800, check-out 1200, all ranks, leave or official duty. **C-(USA) 011-34-56-82-2643**, (SP)956-82-2643. Bedroom, private bath (48). Kitchen, microwave, utensils, A/C, color TV in room & lounge, housekeeping service, cribs/cots, coin washer/dryer. Modern structure. Rates: $52 per unit. Max 5 persons. All categories can make reservations.

TML: BOQ. Building 39, officers and enlisted, all ranks, leave or official duty, C-011-34-56-82-1750/51. Bedroom, shared bath (168); separate bedroom, private bath (43); suites, (VIP) (21). Refrigerator, A/C, color TV in lounge, housekeeping service, cribs, washer/dryer, 2 rec rooms, conference room. Modern structure. Rates: $8 per person, $18 per person (DV/VIP). Duty can make reservations, others Space-A.

TML: BEQ. Buildings 36-39, enlisted all ranks, leave or official duty, C-011-34-56-82-2460/2680. Bedroom, common bath (298); bedroom, hall bath (E7+) (54). Refrigerator (22/1-bedroom only), color TV in lounge, housekeeping service, washer/dryer. Modern structure, remodeled. Rates: $4 per person, maximum 1-4 persons per unit. Duty can make reservations, others Space-A.

DV/VIP: Protocol Office. Building 1, 2nd floor, C-011-34-56-82-2744. O6+. Retirees Space-A.

TML Availability: Good, winter months. Difficult, Jun-Sep.

CREDIT CARDS ACCEPTED: The Navy Lodge accepts Visa, MasterCard and American Express.

Gate security is strict (administered by Spanish Military Police). Commissary and NEX unavailable to retirees. Inquire at Navy Family Services about tours of Cadiz, a shopper's delight. Inquire at Osborne and Terry Bodegas for a tour of sherry facilities.

Locator 2222   **Medical 3305**   **Police 2000/1**

Temporary Military Lodging Around the World - 323

TURKEY

Incirlik Air Base (TU03R9)
39 SVS/SVML
Unit 8915, Box 165
APO AE 09824-0165

TELEPHONE NUMBER INFORMATION: Main installation numbers: C-(USA) 011-90-322-119062/111285, (TU) 322-119062/111285, D-314-676-1110.

Location: From Adana, east on E-5 for 3 miles, left at sign for Incirlik. Base is clearly marked. NMC: Adana, 3 miles west.

Lodging Office: Building 1081, 7th St, 24 hours daily. Check in facility 1300, check out 1100 (Space-A), 1200 hours (all others) daily. C-(USA) **011-90-322-3161774/80**, (TU) 322-3221774/80-EX-66709. D-314-676-937, DSN FAX 314-676-9341. Government civilian employee billeting.

TML: TLF. Building 1066, **Hodja**. All ranks, leave or official duty. Separate bedroom, living room, dining room, private bath (49). Kitchen, complete utensils, microwave, A/C, color TV in room & lounge, housekeeping service, cribs/cots, washer/dryer, ice vending, facilities for DAVs, irons, clock-radios. Modern structure. Rates: $32 per unit; $50 double. TDY/PCS can make reservations, others Space-A.

TML: VOQ. Buildings 934/36/38/40/52, 1010/12, officers, all ranks. Leave or official duty. Bedroom, shared bath (24); bedroom, private bath (64); bedroom, 2 beds, private bath (may be reserved for air crews) (12). Refrigerator, A/C, color TV in room & lounge, housekeeping service, washer/dryer. Older structure, renovated. Rates: $14 per person. Duty can make reservations, others Space-A.

TML: VAQ. Buildings 1004/42/44/46/48/50/52, 902/04/06/08/18/20, enlisted, all ranks, leave or official duty. Bedroom, 2 beds, private bath (may be reserved for air crews) (36); bedroom, 2/3 beds, common bath (E1-E6)(no females or children due to common bath) (156); separate bedroom suites, private bath (E7-E9) (7 day limit) (2). Refrigerator, A/C, color TV, housekeeping service, washer/dryer. Older structure, renovated. Rates: $8 per person. Duty can make reservations, others Space-A.

TML: DV/VIP. Building 1072, officer O6+, leave or official duty. Separate bedroom suites, private bath (6); bedroom, private bath, contract quarters for TDY, funded travel orders only (95). Kitchen, limited utensils, A/C, color TV, housekeeping service, washer/dryer, ice vending, alcoholic beverages and soft drinks stocked in room on "Honor System." Older structure. Rates: $14 per person. Duty can make reservations, others Space-A.

DV/VIP: Protocol Office, 39 TACG/CCE, C-EX-6347, E9, O6/GS-15+. Retirees and lower ranks Space-A.

TML Availability: Fair all year.

CREDIT CARDS ACCEPTED: Diners.

TURKEY
Incirlik Air Base, continued

Historic sites near Adana include Misis (Roman), Yilanlikale (Castle of Snakes), Karatepe (Hittite) and Payas (16th Century and Alexander the Great). There's much more to see and do. A tour here is "no turkey"!

Locator 6289   Medical 6666   Police 3200

Izmir Air Station (TU04R9)
Military Lodging Office
Izmir Air Station
Facility 77, Room 104
APO AE 09824-5000

TELEPHONE NUMBER INFORMATION: Main installation numbers: C-(USA) 011-90-232-484-5360, (TU) 232-484-5360, D-314-675-1110 EX-3379, FAX-011-90-232-484-5564.

Location: In the center of Izmir on the central west coast of Turkey. HE: p-82, G/6. NMC: Izmir, in the city.

Lodging Office: Pullman Hotel. C-011-90-232-4890 Ext 256, D-314-675-1110-EX-33379, 0700-2300 daily. Check in facility, check out 1200 hours daily. Government civilian employee billeting.

TML: TLF. Pullman Hotel, all ranks, leave or official duty, handicapped accessible. Bedroom, private bath (63). Refrigerator, A/C, color TV in room & lounge, housekeeping service, cribs/cots, washer/dryer, ice vending (The 63 rooms are leased in a 5 Star commercial hotel). Rates: $28-$44 per room. Maximum 3 per unit. Duty can make reservations. TDY/PCS have priority, others Space-A.

DV/VIP: Protocol Office, 7241 ABG/CCE, facility #48, room 603. D-314-675-1110-EX-3341, O6+/E9. Retirees and lower ranks Space-A.

TML Availability: Good, except May-Oct.

CREDIT CARDS ACCEPTED: Visa, MasterCard, American Express and Diners.

Visit the tours desk, MWR for one day, overnight and multi-day excursions to Ephesus, Pergamon, Pamukkale, Aphrodisias, Istanbul, and the Greek Islands. East and west meet here, don't miss the fascinating consequences!

Locator 3431   Medical 3357   Police 3222

Temporary Military Lodging Around the World - 325

UNITED KINGDOM

RAF Alconbury (UK01R7)
423rd SVS/SVMH
Bldg 639, Texas St
APO AE 09470-5000

TELEPHONE NUMBER INFORMATION: Main installation numbers: C-(USA) 011-44-1480-82-3000, (UK) 01480-82-3000, D-314-268-3000.

Location: From London, take A-1 North to A-14, exit marked RAF Alconbury, follow signs. Approximately 65 miles north of London. HE: p-13, D/3. NMC: Huntingdon, 4 miles east.

Lodging Office: Building 639, Texas St, C-(USA) **011-44-1480-6000**, (UK) 01480-82-6000, FAX 011-44-1480-45-4127, 24 hours daily. Check in facility 1400, check out 1000 hours daily. Government civilian employee billeting.

TML: VOQ. Buildings 639, 640, officers all ranks, leave or official duty. Bedroom, shared bath (44); suites, private bath (DV/VIP) (7). Refrigerator, color TV in room & lounge, housekeeping service, cribs/cots, washer/dryer, telephone. Modern structure. Rates: room $10 per person, suite $14.50 per person. Maximum 2 per suite. Duty can make reservations, others Space-A.

TML: VAQ. Building 652, 692, enlisted all ranks. Two bedroom, shared bath (38); bedroom suites, shared bath (4); separate bedroom suites, private bath (3). Building 692: two per room, central bathroom (22). Refrigerator, color TV/cable, housekeeping service, washer/dryer. Modern structure. Rates: $8 per person rooms; $10-$14 per person suites. Duty can make reservations, others Space-A.

TML: All ranks TLF also available. Suites, private bath (20). Rates: $21 per unit.

DV/VIP: Hq 423rd ABW, C-EX-3111/3112, O6+. Retirees and lower ranks Space-A.

TML Availability: Good, Aug-Mar. Difficult, other times.

CREDIT CARDS ACCEPTED: Visa, MasterCard and American Express.

East Anglia, Essex, Suffolk and Norfolk is full of historical sights. Start with the village of Little Stukeley (interesting church with carvings), and pass on to Huntingdon, where Romans first settled.

Locator 2565   Medical 116   Police 114

Diego Garcia, U.S. Navy Support Facility (UK05R7)
Combined Bachelor Quarters
PSC 466, Box 31
FPO AP 96464-0031

TELEPHONE NUMBER INFORMATION: D-315-370-011 (No commercial phone service).
Location: In the Chagos Archipelago, approximately 1000 miles off the southern tip of India in the Indian Ocean. NMC: Colombo, Sri Lanka, 900 air miles northeast.

UNITED KINGDOM
Diego Garcia Support Facility, continued

Lodging Office: Billeting Office. D-315-270-4415, 24 hours daily. Check in billeting, check out 1200 hours.

TML: BOQ/BEQ. All ranks, active duty/contractors on official business only. Shared room, private bath (150). Refrigerator, TV in lounge and rooms, housekeeping service, essentials, washer/dryer, ice vending. Rates: enlisted $2, officers $6.

DV/VIP: D-315-370-4415, O6+.

ALL PERSONNEL MUST APPLY FOR "AREA CLEARANCE A MINIMUM OF 30 DAYS PRIOR TO TRAVEL TO DIEGO GARCIA. ACCESS IS AVAILABLE ONLY VIA AMC OUT OF NORFOLK OR YOKOTA, JAPAN. NO FAMILIES ARE PERMITTED ON THE ISLAND.

Locator 4830   Medical 4748   Police 95

Edzell Naval Security Group Activity (UK06R7)
Bachelor's Quarters
FPO AE 09419-5000

TELEPHONE NUMBER INFORMATION: Main installation numbers: C-(USA) 011-44-1356-64-2218, (From UK Edzell 0356-64-2218).

Location: From Aberdeen take A-90 South, follow Perth/Dundee signs. Last town before Edzell is Lawrencekirk, look for RAF Edzell signs to base. HE: p-6, G/6. NMC: Aberdeen, 40 miles north.

Lodging Office: Campbell Hall, C-(USA) **011-44-1356-64-2218,** (UK) 0356-64-2218, 24 hours daily. Check in facility, check out 1000 hours daily. Government civilian employee billeting.

TML: Navy Lodge. All ranks, leave or official duty, **C-(USA) 011-44-1356-64-2633,** (UK) 0356-64-2633. Check in 1500-1800, check out 1200. Two queen beds/private bath (15). One handicapped accessible unit and four (4) non-smoking units. Kitchenette w/microwave, utensils, CATV, clocks, complimentary coffee/tea, cribs, cots, dining table, hair dryers, high chairs, washer/dryer, ice, irons/ironing boards, housekeeping service, playground, snack machine. Rates: $70. Duty can make reservations, PCS priority, others Space-A.

TML: BOQ. Officers' Open Mess. Officers all ranks, leave or official duty, **C-(USA) 011-44-1356-64-2218,** FAX 011-44-1356-64-2377, (UK) 0356-64-2218, D-314-229-4218. Separate bedroom, private bath (3). Kitchen, limited utensils, housekeeping service, washer/dryer. Modern structure. Rates: $8 per person, VIP suite $15 (must be booked through CO's secretary). Maximum 2-3 persons per unit. Duty can make reservations, others Space-A. Three transient BOQ rooms available.

TML: BEQ. Enlisted Mess. Twelve (12) rooms available, microwave, coffee pot, TV, housekeeping service. Active duty can make reservation, others Space-A.

DV/VIP: PAO, Building 22, C-(USA) 011-44-1356-64-2237, D-314-229-43337, O7+.

TML Availability: Good, Nov-Feb. Difficult, other times.

UNITED KINGDOM
Edzell Naval Security Group Activity, continued

Edzell has become a resort, with golf course, tennis and bowling green. Beautiful walks in every direction, and castle ruins are nearby. Aberdeen and Dundee, both large cities, are within an hour's drive.

Locator 2351　　　　　　Medical 2264/5　　　　　　Police 2880/2882

RAF Fairford (UK11R7)
Stirling House
ATTN: 720th ABG/SBVH
APO AE 09456-5000
(This is a contingency base)

TELEPHONE NUMBER INFORMATION: Main installation numbers: C-(USA) 011-44-285-714000, (UK) 0285-714000, D-314-247-1110.

Location: Eighty miles west of London and 10 miles east of Cirencester. Take A-417 from Cirencester to Fairford. HE: p-13, B/12. NMC: Oxford, 18 miles east.

Lodging Office: Stirling House. Building 551, C-(USA) **011-44-285-712784**, (UK) **0285-712784 or 0285-714962**, d-314-247-4272, FAX-011-44-285-714150, Due to being in care-taker status, call ahead to check availability for Space available. Reservations taken for O6 and above for space available. M-F 0730-1700. Sa-Su 0800-1200. Check in lodging, check out 1200 hours daily. Government civilian employee billeting.

TML: TLF. Building 551. All ranks, leave or official duty. Bedroom, private bath (8). Kitchen, utensils, color TV in lounge, cribs, washer/dryer, ice machine. Handicapped accessible facilities. Modern structure. Rates: $20 per night per person. Duty can make reservations, others Space-A.

TML: VOQ. Building 551. All ranks, leave or official duty. Bedroom, private bath (38). Kitchen, utensils, washer/dryer, ice machine. Modern structure. Rates: $8 per night per person. Duty can make reservations, others Space-A.

TML: VAQ. Building 551. All ranks, leave or official duty. Bedroom, private bath (6). Kitchen, utensils, washer/dryer, ice machine. Modern structure. Rtes $8 per night per person. Duty can make reservations, others Space-A.

TML: DV Quarters, building 551. O6+, leave or official duty. Suites, private bath (4); SNCO suites, private bath (1). Kitchen, utensils, washer/dryer, ice machine. Rates: $10 per night per person.

DV/VIP: Command Section, building 2. EX-4200/4800.

TML Availability: Fairly good. Best Nov-Mar. Difficult other times.

The Cotswolds is one of the most beautiful parts of England. Fairford boasts a 15th century church with magnificent stained glass windows, Cirencester, 10 miles west offers shops and services, a sports center and the Cornium Museum.

Locator 4477　　　　　　Medical D-314-263-5224　　　　　　Police 4477

UNITED KINGDOM

RAF Lakenheath (UK07R7)
SVS/SVML
Unit 5185, Box 70
APO AE 09464-5000

TELEPHONE NUMBER INFORMATION: Main installation numbers: C-(USA) 011-44-1638-52-1110, (UK) 1638-52-1110, D-314-226-1110.

Location: From London, go north on the M-11 to the A-11 to A-1065. HE: p-13, E/1. NMC: Cambridge, 30 miles south.

Lodging Office: Liberty Lodge, Building 955, **C-(USA) 011-44-1638-52-1844/2172,** FAX 011-44-1638-52-6717, DSN FAX 314-226-6717, D-314-226-1844/2172, (UK) 0638-52-1844/2172, 24 hours daily. Check in facility 1300 hours, check out 1000 hours daily. Kitchen, complete utensils, color TV, housekeeping service, cribs/cots, washer/dryer. Modern structure. Rates: $28-36.50 per unit, per night. Duty can make reservations, others Space-A. No pets.

TML: VOQ. Building 978, all ranks, leave or official duty. Bedroom, private bath (56). Shared kitchen, housekeeping service, color TV, washer/dryer. Rates: $8 per person. Maximum 2 per unit. Duty can make reservations, others Space-A. No pets.

TML: VAQ. Buildings 955, 957, 980, all ranks. Shared bedroom (E1-E4), shared bath (39); shared bedrooms (E5-E6), private bath, shared kitchen (30); SNCO suites (E7-E9) with private bath, private kitchen, (9), color TV, housekeeping service, washer/dryer. Rates: $8 per person shared rooms, $17.50 per person SNCO suites. Maximum 2 persons. Duty can make reservations, others Space-A. No pets.

TML: DV/VIP. Various buildings, officers O6+, enlisted E9, leave or official duty. C-0638-52-3500, D-314-226-3500. Enlisted separate bedroom, private bath (3); officer separate bedroom, private bath (4). Kitchenette, cribs, color TV, housekeeping service, washer/dryer. Older structure. Rates: $14 per person, maximum $28. No pets. Duty can make reservations thru 48 FW/Protocol, ext 2444, others Space-A.

DV/VIP: 48 TFW/CCP, building 1156. C-EX-3500, O6+ & E9. Retirees and lower ranks Space-A. **Note: all numbers are C- or D- extensions.**

TML Availability: Limited.

Don't miss seeing Cambridge College, which attracts thousands of tourists each year. Visit the ITT Travel office for information on the many attractions of London. Lakenheath is the largest US Air Force operated facility in England. Shuttle bus to Mildenhall departs 50 minutes after the hour 0650-1450.

Locator 1841   **Medical 116**   **Police 114**

Temporary Military Lodging Around the World - 329

UNITED KINGDOM

London Service Clubs (UK13R7)
Union Jack Club
Sandell Street, Waterloo
London, SE1 8UJ, United Kingdom

TELEPHONE NUMBER INFORMATION: C-(USA) 011-44-171-928-6401, (UK) 0171-928-6401, FAX 011-44-171-620-0565.

Location: Opposite Waterloo Station (train), central London. HE: p-13, D/3. NMC: London, in the city, opposite Waterloo Train Station.

Lodging Office: Address as above. Advance booking office C-(USA) **011-44-171-928-4814**, (UK) 0171-928-4814, FAX 011-44-171-620-0565, the club embodies the original Women's Services and Families Club. *Allied Forces are welcomed and granted Temporary Honorary Membership, 24 hours.* Check in 1300 hours, check out 1000 hours daily.

TML: Club/Hotel. **All ranks, leave/vacation only.** Reservations accepted above number. All charges include VAT. Check accepted when supported by cheque card. Visa, Access and Switch cards accepted. Meals paid for when taken, 10% discount for 7 days booking or more, deposit of one night when booking, refundable if canceled 48 hours in advance of arrival.

Other: Rooms, single (208); rooms, twin-bed (60). Wash basins, H/C water, with baths, showers, and bath (WC) centrally located on each floor; rooms, private shower, WC (65); twin-bed rooms, private bath (25); family suites, twin beds (35), double bunk-bed, private bath and WC (10). Bar, color TV, launderette, reading and writing rooms, conference and banqueting areas. **Rates:** Single, £20.00-£28.10. Double, £36.30-£52.40. Family suites from £53.20. Excellent public transportation service, limited car parking facilities. Club will provide rates and other info upon request. **An Officers' Annex recently opened consists of a bar/anteroom, a dining room, and bedroom accommodations for individuals and families. All serving and retired officers are eligible.**

Note: This is a private club and is not government/military billeting.

TML Availability: Good, but book early.

CREDIT CARDS ACCEPTED: Visa, MasterCard, American Express and Diners.

A ten minute walk takes you to the West End, Theaterland and the Savoy (for high tea - necktie and jacket required!). All of London is easily accessible by bus or train. Don't miss a trip to Buckingham Palace, the Tower of London and all the history of London!

Victory Services Club
63/79 Seymour Street
London W2 2HF, United Kingdom

TELEPHONE NUMBER INFORMATION: C-(USA) **011-44-171-723-4474**, (UK) 0171-723-4474, D-none, FAX 011-44-171-724-1134.

Location: Two blocks from the Marble Arch station, easy walking distance to the American Embassy, Navy Annex, Mayfair and Oxford Streets. HE: p-13, D/3. NMC: London, in the city.

UNITED KINGDOM
Victory Services Club, continued

Lodging Office: Same as above, reservations as above. **This is a members only club.** The following are eligible to join. A) serving and ex-service personnel of all ranks of the Armed Forces of the Crown, including those of the Commonwealth and members of NATO Forces; B) spouses of members of the club; C) widows and widowers of ex-service personnel. **The membership year is from 1 April and 31 March. Membership Fees: £10 annually, £200 pounds lifetime.** Write to the club for an application and further details. **Serving personnel are not required to pay membership fees.**

TML: Club/hotel. All ranks. Bedroom accommodations for 300 members with 753 twin/double bedrooms, some with private bath. Checks accepted when supported by a cheque card. Club facilities include a modern buttery, grill room, bar lounge, game room, television rooms and library. Rates: twin rooms £44.50; single rooms from £19.50. Twin rooms with private baths available at £55. All categories can make reservations.

TML Availability: Good, but book early.

CREDIT CARDS ACCEPTED: Visa and MasterCard.

Founded in 1907, the present magnificent site was opened in 1948. In WWII it was the site of the American Red Cross Columbia Club - the largest in Great Britain.

RAF Mildenhall (UK08R7)
100 SVS/SVML
Unit 4905, Box 400
APO AE 09459-5000

TELEPHONE NUMBER INFORMATION: Main installation numbers: C-(USA) 011-44-1638-54-6000/1844, D-314-238-6000/1844, 24 hours.

Location: From London or Cambridge follow A-11(M) to Newmarket and Barton Mills. Take A-1101 for 2.5 miles through Mildenhall Town to Beck Row Village and the AB. HE: p-13, E/1. NMC: Cambridge, 30 miles southwest.

Lodging Office: Building 459, Reservations: **C-(USA) 011-44-1638-54-2655**, FAX 011-44-1638-54-3688, (UK) (01638)-54-2655, D-314-238-2655. Open 24 hours daily. Check in facility 1500, check out 1100 hours daily. Government civilian employee billeting. Lodging manager, building 438, 100 SVS/SVL, C-(USA) 011-44-1638-54-3044, (UK) (01638) 54-3044, D-314-238-3044, open Mon-Fri 0730-1630 hours.

TML: TLF. Building 104, all ranks. Bedroom apartments, private bath (40). Kitchen, microwave, complete utensils, CATV/VCR, complimentary video rental, housekeeping service, cribs, washer/dryer. Modern structure. Rates: $23 per unit. Maximum 4 per room. Duty can make reservations, others Space-A.

TML: VAQ. 100, 200 and 400 area, enlisted all ranks, leave or official duty. Shared rooms with open bay rest rooms, some bedrooms, private bath (46). CATV, housekeeping service, washer/dryer. Rates: $10 per person. Duty can make reservations, others Space-A.

TML: VOQ. 200 and 400 area. Officers all ranks, leave or official duty. Bedroom, private bath (42). CATV, housekeeping service, washer/dryer. Rates: $10.00 per person. Duty can make reservations, others Space-A.

Temporary Military Lodging Around the World - 331

UNITED KINGDOM
RAF Mildenhall

TML: DV/VIP. Officer O6+, leave or official duty. Bedroom suites, private bath (3). Rates: $14. Duty can make reservations, others Space-A.

DV/VIP: Protocol Office, 3rd AF, building 239. C-011-44-1-638-54-2777, O7+. Retirees and lower ranks (O6) Space-A.

TML Availability: Extremely limited. Best, Nov-Dec. Note: All numbers C- or D-extensions.

CREDIT CARDS ACCEPTED: Visa, MasterCard and American Express.

Shopping and antique hunting is popular in the area. Discover the story of Mildenhall Treasure in the Mildenhall Museum on High Street. Most active Space-A airport in the UK. Daily Bus to RAF Lakenheath and AMC Terminal.

Locator 2669   **Medical 2657**   **Police 2667**

Portsmouth Royal Sailors Home Club (UK10R7)
Queen Street
Portsmouth Hampshire
PO1 3HS
United Kingdom 01705 824231

TELEPHONE NUMBER INFORMATION: C-(USA) 011-44-170-582-4231.

Location: The club is conveniently located near the Portsmouth HM Naval Base. Take Motorway A27/M27 to M275, follow signs to Portsmouth HM Naval Base and the Home Club.

Lodging Office: Queen Street, Portsmouth, PO1, 3HS. **C-011-44-170-582-4231**, FAX (USA) 011-44-170-529-3496.

TML: Residency club. All ranks. This club has 46 single rooms; 34 double rooms; 7 family rooms; 1 DV Suite, and 31 smaller rooms. Color TV, essentials, housekeeping service, coin washer/dryer, cribs. Handicapped accessible. Rates: £47 for double includes breakfast, £22-25 for single. There is a £5 membership fee and the Value Added Tax is 17.5%. Payment in cash or with an English bank traveler cheque.

The Carvery Restaurant is open from 1200-1400 hours and from 1800-2300 hours daily. Entress range from £2.70 to £5.50. This is a high quality restaurant with full menu and excellent service at moderate prices. The club bar has good selections of beers, wines and spirits. Bar hours are 1000-2300 hours daily.

Visit Naval Heritage and D-Day Museum.

CREDIT CARDS ACCEPTED: Visa.

Too Late To Copy
Other non-government TML in England is available at the **Royal Fleet Club**. See page 348 for more information.

APPENDIX A

Country and State Abbreviations Used in this Book

COUNTRY

AN-Antigua
AU-Austraila
BE-Belgium
CN-Canada
CU-Cuba
GE-Germany
GR-Greece
GU-Guam*
IC-Iceland
IT-Italy

JA-Japan
NT-Netherlands
NZ-New Zealand
PN-Panama
PO-Portugal (Azores)
PR-Puerto Rico*
RK-Republic of Korea
TU-Turkey
UK-United Kingdom
US-United States

* United States Possession

STATE

AK-Alaska
AL-Alabama
AR-Arkansas
AZ-Arizona
CA-California
CO-Colorado
CT-Connecticut
DC-District of Columbia
DE-Delaware
FL-Florida
GA-Georgia
HI-Hawaii
IA-Iowa
ID-Idaho
IL-Illinois
IN-Indiana
KS-Kansas
KY-Kentucky
LA-Louisiana
MA-Massachusetts
MD-Maryland
ME-Maine
MI-Michigan
MN-Minnesota
MO-Missouri
MS-Mississippi

MT-Montana
NE-Nebraska
NC-North Carolina
ND-North Dakota
NH-New Hampshire
NJ-New Jersey
NM-New Mexico
NY New York
NV-Nevada
OH-Ohio
OK-Oklahoma
OR-Oregon
PA-Pennsylvania
RI-Rhode Island
SC-South Carolina
SD-South Dakota
TN-Tennessee
TX-Texas
UT-Utah
VA-Virginia
VT-Vermont
WA-Washington
WI-Wisconsin
WV-West Virginia
WY-Wyoming

APPENDIX B

General Abbreviations Used in this Book

This appendix contains general abbreviations used in this book in order to save space. Commonly understood abbreviations and standard abbreviations found in addresses have not been included.

A
AAF-Army Airfield
AAFES-Army & Air Force Exchange Service
AB-Air Base
A/C-Air Conditioning
ACS-Army Community Services
AD-Active Duty
ADT-Active Duty for Training
AF-Air Force
AFAF-Air Force Auxiliary Field
AFB-Air Force Base
AFCENT BX-Allied Forces Central Europe Base Exchange
AFRB-Air Force Reserve Base
AFRC-Air Force Reserve Center
AFRC-Armed Forces Recreation Center
AFRES-Air Force Reserve
AFS-Air Force Station
AIRVAC-Air Evacuation
AMC-Army Medical Center
AMC-Air Mobility Command
ANGB-Air National Guard Base
APG-Army Proving Ground
APO-Army Post Office
APT-Airport
ARB-Air Reserve Base
AS-Air Station
ATM-Automatic Teller Machine

B
BAQ-Bachelor Airmen's Quarters
BEQ-Bachelor Enlisted Quarters
BOQ-Bachelor Officers' Quarters
BQ-Bachelor Quarters (Navy)
BX-Base Exchange

C
C-Commercial Telephone System
CATV-color cable television
CBQ-Combined Bachelor Quarters
CG-Coast Guard
CGAS-Coast Guard Air Station
CGES-Coast Guard Exchange Service
CMDR-Commander
CO-Commanding Officer

CO-Commanding Officer
CP-Command Post
CPO-Chief Petty Officer
CPOQ-Chief Petty Officer Quarters
CSM-Command Sergeant Major

D
D-Defense Switched Network
DAV-Disabled American Veterans
DM-Deutsche Mark
DoD-Department of Defense
DSN FAX-Defense Switched Network Fax
DV-Distinguished Visitor
DVOQ-Distinguished Visiting Officers' Quarters
DVQ-Distinguished Visitor Quarters

E
ETS-European Telephone System
EX-Telephone Extension Number

F
FPO-Fleet Post Office
FT-Fort
FTS-Federal Telephone System
FY-Fiscal Year

G
GH-Guest House
GM-General Manager

H
HE-Hallwag Europe Road Atlas
HQ-Headquarters

I
IAP-International Airport
ID-Identification
ITR-Information, Ticketing and Registration
ITT-Information, Tickets & Tours

K
Km-Kilometer

M
MC-Marine Corps
MCAS-Marine Corps Air Station
MCB-Marine Corps Base
MCLB-Marine Corps Logistics Base
MCRD-Marine Corps Recruit Depot
MCX-Marine Corps Exchange
MEDEVAC-Medical Evacuation
MP-Military Police
MWR-Morale, Welfare and Recreation

N
NAB-Naval Amphibious Base
NAS-Naval Air Station
NAVSTA-Naval Station
NB-Naval Base
NCO-Noncommissioned Officer
NEX-Navy Exchange
NG-National Guard
NMC-Nearest Major City
NOAA-National Oceanic & Atmospheric Administration
NS-Naval Station
NSA-National Security Agency
NSB-Navy Submarine Base
NSO-Navy Security Office
NSWC-Naval Surface Weapon Center
NTC-Naval Training Center
NWC-Naval Weapons Center

O
O'Club-Officers' Club
OD-Officer of the Day
OIC-Officer in Charge
OOD-Officer of the Day

P
PAO-Public Affairs Office
PCS-Permanent Change of Station
PMO-Provost Marshall's Office
PX-Post Exchange

R
RAF-Royal Air Force
REC-Recreation

S
SATO-Scheduled Airlines Ticket Office
SDNCO-Senior Duty Noncommissioned Officer
SDO-Staff Duty Officer
SNCO-Senior Noncommissioned Officer
Space-A-space available

T
TAD-Temporary Attached Duty
TAQ-Temporary Airmen's Quarters
TDY-Temporary Duty
TEQ-Temporary Enlisted Quarters
TFL-Temporary Family Lodging
TLA-Temporary Lodging Allowance
TLF-Transient Lodging Facility
TLQ-Temporary Living Quarters
TML-Temporary Military Living
TOQ-Transient Officers' Quarters
TQ-Temporary Quarters
TVEQ-Temporary Visiting Enlisted Quarters
TVOQ-Temporary Visiting Officers' Quarters

U
US-United States
USA-United States Army
USAF-United States Air Force
USAREUR-U.S. Army Europe
USCG-United States Coast Guard
USEUCOM-U.S. European Command
USMA-U.S. Military Academy
USMC-United States Marine Corps
USMRA-United States Military Road Atlas
USN-United States Navy
USNCOQ-Unaccompanied Senior Noncommissioned Officers' Quarters
USO-United Service Organization
USPHS-United States Public Health Service

V
VAQ-Visiting Airmen's Quarters
VAT-Value Added Tax
VCR-Video Cassette Recorder
VEQ-Visiting Enlisted Quarters
VHA-Variable Housing Allowance
VIP-Very Important Person
VOQ-Visiting Officer Quarters
VQ-Visiting Quarters, all ranks

W
WO-Warrant Officer

Temporary Military Lodging Around the World - 335

APPENDIX C

Temporary Military Lodging Questions and Answers

Answers below are based on information available to us at press time. Due to the fact that policies differ from installation to installation, these general answers must be accepted only as guides...not rules. Specific questions should be directed to each individual installation at the time of your visit. Policies often change.

1.) What types of lodging are available on military installations? There are numerous types of lodging available on military installations. They range from very modern, modular-constructed, complete housekeeping units which will sleep a family of five with all the amenities found in a good motel (plus a furnished kitchenette) such as found in Navy Lodges, to the old faithful guest houses...relics of World War II, which are often barracks-type buildings. Some may have been improved while others are definitely sub-standard. Some are the modern hotel type such as the Hale Koa Hotel AFRC (Hawaii), the New Sanno U.S. Forces Center (Japan) and Dragon Hill Lodge (Yongson, Korea). There is also the modern motel type lodging such as the Super 8 Motels at Governor's Island, and another lodging chain at Fort Bliss. Somewhere in between, you will find the VOQ type accommodations that usually consist of private rooms with a shared bath between rooms. If you are the "picky" type, we suggest you take a look before signing in, if possible.

2.) Were the units mentioned above constructed with tax dollars? According to information given TML, the answer on most of the lodging is an emphatic "NO." The newer construction was built from non-appropriated funds or grants from welfare funds, generated from profits from military exchanges, etc. The exception to this is in cases where old unused family housing initially built with appropriated funds has been converted into temporary lodging facilities. Also, TML is frequently available in bachelor officers', NCO and enlisted grade quarters which have been constructed with appropriated funds.

3.) What does space-available (Space-A) mean? The purpose of having lodging on military installations is to accommodate duty personnel and those arriving or departing an installation on Temporary Duty orders (TDY) or permanent change of station (PCS) orders. Those on orders generally have first priority on all lodging. After these needs have been met, if there is any space left over, leave personnel (including retirees and their families) may utilize the facilities on a Space-A basis. During the summer months, Space-A lodging may be more difficult to obtain than during the spring, fall, and winter.

4.) How about advance reservations? While many installations will accept reservations from those on duty, leave and retired travelers will generally find that they cannot make reservations in advance but are accepted on a Space-A basis on arrival at the billeting office. Navy Lodges do accept reservations from all categories. As we are listing the lodging of five (USA, USN, USMC, USCG and USAF) different services in this book, the rules may vary greatly from place to place. Please check each listing in this book or call in advance to check on specific policies on making reservations at the time of your trip. You may be surprised and find that the place you want to visit will accept your reservation.

5.) Can retirees use military lodging? Definitely...usually on the same Space-A basis as active duty on leave. Retirees will also find that they are welcome to use the lodging on many

APPENDIX C, continued

installations overseas, even though they may be restricted from using the commissary or exchange in most overseas areas due to the Status of Forces Agreement. The rules are different for the use of support facilities in each foreign country.

6.) Are Reservists eligible for TML? Many favorable changes have occurred for reservists as a result of the war in Southwest Asia and the Persian Gulf War. Reservists and accompanying dependents may now use Navy Lodges and most recreational lodging such as that listed in our book, *Military RV, Camping and Rec Areas Around the World*. This includes the popular Hale Koa Hotel and AFRC in Hawaii. We have not seen any new information on the use of TML at other services' lodging facilities, however, for Space-A lodging. If we receive new information on the subject, we will include it in our all ranks travel newsletter, **Military Living's *R&R Space-A Report*®**.

Other rules have changed. Reservists now have full time use of the exchanges, and commissary use has been extended, so they may use commissary facilities 12 times during the year, rather than only during their active duty training. There is a proposal in Congress to grant unlimited commissary privileges to reservists. **Reservists on active duty for training and their families are eligible to use all lodging at that time.** Readers of our publications who are in the Reserves have reported to us that they have occasionally been allowed to use TML. Since rules can differ from place to place, we recommend that you inquire at each location if interested.

7.) Your book often refers to Defense Switched Network (DSN, or D-) phone numbers. What are they? Defense Switched Network numbers are military phone numbers which are to be used only by those on **official business**. Such numbers can normally be dialed only from a military installation and are monitored to assure their use is not violated. As many of our readers use military lodging and facilities while traveling on duty, and many government offices use our book as a reference guide, we publish the DSN or DSN-E (Defense Switched Network - Europe) numbers, when available, as a service to them.

8.) What is DV/VIP lodging? It is lodging for distinguished official visitors. Some installations will have a few rooms or a small guest house available for them. If these facilities are not being used by official visitors, many installations will often extend the courtesy of their use to qualified active duty personnel on leave status or retirees on a day-to-day Space-A basis. Most military installations we surveyed referred to DV/VIP as grades O6 and above. Just a few included lower officer grades (O5) and senior NCO (E-8/9) in this category. The Marine Corps calls their distinguished visitors lodging Distinguished Guest Quarters (DGQ). Since 1977, we have noted that many more Air Force bases are providing DV/VIP lodging for their senior NCOs. Those in the DV/VIP category should check our listings in this book for more complete information and inquire at each installation upon arrival. Distinguished visitors will usually find that it is best to make advance reservations through the Protocol Office or Visitor's Bureau of the installation concerned. In some cases, the billeting office has authority to place personnel in the DV/VIP lodging and coordinate the visit for the traveler.

9.) My husband is enlisted. What chance do we have at staying in military lodging? Better than ever. In the past few years, concentrated efforts have been made to provide more temporary lodging for enlisted members. Please notice in our listing the numerous references to quarters for all ranks. In the newer Air Force Transient Living Quarters, Navy Lodges, and Army Guest

APPENDIX C, continued

Houses, rank has absolutely no privileges. All ranks are accommodated on an equal basis. Policies may vary on other types of lodging. At some facilities, enlisted have priority.

10.) May 100% DAV use TML? Most military lodging units accept 100% DAV (Disabled American Veterans) on a Space-A basis if it is possible. In fact, the Hale Koa hotel AFRC specifically mentions 100% DAV in their brochure as being eligible. One problem that 100% DAV have encountered has been caused by the color of their ID card (DD1173). It is the same color (buff or butterscotch) as carried by family members. Many times 100% DAV are turned away from facilities which require family members to be accompanied by their sponsor. The "ID card-checking authority" assumes this military member is not a military member but a "dependent" or family member. Watch for more info on this subject in **Military Living's R&R Space-A Report®**.

11.) How about Navy - Bachelor Quarters (BQ)? We are told that a few Bachelor Enlisted Quarter (BEQ) locations have unsuitable facilities for family members - central baths (latrines), etc. However, most Bachelor Enlisted Quarters (BEQ) have suitable facilities. Also, Bachelor Officers' Quarters (BOQ) are almost always suitable. They will generally accept family members accompanying their sponsor. Rules can vary from installation to installation. If a Navy Lodge is not available, always ask about the possible use of the BEQ/BOQ.

12.) What about widows, widowers, and unaccompanied dependents? The news gets better each time we report in our new TML book. Dependents of active duty personnel who are involved in a PCS move may now use TML and may make reservations at the installation they are leaving and at the new one to which they are assigned. They may also use TML en route on a Space-A basis. This includes TML in TLF and in VOQ or VAQ.

Unaccompanied dependents of military members on leave and also widows/ers of deceased members may use TML on a Space-Available basis in VAQ or VOQ if this policy has been approved by the base commander. (Therefore, this may NOT be in effect at all Air Force installations.) This does not include the use of TLF.

Other services generally have always allowed unaccompanied military family members to use TML on a Space-A basis. This, of course, has and will continue to differ from installation to installation. Navy Lodges, however, welcome dependent children, and non-ID card holders when accompanied by a parent or guardian authorized to utilize Navy Lodges.

13.) What's a Fisher House? Families of seriously-ill patients at Veterans' Administration (VA) Hospitals and some Army, Navy, and Air Force Medical Centers now have a "home away from home" thanks to the generosity of Zachary and Elizabeth M. Fisher. As of spring, '95 the Fishers have paid for 21 such houses at military and VA installations around the United States. A total of 22 are planned. Standard design includes eight bedrooms, a common use living room, kitchen, fireplace and playground. Families may stay while visiting patients requiring treatment, and are referred by physicians or social workers based on a variety of priorities. Generally priorities are: lack of family in the immediate area; severity of illness; financial need. Different hospitals may have varying criteria. A note in the various listings and local phone number are provided should readers be in a situation warranting the use of such facilities.

APPENDIX D

BILLETING REGULATIONS AND NAVY LODGE POLICIES

The Department of Defense has issued several instructions which outline for the Military Departments the broad guidance for the organization, operation, management and reporting for several broad categories of Temporary Military Lodging (TML). **(Please see: DoD Instruction 1100.16 and 4165.63 and DoD Manual 4165.63-M).** The Military Departments within the Department of Defense and the United States Coast Guard within the Department of Transportation have issued more specific policy and procedure directives covering the organization, management, and reporting for their respective categories of TML. **There are some consistencies among these Military Department directives but they are not identical or uniform in their content.** As a special service to our readers, we have synthesized each Military Department and Navy Lodge directive below. In each case we have selected the items from the directives which we believe would provide the greatest benefit to our readers. We have provided the reference for each directive and the reader may request to see the complete directive at the respective Military Department lodging facilities or at their personnel offices.

Army Installation Housing Management

This regulation condenses regulations in the 210-series that govern the management and operation of the Army's family, unaccompanied personnel and guest housing programs and their related furnishing programs. This regulation **Installation Housing Management-AR-210-50** is effective **24 May 1990** and has several changes since that date. The regulation is applicable to the Active Army, Army National Guard and U. S. Army Reserve.

The primary consideration in the management of billeting activities is to promote the use of housing assets. This must be done to ensure that housing that is available is used for its intended purpose, and meets the housing needs of authorized personnel in the performance of their duties.

Billeting activities include the following:

1-Unaccompanied Personnel Housing (UPH) (PP) (Permanent Party). **2**-Officers Quarters (OQ). **3**-Senior Officer Quarters (SOQ). **4**-Enlisted Quarters (EQ). **5**-Senior Enlisted Quarters (SEQ). **6**-UPH (TDY). **7**-Visiting Officers Quarters (VOQ). **8**-Visiting Enlisted Quarters (VEQ). **9**-Distinguished Visitor Quarters (DVQ). **10**-Guest House (GH).

Authority to occupy Transient Facilities:

A-Personnel authorized to occupy TDY housing.

1-**The following personnel with a confirmed reservation:**

a-TDY military and TDY DoD civilians. **b**-PCS military personnel when GH not available. **c**-U. S. and foreign guest of the Military Services. **d**-USAR, ARNG and ROTC on Active Duty Training. **e**-Foreign military personnel TDY. **f**-Military family members on medical TDY orders. **g**-Guest of Armed Forces as determined by installation commander.

APPENDIX D, continued

2-When space is available, the following personnel may occupy TDY housing:

a-Retirees (including Reserve Grey Area), military personnel on leave, family members and guest of military personnel assigned to the installation if GH space is not available.
b-Non-military uniformed personnel of USPHS, NOAA, USCG personnel traveling on official business and foreign military personnel.
c-Within the categories listed in 1 and 2 above, personnel will compete on an equal basis for TDY facilities.
d-Members in promotable status may be assigned to housing of the next higher grade upon presentation of proof of pending promotion.
e-Personnel listed in 2 above will pay the fair market rental rate.

B-Personnel Authorized to Occupy GH Facilities.

1-The following personnel with a confirmed reservation may occupy Guest House (GH) facilities.

a-PCS service members and their families accompanied or alone. **b**-PCS DoD civilian personnel and their families accompanied or alone in an overseas area. **c**-Families, relatives and guests of hospitalized service members or their families. **d**-Active and retired military personnel and family members undergoing outpatient treatment at a medical facility and must remain overnight (RON). **e**-Official guest of the installation. **f**-Families of a soldier visiting an installation incident to internment of the soldier or family members.

2-When space is available, the following personnel may occupy GH facilities.

a-TDY service members and TDY DoD civilian personnel when UPH(TDY) facilities are not available. **b**-Retired service members (including Reserve Grey Area) with or without family members. **c**-Members of USPHS, NOAA and USCG. **d**-PCS DoD civilians with or without family members in CONUS. **e**-Service members on leave not incident to PCS with or without family members, relatives and guest of service members assigned to the installation.

3-Within the categories listed above, personnel may compete on an equal basis or the installation commander may establish priorities within the categories to meet the needs of the installation.

Medal of Honor recipients of all services are authorized transient facilities at the discretion of the installation commander. Medal of Honor recipients may receive priority placement and confirmed reservations in the VOQ, VEQ, DVQ or GH. A DVQ may be assigned regardless of military pay grade.

Reservation System

A-TDY Housing

1-Billeting offices will establish a reservation system that will enable TDY travelers to confirm reservations at least 15 days prior to actual travel. A reservation number will be provided to the traveler.

APPENDIX D, continued

2-TDY travelers who receive confirmation of non availability of housing may live off the installation.

3-TDY students who have confirmed reservations must reside in transient facilities.

4-Reservations should not be held beyond 1800 hours unless the TDY traveler notifies the billeting office of late arrival.

B-GH Facilities

1-Reservations will be on a first-come basis without regard to rank, race, color, religion, gender, national origin or handicap. Reservations should be accepted up to 30 days in advance of requested date. Confirmation should be provided as early as possible.

2-Reservations should not be held beyond 1800 hours unless the billeting office is notified of late arrival. The normal duration of occupancy for all lodging categories is 30 days unless a hardship extension is approved by the installation commander.

NOTE: The Army will begin operation of a worldwide access reservation system by March 1994, located in Huntsville, AL. This central reservation system will serve Army Temporary Military Lodging worldwide. **The toll free reservation number is 1-800-GO-ARMY-1 or 1-800-462-7691.** This central reservation number does not serve all Army Temporary Military Lodging locations.

NAVY BACHELOR HOUSING

The Navy operates bachelor housing and Navy Lodges as Temporary Lodging Facilities. The bachelor housing facilities are operated for both permanent party and TDY/TAD personnel. The Navy Lodge program is administered by the Navy Exchange Service and provides Temporary Lodging Facilities for a wide category of personnel (See below).

The Navy bachelor housing program is covered in **BUPERS Instruction 11103.1B, Activities With Bachelor Quarters, (to be issued Sep 1993)** which promulgates the basic Navy policy covering among other things, the utilization and occupancy of BQ and the related management of this program. This instruction applies to the Navy worldwide.

The instruction applies to active duty and reserve personnel, DoD civilians, civilians authorized by SECNAV, National Guard personnel on active duty for training or active duty, retirees and dependent personnel.

This instruction applies to the following quarters:

1-Bachelor Enlisted Quarters (BEQ). **2**-Bachelor Officers' Quarters (BOQ). **3**-Bachelor Civilian Quarters (BCQ). **4**-Recruit Training Quarters (RTQ). **5**-Reserve Component Quarters (RCQ). **6**-Quarters for duty personnel. **7**-Discipline and legal hold quarters. **8**-Medical holding units. **9**-Ashore Quarters for Afloat Staffs. **10**-United States Marine Corps Barracks. **11**-Leased or contract Quarters. **12**-Temporary Lodging Facilities (TLF Navy Lodges). **13**-Transient Visiting Officers Quarters (TVOQ). **14**-Transient Personnel Unit Quarters (TPU).

APPENDIX D, continued

The Navy has a new program to assign bachelor quarters to their "geographic bachelors" for the entire length of their tour of duty. The implementation of this program **may considerably reduce the availability of bachelor quarters to active duty (TDY/TAD), leave, retirees and Reserve personnel.**

The Navy has priority for use of quarters and reservation systems similar to the other services. When the new instruction is available we will publish this information in later changes to this TML book and in **Military Living's** *R & R Space-A Report*®. Please see the Central Order Coupon in the back of this book.

NAVY LODGES

Navy Lodge Mission. The Navy Lodge mission is to provide United States Uniformed Services personnel accompanied by dependents under Permanent Change of Station (PCS) orders with temporary lodging accommodation, and to provide lodging for all other authorized quests.

Reservations

ANYTIME: Accompanied PCS personnel may make reservations at any time in advance.

SIXTY DAYS: Active duty and Reservist personnel on orders may make reservations up to 60 days in advance. Includes: Unaccompanied PCS, TAD, TDY, Official and Unofficial leave.

THIRTY DAYS: All others may make reservations up to 30 days in advance. Includes: Retired personnel, Reservist, DoD Associates, Official Guest of the Command.

Naval Hospital Lodge mission is to provide authorized guests with temporary accommodations with the following priorities. Priority I: Members of the immediate family of in-patients who are seriously or critically ill and sponsors of children who are undergoing or convalescing from serious surgery. Priority II: Members of the immediate family of all other in-patients.

Reservations: Reservations will be held only to 1800 (6:00 pm) hours without advance deposit or credit card guarantee. Check-in time is 1500 (3:00 pm); however, earlier arrivals will be accommodated according to room availability.

PCS may make reservations anytime in advance of the date of arrival. Active duty, spouses/dependents of POW/MIA, hospitalized and deceased military members' dependents may make reservations 60 days in advance. All other authorized guest may make reservations 30 days in advance.

Navy Lodges do not bump registered guests to accommodate other guests. There is no preferential treatment in regards to rate or rank. Rooms are standard with no special quarters.

APPENDIX D, continued

To assist guests in making reservations, the Navy Lodges provide a central reservation center for all CONUS lodges. Reservations can be made anytime by calling a Toll Free Reservations Number **1-800-NAVY-INN/1-800-628-9466** or DSN 942-3301. Reserved accommodations have priority over guests who wish to extend the length of their stay. Navy Lodges accept MasterCard, Visa, Diners Club and Discover for payment and also guarantee a reservations if arrivals will be after 6:00 pm. Overseas reservations currently must be made by contacting the individual lodge. **OCONUS Navy Lodge numbers are in the individual listings, or you may call the toll free number for these overseas numbers.** Current plans call for overseas lodges to be included on the 1-800-NAVY-INN line by the 1995 time frame.

Marine Corps Housing Management Manual

The following has been extracted from the **Marine Corps Housing Management Manual, MCO P11000.22, dated 14 February 1991, with changes.**

Transient Quarters Management. Transient quarters are operated primarily to provide a service to duty transient personnel and TAD students. Adequate quarters shall be set aside to accommodate TAD transient personnel. When designated transient quarters are fully occupied, transients may voluntarily occupy permanent party quarters.

The following personnel are entitled to designated TAD transient quarters on a confirmed reservation basis: a-Military personnel and DOD civilians on TAD orders. **b**-American Red Cross and Navy Relief Society on official business. **c**-U. S. and Foreign civilians traveling as guest of Armed Forces. **d**-Reserve personnel in TAD status, unit training status, and annual trainees on individual orders. **e**-TAD foreign nationals or foreign military trainees engaged in or sponsored by military assistance or similar training programs unless prohibited by the Status of Forces Agreement (SOFA). **f**-Family members on medical TAD orders. **g**-Military personnel with or without family members, arriving or departing for overseas installations on PCS when TLF or permanent housing is not immediately available. **h**-Official guests of the activity commander.

The following personnel may occupy designated transient quarters on a space-available basis: a-Retirees, military personnel on leave, family members, or guests of military personnel assigned to the activity if TLF space is not available. **b**-DOD civilian employees and their families arriving or departing incident to PCS when TLFs are not available. **c**-Guests of the activity commander.

Non-duty transients shall be advised at the time of registration that occupancy is strictly on a day-to-day, space-available basis and that they must vacate not later than the following day if the quarters are required for duty transients.

Distinguished Guest Quarters (DGQ) are also available to accommodate the frequent travel of high ranking officials, both civilian and military. DGQs are under the control of the installation commander.

APPENDIX D, continued

Coast Guard Temporary Guest Housing Facility Policies

The following has been extracted from **Coast Guard Recreation Areas & Temporary Guest Housing Facilities Guide, Publication P1710.14 dated 18 January 1989, with changes.**

Most large Coast Guard installations have developed guest housing in response to the need for temporary lodging for Coast Guard members and their families. These facilities are operated and managed by the Coast Guard Exchange System (CGES). Since each installation manages its own GH, each has its own rules and regulations regarding usage.

Guest housing was developed mainly for use by active duty Coast Guard members and their families traveling under PCS orders; however, Coast Guard personnel in other than PCS status and members of the other uniformed services are allowed to use some Coast Guard guest housing facilities. It is always advisable to call the facility you intend to visit to determine your eligibility and reservation policy. Most of this essential information is listed in each Coast Guard listing in this book.

Air Force Billeting Operations Regulations

The following has been extracted from **Air Force Regulation 34-601, Air Force Lodging, dated 24 May 1993.**

Transient Quarters Operation. Transient Quarters are operated to provide a service to duty transient personnel and TDY students. The operation of transient quarters is based on the need of the services and the availability of quarters at an installation.

Personnel Eligible for Transient Quarters: The following personnel are eligible to occupy Visiting Officer Quarters (VOQ) and Visiting Enlisted Quarters (VEQ) **commensurate with their grade on a space-confirmed basis. The order in which the following are listed does not indicate a priority: a**-TDY personnel, including crew members. **b**-TDY U.S. civilian employees, and civilians traveling under competent authority. **c**-Members of the Air National Guard and Air Force Reserve on annual tours, school tours, special tours of active duty, or active duty for training. **d**-Members of the Air National Guard and Air Force Reserve on inactive duty training. **e**-TDY or TDY student, foreign military, or civilian personnel sponsored through security assistance, allied exchange, or foreign liaison programs. **f**-USAFA and AFROTC cadets traveling on official orders. **g**-Aircraft passengers on official orders or emergency leave at aerial ports of embarkation, if aerial port quarters are not available. **h**-Dependents on medical TDY orders. **i**-Military and civilian personnel using military aircraft in TDY or PCS status who, for reasons beyond their control, remain overnight (RON) at locations other than their TDY or PCS location. **j**-Contract engineering and technical services personnel (CETSP). **k**-Guests of the armed forces as determined by the installation commander. **l**-Applicants for an Air Force commission. **m**-Active duty personnel on emergency leave. **n**-Unaccompanied personnel, including civilians, entitled to permanent quarters who are temporarily without permanent housing due to PCS travel orders. **o**-Military and civilian personnel and their families arriving or departing an overseas location incident to PCS, if no other government temporary lodging is available. **p**-Military and civilian personnel in a TDY status to nearby locations who desire government quarters in lieu of commercial quarters. **q**-Personnel on permissive TDY orders.

APPENDIX D, continued

The following personnel are eligible to occupy VOQ/VEQ on a space-available basis. Maximum stay is 30 days during any one visit. Extensions must be approved by the installation commander. The order in which the following are listed does not indicate a priority: **a-**Dependents accompanying official TDY personnel. **b-**Married military and civilian personnel with their families in CONUS who are temporarily without permanent housing due to PCS orders, only when TLFs (see below) are not available. **c-**Unaccompanied personnel entitled to permanent quarters who arrive or depart incident to PCS and are temporarily without permanent housing. **d-**Dependents of members who are patients in Air Force hospitals, only if TLF not available. **e-**Retirees and retirement eligible Reservists in a non duty status (who have DD Form 2 AFRES with a copy of ARPC certificate of retirement eligibility) and their dependents. **f-**Active duty members and their dependents on ordinary leave, environmental and morale leave (EML), or travel status. **g-**U.S. civilians and their dependents on EML orders from overseas duty assignments, only if TLF is not available. **h-**Active status and/or in training Air National Guard and Air Force Reserve members and their dependents. **i-**Space-available passengers aboard military aircraft interrupted short of destination, or passengers arriving at ports for space-available travel on departing military flights. **j-**AFROTC cadets, organizations, and youth groups when approved by the installation commander. **k-**Civil Air Patrol (CAP) members on official visits.

Note: transient dependents of deceased military members and dependents unaccompanied by their active or retired military sponsor, or U.S. civilian sponsor in overseas areas, may occupy transient quarters when approved by the installation commander.

Personnel requesting space-available lodging will be assigned lodging upon arrival, unless all rooms are occupied or reserved by priority 1 personnel.

Temporary Lodging Facility Operations. Temporary Lodging Facilities (TLFs) are operated to provide temporary housing to authorized personnel at the lowest possible cost consistent with giving good service.

Eligibility for and Assignment to TLFs. Personnel listed below are eligible to occupy TLFs. Assignments are made without regard to rank and on a first-come-first-served basis. Following personnel have priority 1 status: a-Active duty military members accompanied by their dependents or their dependents alone, incident to PCS, separation, or retirement. **b-**Civilian and military friends and relatives of patients in Air Force hospitals. **c-**Hospital outpatients. **d-**Personnel who are accompanied by dependents and in permissive TDY, ordinary leave, or terminal leave status, and traveling for the purpose of house hunting in conjunction with PCS, retirement, or separation. **e-**Displaced Military Family Housing occupants required to temporarily vacate their assigned lodging. **f-**Official guest of the installation commander.

Following personnel have priority 2 status: a-Military members and dependents on leave or delay en route. **b-**Military and civilian personnel, whether or not accompanied by dependents, on TDY when VOQ or VAQ facilities are fully occupied. **c-**Retired military members and dependents. **d-**Unaccompanied married personnel and unmarried members being joined by or acquiring dependents. **e-**Unaccompanied married personnel and unmarried members incident to PCS, if neither transient nor permanent party government quarters are available. **f-**Civilians accompanied by their dependents incident to PCS, active status Air National Guard and Air

APPENDIX D, continued

Force Reserve not in a duty status and their dependents. **g**-Air National Guard and Air Force Reserve members not in a duty status. **h**-Members of USCG, USPHS and NOAA.

Following personnel have priority 3 status: a-Friends and relatives of assigned military personnel. Note: Personnel in priorities 2 and 3 are accommodated on a space-available basis and are required to vacate quarters no later than the next day after quarters are required by personnel in priority 1.

Reservations. Only personnel in priority 1 may request advance reservations. Reservation request should include expected arrival time and date. Reservations will not be held beyond 1700 hours unless the billeting office is notified in advance of personal needs for a later arrival time. Normal check out time is 1200 hours.

Recent change to chapter 4, Transient Quarters. 4-1c(2) ------- Travelers requesting quarters on a space-available basis should be assigned quarters upon arrival and should not wait until 1800 hours in the event of "no-shows." Upon assignment, travelers desiring space-available quarters for more than one night's stay must be advised to check at the billeting desk prior to check-out time the following day. If known requirements indicate that quarters are not needed for priority 1 personnel, the traveler should be confirmed for another night's stay at that time.

Central Reservation System for Bachelor Navy Quarters

Effective June 1996, "all Navy military and many civilian personnel on official temporary duty travel will be required to make lodging reservations through BQCRS when they make transporation arrangements.

Reservations can be made through the servicing commercial travel office, currently the Scheduled Airline Travel Office (SATO). Privately owned vehicle travelers, or those using organic airlift requiring lodging reservations only, may use SATO travel's toll-free number to make reservations (1-800-576-9327).

Prior clearance is required for using BQCRS in Naval Support Facility Diego Garcia, Naval Air Facility Kadena and Commander, Fleet Activities Chinhae. At those locations traveleres should contact the bachelor quarters directly.

The only activities in the continental United States not covered are Naval Base New London and Naval Education and Training Center Newport.

More information is available in NAVADMIN 092/96 or contact Lieutenant David Donnelly at DSN 224-2924/ C (703) 614-2924."

Too Late To Copy

CALIFORNIA *(Continued from page 53)*
Presidio of Monterey, Presidio of Monterey, CA 93944-5006. **C-408-242-5091, D-312-878-5091.**
San Clemente Island Naval Auxiliary Landing Field, P.O. Box 357054, San Diego, CA 92135-7054. Billeting Office, **C-619-524-9202.**
San Pedro Coast Guard Support Center, Local Housing Authority, PCS, Base PO Box 8, Terminal Island Station, San Pedro, 0700-1600 daily. **C-310-514-6450.** BEQ only at CG Support Center. All ranks. DV/VIP 310-514-6450.
Seal Beach Naval Weapons Station, Seal Beach, CA 90740-5000. BEQ, **C-310-594-7137.**

FLORIDA
Corry Naval Station NTTC, Pensacola, FL 32511-5000. BEQ/DV **C-904-252-6609.**
Homestead ARS, Homestead Inn, 29050 Coral Sea Blvd, Homestead ARS, Fl 33039. **C-305-224-7168**, D-312-791-7168, FAX 305-224-7290, DSN FAX 312-224-7290. Hours of operation are from 0700-2100; holiday hours are 0900-1800. There are 200 rooms and 5 suites. Suites come with stocked bar, microwave, refrigerator, full bath, TV, telephone. Rates: $8 VOQ, $5 VAQ, $14 suites. *A new facility is scheduled to open in Spetember of 1996.*

INDIANA
Camp Atterbury, Billeting Office, Bldg. 506, Edinburgh, IN 46124-4096. **C-812-526-1128** (FAX number also), D-312-526-1128. There are approximately 160 rooms ranging from $6 to $8.

PENNSYLVANIA
Pittsburgh Air Reserve Station, Bldg. 206, 2275 Defense Ave, Corapolis, PA 15108-4463. **C-412-474-8230**, D-312-277-8230, FAX 412-474-8752, DSN Fax 312-277-8752. 0700 - 2300 daily, check out 1200. Rates: $6 - $8. Visa, MasterCard and American Express are accepted.
TML: VOQ/DV, building 206, Officers, all ranks. Bedroom, semi-private bath (20), bedroom, private bath (2), two room DV suite, private bath (2). Telephone, refrigerator, color TV, VCR, AC, housekeeping service, ice vending, microwave in lounge.
TML: VAQ/SNCO suites, buildings 209, 216, 217, 218, 219. Enlisted, all ranks. Bedroom, two beds per room, common bath (72), bedroom, private bath (44), two room SNCO suite, private bath (10). Telephone, refrigerator, color TV, VCR, AC, housekeeping service, ice vending, microwave in lounge.
Locator 474-8000   **Medical 474-8117**   **Police 474-8250/8255**

UTAH
Ogden Defense Depot, Ogden, UT 84407-5000. *Scheduled to close in 1997.* **C-801-399-6030**, D-312-352-6030.

VIRGINIA
Armed Forces Staff College, Terminal and Hampton Blvd, Bldg. SC407, Norfolk, VA 23511-5000. Officers only, **C-804-444-5311**, D-312-504-5311.

Continued on page 348

New Air Force Lodging Policy effective 17 October 1995

- Lodging offices will accept and confirm reservations for space available customers 24 hours in advance of their arrival.
- Reservations may be confirmed for up to a 72 hour (three day) stay space permitting.
- Duty travelers will not bump space available guests with confirmed reservations, nor will they bump them once they have been assigned quarters for a specific period of time (generally three days).
- Lodging facilities should attempt to negotiate reduced rates for their space available guests under their commercial lodging contracts.

Reference message HQ USAF 17 Oct 95.

CENTRAL ORDER COUPON
Military Living Publications
P.O. Box 2347, Falls Church, VA 22042-0347
TEL: (703) 237-0203 FAX: (703) 237-2233

Publications (Prices effective 1 Aug 1996)	QTY
R&R Space-A Report®. *The worldwide travel newsletter.* 6 issues per year. 1 yr/$15.00 - 2 yrs/$24.00 - 3 yrs/$33.00 - 5 yrs/$49.00 (Shipped by 3rd class bulk rate)	
Military Space-A Air Basic Training. $13.95	
Military Space-A Air Opportunities Air Route Map. (Folded) $13.95	
Military Space-A Air Opportunities Around the World. $18.95	
Temporary Military Lodging Around the World. $15.95	
Military RV, Camping & Rec Areas Around the World. $13.95	
U.S. Forces Travel and Transfer Guide, USA and Caribbean Areas. $13.95	
U.S. Forces Travel Guide to Overseas U.S. Military Installations. $17.95	
U.S. Military Museums, Historic Sites & Exhibits. (Soft Cover) $17.95	
United States Military Road Atlas. $18.95	
U.S. Military Installation Road Map. (Folded) $7.95	
United States Military Medical Facilities Map (Folded) $7.95	
COLLECTOR'S ITEM! Desert Shield Commemorative Maps. (Folded) $8.00 (2 unfolded wall maps in a hard tube) $18.00	
Assignment Washington Military Road Atlas. $10.95	
California State Military Road Map - (Folded) $5.95 Florida State Military Road Map - (Folded) $5.95 Mid-Atlantic States Military Road Map - (Folded) $5.95 Texas State Military Road Map - (Folded) $5.95	
Military Living Magazine, Camaraderie Washington. *Local Area magazine.* 1 year (4 issues) 1st Class Mailing $8.00	
Virginia Addresses add 4.5% sales tax (Books, Maps, & Atlases only) **TOTAL $**	

*If you are an R&R Space-A Report® subscriber, you may deduct $1.00 per book. (No discount on the R&R Report itself or on the maps or atlas.) Mail Order Prices are for U.S. APO & FPO addresses. Please consult publisher for International Mail Price. Sorry, no billing.
We're as close as your telephone...by using our Telephone Ordering Service. We honor American Express, MasterCard, and VISA. Call us at **703-237-0203** (**Voice Mail after hours**) or **Fax 703-237-2233** and order today! Sorry, no collect calls. Or...fill out and mail the order coupon below.

NAME:_____
STREET:_____
CITY/STATE/ZIP:_____
PHONE:_____ SIGNATURE:_____
RANK (or rank of sponsor):_____ Branch Of Service:_____
Active Duty:_Retired:_Widow/er:_100% Disabled Veteran:_Guard:_Reservist:_Other:_
Card # _____ Card Expiration Date:_____

Mail check/money order to Military Living Publications, P.O. Box 2347, Falls Church, VA 22042-0347 - **Tel: 703-237-0203 - FAX: 703-237-2233**.
Save $$$s by purchasing any of our books, Maps, and Atlases at your military Exchange.
Prices subject to change. Please check here if we may ship and bill difference.......... ☐

Too Late To Copy *(Continued from 346)*

VIRGINIA *(Continued)*
Cape Henry Inn, Bldg. 1116, Fort Story, VA 23459. **C-804-422-8818**, FAX 804-422-6397. Open to all service members, family members, Department of Defense civilians and retirees; reservations are on a first-come first-served basis. The 50 rooms available sleep four and the cottages sleep six to eight.
TML: The Sandpiper. Suites, with two full-size beds, full bath, TV, and balcony. Rates: $40.
TML: The Dunes. Two full-size beds, pull out sofa, full bath, kitchenette, TV, balcony. Rates: $50.
TML: The Chesapeake. Two bedroom cottage with full kitchen, living room, full bath, TV, balcony. Rates: $60.
TML: The Tidewater. Three bedroom cottage with full kitchen, living room, full bath, TV, balcony. Rates: $65.
Chesapeake Naval Security Group Activity Northwest, 1320 Northwest Blvd, Suite 100, Chesapeake, VA 23322-4094. BEQ/BOQ & DV/VIP **C-804-421-8331**, D-312-564-1336, Fax 804-421-8235 Code 32.

WASHINGTON
Everett Naval Station, 2000 West Marine View Drive, Everett, WA 98207-5001. BEQ **C-206-304-3111/2**, BEQ **C-206-304-4660**.
Jim Creek Naval Radio Station, 21027 Jim Creek Road, Arlington, WA 98223-8599. **C-360-304-5315**.Lodging to be completed in Fall of '96.
Seattle Coast Guard Support Center, 1519 Alaskan Way South, Seattle, WA 98134-1192. BEQ **C-206-217-6410**, 0730-1600 daily.
Whidbey Island Navy Lodge, 2125 N Coral Sea Ave, Oak Harbor, WA 98278. **C-360-675-0633 or 1-800-NAVY-INN**. Check in 1500-1800, check out 1200hours. Two bedroom modular units (23) with kitchen, full bath, AC, TV, hairdryers, iron, ironing boards, rollaways, housekeeping service, playground. Rates: $46. Maximum six per room; seeing eye dogs, fish, and caged birds OK. Visa, MasterCard, American Express and Discover are accepted.

WEST VIRGINIA
Camp Dawson Army Training Site, 240 Army Road, Kingwood, WV 26537-1077. **C-304-329-4420**.
Eastern West Virginia Regional Airport, Martinsburg, WV 25401-0204. Very limited TML, **C-304-267-5174**.
Sugar Grove Naval Security Group Activity, Lodging Office, Bldg 63, Sugar Grove, WV 26815-5000. **C-304-249-6352**, D-312-564-7276, 0730-1600 daily, FAX 304-249-6307.

DENMARK
Thule Air Base, Lodging Office, Bldg. 97, Unit 82501, APO AE 09704-5000. **C-011-299-50-646 EX 3276**, D-314-268-1211 EX 3276.

HONG KONG
The Missions to Seamen, operates two clubs in Hong Kong. They are not a military installation, but a Seafarer's Club primarily for the use of Merchant Seaman, however they do welcome the Armed Forces. **Hong Kong Mariners' Club**, 11 Middle Road, Kowloon. C (USA) **011-852-2368-8261**, (HK) 2368-8261, FAX 011-852-2366-0928. **Kwai Chung Mariners' Club**, 2 Container Port Road, Kwai Chung. C (USA) **011-852-2410-8240**, (HK) 2410-8240.

UNITED KINGDOM
Royal Fleet Club, 9-12 Morice Square, Devonport, Plymouth, Devon PL1, 4PG, C (USA) **011-44-1752-562723**, (UK) 0752-562723. Rates: Deluxe Accommodation, single room £21-£22, double room £42-£44; Family Accommodation, double room £42-£44, for adjoining bunk beds add £8-£9; Standard Accommodation £33-£35. All rooms have tea/coffee making facilities, charges include full English breakfast. Check out 0930.